FROM
Alcatraz
White House TO THE

AN AUTOBIOGRAPHY

BY

NATHAN GLENN WILLIAMS

ISBN 0-9630070-0-9

Library of Congress Number 91-65906

Cover design by ADRIAN KALAR, Seattle, WA

WILLJOY Publishing
Nathan Glenn and Lorna Joy Williams
PO Box 17048
Seattle, WA 98107

DEDICATED TO MY WIFE, LORNA JOY WILLIAMS

For six years, Lorna labored at my side in the researching, writing, editing and typing of this autobiography. In addition to these manual chores, she exhorted me through periods of self-doubt and discouragement. Without her contribution, this book would never have reached the publisher.

ACKNOWLEDGMENT

So many friends have assisted me in the writing of this book, it would be virtually impossible to acknowledge each one individually. You know who you are. I want to thank you from the bottom of my heart for your assistance.

PREFACE

My purpose is to write a narrative autobiographical history, based on the conviction that the truth of my life story is better told exactly as I had lived it. To recreate the feelings, atmosphere and reality of the people, events and places described therein, I have intentionally employed language that may seem unduly harsh, or at times even offensive. For that I beg the reader's indulgence. I am especially concerned, for example, that certain epithets used to describe individuals of different sexual preference, ethnic background or racial groups might be construed as prejudiced. Language in this narrative history is used not so much for effect but rather to more vividly portray the world I lived in, and particularly the harsh realities of incarceration in several penal institutions. One reviewer, an English professor at the University of California, Berkeley, gently reproved me for an earlier draft that omitted such language with the following admonition: "Glenn, don't write it in the King's English!" To be faithful to the record, I have endeavored to heed his advice.

TABLE OF CONTENTS

1

IN THE BEGINNING

In 1938, at 23 years of age, I was involved in a trial which could mean a life sentence in the Washington State Penitentiary. I had already experienced a brief taste of confinement in that filthy hell-hole and the very thought of returning there for the rest of my natural life sickened me. Before this trial had begun I made the decision to die, if necessary, in a final escape attempt. I knew that I was at the end of the line this time. God help anyone who stood in my way! These were the thoughts running rampant through my mind as the selection of the jury was progressing.

The trial was taking place in Wenatchee, Washington. It was in the midst of the Great Depression and this small burg was devoid of money, employment and even the will to live. A pervading malaise reflected the utter despair of the populace. Literally, the town was in a moribund state, empty of any trace of vitality. I was not aware at this time in my life that such a setting was extremely dangerous to a defendant in my position. The citizens were angry at the government and at themselves, eager to strike out at any given opportunity just to "get even" for their miserable existence. I was a natural victim. Most of my life had been spent in Wenatchee. Throughout my youth I had been involved in all types of juvenile escapades; some quite serious. I had been convicted of burglary, car theft, robbery, assault and criminal vandalism before I was fifteen years old. In my school I had earned the reputation of being a trouble maker. It came as no surprise when I began to feel that every eye in Wenatchee was carefully watching me.

I decided to broaden my horizon and quickly fled to the Atlantic Seaboard. Upon arrival in that new locale, I wasted no time in continuing a life of crime. Ultimately, these years culminated in Montana where I was arrested for kidnapping, assault, forgery, car theft and discharging a firearm in the commission of a felony. The officials from the state of Washington assured the authorities in Montana that if I were released to Washington state I would be given a life term as an habitual criminal. Montana was more than happy to release me to the police from Wenatchee. Once again I found myself in the town where I had been raised, now on trial for my life.

The prospect of my hearing had created much excitement, presenting an opportunity for free entertainment. The impaneling of an impartial jury was almost an impossible task. I knew each and every face in those seats. They were the usual small town substantial citizenry; smug, satisfied and happy to be the center of attention for the first time in their otherwise drab existence. Worse yet, many of them had even been victims of my marauding.

1

I knew I could expect no empathy and that each one of the jury would be comfortable if I were removed from their midst. I will never know why my attorney, Lawrence Leahy, did not ask for a change of venue. Under the existing circumstances and in this locale, an unbiased hearing was impossible. Nevertheless, the trial was underway and it was far too late to waste time on regrets. As the prosecuting attorney, Lynn J. Gemmill, began his opening statements to the jury, I glanced around the court room. The faces of the judge, sheriff and the prosecutor were as cold and gray as stone. As I had expected, the members of the jury were also grim-faced. The one exception in the jury box was an elderly, grey-haired lady. When she saw me looking at her, she smiled encouragingly. An image of my own mother flashed through my mind, flower fresh in a dusty and arid setting. The elderly woman in the jury suddenly became like an angel of light and hope. Maybe, just maybe my outcome would not be as bleak as I feared.

Lawrence Leahy proved to be an excellent defense counsel. He fought intelligently and with a tenacity that surprised the prosecuting attorney. He was a young man and was determined to give his best to his client. In his heart, he knew I was guilty. The prosecutor fought like a seasoned boxer in the ring. He knew his opponent had little chance of being victorious and he meticulously presented his case point by point. He possessed damaging evidence and presented it to the jury in a manner that assured their verdict of "guilty". It was a bitterly contested trial. When the district attorney's final rebuttal had been made and the judge's instruction given to the jury, the hearing came to an end. The jury was sequestered. I was completely exhausted and felt that all hope was lost. My attorney looked at me and simply stated, "Don't give up, Glenn. No one can foretell the verdict of a jury."

Two deputies hustled me into the hallway, swathed me in chains and rushed me to a maximum security holding cell. I was overwhelmed with despondency, realizing fully the extent of my guilt and knowing that I was going to be convicted. The minutes passed slowly as I waited in my cell alone with my dark thoughts. For the first time in my life I recognized what a horrible shame I had brought upon my family. My mother, a refined and delicate lady, had not been able to face the ordeal of the trial. She had stayed home, as did my brothers and sisters who had been humiliated and embarrassed before their peers. My thoughts were briefly interrupted as a meal was brought to my cell, but I could not force myself to eat. Knots had formed in my stomach and I began to weep uncontrollably. Five hours after the jury had been given their instructions, the deputies returned to my cell and announced, "The verdict has been determined, Glenn. We are going to return you to the courtroom to hear the jury's decision."

Once again I was trussed like a mad dog and taken back to the courtroom. My father was standing inside the door as I entered and I felt his reassuring hand squeeze my shoulder. I had been in enough courtrooms to know that my only hope now lay in the quality of mercy and not in justice. The bailiff brought court attaches and spectators to their feet by rapping sharply with a gavel to announce the entrance of Superior Court Judge Jeffers. I refused to stand as fear, rebellion and bitterness welled up within me. My attorney sharply prodded me, but I remained adamantly determined to show no respect for Judge or court. The robed jurist, tall, gray and erect, straightened the legal documents spread before him, glanced around the courtroom and then ordered the jury brought in.

All eyes were on them as they filed silently into the jury box. My own gaze sought out the elderly lady who had smiled at me occasionally during the trial. She avoided my eyes and looked straight ahead. Her lips were pursed in a look of grim determination, ready to perform her unpleasant duty. Other members of the jury almost appeared to glow with a look of fatuous righteousness. They, at least, had done their duty by disposing of one of the country's numerous badmen. The attitude of these worthy burghers told me more clearly than words that my fate had been precisely determined. My Father said, "Take it like a man son. Don't forget that I will stand by you no matter what happens."

The words of the jury foreman droned in my ears. I straightened drooping shoulders as he finished, "...of being an habitual criminal we find Glenn Williams guilty as charged." My glance roved to Prosecutor Lynn Gemmill. He nodded his head in approval at the words and looked me straight in the eye, a look of jubilance spreading over his stern features. In the game of law he was a winner, I a loser. As in any game the winner has little sympathy for the loser, so I knew that his interest was not personal.

I became vaguely conscious that there must be two of me. I simply could not be the same boy who, a scant few months previous, had run the gamut of crime from forgery to highway robbery and kidnapping. I couldn't be the same person who had no compunction about swindling the solid, honest families who had given me their faith and confidence. Could it be possible that I was now in the position of feeling sorry for myself and looking for sympathy? All of these thoughts flashed through my mind. Slowly regaining my composure, it came to me that I must not let any of these men discern my inner feelings and weaknesses.

When my attorney was at last satisfied that the jury had actually found me guilty and I again was ordered to stand for sentencing, I assumed a broad grin. Judge Jeffers' gavel rapped sharply. Looking directly at me he ordered, "The defendant will rise." I remained seated, staring contemptuously and feeling a small flicker of satisfaction as the Judge's face turned a deep red. He turned to the bailiff and in an angered voice demanded, "Bailiff, bring the defendant to his feet."

The bailiff motioned to police officer Butts and the two descended on me. One on each side placed his hand under my arms and then proceeded to hoist me to my feet. I brought my knees up to my chest and refused to place my feet on the floor. This action made it necessary for the two officials to support my full weight for the remainder of the sentencing procedure. The judge found it very difficult to continue with any dignity. Finally he asked, "Glenn Williams, do you have anything to say before I pronounce sentence?"

I maintained my silence, still stubbornly refusing to stand. Without further hesitation, the judge intoned, "Glenn Williams, you have been found guilty by a jury of your peers of being an habitual criminal. It is now the duty of this court to impose sentence. I, therefore, sentence you to spend the rest of your natural life in the state prison at Walla Walla. You are remanded to the custody of the sheriff who will deliver you to the warden of that institution. I have known your father, your mother, brothers and sisters for many years and I have the utmost respect for them. It sickens me to have to send a young man to prison for such a long time. Records reflect that you are the youngest person in the United States to have been convicted of being an habitual criminal. However, your record clearly indicates that you are an extremely dangerous person and society must be protected from criminals like you." When he finished I still forced the broad grin, but in the back of my mind was a clear picture of brick walls, bars, steel cells and armed guards. Ahead of me there was nothing but an endless stretch of interminable years. At last I must pay the piper. Only a few days before I had passed my twenty third birthday in the Chelan county jail. Now, if I lived to be sixty, I would still be in jail. Perhaps I would be unlucky and live to be seventy, increasing my time behind the bars to fifty years.

Turning, I shook hands with my lawyer and thanked him for his efforts. I then embraced my father, whose eyes had welled with bitter tears. There was nothing left for us to say to one another. Chief Criminal Deputy, Ray True and Officer O.M. Bice led me to the hallway leading to a cell in the jail. I realized that within just a few moments I would be sealed up tight in a steel cubicle and would have little chance of escape. If I was to make my bid for freedom, it had to be here and now. Without a moment for thought, planning or consequences, I turned on Deputy True and drove my fist into the pit of his stomach. I turned to run down the hall but was stopped cold by Deputy Bice who smashed his fist on the bridge of my nose, breaking it. We slugged it out, toe to toe, but I was no match for this powerful officer. He proceeded to knock me unconscious with the butt of his pistol.

When I regained consciousness I was dimly aware of many people milling around. Bice was standing over me with the muzzle of his 38 Police Special pointed between my eyes. He muttered menacingly, "One move out of you and I'll kill you." I snarled, "You had better do it now, you son-of-a-bitch, because I'm going to live for the day when I can snuff you."

By this time three city police had joined the melee. They turned me over on my stomach, wrenched my arms behind my back and clapped handcuffs on my wrists. I felt my right shoe being removed and a bulky heavy brogan being placed on my foot. I instinctively knew I was being fitted with the cruel Oregon Boot*. My fears were realized when I was jerked to my feet and hustled to the jail's padded cell. My face was smeared with my own blood. It was determined that I was far too dangerous to be housed with the other prisoners. I was consigned to a maximum security single cell.

The following morning when I was awakened, I could not breathe through my nose. It definitely had been broken. The pain was excruciating. I called the jailor, telling him that I needed a doctor. He took one look at my

*A device invented by a con in the Oregon prison. It consisted of a large work boot. Riveted around the ankle was an inch thick band of steel, hinged in the back, enabling it to open and shut like a shackle. Down each side from the steel collar and going under the foot was a steel band. Welded to the bottom of the band was a steel ball. It weighed approximately seventeen pounds.

face, which was black and blue and encrusted with blood. Without hesitation he called in reinforcements to take me from the cell. He then called Sheriff Tom Cannon and asked permission to transport me to the Deaconess Hospital. There was little doubt in my mind that they would have gladly left me in the cell to survive as best I could had they not been fearful of my family's reaction.

When I arrived at the emergency room I was approached by Dr. Sawyer who was a neighbor of my family. He probed my nostrils with an instrument that had a cotton ball on one end. When the probe would run into bone and cartilage in my nostrils, he would continue to probe to clear the passageway. He performed this procedure without benefit of an anesthetic. I screamed in pain. When I felt that I was going to pass out, he finally stopped probing and inserted a roll of gauze into each nostril. Before returning me to the deputies he said, "Normally I would have injected you with morphine. However, the pain and suffering you have caused your family and your friends is something I shall never forget. It is about time that you learn what suffering is about." Only then did he inject me with a painkiller.

A week later when the gauze was to be removed from my nostrils, a nurse was called to my cell. She simply yanked out the gauze and I bled profusely for a brief time. At no point during the following weeks did I cease to plan the death of Deputy Bice and Dr. Sawyer. I was obsessed with the belief that they, among others, were responsible for my predicament. If I had stopped to count the number of persons whom I had mentally consigned to death, it would be an imposing list.

Shortly after the hospital incident I was visited by my attorney, Lawrence Leahy. He told me I was to be delivered to the warden at the state prison within a week. I realized that once they locked me in that institution, escape would be extremely difficult. With this realization in mind I decided to devise a plan of escape before the week was out.

When the jailor brought my breakfast of lukewarm oatmeal and two slices of bread, I asked him for a cigarette and a match. If the jailor had been alert he would have realized that I did not smoke; however, I believe he felt sorry for me and was happy to bring the articles I requested. I was not interested in the cigarette, but I had to have the matches. The only utensil I was allowed to eat with, other than a tin bowl, was a spoon. As soon as the jailor left, I gulped down the oatmeal and bread and then immediately put my plan into action. It was my intent to sharpen the spoon handle by rubbing it on the heavy canvas wall of the padded cell. I worked laboriously the rest of the day sharpening the utensil. I intended to dig the padding from behind the canvas, touch a match to it to create a lot of smoke, then I would call the jailor and tell him my cell was on fire. I believed that he would open the door immediately because of the danger of my burning.

Everything went according to plan with the exception of one major hitch. The padding caught fire and began to burn out of control. At this point I was fearful for my life and I screamed loudly for the jailor. He did not respond immediately and I quickly succumbed to the smoke. I awoke in the Deaconess hospital. Two nurses were administering oxygen. For four days I did nothing but vomit. Sheriff Cannon advised the hospital administrator that I was very definitely an escape risk, and convinced him that restraints were necessary. Reluctantly, the administrator permitted the sheriff to padlock a length of dog chain around my waist and extend it to the chain binding my legs.

For a few days I was too ill to give thought to running. On the morning of the fifth day a nurse came in to give me an alcohol rub. She observed that my ankles were chaffed and bleeding from the chains. She examined my stomach and saw that the waist-chain had left deep impressions in my flesh. She didn't say a word to me but left the room slamming the door behind her. About fifteen minutes later she returned with the administrator, threw my blankets back, and in a cold voice said, "Mr. Burney, I want you to see what the chains have done to this patient. Look at those ankles and then see how tight the chain is around his waist. I refuse to attend him under these conditions. This is a hospital and not a torture chamber. Other than the question of morals, what do you think his family is going to do when they see how irresponsibly we have treated this boy? They would have a perfect lawsuit against the county and this hospital. Unless something is done immediately, I am prepared to resign!" The hospital official simply said, "Nurse, I will call the sheriff right now and demand that the patient's chains be removed. If he refuses, I will discharge the patient, I want you to know how much I appreciate your bringing this deplorable condition to my attention." Later in the day the nurse came to my bedside, "Glenn, they are going to return you to the county jail tomorrow afternoon. Other than to rub your ankles and stomach with a salve, there is nothing I can do for you."

This was a turn of events I had not anticipated. As sick as I was, I forced myself to concoct another escape plan. I was aware that I had to make my break from the hospital for I knew that once I was returned to the maximum confinement cell my opportunities for a crash-out were nil. My devious mind, never still for a moment, was soon devising yet another scheme to escape, or to at least delay my transfer to the state prison. Finally, I decided that I would feign an appendicitis attack, which I did early in the morning on the day I was to be taken back to the county jail. My phony symptoms must have had a ring of authenticity. The head nurse came to my bedside, asked me a few questions, took my pulse and probed gently on my lower right abdominal area. When she did this, I doubled up in feigned pain. She left the room and returned with the doctor. He took a blood sample and probed in the same manner as the nurse did, eliciting the same practiced response I had used on the nurse.

I certainly was not ready for the rapid sequence of events that followed. I was placed on a gurney, prepped, wheeled into the operating room and was given ether all within a matter of an hour. When I awoke my appendix had been removed. For two or three days I was so sick from the ether and operation that I gave no further thought to taking it on the lam. Somewhere along the line, Prosecutor Lynn Gemmill smelled a rat. He summoned Sheriff Tom Cannon to his office and bluntly told him, "Tom, we've got to get rid of this miserable bastard. Make arrangements to transfer him to the state penitentiary as soon as possible, like tomorrow morning. Get him on his way!"

The following morning I was awakened by a nurse who was accompanied by the sheriff and his deputy. They removed my fetters. I was pulled to a sitting position on the bed and leg irons were fitted to my ankles. Once again, the dreaded Oregon Boot was placed on my foot. A few minutes later an orderly brought me a bowl of oatmeal and a glass of milk. My groin area hurt but I was too damn stubborn to utter a word about my discomfort. After I had finished eating, I was wheel-chaired to the elevator and hustled down to the emergency floor. A police car was there waiting. I was placed in the back seat and our trip to the state prison began. It was undoubtedly the longest journey I had ever made.

Not one word passed between me and the officers in the front seat. About an hour later we stopped at a roadside cafe for lunch. When I saw they were preparing to march me into the restaurant in front of dozens of diners wearing my boot and chains on display, I refused to budge. I demanded that they take off my fetters. I suggested it would be agreeable to handcuff me to one of them and we could go in in that manner. Sheriff Cannon refused to give in to my demands. He turned to his deputy and instructed, "Link, you go on in and order three sandwiches to go. I'll stay in the car with Williams." About an hour's ride from the penitentiary, I realized I had to urinate. I felt as if my bladder was going to burst. Suddenly an idea hit me. I quietly urinated in my pants and all over the car seat. I sat there throughout the rest of the trip smug in what I had done.

The odor in the enclosed vehicle became unbearable. Finally, Tom Cannon whirled in the front seat and screamed at me, "You rotten bastard! I ought to blackjack your head." I laughed uproariously. In my warped way of thinking, I had evened the score to some extent. I could stand the misery of riding in a urine-soaked car as long as they, too, were miserable. I gleaned much pleasure from the knowledge that those vermin had to ride all the way back to Wenatchee with the stench I had created. It was comforting to me for many days to realize how long it would take to rid that vehicle of the smell of urine. Oh, happy day!

At long last, the car pulled onto the prison grounds. What a horribly bleak scene; high walls and gun towers. We pulled up in front of the first tower. The guard called down from his little nest and said, "Officers, I am going to lower a bucket in which I want you to place your weapons. You cannot enter the main gate carrying guns." After he had pulled the bucket up, he instructed them to proceed at a very slow pace to the main entrance. We were met by the captain of the guards, M.E. Ellege. I was helped from the back seat of the prowl car. The captain took one look at me and said, "What the hell has happened here?" The deputy told him the complete story, adding, "Here is one of the meanest sons-of-bitches we have had to deal with. Thank God, he's your problem now." The captain stepped back, looked me over for a full minute and drawled, "When we get through with him, he will be a pussycat and will purr when we give him an order." At no time in life could I envision myself living with a broken spirit. Thus began my life sentence.

2

BRUSH WITH DEATH

When most boys have reached the age of 11, they are consumed with the idea of being a fireman or a policeman. Not Glenn Williams. From the time I was about 10 years of age, my burning desire was to be a gangster; preferably a machine gun-carrying hood. I had seen enough movies to convince me that that style of life would be beyond my wildest dream. To the distraction of my family, I emulated all the characteristics of Al 'Scar-Face' Capone, Machine Gun Kelly, Alvin (Creepy) Karpis, Legs Diamond and a legion of other infamous mobsters. I would affect a strut that my young mind conjured as being the way Hit Men would walk. If I had been able to, I would have dressed as they did. I read every story I could get my hands on that portrayed the activities of gun runners, drug smugglers and bank robbers. Such movies were forbidden to me by my mother and dad. Often I would lie to them about what show I was going to see at one of the town's two theaters. At this time they were not aware that I was a devious boy, and that I would go to the type picture they objected to.

It was during this period of time that I developed an unreasonable hatred of uniforms. That kind of dress represented authority and discipline. It was during these formative years that I found myself hating cops. Teachers were another form of authority that I could not tolerate. My resistance became so ingrained in my psyche that I would take umbrage and strike out with my fists at any teacher who attempted to control my behavior. It wasn't long before the inevitable occurred, my confrontation with the police. At first my pranks amounted to juvenile escapades which were attributed to as 'that Williams youngster sowing his wild oats'. They would pick me up, give me a lecture and return me to my parents. My father would administer his usual punishment, a harsh whipping with a limb from an apple tree. That action did not deter me.

Before I reached my twelfth birthday, I became the target of a 'shoot-crazy' deputy sheriff, Ky Baker. It was an experience that could have easily resulted in my death. Beyond any doubt, that incident catapulted me into a career of unbelievable criminal activity that extended over the next four decades. It included forty years of robbing banks, financial institutions and grocery stores, smuggling guns and a number of shoot outs with my natural enemies, the police. And finally a cell in Alcatraz where I was lodged alongside the dangerous criminals I had copied from my early youth. The incident to which I refer occurred in Wenatchee, Washington. Even existing in that village was a nightmare. It was a poverty-stricken, moribund

9

town well before the Hoover-created depression of 1929. With the exception of a brief seasonal transfusion of financial blood, which occurred when the fruit crops were harvested, there was nothing to sustain life. What little vibrancy there was, it was extinguished when the fruit warehouses signaled the end of life for the winter months by discharging the workers and closing down, a ritual that was as certain as the rising of the sun. And there were other inevitable certainties in the form of hunger and cold throughout the terribly frigid months that followed, months when fuel for heat was as scarce as sufficient food.

The only fuel company worthy of note was owned by a congenial fellow named Harry Whiteman. Behind his little office building were three sheds. In these sheds, Harry stored his supply of coal. The railroad tracks ran alongside the sheds. Each fall and winter iron coal cars would line up waiting for Harry's men to unload them. This was accomplished by placing a long metal chute from the cars into the shed's coal bins. Then laborers would start shoveling the precious cargo into the chutes. Some chunks of coal would fall from the chutes and land on the ground. For years, the poor would gather beside the chutes and pick up what little fell off and take it home for burning in their kitchen stoves. Normally, the homes of the poor would have a single stove and, logically it would be in the kitchen in order to create heat for the cooking and, at the same time, heat the rest of the home. The affluent who, of course, were not relegated to scavenging, could boast of possessing two stoves. And the coal bins in their basements were well filled. Those who gathered coal from alongside the tracks had no other source of fuel. What they amassed was truly a Godsend in this poverty-stricken burg.

For nothing better to do, I would go down to the coal yard and watch the men, women and children scramble for their pittance. It wasn't long until I detected the shovelers deliberately tossing sizeable chunks off the chutes for future recovery. This had to be done carefully because Whiteman's foreman was ever on the alert to protect his employer's interests. Somewhere along the line a stool pigeon informed the owner of this practice. Eventually a man was stationed alongside the chutes so he could pick up the larger pieces and toss them into the bins. As soon as the cars were emptied, as if on signal, people would jump into them and sweep up the remaining coal dust. As the years have passed, I look back and think of how demeaning and pathetic it must have been for the underprivileged to be reduced to this station just to exist. Adding insult to injury, Whiteman conferred with his attorney concerning the people who hopped into the coal cars. In answer to his query, the lawyer assured him that the folks were, in fact, trespassers. Apparently, he decided it would not be in his best interest in the community to charge the transgressors. After all, it was a small village and there was bound to be a repercussion. My father had learned of Whiteman's consideration in this matter from the local superior court judge, W.O. Parr. I never forgot my father's comment when he said, "Everyone who walks down the street greeting everybody with a smile and handshake is not necessarily a good person. Such indiscriminate greetings are not from a man who loves his fellow men."

I was an aggressive and enterprising youngster whose energies were not always directed toward worthy deeds. Some friends told me that all the persons who gathered coal were not always disposed to using it for cooking, but were actually peddling it for twenty five cents for each gunny sack full. This bit of information fueled my inquisitive mind. Why couldn't I gather that valuable commodity and make a bit of money? And this I did. However, it was a lengthy task to pick up a gunny sack of coal. Sometimes it would take all day to accomplish this feat; and for a measly quarter. I devised a scheme by which I could do much better than pick the fuel up from the ground in competition with a dozen other scavengers. I met with two friends, Timmy and Robert and shared my plans with them. "Listen", I started out, "why can't we go down to the fuel yard at night, break into the shed and take all the coal we need and then peddle it?" My enthusiasm was contagious so we formed an evil alliance. We met by the railroad tracks that night and decided the best way to get into the shed. Timmy spoke up, "Glenn, we can pry the shed door open and squeeze you through. You can fill the sacks from within and pass them out to us." We had no trouble filling three sacks within fifteen minutes. They were loaded onto our coaster wagon and we were in business. The following day we disposed of the coal at one house. Imagine, each of us had two bits, and the work was easy and somewhat thrilling. We repeated our first night's task again and again. Greed soon took over. Why take three sacks when it would be just as simple to take six sacks? We would have taken more but our wagon was not designed to carry that weight. We decided it would be a good idea to steal a larger and stronger wagon. And we planned to do just that. But unseen events shot our plans to hell.

Our customers were getting suspicious. Here were three kids who had developed a regular route with steady buyers. Where was that amount of coal coming from? An older boy, Carl Richardson, figured what we were doing, and threatened to beat hell out of me if I didn't cut him in on the take. I told him to go f—k off, and the fight was on. It was only a matter of a few minutes before I had taken all the beating I could stand, so I agreed to take him in as a partner. However, in my mind I was determined to get even with Carl. One evening in the local ball park, I challenged the tough to another encounter. Both Timmy and Robert begged me not to fight Carl again. They were afraid for my welfare, but they did not know of my plan. The night we met in the park to settle our differences, I was carrying a lead pipe about 10 inches long. It was concealed under my belt. Even with this advantage, I was afraid. Nevertheless, the fat was in the fire, and the donnybrook started hot and heavy. Carl rushed me off balance and started hitting me in the face. He took about three swings when I brought the pipe into action. One swat above his temple and it was all over. Carl collapsed to the ground. I had inflicted a cut over his eye. He immediately called it quits. As he left the park, he called out. "I'm going to get you for this." In my new found bravado, I took after him menacingly, but he had had enough and fled.

Our good luck with the coal business collapsed. Somebody called Mr. Whiteman and told him the whole story; that Glenn Williams, Timmy

Weathers and Robert Teas were burglarizing his establishment, stealing coal and selling it to regular customers. The sheriff's office was informed and a trap was set. On that fateful night, Timmy, Robert and I were loading our purloined loot into the wagon. Just as we were preparing to trudge up the road with it, a voice bellowed out, "Hold it right there!" With a sinking heart, I recognized the voice as belonging to Sheriff Pete Wheeler. He was accompanied by two deputies, Ray True and Ky Baker. We were blinded by powerful flashlights. In a town as small as Wenatchee, everybody knew everybody else. The officers knew us, had observed our activity and were fully aware we were pre-teenagers. Yet each held a fully loaded pistol aimed directly at us. Timmy and Robert obeyed the officer's command. On an impulse I decided to make a break for it. I bolted toward an apple orchard across the railroad tracks. I knew that once I reached the trees I would be safe. It was pitch dark and there was no way they could spot me among the trees. Their flashlights would prove useless. I had just reached a shed at the edge of the orchard and was starting to put that building between me and the cops, when the quiet of the night was shattered by gun fire. I was horrified. Just as I darted around the building, I heard a bullet slam into the boards of the shed. Whoever was firing was shooting at me. He had to be firing at the noise I was making. Thank God it was too dark for the gunman to shoot accurately.

As soon as I reached the security of the trees, I fell face down and lay perfectly still, listening for pursuers. Someone yelled out, "For Christ's sake, Ky, stop that f—king shooting! Do you want to kill that kid? Let me run him down." I could hear one of the deputies as he took off in my general direction. Had I not panicked and got up to flee I would have been safe. There was no way he could have located me in the dark of night buried in tall grass. But I was fearful and used poor judgement in resuming my flight. The cop was hot on my heels, but he was no match for a fleet-footed fear-driven youth. I headed in the direction of the Columbia river. About six blocks away, I saw the outline of an abandoned fruit warehouse. I sought refuge inside. I waited for what seemed like an eternity before I ventured out. There was no noise so I stealthily crept out and started in the direction of my parent's house. I hadn't gone 30 feet before I was swept into the arms of the waiting officer. He held me in a crushing bear-hug until I stopped struggling. "Now you stand real still. Quit fighting me or I'll split your head open with this flashlight." I meekly surrendered. He tightened a pair of handcuffs on my wrists. Only then did I recognize my captor as deputy Ray True. There was no resistance left in me. Together we marched back to the others. I could see that Timmy and Robert were cuffed also. As I write this, I look back and laugh at what ridiculous fools the local cops made of themselves. They knew who we were, and could have gone to our houses the next day and picked us up. In fact, our parents would have taken us into police headquarters if the cops had requested. I now can only believe that they got their kicks out of making a big town case of the incident. We were loaded into a prowl car and started our journey to the county jail.

About eight the next morning, someone decided that, inasmuch as our crime was committed in the city, we should have been lodged in that bastille,

12

so they transported us to the custody of the city's lock-up. A concern entered our minds. What must our parents think when we failed to show up at home last night? About nine o'clock, the cell door was opened and a jailor summoned us to follow him. We were led down a narrow hallway to an isolated room. It was bare with the exception of a swivel chair sitting directly in the center under a single bright light suspended from the ceiling. Sheriff Wheeler and his deputies Baker and True were with him. Each of the cops smiled with that sort of 'well, we captured them, didn't we' look. The sheriff opened the comments saying, "Now listen, boys, we caught you red-handed so all of us know you are guilty of burglary. In addition to getting a confession from you, we want the names of all the people you sold the coal to. If you cooperate with us, we will see you get off pretty easy. If you get stubborn, we will send you to the reformatory. Let's start with you, Glenn. Tell us what we want to know." Oddly enough, this was the way the flatfeet did their questioning in the movies I had seen. Apparently the officers had watched the same features. My mind was so conditioned to the scene I was experiencing, I really thought the old third degree methods would be employed. It did not dawn on me that these goons would not dare physically abuse us. Our parents would crack their asses in court. Another part of the scenario was the one that had appealed to my imaginative mind, and that was the fact that real gangsters would not stoop to being a stool pigeon. With this foremost in my mind, I reacted as I was certain Al Capone would. I blurted out, "To hell with you, pig dung, I ain't snitching." Timmy and Robert stood with their mouths agape. Ky Baker grabbed me by the collar and dragged me to the doorway. "I'll slam this one in an isolation cell, Pete, and you get the information from the other two." Timmy and Robert, seeing how roughly I had been handled spilled their guts to the satisfaction of the cops.

I had fallen asleep in the solitary cell. The clanging of the door awakened me. Standing in the entrance was my dad. His face was beet-red. "Get on your feet, Glenn, and come home with me." When he got me home, he followed me to my bedroom. The switch he was carrying came down across my back and shoulders dozens of times. He quit punishing me only when he was exhausted. Before he left my room, he said, "There will be a continuation of this tomorrow and each day thereafter until you learn to behave."

Confinement to my room for a week was part of the disciplining process my dad and mother imposed on me. Before the week had passed, my folks had mellowed somewhat and we started communicating. I don't know what prompted me to approach my dad on a subject that had begun to wear on me. It was the shooting that took place the night of my arrest. In that week, I grew up a great deal. I realized what could have happened. I could have been killed. Imagine what my family would have had to withstand had that occurred. For the first time in my life, I was beginning to consider others. When I had an opportunity to get mom and dad alone, I told them I had a very serious matter to discuss with them. We went to their bedroom and I opened up. "Folks," I started out, "I'm sure you remember the rumor going about the shooting taking place about a week ago. Well, I have to tell you that Ky Baker tried to shoot me at the time of my arrest." My parents stood there dumbfounded, not uttering a word. This encouraged me to continue. "I started to run when the police ordered us to come out with our hands up, and I heard the firing a minute or two later." Dad interrupted, "Did it dawn on you, Glenn, that whoever was doing the shooting could have fired overhead to scare you? You mentioned Ky Baker. How do you know it was him?" I replied, "I heard one of the cops, either Ray True or someone else, call out to Ky and order him to stop shooting." Dad thought this over for a minute and continued, "In all probability, he was aiming in the air and hoped to scare some sense into you." I became angry and shouted, "No, Dad, that isn't the way it was. I was going around a shed at the end of the orchard, when I heard a bullet splat into the board near my head." Then my mother interjected, "I'll tell you what, son, let's mark this up to a worthwhile lesson for you. If what you say is true, a terrible tragedy could have happened. You must realize that you alone are responsible for this whole affair. Now you go out and play. I want to discuss things with your father."

Later, my brother, Dan, told me that dad and he went down to Whiteman's fuel yard and retraced the route where I had attempted to escape. When they came to the shed, both of them examined the boards carefully. Finally, Dan called out to dad, "Look here what I found. It sure as hell is a bullet hole." He told me that dad came back and carefully examined the hole. Without a word dad paced off about thirty feet from the shed, pulled his 38 Police Positive from a holster and fired a bullet next to the one Dan had discovered. It matched perfectly. Dad simply stared at the hole for a minute or two and faced Dan. "Son, I want your word that this will not be mentioned. You rest assured I will confront the sheriff and Ky Baker in the near future, and there will be hell to pay."

Some months later, Ray True, who had always been a friend of my father's came to the house to see dad. Had it not been for the fact that Dan always enjoyed the confidence of dad, I may never have learned the details of dad's investigation. And certainly what Ray told him that evening confirmed what dad had suspicioned. The deputy asked my parents not to reveal the nature of their conversation. Otherwise Ray would have been fired. In essence, what Ray revealed to dad, was exactly what I had told him. Ray did not know that dad and Dan had gone down to the scene of the fracas and had discovered the bullet hole. Dan later learned that my father had returned to the shed the following day and measured the height from the ground to the hole. He later measured my height. He was horrified to determine that the slug had entered the shed at a level with my head. His temper smoldered for days. It got to the point where he could contain himself no longer. He called Pete Wheeler and asked for an interview with him and Ky Baker. The sheriff was wary of my father's request and tried to put him off. Dad was not one to be stalled. He demanded an immediate interview, or as he put it to the worried official, "I will go to the local paper and reveal an incident that will embarrass you, and you cannot afford adverse publicity so near your running for office again." The meeting was set for the following day. Dad took Dan with him as a witness. Dan observed dad putting his revolver in his holster and buttoning his coat.

They met in the sheriff's office at the courthouse. Wheeler, ever affable, offered his hand to dad. Ky did likewise, but he was ignored by the obviously irate parent. Dad came to the point. "Pete, my son tells me that one of your officers opened fire on him the night he was arrested for stealing coal. The sheriff, already quite sure why dad had demanded the interview, responded quickly. "Yeah, Merritt, I knew you would be wanting an explanation. Let me tell you what Ky did. In an effort to scare the hell out of Glenn, he emptied his gun into the air. Both of us figured that that would be a lesson your kid would never forget." My dad simply stared at the officer. Finally he said, "Pete, I figured your answer out a week ago. It is logical but you are full of bull shit. This miserable coward sitting here to my right fired at my boy." With this, Ky jumped to his feet, as did Dad. Both faced one another ready to shoot it out. Ky's face was flushed. He sat down. "What's the matter, afraid to confront an armed adult?" my father taunted. While this was taking place, Wheeler jumped up and yelled, "Merritt, you are making a serious accusation. Can you back that claim up?" "You're Goddam right I can. My other boy, who is standing right here, and I went to the area where the shooting took place. About four feet from the ground there is a bullet hole in one of the boards. The bullet, had it hit Glenn, would have entered his head." Ky was as white as a sheet. Pete Wheeler just fastened his eyes on Baker. Dad and Dan walked out, and the incident was never mentioned again.

About six weeks after that dangerous confrontation, Dan called me out to the back yard. Without a word, he drove his fist into my face. I was flattened on the ground, blood streaming from the cut over my eye. I started to get to my feet but was floored again. I figured the better part of wisdom was for me to remain down. My brother stood over me with his fists still clenched, and in a cold voice, said, "Why don't you get out of town? You're a worthless bastard who has embarrassed every member of this family. You're a liar, a thief and a coward. You haven't got enough brains to realize that your father could have been killed a few weeks ago, or that he could have slain a cop and would have spent years in prison. Mom would have lost a husband and us kids would have lost a loving dad. Frankly, I wished Ky's bullet had split your skull in two." Dan was never very friendly to me for years afterward.

I recognized in Dan many of my father's characteristics. Like Dad, he never forgot or forgave. My father was never satisfied with his confrontation with Pete Wheeler and Ky Baker over the shooting incident. He was indiscriminate in his attacks on Pete Wheeler. He publicly declared that a recall of Pete Wheeler was in order. When questioned about his accusations, Dad would simply say, "If what I am stating is not true, then Wheeler and Baker have grounds for a suit. I have been calling them liars and thugs. Doesn't it seem peculiar to you that neither of them has confronted me, nor have they denied the charges that I have laid at their doorstep?" Wheeler tried to leave the impression that my parent was unreasonably irate over the fact that the sheriff had had to arrest his son. My father was relentless in his attack. Finally, the sheriff sent word to dad that any further such comments would lead to a confrontation in court. Dad was not impressed by the threat. He mounted a still more vitriolic attack accusing the sheriff of being involved in boot- legging, pimping and controlling criminal activities throughout his bailiwick. It appeared to many people who knew my father well that he was trying to bait the law enforcement officer into a physical confrontation. At one point, the prosecutor called my father and told him that Wheeler was preparing to file a suit for defamation of character. Dad's response was so typical of my father: "He has no character to defame."

In the summer of 1928, Federal Prohibition Agent, Ludwig P. Johnson of Spokane, lay in the Cascade Sanitarium at Leavenworth, Washington mortally wounded by Sheriff Wheeler and Deputy Ralph Hand in a gun battle on Mountain Road near the town of Leavenworth. According to the account of the accidental shooting—or deliberate execution, as some believed——given by Wheeler to the Wenatchee Daily World, the sheriff had known that a still was running above Leavenworth and his deputies had been watching it for several days. On the evening of July 25th, they decided that it was about time for the operators to begin drawing off their liquor. The officers went there to apprehend them. Sheriff Wheeler stated to the press, "We, Hand and I, went to the place after 10:00 o'clock last night, but in the darkness we were not sure of our location and went back to the city reservoir to locate ourselves. After doing this, we proceeded at once in the direction of the Icicle Canal. The still was located about a quarter of a mile above the canal. Hand and I dismantled the still and started carrying the apparatus back to our car. Just as we reached the car, I heard someone say, 'Throw up your hands or I'll shoot hell out of you'. I swung around to see a man jabbing a gun in Hand's face. The deputy reached out with his left arm and swept the gun downward, his assailant firing. Ralph drew his gun and began to shoot, and I did also as soon as I could get my gun out. Just as I squeezed one round off at Ralph's assailant, I heard the crack of guns from up the canal. All this took place quicker than I can tell it. Johnson, who was opposite to Ralph, shot three times as Ralph emptied his own gun. A number of shots rang out from unseen persons behind a bunch of boulders. Their first slug grazed my wrist and, as I jumped behind my car, a second bullet creased my neck. Just then Johnson fell, saying as he did so, 'You've shot me and I am a federal officer'. From up the ditch in the direction of whoever was firing at Hand and me, a voice called out and identified themselves as federal agents, Gerald Church and Arthur G. Means, and ordered us 'to stick 'em up.' I shouted back and told them I was the sheriff of Chelan county. The firing ceased. The four of us loaded Johnson into the car and drove at once to the Leavenworth hospital. From there I called Dr. Condon of Wenatchee and he came as quickly as possible. I had fired once at Johnson but three times at Church and Means, neither of whom was hit. I would not have fired at them except that I thought they were bootleggers. We did not know they were federal agents until Johnson fell."

The federal agent died three days later of five bullet wounds. Rumors were flying thick and fast. Some said the agent had stopped thirteen slugs which, if true, meant that Wheeler or Hand had to reload his weapon. The most consistent rumor of all insisted that the sheriff and his deputy were removing a still that belonged to them, contending that they might otherwise have destroyed it. The furor that came from the federal government was loud and long. An immediate investigation took place. When the government agents presented their evidence before a grand jury, Sheriff Wheeler and his co- defendants were indicted on 31 separate charges including everything from the possession of liquor to kidnapping. Their trial took place in January 1931. The jury deadlocked after 65 hours of deliberation. Federal Judge L. Stanley Webster discharged the defendants. Wheeler ran for office again but was roundly defeated. He faded from public life and died at 94 years of age.

3

LEATHER ASS

Let me explain how I earned the title "Leather Ass Williams". Despite my father's conviction that my first encounter with the law would be my last, I didn't remain under wraps for long. A rash of burglaries prompted the local newspaper to carry an article informing the citizens of these crimes. The hapless police were going out of their minds trying to arrest the responsible parties. Many older known criminals were picked up and interrogated mercilessly. Some were framed and sent away. I know this because the very crimes for which they had been convicted, were jobs that I had committed. Although I knew they were innocent, I wasn't about to come forward and cop-out. The police were certain that those imprisoned were not guilty. The victims were without funds with which to hire counsel. Deputy sheriff, Link Seibert, once told my father that it was necessary to convict someone to assuage the public's outrage, and to get the cops off the bite-of-the-line. The part that bothered them was that though some of the crimes were 'solved', why did they, with the same modus operandi, continue to be committed? I don't think John Q. Public gave this much consideration.

Just why I became involved in acts of vandalism and theft would be difficult to determine. I have given it much thought, and as closely as I can recall, the idea occurred to me when I was playing in a vacant house. I would find things of interest and steal them. My parents were both moral and strict, and they impressed upon all of us children that we must observe the Golden Rule. My brothers and sisters never became involved in illegal activities. Out of six children, why me? I best answered this by saying, "How in the hell do I know, or give a damn." That was my attitude for as long as I can remember. I always experienced a feeling of excitement and exhilaration; an anticipation that invariably overwhelmed me. To violate the law and get away with it became a challenge. Even at this tender age, I prided myself on being an expert on a 'job'.

Entering empty houses became a bore. There was very little to be taken from an unoccupied residence. I thought this over and decided to burglarize houses when the occupants were out. There was always some kind of loot in a home where people lived. It wasn't unusual for me to burglarize three or four homes a week. What was valuable to a young boy? Sometimes a knife, small coins or a trinket that would normally interest a kid. The night I came across a loaded revolver will never be forgotten. A feeling of euphoria consumed me. I had in my possession the very instrument that was essential to my role of becoming a Hood. It was the difference of being at the mercy of an arresting officer, or finding myself in full control. In my aberrated thinking, it was the difference between life and death. For the first time in my life, I was totally fascinated with an object, a deadly weapon. I spent hours in the mountains practicing marksmanship. It was amazing how accurately I could shoot after a few weeks constant practice. As I look back, I wonder why the clerk in Wells and Wade Hardware did not become suspicious of a mere lad buying boxes of 38 caliber shells.

One day, while at recess at school, the gun fell from under my pants onto the ground. At least a dozen kids saw it. I became the center of attention as they gathered around me to examine the pistol. I showed them how to unload and re-load it. As I was reveling at the attention I was getting, I glanced up and saw my teacher, Gladys Holcomb, coming in my direction at a dead run. Without thinking, I immediately took off running from the grounds. She did not attempt to pursue me. Realizing there was a strong possibility of losing my beloved 'plaything', I carefully wrapped it in a piece of canvas and concealed it under an elm tree on a corner lot. I skipped school for the rest of the day. When I returned home, my mother grabbed me by the ear, dragged me into the kitchen and demanded. "Give me that gun!" I pretended I didn't know what she was talking about. She took a long piece of wood from the fire box and proceeded to beat me over the back and legs. I was obdurate and would not admit I had a pistol. After she was exhausted from administering the whipping, she said, "You go straight to your room and don't budge until your father gets home." I laid on my bed petrified with fear. My dad was a person you couldn't bluff. I heard him come in the front door. I shuddered. After a few minutes I heard him climbing the stairs. He walked into my room and simply stared at me. After what seemed an age, he spoke with carefully measured words. "Son, you know why I am here. Without any problem between you and me, I want you to take me to the gun. If you do, I will not punish you. We will have to, however, return it to where ever you got it, but I will not punish you. You must understand how dangerous this situation has become. You don't seem to understand what might result from having a firearm in your possession. Where is it?" I knew full well what dad would do if I did not tell him, yet I couldn't bear to part with what I considered to be a part of me. From out of nowhere a spontaneous reply came to my lips. "Dad," I lied, "that was not a real gun. It was a cap gun I found on my way to school this morning." A look of relief come over my father's face. "Glenn, I want to believe you. In the first place, where would you get a real gun? I want you to show me the cap gun." "It is in the irrigation ditch. I threw it there before I got home." I replied. "Why," he asked, "would you throw it away if it was a plaything?" My response came easily. "I knew you would whip me for the trouble I caused at school." He peered at me intently for a full minute, walked to the door leading downstairs, turned and said, "I want to believe you, but if I ever learn that you have lied to me about this incident, I'll make you wish you had never been born." I waited a few days before going to the base of the elm tree to retrieve the weapon. To my dismay, it was gone. Apparently someone had observed me concealing it and picked it up later. I never saw it again. I was heartbroken.

I began staying away from home until late at night, refusing to give my parents a logical alibi; there simply was no alibi. I had diversified my unlawful activity. I learned that sometimes, people would foolishly leave personal items in their cars overnight. And to make it easier, they failed to lock the doors of the vehicles. Neither my mother or father suspected that I was stealing. They could not understand why I kept running away, but they refused to attach my waywardness to an illegal act on my part. Both parents had tried everything they could think of to straighten me out. Nothing worked. When they would withhold my privileges and confine me to my room, I would find a way to escape from the house. In my own peculiar way, I adored them, but my love was no match for a strong will and abnormal contempt for discipline. My insatiable desire to be a gangster defied all treatment. I could not wait until I was old enough to go east, and join ranks with the scum of American society, Hoodlums. It surprised me that so many persons would keep guns in their automobiles. But what a pleasant surprise. Within a month, I had a number of guns; rifles, shotguns, pistols and ammunition.

My downfall started long before 1927, but it was in that year that my folks were fully awakened to the fact that their offspring was well on his way to becoming a confirmed criminal. It happened one Saturday morning when my mother came into my bedroom to clean. She began to peel the blankets off my bed when she found that under the blankets were a couple of rifles. I had put them there and tightened the covers so the outline of the weapons wouldn't show. My brother Dan, who was with her at the time, later told me that she didn't say a word. She simply sat in a chair and gazed at my personal arsenal. A few minutes later, she obviously decided to clear the air once and for all. She lifted the lid of my foot locker, removed some old newspapers and saw loot that must have dazed her. She found coins and trivia I had stolen. Under a shoe box she located another loaded revolver. Shocked and sickened, she realized that it was her son whom she had been reading about in the local paper. She bravely resolved that it was imperative that she take a drastic action here and now. She gathered up the ill-gotten gains, walked into the parlor, took me by the arm and marched me out the door. I started to jerk away from her and run out the door, but Dan tripped me and held me to the floor. He twisted my arm behind my back in a very painful hammerlock. When I quit struggling he calmly stated, "You are going with us, either calmly or with your head busted. Make up your mind."

The sergeant behind the desk at the police station stared at the three of us as we marched in. "What's the problem here?" he asked. My mother simply told him the whole story. He looked at me, dumbfounded. He kept staring at the stuff mom had deposited on his desk. "I want to personally see Bob Cochrane, the chief," the irate woman demanded. The officer walked from behind his desk and led us down the hall to the chief's office.

Cochrane couldn't believe his eyes when he saw what she had brought in. "May I talk with you alone, Mr. Cochrane?" my mother asked. He motioned her to a room beside his office. Before she closed the door she looked at Dan and instructed, "If he tries to dash out the door, Dan, I want you to thrash him within an inch of his life." I was always afraid of my older brother, so I caused him no trouble. It seemed to me like they were in that room for hours. The chief came out alone and just scowled at me. He didn't speak to anyone but the sergeant. "Troy, take this punk up to a regular cell and lock him up. Give him no food nor anything to read. Just lock him up and keep him in solitary until you get different orders from me. No one is to visit nor speak to him. Understand?" I was lead away to a cold and narrow cell. I stayed there all day with nothing to eat, seeing no one.

When it started to get dark and my hunger pangs began. I called to the jailor. No response. I started to get panicky. I was awakened from a fitful sleep to find the chief standing outside my door. Beside him was my father. "Glenn, you're going to have to stand trial for many burglaries and related crimes. Even if I could do anything for you, I wouldn't. Your dad is going to take you home, and will return you to the juvenile court when ordered to do so by the judge."

The local papers made small mention of the arrest and recovery of some of the stolen items. Later, I learned that Rufus Woods, editor of the Wenatchee Daily World, out of deference to my youth and respect for my family, did not make banner headlines. The local police were happy with my arrest, though it was accomplished by no effort of their own. The prosecuting attorney 'bargained' with me to cop a plea. He stated that if I pled guilty to the list of crimes the police had compiled, he would make it easier on me when I came to trial. He told me that the judge would take my cooperation into consideration, and would lighten my sentence. I examined the list presented by the cops. There were many crimes contained in it of which I had no part, and I pointed this fact out to him. "It really doesn't matter, Glenn. The list to which you have admitted complicity is a lengthy one. A few more are not going to affect your sentence." Very foolishly I admitted having done them all. The police, therefore, could tell the citizens that they had solved them all.

Again, my family was humiliated by having to be present when the arraignment and sentencing took place in superior court. We agreed to dismiss the usual preliminaries, and I pleaded guilty to three counts of burglary, four of car theft, and nine of malicious vandalism; quite a record for a kid. The most dreadful part of this whole goddamn procedure was my having to listen to the admonitions of this truly compassionate jurist. He mentioned the fact that I had good parents, and that my brothers and sisters were never a source of worry to the officials nor my folks. After his lecture, he sentenced me to an indefinite term to the Washington State Training School.

The unsavory reputation of this vicious institution was well known. The word T O U G H described it perfectly; tough kids, tough staff, super tough discipline. Other rumors seeped from the confines of the "College On The Hill'. Most of the kids whom I met after their release had become confirmed criminals. Actually, as in most penal institutions in this country, it was just another preparatory course for more advanced criminal training. Even today, it never ceases to amaze me how easily the public is deluded into thinking that our prisons serve any purpose other than to dehumanize, degenerate and degrade. The system is nothing more than a commercial venture to warehouse men, women and children. The funniest, and saddest word in the whole criminal justice system's vocabulary is spelled r-e-h-a-b-i-l-i-t-a-t-i-o- n. If you want to get punched out, use the word in front of some bloke whom the guards have rehabilitated.

The good citizens and the hacks were delighted when word got out that I was being transferred to the joint. The traveling guard, Garfield Davis, was to arrive in a day or two to pick up a number of kids and transport them out. The deputies loved to tell me how mean this guard was. "Pull your bullshit on him, boy, and you'll arrive at the school on a stretcher." Another bull chimed in, " Maybe there would be some peace and tranquility in the area; not to mention a degree of safety for citizens' homes, cars and property." From their expressed attitude, you would have thought I was the only trouble-maker within 500 miles. The traveling guard responsible for removing the plague from the burg was well known. His responsibility was to travel to all the towns in the state who had prisoners convicted and ready to be transported to one of the three state institutions; the penitentiary, reformatory or training school. In the many years he had had that job, I had never heard of his losing a prisoner through escape. He was as humane as possible under the trying circumstances. Regardless of age, he thoroughly cuffed and manacled each transferee. He often stated that he had to secure each person in that manner for their and his protection. Years later I heard him defend his tactics when he was addressing a group of Kiwanians. "I have carried men who were homicidal maniacs and others who were determined not to arrive at the pen with me. If they were able to free themselves from the restraints, I would have had to shoot them. If I failed to do this, they might take my life and my weapons. In a situation like this, I have a grave responsibility to society," he concluded.

One morning before daylight, I was roused from a fitful sleep by the jailor who told me that Garfield Davis was there to pick up four other kids and me for the trip to the 'place for intractable kids'. "And let me tell you something you should bear in mind," he said. "Don't f—k with this bird. He has a job to do, and he'll do it. He is determined to deliver you to the superintendent of the school. He has dealt with all kinds of toughies, and you'll be a piece of cake for him." I was ushered into a room and there he stood. He appeared to be a fatherly sort of man, about fifty years of age, grey and stout. As soon as Garfield finished with the other kids, he turned to me and started cuffing me. After he had fitted them, he asked. "Are they too tight, boy?" I assured him they weren't. I was surprised that he was concerned about the comfort of the cuffs. He then adjusted the leg irons asking the same question. After each had been secured, he padlocked a chain around each prisoner's waist, and then threaded a length of dog chain through the waist chains. When we were ready to be loaded in his van, he faced us and said, "Boys, my job is to deliver you to whatever destination is indicated on your transfer papers. I want you to know that that is exactly what I am going to do. If you slip your fetters and make an effort to ramble, I'll have to shoot you. Is that clear? Each of you told me that your cuffs and leg irons were not too tight. I'll not stop and readjust the restraints. The trip should take us about six hours. Our first stop will be at North Bend where we will eat and you'll be permitted to use the bathroom. There will be no other stop. Are there any questions?" No one said a word, so he signaled the jailor to pass his revolver through the bars. I don't know if it was for show or not, but he carefully checked the six bullets in the chamber, slipped it into a holster, buttoned his coat and took us down the stairs to his paddy wagon. It was simply a van with wooden benches on each side. The windows were covered with a cyclone-type screen.

After we had been riding for an hour or so, I whispered to the fellow next to me, "Where you from?" "Ephrata," he shot back. "And the others?" I pressed. "The other three came in from Spokane last night," was his response. My mind was constantly thinking of a way to hit the road before we got to that damn joint. It was a cinch I couldn't break out of the vehicle. Finally, my mind snapped back to what the traveling guard had said after he had us secured. He did say that we would not be stopping until we had reached North Bend, and then we would be fed and permitted to go to the bathroom. I made up my mind to make a break for it when we stopped. I did not know how this could be done, but I figured I would play it by ear. Maybe I could overpower the guard. No, that was stupid thinking. That guy could snap my back with little effort. In that case, I reasoned, I will have to have help. I quietly asked the fellow seated next to me if he was interested in making a getaway. He showed enthusiasm and asked me what plan I had in mind. I told him I wasn't sure, but it would have to be at the time we stopped for lunch. "Here is what we could do if you will help," I suggested. "He will have to take us into the bathroom. When he does, it will be five of us and one of him. I'll jump him and right away you will have to get into the fracas. We'll have to disarm the geezer. Once that is done, we'll take the cuff key and his gun. We will cuff him to something in the toilet, and head out to the van. How does that sound," I asked. "Pretty good", he answered. "I'll spread the word to the others." There was a great deal of low talking among us. We looked at each other and nodded our approval.

It seemed to take forever to reach North Bend. When we did, Garfield pulled the prison van up behind the cafe. He got out, opened the back door and ordered us to step out. I was sick at the sight that greeted us. It was apparent he had called ahead from Wenatchee and asked the state patrol to have reinforcements ready when we pulled up. Damned if there weren't three heavily armed state patrolmen waiting for us. Garfield led the way into the back door of the eatery. Following at the end were the other two cops from the patrol. I was so dismayed I could hardly eat. We were led into the toilet. Two uniformed men stood inside while we relieved ourselves. Garfield and another cop stood outside the door. " Son-of-a- bitch", I muttered to myself, "this Garfield is a smart cookie."

An hour later we were rolling on toward Seattle and the end for us. I don't know how long I slept on the hard bench, but when I woke up we were pulling into the village of Chehalis, the home of the Training School. When we reached he school, it was about three o'clock in the afternoon. We had to drive up a road that had dozens of trees on each side. Looking out the van window, I saw a large group of kids drilling to the beat of a snare drum. Jesus Christ, I thought, military close-order drill. I had heard that they were fruit for this kind of discipline. Also the guards used excessive drilling as a punishment.

Without wasting any time, the guards hustled us to a basement barber shop where they had another inmate shave our heads. From there we were forced to take a cold shower. We were ushered into a room adjoining the shower-room. It was a clothing room, and there we received the issue to be worn by the inmates until the day they were released. Blue denims. The fit was terrible but who gave a damn? After we were dressed, the hacks led us to the dormitory. On each bed were two blankets (no sheets) and a pillow without a cover. Again, the old bull-necked bastard roared out, "Listen carefully, punks, because I won't repeat this. Your name will be on the head of your bed. Never lie on or sit on another bed. Lights are out at nine o'clock. When they go out, if you mutter one word after that until morning, your ass is mud. The bugler will let go at 5:30 AM and you will have five minutes to get to your squad room dressed. That means you will have to hustle your ass. In fact, you will hustle every waking minute you are in this hell-hole. Get used to it." The next stop was downstairs to the squad room. There were rows of hard benches lined up across the room. He seated us there and told us to remain put until it was time to eat. The food was fair, the rules rigid and unreasonable. That night I went to sleep with more mental disturbance than I had ever experienced. I must have awakened a dozen times beset with horrible nightmares. The next morning I was so homesick I felt I could not endure the day.

When the new arrivals were integrated into the main population, they were subject to unbearable vocal abuse, ostracization and physical mistreatment by inmates and staff alike. In my wildest imagination, I never thought such conditions existed. We were reduced to animalism of the most barbaric kind. When I wrote to my parents and told them of the maltreatment, my letters were censored and destroyed. "I'll tell you something," the mail censor informed me. "Keep up this agitation and we'll show you what treatment we can dish out. Keep that in mind, fish." For once in my life I was unable to turn to anyone for help or advice. My style, prior to being penned up here, was to run away. Such an action from this place seemed impossible.

During the first two weeks of my thirty day indoctrination period, I met two staff members whom I vividly remember to this very day. One was superintendent Gilbert whom we called "Father". Upon my first encounter with him, I could understand the sobriquet "Father". He earned that title not because he was a man of the cloth but because a paternalistic manner emanated from him. It was his policy to talk with every new arrival. When I was herded into his office he motioned me to stand in front of his desk. His disarming manner was a perfect cover-up for his Dr. Jekyll and Mr. Hyde personality. He smiled benignly and asked, "What is your name." This question threw me off guard because he had my dossier lying on his desk. I answered his question and he continued interrogating me with questions for which he already had the answers. It was a disconcerting experience for me, but not nearly so disturbing as his next move. He asked me to come around the desk, which I did. He then ordered me to drop my trousers and underwear and to turn around. I stood there naked and embarrassed for what seemed an eternity. He did not put his hands on me. Suddenly he stood up, told me to dress and return to my squadron. When I related this experience to other kids in my squadron, they told me they had experienced the same sick routine from this "Queer". Apparently he went through the ritual with all new arrivals. Months later his inmate orderly told me that he never made an advance on any boy if that youngster had parents living within the state who were apt to pay their son a visit. If a youngster was from out of state, an orphan and obviously without anyone interested in him, this lecherous man would make vile demands upon his victim's body.

The second person I met was Pop. He was an ex-Navy man. He stood nearly six feet tall and weighed approximately two hundred pounds. He had been a boxer in the Navy and always carried himself with the grace of a man who had spent many years in the ring. Like Gilbert, he was a handsome man of approximately fifty years of age. And like "father", he was a sexual degenerate. I was not aware of his sickness until I learned of it from a number of boys on whom he had committed sodomy. Pop was the most feared and hated guard at the institution. He reveled in this reputation. One of his most prominent displays of sadism was his arrangement of boxing matches between inmates. It was always a deliberate mismatch. Today I can still see his face with a vicious grin across it while he watched one fighter beat the other to a pulp. If either contestant would not fight until he was totally unable to, Pop would yell from the ringside. "Keep fighting, you bastard, or I'll make mincemeat out of your ass with Mary Anne."

A few days after my arrival at the fish tank, the "skin heads" were herded into the basement of a large building. We were instructed to stand at attention, keep our eyes straight ahead and our mouths shut. A large hulk of a man entered the room from a side door. Without hesitation he began, "Boys, I want you to meet an important member of our staff. You will become closely acquainted with this member throughout your stay here. She wields great power and authority as you will learn if you violate any rules of this school. I know, from experience, that after you have met her you will get her message clearly from the beginning, painfully so. This is one Bitch who f—ks you, you don't screw her. Either way, she leaves your dick soft." With that final remark, he reached under a counter and withdrew a heavy length of harness leather. It was about 48 inches long, 1/2 inch thick with a heavy wooden handle riveted to one end. The handle also served as a billy club in the event one of its victims became obstreperous. Again, he began to talk, "Now boys, the staff member I hold in my hand is known as Mary Anne. She is the only female here. Occasionally she will demand a piece of ass from you." With this, he laughed uproariously, then continued. "You will observe she has been soaked in oil to keep her pliable. Do I make myself clear? In addition to this bitch I just introduced you to, we have other equally unpleasant 'rehabilitative measures' such as making you squat down with a broom handle behind your knees. If you become too goddamn tough, we'll take you to the boiler room and handcuff you to a pipe about four inches off the cement floor." Since that time and today, some of the above measures of rehabilitation have been abandoned, and others added.

26

According to an article in the Seattle Times, February 9, 1988, they still maintain a solitary confinement cell that is dubbed as 'the hole' or 'the dump'. It is a dimly lit cell totally bare except for a mat and a toilet with no seat cover. Inmate Laris Gratton described 'the hole' as "like being away from the world. No one to talk to, and you lose track of time. It's like a closet." Phil Kassel, Evergreen Legal Services attorney, charges the state with using the isolation cell indiscriminately and as a 'first resort'. He cited one instance of a recalcitrant youngster spending five months in isolation at various times.

That was our indoctrination to the Training School. If you wonder at this point why so many youngsters come out of our institutions disillusioned, confused, angry and dangerous, look to their treatment while incarcerated; look to the administrators. Bear in mind that psychological abuse, while more subtle and insidious as it leaves no obvious physical scars, can leave an individual equally as traumatized as those who suffer physical maiming. It would behoove society to take a more active interest in the persons who are placed in such defenseless positions.

I lived in mortal fear of breaking the rules. I was convinced that Mary Anne was in complete control of my life. I had been whipped with switches, but never brutalized by such an awesome looking weapon. At this point, I did not realize that within a month I would be horribly punished with the same strap. Nor did I know that the administrator of the beating, the man who had introduced us to Mary Anne, was a totally insensate individual who enjoyed a degree of sexual gratification from abusing the boys under his thumb. After 53 years, I still remember his name with revulsion. I have never known a more sadistic brute than Pop. After I had been in the fish tank for two weeks, our squadron, along with the other three squadrons, was ordered to report to the same basement where we had first met Mary Anne. One of the older boys told me that we were to witness a "disciplining" of a youngster who had been caught stealing an extra doughnut from the mess hall. Pop wanted the whipping to be observed by the rest of us to serve as an object lesson. He always referred to the strapping as a disciplining - never as punishment. It was a fine line of semantics, and at that time I was not aware that it was for the purpose of satisfying outside investigators who might learn of the vicious brutality practiced at this school.

A boy about thirteen years of age was brought into the room. He was a frail lad and I will never forget his fear-filled whimpering. Without a word, two husky inmates grabbed the lad, stripped off his pants and shorts, bent him over a table and held him down. Pop picked Mary Anne up from the table, caressed it lovingly and stepped behind the crying boy. He took a stance like a batter preparing to hit a home run. Without hesitation he brought the strap across the buttocks of the boy who screamed out in his agony. I carefully counted the strokes; there were ten in all. By the time Pop was through delivering his message, the boy had fainted. His buttocks were a mass of cuts and bruises, the pale skin stained black and blue. Fear and a burning fury rose in my throat like a bitter bile. To this day, in my dreams, I can hear the whistle of the strap through the air, the sharp swat as it made contact and the accompanying screams. A half century later that scene

27

haunts me in my waking hours, so much so that I want to weep when it passes through my mind: in reality, it has never passed through my mind but is etched indelibly in my psyche.

Logically you would wonder why the youngster did not tell his parents. You underestimate the cunning duplicity of the officials responsible. About three years after I escaped from Chehalis, I met a former school teacher from the training school. He carefully explained to me how the superintendent would handle parents whose children told them of the brutal treatment. When a parent whose child had told them of the vicious chastisement would confront Superintendent Gilbert, they would meet a master of deceit. Gilbert was a very sanctimonious Christian. He would patiently listen to the parents and would immediately send for Pop. While they were waiting for this beast to make his appearance, the superintendent would read the infraction report to the mother and father. His story usually ran like this:

Gilbert would call the boy in before his parents and ask him, "Did you steal a doughnut from the mess hall as you were charged?" "Yes, I did". "I want you to pull down your pants so that your parents can see if there are any marks on your body." Naturally, by this time, the bruises would have healed. Then in his paternalistic voice he would direct his remarks to the distressed parents, "Folks, we do discipline boys here for infractions of the rules, never inhumanely. It is true that we demand good behavior and obedience. Surely you can understand the necessity of such discipline. But you must believe me when I tell you we do not mistreat any of the charges entrusted to our care. The records reflect that your boy was a troublemaker at school and at home. In fact, so much so that the courts felt he should be put under our jurisdiction in order to teach him to conform to the laws of society. It is my duty to send him home as a responsible lad. I want you to know that I truly appreciate your coming here to see me. If you have any concerns, please know that my office is always open to you." Gilbert had had many years' experience in playing this game.

What the parents did not recall was a letter sent to them right after the boy had been beaten. The letter would contain a report of the boy's infraction. Invariably, each letter ended with this sentence, "Because of this infraction, your son will be denied visitation rights for thirty days." During that time, of course, the evidence of the abuse would disappear. When Pop would enter the office he would be questioned sharply by Gilbert in the presence of the parents. It was a game rehearsed many times before. The scenario never changed. It went like this: "Pop, will you please tell me to what physical extent you disciplined the child of these parents?" Pop's answer was always the same, "I was called in to discipline the lad in question. He was given ten sharp swats across the buttocks and sent back to his squadron". It never failed that the parents left convinced that the boy had deserved the strapping and had lied to them to the extent to which the beating had been administered.

I knew that any infraction of the rules on my part would quickly result in a personal introduction to Mary Anne and for a short time this threat worked to successfully keep me in line. My recalcitrant and stubborn nature was not easily subdued. It seemed that I was forever getting into fights and the guards were cautioned to watch me carefully. In my young mind I knew that the beatings went beyond punishment and bordered on barbarity. Often I was completely stripped of my clothes, bent over a bench where I was held by two husky guards or inmates and severely beaten with that heavy piece of harness leather, Mary Anne. I cannot recall how many times I went to bed with my buttocks black and blue.

One the harshest beatings I received was the result of my breaking the nose of a guard in a fit of anger. I lost track of how many times Mary Anne came in contact with my posterior; the pain was so great that I fainted. When I regained consciousness I found myself handcuffed to a bed in the institution's hospital ward. After my handcuffs had been removed, the officials felt that I was able to withstand the rest of the punishment. Striking a guard was considered the worst violation of all and it was their intent to impress upon me and the other boys that one thing you never did was to raise a hand against a guard.

The final punishment was forcing me to walk in a circle carrying a metal bar weighing about twenty-five pounds across my shoulders. Out of each hour I was permitted to sit down for fifteen minutes. This treatment was called "Time in Circle City". My sentence for this occasion lasted fifteen days. By the end of that time I was a physically fit young man without an ounce of fat, but heavy with a hatred I carried for many years - a hatred directed toward all forms of authority. I had by now convinced myself that I was destined to lead a life of criminality.

Nothing seemed to keep me from disobeying the rules. In time I found that each succeeding strapping hurt me less than the previous one. One of the "honors" that a fellow inmate could bestow upon another was the name "leather ass". This meant that you were able to take the full measure of the lashes without crying out. From the beginning I had heard there were a number of leather asses among the three squadrons of boys. When I first heard the expression and learned what it meant, I doubted that any person could take that type of brutality and not cry out. In just a short time I had earned the title so coveted among my peers, "Leather Ass Williams".

4

RETURN TO THE WHIPPING POST

After I had been at the Training School for about a year, the superintendent called me into his office and informed me that my release had been ordered by state officials in Olympia. Amazement must have shown in my eyes because the superintendent said, "You're not the only one who is surprised, Williams. You are one person who does not deserve any consideration for early release. I heard that your father had political juice, and now I believe it. The way I have it figured is that we needed to have you under our jurisdiction about another year." I stared at him in disbelief. Here was a guy who committed sexual acts on helpless kids, and the bastard was telling me how much more time he needed to effect the rehabilitation of Glenn Williams. I was about ready to vent my feeling when it came to mind that he might, in some way, cause me to remain incarcerated longer, and all I could think of were the streets, good food and the freedom to come and go as I saw fit. It wasn't until I was well on my way to Wenatchee that it struck me why I had been released. I was constantly causing trouble for the staff as well as the other inmates. With a malcontent such as me, it was too difficult to keep the others tractable. Another thought came to mind; maybe dad did pull rank in the governor's office.

An exuberant family was on hand to greet me when the bus arrived. To a member, they assured they were happy to have me back in the fold. I had never been shown so much affection as was showered on me that day. Inasmuch as my release took place in April, my folks thought it would be a good idea for me to wait until the fall to enter school. I was pleased with their decision because I was reluctant to face my friends. Of course, in a town as small as Wenatchee, word had spread quickly that I had returned. Throughout the hot summer months, I alternated between lazing around doing nothing or going horse back riding. One of the sports I had missed most was the freedom I always felt when I was riding a horse bareback, racing through the hills. Just being free was a luxury that took getting used to. I can't remember how long this good feeling lasted. I do recall, however, that inevitable restless sensation gradually coming over me. I felt sorry for my mom and dad and my brothers and sisters because I knew I could not adjust to a normal existence in a family unit. Since my return, my parents were beginning to think I had straightened up. In the latter part of August, the overwhelming urge was more than I could resist. I convinced myself that for just one more time I wanted to burglarize a house or business to see if

I had lost my touch. The first breaking and entering occurred in the Whitman grade school. My take consisted of a typewriter, pencils and other odds and ends, all of little value. The entry was clean and fast. So was my exit. It was a thrill. I again became obsessed by my return to a life of crime. During the following ten days, I robbed a half dozen other homes and establishments. When this routine became monotonous, I had to do something more thrilling, dangerous. After all, my calling to become a full fledged gangster could never materialize pulling small-time, penny ante crap as I was doing. I simply had to head for the windy city, the mecca of criminals, that magnetic metropolis, Chicago.

For a week I refrained from all criminal activities. I simply wanted to take some time out, make some decision as to where I was going from here. One morning I woke up with a novel idea that I thought would be interesting and would take me ever nearer to my beloved city in the Midwest. I decided to rustle some horses and take them from Wenatchee to Ellensburg. In Ellensburg I would find a market for the horses and would have the bus fare to head east. Going it alone was not my style. I was a gregarious sort of kid who liked to have kids my age accompany me on my nefarious doings. It didn't take me long to locate two former friends, Bob and Gary, and to convince them what a good time we could have implementing my plan. Gary came up with an excellent idea. "Why, he asked, "couldn't we head over the Clockum Pass, ride to Ellensburg and see the annual rodeo? We will have six days to ride less than 100 miles." The idea appealed to Bob and me. About a week later, after we had finalized our plans, we went to a local riding academy late one night. We selected three magnificent animals, saddled them up and took to the hills. All of us had been raised in that area and we were fully acquainted with the terrain. We rode most of the first night and slept during the day. We wanted to get out of the immediate vicinity before riding in the daylight. On the evening of the fifth day, we could see the lights of Ellensburg a few miles away. By this time, however, we were without food and money. After we had unsaddled our horses and tied them out to graze, we made plans for our next move. "Listen", I said to my two companions, "let's go down near town tonight on foot until we come to some farm houses. We'll wait until we find one that has no lights. After we make certain there isn't anyone home, we will burglarize the place and load up with food." Motivated by hunger, the others thought it was a great idea.

The three of us took off across the farmlands toward town. We knew we would come across a road and if we followed the road it would eventually lead us to some houses. After all, Ellensburg was only about three miles away. Before we had hiked a mile, we saw the silhouette of a house and barn. Nothing showed up that indicated the family was on the premises, so we moved on toward the buildings. Suddenly we were confronted by a large barking dog. He came within a dozen yards of us and stopped, still snarling. Gary said, "Let me approach him. I have a way with dogs." Bob and I were only too happy to let Gary try his luck. We wanted nothing to do with a mean dog. Gary walked toward the animal, all the while talking softly to him. As he advanced, the dog would retreat. Gradually, however, he would bark less frequently and with shorter yelps. Sure enough, within a few minutes Gary had the dog siding up to him to be petted. Finally, Gary called out, "Come on you fellows, this is a pet. He won't bite." Five minutes later the three of us and the dog were in the farmhouse. "Bob, you and Gary go to the bedroom and get a couple of pillow cases to put the loot in," I ordered. Surrendering to our hunger pangs, the first place we raided was the kitchen. We wasted no time in loading the food into the pillow cases. I took a butcher knife from one of the drawers and cut large pieces off a ham we had run across. Each of us ate ham and worked at the same time. Occasionally, we would stop long enough to wash the ham down with a glass of cold milk. We filled the cases with food and set them near the door. Bob, Gary and I split up, each taking a separate room to burgle. It took us about half an hour to finish our job. In another hour we were back to where we stashed the horses. Each of us dumped our case on the ground to survey the take. "Good Christ", I exclaimed, "we hit the jackpot." In addition to the food, we had come up with two rifles, a pistol and enough ammunition to stand off an army. "And that ain't all," exclaimed Gary, "I found this in one of the drawers." He held out his hand. He had a bull durham sack filled with money. There was over $50.00 in it. Weariness overtook us and we slept.

The bright sunlight awakened us early the next morning. We were elated and ready to tackle the world. As we approached the town, our attention was drawn to a large billboard alongside the road. It read: ELLENSBURG ANNUAL RODEO! ENTER THE BAREBACK RIDING, STEER ROPING, BARREL RACING AND A DOZEN OTHER CONTESTS. EARN BIG MONEY ON EACH EVENT. I excitedly told my friends that we should sign up for a few of the contests. After all, the mounts we had stolen were exceptionally fine animals. "What say?", I asked my buddies. "Hell, yes!" responded Gary. "If you want to do the riding, it's okay with us." It was only logical that I do the riding. I was the lightest one and was an excellent horseman.

The three of us brazenly rode our horses up to the main office, and asked where we should sign up to qualify for the rodeo events. "What event are you interested in?" queried the man in a booth. "I want to ride in the bareback contest", I answered. The fellow looked me over for a full minute. Then he got up, walked to a window and looked Gary and Bob over very carefully. I became suspicious and nervous, but I made up my mind to follow through with our plans. He turned to me and asked, "How old are you son?" I looked him straight in the eyes and snapped back, "That is none of your business." "Yes it is. You have to be eighteen years of age to sign up." Not to be bluffed I immediately came back, "Well I am eighteen and over." He appeared to relax. "If you are that old, we'll accept your application. Go over to the young lady at the desk in the corner and pay the $5.00 fee." I did not notice him casually sauntering out the door. I was intrigued with the idea of riding in a rodeo. When I was about half way through filling out the form, Bob came over to me and whispered, "Glenn, the police are pulling up outside. They are with the guy who asked you your age." I ran to where Bob was pointing and I could see two men in sheriff's uniforms walking briskly toward the building. I, too, noted they were with the man who had left us in

33

the office. Without hesitation, Bob and I streaked through the rear door. We dashed into the milling crowd where Gary had already disappeared. The adrenaline was pumping furiously through my veins. "Follow me, Bob", I instructed, and headed for the parking lot.

My intent was to grab a car, any car. It had to be a car with a key in it. As we looked back, we could see the two cops heading in the direction of the parking lot. They probably thought we had a vehicle in the lot, and they were intent on cutting us off. So we had to circle and go back to the protection of the large crowd. We came across a car near the building we had first entered. We saw a dark blue sedan and recognized it as the police car. "Come on, Bob," I urged, "let's take a chance." Damned if we were not lucky. The cops had left their key in the ignition. I jumped behind the wheel and kicked the motor to life. Oddly enough, no one seemed to pay any attention, which pleased me. I started to circle around behind the building where all the trouble started when Bob yelled, "Where the f—k are you going? Get your ass out on the road and let's split." "No", I replied, "I want to try to locate Gary." The officers would be telephoning for a back-up. I drove carefully, not wanting to draw the heat on us. When we got on the road, Bob and I saw Gary streaking across the road in front of us. He was making his own getaway. I stepped on the gas to overtake him. He bolted out across a field. He had seen us and, thinking we were the law, he wanted to get where a car couldn't go. I realized we would lose him if I could not get close enough for him to see us. I took off the road and cut across the field in front of our friend. When I got near him, I rolled down the window and called his name. He came to a full stop and simply stared at us. "Gary, hop in for Christ's sake, and hurry," I screamed. He hesitated for only a second then ran to the car. We took off at a high speed in the direction of Pendleton, Oregon. The police in the small towns did not enjoy the new luxury of having radio contact. How lucky for us. We drove for about an hour. When I saw a ravine off the highway, I pulled in far enough to conceal the police car. The other two seemed to read my mind. We talked for awhile and agreed we would have to travel by night. The rest of the very long day was spent making plans.

When it was dark enough to make it difficult to identify the car, we took off again. The prowl car had no distinctive markings other than the familiar twin-mounted Appleton spotlights. Of course, the license had the usual exempt plate that identified it as an official car. These could not be seen when facing an oncoming vehicle. However, a car approaching from behind could easily tell it was a state car, and if they were on the lookout for us we were dead ducks. We agreed that it would be safer traveling at night.

It dawned on us that it would be wiser to ditch the cop's car and steal another that wasn't so hot. But, to tell the truth, it gave us a sort of thrill having an official vehicle under our command. And this was especially true when we realized that, being a prowl car, it should have a siren. Gary, who was driving our first night out, tried all the buttons and switches he could reach from the driver's seat. He was pulling here and pushing there when the night quiet was split with a loud wailing noise. Gary had struck gold, and like a bunch of immature kids, we howled with delight. "Hey, buddies", I yelled,

"I have a good idea. We can make money from it as well as have a thrill."
"Spit it out, Glenn", yelled Bob. I felt extremely important when I replied,
"Okay, here's the plan. When we come up alongside some joker, we will hit
the siren, pull him over and take what loot we can get from him." "Jesus
Christ, but you're a dumb f—ker", was Bob's response. "What is going to
keep the victim from going on to the next town and bringing the heat on our
asses?" I glared at Bob, and in utter disgust, I calmly said, "We will disable
his car or take his keys. Now speaking of dumb, you ignorant bastard, why
couldn't you have figured that out? In fact you are so stupid, Bob, I kind of
feel you are out of your class dealing with Gary and me." Finally Bob came
around to agreeing it was a pretty sharp scheme. However, an immediate
problem arose right then. Gary calmly called out and informed us that the
car was about out of gas. Luckily, the skyline of the little town of Vantage
showed up. It seemed we were about five miles away. There was no way we
could pull into the only service station in town with a hot car - a cops' car to
boot - and fuel up. "Pull alongside the road, Gary," I ordered. Let's figure
this thing out." It was not a matter of our not having the money to pay for
the gas; it was how to pay.

Bob came up with an idea. "Let's park the car here and two of us will go
down on foot and tell the operator we ran out of gas." Inasmuch as Gary was
driving the prowl car, it was decided that Bob and I would hike for the fuel.
However, I urged Gary to drive within less than a mile from the station so
we would not have to walk far. When we got to the little grocery store-
gasoline station, there was a single man running it. He was surprised when
he saw us walk up in front of the building. Few people ever stopped in this
out-of-the-way place for service. "What can I do for you, boys," he asked in
a friendly manner. We told him of our predicament. "Well, he said, "I have
only a two-gallon can here, which I can fill up for you. I'll need a quarter for
a deposit on the can in addition to the quarter for the gas." I gave him the
required cash, and we were on our way back to the stranded vehicle. Before
we started the car to go on to the station, we realized that we had a major
matter to deal with here. "You know damn well that the word is out around
here about this cop car being stolen, particularly, at a crossroad junction like
Vantage. So when we go down and fill this beast up and drive off, that
geezer is going to bring the heat down on us." Bob stated. "I've got a
scheme, fellows. Drive on up to the joint and let the guy fill our tank." "
What then," I asked. "Shit, Glenn, give me some credit for having a brain,
will you? Let me run this circus for awhile." I simply sat back and let Gary
start the short trip to the little business enterprise.

When we pulled up to the single gas pump, Bob hopped out and cheerily
said, "Fill 'er up." After the operator had filled the tank with about 15
gallons of gas, he asked for $3.00. He took a double take at the license plate
and then leisurely sauntered into the building. Gary and I must have had the
same idea simultaneously. He bailed out of one side of the car and I the
other. We burst into the little office just as the fellow was picking up the
phone. I knocked it from his hand as Gary placed his pistol against the guy's
head. "Oh, God," he cried, "don't kill me." "I'll blast your brains all over
that wall if you as much as move." The old man started crying hysterically.

I wheeled on Bob, "All right you wise punk, now what?" "Easy," was his reply, "we'll rob the till, take the old boy with us until we get out in the middle of nowhere, tie him up beside the road, and drive on. We'll have to drive like hell, because the real heat will be bearing down on us. Stealing horses and a car is one thing, but armed robbery and kidnap is another." For once in our crazy thinking, we started to realize the magnitude of our actions. I felt a sense of fear, but I would not admit it to the other two. We forced the quaking man into the back seat. Gary had cleaned out the till of less than fifteen dollars, and we were on our way driving like madmen.

All that country was a flatland of sage brush, coyotes and jack rabbits. When we had traveled about ten miles, I pulled off the road and we dragged the sobbing prisoner out of the car and into a ditch. We tied the man up by using all three of our belts. "Now, you listen, fella," I said in a quiet voice, "We aren't going to hurt you. Understand that! You'll be able to work yourself free in a very short time. When you do, crawl up to the road and some motorist will rescue you." And we left him that way.

At the sign of daylight, I pulled off the road. The car was well concealed from the road. The three of us were exhausted, so sleep came quickly. I would wake up periodically throughout the day and listen as the traffic passed. We woke up and one at a time left the vehicle to stretch our legs and relieve ourselves. After we had gotten the kinks out of our aching limbs, we laid down on the ground and decided we had better do some damn straight thinking. About a half an hour later, Bob broke the silence. "I can see no other way out of this fix but to continue with our original plans. Let's use the siren, drag some suckers off the road, rob 'em until we get to California, then get this damn car out of our possession." Gary thought that that would be the logical thing to do at this stage of the game.

Waiting daylight out, the lack of activity and doing nothing but eating the cold ham was a bore. All of us were edgy and short of temper when we pulled up to the highway and went on our way. We were a good twenty miles out of Pendleton when our first opportunity to use the siren arose. Bob was at the wheel when a man passing us honked and blinked his lights. "Hit it, Bob," I yelled. "Let's get our first victim." The police car was powerful and responded to the pressure of Bob's foot. The man who had passed must have thought we wanted to race so he poured the power to his speeding automobile. For a brief time, he pulled away from us, but not for long. When we were about 500 feet behind him, Bob hit the siren. Immediately the car slowed down and pulled off the road. We pulled up beside him, and the three of us leaped from our car and surrounded him. I came up to the driver's window, stuck my weapon in his face and ordered him out. By the time he was aware that we were young kids, he tried to start his car again. I stepped back and shot his left front tire out. "What are you going to do?" he cried. "Not a goddamn thing, if you do as you are told," I snarled. "Walk over to that ditch on the other side of your car and lay down in it." He jumped with alacrity. Gary stood over him and relieved him of his wallet and loose change. He then took his keys and tossed them out into the field. We went back to the car and observed there were many shoe boxes in the back seat. We took the tops off two or three and found they contained new shoes.

"Hell", Gary called out, "this man is a shoe salesman". When we were ready to leave, Bob instructed the fellow to start walking out into the field. He told him, "If you stop before you get out of sight, we'll stop you permanently." We hopped into our car and continued our way on to Pendleton.

When we arrived we drove to the middle of the town until we found a row of warehouses. We parked the police car inconspicuously between vacant sheds. We located a hotel restaurant and ordered a large meal. After our bellies were full, we checked into the hotel. It was about 2:30 in the morning. About 10:30 we awakened, fully rested and at peace with ourselves. After a hearty breakfast we walked toward our parked car. We knew there was a possibility that the car had been spotted and picked up, or at least there was a stakeout on it. "Okay, fellows, here's what we'll do,' I told them. "Let's separate, and one at a time, about three minutes apart we'll walk by the car. If any one of us spots anything funny we will split up and meet in the lobby of the hotel. If everything seems normal, I'm going to get in the car alone and circle the block. As I drive past you I want you to get in one at a time." As I walked toward the car I was very apprehensive. I could imagine police were watching me from the windows of the warehouse. It took all the guts I could muster to walk up to the car, open the door, start the engine and slowly pull out into the street. I made a left turn, circled the block driving at a modest pace. The first person I picked up was Gary and then Bob. The Pendleton police had a stolen police car right in the midst of their fair city, and they hadn't observed it. I knew damn well that the word had reached the police throughout the northwest. And surely the desk man had issued a copy of the events of the night to all police going on duty. Well, it was our good luck. We took the credit for our getaway, and attributed it to our intelligence. When I contacted the big-time hoods in Chicago and told them of my capabilities, they would hire me right away. How sick I was becoming, dangerously ill; mentally so.

I brazenly drove up to the front of the hotel where we had spent the previous night, and parked. Bob went in and picked up our make-shift pack. We had a glass of milk and hit the highway for The Dalles, Oregon. We were in excellent spirits. Everything we needed was in our possession; about fifteen bucks, two pistols, two rifles, plenty of ammo and heads filled with insanity. As we drove down the highway, we sang songs, yelled at pretty girls and generally behaved like the teenagers we were. We dallied along, stopping every few miles, enjoying a milkshake and playing in the streams which ran alongside the road. Getting fuel was no problem. The thought of running out of money didn't worry us. After all, we had guns and all we had to do was siren some pigeon off the road and replenish our wallets. We talked about our venture. To hear us, you would have thought we were of the mobs. Because I had been in an institution, it was more or less natural for the others to look up to me as the leader, and I reveled in this honor. I found myself barking unnecessary orders simply because that was the manner in which the gang leaders conducted themselves in the movies and books I had seen and read. Night fell, and it was time for us to go to work.

As the three of us rolled along, I decided to let my experience show through. "Gary," I ordered, "you take up a station in the back seat with your rifle and pistol so you can cover us from the rear. Bob, you ride up here with me." When we were about half way to The Dalles, we agreed it was about time to pull another job with the siren. I can't describe the pleasure and authority I felt in my new role. Gary called from the back seat, "Hey, we are being over- taken by a car coming up from the rear. Let's pull the goon over and do a job on him." My rear-view mirror confirmed Gary's warning. I let the car get about a dozen yards ahead of me before I picked up speed and caught it. It is amazing how quickly people will acknowledge a siren and pull to the shoulder of the road. And this was no exception. When we pulled up beside the vehicle, all three of us got the surprise of our lives. The driver was a woman. In those days, women rarely ever drove, and much less at night. As soon as the woman saw we were not police, but three unshaven kids, she begged, "Please don't hurt the children." I looked in the back seat and saw three sleeping children. I wanted to get out of this mess quicker than she. This was a hitch I could not have foreseen. I knew we could not just stand there in the highway, so I said, "Ma'am, we aren't going to hurt anyone. You hand me your purse and keep on going." She threw the purse to the pavement, and sped off. Bob was the first to recover. "You idiot bastard. That dame will have the police on our tail in an hour. Let's push our ass into high gear and get to The Dalles and ditch this car. It's hotter than a doe rabbit in heat." I was angry with Bob but I knew he was right. I blew it. I'd leave this part of my escapade out of my story to the big boys.

Within a matter of minutes, the prowl car was speeding down the road. We had to get to the security of the town before the alarm was sounded and a roadblock set up. I drove at very high speeds. After we had traveled about ten minutes, there was a loud bang and the heavy car swerved out of control. It careened off the highway and headed into a field of baled hay. I finally got it stopped. There was nothing to do now but hitch a ride into town, the sooner the better. It wasn't long until a farmer in a flatbed came by. I was waving the flashlight like mad for fear he wouldn't see us in time. Thank God, he stopped. "What are you doing out here at this time of night." he asked. I told him of our blowout and pointed to where our car was sitting. He was convinced and took us right into the city center. The elation we had enjoyed for a brief time was dispelled. Little did any of us dream that we had set up the scene for our eventual capture. We were hungry and disoriented. The bright lights of a diner drew our attention. The meal we were eating was not really appreciated. "Buddies," I whispered, "as soon as we are through eating, we have to get a hotel room and get off the streets. We won't last an hour after daylight." It seemed to me that all the people in the cafe had their eyes on us, or maybe I just thought so.

When we had finished, we arose at the same time and went up front to the cashier. What happened next was too fast for me to follow. Two burly uniformed men broke through the front door with pistols drawn and aimed right at us. I glanced toward the rear, planning to make a break for it. As if by cue, two other officers came through the back door. Each held the dread of all men, double-barreled shotguns. They were leveled at our bellies. "Boys," roared one of the cops, "If you make one little move, you are dead. Sit down on the floor one at a time. Now put your hands behind your necks and don't budge. We know you are armed so it will be necessary for us to open fire if you make a false gesture." The cops who had come in from the rear door positioned themselves behind and to one side of us. It was apparent they did not know what to expect, so they wanted the advantage in the event of a shoot-out. A flat foot behind me grabbed me by the collar and roughly yanked me to my feet. His expert hands found my gun immediately. He spun me around, pulled my arms behind my back and snapped those ever familiar cuffs on my wrist. The other cops followed the same procedure with Gary and Bob. Without a further word, we were hustled into a paddy wagon and taken to the local jail, which was a beehive of action. This activity was the result of our escapades beginning at Ellensburg and ending at The Dalles. This little town had never experienced such excitement since the citizens were called to mobilize for the World War.

Newsmen with cameras were running around taking snapshots and asking questions of the officials. When they tried to talk to us, they were told not to speak to the prisoners. Of course, the arresting officers were jubilant over having made such a big capture; three teenagers who were scared to death. Before we were placed in a cell, a skinny, long-necked, sharp-eyed character walked into the police station. With him was the chief of police. Both were trying to put on an air of importance. I am certain they had in mind that a great deal of publicity could be milked from this incident. Everyone got in on the act, except the burg's chief of dogcatchers. I was too young at that time to understand the interest, but it wasn't long before I understood, to some extent, the mind of a conniving politician. The mayor whispered to the police chief and gestured toward Gary, Bob and me. The chief called to one of the reporters and told him that he wanted some photos of 'those three robbers' and that they were to be taken with the mayor and chief standing beside the three of us. During this hubbub, the people we sirened off the road came in and positively identified us. The crying shoe salesman yelled at the chief and said, "Put me in a cell with those motherless, yellow-bellied scum and I will save you the expense of a trial." He was the one who whimpered and screamed for us not to shoot him. We were taken to a long row of cells. Each of us were jailed singly. Almost immediately, I fell asleep.

I don't know how long I had slept before I was awakened by a jailor and told to get dressed. I was led out to the chief's office. I was ready for the third degree, but he put my mind at ease. "Glenn," he began, "I've been on the phone for the past four hours trying to tie you kids in with the officials in Ellensburg and Wenatchee, Washington. Holy Christ, what a trail you left. And, we learned that you are not sixteen as you told us, but are about fifteen. Have you any idea of the seriousness of the crimes you have committed? You three are wanted for horse theft, burglary, robbery, kidnap, assault and car theft. There are enough charges here to put you away for twenty years. It's obvious that a youth of your age and reputation, and the propensity you have for violence labels you as a potentially dangerous criminal - and at fifteen years of age. After our interrogation of Bob and Gary, it is apparent that you are the ringleader. The officials in your home town have given me these facts. They state that the other two have no police record whatever. Their parents are coming after them tomorrow, and they will have to face the consequences of their acts when they get home. It's a different story about you. They insist on loading the book on you. We have another problem here to iron out before we turn you over to either Ellensburg or Wenatchee. There is no doubt that you could wind up in an Oregon penal institution until you are at least of age. And after that, you have to face the prosecutors in the other towns. I can't imagine what the outcome of this mess will be. Go back to your cell."

I was kept isolated for five days. My predominate thought was to escape. I searched for every opportunity, but there wasn't any. On the sixth day I was advised by the prosecuting attorney that I was to be returned to Wenatchee. The Dalles' officials had made this decision knowing full well that Washington would put me away for a long time. Ellensburg concurred.

Three days later, Deputies True and Bice from the Wenatchee Sheriff's office and the police department arrived in The Dalles, swathed me in the familiar chains and drove me back to the Apple Capitol. Mr. Bice talked with me for a long time and his entire conversation condensed to the fact that I had a good family, was given every opportunity to straighten up and that by my conduct I had rejected society and my family. His last remark is the one I shall never forget. He said, "Glenn, you are going to wind up in a death cell awaiting execution before long." My typical air of bravado and my response to Officer Bice was one of false confidence. Instead of responding in a normal manner, I had affected a snarling attitude. To me this was the way the tough guys acted and talked. With a sneer on my face, I hissed to Officer Bice, "Let me tell you something, Mr. Son-of-a-Bitch. I have no intention of ending up in a death cell. I intend to shoot it out with any copper who tries to arrest me after this. And let me tell you something else - you had better not make the mistake of giving me an opportunity to blast your God damn guts out."

Throughout the rest of the trip Bice and True didn't speak to me again. I was not permitted to eat with my handcuffs removed, I even had to go to the toilet wearing the steel bracelets. The officers were taking no chances with me and, thinking back on it now, I realize that I was fully capable and willing to kill at the slightest provocation. It was a long trip back to Wenatchee and when we finally arrived at the Chelan County jail my wrists were sore from the cuffs and my ankles were rubbed raw by the leg shackles.

When my father came to visit me the next morning, I became aware that his shoulders were starting to slump and that he no longer carried his head in a proud manner. I have never seen parents who were so blindly loyal to their offspring as were my parents. During that visit in the Chelan County Jail Dad made a statement I shall never forget. "Son, you are at the point in life where you will receive no more opportunities. I am financially and emotionally incapable of going much further in your camp. Your mother is devastated. No member in our family can hold their head up. We are filled with shame, humiliation and grief. This is the final time you can expect any cooperation from us. I am going to appeal to the prosecuting attorney to drop the charges and have you returned to the Training School as a parole violator. I pray to God that I will be successful in this endeavor." And he succeeded.

The juvenile authorities in Wenatchee got together with the parents of the boys who had accompanied me on our horse rustling venture. It had been agreed by the officials and the prosecuting attorney that Glenn Williams was the leader of this youthful gang. They reasoned that the other youngsters should be placed on strict probation. In my opinion they used excellent judgment; however, their next ploy backfired. It had been determined by the police and the parents of these youngsters that it would be a good object lesson if they were kept confined a few days under lock and key. It would teach them a lesson, particularly when they could see what was going to happen to me. Neither the parents nor the officials could possibly have foreseen what was going to happen two nights after the boys were placed in the same confinement area in which I was being held.

The juvenile tank was simply a large rectangular room with two windows that overlooked the city park. The windows were covered with a very heavy screen on the outside. It was a framed unit separate from the windows. It was hinged on one side with a padlock securing it on the inside. Accessibility to the padlock was made by simply raising the window. As always before, I was seeking a means of escape and this setup was a real crackerbox.

I had a plan that I felt was sure-fire and I told the others. In their youth and inexperience, Gary and Bob agreed that this would be a grand finale. We could already see our names in the headlines in the Wenatchee Daily World reading "DANGEROUS GANG ESCAPES FROM COUNTY JAIL." The thought of this kind of publicity pleased me immensely. Our finalizing of the plan lasted far into the night. It was agreed that we would take one of the table knives that was given to us at each meal and insert it in the hasp of the lock on the window. We would spring the lock and let it hang in its original position, hoping it would not be closely observed by the jailor who brought our meals. Our room was four floors above the ground, but this posed no problem for us. We would simply braid our sheets into ropes and lower ourselves to the ground.

The following morning about 9:00, our breakfast was brought to us. The jailor made his usual comment, "All right boys; eat your breakfast, wash up your utensils and place them here on the table. I will be back to get them in one hour."

The one utensil that we were most interested in was the standard table knife. It had a handle about four inches long and the blade was of equal length. It was very sturdy, and I was certain that it would suffice to spring the lock. While the other boys stood by the door prepared to warn me if the jailor returned, I inserted the handle in the hasp of the lock. I made two or three attempts to open the lock but could not do so.

Calling Gary over to the window, I asked him if he could break it. He was much stronger than I, and within two minutes he let out a yelp, turned to Bob and me and held up the lock on his forefinger. He had accomplished the first phase of our plan. Placing the lock back on the screen, he positioned it so it would take close observation to determine that it had been tampered with. After we had eaten our breakfast, we did as the jailor had instructed, and when he arrived to pick up our utensils, we were sitting on our beds subdued and well-behaved. As he started to leave the room, he suddenly turned and looked directly at me. "Glenn," he said, "who in the hell bent this knife?" All of us froze in fear. I tried to bluff it out by saying, "No one bent your goddamn knife. It was that way when you brought it in." "Bull shit," he roared, "I'll find out from the cook, and if he tells me that you bent the knife, the three of you punks are headed for solitary."

We spent the rest of the day fearful that he would return and cart us off to the little "darkroom for bad boys." When dinner was served and the jailor gathered our utensils for the last time that day, our spirits arose. After all, we hadn't planned to escape until it was dark anyhow.

As soon as the city lights began to twinkle and we could no longer distinguish people on the sidewalk below, we knew it was time for us to pull our "Houdini." We had passed the long daylight hours by carefully tearing our sheets in strips and braiding them together. It was questionable as to whether or not they would be long enough. After the braided sheets were completed, I decided to place them in the shower and soak them. Somewhere in the back of my mind I had read of an escape in which bed sheets were used. They had been soaked because the escapees determined that soaking them would increase their strength. When it was pitch black outside, we carefully let the rope down the side of the building. It stopped short a few feet from the ground, but after looking the situation over I decided we could easily drop to the lawn below. "You go down first", I ordered Bob. Without a word he slid over the window sill and down the sheets. Gary followed quietly. He had no more disappeared from my view than the gate opened to the room. Two jailors came rushing in. "All right Glenn, we've got you! We knew damn well you were up to one of your shenanigans as soon as we saw the bent knife." I leaned out the window and screamed down to the two below. "Hit the road! Don't wait for me. The bulls......" Before I could finish the sentence I was thrown to the floor by one of the deputies. He quickly handcuffed me to the handle of the steel gate. The other two boys had gotten away and I was still here trapped in this rat hole. I later learned that police were stationed around the building and across the street, just waiting for the signal from the jailor. I didn't see Gary and Bob again until we were chained together and were on our way to the Training School.

Somewhere along the line, it became the policy of the training school officials to administer a lashing to all inmates returned to the institution as parole violators. Someone in the hierarchy of the science of penology felt that the certainty of punishment would deter ex-inmates from continuing a life of crime. Well, here I was being sent back to WASHINGTON'S WHIPPING POST. The inevitable reception caused me many hours of apprehension. As was customary, the flogging would be witnessed by the company to which the violator had been assigned; in this case Company C. This fact concerned me because I knew it would be witnessed by Bob and Gary among others. When I left the joint, I was known as one of the leather asses. But it had been months since I had been subjected to this form of rehabilitation and my butt was no longer calloused. The Saturday after my return, I was told by the company commander that I was to receive ten lashes by Mary Anne, and that this incident would take place right after breakfast. I lost my appetite. When the boys returned from the dining hall, they were instructed to form a semi-circle around the pool table which was in the center of the squad room. "Williams, step up here, drop your pants and bend over the table," Pop called out. Without any show of emotion I did as ordered. It was over in about three minutes; that is, all but the humiliation and suffering. Little did these learned men know or care that all they accomplished by that mistreatment was to make me more vengeful and dangerous.

Only one good thing happened to me from that day until the night I escaped and that was the firing of Superintendent Gilbert under circumstances that certainly destroyed his career and reputation. Albert, a fifteen year old boy who had become involved in a fight, was called from the dining room where he worked and was told to report to Pop for a 'session with Mary Anne.' When he was told to drop his trousers, he panicked and struck Pop in the face. Immediately, two inmates overpowered him and forced him to bend over the table after they pantsed him. I wasn't there, but I learned the following from Gilbert's secretary. She was so disgusted and sick over the mistreatment of the boys in Chehalis that she resigned two weeks after this incident. Pop had beaten the boy into unconsciousness. The leather strap had ranged from his back above the hips down to his thighs. It was even too much for the inmates to witness. One of them begged the bull to quit the inhuman beating. The brute stopped, more from his own exhaustion than from mercy. Even the doctor was sickened at the sight of this youngster laying face down on the examination table in the infirmary.

Little did anyone realize that Albert's best friend was being released that afternoon. He returned to the city of Tacoma where Albert's parents resided. As soon as he arrived at the bus depot, Albert's buddy phoned the lad's mother and told her what had taken place. She asked him to wait right there, that she was coming down to pick him up. Before she went to the depot she stopped by her husband's office and the two of them together picked up Albert's friend. He repeated in front of the father exactly what had happened. By ten o'clock the next morning the infuriated parents were in Gilbert's office demanding to see their son. Gilbert panicked. He resorted to a bluff. "You can't barge into my office and insist on special visiting privileges," he shouted. Not in the least daunted, the father leaned across Gilbert's desk and in a cold flat voice said, "Mr. Gilbert, if you do not let me see Albert right now, we're going downtown and get a court order. We have irrefutable proof of what happened yesterday and a court order, based on what we know, will be a simple document to obtain. In the event we are denied, my lawyer is waiting in Seattle and has been instructed to call the governor. We will not dally with you another minute." The superintendent was thoroughly cowed. He lifted his phone, called the infirmary and told them to escort Albert to his office. He was visibly shocked when the doctor said, "Mr. Gilbert, this inmate is in no condition to walk. He has been severely flogged." Gilbert put the phone down and just stared out the window. Finally, he turned to the distressed mother and father and said in a very weak voice, "I do not know what has taken place. I want you to accompany me to the hospital where your son has been admitted." Albert was laying on his stomach covered only by a bed sheet. The father walked over to the boy and lifted the sheet. The mother took one look at her son and screamed. The father turned on the superintendent and yelled, "You miserable bastard, what have you done to my boy?" In an effort to placate the angry parents, Gilbert said, "I'll demand an investigation into this matter and the guilty person will be discharged." Albert's mother asked the doctor if the lad was able to travel. "Yes, if he is handled carefully. He is not seriously injured but, as you can see, he is in a lot of pain. No bones have been broken." The guards offered no resistance when the lad was carefully escorted to his parents' car.

There was great rejoicing among the inmates of the training school one week later when superintendent Gilbert and Pop were seen leaving the administration offices with their suitcases.

5

ESCAPE

Each waking hour was spent dreaming of perfecting the smoothest escape that had ever taken place from this joint. I made up my mind to go it alone because I was fearful of betrayal if I confided in anyone else. The old adage, 'He Who Travels Alone Travels The Furthest' was constantly in my mind. Those who had tried to escape and were caught invariably came back with an excuse for their capture, and most were valid reasons. I recall when Ned Jensen was dragged back. After he was beaten brutally, I questioned him at length. "What happened, Ned," I inquired. He shot back sharply, "What do you want to know for? Do you want to try your hand at rambling?" In order to drag a response from him, I felt it was necessary to tell him of my intention, and I did. "You are crazy, Glenn", he said. "It ain't worth it. Not only did I get my ass scorched to a crisp. I've lost all the good-time I accumulated. On top of that I have to walk Circle City for ten days." "Let me tell you something, Ned, "I retorted. "I don't intend to be a slave. I would rather be dead." The boy looked at me in an understanding manner. I was speaking his language. "You know, Glenn." He said, "When one of us winds up missing, the screw in the powerhouse blows the whistle, and that son-of-a-bitch can be heard for five miles. That is a signal to the farmers letting them know that one of the boys on the hill has started running. There is a cash reward of fifty bucks for anyone who captures the escapee. Now fifty dollars to one of these hay boys represents more than he is capable of earning in a month, so he grabs his shotgun and goes coon-hunting. You know there ain't too many directions you can go. Logically, Seattle or Portland are the best bets. If you take off southbound like I did, and decide to walk along the road, you can damn well wager that one of the farmers will be in the brush waiting for you. The hayseeds in this town have been netting kids for a long time. They know every inch of this territory. Okay, you have another choice, and that is to take off along the railroad tracks. The same thing happens on that route. There is another problem. It gets colder than hell out there. Also, you get so damn hungry, you would eat the rear end of a skunk. Overcome those obstacles, Buddy, and you're free."

I had my plans well thought out. The fog in that area was so thick at times, you couldn't see ten feet in front of your nose. Quite a few guys made a break for it in the dense fog. It offered such an ideal get-a-way blanket that we referred to it as 'parole dust'. Of course, the hacks were aware of the fog problem, and would not take the inmates out to work in such conditions. Sometimes, after we were already on our assignment, the weather would change suddenly and in minutes the institution would be shrouded in fog. As fast as they could, they would round up the boys and head for the squad rooms.

I did my time with a calculated docility. Conditions had to develop in my favor soon. After all it was early spring, and this was the time of year when weather conditions could alter to benefit my plan and me. After dinner one evening, as we were waiting to go to the gym, I happened to hear the radio weather forecast. I couldn't believe my ears. Here was the announcer saying that a heavy mist and fog was expected. This was it, and I was ready. I went to my food locker and took out six candy bars and a packet of soda crackers. I pulled an extra sweat shirt over my head and picked up a navy pea jacket. When I had completed this overt preparation, the bull in charge of Company C called out, "OK you punks, line up for the gym." I was surprised. Surely he had heard the weather prediction. As we left the building, he called out again, "Keep the ranks closed up tight or we will head right back to the squad room." The fog was not as thick as I had hoped it would be. Should I wait until we were herded back? Maybe it would be more ideal for my escape. No, I decided. What if it lifted? I had arranged myself to be in the middle of the line. There was a guard heading the line and one bringing up the rear. I knew the bulls would not break away and chase me. Without waiting another second, I struck the fellow alongside me. He fell out of line. This was the diversion I wanted. The guard ran up to see what was causing the confusion. When he did, I took off like a scalded cat. I ran to the thickest part of the fog. I wanted to get a building or two between me and the screws. No sooner than I had made a break for it, when the stoolies, of which there were many, started calling to the officers, "Williams is rambling." I heard the number one bull yell, "All of you double time to your company." Like good little spineless sheep, they obeyed.

I knew the hacks would not take off after me before they secured the other inmates and called the powerhouse to order the screw to blow the whistle. In the meantime, I was running like a watermelon thief, keeping the building between me and the direction I knew my pursuers would be coming from. In about two minutes I heard that shrieking whistle. One effect it had was to motivate me to pick 'em up and put em' down much faster. As soon as the dairy barn loomed in front of me, I put the second phase of my plan to work. I circled the barn, then came up from the rear, opened a side door and immediately crawled up in the hayloft. It was a huge barn and the loft was full of hay. When I got to the base of the pile, I did not scramble to the top, but burrowed from the bottom to the center of the stack. I made my entrance slowly not wanting to disturb the hay too much and draw attention to searchers that something had left an obvious hole in the stack. About every two feet going in, I would carefully reach back and attempt to settle the pile. It took me about ten minutes to reach my haven, the very center of my hideout. I curled up into a ball, settled down and waited.

I did not have to wait but a few minutes before I heard loud voices coming from the front door. The dairy boss was leading a few guards to make a shakedown of his domain. "The chances are that Williams is long gone off the property, but we have to search all possible places on the grounds. Double up and look into every nook and cranny big enough to conceal that runaway. I want two of you to follow me to the loft. When you get there, take a pitch fork and drive it in the haystack as deep as you can. Don't worry about hurting him." Sure enough, two of them scrambled to the top of the pile. I could hear them jabbing away. During this time, others were circling the base of the stack looking for anything unusual. After about a half an hour of trying to locate me, the dairy boss called out, "OK fellows, come on down. I'm sure he isn't hiding in there." After much shuffling of footsteps and grunting, I heard them head out the front door. My mind told me to stay concealed. Don't move or make a sound. It could be a ploy. I simply curled up. I was tired and fell asleep.

I was awakened by the voices of the dairy crew coming to work early the next morning. I recognized some of the kids by their voices. Of course, their subject was about Glenn Williams. Fred Cary, a close friend of mine, said to one of the inmates, "I wonder where Glenn is by now?" The reply was quick, "I'll bet he'll get caught by noon today. Some farmer will be marching him into the super's office, and then down to get greetings from Mary Anne."

Laying still for the rest of the day was very difficult for me. It seemed forever before I heard the detail whistle blow indicating it was four thirty and time to call it a day. Even after all had quieted down, I refused to make any noise. I ate another bar and a few crackers. I don't know how long I laid there before I fell asleep. It must have been early morning because I heard roosters crowing. I decided to stretch out at full length to relieve my aching body. The crackers had caused me to be thirsty. There was one thing I had overlooked; water.

In about an hour, the kids working at the dairy started coming in. The talk was about Glenn Williams again. Some indicated their elation over the fact that I had not been caught. They joked and laughed about it for hours. Eventually, the dairy boss took umbrage at the obvious happiness created by my disappearance. He exploded, "If I hear another comment about that dirty stinking Williams, I'll burn some rump. Keep your mouths shut and finish your work." Other than an occasional snicker, nothing more was said about the successful rambler. I, at this time, did not feel successful. I was holed up in a barn, feeling like I was going to die of thirst, and was less than three blocks from my quarters. If I were not captured by the next day, the officials were aware that my rambling would cause a copy-cat reaction among the itchy-footed residents. A positive method they loved to employ when an escapee was caught was to bring him back into the compound in chains, parade him before the kids, and then force them to witness the barbaric mistreatment of the hapless boy. They knew it would make any other potential rambler think before he took the chance. So the guards, from the superintendent on down, were angry.

By the third day, I was afraid and thirsty and my candy bars were depleted. I was so discouraged that occasionally I would contemplate surrender. That morning when the usual crew showed up for work, little were they aware that I was fighting a strong urge to crawl out of my hiding place and toss in the towel. I dwelled on this thought for hours. Sleep came to me easily, and I must have slept all day, because when I awoke there was not a sound in the barn. I laid there for an hour or so listening. I made up my mind to crawl out and determine if it was dark. I emerged slowly and quietly, inching my way out. When I reached the edge of the hay, I carefully peeked out. Thank God. I let out a sigh of relief. I stood on my feet for the first time in four days. Damn but I ached. From this time on, I really did not have a scheme to utilize. My original plan had been shot to hell because I had not anticipated such a long 'hide-out' time. I had another reason to thank God; it was raining, and my throat was parched dry. I climbed down the ladder watching ever so sharply for one of the staff. Later, I learned that the head bulls conceded that I had made my escape good after the second day, so they called off the search locally. I quietly opened the barn door and stood in the rain with my face turned heavenward gulping the delicious rain drops. I could not get enough that way, so I made my way to an outside faucet and drank until my belly ached. My next step was to walk to a near-by lean-to and sit down out of the rain. I needed time to think. I lost track of time, but I knew I had to start my journey to whatever lay ahead. Not taking another minute to try to decide what to do, I headed across the field toward the highway. I walked until day started to break. I sought a secluded spot to hide throughout the day. A large grove of trees stood about a mile from the road so I hid in the cover of the underbrush. By nightfall I was so damn hungry. I doubted I would survive. I was unable to sleep during the day. I was wet to the bone and cold as hell. Nevertheless, I stayed concealed until it was safe for me to start hiking south toward Portland. When I first started down the road I would jump like a jack rabbit whenever a car approached. Now I was just continuing on my way and let the cars come as often as they would. I did not seek cover.

As daylight started to break I decided to go to the first house and beg for something to eat. I was surprised when a car pulled up alongside of me. The driver rolled his window down and called out, "Want a ride?" My initial thought was to run, but I was too weak and tired. Without a word I crawled in beside the driver and simply sat there. We had gone for a few minutes when he asked, "Where you from? Where are you going?" I mumbled something about leaving home in Tacoma and heading for my aunt's house in Portland. He must have sensed my exhaustion. I fell asleep. I opened my eyes as we were pulling into Portland. "Boy," he said, "You must have been really tired. And I'll bet my bottom dollar you're starved. I'll pull into a truck stop up ahead and treat you to a meal." It seemed like an hour before we parked among a dozen trucks and walked over to the little cafe. We managed to get a couple of seats in the rear. I was happy with this position because it kept me away from peoples' eyes. I thought everyone was a cop and those who weren't knew I was a wanted youngster. I ate a hearty meal and was ready to continue on when my companion said, "Ready, Kid? "I'll have to let you off at Klammath Falls. I'm going on to Weed, California in an hour or two. If you want to continue with me, that's OK. If not, so long, and take care of yourself." I assured him I would wait and go south with him. I crawled into the back seat of his auto and fell asleep again. I was awake about the time the driver returned to his vehicle. This time he was carrying a suitcase. Without much conversation we started on our journey. I had escaped, my belly was full and I had all the sleep I wanted.

After we got to Klammath Falls he suggested we eat again. I was a healthy boy with a constant appetite. When the meal was over he fueled up and we were on our merry way. When we were about a mile from Weed, he confessed he was very weary from all the driving. "Tell you what, Kid," he said, "let's take a motel for the night, and take off early in the morning." I agreed. He located a run-down hotel and we registered. "So we won't create any suspicion, I'll sign us in as father and son." At the desk he gave a name that I knew was not the real name. I had read a different name on the registration of the vehicle while he was taking care of his business in Klammath Falls. When he gave my name it was the same last name under which he had registered. This bothered me. I was not against his lying but I wondered why he felt it necessary to do so. I was nervous when we entered the room. It had a single bed. After he had unpacked he said, "Well, let's fall in. We have a long trip tomorrow." I asked myself, why the long trip tomorrow? He had said he was going as far as Weed and not any farther. Just as I started to doze off, he told me point blank that he knew I was wanted back at the institution. "I had been staying with my uncle when the warning whistle sounded during your break. In fact my uncle searched for you. The radio gave a full description of you. As soon as you got into my car I knew you were the runaway." I wondered why he had not reported me to the police if he knew who I was. He could have collected fifty dollars. But no, he let me sleep and he paid for my food and lodging. I had an impulse that dictated I should make a break from the room. "I know what you're thinking, kid," said he, interrupting my thoughts. "You don't have to be afraid. I'm not going to report you." It was a long time before I could relax enough to sleep.

In the middle of the night I was suddenly jerked out of my slumber. The fellow next to me was trying to pull my undershorts down. I struck out at his face with all my strength. My youth and excellent physical condition served me well in this time of need. He cried out in pain as he jumped out of bed. Before his feet hit the floor I was facing him and driving both fists against his mouth and chin. He was caught off guard and, by the time he recovered, blood was pouring from his face. Finally he broke free and ran into the bathroom where he barricaded himself. I stood outside the door and heaped the most filthy language upon his head. After I quieted down he called out, "Hey kid, can we talk?" "What is there to talk about, you filthy bastard?" I called back. For a minute he didn't respond. "I'll tell you what," he eventually answered. "I'll give you a fin if you'll just take off and forget this whole deal. After all, I could call the police and report you for being a wanted felon." This threat angered me still more. "Let me tell you something, you creep," I screamed, "You go ahead. I'd rather be back in the joint than to take crap from you. On top of that, I am trying to decide if I should not call the cops and tell them what you tried to do to me. And you know damn well that if I do you're headed for San Quentin." He started talking in a placating manner. "If I open the door will you agree not to attack me? All I want to do is get in my car and be on my way." I played my trump card, "I'll tell you what I will do," I called in to him, "You give me a ten dollar bill, drive me to the bus depot and I'll cause you no more trouble." He agreed. We parted company an hour later. I bought a ticket to Seattle and was in that city by nightfall.

A place as big and busy as Seattle left me confused. I knew no one in Seattle. Trying to burglarize a house in a strange area was much different than pulling a job in a village the size of Wenatchee. After much thought, I decided to hitchhike to Wenatchee. That night I slept in a boxcar. Early the following morning I started thumbing my way to my home town. It was an easy way to travel. I guess it was because of my youth that I was picked up twice. The first time I was dropped off at Leavenworth. The next drive, a woman carried me on into my destination. I was hesitant to go to my folks house, but I was puzzled and really lost. There didn't seem to be any direction to my young life. I had never experienced such mixed emotions before. When I knocked on the door, I was greeted by my sister, Midge. She was shocked to see me and right away asked, "Glenn, what are you doing here?" I was surprised by this question. Surely news of my escape five days before had reached the family. I avoided a reply and asked for something to eat. "I'm on my way to school so you'll have to fix something for yourself," she said as she walked out the door. "Where are Mom and Dad?" I yelled as she started to leave. "They got a phone call early this morning and both went to town. They said they'd be back shortly." Before I could prepare my breakfast, Mom and Dad walked in the front door. When they saw me they simply stared. Mom was the first to react. She ran to me and took me into her arms. Dad stood patiently until she released me. "Glenn, I'm going to turn you over to the police," he said. "You get a bath and eat a full meal, and when I get back you and I will go to see the chief." Apparently I showed my deep disappointment. He continued, "Don't you see, Glenn, I cannot let you start your life from this point on the lam. If I do, you'll be running forever. Truthfully, I am in fear for your future, your very life." Even to this day, I can see the hurt in his eyes. "Dad," I pleaded, "I can't go back to that brutal treatment. I will be flogged like you wouldn't believe." He turned his back on me and on the way out he said, "You've chosen the style of life you want to lead. It's your choice. You want to be a tough fellow, then you will have to learn that you have to bear up under the consequences. You cannot always turn to us for solace." Mom prepared a meal for me while I showered. After I had eaten I turned to her and said, "Mom, I am really sorry, but I will not wait for Dad. He is asking too much of me." I embraced her, heard her sob, and I walked out.

As I walked aimlessly down the street, an awful feeling engulfed me. I felt truly alone for the first time in my life. Only then did I realize that, subconsciously, I had always gathered strength from my family. When the going got too tough, I could always go home for a meal and a place to sleep. But now it was a different story. My parents had made it clear that they would not help me unless I made a clean breast of things and made a genuine effort to start my life anew. Here I was, in a town where I was well known, alone and hunted as an escapee. Naturally, the police would be casing my folks' house. The idea came to me that I had better seek out one or two of

50

my old buddies and shack up with them until I made a good score.

I walked about a mile to my friend Raymond's house. When I knocked on his door, he appeared amazed to see me standing there. "Jesus Christ," he exclaimed, "Go to the woodshed in the backyard and stay there until I can come out." I wondered what the hell had gotten into him. Usually I was invited in, but not this time. By this time I was puzzled and angry. "What the hell did you send me back here for?" I demanded to know. "Man, your name has been on the radio for three days. They say you escaped from the training school, hitched a ride with a guy and forced him to drive you to California. And when you got there you beat him with a shoe, robbed him, stole his car and disappeared. And you've got the guts to show up in Wenatchee?" I started to tell him the truth about the queer in California, but gave it up as a lost cause.

I strode from his yard and decided to hide out until dark. My best place was in an orchard. I found a pile of apple boxes stacked between some trees and proceeded to make a shelter for a few hours. I slept until night came. During my isolation among the boxes I made up my mind as to what I had to do. I needed a gun, for certain. From this point on, I was going to abandon the burglary route and go for armed robbery; get the cold cash, not something I'd have to fence for a dollar or two. As I was walking up an alley, always staying away from lighted streets, I found myself beside the National Guard building. I had been in there watching the men drill and I knew there were weapons stored inside. What a beautiful place to hit. I knew that if I had burglarized the guard the heat would be awful. How would I get out of this rotten town? As I was trying to think of a way to do this an idea struck me. Right across the street lived a fellow who used to steal stuff with me. I made up my mind to approach him and ask him to join me. When I neared the house, I decided to look in the window and see if I could locate him; otherwise I might get the same reception I got at Raymond's place. As I walked around to the rear of his place, I heard the back door open. I jumped behind a bush. Out came my friend, Karl and his sister. They started to go across the neighbor's lawn, when I whispered loudly, "Karl, over here." He jumped with a start, peering in the direction of my voice. "It's me, Glenn," I spoke in a low tone. Recognizing my voice, he walked toward me. His sister continued her trip to visit their neighbor. I was fearful his sister would tell their friends that I was standing right outside, so I pulled Karl to the other side of his house. "Karl," I said, "I've got a cinch way to make some real easy money and have fun too. Are you interested?" "First, Glenn, I want to talk with you about what I heard a few days ago," he countered. "Let's get out of this area and go somewhere we can gab." "Follow me," I ordered and led him to my apple-box hideaway. We crawled in among the crates and settled down. What he told me was unbelievable. When he finished, I interrupted. "Karl, most of that is plain bull shit. Yes, I escaped and hitched a ride to California with a guy who tried to put the make on me." I told him the details and he took it to be the truth. I told him about my plan concerning the National Guard Armory and what a cracker box it would be to bust. I painted a vivid picture of us getting guns and streaking for the big cities where we would join up with established mobsters. He bought the promise of money and big time. "That's a good idea, Glenn. I'll go home and get some food and blankets. Then we'll crack the armory and head for Yakima. From then on it will be easy street." He and I went to his house. I waited in the dark until he emerged from the house with a load of grub and blankets. Back to our hideout we went.

In the rear of the armory there was a coal chute covered with an iron plate. Karl lifted the cover and both of us entered the basement. From there we went up the stairs and were in the main drill room. The doors to a number of adjacent rooms were unlocked. Some contained file cabinets, desks and other office paraphernalia. The last door we tried was locked. However, there was an open transom above the door, and it took me less than a minute to scamper up and into the room. From the inside I unlocked the door to admit Karl. Along one wall was a cabinet. It too was unlocked. I slid the heavy glass panel to one side and there in front of our eyes was a glorious sight. Rifles were stacked the full length of a gun rack. Under the weapons cabinet were three or four very wide and deep drawers. "Holy Jesus," Karl muttered. "Look at that." My eyes were bugging out of their sockets. The drawers were filled with 45 automatics and clips of cartridges. "Let's bust our ass from this place and get on our way," I said. Each of us took two 45's and one rifle. We loaded up on ammunition.

As we walked up the dark alley a police prowl car swept around the corner and pulled up in front of the armory. Three bulls jumped from the car with their guns drawn. Karl and I laid low and watched from our darkened position. The cops disappeared in the front door which we had left unlocked on our departure. They were inside for about thirty minutes before they appeared in the doorway. "Butts," shouted one of the men in blue, "you go around the left side and I'll take the right side. Be careful, this has the appearance of a big-time caper, and you may run into resistance. Be ready to shoot if necessary." The third cop stood in the lighted doorway until his companions came back. They talked for some time until an army sedan drove up. A uniformed officer hopped out and queried, "What has happened?" One of the cops replied, "We just got a call that the lights were on in the building and had been on for a half an hour. We thought it must be one of you, so we ignored it. Then another call came in, so we came over to investigate." With that all the men walked back inside. Karl and I very carefully sneaked alongside the warehouse and took off for our hideaway. By this time it was well past midnight, so we decided to take off for a cabin in the foothills of the town. It was a place that lots of kids visited when they went hiking. That was one of the longest hikes I had ever taken. It was harder on me than it was for Karl. He was four inches taller and out-weighed me by twenty five pounds. Yet he was utterly exhausted when we fell to the floor of the shanty.

How long we slept is anybody's guess, but the sun was shining brightly when we woke up. Karl broke out some bread and wieners from the pack he had taken from his house, and we stuffed ourselves. Our plan was to take off under cover of darkness that night. We intended to steal a car in town and split for Yakima. The next morning, in order to pass the time, we did a great deal of target practicing. We gave little thought to the nearby ranchers who were bound to wonder what all the shooting was about. It wasn't hunting season and they were concerned because they had horses and cattle grazing in the vicinity. Just as soon as it was dark, we toted our loot toward town. When we were at the outskirts, we hid our stolen property in a ditch and covered it with sagebrush. It took us more than an hour to locate a car with the keys in the ignition. It was parked in front of a darkened house. An idea hit me. "Karl, this place has no one home. Let's rip it off." He agreed and we proceeded to break a windowpane and slip in. There wasn't anything worth taking so we started to leave by the rear door to avoid the possibility of being seen by the people next door. I stepped out on the porch when a flood of powerful flashlights blinded me. I dove off the side of the porch right into the arms of a burly cop. Two others darted inside and captured Karl. Off to the hoosegow we went. Damn but I was mad at myself. Why hadn't I tucked a gun into my belt? Karl was secured in one cell and I in another.

At eight o'clock the next morning in walked police officer, Butts. He got right to the point. "Glenn, where did you hide the guns you got from the National Guard Armory?" I sullenly replied, "I don't know what you're talking about." Butts simply looked at me with disgust and snorted, "Maybe you don't, but Karl sure does." I glared right back at him and shouted, "If he knows so much and you're so bright, why don't you know where the guns are?" He slammed the heavy steel door behind himself as he left. He returned within the hour accompanied by Karl. My buddy, looking sheepishly at the floor, wasted no time in telling me why he was there. "Glenn," he started, "I told them the whole story about the guns, the burglary and all. I thought I could remember where we ditched the guns and ammo but I can't locate the exact spot." "What in the hell do you want me to do?," I shot back sarcastically, "lead them to the loot?" A deputy for whom my dad had a great deal of respect spoke out, "Dammit, kid, let's get this crap over with. You have nothing to gain by being uncooperative. You're going away for a long time whether or not you reveal the location of the stolen weapons. Everybody connected with you is sick of having to deal with such a miserable misfit. Now, I want you to come with me and we'll pick them up. Think it over until tomorrow, Glenn." During the rest of the day and most of the sleepless night that followed I thought of the impossible predicament I was in. A new sentence for escape, two new charges awaiting me, an alienated family and one hell of a reception in store for me when I got back to Chehalis.

Early the next morning the turnkey unlocked my cell and told me to follow him to the sheriff's office. Once there he handcuffed me. "What the hell makes you think I am going to tell you anything?" I demanded. The next thing I recalled was sitting on the floor holding my hand over a bruised jaw. The deputy was standing over me. "Get up, you moron, and start for the door. Try to run and I'll rip your worthless skin off your entire body." It was an amazing turn of events. "My dad will hear about this," I screamed. "If you're so tough, why don't you do your own fighting? Are you going to cry for your mom and dad for the rest of your life?" Nothing hurt me more than that remark. He was questioning my manhood. He wasn't through. "I talked with your parents last night and told them what you were faced with. Both of your folks know you are at the end of the rope. I asked for their OK to handle you any way I saw fit to make you come up with those hot guns and they both told me to do what I had to do. God, what a pleasure it was for them to give me permission to slap your juvenile rear end off. And I'll tell you another thing. I'm prepared to beat your face to a pulp if that's what you want." I knew he was telling the truth about his conversation with my parents. "All right," I sobbed, "I'll take you to the stash." By noon we were back to the jail with all the loot.

A week later I was taken before Judge William O. Parr and was accused in open court. However, the only charge brought down on me was the burglary. I couldn't understand this, so I asked the D.A. if there were any other offenses. "No, not at this time," he replied. The armory matter is a charge the US government will have to consider." So far as we're concerned, we will simply try to sentence you with what we have on you now." About three days later I was taken to Judge Parr's courtroom to make my plea. I was overwhelmed to see my dad and mom in the room. I choked up and started to weep. This action did not move my parents to any display of parental concern. Again the charge of burglary was read and the judge asked me how I wanted to plead, guilty or not guilty. My head was bowed. I was truly beaten. "Guilty," I muttered. "Glenn, do you have anything to say before I pronounce sentence?" Judge Parr asked. I refused to answer. The judge asked me the same question again. He waited a full three minutes. His gavel rapped on his bench. "The defendant will stand." I did as he intoned, "It is the judgement of this court that you be incarcerated for a term of three to five years. I have been in contact with the authorities at the Training School and they advise me that you are too difficult to handle and they have asked me not to return you to their custody. A review of your vicious conduct convinces me that you are too hardened to be imprisoned with younger prisoners. I have no alternative but to instruct the traveling guard to deliver you to the superintendent at the State Reformatory. Court is dismissed!" With that he stood and walked to his chambers. I turned to my folks. Dad's head was bowed, defeated. Mom was being held by my aunt. I still hear her crying fifty-five years later.

No sooner had the judge disappeared from the courtroom than two deputies cuffed and chained me securely. When we reached the fourth floor where they house the hardened criminals, I was placed in a big tank with a dozen other inmates. All were obviously much my senior. I feel certain that the escorting officers were relieved to have me under more secure circumstances. By virtue of the fact that Judge Parr had sentenced me to an institution for the more sophisticated criminals, my keepers felt comfortable placing me among those with whom I would be serving time. This time I was surrounded by men, not kids; men who had committed all kinds of heinous crimes. They were not people who stole cars in which to joy ride or burgled homes for trinkets and vandalized other people's houses. My cellmates were men who stole, robbed, kidnapped and killed for profit. It wasn't a youngster's game to them; it was their livelihood. As I stood in the center of the steel cage with my gear rolled in a blanket, they all stared at me. No one smiled or invited me to take one of the cells. They just fixed their gaze on me. Before the cops could close and lock the main door one of the fellows roared out. "Hey, jailor, what in the f—k are you doing putting a kid in here?" One of the hacks responded, "Keep your shirt on, Pete. This 'kid', as you call him is young in years but old in criminal ways. He is heading to the reformatory with you next week, so get acquainted." Pete looked me over carefully. "Well, whatever your name is, take the vacant cell at the end of the lower tier. You can relax. No one will bother you as long as you keep your nose clean."

The expression 'Soul Searching' was not a foreign one to me. It was forever being interspersed throughout our pastor's sermons. It never meant too much to a youngster with the proclivities for outlawry such as I possessed. In fact, most of his sermons were boring and inane so far as I was concerned. We were all going to hell anyway; that is, unless we tithed heavily. There weren't too many people able to tithe at all, so you can see how I came to the conclusion that if I went to hell, many of Wenatchee's stellar inmates would be there to greet me. I reasoned that I could not tolerate them on earth, so what would I do associating with them assigned to a coal-shoveling crew along the river Styx? Lo and behold, the true meaning of soul-searching crashed in on me that first night in a forlorn cell among many thugs. Many resolutions were determined that evening; none maintained for more than a week. No night was ever longer nor darker.

Throughout my juvenile career, I was treated with some deference due to my tender years and the fact that I had a close and loving family. Many had warned me of what I could expect 'over the hill and down the road'. Suddenly it was present. I now was incarcerated with full-fledged criminals. I realized quickly I must develop from a juvenile delinquent to a neophyte member of the society of convicts; a society in which no man ever gained respect. A society which would indelibly leave its taint and stench etched in my psyche. A society with a deadly set of rules; one of no compassion or forgiveness, or code of ethics; a society that only the deluded seek to join. What is the attraction of such an unholy brotherhood? Would I ever be able to figure it out? Exhausted from attempting to find an answer to these questions, I finally fell into a fitful slumber.

The following morning I was shocked into consciousness by the most horrendous noise. Startled, I leaped from my bunk before I was fully awake. I looked toward the front of the tank and saw the creators of this terrible din. A guard and two trustees were raking large pans across the steel bars, a sort of ritual practiced for many years in prisons throughout the country. The guard started yelling, "All right, hit the deck if you want your morning swill." He described it rightly. I lined up at the bars with my tin plate, cup and a table spoon. As hungry as I was, it was nearly impossible to swallow the slop that had been dished up. I sat at a steel table and gazed at the conglomeration in front of me. Until he spoke, I did not even notice Pete as he shuffled into the seat next to me. He muttered, "Here Kid, try a cup of Kentucky Stud Horse Piss". He referred to the coffee. He could tell by the look on my face that I was ready to vomit. "What's your name, Kid?" "Glenn," I replied. Without looking up from his tray he said, "You better get used to this and worse, Glenn. You hired out to be a tough guy, didn't you? I am going to give you a speech and I want you to listen. You are pretty much of a youngster, and a dumb one at that. Your kind are three cents apiece and at that are overpriced. If you have any smarts at all let what I have to tell you sink in." He stopped just long enough to gulp down some coffee. He continued to give me the best advice a man could give a kid. "There are some damn good men in these joints. Why, in my twelve years of living behind bars, I have actually met two or three, maybe four, but no more. In the main, they are the sorriest individuals you'll meet this side of hell. They have chosen this filthy life style because they are too ignorant to be able to feed and clothe themselves by any other means. And the more they wallow in this mire of degeneracy, the scummier they get. As I see it, you're just starting to get scum on you. Get it straight, cons are a bastardly bunch. They're the puke and vomit of the earth. Their society is compiled of those who rape babies and beat aged and infirm people for a few dollars. Most of them would snitch on their mother if they could earn one day's good time. They steal from each other. They rape the weak and helpless and kill those who cannot conform to their methods." He pounded my ears with that battery of diatribe for an hour. He ended his denunciation of criminals by saying, "The only shit worse than a professional criminal is the person who takes the job of being his brothers' keeper; the guard. I tell you this for one reason and that is I don't want to see you ruin your life like I have done." Here was this old timer downgrading the very class of men I wanted to emulate. He made a liar of the books I had read about the Mafia and all those movies I had seen where the gangster was the hero. For a brief minute I hated Pete. I started to get up. When I turned around there was a huge black standing over me. "Better heed the best advice you ever heard, punk."

All the grandiose ideas I had of being a gangster had exploded and I suddenly became a scared brat. The stories I had heard of the Northwest Penitentiary, as the reformatory was originally known, had been horrifying. Rampant brutality by the guards and even worse maltreatment by the inmates on one another were rife. Authentic evidence had leaked from those formidable walls. Unbridled rape was not the exception, but the rule. I had heard that the food was not bad, it was plain rotten. And here I found myself on the doorstep of that imposing edifice of hell after begging for three years to be admitted. Who in the hell else was to blame for my predicament? The courts, police, family and friends had done their best to redirect me. I would brook no curtailment of my illegal activities. A person couldn't be more petrified than I. But damned if I was going to display my abject fear. At night I had sickening nightmares of being attacked by other cons and the screws. I remembered the lashings I had experienced at Chehalis and wondered if a like punishment was in store. To myself I admitted that I was, in reality, a coward and that the consequences of my misbehavior were more than I could bear. But it was too late. Soon I would be chained up again and hauled like a pig to the slaughterhouse.

Rumor had it that the chain to the reformatory was to leave in a few days. Instead, the following morning right after swill time, a deputy came into the tank and called out, "When I read off your name, gather your things and be ready to make that journey to The Grey Bar Hotel." My name was the first called. He droned eleven other names, and one by one, we lined up at the door. For security reasons, only one man at a time was permitted to step into the hallway. I was number one. They marched me to a room down the hall. When I stepped in, I don't know why I was so surprised to see Garfield Davis, the traveling guard, standing beside a pile of handcuffs, leg irons, shackles, and crotch chains. As he was adjusting the hardware he quietly said, "Glenn, I told you quite sometime ago that I would be toting you to another more secure institution. Like most of these men, you're incapable of thinking." It took him about a half an hour to secure all twelve of us. We were marched to a prison bus in single file. He had placed a chain around the waist of each of us. Then he attached another twenty foot length of dog chain to the lead convict. He passed that chain between the legs of each of us. A guard brought up the rear holding firmly onto the crotch chain. If we got unruly, or tried to run, the rear hack was prepared to give a yank on his end of the chain. It wouldn't take an Einstein to figure out what would happen to the testicles. Believe me, we were a sight to see as they marched us down the street to the bus. Every man walked gingerly. The thought of becoming a eunuch was upsetting.

The vehicle used to transfer us that morning was nothing more than a converted bus. Between the driver and the inmates was a steel webbing, making it impossible for one of us to get to the driver. The last two seats of the bus had been removed and a guard post had been rigged up. Behind another steel fence sat another armed guard. A bucket was used as a toilet. It sat in the aisle where everybody's necessary functions could be observed. Lunches had been prepared for the trip of 165 miles. Once or twice the bus would stop at a roadside eatery and one bull at a time would go in to eat and use the lavatory. At each of these scheduled stops the prison van, known as the 'Hearse', would be met by policemen from that locality.

Five hours later we pulled into the farming town of Monroe, the town that was blessed by having a prison to help support it. All of us riding in the hearse were trying to spot the institution. Our vision was impaired because the windows probably had not been washed since the vehicle rolled off the assembly line. I was craning my neck in all directions trying to get a glimpse of my future home. About a mile after we had entered the town the bus turned into what apparently was a private driveway. About four blocks up the driveway we passed between two brick pillars. At the top an arch extended across the driveway. There was a sign printed across the arch which read: ABANDON ALL HOPE YE WHO ENTER HERE.

What a horrible thing to be read by men starting a prison term! The effect it had on me was devastating. The memory of it existed for my full period of confinement, and will continue to haunt me for the remainder of my life. The very word 'Reformatory' connotes a place wherein there is an opportunity for reformation. Only a brief time after I was locked up in that institution I realized what a joke that was.

Crime during the 1930's was on the rampage. From the highest officials to the lowly flatfoot on the beat, the majority could be bought. Common security guards could demand big payoffs for looking the other way. Some honest men in the upper echelon of the US Department of Justice were genuinely concerned. This concern reached into the Congress. One of the results was that a committee was formed to investigate crime and prisons in this country. Congressman George Wickersham was chosen to head the investigative branch of the committee. He had been a former Federal Judge so he was the logical selection. He surrounded himself with capable assistants. Congress allocated the necessary funds and the job was tackled. It was 1930-31. From then until the committee was dismissed, the radios and newspapers carried dozens of sordid stories of the cancerous conditions of the law enforcement branches which were working hand in hand with the most despicable criminals.

Of local interest at this time was the revelation of the decay that had set in in the Seattle Police Department. For the proper consideration the department would make certain that few arrests and fewer convictions ever took place. Prior to the commissioning of the Wickersham Committee, the State Reformatory was known as the Northwest State Penitentiary. After the Committee's investigation, that institution was the subject of a scathing denunciation by Mr. Wickersham. It would require dozens of pages to detail the charges brought against that institution, the guards and the state for allowing such a shocking state of affairs to exist. In a compendium, the pen was declared to be one of the worst places of confinement in the United States.

A broad range of recommendations was submitted in an effort to clean up the whole nationwide disaster. The media had a field day for weeks. As all committees, the Wickersham Commission was praised for their fact finding and the wholesome recommendations tendered to Congress. As usual, the committee and its recommendations were filed and forgotten. After all, the Great Depression had engulfed the world, and time and finances could not be wasted on trivial matters. Of course, John Q. Public was trying to survive, so it wasn't practical for him to worry. One change did transpire as a result of the investigation. The state declared that the facility would hereafter serve as a reformatory and would have the title of Washington State Reformatory. The gun towers did not come down, nor did the walls, nor were the solitary cells and accompanying brutal conditions removed. However, we now could boast of having a reformatory. And it was into this setting which our prison bus arrived.

6

The Big House

The hearse, with its uneasy cargo of prisoners, crept further up the incline toward its goal. As soon as we topped a slight knoll, the ugliest of ugly sights burst into view. It was a grey building about one thousand feet long. In the center of the structure was a rotunda shaped building which I later learned was the nerve center as well as the visiting room. This was my first sight of a full-fledged big house (prison). Ever since the judge had sentenced me to this place, I had been nervous and fearful. Little did I realize that the emotions that were tearing me apart were the same as those of each person in the bus. To look at me one would never know of my anxiety. I carefully scanned the countenances of each of my cohorts. They, too, were putting on airs.

The vehicle came to a sudden stop right up against the highest wall I had ever seen. Directly above us was a gun tower. A guard was standing on the towers catwalk. He was holding what appeared to be a sub-machine gun. It was partly cradled in his arms and, at the same time, seemed to be covering the bus. I heard a heavy clanging and turned in time to see a huge iron gate open in the side of the wall. Immediately our bus moved into the enclosed yard. And just as quickly, the gate shut with a resounding finality. Once I had seen a picture of a boa constrictor swallowing a baby deer. And I related the closing of the gate to a reptile swallowing the hearse and its occupants. The door of the bus opened and a dozen guards walked inside. A man who was obviously in charge called out, "Fellows, we are going to remove your fetters. You're not going anywhere but to the dress-in quarters. So, follow me as soon as I give you the signal." The guards were on each side of the line and bringing up the rear. Someone had the showers turned on and ready for us. "OK, you guys," roared a fat, squat screw, "Strip, come over to the nurse here, bend over and spread em." I had never in my life felt so violated and degraded. Each cavity of our bodies was subjected to search. After we had showered, we were given prison issue clothes and marched into the main cell block. No sooner had we entered that segment of the joint than the cons who were locked into their cells started screaming, whistling and calling us all sorts of vile names. I learned that that conduct took place in all penitentiaries. We were a new 'chain', and such an event breaks the monotony of life behind the bars. New faces, new names and new stories ABOUT THE OUTSIDE WORLD. Sure enough, after I had been there a few months, I joined the rest in the cat-calling. There is a section in all joints that is set aside for new incoming men.

59

It is called the 'fish tank', and recent arrivals are locked in these tanks during a quarantine period of thirty days. During that period of time, we were referred to as 'fish'. While confined in these cells, we are vaccinated and blood tested. From there we are herded into an indoctrination room where a number of the staff addresses us for the purpose of letting the men know what is expected of them.

The most disturbing part of the indoctrination was when we were told that on the following morning our heads would be shaved. We were not permitted to eat in the main dining hall. Our food was brought to us on a cart from the kitchen. The chuck was unappealing in appearance and in taste! And as always, the coffee was lukewarm. I thought the indoctrination period would never pass. On the last day, word spread that our final ordeal would be in the form of the Captain of The Guards, Jack Brady. Rumors had drifted in to us that he was a son-of-a-bitch; a terror, a man feared by the hacks and the cons alike. I don't recall all the stories that I had heard about this fellow, there were so many. Naturally, all of us were not pleased to have to face this ogre, but it was a must before we were admitted into the general population.

The last night was a miserable one. I laid awake wondering if this was what all gangsters experienced. How did they stand the slop, the unreasonably strict regimen and the deprivation. I comforted myself with the knowledge that all mobsters were not caught, and that most never saw the inside of a place like this. I really believed they were too cunning to be caught; that I was here only because I was a novice, and that I'd never get snared again. From now on, I was going to outsmart all law enforcement people. It is amazing how naive I was, how much I believed the trash shown in the movies and printed in cheap magazines. I cannot remember when I fell asleep, but I damn well remember being jerked awake before daylight the following morning. It was dark outside. I wondered why we were roused so early. Breakfast hadn't even been served. I heard a rattling of keys near the automatic sliding barred door. I peered out as the door slid open. A half dozen guards were standing at attention.

One of the men in a cell next to me whispered, "Glenn, what the hell is going on?" "I don't know", I called back. His question was answered within the next ten seconds. A man in a business suit stepped through the doors and, without a second's hesitation, he walked directly to the front of the group of fish cells. He snapped to the screw who operated the central lever which opened and closed the cages. "Open the doors." They were opened immediately. We were puzzled as to what was expected of us. We simply stood in front of the doors like well-trained animals. Already, we had been indoctrinated not to budge unless instructed. This had to be Captain Jack Brady. He was a short individual of not over five feet six inches. To compensate for his stature, he held himself unusually ramrod stiff as if to emphasize that he was all man notwithstanding his height. He was a well-knit person. Very coolly he eyed each one of us. He was without expression. When his eyes locked on mine, I was forced to divert my attention. Eventually, after what seemed to be an hour, he stepped back, militarily. "Fellows, I want you to step three paces out from your cell doors and stand at attention

60

until I dismiss you." As one, we did as he bade. He came right to the point. "I am Captain Jack Brady. I control the entire custody of this institution. There are some things I want you to understand from the beginning. If you do, you will have no trouble. If you don't, your ass is mud. I take no bullshit from you or the guards. By now you must have read the rule book. If not, read and memorize it between now and lunch time. The reason for that order is simple. If you get busted for an infraction, I don't want you to whine and say I did not know the rule. Do as you are instructed by the officer under whose charge you are placed. If you don't understand me, say so now." He waited for a full minute, but none of us spoke. In one minute he was out of the fish tank area.

I figured I had better review the rule book and was doing so when a trustee came by pushing a broom. I called him and asked, "Is that guy for real?" The old baldheaded con looked at me and smiled. He muttered, "They have three names for Captain Brady. He is called the Little Tin Jesus, the Man With the Brass Balls and Napoleon. And let me tell you another thing, kid, he is as tough physically as any man in the place. He would as soon fight you as look at you. He is mean, mean, mean."

Our last tour of the facility took us to the Department of Education. The rooms were dimly lit, in need of paint and, of course, the windows were barred. Not an atmosphere conducive to enlightenment. We were led into the superintendent's office where I knew we were going to be subjected to another boring speech. This guy was in love with the sound of his own voice. He could have said in ten minutes, what he droned on for an hour. His last pitch was the one that interested me. "You guys can sit in this place during your entire sentence and vegetate, or you can improve your minds and prepare for the day the front gate opens. If you don't enroll for schooling while you're here, you'll be assigned to hard labor. We get a lot of rain and cold weather here. Regardless of the condition outside you will be called to cut brush, bake bricks or weed the gardens. This will be your last opportunity to sign up for classes." As I saw it, his motive for the hard sell was to ensure his job. Before he had finished his speech, I had decided to spend my time in the comparative comfort of a heated school room as opposed to the hard labor routine. There was another ulterior reason for my decision. One of the inmate teachers had let it slip that a prisoner who was attending school when his parole hearing came up for review stood a better chance of early release. I was covering all bets. Getting an education didn't enter the picture. This same teacher also strongly urged me to get religion and assure myself of the pastor's support. He added, "Go to mass because the warden is Catholic." These guys didn't miss a bet. What a bunch of connivers, I thought. Sort of like politicians making certain they appeased all factions, kissing all babies. They were playing the get-in-game; I was playing the get-out-game, and everything was fair in politics, love, war and sway-the-parole-board charade.

It took the associate warden a week to approve my school application. I began to sweat. What if he rejected my request? He didn't, and a week later I was standing before an English instructor who was to have a tremendous impact on my life. When I walked up to his desk he didn't even bother to acknowledge my presence. He just waved his hand in my general direction and said, "Be seated." Anger welled within me. I resented his attitude. When he finished reading the papers I filled out he looked up and through me. In return, I stared down and through him, a sort of you blink first game. He then disarmed me with the nicest smile anyone had wasted on me since I had left home. He stood up and extended his hand. Holy balls on a cow, I thought, this officer is a regular person. "Glenn, I am Richard Culp, who will take over the direction of your scholastic development while you are here, which I hope will not be a lengthy period." Never in my life had I taken such an instant liking to another human being. He had the most magnetic personality of any man I had ever met. I didn't know what to say in response to his friendly overture. I stuttered, "Thank you, Mr. Culp. I......." That was as far as I got. An expression of bewilderment and embarrassment spread over his gentle countenance. He placed a hand on my shoulder, looked me directly in the eyes and said, "Young man, I am not Mr. Culp. I am inmate Culp, Richard to you." I stepped back and looked at him in amazement. "Does that bother you?", he continued. I was at a loss for words. He could see I was uncomfortable. He walked to the door. "Meeting you has been a pleasure, Glenn. I'll be expecting you in class at 8:30 tomorrow morning." While in the yard later that afternoon, I talked with new acquaintances about Richard. There was a general feeling of goodwill toward him. However, I sensed a reservation on the part of the fellows to discuss him at length. I could detect a reluctance of many of the men to associate too closely with my new-found friend. This attitude bothered me, but I decided not to pursue the matter further. You don't have to be among this element very long to learn that you don't push yourself on them. Convicts are a rare breed of cat, unpredictable and ready to strike out.

The following morning was the beginning of a relationship which I treasure in my memories. I showed up for class with about eight other thugs. Try to imagine what a motley crew we presented. One always thinks of students as being fresh-faced youngsters, unlearned in the ways of the world. My fellow students were beyond description. They weren't necessarily bad appearing, but their demeanor was something else. Nowhere in the world could they be matched for their disrespectful attitude or brash response to the teacher's efforts to enlighten them. Richard was painfully aware that most were present for the very purpose I was; avoid at all cost the slave labor conditions that were the only alternative. I would have thought it must have been discouraging to the teacher. If it was, he concealed his feelings well.

A surprising experience occurred during the first month of my resident schooling under the dismal circumstances. I actually became interested in my studies. The subjects were presented in an interesting manner. My friend was indeed an excellent instructor. Unbelievably, I studied at night in my cell, foregoing the movies and other entertainment. I looked forward eargerly to going to class. Richard was aware of my keen interest. He pressed me hard with my studies. He gave me less latitude and demanded more in effort from me. During the first six months, I realized what a jewel I had in this man as a mentor and friend. He became a sort of father figure to me and showed this in response to any propensities I exhibited toward bad conduct, both in the classroom and other areas of the institution. On a number of occasions, I had been on the verge of challenging him when I felt he was riding me. My respect for Richard prevented me from bad-assing him.

One evening while we were walking in the cellhouse corridor, on an impulse I asked him if I could move in his quarters with him. We walked for another two minutes before he answered. "When I first met you, Glenn, I had little hope that I could do anything for you. Your record was a signal to me that you were a bad apple. I knew in my heart that you went to school to avoid work and to impress the authorities with your new leaf image. The only thing you had going for you was your youth. Frankly, I had you judged as the most ignorant smart-ass in the joint. But, you were a challenge to me. You have done more than prove me wrong. I now find you a good student as well as a friend. So far as I am concerned, you're welcome to be my cell-mate, but there is one thing of which I don't think you are aware, and I owe it to you to enlighten you. Often you have asked me where I got my education and, while you had too much class to ask, you wondered what I was doing in a place like this. In one statement I will answer your questions. I am a graduate of the University of Southern California and, prior to coming here, was a professor of English at the University of Washington. I became sexually involved with one of my male students, was caught and sentenced for a term of four to ten years." The first answer I easily believed; the second shocked me. He didn't look at me until I found my tongue. "Gosh, Richard", I stammered, "that's difficult to believe."

His explanation cleared up a number of things. First, you will have to understand that sex criminals are looked upon as the most despicable of all inmates. Other legitimate cons avoid them like the plague. As well liked as Richard was, very few inmates would associate with him. He was smart enough to know this, so he wouldn't impose himself on others. While he normally was a gregarious individual, he had to control himself from making normal overtures. This also told me why he seemed to be a lonely, with-drawn person, always keeping to himself. He interrupted my solitude to say, "I personally am honored that you would ask to be my cell partner. But you had better think it over. There will be those who will dislike you for your association with me. They will start rumors that you're queer, that we are lovers. Your world could come crashing down on you if you are subjected to the inevitable consequences of such a move. I want you to think this over for a week or two. Then if you want to join me, all I can say is welcome."

The following two weeks were tough ones for me. I was torn between what I wanted to do and what would be the best for both Richard and myself. Each day in class there seemed to be a strain between the teacher and me. Maybe the strain was within myself. This proved to be a growing experience for me. I learned that men imprisoned together become distrust-ful of one another. There is very little outlet for natural expression. The end result is that you have a group of men having different degrees of paranoia. Considering the instability of most of us, it is prudent to assume we are potentially dangerous. There must be an outlet and that outlet, more often than not, manifests itself in a violent explosion. The more I thought of my dilemma, the more uncertain and fearful I became. Eventually, when the burden became too much for me to bear, I decided to seek the counsel of the chaplain. Prior to seeing him, I felt I owed it to Richard to tell him of the coming interview. As usual, he was an understanding person. "The pastor is a good man, Glenn. You talk to him and listen carefully to his advice."

The Reverend Smalley was a short and very fat geezer. I guess his wheezing, which I found to be disconcerting during our conversation, was due to his being so obese. The lens on his spectacles were so thick it appeared he was looking through the bottoms of coke bottles. As he wore trifocals, he was always tilting his head backward to bring you into focus. Without asking me to be seated, he asked, "What can I do for you, Williams?" I was extremely uncomfortable with both the preacher and the subject I had come to discuss. Eventually I screwed up the courage to broach the reason for my visit. I laid the whole scene out to him. When I got through, he peered through those thick lenses so intently I thought he was angry. "You're old enough to solve your own problems. If I approve the cell move and something goes wrong, then you'll blame me. You said you have given it about ten days consideration and haven't made up your mind yet, and you want me to give you an answer in five minutes. I won't walk into that kind of trap. Anything else?" he asked as he stood up indicating the interview was over. I was infuriated. Without acknowledging his question, I turned my back on him as contemptuously as I could and stalked out the door.

I didn't consult with Richard about my next move. I simply made out a request to the associate warden asking permission to move into Richard's quarters. I was approved and my teacher and I were sharing our living area, our hurts, desires and dreams. During our acquaintanceship, he never once made a move or suggestion that indicated he had a sexual interest in me. In the eighteen months I was closely associated with Richard, I matured very much. I developed a sense of responsibility and respect for others. I became more considerate, compassionate and understanding. Apparently he had quietly decided to see what he could do to straighten this crazy-acting boy out. He never showed impatience. His method of disciplining me was never abrasive. I was not aware of the change that had come over me, but my parents recognized a different son when they visited. My letters made much more sense to them. In fact, while I was away from them for nearly two years, I actually became closer to them. The truth to the expression 'all good things must come to an end' struck home with a devastating blow late one night. I woke up to hear a heavy gasping coming from Richard's bunk. I leaned over to see what was wrong. He was writhing while attempting to gulp air into his lungs. I leapt off my bed and was beside him in a second. "Richard," I cried out, "what's wrong?" It was obvious he couldn't respond. I grabbed my heavy metal cup and started running it across the bars, a universal method of calling guards' attention to the fact there is something radically wrong. When the other inmates are roused to this noise they too grab their cups and join in the cacophonous explosion. The single hack on duty immediately pressed the riot button. In a few minutes the ever anxious goon squad was on the run to my cell. To the credit of the officer-in-charge, he didn't waste time asking questions. He ordered the control guard to open the cell. "Get the chief nurse down here, NOW," one of them yelled. Another, who had placed his ear to my friend's chest, quietly said, "It is too late. This man has been pardoned by the King of Kings."

Coping with the loss of Richard was indescribably difficult for me. I had once read that death was a part of life. Prior to my friend's departure those words were meaningless to me. Now the meaning was clear. School was cancelled for the remaining part of the week. So far as I was concerned, it was cancelled forever. Richard had mentioned very little about his family. Once or twice, he made passing reference to his mother. I knew he wrote her weekly. A month after they had sent the teacher's body home, I was called out to see the Man With The Brass Balls, Captain Brady. "Williams, I have a letter from Mrs. Culp for you. I am going to relax the rules for this one single time and let you have it," he barked. I was dumfounded; a letter from Richards mother.

My hand trembled as I read the following words: "Dear Glenn; Needless to say I am broken-hearted over the loss of my beloved Richard. Until his indiscretion nearly three years ago, he had been a model son. He was blessed with an excellent mind, good character and an all-consuming love for his fellow men. When he was fifteen he lost his father to a heart attack. From that day on Richard lost himself in his studies. He was not a gregarious young man and had few friends. During our separation I sensed he was dying a little each day. No mention was ever made to that effect in his letters; I simply knew. About a year ago, he wrote about you. He said he had agreed to take this wild, bull-headed and crazy kid into his quarters. He stated that, while you were a totally irresponsible young man, he detected a basic good character, a person of good breeding. During the months that followed he wrote of you as his son and told me that you were a beacon of bright light to his otherwise drab existence. He was proud of your growing up and your interest in school I want to thank you for the happiness you brought into his life. I am going to write your mother and share his letters with her. They best describe you and I know they will comfort her. Please continue your studies. My Warmest Personal Regards, Bessie Culp."

I carefully folded the letter and buried my face in my pillow and sobbed. I didn't want the men in adjacent cells to hear me cry, the unforgivable sign of weakness in prison. The part of that letter that cut most deeply was where she said she wanted to thank me for the happiness I had brought to his life. She would never know what this guy had done for me. The segment of the letter that bothered me was the part which read; please continue your studies. I knew I would never go to school in that institution.

I don't know whether it was the loss of Richard or what, but I began getting into trouble with both the other inmates and staff. Shooting off my mouth was a mistake in a place like this. There was always the guy who was willing to try to shut your mouth. It seemed I was involved in a fight at least once a week and the results always were disastrous for me. I was a small fellow of about five feet seven inches and weighed not more than one hundred thirty pounds. Consequently, I was forever on the receiving end of a handful of knuckles. This got kind of tiresome and painful. One day while in the yard, I watched the boxing team working out. An idea struck me. I approached one of the trainers and told him I wanted to learn to fight. The big black looked me over and drawled, "Fellow, I don't teach men to fight. I teach them to box. Any fool can fight, but it takes an artist to learn to box. You ain't got much beef on your bones, but I'll take you over if you will listen to me. I take no shit from any of my students and you bear that in mind."

For the first month of assiduous training all I got was guff from Big Blue, the teacher. He would not let me enter the ring in competition until I had developed a few skills. He once told me, "I don't want my men to get in that ring until they have some capability of defending themselves. When you're ready, I'll select someone of your approximate size and let the two of you go at it." For about two more weeks I had been punching the speed bag, the heavy bag, skipping rope and shadow boxing. I became interested in what I was doing. About three weeks before the 4th of July, the boxers who were to be on that card were paired up. Being on the program of trainees, I was given a ringside seat. The training was in earnest now because each was determined to be a winner. There was an excellent fighter in my weight class who had been chosen to box another fellow of the same weight and experience. His ring name was Tiger Bud. A few days before the program was to be put on, Tiger Bud broke his thumb and was withdrawn from competition. I saw my chance and approached Big Blue and asked to substitute for Tiger Bud. I expected to be denied and was surprised when he replied, "OK, Glenn, you're on." I was both elated and afraid. I caught myself watching my opponent more often. He could really box and I had never had a match. My mouth was always getting me in inextricable situations. My fear prompted me to work even harder during the training sessions. The night before the big event came I was unable to sleep. When I confided this to Big Blue, he said, "Maybe your opponent didn't sleep either." I was pleased with that response.

On the morning of the 4th I was so nervous I couldn't eat breakfast. To make matters worse, my opponent, who was sitting across the table from me ate heartily. He laughed and talked with his friends as though the upcoming event was nothing more than brushing his teeth. My mind worked tricks on me. He seemed to be bigger and huskier than I had ever imagined. Well, it was too late to dodge it and I would not have backed out if my life depended on it. The fight was to begin at 10:00. At 9:30 I walked slowly around the exercise area and then returned to the weigh-in table to get my weight recorded and my hands wrapped.

Because this was our first fight, Ken and I were to be the curtain-raisers. I began warming up by shadow-boxing and light calisthenics. This distraction worked wonders on me. Suddenly my confidence came back. I was anxious and ready to go into combat. I had psyched myself into believing I was going to KO Ken. Oddly enough, I truly expected to accomplish just that. I heard the announcer's voice as he yelled into the mike, "Gentlemen, the contest will start off with two welterweights. Will Glenn and Ken enter the ring?" I hopped in and took my corner. Both of us were doing a bit of footwork to warm up when the announcer again yelled, "Gentlemen, we have in the number 1 corner, Killer Ken, weighing in at 133 pounds. His opponent is Glenn Williams, weighing in at 130. They will go six rounds unless there is a knockout or the fight is stopped by the referee." The ref called us to the center of the ring and gave us our instructions. We shook hands and came out for action. Ken out-boxed me. It seemed he hit me three times to every one I hit him. By the time the fourth round came about my second asked, "Are you hurt, Glenn?" "Hell no," I answered. The second's next words shocked me. "Then get in there and fight. He's out-pointing you. If you're sure he can't hurt you, why the f--k are you dancing away from him so much? Get in there and start hitting. Otherwise, I'm going to toss in the towel." With his words burning in my ears, I walked to the center of the ring to meet Ken halfway. I immediately took the initiative and began punching with all my strength. My foe was startled with my aggressive manner and began backing away. I never stopped punching for the full three minutes. To my surprise, Ken's knees buckled and he went down at the bell. I was elated. I had decked my first opponent. I couldn't wait for the fifth round to begin. I fully intended to win by a KO. When the bell rang I ran to meet Ken. He didn't stand up. In a very brief time his second tossed in the towel signaling that Ken was unable to answer the bell. The crowd went crazy and I drank in the sweet taste of my accomplishment. My hand was raised in victory. I went to Ken's corner to embrace him. I saw then that an ugly gash had opened over his right eye. Oddly enough, I felt badly.

As the months passed, I grew taller and put on solid weight. I boxed many times after that. I won some and I lost some. I never became really proficient. I became deeply involved with types of martial arts, wrestling, judo and savate. Learning to fight became an obsession with me. While I was nowhere near the best in the institution, I became a formidable foe to be reckoned with. Those who were inclined to abuse me before were no longer anxious to contest me. The bullies chose to seek out victims who were more vulnerable. I became confident in many areas. I guess I was becoming too damn cocky for the guards. They sensed my intense dislike for all of them, and I spent no time trying to conceal that hatred. At the slightest provocation, I would cuss a screw out. Only God knows how many days and nights I spent in the hole on bread and water. On a number of occasions I fought with them. They always won on these encounters because they operated as a team. I must have been a stupid bastard. It took me a dozen whippings and months on end in the dark hole before I decided I was on the losing end of this stick. I was losing my good time as soon as I had accumulated it. At this rate I'd die in this miserable place. So, with a calculated docility, I slowly backed away from my former stance. It took the dumb bunnies months to recognize my change in behavior. Getting into the good graces of a segment of society which I truly detested was a tough task for me. Gradually, living in this environment became easier. In the back of my mind I knew I could not win while confined. Just wait until I get on the streets and then, with a gun in my hand, we'd see who was a tough guy. I dreamed of the opportunity to meet them man-to-man, gun-to-gun. There was no way I could understand at this time in my life that I was setting myself up to be executed by legal means or die at the hand of some other sick criminal.

My good-boy-ploy was hard to live up to. Occasions arose when I was tempted to resolve my problems with fisticuffs. I controlled myself admirably. The most difficult testing would arise when some badge carrying bull would give me lip. I learned to say nothing; to go on about my business. This new demeanor was tough to maintain, but the more I practiced it the easier it became. Within three months the staff and cons started commenting about the change in Glenn Williams. I developed a sense of pride at how easily I had deceived them into believing I was on the road to rehabilitation. I enjoyed the role immensely. It paid off sooner than I had dared hope. One Sunday morning I thought I had better add the clergy to my support, so I joined the sparse line of Christians who marched off to the chapel. The pastor was surprised to see me in the congregation of twelve repentant convicts. I listened for its lake of fire. Every other expression was laced with hell and damnation. How I lived through the sermon I'll never understand. When the hymns were sung I would let my tenor voice ring out loud and clear, if not out of tune. The favorite song of cons in prison seemed to be 'Bringing In The Sheaves.' Don't ask me why. Instead of following the words as written in the song, I would sing a parody that I had made up. "Bringing in the thieves, bringing in the thieves, the warden will come rejoicing, bringing in the thieves." It wasn't too many Sundays before the complete congregation was singing my version of the hymn. The pastor was greatly incensed with our sacrilegious actions. The song was, thereafter, deleted from our choice of hymns.

About every six months, the heads of all departments were instructed to write their opinion of the progress, or lack thereof, of all inmates who were scheduled to appear before the parole board. Those august persons then would decide who was a favorite candidate for parole. They depended to a great extent on the merits of these reports. Not knowing the inmates personally, they had no other criteria by which to make a judgement. I was amazed when the pastor's clerk stopped me in the corridor and informed me that the man of the cloth had sent a long and glowing account of the turn-around of Glenn Williams. He urged them to give me favorable consideration. I couldn't believe my ears. I had other connections so I contacted the inmate secretary of the Board and asked him about the chaplain's progress report on me. During lunch he whispered, "Hey, Glenn, the man with the halo practically told the Board that you walk on water." This I could not figure out. Three weeks later I was called before the Board to plead my own case. Because of my past and my former obnoxious behavior, I felt I didn't have a chance in hell of being considered for release. The chief of the Board did the interrogating and started on me by asking why I should be released. I lit into a long well-rehearsed spiel about my seeing the light, wanting an opportunity to prove myself and ending by telling them I would never be able to redeem myself as long as I was penned up. Unbelievably, they bought my tale and ordered my release effective three weeks hence.

That night I wrote my mom and dad of the good news. Their response was one filled with elation and hope. Mom told me she had prayed for me every day and that the Board's action was a result of God's intervention. She finished her letter by writing, "and be certain, Glenn, to get on your knees and thank the Creator." There was no sleep for me that night. It wasn't the excitement of knowing I was going to be on the streets very soon. I simply couldnt bring myself to face my mother, who was a Christian, and deceive her. I tossed the whole night. I knew my intent was to return to the crooked path as soon as I got a taste of freedom. The thought of the trust and confidence my folks placed in me and the despicable manner in which I cruelly deceived them cut into my guts. And here, nearly a half century later, this knowledge returns to cause me continuing discomfort. To make matters more unbearable, it is too late for me to beg their forgiveness.

Not wanting to wait for me to come home by bus, the entire family drove to the reformatory to welcome me back into the fold. The ride home was a joyous occasion. I was rid of all fetters, bars, concrete, screaming convicts, sullen keepers and bad food. What a glorious feeling.

There was a noticeable lack of acceptance from the townspeople in Wenatchee. They remembered me and my criminal activities, naturally. I got the impression that it would be impossible to prove myself to them. The burg was too small and the citizens were of no stature. Former friends avoided me. It was still a depressive community. Very few jobs were available. When a job did come up I found the prospective employer wouldn't even talk to me. I became discouraged. My parents were aware of the hardship I was facing. Their concern was that I would return to a life of crime. Their worries were justified.

After one year I was a pressure-cooker without a release valve. An explosion was inevitable. Many things galled me; lack of work and a refusal of young people my own age to ask me to join them in their activities, of which there were damn few. When I wanted to go to a show or swimming it was necessary for me to ask my folks for a handout. They were more generous than they could really afford to be. I grew more restless. In the evenings I would take to wandering the streets. The most challenging thing in my town was to simply exist. I demanded a more exciting life, one of total abandon, not being responsible to a living soul. To me that would have been utopia. I longed for the feel of a fast car under my reckless control. I found myself chaffing more and more at the confines of a small town where everyone knew everyone else and everything about their personal and private business. I needed to be in fast moving company, a group where they did as they saw fit and to hell with what others thought or the consequences of their lifestyle. I didn't want to have to concern myself with my mom's great aunt, thrice removed, telling my neighbor's grandmother what her cousin had heard. In that tiny town you didn't need a newspaper or a telephone. The citizens gossip-wire couldn't be surpassed for speed and inaccuracy. In a capsule, my problem was really mine and not that of Hicksville and farmer John. I dreamed that another community among other people would prove to be paradise. This attitude on my part fueled the pressure-cooker to a more explosive point. Along the line at some time it blew its top; and mine.

7

The Big Time

In the mid thirties, my life crashed in on me like a cyclone, bringing armed robberies, forgery, kidnapping and bank robbery indictments. When I think of the serene community from which I wanted to 'escape', as opposed to the excitement I had sought and found, there were many times I longed for the safety of my hometown. I found all the glitter of a life of crime exciting all right, but I also learned that it was sordid, vicious and lethal. The die was cast and it was too late for me to reconsider the options; in fact there were none. I was determined to live by the "Golden Gun Rule" of outlawry. I became aware that it was the police who always called the shots. Being branded an outcast and being sought night and day damn soon lost its appeal.

The last day I was to live as a free man in Wenatchee started early one morning. My determination to leave that cloistered conglomeration of narrow-minded people was so overwhelming that it clouded my reasoning. I needed a gun, and the method by which I was to obtain it did not bother me an iota. Fortunately, I came upon a plan that did not involve strong-arm robbery, a choice I seriously considered. I had made up my mind to burglarize houses or cars until I found a weapon. In that area guns were commonplace. Late that evening I went on the prowl, a lonely and some-what desperate and dangerous individual. As luck would have it, I found a fully loaded 38 Police Positive in a car. How lucky could I be? In addition to a loaded life-saver, it was encased in a shoulder holster. The average person will never understand the power one feels when he is armed, particu-larly if he is criminally inclined. I experienced inexplicable feelings of euphoria and invincibility, a dangerous combination. Defiantly I thought, "Let some badge-carrying, flat-footed cop confront me now."

That night I checked into the Columbia hotel, determined to stay off the streets during the night hours. I arose early the following morning, went to the Red Apple cafe and ordered my breakfast. Notwithstanding I had less than a dollar left over, I comforted myself with the knowledge that my pal in the holster and I would never worry about finances again. Impetuosity was a second nature to me. As I walked up to the cash register to pay for my meal, I pulled the pistol from its holster, aimed directly between the eyes of the cashier and quietly advised him that he had no other choice but to give me all the cash in the register. "If you call out or go for the gun you keep under the counter, I'll be responsible for your wife collecting on your insurance policy," I assured him. Without hesitation, he scooped up the bills, put them in a sack and handed it to me. If he had decided to make a move for his gun, I am confident I would have paid all my debts to society with my neck broken by the hangman's noose above 6 Wing in the state penitentiary. Other patrons were not aware what was taking place in the eatery. "Walk alongside of me," I commanded in a low voice. "When we get to the street, you walk across to the other side. Make a fuss in any way and I'll give you a speedy exit to hell."

I walked hurriedly down the alley and worked my way back to the hotel. As I was walking between two buildings, I heard sirens approaching. They sped on by and headed for the main street toward the cafe I had just heisted. When I was in the safety of my room, I emptied the sack of loot on the bed. To me, who had never seen much money, the pile of bills appeared to be two feet high. I totaled it up and it came to a little over two hundred dollars. That was one hell of a lot of money in those times. Sirens kept up their wail on the main street. Damned if I hadn't created some excitement for the residents of "Sleepy Hollow". Normally I would have been in the streets chasing the police cars to determine what had happened. At this time, I was really proud to realize that it was I who afforded the citizens with something else to do but listen to the radios. I had the insane desire to walk into the cafe to watch the police fumbling around trying to look professional. However, I was fully aware that it would be folly for me to show my face around there. As monotonous as it was going to be, I knew I had to stay in the confines of my hotel room. I had to spend more than ten hours cooped up in the dingy room. For something to do I turned on the radio and darned if it wasn't some excited announcer telling about the man who had just robbed the cafe. They described me as being about six feet tall and weighing nearly 185 pounds. Actually, I was less than five feet seven inches tall and I weighed not more than 140 pounds. I was so happy to think how slick I had been. No mask or other disguise whatever, and they still were way off in their description. Until they mentioned sealing off the bus station and railroad station, I had not given any thought to getting out of town. What a dilemma. I cursed myself for not taking this into consideration. I could easily be trapped here. I comforted myself with the thought that the pussy-footers had no idea it was Glenn Williams.

I fell asleep and did not wake up until it was dark. I had to make my move, and do it right now. Just as I started to leave the room, a news bulletin came over the radio. It seemed that witnesses had a better description of the robber than had been given originally. They did not offer too much information, only to say that the police had what they considered a lead on the identity of the stick-up man, and they expected an arrest to be made shortly. I was truly scared now. I reasoned that, in a small town like this, someone was certain to have recognized me. Instead of going out the front I went down the back stairs and out the rear door. The buildings were darkened. I was happy to be encased in the security of night. I sought the comfort of a doorway as I pondered my next move. How in the hell was I going to get out of town? I seriously thought of stealing a horse and riding through the mountains. I had no food nor blankets so that option was abandoned. The solution seemed to be to snatch a car and head east until

I got far enough away for it to be safe for me to take a bus or train. From experience, I knew it was not always an easy task to find a vehicle with a key in the ignition. Before, when I had tried to purloin a car, it wasn't unusual to spend hours locating one that had a key. As a last resort, I decided to commandeer an auto.

Walking nonchalantly up Mission street, a block off the main avenue, I headed south. During my stroll, I was passed twice by a prowl car. The cops scanned me carefully and cruised on by. I tried to appear calm, but I was ready to hit for the tall timber if they had stopped to question me. I had forgotten the gun I was carrying and my promise to shoot it out with the flatfeet if they attempted an arrest. A couple of minutes after the last police cruiser passed, a car with a lone individual pulled into a driveway across the street. This was my opportunity. I immediately ran up to the car as the man was starting to get out. Later I read his account of the gunman and subsequent abduction. He told the investigators, "I did not know anyone was behind me until I felt a hard object poking at the base of my neck. At the same time, I heard someone whisper. 'Don't make any noise and slide back under the wheel. Do as I say and you'll be okay. Move quickly,' I slid back under the wheel as the gunman jumped in the rear seat." Just as he had told the investigators, I positioned myself directly behind him in the rear seat and ordered him to head for Spokane. He did as he was told. Fortunately he had a full tank of gas, so I had no worries on that issue.

Neither my hostage nor I spoke more than a dozen words throughout the four hour trip. Mixed emotions were running rampant in my mind. The big puzzle to me was where I was going to drop the driver. If I let him out of the car on the streets of Spokane, he would streak for the fuzz and this would complicate my escape. Still, I couldn't have him taxiing me around the town. I had to assume the alarm would be out asking the coppers to be on the watch for the car. Two facts faced me; I had to get rid of my prisoner and find a safe place to hide for a few days. In a strange town I could not figure how I would accomplish those tasks. We would be pulling into Spokane about 5:00 AM. It would still be dark, but not for long. During the long trip I had managed to keep my face pretty well covered so the guy I had kidnapped could not give an accurate description of me. This meant I had to be rid of the fellow before daylight. I toyed with the idea of stopping along the desolate road leading into Spokane, tying the victim to a tree and taking the vehicle on into town. Suddenly the terrible thought came to mind. What if we ran out of fuel. I looked at the fuel gauge and was shocked to see it was on empty. That left me with one choice; race on toward the city and hope I could reach a populated area before it was too late. About ten minutes down the highway we pulled into Spokane. I was truly panicky at this point. On an impulse I ordered the driver to turn into a dark alley in the seamy end of the town. I had seen a few crummy hotels. At least one of them would offer a haven. At the darkest spot in the alley, I told the guy to come to a stop. He was white with fear when he blurted out, "God, don't kill me, mister. I won't run to the police, I promise." I replied, "Hell, I'm not going to harm you if you do exactly as I tell you. If you try to call out or run, I'll be forced to blow your head off." An idea came to mind. "My buddies will be up the street waiting for me," I lied, "so all you have to do is remain quiet. I am going to tie you up and put you in the trunk. You will be able to kick off your ropes and yell for help. I want you to lie face down across the front seat. I'll use your belt and mine to secure you. Do not make a phony move or I'll blast you to kingdom come." After he was securely trussed, I helped him into the trunk. Before leaving, I tied a dirty oil rag over his mouth and cinched it up tightly. I only hoped he would be secured long enough for me to find a hotel to check in. As I came out of the other end of the alley, I couldn't believe my eyes. A taxi was cruising by. I hailed it and asked the driver to take me to a hotel. He dropped me off in an older area of town. There were a number of hotels within a five block radius. I selected one and signed in as Paul Gregory, an alias I used from that time on for forty years. For four days, other than to go out for a snack, I stayed in the hotel throughout the daylight hours.

The evening of the fourth day, I took a taxi to the train depot and bought a ticket for Minneapolis. I don't know why I selected that city as my destination. On my arrival in Minneapolis, a porter at the railroad station directed me to a rooming house on Hennepin Street. The lady who owned the house was a kindly soul who saw that her tenants were well-fed and comfortable. I had been spending my money too rapidly, and it wasn't long before I had only a few dollars remaining. This fact necessitated my looking around for a job to pull. However, I made up my mind that this time I was going to plan the caper from A to Z. After all I was now in the big-time, and I had to start using my head. This wasn't a small apple-picking community. These cops were a hell of a lot smarter than the clowns I had just left behind. One thing for sure, I had to start using a disguise or a mask. Then there was the matter of fingerprints, meaning that gloves were an important part of my gear. I realized that a gun was a small part of the essential accouterments. But all this preparation was to no avail if I didn't use my brain. It was at this time I also made up my mind that there would be no more 'small-time crap'. When I had successfully robbed the cafe and kidnapped a man, I reasoned it propelled me into the upper class category of crooks. And too, hadn't the stick-up of the cafe netted me much more than all the breaking and entering of my young life?

During my daydreaming, I made up my mind that I was going to special-ize in robbing banks. The old adage "Go where the money is" was certainly applicable. Dillinger was out there reaping large sums from each bank. Creepy Karpis shoveled in the loot. At what? Banks, of course! I realized that I needed a name if I was to crash into the elite of gangsterdom. Punks and goons were a dime a dozen. With this "Impossible Dream" foremost in my mind, I set out looking for my first bank heist. I didn't have a car so it was necessary for me to take the trolley to the business district of Minneapo-lis. On the fifteen minute ride, I would subconsciously case the districts for a good bank to hit. On the outskirts of town there was a small combination cafe and tavern where I would occasionally stop for a bite to eat. On this particular afternoon, while I was seated at a table near a front window, I saw something that had avoided my sight before. Right across the street was a small bank; exactly what I had been seeking. As I sipped my coffee, I sized up the building, surroundings and the best route for a hurried exit. So far as I was concerned this was to be my first baby. I left the restaurant, walked two blocks up the street, circled the bank, all the time observing my proposed route of escape. For the next three days straight, I ate two meals a day. I spent about twenty minutes watching every detail of my prey and about the same length of time eating food I didn't even taste. The excitement of just the planning caused my appetite to abate.

One afternoon, I was lost in my thoughts while in the eatery, when a gruff voice from behind me rasped, "Where you from, Kid?" I must have jumped from surprise. Instantly I thought, "This guy is a Dick." I turned around to face my questioner and coldly responded, "None of your f—cking business." The man standing before me was a dark complexioned person. He was very powerfully built and was quite handsome. He scowled at me intently and then walked off. It was at this time that I observed him pushing a broom and bussing tables. I recalled having seen him there before, but I had had no occasion to speak to him. After he disappeared behind the swinging door leading to the kitchen, a young waitress who had waited on me for some time stopped at my table. She looked me over carefully, then spoke. "That guy you snapped at is very much respected in this establishment, Buster, and I for one resent your attitude toward him." I was taken by surprise, but wasn't going to apologize or back away from my stance. As I stood up to leave, I commented, "I am not accustomed to having strangers get personal with me." She followed me to the cash register and as she made change said, "That man is my father and if I hadn't been there, he would have tossed you through the window. If you want to get along in this life, Buster, you had better get off your high horse and get control of your stupid mouth. Big J can be mean."

Before I fell asleep that night, I realized that I had made a gross mistake. I had eaten in that joint for nearly two weeks, so naturally the waitresses, cooks and the bus boy could identify me easily. Here I was on the verge of knocking off the bank across the street, and I had to draw unfavorable attention to myself. What a stupid bastard I had been.

The next five days I ate elsewhere. I wanted the folks at the cafe to forget me. Yet, I was not through with my observation of the 'victim'. It might be the better part of wisdom to go back to my favorite eating place and apologize. The very thought of such an action on my part galled me. I always thought that an apology was a sign of weakness. To this day, I thank God that I did return to the restaurant, seek out the bus boy and his daughter and ask them to forgive me for my rudeness. When I finished my stuttering apology, the girl hugged me. Her dad looked me over for a full minute and blurted out, "You dumb asshole, I just wanted to tell you that every time you came in here, I could see you were carrying a gat in a shoulder holster. And I wanted to warn you that this place crawls with cops every noon. I don't know your reason for packing heat, but I can tell you one thing you had better remember. You only carry a gun when you are ready to use it." He walked away not bothering to accept my apology. I went to the restroom and took a careful survey of my appearance. Sure enough, it was obvious I was packing a bucket of six bolts. Why had the bus boy saw the familiar bulge?

The next day, when I came in to eat, I spoke to him. He was congenial and asked if he could have a cup of java with me. I was pleased to think he had accepted my overture. He sat at my table and we chatted for a full hour, all trivial nonsense. For the next four days, we ate together and became friends. I noticed his good manners, direct way of speaking and the very quiet way he spoke. A person six feet from him could never have heard a word he said. The daughter was really fond of him. She would scold him for not wearing a coat. She chided him for wearing clothing that didn't match. He took her disciplining in stride. You could feel a sense of devotion between them.

Time and my finances were running short. I had to make my bid and was determined it would be the following Wednesday. I wanted to steal a car and park it near the rooming house. Also, I wanted to get a ticket to Jacksonville, Florida. Everything had to go like clockwork. On Monday, just as I was getting ready to pay for my meal, I saw Big J parking his car in front of the bank. I wondered why he didn't park in the lot behind the cafe. As he left the car I noticed he was wearing a dark blue suit. It dawned on me then that he was a fine figure of a man. He spotted me through the window and waived jovially. Marie saw him as soon as I did and had a cup of coffee ready for him. He sat down with me. In his soft voice he said, "Kid, can you join me for a drive this fine day?" I was only too glad to break my routine and go with him. When we had finished, the two of us got into his car and drove in the direction of St. Paul. Once across the bridge, he made a U turn and returned to Minneapolis. He repeated this trip again, the same route. Then he asked me if I could remember the exact route he had driven. I assured him I did. Without a word, he vacated the driver's seat and told me to take the wheel. I took him over the route and parked behind the cafe. As I was shutting off the engine, he asked, "Why did you park here?" I faced him and said, "Don't ask me some stupid question!" He didn't look at me when he replied. "I was hoping you'd be sharp enough to realize that that route, the one you are planning to take, is a dead mortal cinch to wind you up in the state prison." I simply stared at him slack-jawed. I didn't bother to start denying what to him seemed to be an open book. "How did you know?" was all I could ask. "We don't have time to sit here and talk", he stated. "Tonight I want you to spend a few hours with me at my apartment. It will be the best learning experience you will ever have." I was so shaken on the way to my room that I rode the trolley three blocks past it before I got my wits about me. I kept asking myself, "Who the hell is this Big J and how did he know of my plans?" By the time he finished his shift, I was waiting for him at his car. His living quarters were only about a mile away. Typically bachelor accommodations consisting of a living room with a Murphy bed in it, a bathroom down the hall. It was neat and clean as I somehow knew it would be.

To my surprise, Marie was sitting at a table when Big J and I walked in. I began to get suspicious. By nature I didn't trust people and here I was alone with two strangers, so to speak. Marie was a pretty young woman of about 24 years of age. When I entered the room she came over to me and hugged me briefly. Big J removed his coat and put on a pot of coffee. I brought the meeting to a head by asking, "What is your object in inviting me over here? Who are you, and why do you think I am planning to do something which requires a get-a-way? I want some answers and I want them now. Otherwise, I'm going to walk out of this place." I was directing my conversation to Big J, but to my astonishment, Marie walked over to my chair, stood in front of me and started answering the questions I had addressed to her father. "Listen to me carefully, Glenn, and you'll be able to understand the conclusions at which my father and I arrived. First, a young man walks into the cafe, obviously a stranger to the city. You started coming in to eat on a very regular basis. Our cafe deals only with local people and a stranger is noticed right away, especially if he continues to come at the same time each day. In your case, you always sat at the same table; the only table offering the best view of the bank, of course. When you would leave the cafe, you would always walk up the street, cross at the corner three blocks away, cross the street again and come back on the avenue that takes you behind the bank. You drew the attention of my father and me, so we tailed you. I parked my car behind the bank on three different occasions and watched you. It was apparent you were casing the bank. Why? Logically, one would think you planned to rob that establishment. It was just as obvious that you were a really ignorant to be so rank in your casing attempts. Once you were so wrapped up looking the bank over, you didn't see two uniformed cops eating at the table next to you. The clincher was the day Big J detected the bulge under your left arm, a tell-tale sign of a concealed weapon. Now do you wonder how we were able to put the make on you?" I glanced at Big J. His features were without expression. He had let his daughter lay the cards on the table and she did a damn good job of it. I sat quietly for a long time. When I found my tongue, I blurted out, "Why are you two are so observant? No one else seemed to censor my movements. Why you two? If you are stool pigeons, you have nothing on me and you sure as hell won't get me to talk."

The story Big J told me was unbelievable. For years he had been a solo operator, specializing in banks. His daughter, when she turned eighteen, was his get-a-way driver. After about ten banks, Big J bought the little cafe on Hennepin street. While he was, to all appearances, just a bus boy, in reality it was his possession. He was hoping to retire with a small business to fall back on. Further down the line he wanted to leave something for Marie when he cashed in his chips. She became the sole waitress and bookkeeper and knew the business inside and out. "If I had not been in the racket before you were born, Kid, I would not have been able to make you." When he finished he just looked at me giving me an opportunity to digest what he had revealed. I finally asked, "Why are you telling me this? How do you know I won't go to the authorities?" He laughed and said, "Prove it! And while you are about it, explain to the police why you're carrying a ten-year hitch under your left arm. I want you to team up with me, Kid." I was shocked at his proposal, but proud. Here was a proposition I liked; an offer to join forces with an old-time hood, a veteran in the trade and a successful one at that. I fired one more question at him. "Why are you are willing to go back into the rackets when you own a good diner?" He flashed that infectious and winning smile on me. "That nice diner you mention is just that, a nice eatery. There is one hitch, Glenn. Marie and I are barely holding our own. I want to launder some money through it and infuse some financial blood into it. When I have made enough to pay the mortgage off, it will be easy sailing. It's the mortgage payments that hurt. I figure one or two more jobs and I'll have a bank roll from which to operate. Another side of the picture is one I don't think you would understand. Once you have been in the business of robbery, you never get it out of your system. I guess you wouldn't understand that aspect of my make-up. Here you come along with the same ambition that I had twenty five years ago. So, why not join up with me? Any more questions, Kid?" Here was my chance to get something off my chest. "Yeah", I started out. "First, quit calling me 'kid'. The second thing is, when do we get on the road? I'm running out of bread." He told me he would need a week to get things set up.

We planned far into the night. In those few hours, I realized that he knew more about the stick-up game than I had ever dreamed. And during that time I got attached to this guy. It was agreed that we would hit the road within a week. I was to tell my landlady that I was going to return to the west coast, and I was to move in to Big J's apartment. Within the week he had secured a car we were to use. It was an inconspicuous older Dodge with a rebuilt motor; hot and fast. It was a decrepit looking thing. My partner said he didn't want to attract attention by selecting a big flashy rig. Our working tools consisted of a sawed-off shot gun and two pistols. We went to separate hardware stores and bought two boxes of shells for each weapon. I was chaffing at the bit. For the next three days we cased a half dozen banks. For one reason or another, he rejected all of them. Too many customers in one, a bum getaway route at nother. Finally, we found one in Minneapolis and another in St. Paul. Big J decided we would hit both the same day, and then streak for the east coast. I insisted we take the one across the street from his cafe. It's too near where I live and work, Glenn", he countered. "Jesus Christ," I replied, "I've cased that cracker box for a month and I know we could take it with no trouble." He lost his temper and yelled, "Get this straight, you dirty-diapered brat. You will learn that a good dog doesn't crap in its own backyard, and this is my backyard. I'm not going to have a f—king thing to do with your stupid idea, is that clear?" It was the first time I had ever seen him so angry. I sat back and shut my mouth for two reasons. One was that I was really afraid of this guy, the other was that I didn't want to lose him as a partner. Finally, I asked him, "Let me do a solo job on the baby. You can be in your diner and have a perfect alibi. If I get nailed, I promise I won't turn stoolie." He leaned back in his chair and scrutinized me for a full three minutes. "OK", he acceded, "You have to get your feet wet before you'll learn what a dumb-assed idiot you are. I have a good feeling about you, and I trust you'll keep your lip buttoned if you fail. That is if you don't get your ass shot off. You'll have to get your own set of wheels and do the entire heist by yourself."

Here was a chance to prove myself. I was going to hit my first bank, and alone too. There was much I had to do before that fateful day. The main necessity was a hot car. The getaway route was well rehearsed. The next morning I set out to locate a vehicle. I didn't want to steal it too early because, when it was reported stolen, the cops would be on the lookout. If I had to get caught on my first caper in this state, let it be for a big-time job. All that day and late into the evening, I searched the town looking for a car with the keys in the ignition. Discouraged, I headed back for our apartment. About six blocks from the cafe, I spotted a car parked behind a church. I scanned the immediate area to make certain I wasn't being observed. I approached the car and stood still for a few minutes. I had made up my mind that if I were accosted I'd simply say I wanted to take a leak. Apparently I was unobserved.

It was too dark for me to see if there were keys in the ignition, so I tried the door. What luck, it was open. I ran my hands up and down the steering column until I found a set of keys. God, but I was lucky! I crawled into the car and put it in neutral and let off the emergency brake. I pushed it onto the street and continued shoving it backward until I was about 500 feet from where it was parked. I wanted to get far enough away so that when I started it up, the owner would not hear the motor. I crawled behind the wheel, pumped the gas pedal a few times and pushed the starter. It sputtered a minute or so and then purred into life. With the lights off, I drove it for a couple of blocks. When I felt safe, I turned the lights on. I checked the revolver to be certain it was loaded and ready for action.

I sauntered over to the cafe and ordered breakfast. Marie took my order without saying a word. My partner was in the kitchen washing dishes. I couldn't tell if they were mad at me or not. If they were, I made up my mind that I would simply hit the bank and head out of town. Inwardly I was hoping for success so they would be proud of me. I had psyched myself up and was not going to be dissuaded. After I had finished eating, I moseyed out and headed for the place I had left the car. I glanced around to see if anyone appeared to be watching my set of wheels. Everyone was going about their business, so I jumped behind the steering wheel and kicked the engine into life. I felt good about how easy it started. The last thing I needed was a balky car. I drove the car about five blocks down the street and turned into a vacant lot behind the bank. I parked it in such a manner no other car could pull in front of me and block my escape. I was satisfied the vehicle could not be observed from the bank or the street. I laid the key on the floor board and left the driver's door unlocked. It was ready! It was a little too early for the jug to be open so I sauntered back to the cafe for another cup of coffee. Up to this moment I had forgotten to get a container of some sort to put the loot in. When I entered the diner, Marie motioned me to a table in a far corner. She placed a cup of coffee in front of me and very quietly said, "Glenn, my father and I are worried. Be very careful." I nodded my appreciation for her expressed concern. "Marie, when you bring me the tab, will you also bring me a large paper sack?" She folded the sack into a square so it would conveniently fit in my inside jacket pocket. I stepped out into the sunlight and gazed across the street at the object of my task.

I was confident as I neared the bank. I put my hand under my right arm for the comfort of the feel of my gun. To myself I kept repeating, "Walk

79

normally, purposefully, and with the demeanor of a legitimate customer. Cover the interior of the foyer to see that things appear normal." When I closed the door behind me, it was too late for me to chicken out. My first setback was when I encountered more than six persons at the tellers' windows. When I had looked it over before there had never been more than two or three persons making deposits and withdrawals. All the bravado drained from me. I was experiencing cold fear. This was the very feeling that Big J had told me that made a novice dangerous. A fearful person would always react irresponsibly and in such cases would start shooting for no real reason. I clamped my jaws tightly, placed myself at an oblique position to the tellers and customers, drew my gun and loudly ordered, "Hit the floor! This is a stick-up! One false move and I'll blast the hell out of all of you!" They fell like dominoes. I leaped over the low counter and walked behind the line of prone cashiers scooping the money in the paper bag.

There were only four cages for me to clean out, but it seemed I was in there an hour before I finished the last one. I was so afraid a customer would walk in while I was in the process of performing my task. No one did. When I was prepared to leave, I shouted out a final warning. "If anyone here sets off an alarm, I'll be cornered. In that case, I'll have no choice but to come back in and blast you." I tried to walk casually out the front door without attracting any undue attention. As I stepped into the street, I sighed with relief. There had not been a hitch. When I turned the corner and headed in the direction of my car, I heard a loud explosion. At that same instant the shattered glass from the bank's window splattered in my face. I was knocked flat. When I arose from the sidewalk under the window, I pulled my pistol, aimed it through the gaping hole where the glass had disintegrated, and opened fire into the interior of the bank. I can only recall how angry I was that someone had tried to gun me down. I became indignant at the very idea. I knew that all hell would break loose in a matter of minutes. Blood was streaming down my eyes, but I felt no pain. I stuffed the bulky sack into my shirt front and ran toward my car. Before I got to the vehicle, three or four men started after me. I stopped in my tracks and reloaded my gun. Without hesitation, I fired point blank at my pursuers. They spread like chickens and fell over each other in their effort to get away from the line of fire. This distraction gave me the valuable minute or two I so desperately needed. Thank God the engine kicked into life. I sped out of the lot and headed down Hennepin Street. It was at this time that I realized my vision was impaired by the blood spreading in my eyes. The more I would try to clear my eyes, the more it would smear. I knew I was not hurt because I felt no pain. I thought maybe a piece of glass had cut me. A glance in the rear view mirror assured me that they had not spotted the speeding car. About a mile from the job I came to an alley and turned in. To this day, I don't know what made me do it, but that maneuver saved my neck. There was an 80 degree turn in the alley and this turn blocked view of my fleeing car. Another block up the alley was a large old barn with a big open door that was half off its hinges. I drove into the barn, shut the engine off and laid down in the seat. It wasn't a minute or two before heard sirens screaming their warning. They did not turn in the alley but continued on up the main street. Intermittently, I would hear police sirens in the general vicinity. Eventually the activity died down.

When I felt safe, I raised my head to see what was in the barn. I took off my jacket and used it as a pillow. Slowly I took stock of my injury. Gingerly I felt my face. It was partially numb. There was no feeling in my forehead and upper lip. I could not even feel my nose. The blood was beginning to congeal and about the same time I began to develop a severe headache. I explored around the sides and back of my head. I guess I was looking for a bullet hole. Then I did another crazy thing. I took the bag of money from my shirt front, spread it out beside me and started to add up the take. It totaled the amazing amount of more than $2,100. To a young fellow like myself, and in those years of the depression, it was considered a magnificent sum. I was pleased. More than ever I had to effect a complete escape. Wouldn't Big J and Marie be proud of me? How could I contact them? Where could I go from here? My face and clothes were blood-soaked and surely the papers would alert the townspeople to be on the watch. There was one damn thing for certain. I could not budge from the security of my hiding place until it was dark. With this realization, I laid back down and made up my mind to just wait. I let my head drop back on my jacket and closed my eyes.

When I opened them again it was dark. I had slept. Having no watch I could not tell what time it was. It really didn't matter. I was happy to be ensconced in darkness. I felt much safer. Slowly I got to my feet, put on my jacket and stuffed the money in the front of my shirt. By this time, my eyes had become adjusted to the darkness. I crept to the open door and peered out. There were houses around but no real activity. A house directly across from the barn appeared to be vacant or the people were out. An idea hit me! I sneaked alongside the building until I came to a window. I looked in but could see nothing. I continued around to the front door. A well-fed cat was laying on a mat. It didn't seem to be disturbed, so I concluded it was a family pet, which meant the house was occupied. I cupped my hands on each side of my eyes and stared into the large porch window. I could make out a piano and other furniture. Instantly I decided to break in, wash up and steal a clean shirt and coat. In a matter of minutes, I was inside the home. Quickly I sought out a bathroom. I dared not turn on the lights. I groped around until I located the wash basin. In no time at all I was rinsing the blood off my face. It was a painful chore. I blotted my face dry with a bath towel and started going from room to room. I wound up in a bedroom. In the closet I felt for clothes to put on. An over-sized coat was the first garment I found. In the bureau drawers I located a shirt. Like the coat, it was two sizes too large, but it had to suffice. When I went through the kitchen I spotted a wall telephone. I made up my mind to ring up Big J's apartment. I could hear the bell ringing. After about five rings, a muffled voice said, "Yes." Very carefully I said, "The Kid here." Right away Big J asked, "Where are you calling from?" It dawned on me that I did not know where I was. "Well, I went down the main drag for a couple of miles until I came to this alley. I turned right and came to an empty barn. I have no idea where it is." "OK, Kid, I know what direction you went, so this is what I want you to do. Get back on Hennepin and stand out of sight until I get there. You will know if it is my car because I will shut off my lights in the middle of every block and turn them back on immediately. As soon as you spot a car doing this, step out in the middle of the road and I'll pick you up. Do you understand my instructions?" I assured him that I did. I hung up the phone and headed in the direction of the main street.

I stood behind a large elm tree and waited. In a matter of five minutes I saw this car about a block away shutting its lights off and on. Relieved, I ran down the center of the street to his car and jumped in. He ordered me to lie down and he drove a circuitous route to his apartment. He parked his car in the backyard and we entered the rear door. When he switched on the lights and saw my face, he said, "My God, your face is a mess. Come on into the bathroom." I looked in the mirror and was shocked at what I saw. My nose was bent sideways and my face was black and blue. Big J phoned Marie and asked her to bring bandages and disinfectant and to get over there right away. He seemed irritated over something she asked because he barked into the receiver, "I've no time to give you a blow by blow description of the damage. Get the stuff over here on the double." He helped me to the divan and told me to strip down to the waist, which I did. "Let me put a pillow under your head. Marie will be here in a few minutes and we'll get you bandaged up." He leaned over me and carefully examined my face. "Hell, Glenn, you're not badly hurt. So far as I can see you have been cut by flying glass. The cuts don't seem to be too deep, but I want to look you over more carefully after we get you cleaned up."

Big J answered a knock at the door. He admitted Marie. She had a sack which contained the items he had requested. She came over to look at me. She was scared as hell, as was I. Her dad calmed her down by telling her that the wounds were nothing to be concerned about. "Get him cleaned up, Baby", he instructed his daughter. In a matter of five minutes all the blood was wiped from my face. Her dad bent over me again to make a more detailed observation. Very tenderly he touched the bridge of my nose. I yelled in pain. "Glenn, when you fell did you hit your face on the pavement?" I told him I was not sure what happened. "All I heard was an explosion and I found myself on the concrete. I don't know whether the noise caused me to trip or if I was hit. It dawned on me that someone inside had shot at me. I was so pissed-off that I got up and returned his fire." "We know all that," Marie butted in. "We watched the whole thing from the kitchen window." Finally, Big J straightened up and matter-of-factly informed me, "I think you caught a slug on the bridge of your beak. It seems to be pretty well flattened. One thing for sure, we have to get you to a sawbones". I sat upright and said, "Bull shit, buster, no doc this side of hell will work on me now. In fact, the hospitals have already been alerted. I'll bet you a C note on that." My buddy ignored me and turned to Marie. "Get the car ready for a run to the Windy City. I'll take him to a quack that specializes in setting bones, removing bullets and generally patching up thugs."

The heat created by my bank heist would not cool off. Apparently there was a paucity of news for the local papers and radio. The sheriff's office was in competition with the police department. Each came up with a different story of whether the job was pulled off by local talent or if it was an out-of-town intruder. Each department announced that several clues had surfaced and that an early arrest was anticipated. I was afraid to go out on the streets because of my damaged face and the fact the pussy-footers would snatch me up. Four days after the caper I confronted Big J and told him I wanted to split under cover of darkness. He sensed my anxiety and gave me an insight to the modus operandi of the cops. "Glenn," he counseled, "Let me tell you how the badge packers work. The mayor is raising hell with the chief of police. The same heat is on the sheriff. The public wants an arrest and are accusing the would-be Shylocks of sitting on their collective asses and doing nothing. Both departments know that the public will soon lose interest because something more newsworthy will break. Of course the media makes its living by dramatizing robberies. It is great fill-in and the gullible citizen eats it up. Just be patient. It will die of boredom. When the officials put all this shit out, the criminal reads it and decides to make a break for it. That is exactly what the men in blue want. They call it 'flushing', like in bird hunting. If the bird stays hidden in the underbrush, the hunter doesn't stand a chance in hell of getting their prey. While you are hiding, they have no choice but to fume, but if you fall for this game and come out from under cover, they have an opportunity if you're out and running. And another thing, Buddy, your face looks like it went through a meat grinder. The cops know you were hit and the man in the street has been reading a detailed account of your injury. That is an edge against you. Stay relaxed here in the apartment for a day or two and then we will hit for Chi and medical help." After that long speech he hugged me comfortingly.

The longest two days in my life passed. On the third day, Big J and his daughter came to the pad with their arms loaded. Breathlessly I waited for my partner to give me the long awaited word, which he did right then. "We're hitting the road tonight, Glenn. The pressure has let up a little." I was one happy Kid. No more solitaire, pacing the floor, listening to the radio and peering out through closed curtains. I was dying for action and here it was. Marie sat on the divan smiling like the proverbial cat. I knew she was waiting for a chance to give me further news but would not do so unless dad let her know it was OK. I glanced at him and back to Marie. "Tell him, Baby," he instructed. She bubbled over and blurted out, "Glenn, you haven't had the radio on for the past few hours, have you?" I admitted I hadn't and told her I never wanted to hear a radio again. "Let me tell you what happened about two hours ago," she continued. "Two goons hit a bank in St. Paul. There was a lot of shooting and the bad boys escaped. So your piddling job is passe as far as public and official interest is concerned. The good guys got the license number and a description of the getaway car. This is a perfect time for you to travel the high road." Of course Big J had to add his two bits worth by saying, "I told you so." He unrolled a blanket he had been carrying. Inside the wrap was a 30-30 rifle, a sawed off shotgun, two revolvers and about six boxes of ammunition. Counting the pistol I always carried, we had one hell of an arsenal, and enough ammo to stand off a brigade of cops. "Marie", Big J ordered, "I want you to fill the car with fuel, check the tires and oil. I want us to put a lot of miles between this town and us by daylight tomorrow."

After Marie left, he turned to me and simply stared into my eyes. Finally, he spoke in a voice and manner that disturbed me. "I want you to sit at the table with me, Glenn. Listen carefully to what I have to say and you might live longer if you heed my advice. Your life is in my hands and mine is in yours. Frankly you are the safest, because I will know what to do to protect you. I am entrusting my life to a novice who doesn't know shit from shinola about this business. I chose you to be my partner because you are young and I think you have guts. If you live long enough, you might learn something. Our chances of success and living in this lifestyle are about one in a hundred. Even if we live, we might spend the rest of our lives in a slimy cell. Myself, I'd rather get my keister blown off. To begin with, I want you to get it out of your head that you're a successful mobster because you pulled off a bank caper single-handedly. You got shot and you shot a teller in return. In a smooth professional caper there is no shooting. Keep that in mind. There is one more thing that you don't seem to be aware of, so if you can keep your mouth shut for a few minutes longer I'll finish this lesson on theory. You know why you got away? Surely you don't think you pulled a solo, do you? If it hadn't been for Marie and me you'd be so goddam deep in the slammer, they'd have to pump sunshine and air to you. Now, I have one thing I want you to bear in mind after we have a cup of hot java."

While he was making the coffee, I thought over what he had said and I was resentful. I wanted to break off our partnership. I rehashed what he had said again. He was 100% right. If it hadn't been for him and Marie I would have had no place to go to hide and recuperate. I realized I owed the two of them a great deal. When he brought the coffee to the table he was all smiles. I concluded he was satisfied with his speech. Both of us sipped the hot drink without making any comments. I broke the silence by saying, "Hey, man, I know that without you two I'd be mud by now. Thanks." He put his hand out and we shook on a lifetime partnership, a partnership that ended with his death in his hometown less than a month later.

When Marie got back, we didn't lose any time in loading our gear in the car. When we had finished, Marie hugged me. Then she turned to her father and embraced him for a long time as though she didn't want him to leave. Maybe she had a premonition. I was aware that she was sobbing against her dad's chest. Nothing was said between them, nothing had to be spoken. Even today I can see Big J as he brushed her hair with his hand. He kissed the top of her head. She turned and ran inside. Big J crawled behind the wheel and we took off for Chicago, one knowledgeable gangster and a dumb befuddled brat who thought he was Jesus Christ with a deadly weapon.

"When do you think we will be in Chi?" I ventured. "I want to travel mostly at night, so I'd guess it will take us three or four days," the driver responded. "I am so glad to be out of that room and on my way. What have you got in mind? Do you want me to drive?" He drove on for another fifteen minutes before saying anything. It struck me that he was doing a great deal of thinking. I wondered if he was having second thoughts about including me in his plans. Yet, he did say we were going to see a sawbones about my nose. "Glenn, I have something to say that might prove traumatic to you," Big J started out. "The fuzz have no idea who we are so we are pretty safe right now. However, there is always a chance of coppers wanting to make some money by giving us a ticket. If we are stopped for any reason, and they see your face in that condition, they may start asking questions. If we are pulled over, it won't be a matter of out-running them. It simply means we are going to have to eliminate them. Be prepared for a pure and simple shoot-out. The sawed-off blaster is on the floor board. If it comes to an ass-for-ass confrontation, and by that I mean our ass or theirs, I want it to be theirs. At my age I can't stand a bust and if you know what's good for you, you won't want a pinch either. You are a cinch to be made if they take us in for anything. We will have the advantage of surprise. If we have to, let's give a good accounting for ourselves, Buddy."

This matter-of-fact lecture filled me with fear and apprehension. The realization that Big J was truly a dangerous and fearless man swept over me. He was a seasoned mobster and I was a green apprentice. When he had asked me to join him as a partner, I was overwhelmed that he would select me to ride shot-gun with him. It was a dream come true. The dream burst like a balloon. Killing cops and maybe getting wasted myself was a scheme I hadn't planned on. If we snuffed a copper and got caught, we were a cinch to do a jig on the end of a piece of hemp. Prior to tonight such a possibility never entered my mind. I was hoping my partner could not see me shaking uncontrollably. I had read of such situations and here I was enmeshed in the same scenario. My reverie was interrupted by my partner's voice booming out. "What the hell has got into you? You've been staring out the window for fifteen minutes. Are you OK, Kid?" "Yeah", I responded. "I was daydreaming."

I must have dozed off. My buddy awakened me by yelling, "Glenn, get this broadcast." I heard the announcer saying that the police were near the arrest of the lone Minneapolis bank robber. They said they were certain it was the work of a local thug. They reasoned he must have lived near the bank because he disappeared too quickly. Citizens had furnished names of suspects. The announcer went on to say that the culprit had shot a teller in the chest, but had not killed him. When the news bulletin was over, Big J shut the radio off. "What a lot of bull shit", he said with exultation. "Those phoney bastards will say anything to appease a bunch of farmers. You know, Glenn, it's too bad you didn't kill that teller. As it is now, he's just another witness to salt you away for twenty years." To play the tough role I agreed with him, but in my heart I was elated to learn that I had not killed a human being. Later in my criminal career I adopted the credo that dead men tell no tales, and the prospect that I might cause the death of another while pursuing my chosen field of endeavor did not panic me. I did not realize I was becoming more inured to violence. It became a sort of second nature for me to prepare a reaction in advance, and in every instance that reaction was the same; shoot first and leave no witnesses.

On the second night of our trip eastward, we arrived at the small town of Aurora, Illinois about forty miles from our destination. Both of us were exhausted and irritable from lack of sleep. We stopped at grocery stores and bought crackers and cheese. We felt more comfortable eating such snacks in the car than in going to cafes. It seemed to me that the farther away we got from Minneapolis the more cautious we became. In addition to the lack of sleep, I was suffering from the wound inflicted by the bank teller's bullet. I found it nearly impossible to lay my face on my arm so I could get some shut eye. I mentioned this to Big J. "Hell, Kid", he cajoled, "I know you're hurting. We'll be at Doc Harris' clinic in less than an hour. I want to call him before we get there. I'll explain the nature of your problem without filling him in on the details. Don't you offer him any information." On the outskirts of Chi, Big J pulled into a nightclub and made his contact with Harris. My partner apparently had been to the clinic before. He drove into an alley and turned in a dark driveway, obviously the rear entrance to the clinic. There was a light in the back room of the building. The shades were drawn. When we knocked, the lights went off and at the same time a door opened and an effeminate voice called out, "Come on in and close the door right away". We had no more than groped our way in the darkness than the room was flooded with light. Before us stood a very tiny man. He had a huge dome-like head bereft of hair. His eyes were pale blue; so pale they appeared to be colorless. What struck me most peculiarly were his hands and fingers. They were more delicate than any woman's. He reached out and grasped Big J's hand. Then he turned to me and asked in his high pitched voice, "Well, what do we have here?" Before I could respond, he held my face between his delicately formed hands and carefully scrutinized the bridge of my nose. He then asked me to lay on an old operating table in the middle of the room. After turning on a powerful overhead light he examined my nose more carefully. When he was through, he turned to my companion and said, "This kid has a busted nose. Apparently the damage was done more than ten days ago and it has set itself. If he wants to be good-looking, I'll have to break it over again and straighten it out."

Before Big J could answer I blurted out, "Hell no, I don't want to go through the pain. Leave it as it is." "OK", he responded, "but you should stay here for a few days. I'll give you some pain medicine. You can eat here with my wife and me and sleep on the veranda. I would urge you to stay off the streets. It will be OK for you to take a stroll after dark for some exercise. In about a week, you will have lost the black and blue patch on your face."

For the next six days the three of us played cards. Occasionally our games were interrupted by a patient coming in for treatment. I noticed they all came in under the cover of darkness. I had to assume they were outlaws in need of treatment. I later learned this man was well-known in gangland circles up and down the Atlantic Seaboard.

Late one evening, I was walking around the deserted clinic trying to pass the time until I was tired enough to get some sleep. Other than being in the operating room and my bedroom, I was not familiar with his layout. During my prowling I was startled when there was a loud banging on the door. My first thought was that the fuzz had learned I was on the premises and I was in for a bust. I hit for the back door, intending to split if it was a pinch. When I reached the safety of a large bush, I crawled under it and lay real quiet. Suddenly the outside lights flooded the yard. Doc's face appeared at the door and he called out, "Who are you and what do you want?" A voice with a very definite Brooklyn accent replied, "Hey, Doc, this is Bootsie and I have my brother in the car across the alley. He's been gut-shot and needs help bad." "Bring him on in and lay him on the kitchen floor until I get a preliminary exam started on him," Doc said. I remember thinking, 'What the hell would he want the guy on the kitchen floor for?' In a couple of minutes three men reappeared carrying a man. After he was taken inside, I crept to the kitchen window and peered inside. The sawbones was on his knees and was cutting the fellow's clothes off. There was blood all over his stomach. In just a matter of seconds, Doc Harris straightened up and announced. "Bootsie, your brother is dead. You'll have to dispose of the corpse yourself. I can't have him on my slab. That will be a C note." Bootsie muttered in a low voice, "God but you're a cold bastard." The medic was inured to insults because of the nature of his practice. Just as soon as the men and the cadaver were out of the door, Doc got a mop and a bucket of water and proceeded to clean up any evidence.

Later I asked BJ what they did with bodies of men who had died under such circumstances. He simply said, "There's nothing they can do, Glenn, but measure him for a pair of cement shoes and drop him in the bay to swim." That reply and the nonchalant manner in which it was given caused me to nearly vomit. I wondered just how many persons over the years have just simply disappeared like that, unknown and forgotten. I also know that this notoriety resulted in Doc's untimely death by a bullet hole in the base of his skull. No one knew for sure, but many of us surmised later that he had been killed to cover up for robbery. It was well known he had large amounts of narcotics and money concealed in his clinic. The other possibility was that he had performed plastic surgery on some wanted desperado and that person disposed of him so the secret would never get out.

Each day of this self-imposed idleness was driving me bananas. My natural color was nearly restored to my face. So why in the hell should I punish myself by hanging around this morgue? In addition to my usual frustrations, BJ took off for a couple of days and left me to wallow in my own damn misery. At least when he was present, I had someone I could rap with. Trying to talk to Doc was like conversing with a morphine-laden parrot. I had thought of wandering over to see a movie but I had given my word that I would not show my face outdoors until we were ready to leave. Late the following night, I heard BJ's car pull into the driveway. I felt a sense of relief to have him back. About five minutes after he entered the building I heard Doc's voice boom out, "BJ, you thoughtless son-of-a-bitch, why did you pull that bank caper in Aurora? I can't stand a bust and you know the rules of my clinic. No illegal capers while you're under my roof." There was a full minute of silence before BJ responded and when he did, I recognized a very dangerous quality to his voice. "Doc, no man talks to me the way you have and eats his next meal standing up. I know that one of your stoolies called you and told you I was in his bailiwick. And of course, any half-witted gazunie knew a bank had been popped by a single operator. So you put two and two together and came up with four. In reality, you have no way of knowing if I was the person who made the withdrawal. Glenn and I owe you a pretty sum of money and if I had not gone out and got it you'd be out a bundle. So shut off your babbling. How much do we owe you?" At the prospect of some of the loot crossing his palm, Doc cooled off. "Give me 500 C's and you and that teen-aged misfit hit the road."In that day and age, $500 was an exorbitant fee, but he had us over a barrel.

When my partner and I were alone, he filled me in on the details of the robbery. I was hurt and angry that he did the job without me and I let him know it. "Kid," he said, "we were down to our last few bucks and we were going to have to hit the trail right away. Actually, I got a little over $1,200 but the bank manager hiked the amount so he could safely rake off a bit for himself. This is a common practice. Well, anyway, we have paid our bill here and have about $750 to help us along. However, out of that I'm going to send Marie $500. Tomorrow you and I will be heading for Minneapolis. Along the road somewhere we should find a jug that is right for easy pickins."

I was happy with the prospect of leaving the dismal atmosphere of Dr. Harris'.

8

BJ

The next morning we loaded our car with our belongings and left the clinic. I could not tell BJ how happy I was to be 'free' again. About an hour down the road we decided to pull into a truck stop and fuel up our bellies. We shared a feeling of relief being on the road in search of another caper to pull. One thing was for certain, our stay at Doc's had given both of us cabin fever. We were so relieved and relaxed, we ate a huge breakfast. As was our natural practice, we selected a table away from other people so we could talk with a degree of privacy. Both of us were a bit paranoid. Thieves become this way for obvious reasons. Don't stay in one place too long, make no confidants. At one point, BJ had counseled me with this bit of advice. "If you have to have a woman, pick her up for a one-night stand. Give her a phony name, and take off the next morning. More cons, far smarter than you, have been executed or sent to some hoosegow for life because they shot their mouth off to a woman."

As the years passed, I began to realize that men who lived outside the law, who existed by their wits and guns, developed the feeling that all people were watching their every move. As this paranoia progresses, each stranger becomes a cop. I was not smart enough to reason that this was a one-way road to the execution chamber, a cubicle for life or endless years in a booby hatch. "Partner", BJ asked, "are you game for another withdrawal?" I simply grinned and nodded my head enthusiastically. He continued, "I have two good finger-men, one in Chi and another in Milwaukee. Chi is hot right now, so what say we take a shot at The Brewery Town?" I heartily agreed to whatever he suggested. "OK, let's hit the road for a few hours. After we check into a hotel, I'll contact Toad." I was not surprised at the unusual name. In the rackets you run into some weird monikers.

As I drove along, I began to notice how rough the car was running. It had no pick-up whatever, and on the hills there was no power. This worried me. Artists in our profession may have nothing else, but they must have dependable wheels and a gun. You are dead in the water without the two. I glanced in the back seat and found BJ was dead to the world. Just inside the Wisconsin border, I pulled into a station to fuel up, check the oil and tires and go to the john. During this procedure, my Buddy continued to slumber. I needed some exercise, so I pulled the car into a vacant lot, got out and jogged around the block. I was in very bad physical condition. The stay at the clinic and the constant driving had left me in bad shape. When I got back to the car, BJ was peering out the window. "Where are we?", he queried.

"Just inside the Wisconsin border," I informed him. "Do you want to put up for the night or shall we keep pushing on?" I was relieved when he suggested we should put up for the night. He reasoned, and rightly so, that it might be a good idea to get off the road after dark. Prowling sneaks were more alert to night drivers. And two men in a vehicle with out-of-state plates would be ripe for an investigation. We located a small clean hotel in Madison. I was dead tired and fell asleep as soon as my head bit the pillow. I had slept for a few hours when I was awakened by a muffled groaning. I snatched my pistol from under the pillow and hit the floor in one motion. I laid quietly for about two minutes, ready to blast away. Unless we had a prowler, the only other person in the room was BJ. From the direction of my Pal's bed, the groaning started again. I eased myself over to the light switch and flipped it on. My partner was propped up in his bed in a half-sitting position holding his left shoulder. His face was white with pain. I ran to him and put my hand on his brow. He was burning up with a fever. "What's the matter, BJ?" He took a long time to respond. "Oh, nothing. I just had some severe stomach cramps." He offered no resistance when I bathed his face and arms with a cold wet cloth. He quieted down right away. I sat beside him for a half an hour. Finally, he fell asleep. I remained awake the rest of the night, sick with worry. I did not realize how attached I had become to this big guy.

By six o'clock the next morning I was under a shower. BJ slept through it all. I decided to slip out of the room and get some breakfast without awakening him. After I had eaten, as usual, all the disturbing thoughts of the night before waned. When I returned to the hotel, I decided to enter quietly so as not to wake my buddy. When I opened the door, I was surprised and elated to hear him under the shower singing his fool head off. He sounded terrible but it was sweet music to my ears. After he had dressed, I walked with him to the cafe where I had been. He ate as though he was starved. My worries were completely dispelled. Back at our lodging we gathered our gear and were soon merrily on our way. Wanting him to experience how the car was acting up, I asked BJ to drive. He wasn't behind the wheel more than a few minutes when he growled, "What the hell has gone wrong with this jalopy?" I told him how badly it drove the night before, and added, "We're going to have to invest in a new set of wheels." He readily agreed. "My contact man owns a wrecking company, and he'll be in a position to steer us into a good deal. You know I sent Marie five C-notes, and that leaves us pretty low on lettuce. We may have to pull our next caper in a hot buggy." His suggestion was tantamount to an order. However, I harbored some misgivings about using a hot get-away car. In the first place, stealing a car was an act that could get us slammed.

He drove on while I read and slept. I lost track of the time and miles, and was somewhat surprised when he called out. "Zip up your pants, Buddy, we are damn near the outskirts of Madison. Let's find a spot to check in. Then we can have dinner before we phone Toad." I noticed that BJ had a knack of always selecting a room that faced an alley. When I asked him why, he glared at me in disdain. "I'm one son-of-a-bitch who wants more than one exit between me and any unexpected welcoming committee." Later in my career, I learned that there was wisdom in BJ's caution in respect to having at least one door and one window from which to flee the scene. I also preferred a lower floor. Diving through windows became a necessity. When we got back from dinner, my pal called Toad. It was agreed that we would meet our finger-man in Milwaukee the following evening. During the same conversation, Toad assured him that securing a car would be no problem. He asked us to check into the YMCA when we hit the big town.

We arrived in the city early in the morning. It was a pleasant town. It was too early to check into the YMCA. BJ came up with a good idea; we'd get some groceries, locate a park and have a sort of picnic. We had a feast of cold hot dogs and cokes under the trees. This respite gave us time for relaxation and talk. We commented how seldom we had the opportunity to slow down and just gab. I was not aware at that time that my life would be one of fast pacing. The atmosphere was so conducive to 'just letting our guard down'. When we had stuffed ourselves, we lit up cigars, laid back on the lawn and forgot our mission for a few hours. There was little talk between us for a long period of time. I dozed. When I awoke, BJ was standing up and stretching. Let's ball the jack," he said. "After we get settled at the YMCA, I'll call Toad and we'll get down to business."

When we got settled in our room for the evening, I asked BJ just who Toad was. "Glenn, the guy used to be a copper in Cicero, Illinois and like many flatfeet he was on the make for side money. He used to finger capers for me. Eventually, greed got the better of him. He and another copper started robbing stores. Inasmuch as he had the inside on the 'luxury jobs' they did pretty good. During one of his heists, he was recognized by a customer in the store. It was necessary for Toad to blast the fellow. Toad's partner could not take the heat, so he quit the force and split. Toad told me that he sweat for months expecting his ex-buddy to crack and spill the beans. So, he informed his chief that he wanted to go west and start a garage and towing company. With that, he disappeared. Very few men knew where he settled. He is one helluva mechanic, so he made good. However, once a thief, always a thief certainly applied in the Toad's case. He contacted some good solid racketeers, and started fingering businesses. He will not personally get involved in the actual crime. He simply puts the finger on a lucrative caper, takes his ten percent and goes back to taking care of his business. Over the past five years, he has set me up with a half dozen nice paying propositions. Rumor has it that he furnished cars for jobs. And, Glenn, with our junker gasping its last, we're lucky to have this local connection." I was absolutely intrigued with BJ's story.

A couple of hours after we had checked in, there was a soft rapping at the door. I drew my gun and stepped to one side of the entrance. BJ had his rod out and was on the other side. We stayed in that position for about a minute. A voice from outside the room called out and said, "You called for a wrecker?" Immediately my pal opened the door, and there stood Toad. He was a man of about fifty years of age, dressed in greasy coveralls. He had a very pleasant face, all smiles. BJ pulled him inside and hugged him roughly. I was beginning to think they must have thought I didn't exist, when BJ turned and said, "Toad, I want you to meet my partner." Toad

91

extended his hand, but he had a quizzical look on his face. Before he could open his mouth, BJ said, "I know what you're thinking. Forget it. This Kid is OK or he wouldn't be with me. He has proven himself. You know I would never bring heat on you, don't you?" The mechanic never answered, but he flashed that infectious smile and relaxed. The three of us sat on the bed and plotted our next job. I was amazed how meticulously they went over every detail. Occasionally, they would stop, look at me and ask, "Understand what we're saying, Kid?" I nodded my head. Frankly I wasn't too damn sure I absorbed the lesson, but I was too damn proud to ask questions.

I wasn't in the same league with BJ and the Toad. It seemed when the two of them talked about old-timers with whom they had worked, I was not included in their conversation. I felt much better when the Toad looked at me and said, "Glenn, I'm going to take you and BJ to meet the crew that set this bank job up. A lot of moxie went into the planning, but I would feel better if you would meet with Coop and Davenport. BJ has known them for years, so he won't need any introductions. I think it would be really good for you to sit with us and listen to them as they lay out their original plan". I felt much better because I was included in the meeting with the brains of the operation. Arrangements were made to meet the following noon in Carl's Beanery, a cafe owned by a former gangster.

When we arrived at the Beanery, the Toad led us into the back room where a table had been set up. Sitting at the table were two men who appeared to be well over sixty years of age. They eyed me suspiciously. I knew in my mind they were wondering what a young man my age was doing in their midst. Toad spoke right up and said, "Boys, I want you to meet Glenn. He's a friend of BJ's, whom you already know. He and BJ have already struck a couple of irons. BJ swears by Glenn, and that's good enough for me. Because this Beanery is so well known by the fuzz, I want us to walk off in pairs and go up the street to Jean's Restaurant. I'll grab a table in the center of the dining room so we can watch anyone who comes in." After we were seated, BJ ordered lunch for the five of us. While we were waiting for the food to be served, Davenport and Coop used their napkins to draw a diagram of the getaway routes from the bank. These men were very meticulous. They knew how many staff would be in the bank, when would be the best time to hit it and the best route for our getaway vehicle. They bowed their heads low over the table, spoke very softly and looked at me occasionally to see if I was getting the gist of their message. We were so intent on what we were doing that we failed to see the waitress who had wheeled in a food cart and parked it next to the table. After we had eaten, the Toad advised us to leave in separate groups. Davenport and Coop walked out first. BJ and Toad followed, leaving me to pick up the tab. When I got to the cash register, a young man tabulated the bill and said, "That will be $18.50 minus 10% for the clergy." At first I couldn't figure what he was talking about and I just stared at him. "Young man", he said "it was refreshing for me to see a group of diners bowing their heads in prayer before they ate." It was then I realized that he interpreted our heads, which were bent in planning a bank robbery, as being heads bowed in prayer.

Later that afternoon, my sidekick, Toad and I cruised around the bank they had set up. We tried every street for the best getaway. Bankers who specialize in withdrawals only always want the jug situated on a corner. Toad had done his homework well. The crazy part of this 'casing' was that we performed our task in an old wrecker. The driver was a fellow dressed in dirty coveralls. His two companions were in slacks and blue shirts. What a perfect set-up. No one in the world would dream that hoods were looking over a job from a rickety tow- truck. When we were satisfied, Toad drove us to a cafe a few blocks from his wrecking yard. And Toad dropped the blockbuster in our laps. "After you guys rip the bank off, drive to my wrecking yard. I'll have the gate open so you can pull in among dozens of old junkers. You'll have to sit in the car 'til dark. Then I'll drive you back to Madison and put you on a train. And, I'll haul you in the wrecker. If the heat is on your ass, don't come to my yard. Try to shake them off if you can. Then head for my place. If the fuzz 'glues' on you, it's your problem. Naturally, I won't be in a position to help you. Agreed?" He felt sure that if they glued on us, and we got cornered, there would be a final shoot-out. While he didn't know me, he was certain that BJ would rather rap on the pearly gates than surrender. I got the feeling that he was quite sure that I would stay with my partner until St. Peter accepted or rejected us.

The three of us drove to within a block of our quarters where Toad dropped us off. In parting, he said, "BJ, when you wake up in the morning, you'll find a green Dodge parked across the street. The key will be on top of the left front tire. It will be fueled and ready to go. It won't be on the police 'hot car list' for a day or two, so don't fret." With that he drove off.

The following morning, BJ and I slept in until about nine. I woke up while my partner was in the shower. This time, there was no singing. I knew he was as tense as I. After I finished bathing, we packed our stuff and checked out. It was our intent to hit the bank between ten and ten thirty, no specific deadline. We ate very little. I was so damn nervous, I couldn't have eaten a larger meal. If BJ was as scared as I, he certainly concealed it well. "Kid, the bank opens at 10:00. We're going to pick up the car and drive to within two blocks of our hit. Now, here's what I want you to do. Neither of us has been in the bank, so we've had no chance to case the interior. From where we park the car, you and I are going to enter the bank about thirty seconds apart. You will go in first and ask the teller for change. When you get it, walk over to one of the tables and pretend to be writing something. During this time, look the inside over very carefully. I'll be coming in right behind you for the same purpose. Ignore me completely."

I was nervous as a cat in a fish market. Nobody seemed to notice me as I went about my assignment. I picked up a deposit slip and simply scribbled some nonsense on it. Pretending to be deep in thought, I looked over the inside of the joint. About the time I was ready to leave, in walked BJ. He went to a different window than I had approached and engaged a young teller in conversation. Then he walked over to the table where I was doing my 'thing'. I ignored him and continued to write on the slip. Finally I sauntered out and went in the direction where we had parked the car. It was a matter of another minute before BJ caught up with me, and the two of us headed for our vehicle. As we strode along he said in monotones, "Now Glenn, when we walk in the bank, we walk in together. You walk straight to the table where you were. I'll split from you and cover the bank manager. From that point on, your job is to keep the staff under your gun and still catch those who might come in to do business. Simply tell them that this is a robbery and that you're going to kill them if they make an outcry. Pay no attention to me. I'll be doing the 'heavy' part. The whole thing will not take more than three or four minutes. One final thing that you must remember, Glenn; don't fire your gun unless you must. If it becomes necessary and we're involved in a shootout, shoot to kill because if they catch us it's curtains. Do you have any questions?" I simply shook my head. The truth was I had so many questions I was afraid he'd think I was a fool for asking them.

We drove around the bank just once. BJ said, "Kid, I'm going to park in front of the jug right away. Remember our plans. Follow them to a T. Let's go?" I pulled a piece of tape across my left cheek and drew it tight enough to distort my appearance. My pal did the same and we moved into the bank purposefully. As soon as we got inside, I positioned myself near a table at the front. Quicker than I have ever seen BJ move, he vaulted the counter, pistol in hand and yelled, "This is a stick-up. If you push an alarm button, you will die immediately." Motioning to the bank manager, he said. "You go to every cage and scoop up the cash. No silver. Move goddam fast." With that he tossed a canvas bag to the manager. That individual moved as rapidly as if he had rehearsed the movements. When he had stripped all five windows, he practically ran up to BJ and handed him the loot. As a matter of show, and to delay hot pursuit, BJ called to me and said, "Cover my ass while I get the car. If anyone moves, blow his f—king head off. All of you bastards hit the floor quick. Stay there for at least five minutes. Otherwise, you go bye bye." With that last remark, he casually strode out the door and got into the car.

In thirty seconds, I was in the seat beside him. I looked at the bank door as we pulled away from the curb. I breathed a sigh of relief; there was no activity. In all probability, the tellers and the manager remained on the floor for the full five minutes we had dictated. BJ drove in a leisurely manner for about six or eight blocks. I kept looking back nervously until my partner snapped. "Keep your face to the front. You're drawing heat on us. There is no one chasing us. So far we're as clean as a nun's face. Just pretend you are talking to me. And put that gun back in its holster." While it was only about five minutes more before we pulled into the wrecking yard, to me it seemed like an hour. As Toad had said, the gate was open and there was no one around. We maneuvered our car among the dozens of wrecks until we were completely hidden from view. We had no more than shut the engine off than Toad walked from his office, closed and padlocked the gate. "Kid", BJ said, "carefully crawl in the back seat and lie flat on the floorboards." Without questioning him, I did as I was instructed. I laid there for a full fifteen minutes before my sidekick made his move. And when he did, he landed on top of the rear seat and stretched out. Eventually he whispered, "I'm going to dump the loot on the floor beside you. I want you to grab all the twenties, ten's and five's and pass them to me. I'll count those and you count the one's and two's. Before I could respond, I was literally buried under a blanket of greenbacks. I sorted the denominations as he instructed. I passed them, handful after handful, up to him. When I could find no large bills, I started gathering the smaller denominations and counting them. It seemed as though we counted money for an hour. BJ finished ahead of me. When he finished, he said, "Well, we got $8600 of the big babies." I did not say anything because I did not want to lose my count. As it was, I had to start over three times. When I finished, I told him I had counted $1100. Goddam, Glenn, we scored about 10 G's. That leaves you and me with about four thousand each after we give Toad his share of 2 G's". I was so happy I could hardly talk. When I got my tongue, I blurted out, "BJ, do you realize we made over two thousand dollars a minute?" He simply muttered, "The stakes are high, but the price is great."

As Toad had instructed, we were to remain in the car until it was dark. I estimated we had about six hours of daylight left. I thought the time would never pass. I wanted to get out of the cramped quarters and stretch, but as soon as I made this fact known to BJ he damn soon put a squelch on that idea. "You have to start using your head, Buddy. The Toad knows where the heat is around this town. While you and I may think we are well concealed, there is a possibility that some cruising snoop might just catch a glimpse of activity in a closed and locked wrecking yard. I don't want some impatient brat jeopardizing me." I resented his calling me a 'brat', and it was my intention to challenge him on it at the appropriate time. I laid back on the floor and daydreamed what I was going to do with my share of the bread.

When I opened my eyes it was almost dark. I listened carefully to detect some motion from BJ. Damned if he wasn't snoring. As difficult as it was, I remained quiet for about another half hour. I was startled into full consciousness by the rattling of a chain. I grabbed my gun and peered into the night in the direction from where the noise came. At that time, BJ also glanced over the top of the back seat. I noticed his ever-ready piece was in his hand. Gradually the form of Toad could be made out. He was unlocking the gate. As soon as he opened it, he walked carefully and noisily toward us. He made certain he did not surprise us. He fully realized that we would be easily spooked and might blast him. When he got alongside the car, he called out softly, "OK, guys, let's get ready to go." The two of us crawled from the car and took about five minutes to stretch and limber up.

As soon as we got into the wrecker, BJ handed Toad a handful of bills. "Here is about 20%; the agreed amount. Is that OK by you, Toad?" "Yeah, that's great. I brought you a damn good car for you to finish your trip in. It's a neat job and in good mechanical conditions. You won't have any problems with the cops. After you get to your destination, phone me and I'll report it stolen. If you get in a jam, burn the son-of-a-bitch. How about giving me a couple of C notes for my trouble, BJ?" Both of us felt an immediate sense of gratitude toward Toad. Our finger-man drove us about five miles out of town to an abandoned service station. Parked in front of the dilapidated building was a nice looking Ford sedan. We walked around it and determined that it had good rubber. When the good-byes were said, my partner and I got in our new found treasure and headed for Milwaukee. The vehicle drove like a dream. After about three hours of moving right along, BJ asked me to spell him. I was wide awake and anxious to do my share. He crawled into the back seat and got about four hours sleep. Even when I stopped at a station to fuel up, he had not stirred. When I finally became exhausted, I woke him up. "I need some rest. Do you feel like herding this beast for a couple of hours?" He nodded and stopped at the side of the road. I got into the back and fell asleep immediately. Somewhere down the line, I vaguely recalled him pulling in to get some gas.

When I did awaken and take stock of our whereabouts, I saw the bright lights of a pretty large city on the horizon. Before I could ask my pal where we were, he said, "Glenn, we're on the outskirts of St. Paul. We'll head right on into Minnie." I panicked. "Listen, you may be going on in to Minneapolis, but you can bet your lead-loaded ass I'm skipping the oven. Have you forgotten that I am hotter than a well-digger's ass in that town?" "Buddy," he asked, "Will you stick with me until I get something off my chest? You surely owe me that much." He continued, "It will still be dark when we drive into my daughter's place. This car isn't hot so we'll have no heat on us. We can get some sleep in a real bed, get a good hot bath, do our laundry and be on our way. And there is something else I want to tell you. For the past week I have had difficulty in moving around rapidly. When I do, there is a sharp pain in the area of my left shoulder. I keep thinking it might be my ticker." Before I could ask any questions, he continued, "I have been talking with Marie by phone every night and have confided in her just what I told you." It suddenly dawned on me that, indeed, he had appeared tired and drawn for the past week. Without another word, we rose together and headed for the car.

Daylight was breaking as we pulled into Marie's driveway. When her dad rapped on the door, she opened it ever so slightly until she was certain who we were. She ran into her dad's arms and they embraced for a long time. I realized the close bond between these two. When they parted, she hugged and kissed me.

Little was said until we finished the breakfast Marie had hurriedly prepared. Eventually she spoke to BJ. "Dad, I know something is not right. Your phone calls were too glib and you kept repeating how great you felt." My partner leaned back in his chair and looked his daughter straight in the eyes. "Baby, there is nothing wrong with me that a couple of nights rest won't cure." Marie wasn't satisfied. "Papa, I want you to get off the road. The two of us can really get this cafe hopping. With the money you have been sending, I have all the bills paid, the pantry is stocked to overflowing and our lease payments are caught up for six months in advance. The diner is doing the best business it has ever. I want you to stay home with me." BJ got up, walked around the table to Marie's side and kissed her. "I'll tell you what, Pumpkin, let Glenn and me get some shut-eye and we'll talk about it. OK?" Without another word, he walked to the bedroom and closed the door behind himself.

Marie and I sat across from each other sipping coffee. Many things were running through my mind. I realized that if BJ decided to stay in Minneapo-

96

lis, I would be without a partner; not just a partner, but a very dear friend, indeed. What would I do? Where would I go? All of these questions overwhelmed me. My reverie was interrupted when Marie asked, "Glenn, would you consider staying on with us?" My reply was quick and to the point. "No. In the first place, the cops would give their life in heaven to get the guy who knocked that bank off across the street. Marie, do you realize what you're asking me?" She looked into her cup a full minute before responding. "I guess I am being foolish, but I like you. Dad thinks of you as a son. I sort of felt we could make a go of it here, the three of us." Without referring to her comment, I made my position doubly clear. "I intend to rest up here for another day. If your father wants to stay, that's OK by me, but by tomorrow this boy will be heading east. I'm going in to say goodnight to BJ, then I'm hitting the hay." As soon as I started to open the bedroom door, I had the strangest feeling. I looked into the dimly lit room at the figure on the bed. I suddenly became ill. For some reason I could not explain, I knew that my old Buddy would be staying home forever. I walked over to the figure curled up with the pillow over his head. I touched his hand. It was lifeless. During this brief interlude, Marie had started doing the breakfast dishes. I simply strode to her and touched her shoulder. I didn't know what to say or how to say it. She looked at me questioningly for a few seconds. I gathered her in my arms and we both began sobbing uncontrollably. She spoke first. "I new he was dying. How can I get along without him? He raised me since I was a baby." She jerked away from me and disappeared behind her bedroom door. I don't know how long I stood at the kitchen sink and just stared out the window, seeing nothing.

Marie made the necessary funeral arrangements. She was planning a memorial service and decided to invite many of his friends. I was afraid she would forget that during his life BJ had made dozens of friends among the criminal element, and it was a cinch the police were well aware of this fact. On occasions such as this, they would have plain clothesmen among the mourners to try to identify the hoods. Some would be wanted, and this would give the cops an opportunity to make an easy 'pigeon' arrest. When I got the opportunity to talk with Marie, I explained my anxiety about being there to pay my last respects. "Glenn," she assured me, "I know what you're saying is true. In fact, I was going to advise against your being there. But will you stay with me for a few days? I don't want to be alone." I assured her I would not leave the city for sometime, notwithstanding I was nervous about being in that town. After all I had just cracked a jug across the street from her place of business.

The news of BJ's death was not a real event in Minneapolis. According to Marie, however, there were more than fifty persons paying their last respects. While Marie was greeting the mourners, I stayed in her apartment. I thought of the death of my very dear friend Richard, who also died of a heart attack. It was difficult to accept my loss, and now I had to accept the departure of another close buddy. The funeral lasted about two hours. I was relieved when I heard Marie's key in the lock. She came up with an idea that certainly pleased me. "I have a good plan, Glenn. You will be a nervous wreck if you lay around here for a week or ten days. Why don't I get my sister to take over the place, and you and I go to Warroad? It's a little town in the Lake of The Woods area near the Canadian border. My friends there won't know you from Adam. How does that strike you?" The arrangements were made. We left the following evening. Inasmuch as BJ's car was ready to give up the ghost, we decided to use her Dodge. It was nearly new and was dependable. Also, I was uncomfortable with BJ's rig.

Three days after we put BJ away, Marie and I were on our way to Warroad, Minnesota. I don't know how many miles that town was from Minneapolis, but I do know we drove endlessly. Neither of us were in the best of spirits. Our loss was painful. She lost her father and a friend. I lost a partner and a mentor. Little time was wasted on idle talk. I don't know what ran through her mind, but my mind was running rampant. Where would I go after I left this state? I had told Marie I wanted to go to Chicago. Why I told her that, I will never know. I did not know a soul in that city. Maybe it was because I related the Windy City to gangsters. It was surely the Robbers' Roost of modern day. And then again, I thought about going home to visit my family. Undoubtedly they were worried sick over not having heard from me. I envisioned the little town from which I had 'escaped' and immediately decided that that was no place for an up and coming bank robber. After all, had I not knocked a bank off solo, and did another job with a pal? This last thought led me to another line of reasoning. Many times, older crooks had advised me against taking on a partner. Harold Babbitt, a very dignified con man once said, "Boy, go it alone. When you have a buddy in the rackets, you increase your chances of being caught. He may be a talker, a boozer, a gambler or an inveterate womanizer. Any one of those combinations, coupled with a life of criminal activity will spell disaster. You take any guy in prison and ask him how he got caught. He'll invariably tell you it was his partner's fault. And the truth of the matter might well be that he himself caused his buddy to fall. Another very important factor that enters the picture is, that no matter how much you get, you will have to split it." It was at this point that I made up my mind to travel alone, and that is what I did with one exception, and damned if I didn't wind up in Alcatraz.

After a long and tiring journey, we pulled into a town so small I quaked with fear. I had a horrible feeling about little towns that shelter little minds. "Marie", I asked, "What in the hell are we doing here?" She did not answer for a long time and when she did I detected a bit of sarcasm in her voice. "It so happens I was born here. I have many friends and relatives still living here. Relax, Glenn, and you'll meet some very nice folks." For the next five days, she and I traveled between a number of equally tiny and remote villages. There was Baudette and International Falls. For the first time I ice skated, tobogganed, skied and square danced. I also relaxed for a brief time. On the sixth day, I told Marie that I had to be on my way. I was anxious to get to bigger and better towns, and to be among a set that traveled high on the hog. The next morning we were on our way back to The Hell's Kitchen. She was looking forward to getting back to the cafe so our return trip was more amiable. Two days later I kissed her good-bye and began my trip to Chicago. As the train pulled out from the depot, I saw her wave forlornly.

9

Love Lost

With all my phony confidence, I felt alone and vulnerable as the train raced toward Chicago. I had no BJ to succor me, no one to whom I could turn for advice and support. Admittedly I was afraid. What the hell would I do when I reached that city which represented itself to me as the most imposing metropolis in the world? You don't walk up to a person and ask, "Could you direct me to some well-established mobster? I want to join his ranks." Why hadn't I asked BJ to give me a connection?

As a matter of fact, I never dreamed that he and I would ever part. I had heard that if you enter another's turf and start pulling capers, eventually, some local man who resents your intrusion will damn soon accost you and advise you to get the hell out of his domain. An out-of-town thug does nothing but draw heat in the area. And then, too, many characters force you out of the city through the 'cement boot' route. I was puzzled and very fearful. After a couple of hours, I fell asleep in the coach. I was awakened by the conductor's voice calling out the name of some town, and telling us that the train would be stopping for fifteen minutes. I stumbled out of my pullman and found myself on the wooden platform of the station. Some people were leaving the train; others were embarking. Fearing I would be left alone in the middle of nowhere, I crawled back into my compartment.

As I groped my way to my seat, I discovered that it was shared by a young lady. She was an attractive brunette whom I judged to be about eighteen years old; near my age. I was unsure how to seat myself next to her. Rather than reveal my diffidence, I walked boldly to my former seat and sat down. I tried to pretend I was a seasoned traveler. I placed my case beside myself, picked up an old abandoned newspaper and started reading it. After about twenty minutes, a porter walked down the aisle calling out, "Sandwiches, cold drinks, candy......"

When he got to our area, the brunette leaned over me and asked the porter for a cold beef sandwich. She smiled at me prettily and said, "Excuse me for reaching in front of you." With that she flashed a dainty smile, and I fell in love. I responded, "Don't give it a second thought. I was just going to order something to eat also." Within a few minutes we were talking as if we knew one another for years. It struck me that I didn't even know this girl's name so I asked her to tell me a little about herself. "My name is Jean Sampson, and I am returning from a visit with my aunt in Minneapolis." I shuddered to think that she had been in Minnie only a short time after I had busted the jug in that town. She continued, "I am from Peoria. I work in my dad's grocery store. I live above the store in my own apartment. My mom died ten years ago, and my dad has raised me. Now I want to know more about you." "Well, my name is Paul Gregory and I was born in San Francisco. My mother is a music teacher and my dad is a lawyer. They had plans for me which I resisted. I wanted to select my own vocation, but they offered me only two alternatives; either a musician or an attorney. So I simply told them I was going to leave the west coast and strike out on my own. There was a bad scene. One evening when they were away from the house, I gathered my clothes and left. Beyond that, I find it too painful to discuss." I was afraid my talk was inane, but if that was the case, she did a wonderful job of covering up. By the time we were finishing our coffee, I was completely infatuated. I noticed her beautiful hands and legs and imagined what a lovely body she must have. Her hair was gorgeous. Never in my life had I met a girl I was so smitten with.

As the night wore on, she fell asleep and leaned her head on my shoulder. Encouraged, I placed my hand over her shoulder. She seemed to snuggle in the curve of my arm. I don't know what time it was when I woke up. The porter was announcing that breakfast was being served in the dining car. I gently shook her and asked her if she would have breakfast with me. If she had rejected me, I would have been humiliated. We went to our respective rest-rooms and washed and groomed ourselves. When we met in the dining room, I was speechless. This darling doll lighted up the entire car with her effervescence. It dawned on me that we would be approaching Chicago. I panicked. My God, would she simply walk out of my life? Out of sheer desperation, I blurted out, "Jean, are you getting off when we reach Chicago?" She leaned across the table and countered my question with one of her own. "Paul, I was going to ask you the same thing." I was ready with my response, "To tell you the truth, I have no definite destination. Being from the west coast, I just wanted to go east and try a new section of the country. Whether I land in Chicago, Philadelphia or New York doesn't matter to me. I just want to get work and settle down." She stared at me for so long I started to become nervous. Finally, she asked, "Paul, how old are you?" I replied, "Oh, I'm twenty-two." She giggled like a school girl and promptly informed me that she thought I was much younger. "I'm twenty-one, but I would have sworn you were about nineteen." I don't know what in the hell got into me. I blurted out, "Jean, I don't want to lose you." The young lady was taken aback by that spontaneous outburst. As she looked at me, I found I couldn't talk. Both of us simply looked at one another. It was I who recovered my composure first. I don't know where I got the courage to continue with, "Jean, I love you." Having said that, I was in seventh heaven. She dampened my spirits a little by replying, "Paul, we don't know each other well enough to talk about love. I really like you, but only time will tell if I can love you." The fact that she did say, 'only time will tell' encouraged me. At least she was indicating that we would not be separated. Without any thought that she might reject me, I put my arms around her and kissed her on the mouth. She did not resist. Both of us seemed to be oblivious to the smiles of the other passengers and the soft laughter that rippled through the diner.

At two o'clock the next morning, our train pulled into Chicago. Both of us were asleep when the engine jarred us awake as it stopped. We had coffee in the station's cafe and made up our minds as to what our next move would be. Jean asked me if I had anywhere to room. "No", I replied, "I'll have to locate a place to crash until tomorrow when I'll have time to look around. I'm a total stranger here." She sipped on her coffee slowly, then offered me a deal I could not very well turn down. "Why don't you stay at my apartment until we can get you settled? I have a sofa on which you can sleep. My place isn't much, but it will do until better arrangements can be made." She hailed a cab. It took us about fifteen minutes to get to her place. Like she had said, it was above a little wooden building that housed her dad's grocery. "You know Jean, I'm nervous about staying here even for one night. What if your dad walks in on us? Trouble is something I'd like to avoid." "You needn't worry, Paul", she countered. "My dad is a great guy, but he is alcoholic, and not too aware of what goes on at the store. He lives about a mile away, and the only time I see him is when he runs out of pocket money. Then he comes in for some booze pennies. He hasn't been upstairs for four or five months. Nevertheless, Paul, I don't want a 'shack-up' situation to materialize between us. You will have your sleeping couch, and I will have my bed." It was agreed. However, within a week, we were sleeping together and comfortable with the arrangement.

Jean would open the store about eight every morning and close it by six each evening. It was during the depression, so she was not very busy. Occasionally, I would help her. My part of the job was to stock the shelves and keep an eye on the inventory. At first, this domestic setting was sort of pleasant. As the weeks dragged by, I became nervous with so much time on my hands. It irked me that Jean put in so many hours for such a penurious income. Some days she would not gross three dollars. When I had moved in with her, I had nearly eleven hundred dollars in loot from the bank BJ and I had hit. I realized what a difficult time she was having to make ends meet. She wouldn't accept any money from me, believing I was stone broke. So I contrived a method of helping her without her knowing. After she would count the day's receipts, I would slip a dollar or two in her hideout. While Jean's situation wasn't the best, at least she had a roof over her head and plenty of food.

As time dragged on she began to ask me questions about my family and youth. I had to be careful with my replies. During one of her inquisitive sessions, I expressed my anger. "Damn it, Jean," I flared, "My family and my past is my business. I wish you would quit trying to bore in on my life." She yelled, "Let me tell you something Mr. Secret, supposedly, some day in the not too distant future, you and I were planning to get married. Don't you think I deserve to know something about you and your family? To me, marriage is a union of two people and it isn't to be taken lightly. I don't know how you view it, but to me it is the most serious step two people can make. You've asked me many personal questions, and I have told you the truth". She stamped out of the apartment and didn't return for a couple of hours. While she was gone, I did some serious thinking. I wondered why I was tying myself down. Wasn't I the one who had carefully planned my life, and wasn't that life dedicated to the rackets? On the other hand, I was really crazy about Jean. Wasn't she everything a guy could ask for? It was time for a decision and there was little time left for me to make up my mind. When she came back into the room, I acted petulantly and did not speak. She made coffee and brought a cup over to me. That gesture melted my heart. I hugged and kissed her. Nothing more was said of the previous confrontation.

One night while I was sleeping, Jean nudged me awake. She had put her hand over my mouth and whispered, "Paul, someone has broken in downstairs." Without making any noise, I rolled out of bed, went to the closet and picked up my equalizer. I crept to the top of the staircase and peered cautiously into the dim light below. I could make out a figure of a man on his hands and knees crawling toward the makeshift cash register. I aimed my gun as carefully as I could, drawing a bead on the thief's head. In rapid succession, I squeezed off two shots. In the quiet of the night the explosion sounded like a cannon. Within ten seconds I heard a crash of glass. The burglar had dived through a window. I chased after him until I was in the street in front of the store. The guy was nowhere to be seen. When I turned around to go back inside I nearly bumped into Jean. She had been right behind me. After we nailed some cardboard over the shattered window, we went upstairs. Both of us were too upset to go to sleep.

When things quieted down, she asked me, "Paul, what are you doing with a pistol?" My retort was unrehearsed and right to the point. "Just for such occasions as this, Baby. I am damn glad I was here and was armed. What would you have done if I had not been here?" She smiled that infectious smile and answered, "I keep a half dozen pint fruit jars on the cabinet right next to my side of the bed. I once discovered a burglar down below. I simply went to the top of the stairs and threw two jars down. The intruder nearly broke his leg getting out. I would have done the same thing this time if you hadn't acted so quickly." I had to smile in admiration for this plucky young woman.

The following morning she broached the subject of my gun again. This time I exploded, "Listen, Jean, I've always had a gun. I've been raised with one. I've found that when you need one, you need it." "Paul, I want to bring up another question. When I count the receipts at night, why do I always find an extra dollar or two in the hide-out the next morning? This never occurred before you came on the scene." I admitted this and told her I simply wanted to contribute to the extra expense of my being there. From that time on, there was an inexplicable tenseness between us. I made up my mind that I was going to leave shortly. I had to figure a way I could make the move without hurting her.

Ever since I have been a very young boy, I suffered from an uncontrollable wanderlust. In my youth, I would simply run away from home and roam the hills around my hometown. When I became hungry and exhausted, I would turn up at home and attempt to continue my life as though nothing had happened. As the days dragged by when I was with Jean, I experienced this compelling urge to be on the road. I knew from the past that the only cure for this urge was to leave and 'do my own thing'... How could I explain such a condition to Jean. She couldn't possibly understand. Finally, when the urge could no longer be denied, I went to her and simply said, "Jean, I have to get to work. I want to be supportive in our joint living arrangement. I won't be gone but for a day or two, and I'll keep in touch with you by phone every night." She was far more understanding and observant than I had dreamed. Her response pleased me because she didn't ask a bunch of questions. "Paul, I've recognized a restlessness in you for the past week. I can appreciate your feelings. Try to find a job near here, will you? I love you and don't want you too far away. You can borrow dad's car. He doesn't use it once in six weeks."

The following morning I packed up one change of clothes and loaded them in the 1929 Plymouth I would be using. When I hit the road, I had no idea where I was going. The only thing I really knew was that I wanted to find a convenient bank to heist. I didn't have an immediate need for cash; I just had a need to keep in practice. I headed southeast from Peoria.

About fifty miles from Peoria, I came upon a town that was larger than the last two places. On the outskirts there was a small sign that read "NORMAL. GREEN LAW ENFORCED!" I knew they also enforced a law against robbing banks. My attitude was that the officials had to capture the wrongdoer before they could enforce the law. Simply because I had robbed one bank alone and had participated in the cracking of two others, I began thinking I was invincible. I recall what BJ once told me. "If you run up and down stairs often enough, you'll stumble and fall at some time. And in this game, you fall just once." As I drove down the nearly deserted main street, I began to think that maybe this town was too small to support a bank. When I got through the village, I decided to circle and come back, hoping to find a cafe. I hadn't gone more than three blocks when I spotted a bank one block off the central drag. I drove past the building twice from each direction, noting the advantages and disadvantages. About fifty feet from the back of the bank, an alley cut through from one street to another. I drove in and out of the alley. I made up my mind to point the nose of the car right up against the alley. Such a position, I reasoned, would prevent another car from cutting me off by parking directly in front of or behind my vehicle. I was pleased to note that traffic was starting to move, and I could move in and out of cars without drawing attention. Satisfied with the set up, I stopped at a cafe and ordered lunch. During my meal, I made mental sketches of the area adjacent to the victim of my intent.

After leaving the cafe, I walked to a nearby drugstore and bought a small roll of adhesive tape and a valise. I had forgotten to bring a container in which to put the money. I sauntered back to my car and pretended to be fooling with the gas cap. In reality, I had cut a few strips of the tape and proceeded to alter the license number. By putting a piece of tape over a part of the numeral 7, I converted it into a 1. I completely blocked out the first number. I hopped into the old Plymouth and headed for the bank. At one part of the alley, a hedge ran along for about twenty feet. Directly across from the hedge, I noticed a dilapidated house that was used as a church. The faded sign read, 'The Church of The Divine Light'. Next to the church was a vacated parking space. A sign across the space read, 'Parking for Rev.

Theodore Blassinggame'. What an opportunity. I would simply pull into that parking spot. It would conceal the car and at the same time let me pull out into the alley, unseen. I left the key in the ignition, pulled a band aid across my lower jaw and casually sauntered into the building.

There were only four tellers, the manager and three customers. I walked over to the manager and told him I'd like to speak with him. He immediately invited me to come behind the counter and sit down at his desk. As soon as I was seated, I drew my coat aside so he could see the handle of my 38 revolver. I spoke quietly in a monotone. "You and I are going behind each teller's cage and tell that person to put all her money in this case. Tell them that an outcry or the setting off of an alarm will result in your death as well as theirs. Just smile and be friendly. One mistake and some people will die here and now. Just nod if you understand." He started nodding and seemed unable to stop. "Let's go!" I stood and he did likewise. Each teller did as she was told. The last girl fainted dead away. I stepped into her cage, scooped the money up and the manager and I headed for the door. By this time, the customers were aware something was amiss. I had to act quickly and forcefully. I yelled, "This is a stickup. Each of you get to the floor and stay there for five minutes. I will be waiting for my driver to come to the front of the bank. Make one bad move and I'll shoot the ass off all of you. Down!" They dropped like ten pins. I told the manager to sit down on a seat near the door and to make no move whatever. I walked out and headed across the lot towards the hedge and my car. At that instant, the bank alarm started ringing. You could have heard it for a mile. I threw the briefcase into the back seat and started to crawl behind the wheel. About the same time, a black man with a minister's collar came out of the church. He saw me and said, "Oh, my God, the bank's been robbed." I had but one choice and that was to play along with him. "Parson, you are right. I hope there isn't any shooting. You and I are so close." He grabbed me by the arm and said, "Let's go inside and watch from a window." I couldn't believe my luck.

From the safety of his living room, we watched as a large crowd gathered. It took the cops about fifteen minutes to get there. They pulled up in typical Keystone style. There were two carloads. By the time they came out, the crowd was pushing, trying to get inside the bank. I turned to Reverend Blassinggame and said, "Pastor, let's join the excitement. The robbers are surely gone by now and there won't be any shooting." His curiosity got the better of him and he joined me. Three of the law enforcement men charged out of the bank and into the crowd. One yelled, "Did anyone see the robbers?" Apparently the employees had told the officials there was more than one. Not a soul came forward to offer information. In about ten minutes the mob began to disperse.

The kindly minister placed his arm over my shoulder and suggested we go back to the church. Once inside he extended his hand and proudly announced, "I am The Reverend Theodore Blassinggame, and you..." I reached my hand out and introduced myself as Paul Gregory from Skokie. I further satisfied his curiosity by continuing, "My mother and I drove here in search of a former school chum who had moved here. She is resting at the rooming house. After we have had dinner we will be returning home." The minister consoled me by saying, "My land, what a reception for a stranger to receive. Usually, Mr. Gregory, this is a quiet law-abiding community. I certainly hope you won't judge the fine people of this city by the terrible thing that happened today. Here, let me fix you a cup of tea to calm your nerves. I can imagine you are really upset." The old gentleman was talkative. We gabbed for about three hours. The immediate heat would be gone very soon, and I could drive leisurely back to Jean's.

As the dusk settled, I announced that I had better go pick up my mother. I was nervous when I saw he was going to walk me to the car. I was fearful that he might have been suspicious from the beginning. Also, I wondered if he might notice the altered plates. Before we got to the car, I asked Blassinggame if he would mind checking my headlights. "If you will go to the front of the car and tell me if both lamps are burning, I'd appreciate it." When he went to the front of the car, I immediately went to the rear and pulled the tape from the plates. For a moment, I seriously considered taking the fellow back into the church and tying him up so I could take off safely. On reconsideration, I realized such a move could mean trouble for me down the road. He had a perfect description of me. As a last resort, I decided on another tack. I opened my wallet, extracted a ten dollar bill and said, "Reverend, I want to contribute this to your work." "Lawd bless you, my boy. Now you hear me, you all come back when you are in this neck of the woods again." In a matter of a few minutes, I was back on the highway heading for Chicago.

While the trip to Jean's was less than two hours, I found it to be a boring driving experience. I realized that I was getting ready to leave the comfort of her bed. The desire to be on the highway to hell overwhelmed me. Planning my next job was a sort of addiction. As the miles rolled by, dreams of the next caper crowded all other thoughts from my mind. Like all thieves, I dreamed of making the 'big one' so I could buy a ranch, retire and raise a family. Deep in my heart, I knew this was never going to be a reality. I loved travel and outlawry. I was not smart enough to see that I was on a dead-end journey, and I mean DEAD-END literally.

As I was pulling into the outskirts of the big city, it dawned on me that I had given no thought as to how much I had netted on the Normal robbery. Oddly enough, I was not too anxious to make that determination. That could be done when I got home. The parking area for the grocery store was in the rear of the building. It was after I had parked that I pulled the valise from the back seat and placed it beside me. I was comfortable counting the money at this spot. The valise was about half full of greenbacks. I began stacking the denominations in separate piles on the seat beside me. All I could see initially were many one dollar bills. Occasionally there would be a few two dollar bills, and fewer fives. I found a half dozen tens and maybe the same amount in twenties. When I finished tabulating the haul, I was livid with anger. There was less than nine hundred bucks. Angrily I stuffed the loot back into the valise and put it in the trunk of the car.

As a matter of precaution I drove around the grocery store twice before I pulled into the parking area in the rear of the store. I could see Jean waiting on a customer, so I loitered a couple of minutes until she was alone before I entered. I expected a warm kiss and hug from her when I entered the store. Instead I was met with a cold stare. I decided to wait for her to get over her pique before I spoke. I walked to the rear of the grocery store and mounted the stairs. A cold wave overtook me when I noted my suitcase and the shoe box in which I had hidden the money lying beside the suitcase. A wave of anger overtook me. I had concealed the money box behind a number of storage bins in the closet. The only way she could have found it was to make a deliberate search. And why would she do such a thing unless she became suspicious? I opened the box. The money was untouched. I counted it and the amount was exactly what I had put in the container. I was tempted to put on an air of resentment for her having got into my belongings. I changed my mind. My thinking was muddled so I sat on the edge of the bed and tried to figure out what had happened in the few hours I was gone. One thing was certain; there was going to be a showdown as soon as she locked up the store.

I didn't have long to wait. I heard her secure the doors. In a few minutes she walked up the stairs and into the room. She walked over to the bed, stood in front of me and said, "Paul, I want a full explanation. I want to know why you have lied to me as to your correct name. I also know that your father and mother don't live in San Francisco, nor is your mother a music teacher and your father a lawyer. So we can come into the open and not waste time, I want you to know that I have been suspicious of you for a number of reasons. And here they are: While looking for some old records in the closet a week or so ago, I came upon the shoe box with more than a thousand dollars in it. On top of the money I found a fully loaded pistol. Among some of your papers there was mention of a town in Washington state. I took the liberty of calling the sheriff of that town. He never heard of a lawyer named Gregory nor a musician of the same name in that town. He said it was a very small village and that he knew nearly everyone in that area. Let me come right to the point, Paul, or whatever your name is. You are a liar! However, that isn't important at this time. What is important is that you are to pack up and get out of my sight. And I mean tonight." With that tirade over, she picked up my suitcase and money box, walked to the top of the stairs and literally threw them down. Many emotions ran through my mind. Where would I go at this time of night? Had she tipped off the police? Just what had the sheriff told her? I knew it was useless to try to strike up a dialogue with her.

In a daze I walked down to the storeroom at the foot of the stairs. In the back of that room was a door which led into an alley. No sooner had I closed the door that I heard Jean lock all the safety catches and shut off the lights. As I stood in the dark, a sense of pity overcame me. There was no doubt in my mind that she was deeply hurt. There had been talk of a future together and now her bubble had burst. In my heart, I knew she was lying on her bed sobbing. It was now quite late. I knew better than to stand in the alley any length of time. As sure as hell, a cop would be driving by, and would want to know what I was doing there.

While I was pondering my predicament and trying to decide my next move, I was blinded by a powerful spotlight. I was either going to be robbed or arrested, or both. I reached for my pistol ready to fight. That is as far as I got. Two huge cops landed on me like a ton of bricks. I started to slug it out but didn't last a minute. My arms were pinned behind my back in a vice-like grip. I lay quietly fearing what might come next. The cop who was straddling my chest told his partner, "Shake this punk down. One more move from him and I'll lay his head open." The first thing they sought and found was my gun. After they had disarmed me, they put cuffs on both wrists. With one cop on each side, they hustled me into the back seat of the prowl car. It was pitch dark. I couldn't even see their faces. Without speaking to one another, they proceeded to search my luggage. They found nothing of interest nor value in my suitcase. The cop in the front seat instructed the other cop to see what I had in the smaller box. "You'll probably find a couple of sandwiches," he joked. I heard the guy rip open the shoe box. Suddenly, he roared, "Pete, this punk's got a box full of money here." My heart sank. They had me, my gun and now my loot. The driver of the car started the motor and drove off. I expected abuse, but was surprised when the captor closest to me released me from the restraints altogether. Suddenly the car pulled off to the side of the road. I had heard how police would catch a thief with money and they in turn would rob the thief. In some instances, they would kill the man whom they arrested, and tell the public they had to shoot the thug because he had tried to grab one of their weapons. I was afraid that this is what was going to happen to me. We sat parked alongside the curb for a full five minutes. As if on signal, both of the men stepped from the vehicle, walked about ten feet away and were talking in voices so low I could not hear what they were saying. For once I realized I was in a deadly game. The two cops talked for what seemed to be an eternity before they sauntered back to their car. The one referred to as Pete opened the back door and called out, "Get out of the car. Bring your suitcase with you. We're going to turn you loose and we want you to get out of town. Is that clear? If you have any idea about going to the police and telling them that you were arrested and robbed by a couple of their brother officers, forget it. It's your word against ours. Also, we have your gun which has your prints all over it. Carrying a concealed weapon calls for ten years in the pokey. We're going to keep your other property. Here is a ten dollar bill. You find your way to the bus depot and get a ticket out of this state. If we catch you around again, your life won't be worth a plugged nickel. Pick up your suitcase and wiggle your ass, buster." With that, he stepped back into the car and the two drove off to do their duty and resume 'protecting society'.

I could see the lights of the town on the horizon so I walked in that direction. After I got nearer the city limits, I began to recognize the neighborhood as being near Jean's grocery store. And with that realization a very comforting thought swept over me. Why in the hell had I not thought of it before puzzled me. Didn't I have about nine hundred bills from the Normal caper? And it was safely ensconced in the trunk of Jean's father's car. On top of that, I still had the key to the vehicle in my pocket. I was so happy, I could have laughed aloud. As I approached the store, I was wary to keep from being seen by Jean if she happened to be looking out of the window. The building was pitch black. I looked at my watch and was surprised to see that it was nearly midnight. In a matter of minutes I had secured the valise of cash from the car and started walking hurriedly toward town. I flagged a passing taxi. Within five minutes I was inside the bus depot. When the ticket master asked me where I wanted to go I replied, "Seattle, Washington." Inasmuch as I had a three hour wait for departure, I settled in a hard seat. I used the valise for a pillow. To be certain some thug did not grab it, I took off my belt, laced it through the handle and wrapped it securely around my arm. Sleep was elusive, so when my bus' destination was called, I was on board in nothing flat. After I settled in the seat in the rear of the bus, I fell asleep and did not wake up for five hours.

Other than an occasional stop for food, the journey moved uninterruptedly toward Denver. The hours were long and tiring. I wondered why I had decided to choose to go to Seattle. I guess it was a subconscious desire to get away from the Midwest. Things were getting too hot for me, and I sensed that distance from Peoria was in my best interest. Seattle was about as far as I could go in the U. S. For a certainty I didn't want to go to Wenatchee. The thought of that town brought memories of my parents, brothers and sisters. I had been gone but a few months, but it seemed like years since I had seen them. I was surprised how lonely I felt when they came to mind. I guess it was a case of good old fashioned homesickness, a condition I would never have admitted to anyone. Maybe I could slip into town unseen and spend a few days with Mom and Dad. I toyed with the idea until I fell asleep. The bus driver's booming voice jarred me awake. "This bus will arrive in Denver in fifteen minutes. Those of you who are getting off here must not forget to gather your belongings before exiting. Those of you who are continuing on to Boise, Spokane or Seattle will have to make your connection here. You will have time to get dinner. Remember, be back on board in one hour." Without any thought or preparation, as was in keeping with my nature, I made up my mind to stop off in this city. My erratic behavior was to be my downfall in many instances in years to come. I had no idea what Denver had to offer. Inasmuch as I was comfortably fixed as a result of my withdrawal in Normal, I had plenty of green stuff to tide me over until I had time to make a decision.

A few blocks from the bus station I located a third-rate rooming house where I took up quarters. It was my intention to lie low for about a week. After I had settled down, I sought a place to conceal my money. Because it was in such small denominations, it was quite bulky. Right then, I made up my mind to go to a bank the next day and have it changed into tens and twenties. I wanted to be able to carry most of it in my wallet. I felt that what I had to hide this evening would be safe if I put it under my mattress. Before doing so, I put about fifty bucks in my wallet. Then I went downtown to find a good restaurant where I could splurge on a T-Bone steak. After a belly full of steak, potatoes and apple pie, I returned to my room to get a hot bath and a real night's sleep. While I was luxuriating in the tub of hot water, I thought of the money I had stashed under the mattress. Naked and dripping wet, I jumped from the tub and ran to the bed. God, what a relief to feel the familiar lump beneath the covers. Years later I learned that concealing valuables under a mattress was a stupid thing to do. A very professional cat burglar once told me that he always ripped the covers off beds, then the sheets, followed by thoroughly slicing the mattress cover to reveal any loot that might be hidden there. He confided, "If you want a safe spot to put your money, roll a corner of the rug back and spread the bills on the floor. Cover them with the rug and then set a chair or other piece of furniture over the area."

Snuggling my hard-earned lettuce under my head like a pillow, I settled down for a few hours in the comforting arms of Morpheus. Sleep would not come to me. Thoughts of Jean kept creeping into my mind. For the first time in my profligate life, a sense of despair overcame me. Jean had been a loyal companion and lover and I had deceived her, and used her badly. I thought of sending her a hundred dollars, but discarded the idea. Such a gesture would have added insult to injury. She would have concluded I was trying to buy her. I knew she would never accept a cent of stolen money. Suddenly a bright idea came to me. Why not telephone her and ask her to forgive me? I would be telling her the truth if I let her know how miserable I felt for the way I had abused her. I spent hours turning and pitching all over the bed.

As soon as the sun rose, I got out of the sack, showered and shaved and headed back to the bus depot where I knew there was a bank of phones from which I could place my call. I was so nervous I could hardly give the operator the necessary information she needed to process my call. After a long wait, I heard Jean's voice on the other end saying, "This is Jean." I replied with a shaking tone, "This is Paul, Jean........." Before I could utter another word, she yelled into the receiver, "Paul, you're a fool to be calling here. The police have connected you with a bank robbery in Normal. They have an accurate description of you in this morning's paper. The article stated that a preacher identified you right down to the clothes you were wearing. I find it hard to believe you would do such a dumb thing as that. Just where are you calling from?" Without a word I hung up the receiver, and made a B-line right back to my room.

Utter confusion left me so disoriented I could not think clearly. The foremost thing in my mind was to get away from Denver. It would take the cops only a few minutes to trace the call, assuming Jean would call them and tell of my contacting her. As soon as I closed the door to my room, I pulled the shades, sat on the bed and forced myself to calm down. As my reasoning returned, I realized that the cops had nothing on me. All Jean could tell them was that my name was Paul Gregory, and that didn't mean a thing. If they accidentally stumbled onto me, it was a cinch that preacher in Normal would put the finger on me. I couldn't stand a pinch. If the officials had traced the call, it would be folly for me to try to escape by trying to take a bus or train out of town. They would seal off all avenues of flight. Instinctively, I went to a window and peeked from behind the curtain. As I glanced out on the street, I saw a cabbie discharging a lady in front of a dress shop across the street. An idea was born. Why couldn't I simply take a taxi to some adjacent town? But where to? All the burgs in Colorado were small ranching communities, and I knew damn well that the denizens of those villages are suspect of all strangers. The name of Reno came to mind. Why not hire a cab to take me from the state, and right now? As soon as it got dark, I would walk toward the depot where I had seen a few cabs lined up.

It seemed the safety of darkness would never come. But as soon as it did, my suitcase, valise and I were on our way. I did not want to enter the station so I approached a cabbie who was standing beside his vehicle. "Say, Buddy," I began, "I have an appointment in Reno and I can't get a bus nor train out of town for three or four hours. Can you furnish me transportation? I'll pay you well." The hack flipped his cigarette to the pavement and quickly said, "You bet. First, let me call the office. We can't go out of town without calling in." When he walked inside to phone, I was tempted to flee. Bad thoughts ran through my muddled mind. What if the word was out and he went to call the police? Before I could make a move, he was walking hurriedly toward his cab. "Let's go. It will cost you a century note in advance." I was shocked that he wanted so much. A regular bus ticket would have come to about nine dollars. Being in no position to complain, I simply said, "That's a pretty stiff fare, but here it is." He smiled and said, "Sure it costs like hell, but you have to consider I have to drive all the way back. And while I am with you, I can't pick up any other fares. And my buggy will be out of commission all the time we are gone." He took my suitcase and valise and threw them into his trunk and we were off. As the miles flew by, I became more relaxed and comfortable with the picture. The only time he spoke on the trip was to ask, "You going to be doing a little gambling? They're trying to make it legal up there, you know." "No", I replied, "My company wants me to look into some real estate. They're convinced that Reno will be a booming town not too far down the pike."

10

On The Lam

I found myself standing in front of a nice hotel in Reno where the cabbie had dropped me off and drove away without a word. Again I was in a strange town without a friend or a place to stay. One comforting thought was that I wasn't broke. I did not want to check into an expensive hotel. I had been taught that such elite hotels always retained their own security police, and that when a stranger entered, he was subject to suspicion. I was still fearful of being traced because of the Normal job. At this early state of my chosen profession, I was not aware that anxiety and fear were thieves' constant companions. Sleep would not come easily, and when it did come, it was a fitful and restless time.

In addition to this unnatural condition, I found I was afraid to make acquaintances. I felt that I could not trust anyone. This bothered me to no end because I was, by nature, a gregarious person. Living many years under these abnormal conditions warped my personality. Wanting to get off the street, I decided to check into the local YMCA. The room to which I was assigned was not much more commodious than a cell. At least it offered me a chance to lay on a bunk and make some plans for my next move. I knew I wasn't going to hole up in this cowboy haven, and that I would be on the run as soon as I determined where to go.

At dinner time, I ate in a truckers' favorite eatery. The place was so jammed that I couldn't find a seat. As I stood near the door looking for a vacant spot, I saw a table occupied by a single individual. When he looked up and saw me standing there, he motioned for me to join him. He was a powerfully built man of about 35 years of age. I liked his rugged features immediately. "Sit down here," he bellowed. "No use waiting for a chair in this place. What's your name, boy?" he asked. He caught me off guard. I don't know why I replied, "My friends call me BJ."

He smiled and said, "That's good enough for me. Where you from?" Instantly I became wary and was on my guard. In a feigned disinterested manner I lied, "I'm from all over. I've been hitching rides westward looking for work." He looked me over closely and went on eating. I ordered a hamburger and a cup of coffee. I was surprised when he suddenly asked, "What kind of work do you do?" The only work I could think of was the type done in my home town. "Well, I pick fruit, thin apples and spray in the orchards." He finished his meal before I started mine. He extended his hand and came up with a golden opportunity for me. "If you want to go to

111

Spokane, Washington, you're sure welcome to ride with me. There are a lot of fruit orchards up there and I'm sure you could find work in that area." I was elated with his offer. I could ride with him for many miles in the direction I wanted to go and I would not have to worry about police who might be covering the bus and train stations. I shook hands with him and accepted his invitation. He asked, "Where can I meet you in the morning? I want to have breakfast and be on the road by 6:00 A. M. My rig is parked right behind this diner. If you're not on time, I'll drive off." I smiled and assured him I would be right there.

By 7:30 the following morning, I was sitting smug and content beside the truck driver. The huge vehicle was roaring down the road at a speed which amazed me. Within an hour I learned that his name was Buck Connely and that he was married and the father of a nine year old boy. He owned his own truck and was based in Spokane, his hometown. Like most knights of the road, he knew every eating place on his route, and near noon we were pulling into a cafe called 'The Chow Hall'. During our lunch I realized Buck was looking me over carefully. Without lifting his face from the plate he startled me with his next question. "BJ, if you have ever worked in orchards, it hasn't been for many months. Your hands are too clean and soft. Have you run away from home?" I didn't even bother to look up when I replied, "Yep." We never spoke again until we were on the outskirts of Spokane. Then he said, "Why don't you go on home. As sure as hell, your parents are worried about you. Where do you live?" Inasmuch as I really did not have anything to conceal from him I confessed that I lived in Wenatchee and had done very little manual labor in the orchards. "When we get to Spokane it's going to be quite late. Why don't you stay the night with me and my family. If you're broke, I'll take you to the bus depot and buy you a ticket home." It dawned on me that here was a grand guy; a real solid citizen, the kind my Dad had often talked about. Tears came to my eyes as I nodded in agreement. Little did Buck know just what I was running from. He would never have dreamed that this kid riding with him had soloed a bank job, took part in two others, had been shot, and, in return fire, had wounded a banker. He wasn't aware that I was carrying a revolver, nor that I had nearly nine hundred pieces of green on my person.

By the time Buck had turned in his manifest at the office and we had entered the driveway of his modest home, it was nightfall. His wife and son greeted him noisily at the door. Right away I could see that this was a close knit and loving family. I was envious of the warmth and understanding between them. When he introduced the youngster to me, I was surprised to be met by such an adult acting boy. He held his hand out and we shook. His wife went to the kitchen to prepare a snack. Buck joined her. His son and I hit it off from the beginning. He showed me his stamp collection. He brought a fruit jar from his bedroom and confidentially told me that he had saved $47 which he had earned from doing odd jobs around the neighborhood. I admired his industry. By the time we had eaten, all of us were tired. Buck was near exhaustion so he retired first. His son and I played a game of checkers before going to bed.

The bright sun shining in my face awoke me the following morning. I could hear Buck's wife preparing breakfast in the kitchen. The smell of eggs and bacon was inviting. I got up, bathed, dressed and sauntered into the kitchen. "Welcome," she said. "Buck and my son are still in bed, but by the time I get this meal on the table you can bet they'll be here. You don't need to wait for them, BJ." When she used the initials 'BJ', I knew they must have discussed me. Buck had not introduced me as BJ the evening before. I wondered how much he had told her. Well, it didn't really matter because he knew nothing of my past. Gosh, how I admired that guy. I went to the living room while the family pitched in to do the dishes. As soon as I had an opportunity, I took a ten dollar bill from my pocket and put it in the hand of a big stuffed teddy bear that I knew was the boy's favorite toy. Buck went to the telephone and called the bus depot to learn what time the next bus left for Wenatchee. All the family went with me to catch my ride. Buck shook my hand, his wife and their boy hugged me as we said our good-byes.

By the time the coach was on its way for a couple of hours, I began worrying about what I would do when it reached Wenatchee. After all, I was not going to receive a hero's welcome. As sure as hell, the cops would know it was Glenn Williams who robbed the cafe and abducted one of the town's citizens. I was a fool to be walking into the spider's parlor.

By the time we reached the town of Quincy, about thirty miles from my destination, I was a nervous wreck. I could jump the bus here, but I had nowhere else to go. About that time, I recalled that the bus always stopped at East Wenatchee just across the bridge from my home town. I would simply have to disembark at that point. I made up my mind I would walk across the bridge and go to some friend's house to learn just how much heat was on me. Crossing the bridge would have to be done after dark. Too many people would recognize me in broad daylight. There was no depot in East Wenatchee. The bus pulled up in front of a small grocery store to pick up passengers. The only person to vacate the vehicle was yours truly. Unnoticed, I walked into the store hoping no person who knew me would spot this fugitive. I needed to stall for time, so I meandered around the market for about twenty minutes, buying a couple of oranges, a pint of milk and a candy bar. When I left, I sauntered very leisurely across the road, walking far enough into an orchard until I was certain no one would see me from the road. The alfalfa was high and offered good concealment. I put my suitcase under my head to serve as a pillow and laid back to pass the time. Always when you're waiting for something, it takes an eternity for it to come. By the time it was dark enough for me to travel, I was fit to be tied. Pretty soon the lights started to come on in the houses and drivers began turning on their headlights. Feeling quite safe, I left my hideaway, walked along the roadside to the bridge and started across at a fast pace. When I reached the other side, it was dark.

As I walked through the familiar streets, I thought of the many boyhood friends I had known. I had to be very careful whom I contacted because there was always a chance that whoever it was might go to the cops. Or if he confided in a member of his family, I would be a dead duck. As I passed a dilapidated old house in the south end of Sleepy Hollow, I remembered a school chum by the name of Justin. He had lived with his aunt in this house for as long as I had known him. A light shined in his bedroom so I crept alongside the building and peeked in. Justin was sitting there on an old chair reading a newspaper. I tapped lightly on the window and got his attention. He came to the window and peered out. It took him a minute or two to recognize who was out there. As soon as he spotted me, he quietly slid the window open and held his finger close to his lips, signifying that his aunt was in the house. I hoisted myself into the room. He was delighted to see me, and indicated he had much to talk about. "Slip back out, Glenn, and go to the park. I'll tell my aunt that I'm going out for a pack of Bull Durham. Give me a few minutes and I'll meet you."

When he arrived at the park, we instinctively sought the darkest and most remote area before we felt safe. Justin and I had pulled many small-time capers together. However, he had never been involved in any major felonies. When I told him where I had been and what I had done, he was amazed. "Shit, Buddy," he whispered, "I never thought you'd wind up in the big stuff. I do remember, though, that one of my teachers told my aunt that Glenn Williams was going to spend the rest of his life in prison, or was going to be killed unless he straightened out." I swelled with pride that he had used the expression 'you'd wind up in the big stuff'. At last, my peers were learning that I was not going to become involved with anymore penny-ante crap. I leaned toward my pal, put my forefinger against his chest, and in my best display of bravado, I told him, "Justin, I can hit a bank and be out and away before you can even break into a house to commit a burglary. And what do you get from a burglary? You and I have bashed in more windows than a hurricane, and what have we come up with? Nothing but a couple of hot radios or a gun or some other small loot that we have to fence for three dollars. In a jug, you come out with one of two things; a sack full of money or a bullet in the guts. If I am going to put my sweet life on the line, it has to be for the whole lettuce patch." To impress him I pulled a case from under my shirt and displayed more money than he had ever dreamed existed. It was a full minute before he could find his tongue, and when he did he croaked, "How much is in the swag?" When I told him, he could not believe it. I said nothing because I wanted the magnitude of my proposition to register with him.

He broke the silence. "You know, Glenn, I don't want to shoot anyone. Stealing is one thing. Murder is another and it's too damn scary for this boy. How about coming with me, and I'll show you what I have set up? I've got the beginnings hidden in our shed. If you'll go along with me, we will stand a chance of coming out well healed, and we won't have to jeopardize a living soul." I followed him back to the house and waited in the alley for him to get whatever it was he had concealed. When he reappeared from the shed, all I could see him carrying was a large envelope. At the park he pulled out a flashlight and shined it on the envelope. "Reach in there and pull out what could be our fortune." I took out the contents and was really puzzled. All I had in my hand was a stack of blank checks. I couldn't believe my eyes. "For God's sake, Justin," I snapped. "What in the hell can we do with these checks?" He eyed me contemptuously. "I'll tell you what we can do. You can see that the checks are put out by the American Fruit Company.

They're payroll checks. There are one hundred blanks here. They won't be missed because I stole them from the back of the check register. You're too hot, but I can start out on a Friday noon and cash checks for up to $25.00 each and keep it up until Sunday night. Then we can go over to Yakima and Spokane and cash dozens more. In three or four days, we can walk out of this state with one thousand bucks apiece. By the way, American Fruit Company checks are honored anywhere on the west coast; good as cash." The mention of a thousand bucks caused me to perk up my ears. I reasoned that after I got my share of the loot, I could simply bid Justin and the town good-bye and head back to the east coast. I turned to my pal, held out my hand and we sealed the bargain.

I didn't mention to him that after the spree, he would have to make himself scarce. There would be dozens of merchants eager and ready to put the finger on him. Apparently, he had planned to skip out anyway, so identity meant nothing to him.

I hid out in his shed for two days and nights. He smuggled food in to me. Friday noon he brought the checks to me to fill out and sign. I had a good handwriting so I set out to fill in and sign the documents by the dozens. Because I was wanted and would be recognized, I stayed in the hideout while he papered the whole town. I knew the stores would be closing at 6:00 P.M. and that he would be coming back to the shed shortly afterward. I waited patiently for him to return. I wondered just how much he had garnered. At about 6:30, I heard him approaching. Instead of coming in, he cracked the door open and motioned for me to be quiet and to follow him. Back to the faithful park we went. Without a word, he opened the front of his shirt and started pouring money onto the ground. "Now, Mr. Tough Guy, feast your glimmers on that pile of money." I had to admit that I was really impressed. We held our coats closely around us so the flashlight's beam could not be seen by any chance passerby, and proceeded to count our blessings. When we were finished, we had tabbed up a tidy three hundred dollars. I was a little disappointed, but I had to agree that this method of thievery did not entail the possibility of violence. Also, this was just one day's take, and we still had two or three other towns we were going to rip off by Sunday evening. If things went according to plan, we should each net about a thousand big ones. I turned to Justin and said, "Well, I guess we're going to split for other parts. How do we get to Yakima? I can't show my face at any depot." I was taken aback with his response. "Glenn, I didn't touch half of the merchants here. I want to stay over and plaster a couple of dozen more. Then we can buy a used car and travel in comfort to the other towns. What say?" I thought it was damn good thinking, and told him so.

The night passed quickly. I settled down for another day's endless hours. When I became too impatient, I would comfort myself with the knowledge that we would be on the road to fat city. I was in for one hell of a surprise. At 6:30 that night, no Justin. I became panicky. What if something had gone sour? Just as I made up my mind to make a run for it, I heard someone approaching the shed. I could tell it wasn't my partner. I slid my gun from its holster, trained it on the door, and waited. I almost jumped out of my boots when I heard my brother's voice whisper, "Glenn, cut out of here quick and head for Jaffee's pasture. I'll be there tomorrow night with food. The cops got Justin, and he told them you and he were in on the scam together. Link Seibert got word to Dad right away." I didn't wait another minute. I left the place like a scared jackrabbit, and headed for Jaffee's pasture. Link was a detective and a good family friend. If it hadn't been for him, I'd be cooling my heels in the local bastille.

When Dan had ordered me to head for Jaffee's pasture, I knew exactly what he had in mind. He wanted me to hide out in the remote hills near Jaffee's so he would know where to locate me the following day. At the far end of the pasture, there was a deserted cabin in which I could find shelter. It was so situated that anyone approaching would be seen long before they could surprise you. I skirted the residential neighborhoods and made my way to my destination. It took me well over an hour to reach the security of my hideout. I knew there would be no one there so I walked directly to the door and entered. I was so emotionally and physically exhausted I flopped down on the dirt floor. As I laid there, I started getting unreasonably angry at myself.

What a dumb son-of-a-bitch I was for listening to Justin. Here I was with nearly a thousand bucks in my pocket and I allowed some petty ante thief talk me into a wild scheme involving forgery, a crime about which I was totally ignorant. On top of that, I never dreamed he would snitch on me if a bust came down. The more I dwelled on my predicament, the angrier I became. I asked myself just why did I come back to Wenatchee? Here I was in these bleak hills, hungry and cold. I wanted so badly to know what Link had told my brother. It was a cinch that the detective had the complete story. One thing I did know was that I was knee-deep in trouble. If I got caught, it was a certainty I would be convicted. After all, I had my handwriting all over the checks. By now, I thought of putting the barrel of my revolver in my mouth and pulling the trigger. I was too big a coward to commit suicide.

I was awakened by the bright morning sun streaming through a dirty window. Having no watch, I had no idea how long I had slept nor what time it was. From the position of the sun, I judged it to be about 9:00 o'clock. I didn't jump right up. I laid there and tried to get my brain functioning. I must have dozed off again. I became wide awake when I heard someone whistling from down the slope. I slid my heater from its holster, and peered out the window. Sure enough, I saw Dan walking toward the cabin. He was smart enough to alert me that he was coming, and he stayed in the clearance so he could easily be seen. He knew I would be trigger-happy. When he got to about fifty feet from the door, I stepped out and greeted him. He stepped through the cabin door and threw a heavily loaded knapsack from his back to the floor. "Dan, am I glad to see that you brought something to eat. I'm famished." He didn't respond right away. He watched as I started emptying the contents of the pack on the floor. When I spotted the paper sacks, I ripped one open and started wolfing down a sandwich. I couldn't believe how good it tasted. I was thankful to see he had two canteens of water strapped to his belt. He, like all members of my family, was a pretty thoughtful guy. He waited until I had finished a candy bar before he spoke. And when he did, I could see that he was really angry. "You're really in a crappy mess this time. Link told me that Justin had tried to cash phony checks in some of the very businesses where he passed a half dozen the day before. Apparently he went back to the Montgomery Ward store and handed a check to the very clerk on whom he had previously passed one. The clerk became suspicious. He stalled Justin while he took the latest check to the manager and told him he felt something was wrong. Immediately the manager called the police. Link took the call and went to Ward's to apprehend Justin. In the meantime, Justin had walked into the Mills Brothers Haberdashery and bought a neck tie. He offered a check in payment. Mr. Mills refused the check. Justin panicked and dashed from the business. Well, he dashed right into the arms of the deputy. As he was being taken to the police station, Justin started running his mouth. He told of the whole scam, and named you as the one who came up with the idea. As soon as he booked your partner, he drove to the Orondo Pool Hall where he knew that Harvard or I would be playing pool. He motioned for me to follow him into the alley where he told me the entire story." Dan paused to let the seriousness of the situation sink in. My brother had told me everything I wanted to know.

I stood up and started pacing the dirt floor. I made one turn when Dan lashed out and caught me flush on the jaw with a vicious hay maker. I dropped to the floor, out cold. As I started to regain consciousness, I heard Dan's voice cutting through my foggy brain. "You're an ignorant bastard! The cops have been looking for you for the past four months. They know, as well as you and I do, that you robbed the cafe and abducted a fellow and forced him to drive you out of town. You were lucky enough to get away, and what do you do? You march your stupid butt right back to the trap. I've got to ask you this; why did you come back? You know they want you bad. Well, I've got to get back home. Dad wants you to hole up here for a few days. I'll bring more food tomorrow. You have enough water, and you have two blankets. Don't try to escape on your own. The police have advised all the cops in a radius of fifty miles. Let us try to smuggle you out of the state."

All day I thought about making a run for it on my own. I was infuriated with him for wounding my ego by downing me with his fist and with his nasty language. I toyed with the idea of confronting him the next time we got together but knew damn well he would give me a good beating. Deep in my mind was the urge to strike out on my own and make my way out of the state. I had the money to take care of myself once I shook the cow manure of this town from my boots. Remembering what Dan had said about the cops being alerted to the fact I was in this area made me think twice before depending upon my ability to escape the trap. Every depot around here would be sealed. Also, they would have my family under close surveillance. I even thought of the idea of hiking across the mountains and catching a train out of Seattle. Every plan I decided on was not practical. Finally, I thought I would have to leave the matter in the hands of my Dad. He was a cool and level- headed customer in whom I had a lot of confidence. I hung pretty close to the shack because I didn't want to be seen by a hunter or hiker.

After dark that evening, I walked to Wenatchee, being careful to avoid contact with anyone. I simply had to do something. I arrived back at my hideout about midnight and fell asleep as soon as I wrapped the blankets around me.

When I woke up, it was noon according to the sun overhead. I immediately became afraid. Where was Dan? He promised to come up to see me. He hadn't said what time I could expect him, but I was sure as hell he would have been here by now. There was nothing I could do but wait, and as the hours dragged on I was positive he had been delayed for some reason or another. As night began to fall, I had made up my mind that I was going to make a dash for it if he did not show up by darkness. I had run out of water and food, so I felt I had no other choice. I sat on the hillside until I saw the lights of the town flicker on.

I realized that it was too dark for me to see Dan if he was approaching. Surely he would make his presence known long before he reached the cabin. It would not have been prudent to surprise me.

I walked back to the shelter and picked up a blanket and threw it over my shoulders. As I returned to my perch, I heard that familiar whistle that identified Dan. I remained concealed in the darkness until he was within fifty feet of me. I quietly called out to him, "Over here, Dan." He veered from the trail and met me on the hillside. I was relieved to see him, but was perturbed that he had taken so long to get back. When I told him of my concern, he said, "They've put a stakeout at our house, so I waited until it was nightfall before I gave them the slip. This puts a damper on our original plans, Glenn. Link is feeding us the latest moves the police are making, so we're that much ahead of them. We know every move they plan." I broke in and asked, "What can we do?" Dan replied, "We have to act quickly. You can't hide out here indefinitely. Dad came up with what I think is a good plan. When I come up tomorrow, it will be real late. If I don't show, you will know that they've tightened their surveillance. If that's the case, I'll drive over toward Castle Rock. When I get in the canyon, I'll simply park and cut across the hills and will come in above here. They will not be able to follow me going in the canyon without my seeing their headlights. Here's what Dad expects you to do. He wants you to cut across the mountains to Cashmere which will be about a fifteen mile hike. The going won't be rough, but you'll have to walk at night. There are a few ranches between here and there. You must avoid being seen. When you reach Cashmere, you're to go directly to Ryan Jackson's house. Paul, Harvard, myself and Dad will be waiting for you at Ryan's. You'll be arriving at his place early in the morning, but you'll have to get some sleep. By nightfall, all of us will drive to Ellensburg. We're going to put you on a bus and send you to Jacksonville, Florida. This scheme may have to change if something happens between now and tomorrow night.

I brought one of your dearest friends with me. You'll feel safer with it." With that he bent over the pack he was carrying and detached a bedroll. He unrolled it on the ground, and snuggled in the blanket was a 30 06 rifle. The rifle was one of my prized possessions. Alongside of the gun was a box of fifty cartridges. My armory was now more complete. In addition to the weapon and extra blanket, Dan had brought a dozen sandwiches, some oranges, apples, a dozen candy bars, and three canteens of water. I was all set for the trek across the mountains. In parting, he said, "I'll be here tomorrow night. Don't get impatient." With that he disappeared in the dark.

The following morning I was more at ease. There was a definite plan that offered me some guidance. I went to the cabin door and was surprised to see rain clouds gathering. In a matter of minutes, there was a regular deluge, something quite rare in eastern Washington. I could see that I was going to spend the full day inside, so I closed the door and wrapped myself in the warmth of the blankets. I slowly ate two beef sandwiches and a candy bar, which I washed down with water.

As the day wore on, I became restless. To pass the time, I examined my rifle and pistol. Suddenly, an idea came to me. Why not get in some target practice? It would be a safe bet that no one would be in the hills in this kind of weather. I knew it was a foolish thing to do, but I did many things that were foolish. I opened the door and methodically fired at rocks and the stalks of sage brush. I didn't want to shoot the revolver because I had only six bullets. When I had expended about a dozen rifle shells, I began to be concerned that I might have attracted attention. For more than an hour I gazed fixedly down the hillside in the direction of town. There was no sign of foot traffic, so I laid down and day dreamed. The downpour hadn't abated in the least. In one respect, I welcomed that kind of weather. I felt safer because of the limited visibility. On the other hand, it was a hell of a mess for Dan to have to trudge through. But trudge he did, and arrived far earlier than the previous evening. He was in a bad mood, and spent ten minutes cussing me out. He had the usual sandwiches. Mom had sent a raincoat, a candle and a letter that made me weep unashamedly. As I read it, my brother stood in the doorway and gazed homeward.

She had written: "My dearest son: I do not know where all this is going to lead. Personally, I would prefer that you surrender and accept the punishment you deserve. Unquestionably, you would be sent to prison, but at least you would be safe. At some time you could come back home, and start your life over again. All of us would visit you so you would not be completely cut off from your family. In prison, you could prepare for the future. By running, you're ensuring endless misery for you and us. You will be unable to write or call us. You will be hunted like an animal. Eventually, you will be captured. There is a possibility you will be shot to death. If that were to happen, my life would be over. I am sad that your father and I do not agree on the subject of your immediate future. I do not know what went wrong in your life. I feel a great burden of guilt. This you must know; I love you as dearly as a Mother can love her son, and I will continue to love you until I no longer live. Lovingly, Mama." I was choking back sobs as I brushed by my brother and walked into the rain. When I returned, sopping wet, Dan softly said, "I'll be back tomorrow night about the same time. If I don't make it, it'll be because I'm being watched too closely. In any event, you're to strike out for Ryan's house as soon as it gets dark. Take good care, brother." Deep sadness and regret hung heavy in my heart as I watched him disappear. In this kind of game, I never knew if or when I would ever see any member of my family again.

I spent the next day planning my future. It was irrational thinking. There wasn't a thought given to a constructive goal, just criminal activities. If I had had an ounce of brains, I could have seen the inevitable result, the result my parents had tried to make me understand. My mother's letter did have a profound effect on my life in later years. My Mother had always been a reserved but feeling lady. She was sensitive and had a deep love for her family. Many times throughout the years, I had to fight back tears as I thought of her. There isn't any doubt that my father was as equally injured by my way of life. He never expressed his hurt to me or anyone else. I grew up thinking he was a tough man and was capable of handling the disappointment I inflicted on him. In later years, toward the end of his life, I was acutely aware of how methodically I killed him. After he was gone, I realized how great a fellow he had been. When these feelings of regret would overcome me, I would force them from my memory, not realizing they would return in my later years to haunt me. I have paid for my insensitivity and selfishness tenfold, and I will continue to pay until I die. It still surprises me how I could have been so unfeeling as to the humiliation and embarrassment I brought down on my brothers and sisters. There were periods of sorrow I felt for my Mother and Dad, but never a consideration of the damage to my siblings. There were a number of instances where I would get caught in the commission of a crime. The arrest and conviction would appear in the local tabloid. In a small town, such juicy gossip was a holiday of reading. My sisters and brothers would be unable to attend school because of the remarks made by their school chums. The alternative was to drop out of school for a few days. Their grades suffered, but not as much as did their feelings. One of my sisters left home and did not return for more than a dozen years. In spite of all the horrible things I visited on them, they have always remained supportive of me. It is a burdensome debt on my shoulders, one I cannot repay.

The trip to Cashmere was endless. The rain never let up. Before I had gone an hour, I was miserably wet and cold. During my youth, I had made the same journey a dozen times, but never in pitch dark, nor when I was soaked to the bone. In addition to these discomforts, I became disoriented and was not sure of my destination. In the inclement weather, the mountain peaks, which had served as guideposts before, became reminders of the vast and endless maze of confusion. Then, too, I was constantly imagining that there were wild enemies stalking me. I knew that cougars, bears and wolves were rampant in the mountainous area through which I was trudging. I was so fearful that I would actually 'see' the beasts trailing me. Finally, I got to the point where I would fire shots at the non-existing predators. All this anxiety tended to exhaust me. Twice I rested against a tree to regain my strength. In each case, I would catch myself falling asleep. I knew that if I permitted myself that luxury, even for an hour, there would be no way I could arrive at Ryan's by daylight. If I didn't show up, all the family would immediately begin a search for me. If such an action should materialize, the whole plan would fall through.

Each mile I would vent my anger on Justin. How could he turn stool-pigeon on a buddy? I prayed that I would have the opportunity to confront him sometime. I mounted a small knoll, and was elated to see a haze of light ahead and to my left. It had to be Cashmere. I felt much better after seeing the beacons. My strength returned. I resolutely picked up my speed. In another hour, dawn made itself apparent. I knew I had to be at Ryan's before daylight.

In the early hours of the morning, just before the sun rose, I reached the house. Dad was the first one to see me. He rushed out and pulled me inside. He hugged me warmly, and complimented me on my ability as a woodsman. Ryan and my brothers, Harvard, Dan and Paul, were still sleeping on the floor. Ryan's wife had a fire going and set about preparing breakfast. There was a real bustling confusion in the small house, which had accommodated seven people. Ryan's wife could see that I was totally exhausted. When the food was ready, she served me first. I was so sleepy I could hardly keep my eyes open during the meal. As soon as I finished, she suggested that I lie down on the davenport and rest.

When I awoke, it was after 4:00 P.M. I had slept nearly ten hours. Right away, she filled the bathtub and told me to clean up and put on a complete change of clothes which my Dad had brought. For the first time in 24 hours, I was warm. When I started to dress, I noticed large blisters on my feet. The small discomforts were nothing compared to the good feeling I had. My Dad asked, "Was the going really tough, Glenn? Did you get lost? Were you afraid?" I looked at him contemptuously and answered all his questions with one lie. "Hell no, Dad. I know these hills like a book."

After we had eaten, Dad told us to listen to every word he was going to say. And when my father spoke, we had learned it was best to listen. "Our plan had been to drive from here to Seattle where we were going to put Glenn on a bus or train. Yesterday I received a call from our good friend, Link. It seems he had learned something of importance that he wanted to convey to us. Rather than chance doing it on the phone, he suggested that we wait here for him to drive up. He gets off at 5:00 P. M., and will take a half hour to get here. In fact, he should be here at any moment. I want to discuss another thing. Each of us must never mention Link's name in connection with this case. He is a grand Kentuckian." That last comment by Dad was the highest compliment he could pay. It wasn't incidental that everyone in that room was a Kentuckian.

Before Dad could continue, there was a soft rap at the door. It had to be Link, but none of us were taking a chance. Ryan called out, "Yes?" A voice with the definite southern drawl responded, "Link." Without being invited in, he pushed open the door and stepped inside. Standing before us was one of the handsomest men I had ever seen. He was about six feet tall, lean and rangy. His eyes were a gentle blue, his features craggy. He wore a sheriff's uniform complete with a gun at the belt. When you looked at him, you would think twice before issuing a challenge. And you had damn well better think twice. All of us had heard what a bearcat this man was. It didn't matter if you fought with gun or knife, you had better be prepared to fight to the end. His reputation had preceded him from Kentucky. Contrary to his reputation, he was a gentlemen, one whom you could trust with your life. If you were his friend, he would die for you. When my father and Link were young men, they were the best of buddies.

That friendship continued to this day. It was that relationship that caused the Kentuckian to go to Dad when Justin was apprehended, that relationship and the fact that Link knew his boss was criminally involved with pimps and bootleggers in Wenatchee.

Link addressed all of us but was really speaking to Dad. "The prosecutor and his staff met with the chief of police yesterday. The prosecutor was perturbed with the police. He reminded the chief that he nor none of the cops had seen Glenn, that they had taken the word of a known thief that Glenn had written the checks. Yet Glenn has not been seen by any of the dozen acquaintances that he would have contacted if he had been in Wenatchee. As you know, Merritt, your place has been staked out for twenty four hours a day. And yet the person they are searching for hasn't been seen. The district attorney reminded the chief of the cost of this surveillance, and suggested they forget Glenn and go ahead with the prosecution of Justin. He also brought to their attention the fact that they had been unable to get a sample of Glenn's handwriting for further identification. He continued by saying that if Glenn was back in this community, he would soon surface, and then could be arrested. As it stands now, the authorities will keep a keen eye out for your son, but they will no longer concentrate on special and overtime cops." When he concluded, he looked to my Dad for comment. Dad appeared to be somewhat relieved, but puzzled as to what course he should follow now. "Link, what would you suggest we do in view of this turn of events?" The deputy locked his hands behind his head and looked at the ceiling for a few minutes. Finally, he suggested, "Merritt, your plan was to take your son to Seattle. Before talking with the DA, the chief had put out a bulletin to Seattle, asking for their cooperation in arresting Glenn. The police in Seattle are ten years ahead of this town. In my opinion, I'd take Glenn to Yakima and send him south from that town. Whatever you decide to do, I'll cooperate in any way I can." He finished with what he had to say and stood up. He walked over to where I was sitting and said, "Boy, you had better get your act together. You aren't smart enough to function as a gangster. Do your family a favor. Get lost and stay lost. You're not worthy of such nice people."

In a matter of minutes, Dad made his decision. "We're going to go back home and hole up there until tomorrow night. We'll hide out in the abandoned warehouse on Emerson street. As soon as it gets dark, the five of us will head for Yakima. We aren't out of the woods yet, so I want all of us to keep our artillery close at hand. If they do locate us and come after Glenn, we are going to shoot it out then and there." I was scared.

All of us stayed at Ryan's place until it started to get dark, and then we started our drive to the warehouse. I laid on the floorboards so I would not be seen. By the time we pulled up to our hideout, it was dark. Dad and my brother, Paul, left to go to our home and pick up some blankets and food. My brother, Harvard, agreed to stand guard for the few hours we were to remain there. The rest of us sat in a semi- circle and spoke in low tones.

These past few days had been a nightmare for all of us. Suddenly, Harvard gave a hissing noise. He shifted his rifle to his shoulder and stood perfectly still. Within seconds, the rest of us were at separate windows peering into the night. Sure enough, across the street was a prowl car with two officers in the front seat. They didn't get out nor did they seem particularly interested in the warehouse. Our concern was heightened when we saw another police car join them. If they knew that five heavily armed men had a bead on them, they would have departed quickly. After about five minutes, the two vehicles drove off. We spread out in the warehouse and covered all sides. We kept the alert up for at least half an hour. Dad had covered the window by which our car was parked. He half expected them to try to disable our getaway vehicle if they were planning to set up a siege. In a few minutes he walked to each of us and whispered, "Three of you walk to the car. We'll keep you covered. After you get in, you cover us and we'll join you. Dan, you do the driving. Head for Ellensburg." Within minutes we were out of town and well on our way.

The city lights of Yakima loomed on the horizon. I was happy because they represented the departure place for me. I dreaded being in the state of Washington. It was a place that would imprison me as sure as hell if the officials ever laid their hands on me. I wanted miles, miles and miles to be between them and me. Dad told my brother to pull into an all-night restaurant where he treated us to dinner. When he finished, he looked at me and quietly offered his final advice. "You have never been one to listen to me, Glenn, but I want you to hang on to every word I have to say. This is the last time I will ever assist you. You have exhausted our finances and patience. You don't deserve further consideration. You'll be in Jacksonville in about five days. If you don't make it in the new location, don't call on any of us. I'm fearful for your future, but I cannot forfeit the rest of the family for you. Bear in mind that if you write or call us, you will be traced, arrested and extradited back here. And the charges they have against you will assure your being in prison for many years. What I have just told you doesn't mean that I don't love you. It simply means that you're going to have to straighten up and live a better life. Here is all the money I can afford to give you. Use it sparingly." With that, he handed me fifty dollars. I refused to accept it because I had much more cash on hand than he did. "Dad, I will get my feet on the ground and, after I have settled down, I will contact you. Give Mom my love, will you?" I handed him an envelope containing one hundred dollars and asked him to open it after we had parted. None of us knew if we would ever be able to meet as a complete family again.

Two hours later, I chose a back seat of the departing bus and cried. I thought the trip would never end. Apparently Dad sent me to the farthest point from Wenatchee for my own protection.

I was asleep when we pulled into Jacksonville. The driver had to come back to my seat to awaken me. He shook me roughly and shouted, "This is as far as this bus goes. Get your luggage and clear out of the car." I don't remember how big this city was at that time. But the first thing I liked about it was that it was ten thousand times as big as the burg from which I had escaped. I didn't have to worry about being recognized, much less being bugged by the constabulary. How long I walked with my suitcase before coming to a hotel, I do not recall. But I saw a lighted sign which read, 'DeSoto Hotel'. I checked in and reserved a room for a week. I figured it would take me that long to get my bearing. I ate at a restaurant chain of cafes called National Cafes. Each day I would wander farther and farther from the hotel. Before long I was pretty well acquainted with the town. Being foolish, I spent a lot of cash on clothes and movies. When I eventually took stock of my finances, I was shocked to see how much I had deleted my resources. I comforted myself thinking that if things got too rough I could very easily commit a robbery, preferably a bank. I didn't want to draw heat to this place, so I figured I would have to locate a town not too far away to go into my act.

I had met a man by the name of Steve, about ten years my senior, at a local pool hall where we played snooker. I had adopted the name Ralph Halscomb. When he asked me where I was from, I told him I had lived in South Dakota, but I left to try to find work in a warmer climate. He was satisfied with my story, and never questioned me further. On one week end, Steve asked me to accompany him to Macon, Georgia where his parents lived. I was glad to get away for a few days, so I accepted his invitation. The following Saturday, we drove to Macon. It was a typical small southern town which I liked, not for the purpose of living, but because I had observed that it boasted of having two banks. By the time we left to return to Jacksonville, I had made up my mind to return and rob one of their jugs. However, I was in a hell of a mess. I needed a dependable car before I could rip off a job like that. All I had to my name was less than fifty bucks.

My only alternative was to steal a car to use on the caper. Such an approach was always a risky venture because I had to commit one felony in order to commit the other. I realized I was double jeopardizing myself. But, I rationalized; what else could I do? That night, I told Steve I would be gone for a day or two because I had heard about a job in Atlanta.

At five o'clock that evening, I was on a bus going to Atlanta. Tucked under my armpit in a snug shoulder holster was my beloved companion. In my back pocket, I had a pair of wire cutters with which to do the hot wiring. In a shirt pocket I had a four inch piece of tape to alter my appearance by placing it across the bridge of my nose. Preparing for a heist had a sort of sedative effect on me. I was never afraid of the possible consequences, like being shot, having to shoot someone or the certainty of years of imprisonment if I were captured. It wasn't a matter of bravery. I was terrified of the thought of injury in a car accident, or of drowning. I can only conclude I was suffering from some kind of aberration during my criminal career.

By the time I reached Macon, it was dark; an ideal time to hot-wire a car and park it in a secluded spot near the bank I had chosen to rob. On the outskirts of town, I walked the streets trying to locate a vehicle that suited my purpose. A late model Dodge, which was parked in front of an unlit drug store, seemed to be an answer to my prayer. I sauntered across the street, walked a block or two on the other side and then headed alongside the Dodge. As I passed, I tried the door. It was unlocked. I jumped in right away, closed the door and laid down on the front seat. I remained down for at least ten minutes to make certain I had not attracted attention. Then I started to cut and rearrange the wiring under the dashboard.

I was absorbed in my work, and did not see the two cops who jerked the car door open. They pulled me from the vehicle, slammed me against the car door and began searching me. Not a word was spoken during this rough treatment. When one of the men discovered my concealed weapon, they became more brutal. I was slugged in the stomach repeatedly until I was on my knees. "Pull that f—ker to his feet, Joshua," one of the men snarled. The other hauled me up and asked, "What you doing in the car, Boy?" I couldn't answer right away because I thought I was going to vomit from the beating I had taken. Apparently, the ignorant southern redneck thought I was refusing to reply, so he slugged me in the mouth. Through bleeding lips I lisped, "I was just trying to find a place to sleep." He grabbed me by the front of my shirt, shoved his face against mine and questioned. "Do you Yankees always carry a gun? Don't you all know that you can get ten years in the jailhouse for that down here?" While he was brow-beating me, I noticed he had shoved my revolver in his waistband. I weighed my chances of snatching the gun from his band and blowing him away. At this instance, he spun me around and took my wallet from my pocket. He stepped back and checked out the contents. "My God, Hacker, "he drawled to his partner, "This Northerner done has plenty of money here. I guess we had better safe- keep it for him." He stuffed my green backs into his shirt pocket and smiled an evil smirk as he directed his next words to me. "We'uns is going to take you to the night court judge and have him pronounce sentence on you." I asked, "Do you mean he is going to give me jail time without a trial? I want to see an attorney." Both cops broke into a loud guffaw. "Yeah, you can see a 'tourney if you got the money to pay him. Has you?" I replied, "You know I have the money. You took it from my wallet." The short fat one turned to this partner and asked, "Hacker, did you find any money on the Boy?" Hacker muttered something about how all the men they arrested saying they had money when they didn't have any. I saw the game immediately, and knew I could never prove they had taken my cash. I had heard from lots of my friends about the tactics southern police used. I had also heard how they would beat prisoners to death if they caused too much trouble. Realizing I didn't stand a chance in hell, I admitted that I had not one penny when I was arrested. The two bullies saw that I had seen the light and that I would not resist any further. "Because we like you, we ain't going to tell the judge about you bringing a gun down here. Of course, if you say you did have a gun, we'll have to produce it. In that case, you'll be salted away for a long time. You understand what we is saying?"

I was taken to the county jail and locked up with about fifteen other hapless souls awaiting the action of the Kangaroo Court. It was a practice in the south to hold petty court trials all night. I asked a black man sitting on the floor what the sentences amounted to. The fellow looked at me as if I was crazy. "Just what did you do?", he asked. I told him my story. "Well," he drawled, "About every crime in the small court mounts to thirty days on the chain gang. If'n you be black, you apt to get sixty days."

I had been in the makeshift cell for two hours before my name was called. A deputy cuffed me and hauled me into another room. Sitting at an old school desk was the fattest man I had ever seen. I estimated him to weigh more than 300 pounds. A man in a rumpled suit must have been the city attorney. Reading from a paper he intoned, "Y'honor, this man had no identification on his person when he was arrested. Therefore, be he known as John Doe. John Doe was loitering around a parked car with the intention of burglarizing same." Without asking me one question, the judge yelled out, "Thirty days on the road gang." I was never so shocked in my life. I opened my mouth to complain, but was yanked off my feet and out the door.

The following morning I, with ten other men, were fitted with ankle chains and loaded on a hay wagon. Two mules were hooked up to pull the human cargo. Before we started on our journey, two blacks fed us a piece of corn pone, a tin of black-eye peas and a cup of chicory, which they referred to as coffee. We were given fifteen minutes to wash the slop down before three mounted men rode alongside the wagon and called to the black mule skinner, "Jason, head them animals down the pike to the prison shed." It was the most incongruous sight I had ever seen.

At noon, we pulled alongside a creek, were ordered off the wagon and told, "If you have to take a crap or drain your tank, get with it." The ten of us, still chained together, performed our toilet as best we could. When we had crawled back onto the wagon, we were fed a tin containing sow belly, grits and corn pone all mixed together. I looked at the garbage and declined to touch it. A tough-looking character chained next to me whispered, "Before the week is over, you all will be begging for your share of this southern cooking." He roared with laughter at his remark. He was right. I was so starved by dinner I cleaned my plate.

We had traveled about fifteen miles when we arrived at a grove of trees. Among the trees was a long wooden shed. Its windows were covered with a heavy metal screen. I knew without asking that this was to house me until my thirty-day sentence was completed. Inside, along each wall were twenty wooden bunks. Each had one blanket and no pillow. At the head of each bed, where a pillow would normally be, there was a black and white striped uniform, so often seen being worn by road gang convicts. Shortly before my sentence was completed, the prison officials bowed to the demands of an irate public and the striped suits were replaced with blue denim coveralls. A bucket which was to serve as a toilet was next to each bunk. The stench made me want to throw up. At the foot of each bed, was a four foot length of heavy chain. Leg irons were attached to the end of the chain. One by one, we were unchained and assigned to a bunk. As soon as each man sat on his bed, a black trustee would fasten the leg irons on his ankles. And that is the way we slept.

In the morning we were awakened by a trustee banging a tin cup on a pail. The typical hog food was fed to us for breakfast. After we had eaten, a hungry looking guard stood in the middle of the room and announced. "You convicts were sentenced to work on my road gang. Do as you are told or face the cat-o-nine tails. Try to escape and we'll drag you back here by your balls; that is if we don't shotgun your ass off. Trustee, unlock the men, load them on the chariot and take them to the section of the pike we worked on yesterday." I smiled to myself when he referred to the wagon as the 'chariot'. Once again, I found myself on the chariot, but this time there were fifteen desolate convicts in their striped monkey suits, looking forward to another slave-driving day breaking rocks. A large kettle of food was loaded in the back of the wagon. I presume it was hot when we started to the work site, but by noon it was lukewarm and tasteless. As early as it was, the sun burned down, miserably scorching our uncovered heads.

I didn't believe in heaven nor hell until I had finished the back- breaking labor on my first day on a road gang. By the day's end, I was half-Christian because I had at least experienced hell. I am still waiting for heaven. From early morning until midday, all I could hear was the sound of rock being crushed, men swearing and the mounted crew guard exhorting the workers to produce more. One of the guards was as rotund as a hog being prepared for the slaughter house. When he had something to say to one of us, he never called out in a voice, he would simply oink. On one occasion, I stopped 'making little rocks out of big ones' so I could stretch. My back was killing me, and I didn't think I could stand it. Hog Jaws saw me lay down my pick. It had no more than hit the ground than his black snake hit my shoulders. The pain was indescribable. Hog Jaws oinked loudly, "You Yankee, pick up that tool! If'n I see anything but your ass and elbows again, you all are going to spend three days in the sweatbox." Without a moment's hesitation, he slid his shotgun from the saddle scabbard. I truly believe I was within a moment of being slain. Later I learned that many convicts were slaughtered by insensate guards for the slightest reason. If a public outcry started, a half dozen of the guard's companions would come forward and tell the upper echelon that the 'very dangerous homicidal criminal had attempted to grab the officer's weapon'. The public was satisfied, especially if it was a black who had unnecessarily perished. I grabbed my fallen pick and bent to my task.

How I ever survived the next twenty-nine days, I will never know. When I was called into the warder's office and told I was free to be on my way, I didn't get any of my property they had confiscated. Only my clothes were returned to me. I was so happy to be free I walked hurriedly down the street, never daring to look back. The experience left me as lean as a hungry bear and twice as sinewy. For years I despised anyone with a southern drawl. I dreamed of the day I could wreak disaster on any law enforcement officer. I bundled them all into one great hate-bag. I left Macon and struck out toward Jacksonville, broke, hungry and without the tool of my trade, a pistol. People in the south rarely picked up hitch-hikers. I survived starvation by stopping at farmhouses and begging food. Somebody, probably a southern member of their Chamber of Commerce, coined the expression 'Southern Hospitality'. To that I say, bull shit! Nowhere in the east, west or north had I ever been so badly mistreated. On my third day from the prison camp, I reached the city limits of Jacksonville.

I located Steve and told him the story of what happened to me. I lied about the reason I had been sentenced to a road gang. "Steve, I was just bumming around Macon when I got picked up as a vagrant. As soon as they found out I was from the north, I was subjected to hell." He retorted, "Ralph, you have to be careful down here. Whenever these bastards want free labor, they railroad any unfortunate man they can pick up. If they haven't got a charge, they make one up. Every crime imaginable calls for thirty days. You can stay with me until we can get you some duds. In a few days, you can get some kind of job until you get on your feet. In the meantime, here is a twenty dollar bill to tide you over." I never told Steve that I wasn't the working type. In my mind I intended to start burglarizing in order to get a gun and some change. Above all, I had to have a weapon because I was determined to hit a bank and head back to God's country.

About a week later, I walked into a gold mine in a home I was burglarizing across the St. John's River in South Jacksonville. The fellow who owned the house was about my size, as I determined when I tried on some expensive clothes I found hanging in his closet. While I was outfitting myself, I noticed a snappy army officer's uniform among the suits. Without hesitating, I threw the uniform, a Sam Browne belt, a cap and a sharp pair of officer's boots into one of his suitcases. Everything fit me to a T. I searched a set of bureau drawers and found a loaded 45 Automatic pistol. Before I left, I called a cab and prayed it would get there before the home owner returned. However, if he had walked in, I would have covered him with his own gun, robbed and tied him up. I sat at a table in the kitchen where I could see the cab when it came. I noticed an envelope on the table, and out of idle curiosity, I opened it. Now I believed in heaven, because there was one hundred and fifty dollars inside. The cab pulled to the curb in front of the house. I hurried out and instructed the Cabbie to take me to the train depot.

Once at the depot, I took another cab and asked the driver to drop me off at any good hotel. After a few days I called Steve and told him that I had my folks wire me some cash, and that I would be buying some clothes before returning to his hotel. The next day, sporting the clothes I had stolen, I showed up at Steve's. That night, I took him out to dinner. I repaid the money he had lent me. I confided that I had a tentative job and asked if he would lend me his car for a couple of hours. Willingly he responded. "You bet I will. Pick it up whenever you want it." Long before I had asked him, I had already planned to get a car somewhere for a quick bank caper. No more trying to hot-wire one after that fiasco in Georgia.

Early the next morning, I picked up Steve's car and headed south. If I had gone north, I'd have found myself in Georgia, and from my experience in that backward state, I would rather be in hell. An hour later, I reached the town of Gainesville. It looked pretty good to me from the viewpoint of a bank heist. Before looking for a soft pigeon, I sought out a good cafe and stopped for breakfast. I spent an hour eating. I figured the banks would be opening their doors by this time. Realizing I might have to make a wild getaway run for it, I made certain there was a full tank of fuel. I always wanted my victim to be on the outskirts of a city. One of the reasons was that if I were being pursued, I'd not be caught in traffic. Another reason was that I didn't want to get lost on streets with which I was not familiar. At the edge of a town, a person is less likely to get confused by being trapped in a dead-end street. I had learned that it's the little overlooked eventualities that increased your chances of being caught. I have known other robbers who would rather rob an establishment in the center of town. They reasoned that, if they became involved with a hot pursuit on their tail, they could create traffic jams behind them, thereby impeding the speed of their pursuers. It was a sort of six of one thing or a half a dozen of another.

I had been cruising the streets for more than an hour before I happened on to a dream of a money-maker. To my liking, it was situated on a corner with at least three avenues of escape less than a half mile from the main road leading north. I circled my find three times and was satisfied with everything I saw. When I parked my car in a place of easy exit, it was about 11:00 A.M. I got out of the vehicle and strode in to the bank for a careful observation of the interior. I walked to a table in the center of the bank, picked up some deposit slips and walked out. The manager was seated near the front door in an open area. I liked that arrangement because it would be easy to approach him and not draw undue attention. I went back to my car and got in. There, where I wasn't apt to be seen, I placed the strip of tape over my nose, folded the cloth money sack and put it in my coat pocket. I took my automatic from its hiding place. As a final check, I made sure the clip was full of bullets and that the action worked smoothly. Satisfied that all was ready, I walked into the bank and directly up to the manager's desk. I seated myself, extended my hand and said, "How do you do. I am Filmore Wilder, and I'd like to discuss a loan with you." He was surprised by my approach, but when he detected a possible business deal with the bank, he smiled warmly, reached out and took my hand. If anyone of the employees had witnessed the scene, they would have concluded that we were old friends. I was extremely pleased with how nicely things had gone so far.

"My name is Henry Morris, Mr. Wilder. We will be happy to consider extending you a loan. How much did you have in mind?" I looked him straight in the eyes and calmly replied, "Every goddamn dollar you have on hand." As I was talking, I opened my coat slightly so he could see the gun in my trouser waistband. I continued, "This is a robbery. If you cause a problem, you will be the first to die. When we go behind the tellers' cages, you caution each one to do as she is told. Tell the others to remain at their desks and not to look up. Be sure no alarm button is pushed. Is that clear?" He nodded his head like a robot. I was afraid he was going to faint so I said, "Just do as you are told and I'll be on my way in minutes. Let's go!" I handed him the cloth bag and told him to stuff the cash inside. As we stopped at each cage, I softly instructed the teller, "This is a robbery. Put all your cash in the bag that Mr. Morris is holding. If you sound an alarm, all of you die." I couldn't believe how quickly we had covered all the tellers' cages. When the bag was handed to me, I marched the frightened manager in front of me to the door. On leaving, I told him once again, "No alarm for five minutes, or I'll come back and blast you." He was so petrified with fear, he could only nod. I threw the bag of money on the back floorboards, crawled under the wheel and moved into the mainstream of traffic.

Forty-five minutes later I drove in to an alley in South Jacksonville. I opened the trunk of the car where my suitcase was. I stuffed the money in with my clothes, slammed the lid shut and drove on a westerly route toward Tallahassee. Other than for a brief stop to eat, I drove straight through to Montgomery, Alabama. I checked into a hotel under the name of Paul Gregory, took a bath and fell exhausted on the bed.

When I woke up, it was nearly noon. Oddly enough, I was not interested in counting the take until I ate lunch. On my way back to my room, I stopped at the desk and checked out. Before rearranging my suitcase, I took stock of how much money I had earned. I had a small fortune in my possession; more than $13,000 dollars. I am positive that the ease with which I got this money created in me a sense of invincibility. And to think, just a few days ago, I was on a chain gang eating swill. And now I was dining on New York-cut steaks smothered in mushrooms and topping it off with Pecan pie. The waitresses addressed me as 'sir'. Hog Jaws kept coming into my mind. I vowed to myself that if ever the opportunity arose, he was one bastard I would snuff. When I was re-packing for my trip to Birmingham, I had a better opportunity to examine the uniform I had stolen. I decided to try it on. It fit quite well, but would require a few alterations.

The ride to Birmingham was uneventful. I was in no particular hurry. There was no heat on me so I was free from worry. I was troubled over the past few days about the way I had deceived Jean back in Peoria. I made up my mind to call her when I reached Birmingham. I realized it might not be a smart thing to do, but in my usual impulsive manner I decided to make the call. In order to avoid a display of prosperity, I sought out a second-rate place and paid a weeks' rent in advance. Again I felt comfortable using the name Paul Gregory.

Two days after my arrival I made a call to Jean's grocery store. I had made up my mind to apologize to her, to tell her that I still loved her and then hang up quickly. The operator got her on the phone and then turned her over to me. My voice sounded squeaky as I said, "Jean, this is Paul." I definitely heard her gasp, but she didn't respond. I tried again. "Jean, this is Paul. May I talk to you for a few minutes?" I could hear her crying over the phone. All I could do was to keep the line open. After an interminably long time, she spoke in a soft voice. "Paul, why are you calling me? Haven't you done enough harm already?" Hurriedly, so she wouldn't hang up on me, I said, "Jean, please hear me out. There is no way I can tell you how sorry I am. I just want to tell you that I love you. I will never see you again, but you must know I did not intentionally play games with your heart. In a few days, I'll be in New York city, and will write you from there." When her voice came across the wire it was more composed. "Paul, you don't have to write. I urge you not to come back here. The officials don't know who you are for sure, but they have a very good description of you. Stay away and good-bye forever." I heard the receiver slam down. From my room, I wrote her a brief note. Before sealing the envelope, I put ten $10.00 bills inside and posted it. I knew that that gesture would never right my wrong, but it made me feel better. I felt the money would alleviate any financial burden she might be under.

There were some excellent pool halls in this City of Cotton. I spent many hours playing pool with the local sports. My time was passed between the movies and the pool halls. Occasionally, I would go to dances, cock fights and boxing matches. There was a racetrack on the outskirts of town where I lost a bundle of money betting on the horses. I remained in that city for several months, and during that time I never once tabulated what I had spent. Like all crooks, I was not too concerned about money. I knew that I could replenish a diminishing purse by making another hasty withdrawal. Finally, sheer boredom caused me to consider leaving this southern town and going east.

One morning I packed my cases and found myself on a train going in the direction of Minneapolis. I realized I was gambling by going back, but I wanted to visit Marie. By the time I had returned, I was nearly a year older, deeply tanned from the sun in the south and I was nattily dressed in expensive clothes. I did not resemble the kid who lost his cherry on his first bank in the Hell's Kitchen city. When my train pulled into the station, I hurriedly took a cab and told the driver to take me to a good hotel. From my room, I called Marie. She screamed with delight on hearing my voice. I did not want to push my luck too far by going into the neighborhood of her cafe, so I asked her to join me in the hotel restaurant. She stayed with me for three days and nights. On the third day, she told me that she had to get back to her place of business. There had been a question on my mind ever since I pulled into town, so I asked her, "Marie, has any heat come down on the bank I hit?" She laughed and replied, "I thought you'd never ask. I knew damn well it was bothering you, or else you were one cool cucumber. Well, it is the same old crap with the police. Every so often, the chief will put out a report stating 'we have a new lead on that robber'. And for want of something to print, the media would re- hash the caper. To answer your question, they are as far from solving the job as they have always been. Unless a stool pigeon tips the coppers off, they're helpless. Then if a stoolie snitches, the cops announce to the papers that they, through good police work, have solved the crime." The next morning she bade me good-bye.

It had been my intention to stay for a few days in the Twin Cities area. I had no particular reason for making this decision except that I had not decided what my itinerary would be. I guess I had no real goal. In fact, other than my family, it didn't matter whether I existed. At one time in my existence, I had the feeling I was only floating in space. Many times at night when I couldn't sleep, I would long for someone to care. But then if they did, I would have responsibilities and I could do without that burden. My greatest enemy was being lonesome, and I never succeeded in overcoming it until I left the life of crime. It was funny that in all the books I used to read about criminals, there was never any mention of the terrible emptiness and isolation that was ever-present. When I began to recognize the symptoms of these moods, I would avoid them by doing something physical. But their avoidance was always temporary, their return inevitable.

I went to St. Paul to seek new places of entertainment. An idea struck me. How about my uniform? Why couldn't I wear it around town for the thrill of it? I felt I could create a totally different person than myself. When I got back to my hotel, I asked the clerk if she could recommend a place where I could get some clothes altered. She directed me to an alterations shop a few blocks from the hotel. A Chinese woman ran the establishment. I told her what I wanted done and, after she took my measurements, she assured me that the clothes could be done over to fit me perfectly. Right after lunch the next morning, I returned to the tailor-shop to pick up the uniform. The lady asked me to try it on before leaving. I looked in the mirror and was well pleased with the new character who peered back at me. Boy, was I impressed with my appearance! I wanted to wear it back to the hotel, but I didn't dare. The staff would wonder why I left in a civilian suit and returned in an army officer's get-up. Also, the grey shoes I was wearing would have created some questions. In my suitcase at the hotel, I had a nice pair of black shoes that would go well with the army outfit.

As soon as I got to my room, I called Marie and asked her to have dinner with me in the hotel's restaurant that evening. She was dumfounded to hear my voice. "Glenn, I thought you had gone. What are you up to? Anyway, I'll be off here at 5:30." By the time she arrived, I was fully disguised in my new role. When I opened the door in response to her knock, she gasped and stood there as though transfixed. "I...I..", she stuttered as she tried to find words. It took her a full minute before she could form a question. "Glenn, what are you doing in that silly-looking suit?" I simply stood there and smiled. "Marie, I picked this uniform up in a burglary in Jacksonville, Florida. It dawned on me that this outfit could serve me a number of ways. It is an automatic pass in this flag-waving society. I pulled off a couple of bank deals down south. I don't know if I am hot or not, so I've been laying low for about three months. You can bet your rear-end that my MO has been well established, so I'm going to keep out of sight in the banking occupation. While I was laying around here, an idea hit me. I figured I could open a checking account and then spread paper all over the country. Of course, after a week or two of this, the word will get out, but by that time I could accumulate some large heads of pretty green lettuce. When I figured it was time to quit, I'd take off my uniform and slip back into street clothes. Say that I can pass 150 checks amounting to $100 each. And all this time, I'll not have to use my gun. How does that strike you, Baby?" She just stared at me for a few minutes before she said, "Glenn, I think you have come up with a good idea. And that idea is going to land your keister in some Iron Bar Hotel for a long time. Remember what my dad told you many months ago? He advised you to decide what corner of the crime field you wanted to play ball in and, when you made up your mind, to stay in your field and keep your ass there. Start diversifying, and you're in trouble. Glenn, my dad knew more in this business than you will ever know. I don't expect you to follow his advice, because you're too stupid. Do me a favor, Glenn, keep in touch with me by phone or letter." She walked out on me. I thought to myself, "Well, to hell with her. When I get back to Minneapolis, whether it's one year or ten, I'll walk into her cafe with a bundle so big it won't fit in a gunny sack. I'll show Marie a thing or two."

11

The Imposter

It was noon. I walked up to the hotel clerk and told him I wanted to check out for a week, but that I wanted another reservation for the day of my return. He looked up from his work, did a double take and commented, "My gosh, Mr. Gregory, I didn't recognize you in that uniform. I had no idea you were an army officer. You look so much different." If he didn't know me after the length of time I had been his guest, it was a mortal cinch I would not be known by those who had had only a casual glimpse of me. I became far more confident in my new role. "Yes," I assured the startled clerk, "I am Lieutenant Paul Gregory, attached to the Intelligence Division. Of course, when I am in uniform, I wish to be addressed as Lieutenant. I am sure you will understand." The clerk actually genuflected. "Mr. er...er I mean Lieutenant, I understand. And your room will be available to you on your return." I thought to myself, 'you obsequious ass'. "Please call a cab for me", I said. As I was pulling from the curb, I saw him staring out the window at me. I would have loved to have heard what he told the rest of the staff.

As my train rolled toward Washington, D.C., I was the center of attention in the pullman. It surprised me how much subserviency people displayed when in the company of a lowly Lieutenant. I was more surprised that I, a young man who hated all uniforms, could enjoy the admiration of those around me, especially the women. I learned on this brief journey that women are amazingly gullible for a uniform. It reminded me of a comment that BJ had made months ago when he stated, "Women will hop in bed with a man in uniform without hesitation."

I fell asleep, and was awakened when a porter came through the pullman announcing, "Dinner is being served in the dining car." When I stepped into the aisle I bumped into a young lady. I tipped my cap and hastily apologized. She was very gracious in her acceptance. As she walked in front of me, I took stock of her chic clothing and her figure. She took a seat at a table. I purposely took a seat across the aisle from her, positioning myself in such a way that it was impossible for either of us to look up without making eye contact. Before a waiter could approach me with a menu, I stood up and walked to her table. She glanced up, somewhat startled. Standing respectfully in front of her, I politely asked, "Ma'am, I am travelling alone and I would appreciate your company for dinner." It seemed she left me on the cooker for an hour before she, with a wave of her hand, indicated I could be seated. I was pleased. I introduced myself as Lieutenant Paul Gregory.

Very sweetly, she said, "My name is Annabelle Harris. And I am pleased to meet you, Lieutenant. Where are you bound?" "I am scheduled to report for duty in Washington, D. C.," I lied. I was in seventh heaven for the next hour. She was a good conversationalist, witty and sharp. When it was time for us to relinquish our seats, I asked if she would like to sit with me. She seemed pleased. We talked about everything from our childhood to our adult life. She stopped me cold with a very keen observation. "Lieutenant, I know you must be of age or you would not be an officer in the army, but you appear to me to be about eighteen. I don't mean that to be a leading remark; you just seem to be so youthful." I made up my mind to carry this charade to the limit. I smiled and laughed. "You aren't the only one misled by my appearance. Actually, Annabelle, I am 24 years of age." She laughed and said, "We have two things in common. I, too, am that very age." After a few minutes of silence, I asked her what was the other thing we had in common. I damn near choked when she replied, "My father is a Major General in the U. S. Army." I muttered to myself. If she were getting off in D.C., and he met her, I'd be in an awful mess. A guy that high-ranking would pick me out as being a phony damn quick. And I knew that wearing a uniform and representing oneself as a serviceman could mean some time in a federal brig. How in hell was I going to get around this predicament? One thing for sure, I couldn't go on to D.C. I waited for the opportune moment, then I directed the conversation around to my itinerary. "Annabelle, I will be getting off in Chicago to spend a few days with my parents before reporting in. After I get into the capitol, may I call you up?" "Oh, Paul," she said, "I am sorry you won't be going on in on this train. My dad is to meet me, and I wanted to introduce you to him. Well, anyway, you may certainly call me when you arrive." Was I relieved!

I found myself standing on the platform in this goddam cold and windy city. Luckily, I had some cash, so there was no financial crunch. I would simply have to follow my plan here instead of D.C. That would not be an insurmountable problem. My scheme amounted to just this: I was going to establish a checking account, wait until some checks were printed bearing my name and a fictitious address. Then I proposed travelling around the country and cashing the spurious checks. I was depending on businesses being gullible enough to accept them. I registered at a hotel in the Loop.

About 11:00 A. M. the next day, I was standing in the lobby of a large bank about six blocks from my hotel. There was a desk in a corner of the lobby which had a sign on it reading 'New Accounts'. In a pompous manner, I approached a young lady at the desk and informed her that I wanted to open a checking account. I was nervous because I had never had an account and was unsure of the proper procedure. She guided me through the affair. Then she asked me to what address I wanted the checks mailed? This stopped me for a minute, so I gave her the hotel address. She reminded me that the printed checks would not be available for ten days. That threw me because I wanted to be back in Minneapolis before that time. "Please mail them to me at the hotel, and if I am out of town, the hotel will forward them to me." She was agreeable to the arrangement. I nearly muffed the whole deal by not having a prearranged address. I begin to wonder if I was out of my field of expertise, and headed for a fall. Well, it was too late to change my plans now.

I hung around Chicago for nearly a week before I boarded a train for Minneapolis. When I went to the hotel to register back in, my friendly clerk was on hand to greet me. "How were things in the Capitol, Lieutenant?" "Boring," I answered. "I'm glad to be in your friendly city. Washington is nothing compared to Minnie." He was pleased with my response.

As soon as I got settled in my quarters, I placed a call in to Marie, and told her what took place and that all seemed to be going ok. Her response was rather salty. "Well, I hope you can tell me that in six months. And one more thing; you will be leaving a trail a mile wide by wearing that uniform. Be careful!" A few days later, a package came for me from Chicago. I was delighted to open it and find six books of checks containing fifty checks in each book. My name printed on them looked so official and impressive. The same clerk who welcomed me back from Washington was at the desk when I came down one evening and announced that I had another emergency call from headquarters and had to leave the following morning. By now I was beginning to believe my own story and I, too, regarded myself as a big shot.

Three days later, I was snug in a hotel room in Des Moines, Iowa, practicing signing my name until I could do so with no hesitation. After lunch, I made up my mind that I was going to start hanging paper from one end of this town to the other. It was Friday noon and I knew that, at the earliest, my checks would not hit the bank until Monday and, by that day, I'd be in another state repeating my fraudulent activities. I was aware that I'd have to move lightening fast, because the cops would soon figure my MO, and they'd have bulletins all over the country. I also knew I would have to zigzag around the country. If I set a straight line of operations, they would jump ahead of me and be waiting. I was beginning to realize that I could do this for only a two week period, so I'd have to keep busy to make it pay. I wanted to realize at least 150 bogus papers at fifty bucks apiece. In some cases I could hike the amount to $75.00, depending on the place of business.

Des Moines proved to be a bonanza. The store clerks would look my uniform over and accept my checks without hesitation. As my confidence increased, I would increase the amount of each check. I learned that it was as easy to cash a hundred dollar check as a fifty. It was necessary for me to make a small purchase with every presentation. I soon ran into a transportation problem. There was no way I could get from city to city using a train or bus. It took too much time. I decided I would have to rent a car. I had no driver's license so renting was out of the question. I hit upon an idea. I could buy a used vehicle. A small down payment with the first monthly payment 30 days down the road. By the time that payment was due, my scheme would be over. When I left Des Moines after a three-day spree, I had bought a 1931 Plymouth. Ames, Iowa was my next target. I had to get it over with in that town in one day. It was too close to Des Moines, where all hell would break loose by Monday noon. I covered Ames for six straight hours and scooted out of town after leaving eighteen unhappy merchants.

I drove south and holed up in Kansas City. My hotel bed was a welcome respite. I didn't realize how tiring my stint had been. Thirty minutes in a tub of hot water left me rested and relaxed. I sent my uniform out to be dry cleaned while I ate and lazed around. My clothes were back by noon the following day. During my idle period, I took stock of just how many bum ones I had dropped. Des Moines was gifted with 23 of my jewels, in exchange for which they gave me many shirts and neck ties and a net of more than seventeen hundred roots of all evil. With the money I had left over from my banking business, I was well healed, having more than thirty three hundred bucks. Not bad for a country boy from the apple capital of the world!

Before I began my rip-off in Kansas City, I had made up my mind to hit another score in Denver, then cool my heels in Butte, Montana. Little did I know that this was the beginning of the end. Kansas City was as ripe as the other two towns. I rolled from that city with another twenty five hundred dollars. I had so many clothes that I dropped them off at the Salvation Army. After a night's sleep, I pointed the Plymouth toward Denver. Before registering in a hotel in the mile-high city, I treated myself to a big dinner. I enjoyed the sleep of the innocent that night. I figured a late breakfast would give the stores time to open up. Before I started my nefarious rounds of the city, I packed my duds and put them in the trunk. The next seven days proved to be a hectic week, a week that saw me chased and captured. I hit four stores with bad checks. At the last one, the manager questioned me closely. That was the first time I had been questioned. Reluctantly, he accepted my check but insisted that it be for the price of the purchase only. When I left the store, he had an employee follow me. I knew the heat was on. I walked about four blocks with that clerk on my tail. I was getting panicky. I stepped into a large western clothier store. As soon as I was inside, I asked a clerk where his restroom was. As he pointed it out, I noticed the guy on my tail step into the shop. I hurried to the rear of the store. About halfway to the restroom, I dodged behind a large rack of suits. Sure enough, the fellow who was following me broke into a run after me. I immediately walked quickly out the front door and crossed the street to my car. I had no more than slid behind the wheel when the trailer ran out the door. He stood in the street looking up and down. He knew I had given him the slip, so he ran back to his boss. I knew I didn't have a minute to lose.

Years later I found out that the cops went straight to my hotel. They laid a trap for me, expecting me to come back for the belongings which I had in the trunk. While they were hiding in ambush, I was streaking north. By the time I reached Casper, Wyoming, both the car and I had had it. It gave up the ghost in back of an old abandoned warehouse on the outskirts of Casper. I stepped into the street and hitched a ride to the center of this little village. By now I dreaded the attention I was getting because of my uniform. I saw an old cab parked by a grocery store. The driver was inside shooting the breeze. I told him I wanted a ride to the bus depot. He drove me about six blocks and dropped me off in front of a feed store. I looked puzzled. He grinned and said that the bus stops here. "Where do you want to go?" he queried. I told him I wanted to get to Billings, Montana. "It'll be here about midnight." This was a serious setback. I was scared. I had a lot of loot in my possession, but it wasn't doing me a bit of good. Again my mind wandered back to what BJ had told me about getting out of my area of capability in the crime field. I had chosen to concentrate on bank robbery, and here I was involved in a forgery scam that threatened my very freedom. What a jackass I was. Standing in front of a feed store in a one-horse town wearing a flashy uniform, I stuck out like a sore thumb. If there had been a hotel, or even a rooming house, I could have gotten off the street. As it was, I feared leaving the bus area. I sat on my suitcase and cussed myself out.

A truck loaded with hay and grain pulled up in front of the store. Apparently he was going to unload at a small dock at the side of the building. The driver walked around to the front door to advise the owner he was there. When the two came out, I heard the driver say, "Jed, I want to get rid of this cargo as fast as I can and get back to Billings." He took off his jacket and the two of them pitched in on the job. Within a half hour, the truck was empty, and the driver was getting his manifest signed. He suddenly seemed to notice me. Smiling, he spoke, "Hi there, Shave-tail. You waiting for a bus?" "Yes, Sir," I responded. "By the way, I heard you say you were heading for Billings. I would be happy to pay you if I could hitch a ride." "Agreed", roared the truck driver, "but I won't accept a penny for the lift. Before I leave, I want to have a meal. Will you join me?" How lucky could I get? I said, "Only if you will let me pay for our dinners." During the meal, I learned he had been in Europe serving with the American troops. I was very careful to steer the conversation away from military talk. Any soldier could trap me as a phony in a short time.

I was fearful that the police in Denver might get in contact with the cops in the neighboring states and towns. I don't know how many hours we drove before we arrived at a town called Sheridan. If I remember nothing else about Sheridan, I will never forget the wonderful venison steak we were served at a log cabin eatery. I felt sorry for the driver. I knew he must be terribly tired, but I could not relieve him. A truck was too much for me to cope with. I had to give the guy credit for tenacity. I slept until he called out, "Shave-Tail, end of the line." He drove up to a rooming house that he had suggested I stay in. The rooming house was my home for the next three days. During that time, I got a haircut and had my clothes laundered, and my uniform dry-cleaned. Good food, good people and lots of rest restored my energy and fortitude. I was prepared to start here and continue my papering business. I planned to tap Billings, Bozeman and Butte before winding up my latest criminal venture. It was my intention to pack up the uniform and go back to wearing civies. I had to let the military gag cool off. In Butte, I would buy another car and go pell-mell for California. On paper and in my mind, everything seemed so simple and catch-proof. Those damn Montana officers were responsible for my downfall, but not before I raised plenty of hell in their communities. As one deputy sheriff told me, "We have not had so much excitement in this state in the past twenty years."

One bright Friday morning, resplendent in full dress army regalia, I strode confidently down the main street of Billings looking for a good restaurant. I had much work to accomplish before that day was over. As I approached the first place of business, there was no lack of confidence when I told the clerk of the stationery store that I wanted to place an order for a ream of good bond paper. I further told him I wanted my name and address printed on it, and that I would be picking it up within the week. "By the way", I added, "will you be so kind as to accept my personal check? I'd like to make it out for more than the amount of the purchase, as I have a great deal of shopping to do and have no ready cash on hand. May I make it out for fifty dollars?" He was very obliging and assured me that it would cause no inconvenience to the establishment. He handed me the change and wished me a happy day. Store after store 'obliged' me. Without giving any thought to time, I ripped off nineteen stores. It was like taking candy from a baby.

Prior to going to work, I found that a train to Bozeman was leaving at 5:25 P. M. A glance at my watch told me that I had a little more than an hour to get my suitcase from the boarding house and be at the depot. I informed the lady where I was staying that I had received an emergency call, and that I had to be in Great Falls the following day. "I will be returning in less than a week", I assured her. "Lieutenant Gregory, let me fix you a bite to eat and I will drive you to the station," she pleaded. "In view of the fact that I want to bathe and change into my civilian clothes, I certainly appreciate your gesture. These uniforms can be stuffy to travel in," I complained. I ate like a horse. "Madam, I will have to pay you by check if that is alright with you. Also, I would like to make it a bit more than I owe. I will need some money to travel on. Would that inconvenience you?" She told me it would be alright; however, she had only about $80.00 on hand at that time. "Thank you. I am certain that will suffice," I stated. I was glad to be out of my disguise. As I purchased my ticket, no one was paying any attention to me. That was the way I wanted it.

It was early evening when I checked into The Bozeman hotel. I was rested, so I decided I'd go to a movie for relaxation, but before doing so, I wanted to take an accounting of just how much cash I had on hand. I couldn't believe my figures when the amount exceeded $5,700.00. That amount scared me. I stuffed $500.00 into my pockets and planted the rest in the water closet above the toilet bowl. I thoroughly enjoyed a Hoot Gibson movie. He took the part of a Wells Fargo detective chasing a band of train robbers. While I liked Hoot, I pulled for the robbers. I felt a sort of empathy with them, but damned if he didn't capture the whole band of about fifty outlaws single-handedly. After I went to bed that night, I had second thoughts about hitting any more towns. After all, I had more money than I had ever dreamed I would have. I had enough with which to buy a new car and play around for a couple of months. Deep down in my heart, I knew that the officials in a number of states would be formulating a plan to corner me and roast my ass. Also, I had to consider the fact that the federal government would soon develop an interest in Lieutenant Paul Gregory.

It was good to wake up the next morning and not be concerned about putting on my uniform. However, by some subtle method, I had to let it be known in this small community that I was not just some person who was

138

visiting. I was an important individual. The use of the uniform served me well in the acquisition of money and attention, but later proved to be my undoing. I was cognizant of the fact that I stole and fraudulently used a uniform, and that alone was a separate major crime. States would want to imprison me if I were captured. And the federal government would want to do the same. On top of all this, I knew that my home state of Washington was patiently waiting for my return to their jurisdiction so they could salt me away for robbery and kidnap. I have never been able to understand what precipitated this abnormal conduct. Surely I was suffering from some type of mental aberration. For a reason I no longer remember, I changed my base of operations to Livingston, Montana. It was a town east of Bozeman and offered no advantages so far as I could see. It was smaller than Bozeman and, by virtue of that fact, it limited the number of checks I would be able to cash. If I had been smart, I would have avoided both those towns because there was only one avenue of escape. True, it was my intent to cool off and stay out of uniform and banks until I felt the heat had abated. My impatience and restless nature demanded action. I listened to the radio regularly to see if there was mention of me and my nefarious activities. I was comforted by the fact that a number of the programs that gave wide range to the 'army officer' who had bilked dozens of businesses out of thousands of dollars in cash and merchandise, were unable to give a description. I was so proud when they made comment that the culprit appeared to vanish in space when a trap was being laid. If I had had an ounce of brains, I would have known that such statements were designed to give the check artist a false sense of security and thereby flush him out of the woods. I had thought of that possibility but was too vain to give the officials credit for having any brains.

I began going to skating rinks and dances where I met youths near my own age. I spent freely, mixed well and was accepted as a 'great guy'. In such a small community, where everyone knew everyone, my presence aroused much curiosity among the parents of friends I had made. The kids were asked such questions as, 'who is this Paul Gregory? Where did he come from? Where does he get the money to always be treating gangs of young people'? The queries were non-stop and captious. In turn the kids would question me. I knew I was going to have to come up with some plausible explanation or an investigation would soon ensue. I made up my mind right then to face the issue head on. I had learned that people were always impressed with unusual responses to questions. The more bizarre the answer, the more acceptable. So I dropped a few words in the ear of a young lady with whom I had been going. She was well known and inclined to elaborate on local gossip. Late one evening when we were returning from an ice skating party, I confided in her some quasi-secretive information. "Loretta, I will be gone for a few days. My superiors in Butte have ordered me to report to the office. I'll be back by Monday. Will you please take me to the railroad station tomorrow?" My announcement had the desired effect. She was inquisitive, and became more so when I cut her questions off with a curt, "There are some things I can't tell you at this time."

At ten o'clock the next morning, I was aboard the train bound for Butte.

Tucked away in my luggage was the main prop for my audience when I returned. Of course it was my faithful uniform. There was nothing for me to do in Butte but read, sleep and go to an occasional show. One evening when I was walking around town, I passed a Railway Express Agency just as the agent was locking up. With no real plan formulated, I stepped quickly into the shadow of a loading dock and watched the fellow through a side window. I saw him take a pistol from a hip holster and put it in a desk drawer. Weapons have always held a fascination for me. They would draw me like a magnet. I stood perfectly still in the dark until the agent had secured the door and walked down the street. Breaking in the office was like taking candy from a baby. I picked up a heavy rock from the ground, carefully wrapped my jacket around it. One sharp muffled thud broke the glass in a window in the rear of the building. Sliding the window was a snap. When I left the building, I had a beautiful 32 caliber revolver in my hip pocket.

The next day, I entered an office supply store and bought a new portable typewriter. The salesman accepted my check without hesitation. As I was walking toward my hotel with the machine, I passed a hock shop which had an attractive display in its window. Among the many interesting items was a pair of handcuffs. Just why I purchased them, I don't know, but later they came in handy.

I telephoned Loretta and asked her to meet me the following afternoon at the depot. When my train was about fifteen minutes from Livingston, I went in the lavatory and switched into my uniform. Strapped to my Sam Browne belt was my holster, complete with the 45. I was looking out the window of the train and was surprised to see Loretta and a few of her friends waiting for me. I disembarked with an exaggerated air of pompous importance. My reception committee stood as though transfixed. Loretta was the first to speak. She rushed up, kissed me and said, "Paul Gregory, I knew there was something unusual about you. You were always a mystery. And here you are an officer. Won't mama and dad be amazed?" Those with her all started asking questions at once. I whetted their interest by playing the mysterious role to the hilt. In a blanket statement to all of them I said, "I'm sure you realize that I can't reveal the purpose of my visit here. There are those from whom I take orders, and my instructions are very clear. I'm exhausted from a three-day ordeal, so I'll have to excuse myself for the remainder of the day. I'll look forward to tomorrow when we can get together again and enjoy ourselves." With that, I crawled into Loretta's car and asked her to drive me to the hotel.

It was going to be a long afternoon and evening. I had no more than finished my bath than the phone rang. It was Loretta and she gushed with, "Mama and Dad are thrilled to hear you are back, and in uniform, too. They want you to come over for dinner this evening about seven. There will be a few close friends to join us." I knew damn well what the score was. The parents had smelled a story that involved an army officer who was in their small village on government business. While I had not stated such a thing, I dropped just enough bait for them to put their imaginations to work. I was very polite in my rejection. I told Loretta I was expecting some long distance calls and had to remain by the phone. "That's all right, Paul. I can understand. I'll look forward to seeing you in the morning. I'll meet you in the lobby before I go to school." I could well imagine the stories that would run rampant throughout the student body and the teaching staff.

Loretta was waiting in the lobby when I came down the stairs. She was dressed prettily. "Oh, Paul, can't we have a cup of chocolate before I have to go?" I wanted to order breakfast while she had a cup of chocolate. "Paul," she said excitedly, "the kids called me until midnight. There was rumor that you were a secret agent here on federal business." Very calmly, I looked her straight in the eyes and whispered, "I see the news is out." She could not leave fast enough to get to school and confirm the very rumor she had planted. The kids accepted my story, but I was concerned that the adults would be skeptical. They might even start an inquiry, and I could not stand that.

About noon I returned to the hotel to have lunch. I had no more than seated myself than in walked Loretta's father with three other businessmen. Her dad walked over to my table simply beaming from ear to ear. He held out his hand and greeted me with a hearty, "Good morning, Lieutenant. May my friends and I join you for a bite to eat?" I arose from my chair and offered my hand. "By all means, join me." He introduced his friends as local businessmen. Other than to address me as Lieutenant, he ignored the uniform. To me that wasn't natural. If he was being coy, I'd play the same game. Our conversation got around to livestock, big game and other subjects native to the Montana area. When he could see that I wasn't going to offer any explanation for my absence from the town, and returning in uniform, he cracked the ice. "Lieutenant, you've set tongues wagging here. You know how gossipy people are in small towns?" I took the bull by the horn and asked, "What is it you want to know?" He was taken aback by my abrupt question. One of the men at his left came to the point. "I'm a reporter, Lieutenant Gregory, and I smell a story. May I have an interview?" I appreciated the fellow's forthright manner. "Sir," I said, "other than to tell you that I am investigating a plane crash that occurred in the area about two months ago, there is little I can say at this point." The ears of every one of them perked up. Finally the reporter continued, "How did the government become involved in the crash of a commercial, non-government plane?" He took out his note pad and was writing as he talked. Without hesitating, I said, "When flights cross state lines, the federal government is involved." I was sweating profusely. What if one of the other men was a lawyer? Loretta's father said, "By God, this is intriguing." With that, I stood up and bid them good day. The reporter worried me. He was persistent and asked, "Lieutenant, will you give me the first shot at the story when it is ready to be released?" I gave my solemn oath that I would. By nightfall, the whole town knew what had been said at the restaurant.

I was resting in my room later in the evening when the phone rang. A lady's voice introduced herself, "I am Mrs. Blodgett, Officer Gregory, the principal at the high school. Loretta, who is a friend of yours, said you might be willing to address the student body tomorrow afternoon. We would most certainly appreciate it if you would take the time to visit us." That Loretta was a conniving one. And her father had done a pretty good job of broadcasting what took place at our luncheon. Getting back to the principal, I asked, "What subject could I speak on that would be of interest to high school students?" She had her answer well rehearsed. "All of us would like to hear about the military. Many of the boys who are not much younger than you are thinking of making the military their career." I agreed to be in the lecture hall at 2:00 PM the next day. For a brief time, I gave thought to skipping out of town. Someone was going to put a hook in me and take off my covers. I knew that my days were numbered in Livingston. I was angry with myself. All I had accomplished in the past week was to bring a lot of heat on my head. A friend of Loretta's by the name of Ginger, called me just before I was ready to go to sleep. "Paul, my aunt, Mrs. Blodgett, called my mother and said you were to be our guest speaker tomorrow. I called some of my friends and told them. We can't wait to hear you." I thanked her, and hung up. I had a natural propensity for getting into trouble. If I could have only foretold the dire consequences of the next week, I would have bought a car the next day and skipped out. I was always blessed with more fortitude than brains, so I remained in Livingston that night and prepared for the confrontation the next day, and a series of very dire confrontations for the next week.

I sat behind the podium in the school's gymnasium and nervously watched the student body file in. Seated on my right was the principal, Mrs. Blodgett, on my left the president of the student body. As soon as the last student took his chair, Mrs. Blodgett rose and said, "Students, we are honored today to have as our speaker this afternoon an officer of the U. S. Army. He is assigned to the investigative branch of the armed forces, better known as G2. There are, understandably, limitations to the extent he can dwell on his private assignment here. However, I am sure you will find his experiences interesting and informative. I am pleased to introduce Lieutenant Paul Gregory." I was paralyzed as I walked to the podium. However, my confidence was fully restored at the loud roar of voices, and the sustained applause and stamping of feet. I talked about my high school days and of my many months of severe training at the Officers' Training School in Fort Benning, Georgia. From that school, I was selected to go to Washington D. C, and take part in the concentrated training of the G2 Division. The talk was rolling so smoothly I raved on for another half hour. I am not too certain what I said in the latter part of my speech, but I must have impressed the kids as well as the staff of teachers. Everyone rose from his seat and clapped for a full minute.

As I started to walk out, I was disconcerted upon seeing the reporter who had asked for my interview. He cornered me at the door and asked, "May I have about an hour of your time this afternoon, Lieutenant?" I told him I would be unavailable until tomorrow morning, at which time I would meet with him in my room. He was obviously disappointed and angered. A sort of sixth sense alerted me that I was nearing the end of my ruse. This feeling was supported by the attitude of the hotel clerk when I asked for my key. He eyed me nervously when he handed it to me. By the time I walked up the stairs, and down the hall to my room, I was sweating profusely. I fitted the key in the door, but before I pushed it open, I drew the 45 from its holster, and was prepared to shoot if necessary. No one was inside. However, someone had been there. The bureau drawers were turned upside down on my bed. My suitcase was lying on the floor wide open. Its contents were strewn all over the floor. Either it was a burglary or an illegal search by the cops. I thought of my concealed money. I raced into the bathroom and took the top off the water closet. My money was gone. I was sick with fear. I gathered up all I had that was worth taking and re-packed my alligator traveling bag. I knew I didn't dare go down the front stairs because they would certainly be waiting for me. I looked from behind the curtain and scanned the alley carefully. Not a soul was there. I started to raise the window and go down the fire escape when I heard a knock on the door. I knew I could not very well run out the back way. In a calm voice I asked, "Who is it?" A man's voice replied, "My name is Marvin and I am one of the students who heard you speak, and I'd like to talk with you." I loosened the flap on my holster and cautiously opened the door. Standing there was a handsome young fellow. I invited him in and asked what I could do for him. He said, "I want to be a government agent and I thought you could give me some tips." Before he could say another word, he was looking at the business end of my gun. The fellow blanched and stuttered, "You're not going to shoot me, are you?" "Not if you do as you are told", I snarled. "If you call out or draw any attention, your life won't be worth a damn. Do everything I tell you or I'll blast your head off. Lie on the floor face down, and don't move." I opened my suitcase and took out the handcuffs I had purchased in Butte. Without saying a word, I put one cuff on his left wrist. I straddled him and placed the muzzle of the automatic against the base of his neck. "I've got to take you hostage so I can get out of this trap. Let me tell you again, you walk with me as though we are good friends strolling along. If we pass anyone you know, you had better speak and keep on walking beside me. I'm going to drape your coat over the handcuff, but I'll have a good grip on the other cuff in case you think of breaking away and trying to make a run for it. After we are out of town and I feel safe, I'll turn you loose. Did you bring a car with you?" He nodded in the affirmative. "Where is it parked?" He pointed to the rear of the hotel. "OK, stand up." I instructed. "You carry my case and walk down the back steps. Go directly to your car. You will be doing the driving." He was very obedient, and in a few minutes we were on the highway heading for Butte.

I had to make decisions as we drove. I knew I could not let him off in a small town. In fact, I pondered, how could I drop him anywhere? Getting out of Montana would be a tough job. I couldn't very well keep him with me for a long trip. There would be the problem of eating, sleeping and going to the privy. Even if we made it as far as Idaho, then what? I even toyed with the idea of taking him on a side road, and tying him up. I dismissed that thought. It was terribly cold. If I trussed him tightly, he would freeze to death. Suddenly, I noticed a Montana Highway patrol car approaching from the opposite direction. I knew that my captive would be apt to make his move now, if ever. I shoved the muzzle of my gun hard into his ribs and hissed, "Don't do it, prick, or you'll be on your way to meet your ancestors."

Despite the warning, Marvin nodded energetically to the cop. He overdid the nodding. When we were alongside, Marvin stuck his tongue out at the trooper. I drove the gun in his rib cage with such force that I thought I heard ribs cracking. He gasped in pain, and nearly collapsed. He was really hurt. I turned and watched the cop. I thought he might turn around and stop us. After we were safely out of sight of the lawman, I told Martin to roll his window down. He was apprehensive as to what I was planning and did not do as I told him. I put the gun barrel in his ear and repeated my order. Quickly, he did as I instructed. As soon as the window was fully down, I put the gun under his chin and fired three quick shots into the hillside. I thought he was going to faint. "Roll that goddam window up, you asshole. That was to let you know this weapon is loaded. The next time I am forced to pull the trigger, you'll never hear anything again 'cause you will be busy turning up your f—king toes."

A sign along the road read 'Butte - 6 miles'. The pressure was building up in me. I was so tired I couldn't think clearly. There seemed to be no way out of this dilemma. An idea came to my mind. Why not pull off the side of the road and blast this nuisance? I could dump his body in a gully, go on to Butte and plan my action from there. It would be days before they would find his body. By that time, I could be in New York. I shuddered with revulsion.

How could I even entertain such a thought? If I were pulling a bank job and someone wanted a shootout, I could easily justify putting a slug in that someone's brisket. But to just shoot an unarmed man, no way.

We pulled into the heart of Butte. I made up my mind that I'd have to get a couple of train tickets to Seattle and take Marvin with me. I had psyched myself to the point that, if everything failed, there was going to be blood spilled. "Marvin", I said, "pull into a parking place. We're going in and get a couple of tickets to Seattle. Play it carefully." The strain was too much for my hostage. He started shaking uncontrollably. I was afraid he was going to collapse. I had to calm him down. "Here, sit down on this bench and get a hold of yourself. You'll be OK", I assured him. Just as I started to seat myself beside him, all hell exploded. I was struck alongside the head and was knocked ass over a tea kettle. I was stunned but not so much that I couldn't get my gun into action. I rolled to my side and brought the gun up and lined a burly bastard's belly button in the sight. Before I could squeeze off a slug, a boot kicked the automatic from my hand with such force I figured my arm was shattered. I found myself laying on the marble station floor. Two cops stood over me with drawn guns. One of them yelled, "Make another move, Lieutenant Gregory, and they'll bury you in the National Cemetery in Arlington." The last I saw of Marvin, a pair of plain clothes men were escorting him to a car. He was sobbing hysterically.

When they tossed me in the Butte city jail, they were anything but gentle. I fully expected them to kick the shit out of me. I knew that whenever an outlaw pulled a gun on a bull one of two consequences took place; either they would blow his head off, or they would beat him half to death when they got him out of the public's view. If there was a stink raised by the victim's family the cops would simply swear that the criminal attempted to grab one of their weapons. Of course they always had the advantage of having two or three witnesses willing to testify that the officers reacted to preserve their lives or the lives of others. Many times the police would get another con to swear that the victim was attempting to assault the authorities. In return they would grant the con special privileges. It was a no-win situation for the wrongdoer. Why I wasn't subjected to their brutality, I'll never know. A day or two after my arrest, I was taken to the emergency ward at the local hospital where a doctor sewed up the gash on my head.

For two days I was kept in solitary confinement. On the third day, I was interrogated by government agents. Among the hundreds of questions they asked were; Where did you get the uniform? The guns? The checks you were cashing? All the questions were pertaining to forgery, kidnapping and car theft. Not once did they mention bank robbery. I was stupid enough to think I was just plain lucky. I didn't give thought to the fact that kidnapping was a crime of the utmost magnitude. After I was exhausted from all the interrogation, the feds brought in my suitcase. It contained nearly all the items with which I had packed it. Nearly, but not all. The money I had hidden was gone. I complained bitterly, but was told, "Don't give us your bull shit. There wasn't a dime around." I retorted angrily, "You are a fucking liar. I had more than five grand in there." They laughed and said, "You never saw five grand in your life. Forget it." I added, "Where's my typewriter?" They ignored me and walked out. I had to accept the fact that the officials, city, county, state or federal government had stolen some of my property. In addition to my loss of typewriter and cash, the filthy bastards had purloined one of my gats. I was absolutely infuriated. I felt that you couldn't trust anyone. The last time I saw the government scum, they told me that I had a series of felony detainers from Illinois, Wisconsin, Iowa, Colorado, Florida and Montana and that those charges were state crimes. In addition, I had federal detainers charging me with representing an army officer, transporting stolen weapons across the state line, transporting stolen cars across the state line and two counts of kidnap.

It took a couple of days for me to realize the gravity of my situation. It took no imagination to visualize that I would die in prison of senility. I asked for an attorney and one came to visit after I had been jailed for about ten days. He was a young fellow by the name of George Killian. I was encouraged by his jovial manner. "What can I do you, Glenn?" I was shocked to hear my correct name for the first time in months. "How did you learn my name?", I asked. George came right to the point. "It took the officials about a week to trace you. They got all the information from the Sheriff of Wenatchee, Washington. My God, Kid, what a trail you left behind. Actually, all the authorities involved in dozens of cities are confused as to which jurisdiction you should be returned. It seems to me that it doesn't really matter because each one could give you life. The Feds will probably get first shot at you. Because of the felonies stacked against you, the prosecuting attorney in Wenatchee says they can give you life under the habitual criminal statute of the state of Washington. The sheriff of Livingston wants you brought back there next week. In my opinion, simply to save money, I'm betting that you will be returned to your hometown. Why Livingston wants you back, I don't know. Back to your request for an attorney, what can I do for you?" "Hell, man, from your attitude, I don't see any need for a lawyer!" I snapped.

It seemed to me that one official after another kept coming to my cell to grill me. Prosecuting attorneys and cops came from four different states in an attempt to identify me as the forger, burglar and car thief. It appeared to be a contest among the various states and cities as to which one could take me back to their jurisdiction to fry me. Conferences were held between the district attorneys of Butte and Livingston to determine which jurisdiction would get custody of me. During their meetings, other prosecutors from states in the Mid-West put in their bid to have me extradited to their domain. Much of this information was brought to me by a trustee whose job was to bring my food. The crux of the question seemed to be which jurisdiction could guarantee to give me the harshest treatment. Each representative promised the others that, under the punishment to be meted out in their state, they could promise to make me non-existent for a term of at least 50 years. In the forefront of the drawing for my rear end, my home town of Wenatchee seemed to be far and away in the lead. The prosecuting attorney of that district assured the state of Montana, and the others, that under their laws, I would get a natural life sentence under the Habitual Criminal Act of that state. That piece of legislation permitted life sentences to be dispensed in all cases where a person had been found guilty of committing three felonies. The legislature agreed that when a person does, indeed, commit three felonies, he is beyond redemption and, therefore, had forfeited his right to reside in a free society. The appeal from the prosecutor of Wenatchee was the most attractive. It was agreed that Washington state should start extradition proceedings. I was advised that I had the right to fight extradition, and that if I chose to resist extradition, the matter would have to be resolved before the Governor's Review Board in the Montana State Capitol. In the meantime, Livingston wanted me returned to their custody while the proceedings were being processed. Being a fighter and wanting to cause trouble whenever possible, I chose to resist them.

Such an action on the part of a criminal creates an added expense to the holding state as well as the state seeking his return. It necessitated having lawyers appear before the governor's Review Board. In reality, I knew that extradition was granted in 99% of all cases. Nevertheless, I intended to be stubborn.

While the wheels of justice were grinding, the cops from Livingston swooped me up exceedingly fast and transported me back to their bailiwick, and promptly ensconced me in the death cell. It took me a few days to understand why they transported me to Livingston and in, of all places, their pride and joy; the death cell. After I had been there a couple of days, I was besieged by reporters wanting stories. The most humiliating visitors of all were dozens of curious school children. Many were the very kids I had spoken to in their assembly. When they showed up, I covered my face with a blanket. And that is when I came to the conclusion that I was brought back to be put on display. An old time deputy said, "Hell, young feller, we ain't

146

had this much excitement since the carnival came through here four years ago. You are regarded here as a real freak."

Before long, I grew tired of the crummy jail and citizens. I had been placed in solitary confinement with no reading material or other amenities. For ten days, I never heard one word about the proceedings that were taking place in the governor's office. Out of boredom, I decided to contact the prosecuting attorney in Wenatchee and tell him I would sign extradition papers if I could be assured I would be taken back to Wenatchee immediately. I sent that word through Livingston's Prosecutor's office. Three days later, I was told that a Wenatchee deputy would be coming after me.

One morning while it was still dark, I was awakened by a guard and told, "Get dressed and gather all your things. You will be given breakfast early. You will be taken back to the state of Washington as soon as you eat. The deputy who came after you says he has known you since you were a youngster. He says you piss a pretty straight stream for such a young fellow. Hurry up now." For more than fifty years, I have wondered what that cop meant by 'you piss a pretty straight stream'.

After I had eaten, I was led out to the sheriff's office. When the door was opened, I was kind of surprised and pleased to see Ray True sitting there. As always he greeted me in friendly fashion. "Well, Glenn, you've cut a wide swath since you left the old burg. I have specific orders to put the Oregon Boot on you, and it is to stay there until I put you in the county jail. I had nothing to do with that decision, Kid. I'll treat you fair and feed you well but, by the same token, it is my job to return you. Your parents are my friends so I don't want to have to do anything that will hurt them or me. If I have to, I will."

I was in awe of the Oregon Boot. The boot was a device invented by an inmate in the Oregon State Penitentiary in 1880. It consisted of a steel cuff about 1" thick. It had a mechanism on one side that was hinged. On the other was a locking device. A strap of steel was attached to each side of the cuff and went under the arch of the foot, sort of like a stirrup. The steel band was riveted to the sole of a heavy leather boot which was a size 13 so it would fit any foot. Once it had been locked on a man, there was not a possibility of getting it off without the key. To try to walk with it was a nightmare. When you did walk, you had to swing your leg very wide to avoid striking your other ankle. On top of all that, this devil's device weighed 18 pounds.

Before we left the office, Ray fitted me with that impediment as well as cuffs, leg irons and a waist chain. He cautioned me to walk carefully. "The BOOT is a miserable and cruel invention, Glenn." Then he turned to three local deputies and said, "I wouldn't put this thing on a dog, but it's the chief's orders." It hadn't dawned on me that we were going to travel by train until all three deputies who had been in the office walked out with us and motioned me toward a Montana State Patrol car. I started to complain bitterly but had struck my free ankle with the steel cuff because I forgot to 'swing wide' as I had been told. It was probably the most excruciating pain I had ever suffered. I cried out and fell to the ground. The cluster of bulls rushed over to help me. "Damn this stupid gadget." A young man standing to one side looked at the cops and said, "Yeah, and that goes for anyone who would put something like that on a mere kid. You must think you're Wyatt Earp." Ray examined my ankle to determine if it was broken. Satisfied that I was just painfully hurt, he assisted my getting in the prowl car.

By the time we were ready to board, a dozen people had gathered at the depot. It was apparent that someone had tipped the action off. Photographers' flash bulbs popped. Others had their note pads out and were scribbling rapidly. More than fifty years later, I read what they had written. Ray was solicitous of my comfort. I knew he felt badly about the accident. He guided me to the rear of a nearly vacant pullman and there we stayed throughout the trip. As the train was pulling out, he carefully examined my leg. About four hours later, Ray commented that we would go eat in a few minutes. I refused to go to the dining room, and as I complained to Ray, "Why in the hell do you want to put me on display?" He took a long time to reply. "Glenn I didn't put you in this position. Get that through your skull. I want to feed you, and the only place we can eat is in the diner." About that time a negro porter came down the aisle. It was obvious that he wanted to see the convict and the Oregon Boot. I never saw more porters, conductors, cooks, waiters, and brakemen in my life. When this particular porter got alongside of us, Ray got an idea. He whispered to the individual, "Porter, I'm transporting this young fellow on a four-day trip. Naturally, we have to eat, and I can't very well drag him through six or seven Pullmans to get to the dining area. Would you please get us some sandwiches, coffee and milk, and bring them here? I'll pay you well." The negro responded quickly. "Yes, Suh, I'll get you both something to eat right away. Just you sit right here." I had to smile. Where did he think we were going?.

In a brief time, the fellow was back with some very tasty food. I kind of liked the guy. Both Ray and I slept fitfully. He was jumpy because he had to be on the alert for any move I might make. I couldn't sleep because my ankle ached so badly, and trying to get comfortable with a hunk of iron dangling from my ankle was not exactly conducive to sleep. By the night of the second day, both of us were plain touchy. Ray became fretful, and was testy to the crew. Each time one of us had to go to the toilet, the other had to drag along. At breakfast the third morning, Ray had reached his limit. He collared a conductor and asked, "Sir, I haven't had a chance to eat a decent meal for nearly three days. Could I hire someone to sit with this prisoner for an hour? I will pay well. And he won't cause any problems because he'll be chained like a mummy." The conductor acted as though an honor had been bestowed on him. "I'll watch this criminal for you while you go to the diner. And don't you worry, if he tries one damn thing out of line, I'll bend this ring of keys around his head. Now you go on." With that he seated himself across from me. I don't think I have ever been so infuriated in my life as I was with this conductor, so I took great pleasure in downing him. I looked him over scornfully. I sneered contemptuously right in his face. I spit at his feet. He jumped up and started stamping his feet like a spoiled brat. I sat staring at the conductor without batting an eye or taking my glare from him. By the time Ray got back, my quasi-guard was insane with anger. Pointing at me, he yelled at Ray, "This man is a dangerous animal." I looked at the deputy, smiled and whispered, "Ray, this conductor is a coward. He is a boy trying to do a man's job." The conductor turned and practically ran down the aisle of the coach. That was the only fun I had experienced for weeks.

Shortly after that incident, the porter brought me three sandwiches, milk and donuts. While I was putting them away, I heard him tell Deputy True that we would be pulling in to the Spokane Depot and, at that destination, it would be necessary for us to make our final change. Our next stop would be Wenatchee. As Ray conveyed that news to me, he must have thought that if I were going to make a break for it or create any unforeseen ruckus, it would be when we changed trains, because he cautioned me, "There will be a railroad officer accompanying us on our transfer, so don't make any problems. We are seven hours from home, and this tiresome journey will be over." After his comment about the railroad officer, implying that they were pretty tough, I snapped, "Lay off the BS, Ray. Bulls are all alike. They're real rough and tough when they have a man chained and helpless. If he says one word out of line, like that sick-assed conductor did, I'll cuss him out like he has never been cussed before." Ray just rolled his eyes upward, and kept on talking. "We're going to have to walk about four blocks across a marble floor so you better prepare yourself for a lot of noise with those chains and that heavy boot thumping along. It's going to be embarrassing for both of us, so please make the best of it." His description created a vivid picture in my mind, and I dreaded to face it.

From the dirty Pullman window, I could see the Spokane sky-line nearing. I sensed someone standing slightly to my rear where the travelling guard had stationed himself. I turned and was pleasantly surprised to find my friendly porter. Throughout the entire trip, he had treated me decently, almost with deference. He addressed Ray True, "Suh, its heavy in my heart to talk with your prisoner. I'd be most obliged for this privilege." Because the weary trip was nearly at an end, Ray was doubly alert. He knew from long experience that, when transporting convicts, they were more of a problem at the end of a journey. They became restive and, if they were going to do something desperate, it usually occurred just before the 'final door' was going to be slammed in their faces. He carefully scrutinized the colored gentleman who stood before him. "What is it you want to talk to Williams about, Porter?" Without hesitation or embarrassment the individual replied softly, "I'm a man of the Lord. And my Creator has put the burden on my heart to tell this unfortunate young man of His everlasting promises. He will be going on his way in a few minutes and I won't have the opportunity to carry His precious word to this creature." I sat there unable to believe my ears. Ray interrupted my thoughts by saying, "Porter, I respect you and all you believe in, but I cannot permit you to deliver your message without the prisoner's approval. Ask him." I was all set to land into that impertinent black, but hesitated. Hadn't he been a caring individual? Did he not bring me extra food and deserts without being asked to do so? He felt he had a mission and maybe he did. Another thing I liked about him was his guts. "Shoot the works, partner," I invited him. There was no searching for words when he spoke in his magnificent voice. "Young man, you are perfect in the eyes of God. He created you and He is pleased with his result. However, Satan has got into your life and is defiling you. I don't know what

149

you did nor where you went wrong, but you ain't done nothing that the Lord can't put right. He is your salvation and your only hope. Please drop on your knees right here and now, and ask His forgiveness. He will heal you and make you whole. You'll be born again." If it had been anybody else but this kind soul, I would have treated him to some choice words. Instead, I simply said, "Man, I want to tell you that I appreciate all you have done for me on this trip. You have been good to me, and you are the only one who has treated me as a human being. But there are two reasons I won't drop on my knees and ask for forgiveness. 1) I don't believe in all that Jesus stuff. 2) I couldn't drop on my knees even if I wanted to. I'm wrapped so tight in chains that I can't move." With a 'Lord Bless you', the good porter moved from my life, but he has never been forgotten.

The train came to a creep and moved like a snake toward the depot. It inched to a such a jerky stop I was nearly thrown from my feet. The deputy grabbed my arm and helped steady me. He kept me near our seat until the majority of the passengers had left the Pullman. When the area was clear, he told me to make my way toward the front of the platform. "Be careful not to fall, Glenn. I'll be directly behind you and will give you a hand if you need it. The man in the wide brim hat ahead of you is the railroad officer sent to assist us through the crowd. Start walking forward and follow him." I began shuffling through the mass of people who parted quickly upon seeing and hearing the prisoner as he dragged chains and boot across the marble floor. The disinterested passengers had suddenly become spectators. They parted into lines and I tried to walk in a dignified manner between them. All seemed to gawk at my face first and then at my fetters. Children huddled nearer their parents and stared slack-jawed. One boy of about five years of age looked up at his dad and said, "Daddy, what has the man got on his feet?" During this parade of shame, the deputy stayed at my right with his hand on my arm. In my seething anger and embarrassment, I forget to swing my booted right foot wide. Again, the iron enforced brogan struck my opposite ankle. Try as I did to stop it, a cry of pain escaped my lips. The original bruise had not healed, and the second injury pained me doubly. My guard realized he couldn't permit me to stop. There was no place to be seated, and he had to be certain that a crowd didn't gather. He pushed me forward. By this time, I was dragging my encumbered leg as though it were a lifeless limb. When it was obvious I could walk no further, Ray True and the other bastard each gripped me by an arm and helped me stand immobile until the pain subsided. The trouble was, it didn't let up. And sure enough, people began to gather around. Unknown to the deputy and me, the railroad officer had signaled company detectives that the potential for much trouble was near at hand. Before I realized what was happening, four train officials surrounded us. We were quickly pushed into an ante room and the door was secured. One of the detectives shoved his face in mine and yelled, "You trouble-making idiot, as soon as the crowd disperses we're going to hustle you to your departing Pullman. If you open your mouth once, we'll put you to sleep with our saps and carry you. Have you got that straight?" I spit in his face just as Ray jumped between us. He was so angry he couldn't contain himself. He turned on the offending hack and screamed, "This man is my prisoner. He has been hurt, and I demand medical treatment for him right now. You have a medical man at this station, and I want him to attend to my prisoner." Here was a case of the king defending the slave, and it dumbfounded the rail employees. They gathered in a knot and whispered among themselves. Two of them left hurriedly. I was seated in a chair where I got a little relief.

Not a word was uttered for fifteen minutes, and then the silence was broken by the entrance of a man dressed in a white gown. Obviously he was a medical man of some degree. He asked the Wenatchee police officer what had taken place. True told him in a matter of a few words. "This man is my prisoner. He is wearing what is called an Oregon Boot, a device used on dangerous escape risks. The prisoner accidentally hit his free ankle while trying to walk. Such an experience is very painful and has been known to break a leg. I don't know to what extent the prisoner has been injured, but I do know he is hurt. Please do what you can for him. We have about thirty minutes to catch our train." The medic started to examine my ankle but couldn't get past the boot. He asked Ray to remove it so he could make a thorough examination.

The deputy refused the doctor's request saying, "I can't do that. He carries the boot until he is jailed in Wenatchee. Can't you give him something for pain until I get to our destination?" The medic's face turned beet-red. "Yes, I'll give him a shot now to help him immediately, and then give you some pills to give him every three hours. And, I will make a full report on this blatant case of barbarity. I can't believe what I have seen and heard here." He told a nearby Redcap to take me to my Pullman in a wheel chair. The morphine took hold within ten minutes, and I was much relieved as I was wheeled to the connecting train.

I don't know how long I slept before I was awakened by a dull throbbing in my injured leg. As soon as my guard heard me move, he asked, "How are you feeling, Glenn?" I answered him in one word, "Miserable." True opened a small box and handed me three pills. "Here is something that will help you until we get home." I looked out the window and saw familiar terrain; sagebrush, jackrabbits and rattle snakes. Sure enough, it was Wenatchee country. Ray glanced at his watch and reckoned we would be in town in an hour or two. As the engine pulled its cargo up along the Columbia River, I was lost in reverie. There was no question, I was headed for the iron bar hotel for many years. Even if I were ever released from the penitentiary, there were countless other charges awaiting me. The picture was grim.

I was not aware how close we were to Wenatchee until the train, its mournful whistle seeming to announce a funeral dirge, began to cross the bridge. Darkness had closed in quite rapidly during the past hour. As we pulled into the depot, I pressed my face against the Pullman window. There appeared to be more people out there than was normal. I had no more than shown my face in the door way than a number of photo flash bulbs burst in my eyes. Four cops swooped in on me. I was carried bodily to an awaiting prowl car. I heard a number of friends call out my name before the car door was slammed, and I was whisked away.

151

In no time flat, I was sitting in the sheriff's office. Fred Mallion, the chief deputy said, "Glenn, we're getting a doctor down here to see you. Deputy True had the doctor call from Spokane, so we were prepared. Let me remove the Oregon Boot, and get your socks off." True knelt with the key and gently opened the steel cuff from around my ankle. For the first time in my life I thought I was going to faint. I had worn that diabolical contrivance for five long days and nights. When it was removed from my body and dropped to the floor with a loud thud, it was like lifting a heavy weight from my entire body and not just my leg. My socks were bloody from mid-shin to soles. The blood had coagulated and caused my socks to stick to the open cuts. At this point, in walked the doctor. He took one look at my leg and said, "I'm going to have to get an x-ray. Let's get him to the hospital." While the doctor was preparing me to be moved, Sheriff Tom Cannon strutted into the room. He boomed out, "Well, what are we doing with Williams?" Without looking up, the doctor said, "I'm taking him to the hospital for an x-ray. There is a possibility he has a broken ankle bone." Cannon wheeled on his chief deputy and told him, "You take another man with you and keep a guard on him every minute he's at the hospital. If he gets away again, you'll be back on WPA on the end of a spade. This kid is as fast as a jackrabbit and as slippery as an eel."

The deputy selected an old retired marshall from the Okanogan country to accompany him while he was on guard at the hospital. He sort of reminded me of the old Dodge City marshalls of which I had read. He stood on one side of the operating table and Mallion on the other while two nurses soaked my blood-encrusted sock off my ankle. They were gentle and kind, and I appreciated them. The x-ray was taken and it was determined I had no broken bones. The flesh was cut and badly bruised. As the nurses were bandaging me up, I heard the old marshall comment to Mallion, "In all my years in this business, I've only seen two men who required 'booting'. In fact, I heard they outlawed the use of this form of torture years ago. I'll bet this kid is the youngest person on record, and the last, to have been 'booted'. Am I right, Mallion?" The sheriff's agent looked embarrassed as he muttered, "I had nothing to do with this. But I'll bet that order returns to haunt someone." Within the hour, I was returned to the cell known as the 'strong box'. Other than my dad, who visited me twice weekly, I was not permitted to see anyone. Orders were issued that I was to have no reading material, except the Bible, of course, and was to write only one letter each week, and that was to be censored personally by Tom Cannon. I had embarrassed the officials of the village, and they were getting their revenge. As each day passed, I was able to walk longer distances, that is back and forth. The pain subsided quickly. The scars remained for months.

Early one morning, I was cuffed and taken to the sheriff's office. The county prosecutor, Lynn Gemmill, had come to talk with me about my upcoming trial. He was a soft-spoken and dignified-appearing man. When I entered the room, he stood and offered his hand. He came right to the point. "Glenn, you know that we have enough evidence to try you on a series of local crimes. It would only take one conviction to be able to successfully try you as an habitual criminal, and have you sentenced to life.

152

I don't want to do this. You're too young to face such a sentence. I have come to you with a proposition. If you will plead guilty to robbing the cafe, I will get the judge to accept your plea. By pleading guilty, we can legally avoid the habitual criminal charge. I am sure Judge Parr will give you about a five-year term. With time off for good-time, you will be released in less than four years. What do you say to this deal?" I couldn't believe my ears. Here was the DA asking me to assure him that I would trade four years of my life just to make his task easier. That guy had to be crazy. In the first place, I was confident they could not convict me. I failed to remember that there were three other charges pending, and it was a cinch they could get at least one conviction. And one was all it would take for me to go bye-bye for life. Probably the craziest answer I ever gave to a question in my life was this classic reply. "Gemmill, I want you two to get this straight. I'll see both of you in hell before I plead guilty. You two small-time, blood-sucking bastards just want to make a name for yourselves. My answer is no!" The sheriff jumped up as though he was going to slug me. Gemmill leaped between the two of us. The uniformed bluff puffed up like a bantam rooster. Gemmill, the more intelligent of the two, stared at me in a puzzled way. "Glenn, I can't understand you. Your family are nice people; well- bred, educated and law-abiding. And look at you. How can you be so different? You need help." With that he left the room. I was escorted to my ice-box.

I think Link Seibert must have told my father what transpired between the district attorney and me, because when Dad came to see me the next day, he admonished me for the manner in which I had addressed the prosecutor. "You could have been a gentleman, Son. As it stands now, you have lowered yourself to his level. I agree that you should not plead guilty. We will fight it out to the end. You don't get a chance to see a paper, but The World has been having a holiday with your story. Their stories are going to prejudice the public. In fact, your attorney, Lawrence Leahy, is going to ask for a change of venue. There is no way you could get a fair trial with all the jury-rigging the officials practice here. We are asking for a judge from another county to sit on your case. When I get the details, I'll be up and tell you." Time must have stood still. Four months after I had been indicted, my trial date was set. I had learned that the presiding judge agreed to have a visiting jurist hear the case. I couldn't bring myself to be too happy. I reasoned that the local citizens would be on the jury, so what did I gain? Even at that age, I knew it would be more desirable to be transferred to a larger city where the small-town biases were not so rampant. I mentioned this fact to my attorney and father. Both agreed that it would be best to transfer the trial to a larger city.

The morning of the trial found me fully awake by 5:00 A. M. I believe that the gravity of my predicament finally registered. In the loneliness of my solitary cell, I was compelled to face some sobering facts. I was being tried on a statute that provided for a lifetime of confinement if found guilty. To make the overall picture more dismal, I knew I was guilty of every offense of which I had been accused. My confidence was shattered. Too often, my parents had pulled me out of scrape after scrape with nothing more than a slap on the wrist. It was at this time in my life I awakened to the fact that

153

the officials in Wenatchee had not treated me as shabbily as I had imagined; that this town had many fine people who had accepted me as one of them. I knew I had blamed all my problems on people and circumstances around me. What could I expect from a jury of my peers at this time? It was I who had alienated them. In a few hours, my judgment day would dawn.

12

Release And A Family

I have no trouble remembering or describing my fish cage* in the Washington State Penitentiary. It was simply that, a cage about five feet wide, six feet long and seven feet high. The bars were of flat steel, laced back and forth to form openings one and a half inches square. In the center of the ceiling, was a 40-watt bulb, so dim it was virtually impossible to read by its light. The bad lighting caused nearly all inmates to have poor eyesight in a matter of a year. My eyes required glasses within the first six months. If you had no one on the outside to come to your rescue in such emergencies, you went without spectacles, and your eyes suffered for the rest of your life. There was no running water. Early each morning, a trustee would come down the landing, calling out, 'water'. Ten minutes later, he would come by with a large bucket of drinking water. At dinner time, he would follow the same procedure. In a rear corner of the cell, was a metal chute that rose to the roof for ventilation purposes. At the bottom of the chute was an opening in which a honey-pot was placed. That was the receptacle in which you defecated and urinated. Once daily you were allowed to take the bucket to a long trough in the yard to empty it. Attached to each side of the wall of your 'house' was a steel bunk with just a cotton pad for a mattress and no pillow. The only reading material was a bible. To keep from going nuts, the cons would read it and, because of their dependency on the Good Book, they learned to hate it. After you were released from the time spent in the fish tanks, you could scrounge up other material to read. During that period, there was no commissary. Your swill was brought to you twice a day. If you had some white-money**, you could buy food and other amenities from a hungry*** guard, and most were hungry. Those first thirty days were depressing. Being released into general population was like being freed to the streets.

The main institution boasted of having eleven hundred citizens. It was a community in itself. To an extent it was governed by the strong cons, not necessarily physically powerful but those who controlled the flow of white money, drugs, punks**** and soft jobs. Often these factions controlled your choice of cellmates and where you worked. In reality, they governed your very life while you were incarcerated. For anyone who incurred their ire, retaliation was swift, often cruel and sometimes fatal. The inmates were the first to scream if their rights were infringed upon. Yet these same people

*cell in which incoming prisoners were placed. **regular currency which is illegal for cons to possess. ***guards with their hands out. ****boys used as girls

would take your life if you stole a pack of cigarettes from them. It was an insane world.

I became involved in the inmate political society. Actually, the different factions amounted to no less than gangs. The most powerful were those who had bought guards. By their connections, they were able to have drugs brought in and letters, which were censored at that time, smuggled out. Whenever there was a drug bust due to fall, the connection guards would tip off the inmate drug lords. I thought it was humorous when a big raid would take place and the officials would feed the media such headlines as, 'Officers break huge cocaine connection in state prison'. The proper officials pictures would appear in the papers. In more than one instance, the guards would say that the visitors were smuggling dope to the inmates. However, the cons knew that for every ounce sneaked in by some guy's girlfriend, the guards were bringing in a pound. Thus, my introduction to the real life of convicts, and their school of criminal practice.

Because of connections I had through having met some of the inmates in the training school and reformatory, I was more readily accepted. I secured a job in which to pass my time, and was able to select a cell partner of my choice. From the beginning, things seemed to run smoothly. My first mistake was to join up with a clique of the tough guys. I found myself having to defend an imaginary turf from an imaginary intruder. As a result I soon became involved in fights and knifings that were with anything but illusionary enemies. The stab wounds and broken bones were real and painful. Those who died in these skirmishes were genuine cadavers. It wasn't long until I had earned and cherished the reputation of a bad con, one not to be fiddled with. When I became aware how treacherous my so-called friends were, I gradually withdrew from them. This act, in itself, proved to be dangerous because if you weren't with them you were against them. Once you chose up sides and established yourself, there was no neutral ground. But I was determined to fight my own battles and avoid those misfits who lived on trouble. People in prisons know every dirty trick imaginable. If they wanted to dispose of you there were three sure- fire methods: kill you themselves, put a contract out on you or, worst of all, hang a jacket* on you. The latter is accomplished by the simple expediency of starting the rumor that you are a stool pigeon. Tell one or two of the most simple-minded cons that you snitched on another inmate. Within 24 hours, the institution is saturated with the rumor that you are a fink. At that point it is no longer a rumor, but a fact. No one will recall who started the tale, nor on whom you are presumed to have informed. Such a story will never die until the stool pigeon has been snuffed. God alone knows how many innocent and unsuspecting men have perished in such a manner.

Certain happenings in the cooler** leave memories with you that never fade. In one instance, I was locked up on bread and water. The cells used for such punishment were on the second tier of a cellhouse. Condemned men were isolated on the first landing. One of these men was a former Seattle fire fighter named Carl who had been sentenced to be hanged for killing his wife. His exercise area was on his landing where he was permitted

*a false record **jail or prison.

156

to bounce a handball against the wall for hours on end. After my thirty day bread and water stint was over, I was kept in the punishment cell for six months longer. During this time, I struck up a friendship with the man due to have his neck stretched. Day after day we would talk about the outside and our families. As his day of execution neared, his talks concentrated on his kids. When it was time for lights out, I would lie in my bed and worry about 'his day'. As was the practice of the officials, condemned men were taken to the death cells in another building 48 hours before their execution was scheduled. When Carl's date came, I heard the horrible sound of keys being fitted into the locks to his cell. The hangman in Walla Walla was known as the Sheep Herder. He and three other guards opened Carl's cell. "Carl, will you please come with us?" For the first time in two years, Carl heard a guard say 'please'. I could not imagine a guard saying please when he was taking a man to his death. When Carl stepped out of his cell, I jumped to the back of mine so I would not have to face him. He called out, "Glenn, take care." After they led him out, and I heard the outer door slam behind him, and I knew he could not hear me, I fell prostrate to the steel floor and cried uncontrollably.

The next day I was released to general population. I was placed in a cell in six wing, directly under, of all things, the death cells. I had heard men tell of lying in their bunks wide awake on the nights hangings were to take place. The heavy trap door would jar the whole cellhouse when it dropped and hit the wall. Men would look at their watches and know exactly when the trap was sprung. The following day, the Walla Walla Bulletin would tell at what minute the doctor pronounced the victim dead. The night after my being put in six wing, I knew that Carl was being prepared for his final journey in life. For once I prayed that I be allowed to fall asleep so I would not hear Carl die. My prayer was not answered. I looked at my watch at exactly midnight. I squeezed my eyes shut and held my pillow over my ears, and even held my breath. I gasped in air at the same second Carl plunged through the trap. I've never forgotten that horrifying moment.

Carl's going did a lot to make me mature. I began to take life more seriously, to realize there had to come a time when I had to accept responsibility and to hold myself accountable. I found it difficult to try to improve myself. A life sentence left no future for planning. On the other hand, I couldn't just sit by and vegetate as so many convicts did. It would have been a small step to becoming stir- crazy. In some respects, life would have been easier to accept. Other cons and the guards ignored those who were stir-crazy. The fear of regressing to that state was my greatest fear. To keep in shape physically, I would box, wrestle and run around the yard until I was exhausted. For my mental well-being, I would study. I made friends with the more intelligent men. I found it rewarding to emulate their mannerisms. Before long I avoided those who sought trouble. I began to settle down and conduct myself as much like a gentleman as I possibly could under such adverse surroundings and circumstances. One of the inmates was a former English teacher at a small high school. For two years, I studied under him assiduously. Eventually, I was assigned to the Department of Education where I taught English to the lower grade students. My class represented an

157

odd conglomeration; a lifer as a teacher and robbers, murderers and arsonists as students. The oldest was 73 years of age; the youngest was l6. He, too, was serving life for murder. If my friends had known I had stolen a book on etiquette by Emily Post, they would have razzed me out of the cellhouse. But I did just that and poured over it for hours. I made up my mind that I might live and die in prison, but I would at least live one grade above my cohorts.

The youthful murderer of l6 whom I mentioned was one of my students. When he was a mere lad of l2, he lived in dire circumstances in a little town in Eastern Washington. Whatever prompted him to break into a grocery store one night was not made public. However, he told me that he burglarized the store in search of candy, so much like the child he was. Someone passing by saw the intruder and called the town's lone marshall. The marshall peered through the store window and thought he spotted a person on the premises. Using his passkey, he entered the building and called out, "Come out of there with your hands in the air." The boy told me that he was crouching behind a counter. The marshall called out again. As the boy scooted down further behind the counter, he saw a pistol on a shelf. He picked up the gun, laid it across the counter and pulled the trigger. The cop's heart took leave of his chest. This boy was charged with first degree murder, convicted and sentenced to spend the rest of his natural life in the penitentiary. The boy served thirteen years and was released.

The years rolled by. My parents, brothers and sisters visited me on a regular basis. I grew older, Mom and Dad's hair turned white and my brothers and sisters aged with me. It was during the latter years of my term that I began to realize that, when a man leads the kind of life I did, members of his family are the true victims. My brother, Dan, during one of his visits said, "Glenn, I've noticed an improvement in your attitude. I have confidence that you will make a go of it when you get out." When he left, I was sick at heart. Didn't he know that I was serving a life commitment, and that a mere five years had passed? All I prayed for was that I would be able to see my parents on the outside before they passed away. I was incapable of thinking in terms of failure or success. All I was striving to do was to survive. I knew that, as the years rolled by, my chances for gainful employment diminished. What opportunity would I have to marry and raise a family? Without those privileges, was freedom any longer important? I confessed to myself that I was afraid to face the challenges of the outside world. I couldn't bring myself to admit that I was fearful of failure. With this kind of attitude and weakness, what were my chances of succeeding? Like any prisoner who had served more than five years under the penal system in this country, chances are nil!

Early one morning, as I was entering my sixth year of incarceration, I was called out of my cell by the captain of the guards. He told me that the warden wanted to see me. I think the captain was as curious as I about the warden's order. Finally his interest got the better of him so he asked, "Wonder what the Big Boy wants with you, Williams?" Even though I was dying for an answer to that question, I enjoyed leaving the captain on the hook. He wasn't the smartest student in his class. In fact a year or two

158

before this, he really showed his ignorance. One of the largest industries in the compound was the license plate mill. About thirty cons were assigned the task of making all the license plates for the state of Washington. One day some cons torched the mill. It went up with a blast. There were hundreds of gallons of paint and thinner in barrels stored throughout the building. From the beginning, it was apparent that the inmate fire department could not control the blaze. The Walla Walla fire department was called in to assist. Between burning itself out and the water being poured onto it, it was finally extinguished. When it was all over, the captain who was standing next to the downtown chief asked, "Chief, what caused this fire?" The chief responded, "Captain, it was set by spontaneous combustion." The captain turned to one of his subordinates and snapped, "Guard, throw that arsonist in the hole, and we'll hold Kangaroo Court on that son of a bitch."

In accordance with the warden's orders, the captain gave me a skin-search. That was normal procedure before an interview was granted to an inmate. He was taking no chance of being assaulted. When I was escorted into the warden's office, I got the surprise of my life. He jumped up from his desk, extended his hand and smiled. What the hell was going on? He said, "Sit down, Glenn. I have a pleasant surprise for you. Your dad is in the outer room and he has a gift he brought to you from the governor's office. Step in there with me." I did, and was happy to see my father. Without a word, he handed me a rolled scroll. I accepted it and proceeded to unroll it. I could not believe my eyes. As big as day were the letters across the top that read; THE GOVERNOR OF THE STATE OF WASHINGTON HAS GRANTED YOU A COMPLETE AND UNCONDITIONAL PARDON. I sat down stunned. My dad did not speak. He simply put his arms around my shoulder and wept, as did I. Discreetly, the warden stepped from the room. When my dad and I recovered our composure, we went into the superintendent's quarters. It was all I could do to keep the tears from blinding me. Dad asked, "When can I take him home?" The warden pressed a button on his desk and summoned a lieutenant. "Gus, take Glenn to his cell so he can gather his property. He has been granted a pardon, and will be leaving us within the hour."

An hour later, with my brother Dan behind the wheel, we were speeding westward toward Seattle and my new home. I can't remember what took place for the next three or four weeks. As each day went by, I became more aware of my surroundings. It was very difficult for me to wake up in the morning and realize I could walk out the door and go anywhere. A prison's purpose is to confine and destroy; not to rebuild and to save a human being. It renders a person incapable of making a decision. Physically and mentally most long-termers, when they are freed, stumble throughout life. I found this condition affecting me after only five years. I hesitated before opening doors or crossing streets. Selecting my own clothes was a major chore. To try to make the acquaintance of a woman was a terrifying experience. To consummate a sexual relationship was impossible for more than a year. It was tough to make it on the outside. It is little wonder that the preponderance of releasees return to prison.

I was blessed with a family who surrounded me with affection. It wasn't necessary for me to locate a job right away. I had a nice home, good food and entertainment. Most of all, I was accepted as a person. Even with all those advantages, it was three months before I could function as a normal human being. I used to think how utterly impossible it was for a paroled convict to live up to the ridiculous terms of his parole agreement. The senseless rules governing his day- to-day freedom were endless. He is advised that: he may be returned with or without cause; he must have gainful employment right away; he must not associate with another ex-convict; he must not leave the community to which he was released without notifying, and getting permission of, his parole officer; he may not get married without an OK from the parole officer; he must advise his parole officer of how much money he makes every month, and give an accounting of the disposition of the money; he must not change his residence without prior approval. This is simply the beginning of the impossible restrictions governing every breath he takes. You must bear in mind that all this is in the interest of 1) society and 2) the restoration of a destroyed individual. I have seen hundreds throw up their hands in futility and make a run for it.

Some who absconded made successes of their lives. In most instances, the end result is a tragedy. There are countless cases which appear in the newspapers every year telling of parolees who have absconded, changed their names and identities, found employment, married and established the 'square John' image in their new-found community. In all too many instances, some of these 'wanted' men are discovered when a traffic cop runs a check on them because of a traffic violation or some other minor infraction, Immediately the culprit is arrested on a fleeing felony warrant. The state from which he fled demands that he be extradited. His new found friends and employer vouch for the individual and, in most cases, promise to support him in every way possible. I have read hundreds of letters in which an unbelievable number of prominent citizens have pled with the governor of the 'injured' state to allow the parolee in question to remain in his adopted area. They cite the years of established work patterns, melding into their new environment, being members of civic clubs. Generally they have married and are the fathers of children, and are buying homes; the very fiber from which solid citizens are formed. In spite of all the opportunities offered the 'victim', I can recall few governors having the courage to defy the vaunted criminal justice system. The man is returned at a tremendous expense and heartache to dozens of people, and slapped back into prison where he is warehoused. In a few years, and after he has lost his family and friends, he will be paroled again, an unending carrousel.

Months rolled by. I became dissatisfied with the lack of money. There was never enough to buy the things I felt I deserved. It seemed that every time I made an application for a better-paying job, I was rebuffed. In my mind, I made up the excuse that it was because of my past and that I was being denied an opportunity to prove myself. I refused to admit that I was untrained for a better-paying profession. Like most cons who are on the road to failure, I found it was convenient to blame society for my ills. We often do this to justify why we fail. Little did I reason that I was

160

building myself to the point where I, too, could rationalize my future outlawry. Deep in my heart, I knew I was going back to my real desire; that of being a bank robber.

Early one morning, I told my boss that I was going to see a dentist, and that I would like to take the day off. By eleven o'clock that morning, I was standing in the lobby of a bank in Auburn, Washington with a pistol in my hand, and seven bank employees staring at it. I committed the robbery with no real planning. The escape vehicle was my brother's pick-up truck. Satan must have been with me because I made a clean pull out. There was no pursuit nor audible alarm. Within a half hour I was back in my apartment counting out more than $8,800 dollars. Right then and there, I made up my mind that I was not destined for labor. I also set down some rules for myself that I vowed not to break. I had violated every rule of the game before, and it resulted in my being put away for life and, had it not been for my dad's influence, I'd still be put away. Some years later, I recalled my brother, Dan, telling me exactly how I got a pardon, and beat the life rap. "Don't give yourself any credit, Glenn. Dad had the connections and the money to put in the right politicians' hands. He didn't tell me just who he bought, but he did say, 'I have never met a politician who was without a price. When I feel that Glenn has been punished enough, I'll find that person', and apparently he did. You know full well that you would have rotted in the clink if it hadn't been for Dad. You show me a lifer that gets a gubernatorial pardon in seven years, and I'll show you the concrete evidence of a pay-off."

My brother, Paul, was a line-driver for one of Seattle's biggest trucking companies. At Paul's urging, I made an application for a spot driving the coastal route. I was asked what experience I had with big road rigs. Paul had coached me pretty well. Looking the road boss in the eye, I said, "I drove for the army for five years." Following the usual procedure when there was no opportunity to verify such a statement, the road boss said, "I'll put you on the road for testing with a couple of seasoned drivers. Either you'll make it or they will wash you out." Naturally my brother had arranged it so I would be assigned to his rig. He and his partner made a line-driver out of me. I drove for nearly five years and by the time I had finished I was a seasoned driver. Little did my brother know that, in connection with my regular chore of driving, I was engaged in hitting an occasional bank in California and Oregon. Following BJ's advice, I did not crap in my own backyard. I kept Washington clean.

To be certain I did not set a pattern that the FBI could follow, I would let a month or two go before striking again. Occasionally I would take a day or two off and ply my trade in Idaho, Nevada and Arizona. If my brother ever suspected I was back in the rackets, he never said a word. He probably reasoned that, because I was unmarried, I had plenty of cash to toss around. I bought a new Buick, stocked my wardrobe and wound up with some pretty fancy jewelry from the proceeds of the Auburn heist. He knew I had taken flying lessons from Kurtzer's seaplane base. He did ask my other brother how I could afford such an expensive pastime. His questioning concerned me, but nothing more was said. Dan, however, began to wonder how I could afford to rent a seaplane and fly into Canada every day I was off work. On one occasion, Lana Kurtzer, the base's owner told Dan that I had paid him $250 in silver and that in all his years operating the company he had never been paid in such a manner. He further commented, "Glenn comes down here and rents a plane and thinks nothing of putting three to four hours flying time on the engine. Of course, that's OK by me but it is rather unusual. Furthermore, he has been seen landing at Lake Wenatchee, a pretty dangerous route for a small plane. That mountain flying can be treacherous." Dan's response was normal for him. "I don't keep tabs on my brother, Lana. As long as he pays his bill, you shouldn't be too concerned."

About a week later, Dan and I met at the seaplane base. When we were in the pilot's shack checking out our gear, Dan approached me and came to the point, "Glenn, I don't know what's going on, but I know you're up to something. The guy in the office is curious about your mode of payment, and the long hours you are out. You had better cover your rear end."

I was never a person to hesitate to take the bull by the horns. I walked into Lana's office and confronted him, "Lana, do I owe you anything?" He shook his head. I continued, "As long as I pay my bill, you have no reason to complain. If I pay it in pennies, that's my business." I started to walk out when Lana called, "Before you go I want to return your change bag." I was concerned as he went to his inner office. He returned and threw down a bank bag that had been turned inside out. Stamped on the bag was the lettering 'First National Bank of Medford'. My stomach turned to ice. How stupid could I be? It was the bag in which I had given him the $250 in silver. I calmly took the bag and strode to my plane. Even as I taxied to the South end of Lake Union for take-off, I was fearful of what Lana might have guessed. I automatically went through my pre-flight check list not really registering the instruments' readings in my mind. I was anxious to get my altitude and fly north toward Vancouver, Canada, my playground away from home. The bank bag was on the seat beside me. Why had Lana waited two months before returning the bag? More important still, why had I been so careless as to hand him the cash in the bag in the first place? Had he told my brother about the bag? By the time I had approached Bellingham, I had determined what I was going to do with the bag. I swung out over the bay and headed out to open sea. I took my thermos of coffee and stuffed it into the offending bag. It was at this stage of my plan that I determined why I had failed to notice the bank name on the bag. When it is turned inside out, the lettering was not visible. I comforted myself with the thought that maybe Lana had not noticed the tell-tale sign. It was a small comfort. I climbed to about 15,000 feet, did a 360 so I could see if any other planes were within sight. It was clear so, while I was still in the turn, I slid the window open and bid good bye to the damaging evidence as it hit the water.

Years later, while my brother was visiting me in prison, he told me that Lana Kurtzer had been suspicious of me ever since I had dumped such a large sum of silver in his lap. He had immediately noticed the bank lettering on the leather bag. About a week after he had received the money, it dawned on him that maybe the silver had been taken illegally. He decided to make a check on that possibility by ordering copies of a local Oregon paper. He ordered it for one week prior to the date he had received the money to one week afterward. And lo and behold, there was a story telling about a bank robbery that had taken place. The description came very close to being that of Glenn Williams. Later, when I had been released and had an opportunity to talk with Lana, he smiled and said, "I have hauled hundreds of passengers across the Canadian border. I am certain some of their briefcases were not filled with bibles. My job was to transport and not butt into their business."

Other than Vancouver being a city in which to let down my hair, it gave me a chance to get rid of the Canadian money I had accumulated in my numerous withdrawals. The one problem bank robbers had with the loot from west coast cities was that lots of the money was in Canadian currency. There was always a different rate of exchange, and getting rid of any amount state-side drew unwanted attention. As I look back on it, I think I rationalized going to Canada as a necessity. Otherwise, why did I always spend so much up there playing the night clubs, horses and women?

About 1950, I decided I was going to leave the rackets and settle down. I had met an attractive young lady of whom I found myself becoming inordinately fond. I courted her for a few months and made the tragic error of marrying her; tragic for both of us. In 1951, I became the father of a beautiful baby girl. We named her Muriel. Never in my life had I been so utterly happy. She stole my heart, soul and mind. She was so delightful to come home to. I bought a five acre mini-farm in the suburb of Alderwood Manor. It was difficult for me to pay too much on the down payment because my wife would wonder where I had come into that amount of cash. As it was, she could not understand how I acquired a purebred Arabian filly, fenced the acreage, did extensive landscaping and acquired a Cadillac and pickup truck. To protect my daughter from any possible danger, imagined or real, I had a cyclone fence erected around our house. In my unreasonable fear that something could happen to my daughter, I concealed my arsenal of two pistols, a shot gun and two high-powered rifles. I would never need them again for illicit purposes; or so I thought. Somewhere along the line, I gathered a goat and a flock of geese; much to the delight of both my daughter and myself, we had a sort of personal zoo. A neighbor unloaded a half-dozen Japanese bantams on us. Within a year we had an almost uncontainable number of animals and fowl disturbing the peace and tranquility of the neighborhood at five o'clock every morning with crowing, honking and neighing.

Occasionally word would come from gangster friends from throughout the U. S. inquiring as to my sudden withdrawal from their midst. Without hesitation, I let it be known that I was no longer involved with that lifestyle. It took months before they realized I was serious. There were a few who had the class to appreciate my decision and they never called except to inquire into the well-being of my family. Once in a while, one or two would drop in and be our guests for a few days. Muriel never knew who her friends were that bought her expensive gifts on occasion.

Line driving to southern California twice monthly became a bore, and it took me away from Muriel. The added incentive for taking the trips, such as keeping my hand in the banking business, was no longer attractive. I had accumulated a tidy sum safely hidden. I requested a transfer from the over-the-road assignment to working city pick-up and delivery for the same company. It was a relief to go to work at eight in the morning and to be home by late afternoon. Week-ends were jealously kept for Muriel and me. My wages were greatly reduced when I started the local job. As the months wore on, I realized I had to curtail my spending. I had not had to be careful before, and it was foreign to me. One day, while Muriel and my wife were visiting her mother, I went to the far edge of my property line and dug up the fruit jar which held the proceeds from a number of business transactions. It was my intent to determine exactly what remained concealed. To my dismay, I counted only $6,000 dollars. I had to cut back spending so foolishly. Also, I had to take the loot and start laundering* it. How I could accomplish this without jeopardizing myself, I wasn't sure. If I had enough to go into a small business, I could push it through the business account.

Nearly every day, I would visit my parents who lived in Seattle. It was a 15 mile trip and, whenever possible, I would take Muriel with me. About once a week, I would take our laundry in and do it at a laundromat near the folks house. The establishment was owned by a nice young couple. As the months went by, I became more and more acquainted with them. They had a daughter about the same age as Muriel, so it was inevitable that our relationship developed into one of close friends. At times, we would baby-sit each other's youngster. It was during this prolonged relationship that I got the idea of laundering my hot money through their business. Often they would let me take care of matters. In so doing, I soon learned the tricks of the trade. After this relationship had lasted about two months, I put my scheme into action. I opened an account for the North End Laundry Ser-vices in a bank near their place of business. The rest was simple. When they had taken in a certain amount in their till, I would take it and then replace that amount with my hot money. There wasn't too much of a cash flow so the laundering was slow, but it was safe. While this plan served the purpose, it accomplished little to compel me to quit squandering the contents of my 'fruit jar' depository. I had the typical thug's mentality. If it ran out, I could easily replenish it. The old easy- come-easy go comforter. It wasn't but a matter of a very few months before I realized that the fruit jar was empty.

During this time, I continued to drive truck. The wages from that job could not keep up with my demand. One evening, I told my wife that I had to take a trip to Pasco, a town nearly three hundred miles from home. I left the impression I was going to drive when I really made plans to rent a plane from a flight service at Boeing Field and fly to my 'job'. For the first time in a number of months, I unpacked the weapons I had put away, took out my favorite 'persuader' and prepared to take off early the next morning. I kissed Muriel and told her I would be back in a little while.

While it was not compulsory to file a flight plan, it was certainly the smart thing to do under normal circumstances. My circumstances were not nor-mal. I wanted to leave no record of my time of departure, destination or ETA. The sun was barely on the horizon when I climbed to the desired altitude and pointed the nose of the Piper east by southeast. Due to a heavy

*feeding it through legitimate businesses

head wind, I did not land in Pasco until nearly four hours later. I landed at a small strip outside the town, taxied to a run-down flight shack where I fueled up, checked the oil and advised the sole occupant that I would be in town for about an hour or so. He called a taxi at my request and, as I drove off, he was tying the craft down. I engaged the taxi driver in small talk, during which I told him I was a Methodist minister and was in town attending a Youth Symposium. As we neared the town's center, I told him to drop me off at the Methodist church. I held my breath for fear he would ask me, "Which one?" He made no comment but drove me to the front of an old weathered church. I bounced from the cab leaving him with the impression I was familiar with my way to the entrance. From the corner of my eyes, I saw him drive off without looking after me.

Instead of going into the sanctuary, I veered off, walked along side the building and headed for the center of the village. It was nearing noon, and the town was just beginning to stir. As was my practice, I sought out a cafe and ordered coffee. I always sat near a window so I could better case the main street and, in this instance, I did not change my habit. I sat my old battered briefcase on the table, opened it up and shuffled a few papers around. When I saw no one was looking at me, I closed the case and walked into the restroom. Once inside I blocked the door with my body, opened the case again and took out my gun. Notwithstanding it had been some time since I had had the weapon on my person, it felt vaguely familiar and comfortable. I was not worried nor overly concerned with my method of operation. It had been rehearsed so often that it had become a second nature to me. The thought of being shot did not enter my thinking. I sauntered down the main street keeping my eyes open for a bank. The town was so small it took me about five minutes to get to the other end. The only bank I saw was so small I had to take a double take to make sure it was a bank. I peered through the window. There were three cages and a teller in each one. There were no customers, but that didn't mean anything. Some- one could walk in in a matter of seconds. I began to have second thoughts. I made the snap decision to go through with it, win, lose or draw.

After that was settled, I came to grips with my immediate problem at this time; that of getting transportation out to the plane after the job was completed. Taking a taxi back was out of the question. The town was too small and surely a cabbie would put two and two together. Also, the guy at the airport would recall a lone flyer landing and taking off within a few hours. There probably hadn't been a strange plane landing there in a month. Making the getaway concerned me more than the actual robbery. Finally, I hit on an idea. I walked up to a dilapidated service station-garage combination. An old man was in attendance. When I approached, he barely opened his eyes. Before I could speak, be asked, "What can I do for you, partner?" I replied, "I want to get to Kennewick and I need to rent a car for the day. Can you help me?" "Nope," was the response. "Maybe my boy out yonder can locate a car for you. How much you willing to pay? You know, Kennewick is nearly ten miles down the pike." I glanced 'out yonder' and saw a young fellow pumping up a tire of an old 1940 Chevy truck. Both of the individuals looked as though they hadn't seen a dollar between them in a month, so I tossed out a carrot. "Well, I have to get there right away, so if you can find a car for me to rent, I'll give you a ten dollar bill." The boy nearly dropped the tire pump. Before he could say a word, the old codger said, "Make it fifteen and its a deal." I cussed under my breath. The old guy was a horse trader. "OK," I answered, "Its a deal if you can get me a car within half an hour."

Turning to his son he ordered, "Rodney, get some air in that tire, put four gallons of gas in the tank and let this feller have your truck. And charge him for the gas." He looked me over carefully and muttered more to himself than to me, "You 'pear to be a honest man. When you going to bring the truck back?" It was getting to be about two o'clock and I knew if I was going to hit the jug before it closed, I'd have to get a move on. "I should be back here by six tonight. If you're closed, I'll leave the jalopy right where it is parked."

In a matter of ten minutes, I was herding the vehicle down the street. After I got out of their sight, I circled the block and went in the direction of the bank. If everything panned out, I'd be back home by six o'clock. If it didn't work out, I'd probably never get back. One thing was for certain, I had to move quickly. I parked the vehicle behind the bank, walked around to the front and entered. I saw I could not pick off the manager. I was the only customer and all their eyes were on me. I pushed open the swinging door between him and the lobby, drew my pistol and covered all four persons. "Don't one of you make a noise or touch off the alarm or every one of you will be singing in the Holy Choir. Get all your cash together and put it in this case. No silver. Be quick." All of them went into action as though they had practiced. Even the manager sped past me to assist in the loading. It was the quickest bank heist I had ever pulled. When I grabbed the case, I yelled, "All of you get to the toilet. Lay down on the floor and keep quiet. I'll be outside the door for a few minutes, and if I hear one sound, I'll start shooting through the door. They almost fought one another trying to be first. Just as I was turning to leave, one of the women fainted half way in the restroom. It was impossible for the others to close the door as I had instructed. I had to move decisively and without wasting time. I barked an order to the others, "Each of you face the wall away from me. If you turn or call out, I'll blast this room full of holes. Stay as you are for five minutes." With that I stepped out the back door and into the old truck.

The airport was about five miles from the vicinity of the bank. The truck putted along without misfiring, and I was at my destination in less than ten minutes. I parked the get-a-way truck behind an old weather-beaten barn, and walked briskly to the pilots' shack. The caretaker came out and before I could ask, he said, "I've got her all ready, sir." I thanked him, and without appearing to be in a hurry, I walked around the craft, testing the horizontal stabilizer, flaps and ailerons and kicking the tires. I wasn't so worried that all might not be well as I was to appear to be in no hurry. There was a certain degree of professionalism required to impress airport personnel. I thanked him and gave him a sizable tip for his services. He cranked her up, pulled the chocks clear and waved me off.

My return trip to Seattle was a fast one. A tail wind boosted me along at a fair rate of speed. By the time I approached Boeing Field, the city lights were coming on. I was home with Muriel, my wife and $1,750 within an hour and a half after I touched down. All had gone well. I knew that it wouldn't be another three months and I would find myself strapped again. And it was a cinch I did not want to keep on tapping the resources of banks. Most of us dream about hitting the 'Big One' and being able to retire. It is sort of like a miner seeking the mother lode. I never heard anything more about the rip-off in Pasco. It got to the point that so many banks were being targeted, it wasn't newsworthy. I settled one thing in my mind after the latest fiasco. I was not going to use a plane in anymore such escapades. Others were beginning to utilize that method of operation, and the police were getting wise to it.

About three months later in Philadelphia, I was having dinner with one of my buddies who did all his 'work' by plane. He fed me a bit of disturbing info that further convinced me that flying to and from jobs was a thing to be forgotten. "You know, Glenn, I read in one of the flight journals that they were going to try to make it mandatory for the pilot of each airplane to file a flight plan at every place of departure, and to close it out at his destination. And that plan has to be on file. You can see what that will do to us. We'd be putting the finger on ourselves. Its getting so a thug can't make an honest living anymore." I had used an aircraft only once, and I had already made up my mind that that style wasn't for me. The handwriting was on the wall. Modern cops would soon be counting on planes to counter planes.

While I had operated on banks alone for some time, I did deviate from my practice when approached by a trusted stick-up man by the name of Julius. He and I hadn't pulled any deals together, but each knew that the other could be trusted. He looked me up in the laundry one morning and put an opportunity before me. I could not reject it. His girlfriend, Cynthia, was the secretary of the manager of one of the biggest Safeway stores in the northwest. She wasn't aware of Julius' past as she confided in him about a payroll shipment coming in each Friday. She brought this up because he had asked her to go away for the weekend. They would have had to leave by four o'clock on Friday. "Julius, I can't make it until after six. On Fridays, the armored car brings in a large sum of money to meet the demand of customers cashing checks over the weekend. I have to be there to help check it in. There are only four of us trusted to do this particular task. Everyone else is sent home at five."

Julius told me that his ears stood up like Rin Tin Tin's when she mentioned a 'large sum of money'. He had to draw the details out of her carefully so she would not rank his interest. He offhandedly commented, "Come on, Cynthia, that store wouldn't cash a thousand bucks in checks on any one week-end, and you could count that alone in five minutes." She jumped for the bait. "Let me tell you something, Mr Wise Guy. Last week we received a shipment of more than twenty five thousands dollars. And sometimes that isn't enough to take care of the demand." Immediately, my pal dropped the subject. This was a caper that would take some going over. Cynthia was no one's fool, so Julius let the matter slip by for two months. However, during that period of time, he garnered information little by little.

He knew that the armored car arrived punctually at four forty five each Friday afternoon. Two heavily armed guards would bring the money into the manager's office safe. It would be counted and signed for in a matter of few minutes. Cynthia was the one who supervised the tabulating. After the guards left, she, the manager and two others would stack the money in several denominations, and divide them into six rubber-banded piles; one for each cash register. They would be wrapped and listed for distribution for the following morning, and secured in the large safe. After this was accomplished, a plan that had been devised by the manager was put into effect. Cynthia and one man would leave by the rear door which was immediately slammed shut and bolted. They would go to their car and drive around the block. All this time they would be on a sharp lookout to determine if they were followed or if anything appeared out of order. If it was clear, they would return and park directly in front of the rear door. In about five minutes, the manager and the other employee would set the alarms and they would walk out. In this manner, they had pretty well assured that no hostages would be taken. Cynthia let Julius know that this procedure had been in effect for more than two years, and they had never been robbed. Julius smiled to himself and thought, 'there's always a first time, Doll'.

I was anxious to be a part of this heist. In the first place, the amount available was greater than one man could hope to take in a bank robbery. Julius and I set about doing our homework. Julius made a remark for which I respected him. "Glenn, under no circumstances is Cynthia to be hurt. She is a fine person. If you blast her, I'll dust you right then and there. If you are not happy with that set-up, say so right now." I simply looked at him and assured him, "Julius, I'll protect that girl with my life. You have my word on that!"

One of the main flies in the ointment was the manner in which they left the store after handling the money matter. It would be impossible to get them together, and thereby control the situation. Taking hostages seldom works, so that procedure was nixed. Finally an idea hit me. "Julius, why don't we pull the old hide-out gimmick? You or I one could conceal ourselves inside the store just before it closes; remain hidden until the armored car people leave. After that, it should be easy to cover the four people, tie them up and pull out." Julius had an immediate response designed to throw cold water on my scheme. "Just one thing wrong with your plot, old boy. You forget that Cynthia would recognize me no matter how well I masked up. The only way I can see us using that approach is for us to bring in a third party, and I'm not too hot on that." This did pose a problem. "Listen, Julius, why don't I do the hide-out routine, get the drop on them and tie each one up and blindfold them? Then Cynthia wouldn't see you." That was the plan and we set it in motion for the following Friday.

On that big day, I pretended to be shopping up to about five minutes before closing time. I stayed near the rear of the store away from the cash registers. When there were two other shoppers left, I edged to the vegetable room in the back. There were dozens of empty lettuce crates stacked at random. I quickly made a sort of cave among them, made myself comfortable and settled down. When all customers had left and the crew was buttoning things up, I could hear their bantering. I kept my ears strained hoping to hear some mention of the armored car. However, what I did hear caused me concern. The manager instructed the crew to walk through the entire grocery and make certain everything was secure. I was afraid that whoever searched the area in which I was hidden might inadvertently discover me. I eased my gun from its sheath and waited. Sure enough, in walked Cynthia. She looked into every nook and cranny, and seemed to spend an extra length of time peering among the crates. I quit breathing until I thought my lungs would burst. At last she left the vegetable section and called out. "Everything is okay here." One after another called in that their areas were secure. I was relieved when the lights were extinguished.

I could hear the group walking to the other side of the building toward the door through which the armored car guards would enter. Things moved so fast from then on out that I had to move fast. I left my nest and eased myself along a darkened wall until I was in an advantageous position. It was a matter of only a minute or two before I heard a loud rapping from the outside of the rear door. The manager peered though the hole in the door, satisfied himself that it was okay, and let the guards in. The sight I witnessed from my cubby hole was too beautiful to be true. Each officer was carrying a heavy money bag. They looked like a pair of Santa Clauses carrying guns and money. The cash was spread on a table and systematically counted. Just as Cynthia had said, they were through and out the door in less than fifteen minutes. I moved rapidly and was on them before they realized what was taking place. I yelled, "Each of you face the wall and do it quickly. Don't make the mistake of trying to look at me. Put your foreheads against the wall. Move!" They obeyed like well-trained soldiers. "Lie face down on the floor with your heads turned away from me. Make no mistakes or you're dead." After they had minded, I walked over to an electric switch on the wall and turned off the overhead lights. As an added caution, I whispered loudly, "Stay perfectly still." I walked over to a bunch of discarded potato sacks and picked up four of them. I then stepped to each of the prone figures and placed a sack over their heads. Very carefully, I said in measured tones, "I'll be out of here in two minutes. When I close the door behind me, if I hear any noise from you, I'll come back in and blast away. It isn't your money, so don't be fools." Julius was ready. As soon as I opened the door he came in so quietly no one could hear him move. I motioned him toward the money sacks which he filled and left. I was on his heels. We were in his apartment within fifteen minutes. We counted more than twenty three thousand dollars. When I left his place, I was walking on air.

Early the next morning while I was giving Muriel a bath, Julius called. He was upset because he had been calling Cynthia since seven o'clock the previous evening, and there was no response. "Something is wrong, Glenn, and I'm worried. Do you think she might have guessed who capered her joint last night? Frankly, it doesn't look good. She and I have been close for months. In fact, we have discussed marriage. We always call each other every morning, and it's unusual that I can't reach her. I'm really concerned, Glenn." In an effort to calm him down, I quietly said, "Just keep trying,

169

Julius. Only God knows where she is or why she hasn't called you. Don't make a move. Just sit tight. If you haven't heard from her in an hour or two, get ahold of me." It was agreed he would call me right after I dropped Muriel off at the baby-sitter's place. By noon, I had not heard from Julius. I began to get worried. The morning paper told of the robbery. There was no mention of possible suspects. By three o'clock that afternoon, I drove over to Julius's apartment. There was no response to my knocking. On my way out, I looked through his window and was surprised to find his place empty. There was no doubt he had flown the coop. Why hadn't he contacted me? Now it was my turn to worry. For days, I was on pins and needles.

Days grew into weeks, and still no word from Julius. There was nothing I could do but wait and stew. At the end of the month I got the idea of calling Cynthia and asking her if she knew where Julius was. I'd have to call her at the store because I had no home number for her. I waited until four in the afternoon and placed the call. A lady answered the phone and I asked to speak to Cynthia. The response surprised me. "She isn't here anymore. She resigned about two weeks ago." Without hesitation, I hung up. Something was amiss. Nearly six months later I got a call from Connecticut. Julius was on the other end. I said, "You do the talking." He told me what had happened. It seems that Cynthia was pretty sure she knew who the robbers were; at least she knew one was Julius. She made up her mind and moved decisively. At noon the day following the stick-up, she drove over to Julius's apartment and told him of her suspicions. She asked Julius if they could go to her folks in Connecticut and be married there. He was happy to comply. She gave notice a week or two later, and they slipped out of town. I never heard from Julius again.

The months flew by. My pastime was watching Muriel grow. Never in my life had I spent a happier time than the three years she and I bonded a solid father and daughter relationship. Nothing pleased me more than to see her with her face pressed against the front window of our home waiting for daddy to come up the drive. As soon as my car appeared, she would squeal for her mother to open the door so she could rush out to greet me. My heart would swell with pride. After our hugs and kisses, she would search through my pockets for a gift which I always brought. After dinner, she and I would go out in the yard and feed the horse, bantams and our geese. Later, I bought a cute little goat which became her favorite pet. During meals, the goat would stand on the porch and look at us through the dining room window. After a few months, this beast grew sharp little horns and developed the nasty habit of butting the plate glass window. At this rate, I knew it wouldn't be long until it broke the glass. Getting rid of it was difficult, but I knew I had to give it away. Shortly afterwards, those cute goslings grew up to be cantankerous and pugnacious geese. They would chase my daughter across the yard pecking at her and striking her with their powerful wings. So they found their way into our skillet. I suppose that we would have had colt fillets if the filly had mistreated Muriel.

After lunch one day, I received a long-distance call from Cob, a former mobster acquaintance in Miami. Little did I know that it was a fateful day and call; one that would destroy my life and separate me from my most

170

precious possession, Muriel. Cob was the only thug I ever knew that I would trust with my life. We had hit a few together and we had a sense of complete confidence in one another. Cob was without fear. His bailiwick was the southeast. Mine was the northwest. If I had a good prospect in this part of the country, I'd finger it for Cob. He would reciprocate in a like manner. Like myself, Cob worked alone. On rare occasions when the job demanded two men, we worked together. So, the call from Cob was appreciated. He was brief on the phone. "Glenn, I'm tired of the sun down here. Would it be OK if I came up to stay a week with you? I've never met your wife or daughter and it will give me a good chance to get acquainted with them." I knew he had something else on his mind, but he was too cagey to make indiscriminate comments on the phone. I told him I would be a pleased to have him as our guest. A few days later, I met him at the airport and drove him home. My family accepted him as a member of the clan.

He was with us for a few days before he cracked his egg. One morning after my wife had taken Muriel to the baby sitter's, and I was currying my Arabian, Cob walked into the barn, sat on a bale of hay and struck to the point. "Glenn, why have you have missed the gold-mine in your backyard?" I looked at him and urged him on. "Cob, what the hell do you know about my backyard? You live four thousand miles from here."

He walked up to the horse's head and began stroking her mane. "Do you remember Bebe who was on the Jacksonville job with me?" I nodded. "Well, he has lived with his brother in Arlington for the past two years. He has been low all this time, so he has contacted no one but me. Also, inasmuch as this is your backyard, he did not want to approach you with the sweet potato he ran into about a mile from here." I laid the curry comb on the shelf, opened the barn door and swatted my filly on the rump. I led the way to the house where we sat down over a cup of coffee.

Cob picked up the subject. "Bebe has been working on his brother's chicken ranch. He does the bookkeeping and banking for him, too. He gets to the First National Bank in Lynnwood every Friday, a little before noon. If he times it right, and he plans it so he does, he makes his deposits at the same time the armored car makes it's drop. From what he says, Glenn, it is one of the best candy stores he has seen anywhere. Lots of sweets around for the picking, and very little security. You know Bebe well enough to know he isn't handing us any bull shit. I want to go into town and see the sights for a day or two. Will you look the caper over and give me your opinion? I'll call you from the Washington Hotel where I'll be checking in under the name of Winston Berryweather. Fancy son-of-a-bitch, eh?" If he ever used an alias it always had to be something outrageously ridiculous. He once told me that his name was so common he hated it. And to add insult to injury, all his friends called him 'Corn'. His first name was Cornelius. In later years he expressed his bitterness over the fact his parents spelled their surname name with one 'B'. It was only natural we called him Corn Cob. He started to comment further on the proposed caper when I interrupted him. "Cob, I'm willing to case the joint and make recommendations, but I'll back away if you contact Bebe on this deal. I simply will not get involved with three people. In fact, I don't want to get mixed up with any person other than myself. I've been pretty successful going it alone. I know the bank you're referring to. I've been in the place a few times. I don't do business there, but I know the inside lay-out, and can give you a perfect drawing of the tellers cage's and the manager's office. For this small of a community, it is quite busy, and employs probably ten people. A good part of the set-up is that it is on a main street with cars and trucks going by night and day. There are a dozen roads leading from the bank and they go in all directions. You could lose pursuit on the country roads. I'll take you there tomorrow, and you do your own landscaping. If you're satisfied, we'll look it over inch by inch. If this hadn't been in my own backyard, I'd have wiped it out months ago."

13

The Beginning Of The End

The next morning, Cob entered the bank to get change for a twenty. A less experienced man than he could not have cased the bank in the few minutes he was doing his bit of business. Since he was preparing to wipe out the bank's resources, the number of exits, the number of employees and their positions, and the visibility from people passing by the bank's windows was of vital importance to Cob. He didn't want anyone to see him long enough to be able to pick him out of a lineup at a later date. My friend walked from the bank with an air of a person who had completed his business. His very manner and appearance drew no attention. I paid my tab and met him three blocks away at the Cressy's service station. As we returned to my house, we talked of everything but Cob's opinion of the layout.

Once in the security of my home, my guest opened up. "Glenn, everything about this setup looks good, but there are a few details to be worked out. From this day on, I don't want to be seen in this neighborhood. All my work outside this house must be done after dark. This brings up another point; how about your wife? If she puts two and two together, my ass will be in a bear trap. I am going to have to ask your help in finding the exact hour and day the armored car makes its delivery and pick up. I can't stake out in the daytime. I'd like to get you to take care of those details. I'll assume the risk and responsibility, and will give you the usual 20% of the take. Let me hear from you?" I had made up my mind to go straight. However, I rationalized, I wouldn't actually be in on the heist. I knew that if he fell, he would never put the finger on me. But, if by some quirk I got involved, I could kiss my daughter good-bye. It was this thought that terrorized me. Neither of us had the haziest idea how much the take would be. The community was bustling with activity, but it was still a question mark. The good side was that, if it was a lucrative pick-off, I would be in a position to sit back and coast. Finally I made the fateful decision, the mark of a weak person. "OK, Cob count me in. We're not in a hurry, so let's take our time and plan this caper with a lot of thinking."

The next ten days were spent covering all foreseeable possibilities. I learned that the armored carrier arrived at the bank's doors at ll:00 o'clock each Friday morning. Every night for a week, we plied the roads between my house and the bank, with Cob doing the driving. The weakest point of our plan was that Cob might not have the route thoroughly fixed in his mind. It was agreed that on arriving at my place with the loot, the car would be parked behind the chicken coop out of sight of the road. I would be given my percentage, and that night we would drive to San Francisco where my buddy would catch a plane to Miami.

One evening after I had put Muriel to bed, Cob and I avoided the mention of any reference to the 'job' because my wife was sitting beside me on the divan. We had a great deal to discuss between us, and little time in which to do so. Never had I planned any robbery as thoroughly as we did this one. He and I had committed a large number of criminal acts but never together. For veterans in our chosen occupation, we were unduly tense; a bad omen. I wish we had listened to our sixth sense. Neither of us confided in the other our profound concern until it was too late.

On the Thursday before D-day, Cob did an unusual thing. He entered the bank for the second time for the purpose of a more intensive casing. Before doing this he confided in me, "Partner, I am going to look this situation over one more time. If necessary, we may have to put the invasion day off until next week." I knew better than to urge him to move into action as planned, or forget the matter. He was a cool customer, and knew what he was doing.

For the rest of the day, we didn't mention what he had learned from his most recent casing. However, that evening, while my wife was visiting the neighbor with Muriel, Cob and I went to a restaurant in Seattle. After we had enjoyed a dinner, we went to the lounge and sat down in a dark and vacated corner. Once there, and after a couple of Harvey Wallbangers, we spilled our guts as to our reservations. I broached the subject first. "Cob, what's your evaluation since your latest looking the bank over?" He wasn't surprised that I hit the subject without too much overture. "Two things are causing me problems," he bounced back. "You've evaded one of the most obvious and important things; what are we going to do for a car on the job? We can't very well grab one off the streets at this late hour. The other will probably force us to cancel the project altogether. In both cases, when I went in to observe working conditions, I was skeptical that I could safely pull it off because of the number of employees. There were at least twelve. We have to assume there were a couple more where I couldn't spot them. As you know, that creates a very dangerous working condition for the robber. A hidden bank worker would feel secure in pushing an alarm, and that almost always results in a shoot-out. Remember the rip-off in Fayettesville? A customer caught a slug in the shoulder, and Pete Zerkov wound up getting free room and board for fifteen years." So, this was one of the considerations that bothered Cob. I was glad he got it out in the open. "Let's take care of your first worry. As for a getaway vehicle, I was prepared from the beginning to handle that. My brother, Dan, who lives a mile from here, has a car I can get. It will be without his knowledge. He has a new Chrysler that he doesn't take to work. It sets in the garage all day except on week-ends. We can pick it up just before the heist and return it within an hour. It's a perfect deal. He lives off the road and his house is completely concealed among trees. He'll never know I borrowed it. The only way I can see to handle the large number of employees is to call in another thug to back you up. I don't know anyone I'd trust that much." Cob's next comment hit me like a bomb shell. "We've put in a lot of time and money looking this over. Glenn, will you join me in the robbery?" I nearly choked on that one. It was the farthest thing from my mind. Some of the old-timers said it was taboo to violate your home, and that those who did so were doomed to bad luck; usually they were caught. Call it superstition, or whatever; many believed it would result in a hex being put on you. Cob continued, "I don't see how we can fail as a team. You know the area, and you're established in the community. What do you say?" I was stunned that he would ask me. He knew how crazy I was over my daughter.

I pondered the matter over the entire night. I convinced myself that the two of us would make an unbeatable team. I don't know why I promised him an answer within twenty four hours when I knew in my heart that we would hit the bank as a team. I never did give him an answer. He simply took my reply for granted when I told him we had much planning to do. For the entire week, I found myself more attentive and loving toward Muriel, if that were possible. Was it an omen that my days with her were numbered? Was I trying to make up to her for the gamble I was taking with her future, her very life? I refused to accept the possibility that I would be captured. If I had any way of foreseeing the future, I am certain I would have ended my life.

Friday morning! It was here, and I approached it with a confidence that was faked. Of all the robberies I had pulled, I never felt as uncomfortable as I did with this upcoming heist. In my other jobs, my stake was mine alone. In this gamble, I had much to lose and it wasn't mine to lose. I was gambling and the stakes were Muriel's future. I had to quit going over this unpleasant reality, and get on with the final sharpening of our plan. The child was taken to the nursery by her mother at 7:30 that morning. By 10:00 AM Cob and I had picked up my brother's car and drove it to my house. We went inside, picked up two pieces of adhesive tape with which to alter our appearances, re-combed our hair in a ridiculous fashion, put on railroad caps, and tucked our pistols in their holsters. I walked into my bedroom, took my sawed-off shotgun from the closet, picked up a box of shells and carried them to the car. I placed them on the floorboard and covered them with a piece of old blanket. In case of a chase, a shotgun is an excellent weapon to shoot out tires. Also, the very presence of that type of gun puts the fear of God in people who might be inclined to pursue us. "Cob, I guess it is understood that I'll drive the getaway vehicle. Unless you have other ideas, here's what I suggest." He listened carefully, as I continued. "We go in together. I'll walk to the rear cage. You go to the manager, announce our reason for being there in a loud voice. I'll repeat it for the sake of the tellers who may not have heard. As soon as I do that, I'll walk to the center of the building where I can see and cover all employees and any customers. Immediately, you are to herd the manager up behind the cages and tell the girls not to set off the alarm. When they look up, they will be staring down the business end of my gat. Psychologically, we'll have the advantage. As you progress with the cash pick-up, I'll ease my way to the front door. When you get the loot, walk to where I'm waiting, and leave ahead of me. I'll cover you 'til you get in the back seat. Pick up the shotgun and cover me as I come out. Let's go."

We entered and took up our positions. There were about four customers. However, we knew more would be coming in. It was my job to see that none left. I held my weapon so anyone coming in could not see it until it was too late for them to retreat to the streets. In less than one minute I was moving toward the front door, our exit. I was amazed to see Cob heading toward me in such a short time. I couldn't understand how he could have completed his end of the chore so quickly. I had the sickening feeling that something was going wrong. I became more alert. I was surprised to see that he was carrying two large money bags. Just before Cob reached me, a crazy thing happened. It was one of those things for which you can't prepare. A tiny grey- haired lady started for the door. I intercepted her and very quietly said, "Ma'am you'll have to wait. You can't go right now." She bristled up like an angry wet hen and snapped, "I'll go whenever I please. Now you stand aside." With that she attempted to brush me out of her way. By this time, Cob was beside me. I had no time to argue, so I simply yelled, "This is a stick-up, lady. You stand still." She stared at me and uttered words that will never leave my mind. She asked, "Does your mother know what you are doing?" I turned back to the frightened tellers and customers and yelled. "If anyone follows or sets off an alarm, we'll come back in here and shoot every one of you." Our car was parked alongside the building where it couldn't be seen by anyone inside. Within a minute, I was under the driver's wheel and Cob slid into the rear seat. As I pulled out, I saw my buddy uncover the deadly blaster and set it across his lap, ready for business.

As we put distance between the town and our car, both of us sighed with relief. There was no sign of pursuit. It was a clean, smooth job and disappearing act. I wove in and out of the wooded streets and ten minutes after we got the loot, I was parked behind the coop. Right away, Cob jumped from the car with the money bags and walked into the house. I never waited a minute. I left my house, drove to my brother's ranch and returned his car. I went in the house and called my place. Cob guardedly answered, "Joe's gas station." I replied, "I need a fan belt and will be there in a few minutes."

When I got to the house, a pleasant sight greeted me. Cob was setting on the bed with heaps of bills surrounding him. I gasped. "My God, Pal, that's a lot of money. How did you pick it up so fast?" He giggled like a love-sick teenager and said, "Hell, Glenn, when I started to the rear of the cages with the manager in tow, here was this cart loaded with the money the armored car dropped off. We're rich!" He buried his hands and face in the pile of money. At that moment, we heard a car door slam in the front yard. He rolled off the bed and came up with his revolver in his hand. I dove into the closet and had my pistol trained on the door. The bedroom door opened. I was ready to squeeze off a round at the figure that appeared in the doorway. It was my wife. I yelled at Cob to hold his fire, but he had seen her an instant before I did. She just stood transfixed, staring first at me with the drawn gun, then at Cob, and finally at the huge stack of money. When she moved her mouth to say something, I was shocked that the first thing she did was to rant and rave about the money soiling the white comforter. I soothingly said, "It's OK. Just relax. We have enough here to buy a thousand comforters." Without another word, she sat on a chair, and continued to gaze at the eerie scene before her. I continued to talk in a quiet manner until she regained her composure.

During this unreal scene, Cob methodically stuffed the money into the original bags. I sensed he was wanting to scram but fast. My wife finally asked, "Where did you get all that money?" I realized that I had better shoot the works with her. She would be reading about the robbery in the evening paper anyway, and surely would put two and two together. I calmly told her, "We just heisted the bank in Lynnwood about an hour ago." Oddly enough, she showed no reaction to my confession. In fact she ignored what I had said and inquired, "How much would you say was there?" I came up with a suggestion. "Let's the three of us count it on the dining room table" Cob simply sat there staring. He had a bag in each hand and looked like he was waiting for a train to pull in. I walked over and pulled the tablecloth off and tossed it on the davenport. Cob took the cue and dumped the swag onto the table. My mate ran her hands through the green stuff and suggested we stack it in separate piles according to the denominations. In about ten minutes we had seven bundles, each of which measured about four inches high. None of us spoke as we started to count. As we would finish one stack, Cob would put a rubber band around it. When we finally tallied, it totaled to more than $50,000, a fortune in our eyes. I yelled out, "Cob, do you realize that we've netted twenty five grand apiece?" He sat back and stared glassy-eyed at the money. He was anxious to be on his way, but I convinced him he should wait until morning. I volunteered to go into town and pick up Muriel at the baby sitter's.

On my way into town I was stopped at a road block. I was unarmed and driving my Cadillac. I felt comfortable about being hailed down. The deputy sheriff signaled me to roll down my window. Before he said a word, he carefully peered into the back seat. I inquired as to the reason for the stop. He excitedly said, "Apparently you haven't had your radio on. The Seattle First National Bank in Lynnwood was robbed less that two hours ago. It is estimated the robbers got away with more than one hundred grand." Inwardly, I smiled. Isn't it like everyone to exaggerate the facts?

Hell, I said to myself, by this evening the figure will be up to two hundred grand. The officer asked, "Do you live in this area?" I responded, "Yes. I live on Locust Way about two miles from here" Satisfied, he waved me on. I couldn't resist a parting comment. "If the robbery took place nearly two hours ago, aren't you a little late in setting up a road block?" "Oh, no," was his reply, "We have every reason to believe the thugs are penned up in this area. We'll keep the seal on until tomorrow morning at least." As I drove off, I thought to myself how lucky it was that I suggested that Cob spend the night. After I picked up my daughter, we returned home via the road where I had run into the block. Considering what the cop had said about keeping the road block until morning, I was surprised to see it was clear of any police.

At the dinner table that night, I told my wife and friend of my experience on the way into town. Cob just smiled and said, "I'm glad I listened to you and didn't head for town." About nine that evening my phone rang. My wife picked up the receiver. Almost instantly her face turned deathly pale.

I jumped up and took the receiver from her hand and asked the caller, "May I help you?" The voice on the other end replied, "I'd like to speak to Corn." I panicked. Who in hell knew he was here? And whoever it was knew Cob well enough to call him by his nickname. Very calmly I said, "You have the wrong number." I hung up. Cob sensed something was wrong. He looked at me in a quizzical manner. I told him what had taken place. He blanched. The phone rang again. My wife reached for it but I stopped her from picking it up. It rang persistently for about fifteen rings. When it quit, I turned to Cob and asked, "Did you tell anyone that you were staying here, and if you did why did you give my phone number?" I was livid with anger, and he could sense I was going to demand an in-depth reply. I could tell that Cob was visibly upset and irritated. "Glenn, you know that Bebe was the one who called me originally and told me about the pigeon. It wouldn't take an Einstein to figure who hit the bank. Undoubtedly he assumed that you would know where I could be located. As for your phone number, it is listed. I can't imagine him being so stupid as to call you so soon after the caper. Certainly, he knew you would be spooked. Otherwise he might try to reach my connections in Miami. What do you say to that?" I nodded and he dialed Bebe's number. He made the connection right away. "Hi, Bebe, Cob here. You called Glenn?" Cob put the phone between both our ears so I could here the conversation. "Yeah, Corn, I called and that son-of-a-bitch slammed the receiver down on me. I don't like that shit." Before he could continue, Cob cut in. "Listen, Bebe, I want to know why you called here for me." Bebe yelled into the phone, "Hell, where else could I reach you? If you were not staying with him, I thought, at least, he could put you in touch with me. What's wrong with that?" Cob looked at me, shrugged his shoulders, and said," "Well, what do you want?" Bebe's response caused the blood in my veins to turn to ice. "Nothing except I heard on the radio where you nicked that bank for nearly 60 G's and I want to remind you that I'm the finger man on the job, so I'll be glad to get my hands on my 20 percent; about 12 thou. Is that right?" Cob looked at me for some sort of support. I nodded my head vigorously. "That's OK, Bebe," Cob assured him. "I'll get back to you tomorrow, and we'll get together for the payoff." He started to hang up, when Bebe dropped a bombshell. "The radio said that you had a partner. Was it Glenn?" Cob hit the roof. "Bebe, Glenn was not in on this job." By the time the phone conversation was over, I was raging. "Cob, we had a perfect setup but for one fact. You and your mouth. Now, we're at the mercy of some hair-brained idiot you trusted. Trusting him is your business, but trusting him with my life is my business. We'll always have this guy hanging over our head. Not only that, it's going to cost us twelve big ones. Not only that, you and I know we didn't get 60 G's. That's the banker's share*." I tilted my head toward the door and said, "Let's take a stroll. I need to think."

After we got away from the house, I told Cob, "We have two choices. Either we pay the guy, which won't solve our problem, or we can pay him

*Whenever a bank is robbed, the manager or whoever else is in a position to do so, will rip off a certain amount of money which he pockets. In his report of actual loss he includes, what we call THE BANKER'S SHARE. Naturally, the robbers cannot complain of the exaggerated amount taken. If they did, whose word would be taken, the banker or the robber?

off by lead poisoning*. I'd hate to snuff the guy because he may have confided in someone who we are. In that case, we'd be looking at the possibility of doing a jig at the end of a rope. Which way do you want to go? This is a matter that has to be attended immediately." Cob was distressed. "Let's pay him off, Glenn. I personally don't want to erase a man unless it is necessary. I'll pay the fink from my share."

That night, after we had retired, I asked my wife, "How did you happen to come home early?" Her reply was, "There wasn't that much work to do at the office so I asked the boss for the day off. It nearly cost me my life, didn't it, Glenn?" It was then that I fully understood how close she came to getting blown away. It was a miracle that Cob or I had not pulled the trigger. I found it very difficult to sleep that night. As I laid there, I could hear my buddy tossing and turning on the davenport.

In the early hours of the morning, I slipped out of bed and brewed some coffee. My mind wandered to Muriel, so I went to her bedside to make certain she was sleeping undisturbed. When I went back into the kitchen, Cob was pouring himself a cup of coffee. He looked awful. I knew he was blaming himself for the faux pas. While I blamed him also, I felt sorry for the guy. "Hey, man, we all make mistakes. Take it easy on yourself. You and I will have to handle it the best way we can. We're going to have to step carefully from here on out. I really don't know this Bebe character. He might be as right as rain. Hit the hay, Cob, we have much to do tomorrow. I want to get you on your way as soon as you pay the third party off. By the way, I want this guy's address before we part company." My friend gave me that info and asked, "Why did you ask for that?" I told him bluntly that if he got pinched, I was going to 'hit' Bebe.

Early the following morning, my guest and I arose at 6:00 o'clock. We counted out Cob's share. In a separate sack, we counted out 12 G's for Bebe. I insisted that we split the unforeseen cost. "I want to take your pickup truck to Bebe's place, Glenn," my partner said. "I'll be back in less than an hour. If it's OK with you, I'd like for us to head for Portland where I can get a flight out." He picked up Bebe's percentage and left. When he returned he acted strangely. I didn't press him for details, but his conduct and attitude made me nervous. As we were sipping coffee, I could hear my wife awakening my daughter. "OK, pal, what's eating you?, I asked. He unloaded, "I'm afraid of the bastard I just gave the money to. He tried to shake me down for an additional 5 grand, and I told him to kiss my ass. He just smiled and said. 'OK, Corn, no hard feelings'. Glenn, I'm going to check in at the Washington Hotel and lay low for a few days." I thought this over and offered a suggestion. "Let's put the rock-a-bye-baby** on this cancer. I mean tonight, Cob. This has gotten out of hand." He replied, "It's too late for that drastic a move. I want you to take me to the hotel. I'll call you twice a day for two days. Then I want us to head south." Reluctantly, I agreed.

He and his money were in a room at the Washington an hour later. I waited until my wife took the youngster to the baby sitter's on her way to work. As soon as she left, I took one hundred $100 bills and concealed them in the ice cube holder in the refrigerator. I covered them with water,

*death by bullet ** assassinate

179

knowing that after it froze the bills could not be readily be seen. They would be available for immediate cash as I needed it. I put ten 50's in my wallet. The remainder, I wrapped in oil-cloth and buried on my property about twenty yards from the house. Normally, I would have been comfortable with those arrangements, but with the specter of Bebe in the background, I was unreasonably edgy.

I went to work in the laundry the next day. I hadn't called Cob. Missing one day without contacting him would not create anxiety on his part. The owner's wife, affectionately known as MacDuff, relieved me for lunch time. As I pulled my truck into the parking lot, I noticed a sedan pull in behind me, bumper to bumper. I stepped from my vehicle to tell the driver to back away. As I went to the rear of my truck, two well-dressed men jumped from their car. I immediately recognized them as FBI agents. Both had wallets in their hands as one announced, "Mr. Williams, we are with the FBI. We would like to talk to you." Laboriously, I examined their credentials. The reason I took so long was so I could gather my composure. To gain more time, I asked, "What do you want to talk to me about?" They knew the purpose of my stalling. They always liked to scare people with their announcement, 'we are with the FBI'. Their tactics were the typical dime-store variety. They were obviously incensed. One spoke up and said, "Could we go inside to talk?" I thought that over for a minute before saying, "No, let's talk right here. If you're arresting me, let me call my attorney. Don't expect me to answer questions unless my lawyer is present." The response was typical. "If you have nothing to hide, why not relax and answer our questions?" I smiled and said, "I've dealt with you before, and I know better than to trust you."

Without any more verbal sparring, the one who was in charge said, "Can you tell us where we can locate Cornelius Cob? We have been reliably informed that he was seen with you this past week." I shrugged my shoulders and casually remarked, "Maybe your informant can tell you where he is. I have no idea." In a thinly veiled threat, the spokesman added, "You might hear from him soon. If you do, it will be to your advantage to call us right away." He pulled his card from his pocket and attempted to hand it to me. I ignored his outstretched hand, turned and went inside the cafe. My mind was churning out irrational signals so fast I couldn't bring reality into focus. I ordered coffee and nothing else. For at least thirty minutes I sipped my coffee. I knew one thing for certain; I had to get word to Cob. I called the hotel from the cafe booth. When the desk clerk answered, I asked for Mr. Randolph. They rang his room at least seven times before advising me that he wasn't in. "May I take a message for him?" "Yes," I said. "Please tell him that Mr. Bull has been looking for him. Tell him that it is of the utmost importance that he contact his business partner." I muttered to myself, "Where in the hell could he be?" I settled down to more rational thinking. He could be out for lunch or could have gone for a stroll. I returned to the laundry and waited until MacDuff left.

For the next three hours, I called the hotel trying to get ahold of Cob. I left the same message as before. Still no response. The following morning, Bebe called me. He advised me that Cob had been arrested at the Washing-

180

ton Hotel late the previous night. I asked Bebe how he knew that Cob had been arrested. His answer was anything but satisfactory. "Well, he gave the FBI my name as his close friend. They charged out here and tried to hook me up to the bank job. Cob told them I didn't have anything to do with it. They're looking for a man about 5'8". I'm more than six feet tall." My first inclination was to pack up and split the scene. Then, after thinking it over, I decided to stay put. I knew that Cob would never snitch on me.

For two days I heard nothing from or about Cob. I reasoned that the FBI was playing a waiting game. Well, I'd play the game with them. I went to work both days. On the third day, I received another visit from the feds. This time, they caught me at the laundry as I was unlocking the door. There were three of them. They introduced themselves, proffering their hands. The one who assumed the dominant role said, "Well, Williams, I guess you know we got Cornelous Cob, and he has confessed." I simply said, "Oh." In his best rehearsed manner, he handed me a newspaper, and asked me to read the headlines. I saw Cob's picture and read one glaring paragraph, One Of The Lynnwood Bank Robbers Captured; Confesses. FBI Expects To Net His Cohort Soon. Without reading further, I handed the paper back and commented, "Congratulations." Another of the threesome, obviously perturbed by my nonchalance, snapped, "We think you could help us clear this matter up right now if you decided to cooperate." I motioned to the newspaper and said, "According to that article, you have the case sewed up. Why waste your time talking to me? I know nothing about the robbery. I want you to quit bugging me." As one, they turned and started to walk out. One gave me a parting shot, "We'll be on you like glue." And they were.

They had a car parked across from my home 24 hours a day. They questioned dozens of my friends. My pastor, Dorr C. Demary, told me that he had been questioned by the FBI. I recognized this as their old game of harassment. During the next few weeks, I never carried my gun, nor did I have any of the bank money on my person. It had been my intent to fly to Canada and pass off some of the Canadian money in Vancouver, B.C. One morning, the local paper carried banner headlines. LYNNWOOD BANK ROBBER GETS TWENTY-FIVE YEAR TERM. IMMINENT CAPTURE OF ACCOMPLICE EXPECTED. I had to give the feds credit; they knew how to keep the pressure on. They realized that they had to flush Cob's partner out of the brush, and get him to bolt. In that manner, they would be able to identify him. In this case, his partner in crime refused to make a break for it. By now, I was confident they suspected Cob and I had worked together on the heist.

One Saturday afternoon as I was shopping in the local Safeway, one of the bank tellers who was a friend of mine gave me some disturbing information. As we walked from the store together, she asked me to go to the cafe where we could have coffee. "I want to tell you something interesting, Glenn." I was becoming paranoid. I instructed her to go ahead, that I would be there after I had put my groceries in my car. My real intent was to watch her as she went into the cafe to see if they had put a tail on her. It even entered my mind that she might have sold out to the FBI. After about five minutes, I followed her to the eatery. She had taken a seat in the center of the room. In one respect, that was a good move. We could see anyone selecting a seat near us. After I had seated myself, I cautiously asked, "What's up, Gayle?"

She was very nervous, and kept glancing around the dining area. Her actions put me on the double alert. "Glenn, the officers who are investigating the recent robbery called all the bank personnel together and asked us if we could identify the person in a photo they passed around. Each of the staff said they had never seen the man in the picture before. When it got to me, I said, 'Yes, that is a picture of my friend, Glenn Williams.' They asked me point blank, 'Was this one of the men who robbed the bank?' I laughed and replied, 'No, this is one of my neighbors. I have known him and his wife for four years.' Frankly, Glenn, they were very disappointed with my reply." I was elated with what she had told me. However, I acted surprised and told her, "Gayle, this is ridiculous. I'm surprised you didn't come over or call and tell me of this before." Her answer was, "I wanted to wait until I saw you. Not one person agreed that you even resembled either of the culprits." I continued to drink my coffee as I said, "Oh, a case of mistaken identity. It's no problem, Gayle. Nevertheless, thanks for sharing this with me. Come on over to see the wife and me soon."

An idea came to my mind, and as soon as I got home, I dialed Bebe's number. When he answered, I told him I wanted to talk to him, and asked him to meet me at the Jolly Roger night club about nine o'clock that evening. He spurted out, "Why? What do you want to see me about? I can't be there. I'm leaving town in a few hours." He was almost hysterical. I smiled to myself. So, it was him who had ratted on Cob, and he must have told the fuzz that I was in on the caper. Before he could hang up, I decided to put the fear of God in him. "It's OK, Bebe, I'm putting the word out on you. One of these days, one of the boys will settle the score. You will be marked all over the country as an FBI stoolie." He slammed the receiver down.

A few days after my conversation with Bebe, as I was folding clothes in the laundry, I spotted a carload of agents parking their car directly in front of the laundry. I tilted one of the washers forward and concealed my revolver under it. Instinctively I looked out toward the rear of the building in time to see another carload of agents parking their car directly behind mine in such a way that I couldn't move my vehicle if I found the chance. This had to be a pinch, or it was a grand display of power designed to intimidate me. I stepped back to the folding table and pretended to be preoccupied. They burst through the front and back door simultaneously. Within a minute, I found myself looking down the barrels of at least five guns. One of the agents called out, "Stand still, Williams, and don't move your hands off the table. We're arresting you for the robbery of the Seattle First National Bank in Lynnwood." My arms were wrenched behind my back and cuffs were snapped on my wrists. They were unduly rough. I felt this was done to vent their anger and frustration over my being so uncooperative. Nothing further was said as they dragged me to one of the waiting cars. In my mind, I knew that Bebe had called the FBI and told them he had been threatened. I was as certain of this as I was that he had been the original stool pigeon. I was crammed in between two of the men in the rear seat of their car. Two others jumped into the front and we were off to the headquarters. As we pulled away from the curb, I saw two more cars pull in behind us. A crazy thought entered my mind. During this whole episode, I noticed that there had never been any evidence of city police involvement. At this time, it was common knowledge that the FBI had always held local law enforcement officers in disdain.

The following day, after a night in the federal holding tank, I was taken to the FBI for grilling. I refused to offer them any information. I would simply tell them that they had the wrong man, and that a jury would exonerate me. They seemed confident that they had me. Ordinarily you can tell when the fuzz are fishing in uncertain waters. However, from the beginning of this session, I got the feeling they were quite certain of their ground. The questions were more relevant and to the point. They were questions that were born of a degree of knowledge of the correct response before they were asked. Coyly, bits of facts concerning the commission of the robbery were dropped as bait. The main goon dropped a bombshell that really hit me in the pit of the stomach by asking indifferently, "Have you ever thought how old your daughter will be before you ever see daylight again if we can get a conviction? On the other hand, if you will cooperate, sign a confession and show us where you hid the rest of the loot, we'll ask the judge to go softer on you. What do you say to that proposition?" To me it was the old, old story used since the beginning of time. I simply looked at the guy and smiled. After a minute of silence on both sides, he told the marshall, "Take this guy back to his cell." And while I was still in hearing range, he said to the others, "Go pick up his wife. Find somewhere to drop the kid while we try to determine if she is an accomplice." Nothing done to this point scared me more than overhearing that comment. The thought of having Muriel taken from her mother and placed in a strange environment was unthinkable. What the hell had I visited on my most precious possession? An innocent child being subjected to this type of treatment all because I was so stupid as to jeopardize her. And for what? Money. Hell, all the money in the world would be meaningless if Muriel were not with me.

I suffered horrible dreams that night. I couldn't sleep wondering if my youngster was home in her bed or in the custody of strangers. How would she react to being awakened in the morning by anyone except her dad? I had known men whom you couldn't break regardless of the vicious treatment visited upon them. I always considered myself as one of those individuals. Yet here I was on the cracking point because of my concern for the care and welfare of Muriel. I would rather have been put to death than subject her to what seemed inevitable.

Early the next morning, I summoned the jailer by banging my metal cup on the bars. When he arrived, I told him that I was ready to admit my participation in the crime. He must have conveyed that message within minutes. A half an hour later I was standing in the marshall's office surrounded by members of the FBI. I told them that my holding out was futile considering that my partner had already confessed, and that I would sign an admission of my complicity if I was assured that my wife would not be arrested and implicated. Little did I know at that time I was duped. A secretary was brought in. I dictated my story to the agents. I was shocked when I was interrupted a number of times and told to stick to the truth. "We know where the money was counted, the amount and the cardboard containers in which it was placed. We know exactly how you divided it with Cob, and the amount you gave Bebe for fingering the job. So, if you want us to live up to our end of the bargain, you had better damn well give us nothing but facts, Williams. And I won't warn you again." I was dumbfounded how well they knew the details. It couldn't have been Bebe because he had not been present at the counting of the money. I was completely puzzled. The informer had to be one of two people; my wife or Cob. I was confident it wasn't my wife. And why would Cob cooperate? He had already been sentenced to the maximum term of twenty-five years and a ten thousand dollar fine. It was too late for him to bargain even if he had been so inclined.

I was told by the marshall that I was to appear before Federal Judge Bowen to enter my plea of guilty three days after my confession had been signed. Beyond a doubt, those were the three longest days of my life. All I had ever wanted had been made available to me and I had blown it away because of greed. I went through a period of seriously considering suicide. Other times, I spent hours contemplating escape. I preferred this latter choice because it would afford me an opportunity to determine who had informed on me. If I could do that, then I would be able to hold my own court in which I would be the judge, jury and executioner. I was convinced I could cleanse my hands of the heavy onus of guilt by washing them in the blood of the informer. I was unable to recognize that I had created my own predicament. My psyche could not accept that.

The day prior to my hearing, I asked my sister to bring Muriel to the jail so I could see and talk to her for a final time. It was a mistake, one that haunted me for thirty years. The visiting conditions then, as they are today, were unbelievably cruel. I was on the inside of a tank* containing fifty screaming idiots. They were oblivious to the fact that visitors were trying to talk to their loved ones. The visitors were herded like cattle to small windows measuring about six by six inches. Twenty holes were drilled beneath each window, and it was through these apertures the visitor tried to converse with the prisoner. My sister tried to talk through the holes loud enough for me to hear. She held Muriel up to the window to see and talk with me. The child was frightened and confused. She could see that it was her dad on the other side. Out of frustration, she cried and hid her face against my sister. I couldn't stand anymore, so I waved my sister away. I was overcome with grief and livid with anger. If I had had a gun, I would have wiped out every one in the tank. I saw her briefly for one last time after I was in the federal prison. As fate dictated the terms, my daughter was lost to me for seventeen years. However, she was in my heart and soul every day of those endless years. When I started on this hell-bound journey of sheer madness, why couldn't I have foreseen some of the consequences? None of them were portrayed in the gangster books and movies on which I had based

*a large steel encased room in which prisoners were kept

184

my entire future, and the future of an innocent child, to say nothing of the endless misery I had visited on my beloved family. My worst enemy could not have hated me more than I despised myself at this time. In my present state of mind, I was a danger to myself and others.

14

The Rock Was On The Horizon

The dreaded first step of the next decade of my life exploded in the early morning hours of September 18, 1953 when a guard started banging on my cell door with his heavy ring of keys.

"Roll out of the sack, Williams" he roared, "Gather up all of your personal belongings. You're headed for the Federal Pen on McNeil Island."

I knew that this was one trip that was going to take years to complete and my depression deepened. At least I had been permitted to see my beloved three year old while in this county jail. What would happen concerning visits at McNeil was anyone's guess. Ugly thoughts raced through my befuddled mind.

An hour after I had been awakened, the jailor unlocked my door and guided me to the marshal's office. There were three other prisoners who were to share my experience that day. It only took minutes for us to be searched and swathed in iron restraints. The four of us were then conducted to a small windowless van where we sat on a wooden bench on each side of the vehicle.

When we arrived at the Steilacoom dock, we were ushered down the walkway to the awaiting prison launch. The guards helped us maneuver down the narrow steps leading into the hold of the vessel. The boat ride to the penitentiary took about 20 minutes. Our arrival was announced by a short blast from the boat whistle. Coming out of the hold proved to be a difficult task, with our chains severely restricting our movements. We stumbled into an institution bus and it labored up a steep incline to the main prison. Not until we were completely inside, and our custody officially transferred to the Feds were our chains removed.

The guards who accepted custody of our bodies were typical; cold, noncommittal, and curt when they ordered us to strip and submit to an orifice probe. As we were guided to the basement shower room we passed many inmates who were on their way to different shop assignments. Catcalls were exchanged.

After our brief session in the damp and chilly shower room, the four of us were ushered into McNeil's fish tanks, where we were confined for a period of 30 days, during which time we were given a physical and an IQ test and were mugged and finger printed. We were also forced to listen to a guard tell us what to expect if we did not behave. He gave us none of the truly sordid details of life in McNeil. We soon learned exactly how the federal government treated its inmates. We learned of the partiality shown to inmates of prestige and wealth. As an example, Mickey Cohen, a mobster out of Los Angeles, was treated with deference and respect. When he was released, he arranged for plush jobs for two guards who had smuggled uncensored letters in and out for him. We were brainwashed and convinced that we were without dignity or worth. One of the deadliest threats, done subtly, was the reminder that you could be sent to Alcatraz at the whim of the officials. Psychologically, that thirty day adventure damaged me more than any other experience I had endured thus far at the hands of guards, and the vicious beatings to which I had been subjected by the Sadistic "Juvenile Counselors" at Washington State Training School. If you injure the mind, it isn't too obvious; in fact, it may never become apparent. That is the modern system of punishment, more deadly because there are no physical scars as evidence of mistreatment.

Late one evening while I was reading a book on my bunk, one of the inmates detailed to mop the corridor tossed a note in my cell. As soon as I determined it was safe to read the scrap of paper, I quickly unraveled it. It was from a long time friend, Harold Keys, and it read, "Nate*, rumor has it pretty strong that you are to be held here for three months and then slated for Alcatraz. It is from a reliable source." Horror washed over me.

ALCATRAZ! THE ROCK! AMERICAN'S DEVIL'S ISLAND! THE GOVERNMENT'S PUKE AND VOMIT PENITENTIARY! THE PRISON DEVELOPED AND CONCEIVED BY CANCEROUS MINDS! THE BLACK HOLE OF CALCUTTA! Call it what you will; by any name it struck terror in the hearts and minds of all inmates in the federal joints throughout the U.S. Alcatraz was a hellhole used as a gimmick by the Federal Bureau of Prisons, the FBI and the ordinary wardens to assure that the convicts under their custody would soon be transformed into vegetable matter; easy to control; mindless robots.

Any official of an institution could conjure up a dozen reasons to exercise the threat. It was a simple procedure to contact the Bureau of Prisons in Washington, D.C. and effect a transfer. The technical reasons used included: recalcitrant, uncooperative, disruptive, threatening, a security risk, can't adjust. The unspoken reasons really were: "I don't like him or his attitude."

Of these prisoners that I later met, few were as dangerous as they had been publicly portrayed. In many cases it was a matter of personality clashes with some guard. Some inmates were very young and didn't warrant the added abuse imposed upon them by insensate prison guards. Of the two hundred inmates incarcerated on Alcatraz while I was there, 150 could have been safely imprisoned at any other federal prison.

Every indication showed that I was going to meet the destiny of which Harold wrote. I was placed under all the maximum security observations in my work assignments and quarters. The picture did not look at all good for me.

One day as Harold and I were talking in the mess hall, he came up with an idea to better determine if I was really 'heading South'. "Nate," he said,

*The inmates in addressing me shortened my first name to Nate. I was known as Nate during the rest of my criminal career.

"here's how you can find out. If they refuse to assign you to anything resembling permanency, you can bet you're here on a temporary basis. Put an interview request in to Phenneger, the Director of Education, and ask him for an audience. For the reason, simply state that you want to attend school to further your education. He'll take that request before the committee. If they put thumbs down on it, you can safely assume you're going to sunny California."

The following morning I wrote out the interview request. It was a week before I got my reply. The interview slip was returned to my cell with DENIED scribbled across the face of it. When I showed this to Harold, we both agreed that my traveling papers were in the mill. The following days were like living in a vacuum. I simply could not function; nothing interested me.

On the visit when I last saw my daughter for an interminable seventeen years, it was all I could do to contain myself. When it was time for her to leave with her mother, I kissed her and told her that I loved her. When she walked out the door I could no longer keep my composure and I broke down and wept bitter tears. I never saw or heard from her for seventeen years. A part of my life died that day.

Satan must have really enjoyed his work that night because he was by me all those tortuous hours of endless darkness. I relived the time from my daughter's birth to the day of my arrest. Until I lost her, I didn't realize how much I adored her, how precious she had become in those brief three years. The thought of not seeing her again left me broken and bereft of a will to continue.

I would comfort myself with the knowledge that she was just a child and would soon forget me; that her memory of me would fade as other interests occupied her life. This thought only lifted my spirits briefly. I was haunted by my memories, and when the lights would go out at night, I would welcome the privacy of my bed. I would lay there ashamed that other inmates might hear me cry out in despair, a certain sign of weakness in the crazy world of convicts. This is what the thought of going to Alcatraz did to me.

And if the visits from my daughter weren't enough to totally devastate me, I was subjected to another very cruel bit of information given me by my brother, Dan, when he came into the visiting room that afternoon with my Mother and Dad. The sight of my beloved parents crushed me. In a few brief weeks, both my folks had aged years. I realized that my parents would not live to see me free. This was one of those rare occasions when words cannot be uttered. We simply embraced until a calloused guard tore us apart and said, "You ain't allowed to have physical contact for more than one minute, and then only when you first greet one another!" Dan was obviously uncomfortable. When he did speak, his statement turned my blood to ice. "Glenn, in case you haven't found out, your wife was the stool pigeon who caused your arrest. She saw an opportunity to get rid of you, and probably collect a reward. If she didn't get a reward, where did the large sum of money go that you put in the freezer of your refrigerator?"

Desperately seeking a respite from my misery, I decided to talk to the

Protestant chaplain. This turned out to be a mistake. When I was telling him my story, he sat at his desk eyeing me imperiously, suspiciously. Coldly he said "Williams, you should have thought of the consequences of your life of crime. I'm appalled at the length of your criminal career. I ask you to drop to your knees and confess your iniquities before God. Those are the only conditions under which I can intercede with Jesus." I left his office without a word, filling slowly with a dangerous hatred. Later that same day, I told Harold of my experience with the man of the cloth. His response was quick and with venom in every word, "Nate, if there is one thing you must learn, that is to avoid any and all persons who tell you they are Christians." With that remark, he walked away leaving me confused.

At noon on April 7, 1954, I was intercepted by two guards at the top of the stairs leading into the basement. One glanced at a small picture he had in his hand and said to the fellow next to him, 'This is one of them'. He took me by the arm and headed me down the stairs. He called to one of the eight guards waiting in the shower room, "Here comes Williams. Process him." When I reached the bottom floor where the shower stalls were, I observed that eleven cons were already corralled there, taking showers.

When our bathing was done, we were all lined up for another orifice probe by an MTA from the hospital. Very little was said by the shivering convicts, but our minds were reeling with questions. By the time the last inmate had dressed, a guard came down with a heavy canvas bag containing many feet of chains, leg irons and handcuffs. We were all very securely trussed in a matter of ten minutes.

Once again I found myself trying to maneuver down into the hold of the prison launch. It was the usual perilous descent, made more difficult because of our chains. Thirty minutes later we were boarding a bus parked at the Steilacoom dock. We were on the first leg of our final journey, and by now all of us realized we were heading to Alcatraz.

When the bus pulled into the train depot in Tacoma, the thirteen of us were herded out and into the main lobby of the station. The noise we made with our chains clanging was horrendous. Hundreds of commuters stopped to gape at us as we clanged our way on marble floors to the awaiting prison coach. Walking ahead, on both sides of us and bringing up the rear, were a dozen or so penitentiary guards. What a sight we must have made!

A number of gleaming Pullmans were aligned behind an engine which seemed anxious to be on its way. The loading platform and the coaches were bustling with passengers bidding good-bye to friends. The only unusual and out of place activity was the presence of a long line of chained convicts. We must have presented an ugly aura among the otherwise happy throng of passengers. Red Caps were in evidence aiding all passengers except those in our group.

The chain moved noisily along the line of rail cars toward the rear. None of us had to be told which coach was ours. It turned out to be the one on the tail end, filthy and in need of paint. The windows were covered with heavy mesh of cyclone fence material. Two Tacoma cops positioned themselves on each side of the only open door to assist the trussed criminals as they struggled to mount the steps. The dragging of the chains could be heard the entire length of the depot, causing many of us acute embarrassment. The free world people kept eyeing us furtively. I felt that some of them were also embarrassed.

Once inside the dilapidated coach, I was treated to a depressing sight. The coach was of World War II vintage and it was immediately questionable as to whether or not it had been painted or cleaned since that time. The interior had originally been painted light brown but over the years it had become darker from lack of any care. The covers over the light fixtures were dirty and encrusted with insects, thus giving off an eerie light. The once upholstered seats were now hard and stiff. The windows were so grimy that visibility was impossible.

At each end of the car a heavy wire gun cage had been constructed. This was for the guard's protection. Two large liquid containers had been placed at the front of the coach. One contained water, the other held coffee. Between the sizeable containers was a large cardboard box. Later we learned it was filled with cold beef sandwiches prepared by the inmate cooks at McNeil.

We were forced to stand in the middle of the aisle until the guards manned each cage. Two guards were left with us in the coach for security reasons. They began to release two of us at a time in order to rearrange our shackles so we could be seated next to one another on each side of the car. The guards in the gun cages were standing at strategic positions with weapons trained on us. It took about twenty minutes to get us seated to the satisfaction of the guards. After we had been secured, the head guard left the cage, came down each line of prisoners and examined the chains to make certain we could not "slip" them. When he had completed this double check, all of the guards retired to the cage.

The seats were very uncomfortable and the restriction caused by tight irons made us even more miserable. The guards anticipated problems arising, so they offered us steaming hot coffee and cookies. This break in routine and monotony temporarily relaxed us. What normally would have taken about four hours to reach Portland dragged into nearly a five hour trip. The only time we were permitted to stand or substantially change positions was when one of us had to relieve himself. It was a major maneuver for one man to go to the lavatory because it was necessary to unshackle his seat partner and take the two of them to the head. We soon learned that if we said we had to go to the toilet, the guards had to go through the routine over and over. Of course, this was an opportunity to get up more often to relieve the horrible tedium.

Our keepers were fully aware of our little game, but there was not much they could do about it. They, too, were experiencing fatigue and frustration and their tempers were frayed. This fact was made evident by the shouting matches that developed between the cons and their tormentors. I sat there and wondered how the guards could be agitated to the point where they lost control of themselves and their demeanor. Little did it dawn on me at that time how enervating the pressure must have been on them.

By the time the city lights of Vancouver came into view, there was a moody and ominous cloud over the occupants of the unholy Pullman. Those on each side of the law had had no sleep. Portland was less than an hour away. The lieutenant in charge of the chain dropped a bombshell by announcing in a loud voice, "Men, we will be changing trains in Portland. I want all of you to cooperate fully to make the transfer run smoothly. We will be in Portland in about an hour so we will start now to rearrange your irons so you can march single file to another train siding."

It took about half an hour to get the men shackled in a single file marching position. When this had been accomplished, we had to stand for another half hour as the train lumbered into the Portland station. To make matters even worse, we had not been fed anything other than the coffee and cookies three or four hours earlier. The guards had not eaten either. It was a dangerous situation, a ticking bomb.

At last the train stopped and the rear car door was opened. At the sight of hundreds of civilians milling around the depot a rebellion exploded among the prisoners. A convict named Ryan, who was the lead man, stopped short of going down the stairs. He simply refused to budge. Despite the barked orders from a lieutenant to move, Ryan refused to be intimidated. The other guards quickly surrounded the recalcitrant man and the possibility for mayhem loomed overhead. Ryan's voice exploded in a stream of angry invectives and accusations, aimed at the guards surrounding him. His sentiments closely matched our own and we began to encourage his outburst with our verbal slugs.

The screws were clearly concerned, and for a few minutes it was obvious that they were beset with indecision. Very quickly a gray- haired senior guard took command. He positioned himself in front of the trembling Ryan and began to speak in a soft voice. "We're not pleased with the arrangements of this transfer, fellows. It was arranged by the Federal Bureau of Prisons and obviously they did not take into consideration that you would be on display like animals in a zoo. To ease the minds of most of you I want to advise you of something. Only three of you men are scheduled to remain on Alcatraz. The other eight are going on to the U.S. Penitentiaries at Leavenworth, Kansas and Atlanta, Georgia. Some of you going on to the Midwest institutions are being sent there at your own request so you can be near your families. If you continue this rebellion, you can bet all of you will be re-tried. Then you will be facing additional time, and you can wager your ass that time will be spent on the Rock. It's up to you. Look outside and you'll see members of the Portland Police Department, the sheriff's office and a dozen U.S. marshals. Rest assured that you're not going to go anywhere. You now have one minute to start down those steps. If you refuse, we'll drag you out by your feet."

A few of us craned our necks. He had told the truth regarding the reinforcements. All of us must have reached the same silent conclusion and that was enough of a motivator to begin our descent down the steps into the custody of the awaiting army. Again the long line of fettered men were subjected to a block-long march on marble floors.

In record time we boarded another prison car and began our southward trek. We had traveled about an hour when the guards decided to unwrap the sandwiches and feed us. The cold beef and hot coffee tasted like a meal served at the Waldorf Astoria.

At seven that night we were fed baloney sandwiches and finished the remainder of the lukewarm coffee. Oddly enough there was very little talk among the men. Ever present in our minds was the big question: Which three of us were going to do our sentences on the Rock? I would find a dozen reasons as to why it would not be me.

At last one of the guards called out, "All right men, we want you to wake up. We will be in San Francisco in an hour." Believe me, that message brought all of us to our senses. A short time later, the lights of the Bay City blinked on the horizon. The guards began gathering their things in preparation to leave the coach. The lieutenant came to the front of the cage to give us his final remarks. "This train will be dropped off at Oakland and I want to warn you against any such display as you did in Portland. You'll be on Alcatraz property and the whole area will be crawling with seasoned guards who are equipped to handle the toughest. Obey every order to the letter. Is that clear?" Actually it was all too clear. No one wanted to tangle with the guards from Alcatraz. They had a nasty reputation.

After some switching of trains, our prison car was put on a siding. It was pitch dark, and with the windows being so grimy we were unable to discern anything outside. About thirty minutes after arriving at this particular destination, our keepers began gathering up their baggage. They then left both gun galleries and entered the main car where we sat. They seemed to be more relaxed and sure of themselves. The reason became obvious as the car door opened and ten guards from Alcatraz poured into the coach. With the regular contingent of guards who had been with us throughout the trip, the cons were now greatly outnumbered. They came prepared to overwhelm us at the first sign of resistance.

An older guard of apparent authority detached himself from the group of guards and approached us about midway down the aisle. He was a fine looking specimen, a man who gave you the impression that he was capable and yet not overbearing. He addressed us in a firm but kind voice. "I realize, men, that you have had a hard trip, that you are weary and hungry. I understand this and will process the rest of your journey as rapidly as possible. Please listen carefully and follow the instructions I give. You will stand so we can rearrange your cuffs and leg irons making it possible to walk single file to the rear door. When you are told to disembark, you will proceed down the steps to the platform where you will stand until the officers position themselves around you. At a given order, I want you to follow the lead man. Start marching."

We had ridden so long under the cramped and fettered conditions that our legs were unsteady. Managing the stairs was a problem. When I reached the bottom step, it took a few minutes for my eyes to adjust to the bright lights. When my eyes were capable of focusing, I was positively amazed by the number of security people around us. I did not have an opportunity to count them. I estimated there were at least ten whom we had not seen before. In addition, there were four San Francisco Police cars strategically positioned.

I had never seen so much fire power in my life. We were faced by shotguns, pistols, machine guns and gas billies. What a reception! Some person among our escorts barked the order to "move out" and we began to shuffle forward like zombies. A distant foghorn belched loudly. Other than that, the only noise was the sound of dragging chains.

To this day I couldn't tell you how far we trod to the awaiting prison launch. I do remember it to be the most exhausting and painful hike I had ever undertaken. The distance was not so great, but the conditions made it seem endless.

As we approached the dock, I could hear the waves lapping against the pilings. The boat had to be right here. Even though the fog had become more dense, I could barely see the outline of the craft that seemed to be about sixty feet long. As we came alongside the vessel, I could read its name; "Warden Johnston". 'Christ's sake.' I muttered to myself, 'Imagine a ship named after him!' What a sick claim to fame! What a lasting memorial! This man's reputation for barbaric treatment was known to every convict in all the joints in the U.S. He was well known among the inmates as "Salt Water" Johnston, a name the cons hooked on him for his practice of turning powerful hoses of saltwater on the particular inmate(s) who had incurred his wrath. The force of the water would knock the hapless man off his feet and batter him against the walls and bars. Under this battering, the inmate would be rendered to a state of complete disorientation, at which time the guards would move in and toss the fellow into the dungeon. By the way, for public consumption, the officials would refer to the 'hole' as an isolation cell. When articles were written about this sadist, the authors would refer to him as a kindly and fatherly gentleman who ran Alcatraz with a firm hand.

The disconsolate human chain trudged to the foot of the prison launch ramp and stopped at the command of the head guard. He should have been called 'dog' because he always barked out his orders. "You cons line up in single file next to the ramp. You can see we have rough waters. Getting up to the deck ain't going to be easy being trussed like you are. I'm placing a guard on each side of the ramp to help you aboard. Let's go!" At no time on this endless journey had I been so close to utter exhaustion as I was then. I was not only weary to the bone, I was psychologically drained; emotionally bereft of any feeling. At this time I would not have cared if I had fallen into the bay and drowned. Men in front of me half pulled me along. Those behind pushed until I found myself on the deck of this miserable ship. I recall thinking how utterly devastated the slaves must have felt as they were being battened down in the hold of the slavers' ships. Again, the 'dog' yelped, "Walk into the cabin. When all of you are inside, you will see a ladder leading to the hold. It is narrow and steep, so you will have to descend going backward. There will be guards to see that you don't fall. Once you start to go down, keep moving because if one of you starts to fall it will have the domino effect and all of you will tumble." I cannot remember going down the stairs. I do recall noticing how small the hold was. How we ever got 13 men in such a small space amazes me to this day. We were standing so cramped together it was difficult to breathe. No guard was in the area below with us. I can understand why. If one had been there, one of us would have contrived a way to kill him.

15

Chain To Alcatraz

ALCATRAZ

Gloomy citadel of defeat
Its cold grey walls a winding sheet
Massive warehouse of despair,
Loneliness is nurtured there.
Grimy edifice of decay
Where social conscience rots away.
Dismal structure of disgrace
Where mankind hides its other face.
Angry crucible, hatred fired,
Where criminality is inspired.
Putrid playground of perversion
Sad, despicable, sick diversion.
Ugly monument to ugly souls,
Hatred driven toward ugly goals.
Cold grey womb where shameful deeds
Are fertilized by hatred's seeds.
Tragic fortressed walls of time,
Built by fear to combat crime.
Wasting place of human lives
Where latent evilness revives.
Brewing sac of all that's vile,
Spewing out its social bile.
Rampart of medieval thought
That men are cleansed as they rot
In catacombs of lonely cages,
Ignorant throwback of dark ages.
Hideous error of our time,
In itself a monstrous crime.
Grim dark shadow upon our lands,
There the modern prison stands.

In the hold of this vile vessel, thirteen miserably cold convicts huddled in yards of chains. When one of us would alter his position, the leg irons would protest loudly. When the guards would hear the rattling of the fetters, they would bring their weapons to the ready position, always expecting a massive and physical resistance from the prisoners, notwithstanding we were completely immobilized. I am certain that their own propaganda concerning the cargo of animals they were transporting added to their paranoia. Each of them seemed to have a permanent grimace etched in his features. I felt they were overdoing their role of protector of all society. In order to qualify as prison guards, I felt there was a page in their primer that read: 'At all times, in the presence of your prisoners, you must impress them with a display of an ominous countenance'.

Suddenly my reverie of hate was interrupted by an obvious change in the noise of the boat's diesel engine as it quieted down. Garrett, one of the cons uttered, "Son-of-a-bitch! Men, we have arrived at the Rock." Before a response could be made from any of us, a red-faced guard shouted, "Keep your mouths shut; you were told not to speak." Garrett stared insultingly at the guard and yelled, "F—k you!" Instantly, three other guards joined the first. They aimed their weapons at the mass of flesh in the hold. Knowing how trigger-happy a prison guard can be, I fully expected a fusillade of bullets. When the first one pointed out the culprit among us, all trained their guns on Garrett. He simply curled his lips in utter contempt and snarled, "Shoot, you son-of-a-bitch." The guards, expecting they knew not what, kept the guns in the recalcitrant's face. Before a further confrontation could take place, the launch jolted against the pier. At this point, three more of the guards came tumbling down the hatch ready for trouble. An old-timer among them recovered his poise first and issued an immediate command. "Two of you guards line up on each side of the ladder. Help each inmate as he starts up. Make certain none falls. Let's go!" Turning to us, he shouted, "Start up to the upper deck, one at a time. Move out."

As we stood and stumbled to the foot of the ladder, our chains made a horrendous sound. Most of us experienced difficulty in maneuvering because the chains had cut the circulation in our limbs. The climbing was double tough. If I live to be a hundred years of age, God forbid, I will never forget the scene that greeted our eyes as we reached the upper deck. In addition to the guards who were in the hold of the boat, there were at least fifteen more awaiting us as we emerged. Actually, there were enough of them to quell a full-scale riot. I don't know whether I was shivering from fear or from the damp cold on that foggy night. My eardrums were assaulted by the horrible noise made by a foghorn. This same horn punctuated the silence of the prison thousands of times in the next few months. After that, I became acclimated to it. There are many conditions of the Rock that the inmates will never forget; the foghorn, the endless fog, the wind and the cold. Garrett whispered to me, "Nate, only Satan could have produced this island."

It was extremely difficult to make out a clear picture of the main part of the penitentiary. In the haze, a dim outline of a building rose 300 feet above us. To our right was a gun tower I estimated to be about 60 feet tall. I could not be certain because the top of the structure hid itself in the mist. There were pale yellow lights all over the area. In this kind of weather, they were ineffective. If there was ever a clear night, I am certain they would have served the purpose of illuminating the dock. When I first stepped on the Island itself, I suddenly recalled my father's saying during one of his many 'admonishing sessions', "If you continue to lead this lawless type of conduct, my boy, one day you will find yourself imprisoned with the likes of such as Al Capone, Baby-Face Nelson, Dillinger and Alvin "Creepy" Karpis and other such human garbage." How right he was!

"Start the line up the hill," yelled a guard, who apparently had some authority. To describe this scene is an impossibility. More than a dozen weary, disconsolate, cold, hungry and heavily manacled men formed a line of living death trying to navigate a very steep hill. I later judged the distance to be about eight blocks. The only sound that emanated from the group was the sound of chains dragging on concrete and an occasional bit of profanity spurting from the mouths of angry men. There was no respite in the form of a brief rest. The obvious paramount concern of the warders was to get us securely ensconced in our cages. Frankly, there was no other wish in the hearts of the cons. We were consumed with total exhaustion. Oh, for a place to lay our heads, whether on cement or steel. Even if we had been unchained, there was not the energy left to make flight or fight.

Out of nowhere, we came up against the wall of what appeared to be a gigantic warehouse. In later years I realized that it was just that, a warehouse for human beings. We were led around to a side of the building, where there was a large solid-steel door. In the center of the door was an opening about 4" X 8". It was covered by a sliding section of iron. One of the guards stepped forward and rapped sharply. From behind the peephole a face appeared. He looked the group over for a full minute before uttering a sound. Finally he said, "Officers, pass your weapons through the opening." The guards did as instructed. The peephole was covered again. It was a full five minutes before the face reappeared. When it did, I heard a loud voice saying, "Will the officer in charge step forward?" It was at this time we saw "Blue Boy" Mitchel, a short heavy man. He must have weighed 250 pounds. Oddly enough, he moved with the grace of Fred Astaire as he strode to the front of the line. Without being questioned, he called out, "Lt. Mitchell here. I have thirteen transferees in this group. We are in complete control and request permission to enter." I thought, "What security measures! No wonder this joint has such a reputation." When he was satisfied that none of the guards had been taken hostage, the face in the peephole again disappeared. Slowly the large gate opened. We were temporarily blinded by the very bright floodlights from within. Our first point of entrance was simply a large cell directly inside the door. When we were secured in that cubicle, the outer barrier slammed shut. It wasn't until we turned around that we realized that none of the traveling guards had entered the holding cell. They had been replaced by a dozen of the regular cellhouse guards. They observed us carefully. Satisfied we were harmless, one of the men opened another door and said, "You cons, walk over to the benches along the wall. Do not be seated until we have removed your restraints." We were a sorry appearing bunch of slaves as we made our way to the bench. We were the result of the Federal Bureau of Prisons; broken of spirit, nothing more than vegetables. The guards lined up along a wall about ten feet from us. They looked us over intently.

The stare-down was broken up by the appearance of a man dressed in a business suit. He had not been seen when he entered the room through a small door at the far end of the building. All of us watched him strut to the benches. When he spoke, it was obvious he was a man of importance. "Your chains will be removed. When they are taken from the last man, you will be seated. Do not talk unless you are asked a question." The man with a canvas bag stepped forward and started removing the chains and cuffs. In a matter of minutes, all of our chains had been removed. Each of us began rubbing the circulation back into our cramped wrists and legs. As I bent over to massage my right ankle, I noticed a trace of blood where the chafing of the leg irons had cut through the flesh. Damn, but it felt good to be able to raise my hands again. One by one we sat down on the hard wooden bench. The man in the suit postured himself grandly, arms akimbo. In measured tones, he said, "I am Superintendent Swope." I thought, "this man is too pompous to refer to himself as 'Warden Swope.'" I hooked the name Brass Monarch on him, a moniker the cons used in reference to him for years to come; not to his face, of course. He attempted to intimidate us with his demeanor, not by words. What a waste of time trying to intimidate a bunch of seasoned felons.

Warden Swope's arrogance infuriated me. I made up my mind to do eye-battle with this arrogant bastard. Before he could begin talking again, we locked eyes. I refused to drop my gaze and give him the satisfaction of belittling me. The longer I stared at him, the more clouded his face became. After a full two minutes of confrontation, he diverted his eyes and began his 'indoctrination' speech. It was almost verbatim compared with the messages I had heard delivered by other wardens to newcomers. "Now, I want you convicts to listen carefully to what I have to say. And I want you to remember every word. I didn't ask you to come here. You are in this institution because you have demonstrated that you can't get along in the free world or in any other institution. You refuse to recognize that rules and regulations apply to you. You have worked hard to impress other cons and the officials how tough you are. We have developed this prison with the thought in mind that one day you would bless us with your presence. Granted, some of you are tough, but we are tougher. Now that you are here, it is our intention to keep you here until you are transferred or dead. No man has ever been paroled or pardoned from the Rock. Oh yes, there is one other way you can win your freedom from Alcatraz, and that is by serving every day of your sentence. We have no printed book of rules. Follow the examples set by the old-timers and you will get by. If you try to hard-ass us, we have a special unit here where we will salt you away so deep they will have to pump sunshine in to you. There are no newspapers or radios. You will be permitted to order a few magazines. They will be severely censored. Any mention of sex or crime will be deleted. There is no commissary for the inmates on this island. We practice the silence system. You may talk in your place of work or in the yard. If you wish to speak to an officer, keep three paces from him, and keep your conversation brief." He turned on his heel and strode out.

A guard stepped from the line of guards and walked over to us. "Follow me", he snapped as he began walking to an adjoining room. Another grilled door blocked our progress. It was opened from the other side and we found ourselves in a shower room, which was also in a terrible state of disrepair. "Strip off all your clothes and line up along that wall with your backs to us." A medical technician dressed in whites and carrying a medical bag approached. All of us knew we were going to get a 'finger wave' as this person searched our anal cavity for contraband. When he had finished his task, the officer-in-charge called out, "Step under the shower. You have three minutes to finish showering". As soon as he had stopped talking, another guard turned on the water. The water was tepid but welcome. On a counter nearby were thirteen bundles of the prison issue of bluish-grey denims, a pair of heavy brogans, sox and a set of underwear. At the end of the counter were thirteen paper sacks. As soon as the last man had picked up his issue, the lead guard started us up a flight of stairs, bare-assed naked.

When we arrived at the top of the flight again we faced a steel gate. There seemed to be no end of locked gates. The head man called to a guard who was in a heavily fortified walkway fifteen feet above the floor. "Pass the key down." Right away a key was lowered on a string to the hack. Before we were allowed to pass through, the walkway guard pulled the key back upstairs, safely away from our reach. This whole procedure from the McNeil Island pen to the very cellhouse in which we stood was designed to show us how escape-proof Alcatraz was. I was impressed with the double double security. And, as the days passed, I became more aware of this security. All that mattered here was complete and total control. We were herded through yet another door and the view that met my eyes left me stunned.

Here we stood at the end of a hallway which measured about 300' long and 15' wide. On each side were rows of small cubicles. There were three tiers of such cages. Each cell claimed one inhabitant. We were treated to our first view of the famed 'Broadway of Alcatraz', so named by the first cons to arrive here in 1934, twenty years before my arrival.

Bear in mind there was no news from the outside world. The cons were starved for some inkling of what was taking place among the free men. Censorship of our letters was unreasonably cruel. Any mention of persons not in your family, of crimes committed on the streets, of arrests or trials was deleted. And the remaining fragment of your letter would be okayed and sent in. Often as not, entire letters were placed in files and never found their way to the con to whom they were addressed. Naturally, the inmate did not know whether he had received a letter or not. The person who had posted the letter assumed it had been delivered. So when a new chain of fish arrived at Alcatraz, it was a monumental occasion. And there were few chains ever entered this government insane asylum. Nothwithstanding it was after midnight, and the silent system was in effect, the cons were on their feet and at the front of their cells to greet us. Each hoped he would see some buddy of the past in the line of nude and shivering men as they made their way to the fish tanks on the first tier of Broadway. They yelled so many questions at us, we could not make heads nor tails of what they were asking. Later on, I learned that the guards gave up trying to control the barrage of inquiries thrown at us. However, after we were secured in our respective cells, they patrolled the landings and ordered each man to 'dummy up'. It was nearly one o'clock in the morning before the cacophony died down, leaving the cavernous structure with an eerie silence, not unlike a mortuary.

I don't know how I managed the past two days. I was so exhausted and discouraged I could not think clearly. It was sort of like being given the third degree for hours on end. When you can no longer concentrate, you are apt to say anything to the cop performing the 'gentle art of persuasion'. Many a suspect has buried himself for long years in prison by virtue of the fact he 'talked' rather than subject himself to the indignities of further abuse. This fatigue caused my brain to spin as it was doing, this first night on the Rock. I did not even survey my cell. I simply threw my blankets on the latticed steel bed which was covered by a thin worn mat, and flung myself face down. A thousand dreams erupted in my brain. Nothing really mattered at this ebb in my morale. Through the remaining hours of early morning, I was awakened a dozen times by some feather-footed bastard as he walked by my cell and shined a powerful flashlight in my face until I moved.

16

Violence

Never in my life, before nor since, have I undergone a more lengthy and nightmarish night than that first night on Alcatraz. I was beset with unforgettable nightmares of my family, especially of Muriel. At that time, I thought that, as the years passed, I would cease to dream of her, but that was not to be. I do not remember how many years I was subjected to all-night thoughts of my girl. However bad the dreams became each succeeding night, none were so vividly cruel as during my first night on Alcatraz. Eventually, I slept.

I had no idea what time it was when I was startled out of a fitful sleep by the horrendous clanging of a bell. I was befuddled for a full minute. Suddenly the entire cellhouse was flooded by bright lights. I could not bring myself to accept life at this point. Directly across from me on Broadway were rows of three-tiered cells. The men in those cages were bustling around, getting prepared for another lifeless day. A con across from my cage called to me, "Hey, Fish, you had better get your ass in gear. The guard will be coming by to take count and you are supposed to be standing in the front of your cell. And stay in that position until the 'all clear' bell sounds." He had no more finished giving me this bit of advice than a skinny cellhouse guard passed my den. He was counting aloud. I could hear other guards on the upper tiers making their count. Years later Alvin 'Creepy' Karpis, chief lieutenant of the Ma Barker gang, told me that Al Capone confided in him why he was sure none of his Chicago gangsters could 'deliver' him from the clutches of Alcatraz. It was because of the count system. He brought to Creepy's attention the fact that in every twenty-four hour day, the officials counted the 'head' of every inmate.

At night, if the inmate appeared to be sleeping, the guard would force him to move so there would be no opportunity to plant a dummy. These official counts took place every half-hour. Many times throughout the day, unofficial counts were made. Scarface estimated that each con was counted more than fifty times daily. Capone realized that if a man did escape from his cell or shop, he would not have time to even get to the water before the guards would tag his ass with a load of buckshot. In about five minutes the all-clear bell rang. After the second bell had rung, the men across the galley from me turned, almost as one, and began dressing and making up their bunks. I followed suit. As soon as I was finished I walked to my sink and began filling it with water. No matter how long I held the button down, the water remained icy cold. It dawned on me that there was no hot water.

Believe me, I was fully awake after I had washed my hands and face. For the remaining seven years I never washed in hot water.

The fourth time the bell rang, it indicated that it was time to go to the mess hall. I watched as the guards opened one tier of cells at a time. In each instance, the men would leave their quarters and face toward the mess hall which was located on the west end of the block. They marched sullenly toward the dining room. As each tier was emptied of men, another would be opened. I could tell by the banging of steel on steel that they were releasing men in the other areas. In about ten minutes a silence settled in the main cellhouse. By listening carefully I could hear the sound of metal trays being taken from the cart and silverware being dropped on the tables. It was amazing how different sounds conveyed exactly what was taking place. Finally, it was the fish tank tier's time to eat. As our doors opened, each of us stepped out on the landing. As though we had been trained, we made a left face and began our trek to the mess hall.

Standing in the center of the wide kitchen doorway was a very fat and squat keeper. We were divided into two lines, each passing on opposite sides of the warder. All eyes, of the guards and cons alike, were on us. It was a big day for the old-time cons, many of whom had been pent up for decades, and their only break in the debilitating monotony came when a 'chain' arrived. If they were fortunate enough to recognize a former acquaintance, they would let out a howl of delight, as though they were happy to have someone with whom to share their misery. I was startled when I heard one of the men already seated call out, "Welcome to the Rock, Nate." It was JB, a young man who had robbed the same bank which had been my downfall. Before I was seated, there were a half a dozen cons calling out my name. There were steam tables at the front of the dining hall. Each was manned by a con. The inevitable guard stood behind the servers to make certain that we were not given more than the allotted amount.

I finished eating before the rest of my companions, so I began to case my surroundings. On each of the pillars that support the ceiling was a rectangular box. From the bottom of the box there appeared to be a half of a large light bulb protruding. A dark visaged prisoner across from me at my table saw me looking at the pillars. He muttered, "Those are gas containers, Fish. They can be remotely exploded by that f—king dog face in the cage above the door." I looked to the front where he had indicated and saw a gun cage protected by bars and steel meshing. A guard was seated on a stool, eyeballing the scene, ever alert for a disturbance. During my time on the Rock, there was never a full-fledged riot in the mess hall. The gas bulbs were never exploded. If there had been, I wonder what would have happened to the guards who were locked up in the mess area with a hundred or so inmates. No evidence of gas masks was visible for the guards to use. As sure as hell, if a riot had taken place, the few guards would have been at the tender mercies of the many cons. I dread to think of what a slaughter would have taken place. From the safety of the gun cages, many cons could have been shot to death, but not before they had butchered some of their keepers.

My mind whipped back to reality when the jailors started moving the men out one table at a time. Before any inmate was allowed to leave, the guard had to account for every spoon and fork on each table. One by one the tables were vacated and the men marched in orderly fashion back to their cells. As soon as the Fish had entered their cells, the doors slammed shut. By this time, I had wished that the cells and doors were made of rubber so they could be closed without that din of steel on steel.

The thirty day quarantine imposed on us was a veritable hell. While 'Time In The Fish Bowl' is a procedure in all penal institutions for new men, Alcatraz deliberately made this period of time particularly odious through the deprivation of books, correspondence with the loved ones, lack of recreation; a total deadlock atmosphere. Obviously the whole scheme was to completely demoralize each man entering 'Hoover's Heaven', so named after the former director of the FBI, J. Edgar Hoover. He was the most powerful police official in the U.S., a man hated by many FBI agents whom I later met, and feared by senators and congressmen on whom he had amassed damaging evidence of immoral conduct. Try as I did, I could not understand what purpose could be served by this isolation treatment. A few years later, a guard whom I had learned to respect told me, "Nate, when I first came here and went through the indoctrination period, I was told that it is better to crush a new man in the very beginning. The Bureau of Prisons referred to this as the 'breaking in period'. This attitude is typical of most government penal procedures. The reasons for the perpetuation of such barbaric treatment has been lost and forgotten for many years. There was one tenet that applied to all who went to work here and that was: 'Don't change nuthin or you'll confuse everybody and everything'.

Each hour became as a day and each day as a month, and so on. The thirty-day period became interminably long. I found myself going through long hours of fantasizing. I'd find myself lapsing into states of deep day-dreaming. If I kept this up, I knew I would soon become stir-crazy. I was terrorized by such a prospect. I decided to occupy my mind by counting the rivets on the steel plating of my cell, spanning my hand and attempting to measure the exact width and length of my cage in inches. I would pace my quarters by the hour and see how many times I could walk back and forth in my cell while holding my breath. I had a hundred ploys I would use to keep from going off my rocker. Many years before I was incarcerated, imprisoned men had practiced the same mental gymnastics in an effort to maintain their sanity. A black man across from my cell seemed to know what I was going through. One evening he called across Broadway and told me, "Listen, Fish, one piece of reading they will give you is a Bible. Ask for one, and then read it night and day. I'm not suggesting you go off your cookie by getting religion. Just read it over and over again. It'll confuse hell out of you, but at least you will have your mind occupied. Otherwise, you'll wind up in the booby hatch one egg short of a dozen." To this day, I believe that was the best bit of advice I ever received from another con. The guard, in response to my request, brought me 'Mr. Gideon's Balm'. Before my quarantine had passed, I must have read most of the good book. The good I derived from the Bible stood by and comforted me many times in the future. It would be correct to say that the Good Book in all probability saved me from becoming a blithering idiot. I found comfort in hundreds of passages. I quit pacing my cell and fantasizing. The days went by more rapidly, more serenely.

Each of us had made requests to shave and to write letters home. For about a week all requests were ignored, a part of the breaking down period I presumed. On the first Sunday in the Fish tanks, a guard came by and told us we would be permitted to write a letter to an approved member of the family only. He quickly announced that correspondence with our family was a privilege, not a right. I later learned that either he was ignorant or a liar. I knew the courts had ruled years ago that no inmate could be denied the right to communicate with his immediate family. About an hour after the hack's announcement, he came by and gave each of us one sheet of paper and the stub of a pencil. I complained that the pencil was so short that it was almost impossible to write a legible letter. He bristled and shouted, "You will not be given a longer one. We are not dumb enough to give you anything you can use as a weapon." I was dumbfounded by his 'reasoning'. "Furthermore", he continued, "you will be allowed to use only one side of the single sheet."

I had so much to say, and could not hope to express myself in so limited space. I wanted to write so badly that I knew better than to spout off for fear I would be denied even the single sheet. I wondered what my mother thought when she got that scribbled mess. When we were finished with our letters, we were told to fold them and place them in the bars where the night guard would pick them up and deliver them to the mail censor the following morning. How long the censor kept them, I will never know. I had to guess it was four or five days because it would often be ten days before I got a response. It wasn't long before I learned that the mail room would arbitrarily keep letters for a week before forwarding them. If the guard who censored them felt they contained a hidden meaning, he would simply toss them in the waste basket. In the meantime, the prisoner would wonder why his family never responded. You would not have to be an Einstein to figure what this kind of treatment did to the minds of the already tense and disturbed inmates. The man in the tank next to mine had been on the Rock before, and he told me that when he was there the last time it was the practice of the officials to rewrite the outgoing letters on plain brown wrapping paper, and to change the wording along with deleting words or expressions he did not understand. Later, the notorious Ma Barker gang leader, Alvin 'Creepy' Karpis confirmed the story. Creepy, who had a hell of a sense of humor added, "Hell, Nate, if the guy who censored the letters substituted words for those he did not understand, we would be in a hell of a mess, because Baker's (the censor at that time) education leaves much to be desired."

On the days we were permitted to shave, we soon learned to bear up under the grim ordeal. The guard would issue the gear which consisted of a razor with a lock-in blade and a piece of soap. Often the blade would be one which had been used by two or three men before. Imagine raking off a four-day stubble of beard under such conditions, and especially when we performed the task using cold water.

In the early morning of our last day in the Fish tanks, we were called out and instructed to follow a jailor to A Block, an old cellhouse behind Broadway. This particular block contained the oldest cells on the Island. It was a unit that had been used probably 50 years before the federal government opened Alcatraz as a bad men's pokey. Near the front of the block, a wall had been knocked out between two units, creating a room about nine feet wide and ten feet long. There was an old desk along one wall. In front of the desk were two old straight-back chairs. Along a wall in front of this room were three benches on which we were instructed to sit. None of us knew what we were in for. However, inasmuch as we had been on the Fish row for 29 days, we assumed that we were going to be assigned to regular population, which was tantamount to the next thing to freedom. After we had been sitting there for thirty minutes in absolute silence, five more guards were ushered into the area. They placed themselves in strategic positions, one at each end of the sitting arrangement and three stood facing us in front of the bench. They took a domineering stance, legs spread about two feet apart with their hands behind them. I judged it was a well-rehearsed pose designed to send us a message of readiness.

Ten or fifteen minutes later, the front door to the cellhouse opened and in walked a man of obvious importance in the echelon of personnel. He was a well-built person of about fifty years of age. He walked over to where we were sitting and came right to the point. "Men, I am Associate Warden Latimer. I did not come here to answer questions or to be interrupted in any manner. I am going to assign each of you to work detail. This will be a temporary place of labor for you. During this period we will be carefully monitoring your attitude and work habits. After a month in this shop, you may want to make a request to a permanent work place. At this time, I am moving you to regular population and a unit in which you will serve your sentence. Line up behind the lead officer and he will take you to your permanent quarters. Dismissed!"

When the guard and I reached the second landing on B Block, he called to another guard who was manning the control lever. "Open B256. Close it as soon as inmate Williams steps inside." Seconds later the very heavy barred door slammed behind me. For a full minute I stood in the center of my new home and gazed blankly around. A hundred mixed emotions raced through my mind. I wanted to scream out, smash my fist into the wall and tear up everything in my quarters. Again, stark reality hit me between the eyes. In this dirty cage I was to remain for twenty five years. To hell with it I decided, I'll take my life at the first opportunity. How? What were my options? Dive over the tier as others had done? Make a rope of my blankets? Why not attack a guard in full view of one of the many armed guards in the various gun cages which dotted the entire joint? Just anything to avoid this horrible torture chamber. I wanted to sit on my bunk and weep but I had to remember that tough Alcatraz cons never cried. I was simply staring at the wall of my cell when my thoughts were interrupted by a guard standing in front of my 'home'. He was putting a piece of cardboard about 3" X 4" in a slot which was attached to the bars of the door. After he had finished, he said, "Williams, get your bed made up and your possessions in their place." It wasn't until I started to obey his order that I took an inventory of my surroundings. My area of freedom was five by seven feet. It had not been painted for years. The predominate color when I occupied it was a vomit yellow. The bunk was a metal frame with slats of steel which were interwoven to form a platform for the 'mattress', which was a two inch pad filled with cotton batting. There were no sheets, nor did I have a pillow. It was then that I noticed a brown paper bag on the single wooden shelf in the rear of my cell. I dumped the contents on my bed. They consisted of a cardboard container of gritty tooth powder, a toothbrush, a piece of polished steel 3" X 4" which served as a mirror, a coat and, of course, the inevitable Bible. The Bible was not kept for reading purposes. I learned that its pages, being thin, were torn out to make cigarette papers. Each inmate was furnished a bag of roll-your-owns, and a book of paper matches. It was decided at this time to issue each inmate a safety razor and two blades. We were ordered to keep both blades on the shelf in full sight at all times. As the guard said when he issued my blades, "If both blades are not on the shelf, openly displayed, we will have your ass before the Kangaroo court." Later that day, I began wondering what was on the piece of cardboard the guard had put on the front of my cell. I took the mirror off my shelf and held it through the bars at an angle where I could examine it. It read:

Nathan G. Williams

1103 AZ

B256

I reflected on my new address, B256. It was not a lengthy one, so there would be no difficulty memorizing it. I had to remember, though, that that house number had to appear on all my letters and other communications. It was my home now and I had to make the best of it. I learned that Alcatraz boasted its own Post Office and its own United States Post Office Cancellation Stamp. In fact, an envelope with the Alcatraz cancellation stamp has now become a much sought-after collectors item. All letters mailed from the Rock contained a stark red stamp on the envelope that fairly screamed, 'ALCATRAZ'! In later years, I was told by members of my family that my parents were terribly humiliated to have the letters sent to their house. Surely the postman saw the return address and wondered who would be writing such nice people as Blanche and Merritt Williams from the notorious Alcatraz. Until I was released, I had never seen the Alcatraz stamp. When my brother showed me one of his envelopes, I was shocked by the sight of it. Why, I asked myself, would the government insist on embarrassing the families of the prisoners? The Federal Bureau of Prisons is that way; cold and calculatingly evil.

After two days pacing up and down in my cell, I began to wonder why I had not been assigned to a work detail. Anything to get out of the deadly confinement. I toyed with the idea of approaching a guard and asking him if he knew when I would be permitted to go to work. Immediately I put that thought out of mind for two reasons; both very valid. No self-respecting convict would want to be seen conversing with a guard, and I was unsure of the response I would get. So, I just continued to pace; three steps forward, three back. The only thing I had to read was my Bible, and I was damn tired of reading of repetitious 'begetting'. It wouldn't have been so bad if only I could have done some of the begetting. There were five verses in Luke that intrigued me. They were verses 39 through 43 in which Christ told the thief on the cross that he would be in paradise with the Creator in later years. I enjoyed reminding Christians who were too 'pure' that Christ personally assured a thief he was going to heaven. Mind you, not a lawyer, judge or doctor, but a common thief.

One day as I was doing my reading of these verses I saw a shadow at the front of my cage. I glanced up, and there was a man dressed in prison blues. He was carrying a board loaded with books. The makeshift shelf was supported by a strap across his shoulders. He was a very handsome fellow of obvious Indian descent. His large brown eyes accentuated his high cheekbones. I judged him to be about 5' 10", weighing about 170 pounds, well-knit and solidly built. He looked at my name on the door tag and said, "Hi, I am Clarence Carnes, known in here as the Choctaw Kid. I deliver books twice weekly from the library. When I pick them up, I take requests for other selections." His voice was soft and his speech was well-articulated. I immediately liked his pleasant and soothing manner. He continued, "You don't have much of a selection from which to choose. Most of the books are plain shit. I'll drop a couple off so you'll have something to occupy your mind until I get around again." If I live to be a hundred years of age, I'll never forget the titles of those books; <u>Little Women</u> by Louisa May Alcott, and Gene Straton Porter's <u>Keeper of the Bees</u>. They were boring and innocuous. If it wasn't that I was starved for something to do, I would have tossed them over the tier. Just imagine how embarrassed I would have been if some of my old gangster friends had caught me reading such books as these. It wasn't long before I learned that the entire library consisted of the most unreadable material ever printed. The guards censored all the material which was sent from other joints. If there was one word about crime or sex, they were burned. Their reasoning? They did not want to corrupt the inmates' morals. As the Choctaw Kid ambled off, he said, "If you want any messages sent to another con, Nate, just slip them to me when I come around again. Some of the boys who knew you on the outside said to tell you hello and that they would see you in the rec yard. I've got to move on. If a jailer sees me standing in front of a cage more than a minute, he'll press the alarm button." He disappeared as silently as he had appeared. Clarence Carnes and I became friends from that day on. And believe me, you don't make friends easily with these paranoid cons. It often proves fatal to do so.

Years later I learned about the tragic history surrounding Carnes' life. When he was just a youngster, he and a friend robbed a service station attendant. During the robbery, his fifteen year-old companion killed the operator. They were captured and sentenced to ninety-nine years in the Oklahoma State Prison. The Indian did not take lightly to spending his life in a cell. He and an accomplice decided to escape. In the attempt, they attacked and severely wounded a guard. During their getaway, they kidnapped a farmer and his wife and took them across the state line. Because they had crossed a state line with their hostages, the crime became a federal offense. They were captured, tried, found guilty and each given another ninety-nine year sentence in the federal penitentiary at Leavenworth, Kansas. At that joint, the Choctaw Kid became a disciplinary problem and was transferred to Alcatraz. At eighteen, he was the youngest inmate ever to be sent to The Rock. He then became a number -714AZ- and ceased to be a human being. He had not been there long before he was duped by wise old cons into becoming involved in an escape attempt.

"Dutch Joe" Cretzer, Sam Shockley, Miran Edgar Thompson, Marvin Franklin Hubbard and Bernard Paul Coy were, beyond a doubt, the most homicidal of all the inmates in Alcatraz. I had not met any of the above men personally, with the exception of Cretzer, with whom I had participated in three bank robberies in Seattle. His cousin, Arnie, had accompanied us on the jobs. Arnie had warned me that Cretzer 'had a screw loose' and was more interested in killing than he was in actually making a withdrawal. Both of us wanted to avoid, at all costs, a shoot-out. We were interested in a speedy and uninterrupted separation of the loot from the bank. Of paramount interest to Arnie and me was not to kill, and at the same time to preserve our own lives, a delicate procedure that can only be accomplished by keeping a cool head. For some reason, Arnie was reluctant to part company with his cousin. His decision proved to be a fatal one. The two of them were caught committing other crimes and were sentenced to prison.

Cretzer and Arnie were securely ensconced on Alcatraz when the Choctaw Kid arrived. Months earlier, Cretzer and his buddies had begun a bizarre and dangerous plan to take over a section of the prison, relieve some of the guards of their firearms and take hostages with which to barter for their ticket to the outside world. For some reason, they took a liking to Carnes, and talked him into joining them in their ill-fated scheme. Many years later, Carnes said he accepted their invitation to the suicidal mission because he was young and fool- hardy.

Thirty years later, Carnes and I, both showing our age, were dining at Joe Di Maggio's on Fishermen's Wharf in San Francisco. We were in a position to view our old home sitting forlornly in the Bay. Naturally, our conversation drifted to events that had taken place during our time on the island. Carnes was in the city in preparation for a Hollywood documentation of men and events which had occurred during his incarceration. "Nate," he reminisced, "it is hard for me to realize that here and now you and I, two over-the-hill thugs, ex-guests of good old J. Edgar Hoover, are enjoying a leisurely dinner in a luxurious restaurant and talking about the sordid and horrible experiences we shared out there". I waited for him to continue because I felt he had some things he wanted to get off his chest. "You know, I am fully aware that the moguls in Hollywood are going to make much wampum on this film. And when they are done with me, those bastards will get rid of me on the first plane back to Oklahoma. And you know, I'll be glad to be out of such an artificial environment." For a long time Carnes and I picked at our salmon dinner, sipped whiskey and tried to put our lives into a truly genuine perspective. I'm certain he was discouraged and wanted to give up life, though he never stated this. "Nate, do you feel in the mood to listen to a segment of my life which I'm sure was the beginning of the end?"

I really wanted to hear what he had to say but was afraid if I vocalized my wishes he might back away. That was a part of Clarence's make-up. It would be safe for me to say that he was 'oiled up' enough to open up, and he did.

"I was barely eighteen when they slammed me in a cell on that bastille in the Bay. I was just like any other kid who truly thought dangerous criminals were a glamorous bunch of he-men. You can imagine how pleased I was to be invited to be a part of such a notorious group of misfits. The fact that I could become involved in a scheme to take over Alcatraz gave me great pleasure. I had nothing to do with the actual preparation. Coy was cunning enough to make me feel I was a major member of his gang. The truth of the matter is, they used me as library runner to deliver coded messages to other participants in separate cellhouses. One time I took one of the messages to my cell and tried to decipher it. It appeared there was a meaningless paragraph widely spaced. I wondered just what the hell all this meant. A long time later I learned that they wrote sentences in the spaces. Instead of using ink, they used urine. When the urine would dry there was no indication anything was there. But if you held a match under the paper a very legible writing would appear. I continued to dream that in years to come I would be linked with this group that had taken over the impregnable Rock and had made an ass-hole of J. Edgar Hoover and the Federal Bureau of Prisons. Before the actual break took place, I approached the apparent leader, Cretzer, and told him I was having second thoughts. He backed me into a corner, put a knife to the pit of my stomach and coldly said, 'Carnes, you know too fucking much. You can back out if you want, but if you try, they'll find your RED-SKINNED ass behind a mangle in the laundry.' You have no idea, Nate, how many times I listened to these sickies try to impress other gullible cons just how tough they were. You know as well as I do what happened after that. When it became apparent we weren't going to succeed in our venture, I had an opportunity to evaluate how crazy Cretzer and Shockley were. Cretzer approached the cell in which the hostage guards were huddled and told them, 'you bastards are dead'. This insane son- of-a-bitch rested the 45 automatic on the cell bars and methodically began his mission of mass slaughter. I could hear the slugs rip into the helpless men. During this carnage, Crazy Sam Shockley was jumping up and down behind Cretzer screaming, 'let me shoot some of them'. When the 45 was emptied, Cretzer turned to me, shoved a homemade gut- cutter in my hand and said, 'Kid, go in the cell and finish off any living man'. I took the weapon, walked into the cell and knelt down among the wounded and bleeding guards. To this day I thank God that Cretzer and the others left the cell area to set up a defense against the onslaught expected from army, marines, navy and prison personnel who had been called in. I took this opportunity to whisper to the cringing hostages, 'Play dead. I'm not going to hurt you'. One of the guards, Mail Censor Baker, squeezed my hand in appreciation." As this presumably stoic Indian relayed the intimate details to me, tears were welling in his eyes.

Thirty-four years after I had met Carnes in front of my cell, B256, he died under conditions that most convicts dread, that of leaving this world while confined in a cage, alone. The newspaper clipping I read simply head-lined, "THE CHOCTAW KID DEAD IN PRISON." No mention of a eulogy nor memorial. No friends to mourn his passing. Twelve words given to the press assured his leaving would go unnoticed. They were issued by his probation lackey: 'Carnes could not adapt to a life in society and its laws.'

I feel compelled to comment further. When Carnes was only fifteen years of age, he was in a warehouse (prison) sentenced to an interminably long term, life plus 99 years. He remained in endurance while under a quarter of a century of horrendously inhumane treatment at the hands of the Federal Bureau of Prisons. The question foremost in my mind is: After being caged for all of his formative years, how could he be expected to 'adapt' to the foreign life in our confused society?

Late in the afternoon of the third day out of the Fish Tanks, a guard stopped by my cell. He was carrying a slip of paper which he read and re-read to himself at least three times before he looked up to be certain the mug shot on the paper matched the mug of the con in B256. Satisfied we were one and the same, he mumbled, "Williams, you have been assigned to work in the prison laundry. Right after breakfast in the morning, when they call 'work detail', you will proceed to the rec yard. Line up along the yellow line and wait until the laundry foreman orders you to march. While you are waiting for that order, you are to keep your mouth shut. Do you have any questions?" Before I could formulate a response, he moved on and repeated the same words to the fish in the cage next to mine.

The message the guard delivered was like a breath of fresh air. I realized that an assignment to the laundry area was not much in the form of freedom, but anything was better than the suffocating confinement of my dismal cubicle. The brief time I had been on Alcatraz had reduced me to an animal who sought just a little more space in which to run. Others had told me that the walk to the laundry area was one block. To me that was like a walk in the woods. For the past five or six weeks, I had walked no more than 100 feet.

As I stretched out on my bunk that night, sleep was difficult to capture. I kept thinking how great it would be to see new faces, structures and a view of the bay. It bothered me to think about what would take place in my psyche ten years from now if such a brief stint of confinement had me so disoriented at this early point of my sentence. It would be pleasant to be able to talk with others in the shop if talking were permissible. Surely I would know some of the laundry workers from other prisons where I had been incarcerated.

The next morning in my cell, the familiar clanging loud bell awakened me rudely. I always felt that the bell had the power to physically yank me from my steel-latticed bunk. The ablutions following, performed in freezing water, had a way of making you face reality; in this case, a numbing reality. At breakfast I caught the eyes of other fish who had been assigned. While we could not talk, a flickering smile delivered the desired message. They, too, were happy for the same reason. However, each of us was apprehensive at the prospect of confronting hostile cons. I say 'hostile' because we are a funny breed of cat. When inmates have worked in a particular shop for years, they seem to develop a sort of "don't tread on my property" attitude, and they damn well resent having strangers trespass. We knew they would be trying to intimidate us by glaring in our direction. It was the better part of wisdom to let them stare us down. If we had responded to their glowering, it would have been tantamount to challenging them to a fight. If you weren't challenged overtly, you would be convinced in your own mind there was a strong possibility that you would be attacked as soon as your back was turned. Cons are always tense, tight and unreasonable. This is more apparent in the men who have been confined in an environment of the strictest nature. They harbor an endless litany of 'I hates' on which to vent their spleen.

I was fearful and made up my mind to tread carefully, work at my detail, keep my mouth shut and my eyes on inanimate objects. Gradually, you will be accepted. When you are accepted, then it automatically gives you the privilege to view the next batch of fish with the same stupid attitude. I learned that prison itself would not be so unbearable if you did not have to serve your time with so many sickies.

Somewhere along the line, the goons who ran Alcatraz made it a practice for all newly arrived inmates to be assigned to the laundry. The purpose of this, I presume, was to give the guards an opportunity to look you over to determine what particular type of risk you might be. After a month or two in this shop, you could put in a request to the captain for a different shop in which to work. On the Rock there were only three choices; the tailor shop, the glove factory and the furniture factory. Each of these shops came under the jurisdiction of the Federal Bureau of Prison Industries. Slave wages were paid. Some paid by the hour, others by piece work. During my stint of about two months in the laundry, I operated the mangle.

The actual working conditions were dull and monotonous. The debilitating routine was interrupted by fights which took place almost on a daily basis. Fights among the inmates on The Rock were not the average types of confrontations. These men fought to kill as a matter of self-defense. The reasoning behind this attitude was, no matter if you were to win in a contest of strength or sheer rough and tumble fighting, the odds were great that the loser would wait for an opportunity to find a weapon and kill the winner. No matter how big or how rugged a man might be, he is nothing to be feared when his head is caved in by a hammer. In some instances, a man challenged to a fight would back down because he knew there was a good possibility he would wind up in the prison morgue.

After two months in the laundry, I asked the captain for a transfer to the tailor shop. He called me out and asked why I chose that particular industry. Among his questions were: Do you know anyone in that section? Do you think you might find a better place from which to escape? Are you a punk or do you have a punk working in that place? By the time he was through with his dumb questions, I was fit to be tied. It was at this juncture I realized that guards who have spent many years dealing with the prisoners become as stir-crazy as their wards.

After a couple of weeks, I was transferred to the Tailor shop. The freedom of movement was a pleasure. I could talk to the other prisoners, about thirty of them. For the next seventy-two months, I made trousers for the army, navy and forest service. I was paid fifteen cents an hour. Then my salary was boosted to about twenty cents an hour when I was put on piece work.

After a few months of this type of work, I became bored and terribly discouraged. On top of the conditions imposed by an insensate system, there was always the twenty-four hour longing for my family, particularly my daughter. When I was in McNeil Island, awaiting transfer to this feces pit of creation, I at least had a photo of her. When we reached Alcatraz, I was allowed to have two pictures in my cell. The bastards who turned the keys here made the decision which two I could keep. I was brokenhearted to find that my snap shot of Muriel was not one of the two. I made repeated requests to Warden Swope that I trade one of the pictures for one of my youngster. There was never a response to my pleadings. It was during this time that I made up my mind to 'forget' that I ever had a child. It was mandatory that I do this or I am certain I would have gone crazy. Try as I did, I could not rid my thoughts of her. Tough men, especially on the Rock, never wept. They went about their daily routine displaying a dark visage and a warped mind.

There were few distractions in our routine. An occasional fight, oddly enough, was an acceptable form of welcome relief. It became apparent that the only thing many of us had in common was a mutual hatred for our fellow man.

The Rock was loaded with homicidal maniacs, schizophrenics and para-noid cons. Further incarceration under such inhuman conditions aggra-vated these symptoms. The slightest reason would trigger some of them into acts of unreasonable violence against whomever might be in their way. In order to impress the mainline population with the fact that they feared nothing, it was not uncommon for them to secure some type of weapon with which to assault anyone near them. They realized that there would be a retaliation unless they permanently injured their victim. As a result, I witnessed three killings. To me it was significant to note that they invariably struck down individuals generally disliked by the others. In this way, they minimized the possibility of a revenge attack from the victim's friends.

I recall one terribly bizarre incident in the maiming of an innocuous convict. There was a Japanese fellow who had been convicted of wartime atrocities against American prisoners of war in Japan. His name was Ikeda. Just before the Pearl Harbor incident, Ikeda visited his native country. He was in Japan when Pearl Harbor was bombed. Immediately he was inducted into the Japanese army. Eventually he became a guard in one of their prisoner-of-war camps and was in charge of hundreds of American POW's. During his reign, he brutalized a number of his wards. He was referred to as MeatBall. Five or six years after the war, one of the former POW's was shopping in a department store in Los Angeles, and lo and behold, who waited on him? None other than Meatball. Unable to contain himself, he dived over the counter and tried to strangle the hated prison commander who had abused so many of his countrymen. Three or four men dragged him from the unconscious body of Meatball and held him until the police arrived. After he had been lodged in the county jail and charged with aggravated assault and battery, he tried to tell the jailers the reason he jumped Ikeda. None would listen to him. The following day, his brother came to visit him and learned what had precipitated the fight. Immediately his brother went to an army barracks and got an audience with the Provost Marshall. Luckily, the Colonel believed him and immediately went to the county jail to interview the accused man. He was impressed with the story that unfolded. That afternoon he went to the department store and conferred with the store's security personnel. Together they went to the section where Ikeda was assigned. Ikeda's supervisor said that the employee was so upset by the unwarranted attack that he asked for a few days off. The city police and the M.P. went to Ikeda's residence, and when he responded to their knock and saw who they were, he slammed the door in their faces. Apparently he realized escape was futile so he re-opened the door. After a few minutes of questioning, he confessed that he was truly the infamous Meatball. The feds tried and convicted Meatball and he was sentenced to death. He spent about seven years on death row in California's San Quentin prison. After many appeals, his death sentence was commuted to life by President Eisenhower. Later he was transferred to Alcatraz where it was hoped he would stay until he died naturally or by the knife of some enraged convict.

A young con by the name of Coe, who wanted to gain a reputation, made up his mind to slay Ikeda. He knew that it would be a popular killing. Ikeda had heard from the grapevine that he was marked for death, so he stayed in his cell that day. Coe was infuriated that his opportunity had escaped him. Those who knew what was going on watched Coe as he raged in the yard, pacing back and forth, frustrated, angry and dangerous. As fate would have it, a harmless and inoffensive con who was alone and friendless crossed in front of the volatile Coe. The victim was known as Dog. I was dismayed by the fact that Dog was walking in my direction and Coe was approaching from an angle. When their paths intersected, Coe pulled the blade from under his coat and stabbed Dog in the mouth. The victim fell to the ground as Coe threw his knife down. He yelled out, "The bastard's gone to meet his Maker." But Dog struggled to his feet and ran toward a guard for protection. Coe picked up the knife and chased the wounded man who was trying to hide behind a guard. The guard was afraid he was going to be knifed, so he stepped aside. Coe moved forward and drove the blade deep into Dog's chest. By this time, other guards rushed forward and grabbed Coe. Dog was rushed to the hospital. Miraculously he lived, but was transferred to another federal prison right away. This as one of many instances in which an unsuspecting and defenseless man was mutilated or slain.

Years later, Ikeda was paroled to Japan. The terms of his parole precluded his ever returning to the U.S. I attempted to contact him in order to get his story about the years he spent on Alcatraz. I wanted him to explain his feelings while waiting for some inmate to kill him. I was successful in tracing Ikeda to Toyko in 1987. I wrote him, identified myself and explained that I was writing a book. Understandably, my letters were never answered. During this search, however, I did run across one of his fellow countrymen who acted as an interpreter throughout the trial. He remembered 'Meatball' and all the details of the crime. He confided in me that he expected Ikeda to be murdered during his incarceration.

The unreasonably severe discipline created most of the problems. The guards, wanting to avoid any hazardous confrontation involving fighting inmates for fear of danger to their persons, would try to ignore such incidents. As in the case of the cons, it was smart to be elsewhere. I can only recall one instance other than the famous mutiny of 1946, which occurred before I got there, in which a guard was slain. In 1938, in an attempt to escape, three inmates left their work in one of the shops and made their way to the third floor of the structure. At that particular time, a guard by the name of Cline met them unexpectedly. The inmates proceeded to beat him to death with a claw hammer. They ascended to the roof of the building where they foolishly attacked a tower guard hoping to take his weapons. Using the hammer with which they had killed Cline, they beat at the bullet proof glass of the cage. From his position in the tower, the guard, named Stites, opened fire on the three desperados. One 45 slug ripped through the brain of one inmate. Another caught bullets in the shoulder and the chest. The impact of the 45 slug knocked him off the roof where he became entangled in barbed wire which had been strung along the roof for just this type of eventuality. The other con surrendered. Whitey, the con who had been shot through the shoulder and chest, told me years later that he felt no pain from the bullets as they ripped through his body. He vaguely remembered rolling off the roof and being caught in the barbed wire. "Frankly, Nate, I thought I was dying. In fact, everything became so peaceful I enjoyed the idea of leaving it all behind. Not only was I serving a life sentence in the beginning, but now, if I lived, I'd be facing the gas chamber for beating Cline's brains out. As I looked at the cement walkway fifty feet below me, I could see my blood dripping on it. I was surprised when I came to in the hospital, surprised and disappointed. Death would have been so sweet."

One morning an argument erupted at my table in the mess hall. I was prepared to jump up and step back because I wanted to be away from the knifing that I felt certain was going to take place. As quickly as the argument started, it quieted down. The other six men at the table quit eating. They were prepared for anything violent. But both the antagonists went on eating. Suddenly, one of the fellows took his cup of boiling hot coffee and dashed it into the face of his foe. The scalded inmate screamed, covered his face, leaped from his seat and stumbled blindly across the mess hall floor. By this time, four or five guards ran toward him. Before they could protect him from further harm, the attacker ran to the blinded fellow and drove a knife into his back. By this time, all hell broke loose. The cons left their tables and sought cover because they were certain the outside guards would open fire. The inside guards jumped the knife wielder and wrestled him to the floor. The remaining milling men were hustled back to their cells. The wounded con was rushed to the hospital, the other one to the hole.

The deadly monotony of the severe routine and the lack of discipline among the guards took its toll in varied ways. Of all the penitentiaries under the control of the Federal Bureau of Prisons, Alcatraz recorded the highest rate of insanity and suicide. Those hapless men were shipped off to the government's insane asylum at Springfield, Missouri.

Others, realizing the futility of their actions, made senseless runs at the fence. In one case, an inmate named Persful flipped his cookie and chopped off the fingers of his left hand. A half dozen others, hoping to attract attention and sympathy, slashed their Achilles tendons. Doctors from the mainland simply patched them up and tossed them in solitary. All they gained by their self-mutilation was the disdain of the inmate population, and the fact that they were crippled to some extent for the rest of their lives. Their time ran on uninterruptedly.

Author at 17, during escape,
hiding in hills; 1932.

Author, age 11, beginning of criminal
career; 1926.

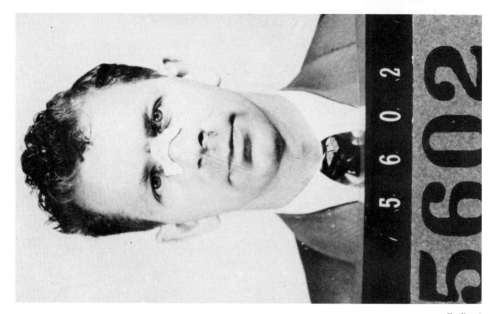

Williams, High School
Graduation; 1932.

Author pictured with broken
nose after fight with police
during escape attempt; 1938.

Author at President Reagan's inaugural ball. A far cry from an Alcatraz cell.

Father and daughter at Muriel's graduation as an RN; 1987.

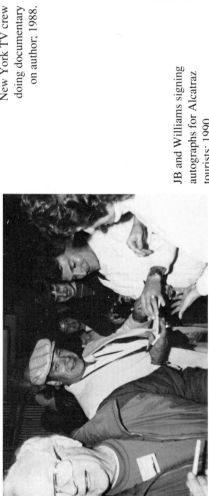

New York TV crew doing documentary on author; 1988.

Author being interviewed for TV by San Francisco TV cameramen; 1988.

JB and Williams signing autographs for Alcatraz tourists; 1990.

Author with Doctor Thomas Gaddis who wrote "Bird Man of Alcatraz"

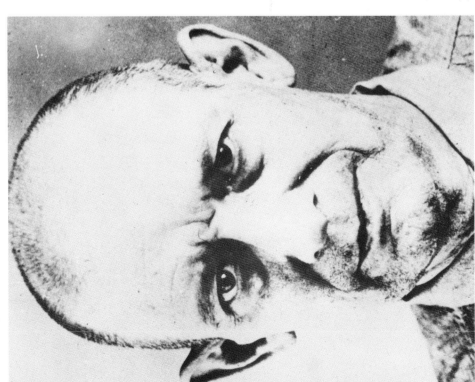

Robert Stroud, Bird Man of Alcatraz

Family picture at wedding; daughter Muriel, Glenn, Lorna, sons, Scott and Don and daughter Natalie.

Author and wife at reception in Governor John Spellman's mansion to receive Governor's Distinguished Volunteer award. State of Washington; 1983.

LIVINGSTON ENTERPRISE

COMPLETE
ASSOCIATED PRESS
SERVICE

LIVINGSTON, MONTANA, FRIDAY MORNING, FEBRUARY 4, 1938.   PRICE FIVE CENTS

Kidnaped by Pseudo Officer

Kidnaps Local Young Man Thursday

Paul Gregory, kidnaper of Marvin Gjerde, 19-year-old Livingston young man, Thursday, appears as an authentic United States army officer in the above picture, found in his room in a local hotel by officers. Gregory is in the county jail facing, in addition to kidnaping, charges of impersonating U.S. army and federal bureau of investigation officers. He was caught at Butte after kidnaping Gjerde while fleeing from local authorities.

MARVIN GJERDE FORCED AT GUN-POINT TO TAKE FAKE G-MAN TO BUTTE

Paul Gregory, 23, who made himself conspicuous in Livingston the past few days with his flashy United States army officer's uniform and braggadocio manner, is in the Park county jail this morning facing several serious charges-including the kidnaping of Marvin Gjerde, 19-year-old local young man.

Gregory was taken into custody on the outskirts of Butte between 5and 6 p.m., Thursday by Butte authorities after kidnapping Gjerde, and forcing him at the point of a gun to drive from Three Forks, west of Bozeman, to the Mining city while fleeing from Livingston officers. Butte officials, acting on a tip from local authorities were waiting for Gregory as he entered that city. He was taken into custody by Deputies Einor Nelson and Joe Boric.

Appeared Here Monday

Gregory who admitted to Butte officers that he was a parole violator from the Washington state penitentiary, appeared in Livingston Monday, dressed in the pseudo uniform of a second lieutenant in the United States army. Sheriff's and police officers, becoming suspicious of his movements, began an investigation Thursday morning.

Gregory, in some manner learning that the officers were checking up on his actions, immediately packed his belongings left in a localhotel, and persuaded Gjerde to drive him to Bozeman. At Bozeman, Gregory left his card at the Hotel Baxter, telling the clerk he was expecting a visitor and would return in a short time. This was but a ruse, officers suspected and immediately notified Butte officials to be on the look-out. Gregory was dressed in civilian clothes when he left here.

Returned to Local Jail

At Bozeman Gregory talked Gjerde into driving him to Three Forks.At that point, Gjerde says, Gregory drew a gun, poked it into his ribs and ordered him to continue on to Butte. Gregory was returned to Livingston early this morning by Sheriff Taylor M. Darroch, Deputy Vern Meigs and Highway Patrolman Lester Black. Gjerde returned with the officers.

In addition to kidnaping, Gregory faces the serious charges of impersonating a United States army officer and representing himself as an under-cover man for the federal bureau of investigation. Gregory told numerous residents over the city, including police officers (1)That he was a United States army officer here on duty. (2) That he was an under-cover man for the federal bureau of investigation and was here on a secret mission. (3) That he was secretly investigating the tragic air crash near Bozeman in January in which ten were killed.

Claimed He Was G-Man

Many discrepancies in Gregory's uniform first aroused suspicion.On the front of his jacket was the insignia of the U.S. Air Corps. Medals and other insignias were from the regular army, but failed to jibe with any regulation uniform in many respects. The uniform was undoubtedly stolen, officers declare.

While in Livingston he had cards printed, carrying his name, the words "G-2, Intelligence Department, Washington, D.C.," together with the telephone number "National 7117," which is the department of justice number in the capitol city. He told Police Officer William O'Hern he was working for Head G-Man, Edgar Hoover. However, when the officer threatened to call Hoover, Gregory rushed away.

The cards were liberally distributed over Livingston, and authorities believe Gregory, following an old game, was building up a "front" before flooding the city with forged checks-probably Saturday afternoon after the bank had closed for the week-end. Word was also broadcast that a large government check was anticipated Saturday. A small bank account was opened Monday upon his arrival, but closed Thursday.

Gregory, friendly and congenial, made many friends during his short sojourn in Livingston-all probably prospective victims of some scheme or other.

The federal bureau of investigation, it was reported, had a "hold order" for Gregory and was on the look-out for him, as a parole violator. Just what disposition will be made with the case whether Gregory will be turned over to the federal government for prosecution or tried in Livingston could not be learned last night.

Author in cell B256 where he served his time; 1970.

Cruel "Oregon Boot" worn by Williams as prisoner at age 23.

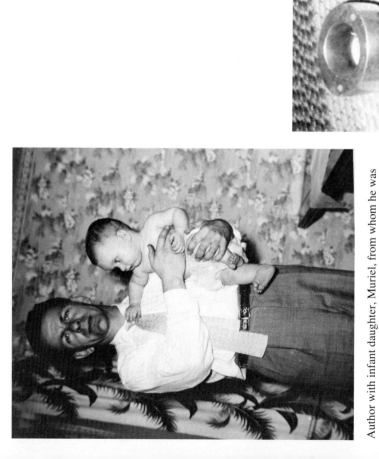

Author with infant daughter, Muriel, from whom he was separated 17 years; 1951.

Alcatraz Island — San Francisco Bay

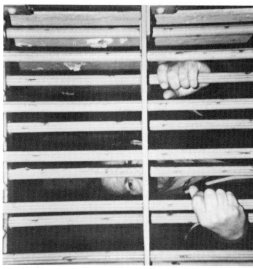

Glenn Williams in cell on Alcatraz

Author in door of dungeon on Alcatraz island; 1970.

Williams at warden's burned out home torched
during indian occupation of Alcatraz; 1970.

Author standing in front of photos of famous Alcatraz inmates; 1988.

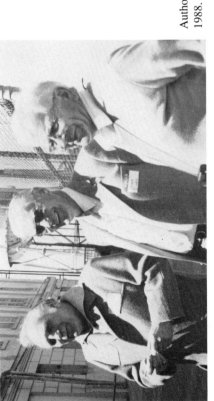

Author with ex-guards; 1988.

Remotely controlled gas bombs in Alcatraz dining room.

Author resting on prison cell bunk in B256; 1988.

Youngest guard ever hired on Alcatraz, Frank Heaney, poses with author and wife ; 1988.

Captain of the Guards, Phil Bergen and author. Alcatraz in happier times; 1988.

Williams in prison boat 35 years after he was chained thereon.

Autobiographer with park ranger, Nancy Bernard, on steep stairs leading to shops and cell house; 1989.

Cake baked as replica of Alcatraz island; 1988.

Elmer Fjermadal, former federal officer and JB at author's 70th birthday; 1985.

Author and wife celebrating 25th year out of Alcatraz; 1988.

JB in dungeon; 1990.

Writer at door of dungeons under infamous "A" block; 1990.

Author and wife with ranger guides Donna Middlemist and Nancy Bernard; 1990.

JB and Author at Alcatraz Morgue; 1990

JB top row 2nd left, posing with former keepers; 1990

Jimmy Carter

PRESIDENT OF THE UNITED STATES OF AMERICA

To All to Whom These Presents Shall Come, Greeting:
Be It Known, THAT THIS DAY THE PRESIDENT HAS GRANTED UNTO

NATHAN GLENN WILLIAMS

A FULL AND UNCONDITIONAL PARDON

AND HAS DESIGNATED, DIRECTED AND EMPOWERED THE DEPUTY ATTORNEY GENERAL AS HIS REPRESENTATIVE TO SIGN THIS GRANT OF EXECUTIVE CLEMENCY TO THE ABOVE WHO WAS CONVICTED

IN THE UNITED STATES DISTRICT COURT FOR THE WESTERN DISTRICT OF WASHINGTON ON AN INFORMATION (NO. 48821) CHARGING VIOLATION OF SECTIONS 2113(a), (b) AND (d), TITLE 18, UNITED STATES CODE, AND ON SEPTEMBER FOURTH, 1953, WAS SENTENCED TO TWENTY-FIVE YEARS' IMPRISONMENT AND ORDERED TO PAY A FINE OF TEN THOUSAND DOLLARS ($10,000); SAID SENTENCE BEING VACATED AND A TERM OF FIVE YEARS' PROBATION BEING IMPOSED ON MAY TWENTY-SEVENTH, 1963.

IN ACCORDANCE WITH THESE INSTRUCTIONS AND AUTHORITY I HAVE SIGNED MY NAME AND CAUSED THE SEAL OF THE DEPARTMENT OF JUSTICE TO BE AFFIXED BELOW AND AFFIRM THAT THIS ACTION IS THE ACT OF THE PRESIDENT BEING PERFORMED AT HIS DIRECTION.

DONE AT THE CITY OF WASHINGTON, DISTRICT OF COLUMBIA
ON December 23, 1980.

By Direction of the President

Charles B. Renfrew

Deputy Attorney General

17

Friendship With A "Good" Guard

Imprisoned men and women go through hell on holidays. The most miserable of all holidays is Christmas. The stress is more than some inmates can tolerate. There are too many poignant memories of previous yule times spent with loved ones, especially if there were children involved. Some of the pitiful reactions I have observed have left me terribly distressed. Under the conditions of incarceration during this 'Season To Be Jolly', the men on Alcatraz practiced every pretense they could muster. The toughies tried to impress their friends with the 'don't-give-a-damn' front. Others pretended to be immune to memories of more pleasant times. There were those, the more violent prone, who went on the prowl looking for trouble with staff or inmates. It wasn't unusual for any number of them to remain in their cells during this traumatic time. As though they were trying to make others share their misery, they penned hateful letters to their loved ones on the outside. More than at any other time, surely, 'misery loves company' applies throughout the Christmas season.

Being away from the members of my family my first Christmas on The Rock was almost more than I could bear. I can't describe how I felt when Muriel came to mind, which seemed to be every waking moment. I envisioned her opening her packages under the tree. I could see her bright eyes lighting up as she tore the wrapping from her gifts. I vividly recall on that Christmas eve when I took a piece of paper from my scratch tablet and figured how old I would be before I would see her again. It was in December of '54, and I had put in only about sixteen months on my twenty-five year term. On a three hundred month sentence, I would get one-third off for good behavior, which would leave me eligible for release in a little over sixteen years. I dropped the pencil in shock. Since no one was ever paroled from Alcatraz, I realized that Muriel would be an adult before I could see her again. I would be unable to share her grade school, junior high school and high school graduation ceremonies. I had to force thoughts of Muriel from my mind. Either that, or dive off the highest tier. That night, I hated Christ and His birthday. Mercifully, I dropped off to sleep.

I was awakened by the discordant voices of convicts singing carols and other religious songs. A lone convict was singing a parody of the old hymn Rock of Ages. He sang ROCK OF RAGES. Considering the location and the pent-up anger he was harboring, his title was more appropriate. This was the most bizarre Christmas Eve I could have dreamed of. Little did I realize I was going to wake up to a more bizarre Christmas day.

217

On Christmas morning, right after breakfast, some of the staff thought they would put a little more of the spirit in this holiest of all holidays. They had managed to smuggle a Christmas tree into the mess hall during the previous night. For about two hours, the guards worked feverishly hanging blinking electric lights, bulbs, tinsel, angel hair and garlands from the tree. At the base they made a small mountain of snow from cotton. Those responsible for the festooning of the tree should have been complimented for their artistic decorating. Years later, a Lieutenant of the guards confided in me about a conversation he had with the Associate Warden. "Chief, I am anxious to see the eyes of the cons when they file in here and spot this tree", he said. The Associate responded, "Yeah, it will be something to witness. Many of these old-timers haven't seen a tree of any kind in years. You never know how an inmate is going to react to a strange situation."

As soon as the guards heard the dinner bell ringing, they positioned themselves in strategic places around the perimeter of the dining room. There was a sense of expectancy in the air as the cons filed into the room, anxious to partake of the turkey, ham and all the trimmings. About fifty men ahead of me had filled their trays at the steam tables and were seating themselves when the silence was broken by the most God-awful scream I have ever heard. It sounded like a wounded banshee. I turned quickly, just in time to see a con break from the line and dash toward the glittering tree. The guards made every effort to cut him off but he eluded them and made his way to that offending, blinking apparition. Before they could capture him, he ripped the tree from its stand, picked it up by the butt and started swinging it in a circle over and around his head. To avoid being hit, the guards retreated a few feet. The Sergeant of the guards realized something had to be done quickly. This was an explosive situation which could easily erupt into a riot. He covered his head with both arms and charged the tree-wielding inmate. As luck would have it, he caught the tree full in the face. By the time he went down, the other bulls dove on the con and wrestled him to the floor. When the sergeant got to his feet, he was the funniest looking sight. Lights, broken bulbs and angel hair adorned his uniform. It was a magnificent break in an otherwise dull routine. The offender was hustled from the mess hall in a matter of minutes. The sergeant, now a walking Christmas tree, called out to the remaining inmates, "Those of you who have your food, sit down and start eating. The rest of you line up at the steam tables, get your dinner and be seated." A con sitting at one of the tables yelled back, "Yes, Mr. Santa Claus, and a Merry Christmas to you." We picked pine needles from our food.

Time continued endlessly for us on Alcatraz. When I refer to time, I don't mean by hours, but measured only in years. No watches or timepieces of any kind were ever seen by the inmates. Such instruments were not of importance to us. We agreed that to have a watch would only serve to slow the passing of time. We were not allowed to have a calendar in our cell. For the men on the Rock, the most accurate timepiece was marking off the years. An hour, a week, a month meant nothing. A year only served to indicate you were 365 days closer to release. For the many who were serving interminably long sentences, even the calendar lost its meaning.

Some of the terms given by judges served one purpose, and that was to show the average citizen how utterly senseless and meaningless those terms were. How could a judge justify a sentence of 150 years plus natural life without hope of pardon or parole? By the average sentencing guideline, a term of that magnitude would mean the convict would have to spend 100 years behind the bars to be eligible for parole, and you have to remember he was sentenced 'without hope of pardon or parole'. These men erased their years by noting each New Year's day. What was the purpose of such a term?

In one case, an accused was found guilty of murdering his wife and two children by burning the house down in which they were sleeping. In pronouncing the court's judgment, the court said to the murderer, "I am sentencing you to life for the murder of your family, and to forty years for arson. While you are serving this sentence, I urge you to apply yourself for the day of your release. Study as much as you can." The convicted man was 38 years of age at sentencing. The soonest he could ever hope to see daylight would be on his 78th birthday. In essence, he was actually condemned to death.

The most anticipated daily event that occurred on this Island was the distribution of mail. For the many who had never had a letter, it was just another time of day. I believe those individuals conditioned themselves to not hear the postman when he walked by.

One evening I received a letter in a business-size envelope. The return address on the envelope read; 'Attorney-At-Law, Gerard M. Shellan, Seattle, Washington'. The enclosed letter was attached to a legal document. It was the document that caused my blood to run cold. It read: 'PETITION FOR ADOPTION OF MURIEL WILLIAMS, A MINOR'. I stared at those words for a full minute, unable to continue. My mind ran rampant. The very thing I feared most was now becoming a reality. My daughter was about to be taken from her mother. Why? And why hadn't my family advised me of this catastrophe? From the legal document, I went to Mr. Gerard's letter. My questions were answered in part. It was many months before I was able to find out what had transpired behind the scenes. Actually it was thirty years later that the full details of the pre-adoption muddle were cleared up. It appeared that there had been a great deal of in-fighting between members of my family and Muriel's mother as to the ultimate disposition of the child. I could not understand how Muriel's mother could possibly put this beautiful child up for adoption. My family felt that Muriel was being neglected. My brother, Dan, Muriel's former baby-sitter and the sister who had initiated the legal action, Denise, were vying for custody of the child. The mother? Apparently they were convinced that she had abandoned my daughter and they were striving to keep her in the family. Denise had retained this attorney to petition the court to approve her as an adoptive parent. It appeared that no member of my family was aware of what was taking place. And through all of this, I sat in a cubicle of unsympathetic steel, completely insulated from what was transpiring. Each family member who could have enlightened me, felt they were sheltering me from a subject far too traumatic for me to cope with. In that respect, they were right. I was sitting in a penitentiary serving a twenty-five year sentence. There was nothing I could do to affect the outcome of this pending battle.

Naturally, after thirty years, I cannot recall the wording of any of the documents, verbatim et literatim. It is difficult for me to describe my reaction to the adoption proposal. I was unable to get its full meaning until I had read it three times. It was a cold and impersonal piece of paper which made it sound like the attorney was dealing with a piece of chattel. He simply told me of my sister's intent to ask the court to approve Muriel's adoption. He asked me to sign the enclosed petition. Late into the night, I composed a response to Mr. Shellan. I agreed to approve my daughter's adoption if I were assured, in writing, that I would be permitted to visit Muriel when and if I were ever released. The attorney's response was quick and final. In essence, what he wrote was this; 'Your sister has refused to give you visiting privileges at any time and, in the event you are released, will petition the court to expressly forbid you to contact your daughter while she is in your sister's custody'. On this date I filed the necessary papers to facilitate the above mentioned adoption proceedings'. I was vulnerable, hurt and confused. About thirty days later, I received notice from the court that Denise had been granted custody of Muriel. In my mind, it seemed to finalize my worst fear, that I had lost her.

Monotonously the years rolled by. From the yard, I could see the Golden Gate Bridge and San Francisco. I would try to make out shapes of cars crossing the bridge. I would watch the tour boats as they came near the Rock. We could hear the tour guide's spiel to the tourists. The loud speakers would carry their messages across the water and to our ears. Often I would be sitting on the cement steps with infamous gangsters and we would listen to the guide tell the tourists all about the men with whom I was sitting. Some of the stories they would relate were laughable. Apparently they were believable, because the boats were always filled to capacity. Finally, I would not stare at the cities across the bay nor gaze at the yachts gliding by. It was too painful.

I was assigned to the 'plum' job of operating the movie projector for our semi-monthly show. It was considered a choice assignment for the simple reason that it offered the operator the opportunity to get out of his cell for a couple of hours, and any break from the deadly routine was a welcome breath of fresh air. The shows that were selected by the staff were third-rate pictures. The film could not contain anything with reference to sex, crime or violence. Naturally, that selection left us with a fair share of Shirley Temple and Boy Scout types of movies. Even those were awaited with great anticipation. The movies were shown in the officers' training center. During the show, an armed guard would be situated in a barred catwalk overseeing the activities below. At first, it gave me an eerie feeling to be watching a trigger-happy guard while I was trying to enjoy the entertainment. Church services were conducted under the same conditions. Once I asked Peter MacCormick, the chaplain, "Doesn't it make you nervous trying to preach a sermon with a guard holding a machine gun over your head?" He smiled, looked up at the guard and replied, "Yes." As the projector operator, I was in a cage at the rear of the room and away from the gun gallery.

Under the federal system, guards were re-assigned to other areas every ninety days. The purpose of this was to discourage a friendship developing between a keeper and an inmate. They had learned over the years that inmates and their warders often became confidants. In such circumstances, the guard might be inclined to bring contraband in to the convict. Even with the switcheroo system, a number of guards on Alcatraz would carry contraband. I used their own system to pull a caper to get to the most confidential records kept on the Rock, records that not even the guards could see. Those records dealt with secret memos between the Federal Bureau of Prisons in Washington, D.C., and the warden of this most impregnable fortress. In addition, there were files dealing with the lives and crimes of every prisoner, and information pertaining to confidential employment records of all the employees, from the lowliest guard to the superintendent. Nothing was sacrosanct as far as my eyes were concerned. I stumbled across this plan purely by accident after I had been working in the projection booth for more than a year.

There was a locked room off the chapel area. I could look through a key hole and see long lines of filing cabinets. Whenever an opportunity would present itself, I would look those filing cabinets over. I had to keep a sharp eye on the guard. I did not want him to wonder why my interest was so keen. There was dust on the floor and tables which were stored in the room. I knew that the files were being actively used because there was no dust on them. In fact it appeared that the chapel and movie area had not been swept nor dusted in many months; certainly not during the eighteen months I had worked there. No one, including myself, gave a second thought to the condition of the rooms. As I thought this over, an idea came to mind. I knew there was to be a re-assignment of staff due any day. If I got a fairly new guard, I would make my play.

The following Sunday, I was called from my cell about a half an hour early and instructed to report to the guard that was to conduct me to the chapel. He was waiting for me at Old Eagle Eye Ordway's station at the lieutenant's desk. Standing beside Ordway was a young guard I had never seen before. Under my breath, I uttered a prayer asking that this new guard be my keeper for the next 90 days. I was confident I could manipulate this fellow if given half a chance. Lieutenant Ordway motioned for me to approach his desk. He turned to the guard and said, "Mr. Ruckels, this is inmate Williams, who has been assigned to operate the projector. You will take him upstairs and directly to the booth, keeping him in you eyesight at all times. You are to search him before he goes into the booth and again just before you bring him back downstairs. Do you have any questions?" Ruckels shook his head. Then my lord and master turned to me and ordered me to do exactly as I had been doing all along. Obediently I followed the guard to the chapel. The movie reel had already been deposited on the floor of the booth. Ruckels stood at my shoulder as I threaded the reels in the old Simplex projector. I knew we had about twenty minutes before the general population would be coming up to watch the show. A little bit apprehensively, I turned to Ruckels and said in my most obsequious voice, "Sir, will you please turn on the ventilation fan? It gets awfully hot and stuffy in here." He responded in a very pleasant tone of voice, "Certainly, Williams. Will you show me which switch activates the fan? Better yet, you pull the switch."

He sat beside me for about forty-five minutes into the feature. It was hot and very uncomfortable in the small booth. Finally, he gave me the opportunity I needed. He asked if it would be OK to smoke in the projection booth. That was absolutely forbidden. I took my Sunday shot at him and replied, "Yes, but the guards usually sit on that low seat below the line of vision of the inmates and other staff. I always keep the fan going in order to carry the smoke out through the shaft." He gave a sigh of relief, took off his uniform coat (another violation of the rules), sat on the seat in a corner and lit up his cigarette. Not wanting to push my luck, I pretended to be concentrating on my task for the remainder of the feature. Inwardly, I was elated. I cautioned myself to 'work' this guy slowly.

As soon as the film ran out, Ruckels stood up and reached for the switch that turned on the overhead lights. Before he could reach the switch, I said sharply, "Sir, may I suggest that you put on your coat first? That Lieutenant-In-Charge is a bear-cat for regulations." The guy actually put his hand on my shoulder and muttered an almost inaudible, "Thanks." Here was a pretty nice bull.

For the next two months, there was a repeat of the first session. Gradually, we talked about our families, politics and many other personal things. I actually began to take a liking to Ruckels. I learned that he had been there only three months and was still on probation. On one occasion he confided, "Nate, I have often wondered why you were put in a place like Alcatraz. You just don't fit the mold." I thanked him for his kind comments and dropped the subject. He began bringing me candy bars, an act for which he could have been arrested. Near the end of his ninety-day assignment, I told him not to make the mistake of trusting convicts. He nodded, knowingly, and said, "During our training sessions, that is one of the subjects on which they placed a great deal of emphasis. I appreciate your concern."

During our preparation to wind the reel one Sunday, I made a leading comment, hoping he would grab the bait. "Mr. Ruckels," I asked, "These rooms are a regular pig sty. Will you ask the Officer-In-Charge if he will permit us to come up here next Saturday so I can dust and mop this joint out? I work in the tailor shop throughout the week, and Saturdays is the only time I can do this." He jumped for the lure. "You're damned right I will, Nate. I have been turning this over in my mind for weeks," he replied.

Two weeks later on a Saturday Morning, I was called from my cell and ordered to report to the front desk. A relief lieutenant was waiting for me when I got there. Standing next to him was Mr. Ruckels. The head man said, "Williams, I want you to go to the mop room and get the necessary tools you will need to clean up the officers' training room. Mr. Ruckels here will accompany you. He will call down a head count on you every half-hour. Get with it." Mr. Ruckels was glad to get away from his tower shift and spend a few hours from under the gun. I was pleased for the opportunity to try my gimmick on him.

For two hours I worked like a mad man. I wanted to finish the main service room so I could bring up my ace-in-the-hole, a shot at the file room. When I had finished the initial chore, I turned to my guard and shot the works. "Mr. Ruckels, I'll change the water in the mop bucket and then I will have enough time to clean up the file room. Is that OK?" I held my breath awaiting his response. "Yes, Nate, that is a good idea." He sorted through the keys and selected the one that opened the door to the forbidden area. I managed to casually pick up the bucket of fresh water, my broom and mop and saunter in among the dozen file cabinets. Before I could start my task, Ruckels asked, "What are in these cabinets, Nate, or do you know?" I gave him an off- the-wall answer. "Well, you know how the government is. There are probably thousands of old records." Wanting him to think I had been in the archives before, I continued, "When I was in here about a year ago, the guard with me spent a couple of hours going through the manila folders. A few times, when he came across something of interest, he would draw my attention to it. I had a lot of work, so I paid little heed to it." I kept on sweeping, but watched him out of the corner of my eyes. Sure enough, his curiosity got the better of him. He slid one of the drawers open, took out a folder and started scanning through it. I worked my way around the other side of the cabinets and kept going until I came up alongside of him. I stopped and mopped the sweat from my brow. Damned if he didn't have a dozen folders stacked on the top of the files. He had the look of a boy who was caught with his hand in the cookie jar. "Look at this inmate jacket*, Nate. It's the whole scoop on Morton Sobel, the guy who sold information to the Russians. I've seen him in the yard and mess hall many times. In fact, I've seen you walking in the yard with him." I glanced at the folder cover and there was a picture of Sobel stapled to it. I opened the record and read some of the detailed entries. It was too voluminous for me to complete. Anyway, I was anxious to look through my own jacket and learn what the FBI had found out about me. I led my keeper into a sucker punch. "If you want to read something, look for the file on Nathan G. Williams, ll03 AZ." Immediately, Ruckels selected my dossier from its alphabetized slot. I pretended to have no concern as to its contents. "Holy God, Nate, you have a long record of some pretty serious crimes," the guard ejaculated. "I can't believe this stuff. You should give it the once-over." I smiled and said, "Mr. Ruckels, you forget; I am the guy you're reading about, so I am familiar with the story." I didn't tell him that I would give my right arm to spend an hour going over the file J. Edgar Hoover's lackeys had compiled. "It's getting pretty near time to head for the main cellhouse, Mr. Ruckels. I am not nearly through, but it will have to wait until next week. Let's replace the files so no one will know that they have been read by unauthorized people."

On the way down the stairs, the guard whispered, "There are some inmates' records I want to see when we come back up here. I want to look over some of the famous cons like Al Capone, Creepy Karpis, Machine-Gun Kelly and members of the Ma Barker gang. Hell, this is a gold mine of information." To whet his interest and keep it alive, I commented, "Some of those characters are still here. Be sure to read the dope on Robert Stroud,

*official inmate information

The Bird Man Of Alcatraz."

For the next week, I could hardly contain myself. I hoped nothing would interfere with our plans. There would never be another opportunity like this. No other guard would have let me within a mile of the confidential information contained in the room upstairs. Only a new guard would have let himself be led by the nose.

While I had maneuvered him, he had not been injured. I really took a liking to this young fellow, and would not have put him in a compromising position.

From that Saturday to the next was probably the longest week I had put in. While I was waiting to be called out for the cleaning job, all sorts of bad thoughts ran through my mind. What if the lieutenant decided to put a new guard on the cleanup detail? While my mind was running rampant, the cellhouse guard threw the lever to my cell door and called out, "Williams, report to the front desk." Even before I got to my destination, I heard Ruckels' voice as he was talking to the lieutenant. I was instantly relieved. After the guard had locked us in the officers' training room, both of us headed to the file room. As he opened the door, I headed for the mop room to get my paraphernalia. By the time I got back, he was already looking through the manila folders. He had selected the particular ones in which he was interested. I pretended to be more interested in my assignment than in the files. It was all I could do to dust and mop while Ruckels was lost in the files. I worked like mad because I wanted some time to browse along with him. Yet, I knew I had to leave evidence that work had actually been done. I finished my job in about a half an hour, took the bucket, mop and broom to the sink and cleaned them up. Immediately, I went back to join Ruckels. I sauntered to the cabinet that held my personal info and took it out. What had been put in my dossier absolutely amazed me. There were letters from people I had known just prior to my capture. Some were designed to help me. Others were of the most condemning nature. People whom I had regarded as my friends made unsolicited statements that were downright false. One in particular intrigued me. It read, in part, 'I knew that there was something shady about Mr. Williams. He had no apparent employment, yet he drove a new Cadillac, wore expensive clothes and jewelry and rented a private plane to make trips to Canada where he entertained lavishly. He invited me to join him as his guest. On more than one occasion, he paid the bills with Canadian money. I talked with other acquaintances about this fellow, and they expressed the same concerns that bothered me. Often he would leave Seattle for a week or two at a time. After his arrest, I realized that his wife was in cahoots with him. If I can be of any assistance to you, please contact me. Yours truly, Russell Rand.' I had known Rand for a period of five years and considered him to be a friend. There were dozens of such letters. However, the piece of information I found to be most disturbing was contained in a letter written by my former wife. Briefly, it was a detailed document in which she snitched to the FBI. I noted that she told the feds where some of the money was cached, but was conveniently quiet about the five G's I had concealed in the freezer compartment of our refrigerator. All who had given 'confidential information' to the government agents had signed their names. There was no way they could have dreamed that I would be reading of their shameless perfidy. Years later I confronted some of those persons.

For the next month, Ruckels and I had a holiday reading 'case work-ups' on dozens of America's Most Wanted criminals. I learned how they managed to corner them, who informed on them and other very pertinent circumstances surrounding their lives, crimes and eventual downfall. I learned of the methods employed by the government to force confessions from accused men and women. I would have given five years of my life if I could have smuggled the files to the outside.

In the few remaining weeks Ruckels had to complete this ninety-day tour, he and I did little cleaning up on those rare Saturdays. He was unbelievably enthralled with the information we were garnering from the government's Confidential Information Archives. One day he said, "Williams, do you realize that the FBI would have solved very few crimes if it weren't for the stool-pigeons they used? The more of these cases I read, the more I realize how they fooled the public with their image of invincibility. They developed a hell of a PR system. In fact, I just read a detailed account of their murder of Dillinger. If it hadn't been for the Woman-In-Red setting him up for the slaughter, he'd still be on the streets. And after all their security, here a prison guard and a bank robber are reading files that were never meant for the eyes of the square John." I simply smiled and replied, "Mr. Ruckels, you are just beginning to see what we cons have known for years."

The guard and I spent the next few weeks scanning the records. On our last day together, he and I just talked about things in general. He made a comment that I treasured, one that I could not repeat to anyone. He was talking about his stint in the army, his marriage and children. This type of conversation, I am certain, was never before exchanged between a keeper and the kept on this miserable, fog-shrouded bastion of hell. A strong and binding friendship had developed between this humane guard and me. This very development was the basis of the prison bureau's rule that read, custodial personnel will be moved from one locality to another in an institution. And these transfers must take place every ninety days. This method will discourage close relationships developing between the guards and inmates. All staff members are cautioned to be alert for any sign of 'fraternizing between guards and inmates'. At this point, he dropped a shocker on me. "Williams, if I had a partner like you on the outside, I'd be tempted to rob banks. The more I become acquainted with some of the guards in here, the more I realize there is a very fine line between the crooks and their keepers." I had a sincere response for him when I said, "Mr. Ruckels, never get involved in anything criminal. Believe me, my friend, if you do, that will be the end of everything."

When his shift was about to end, I told him, "We will probably never meet again or we may see one another in areas of the prison. While we can't exchange signals, you will know that I saw you and will remember you as a great guy." I was amazed that I would ever make such a statement to a guard, a segment of humanity I had vowed to hate. When we stood up and were heading for the gate to the control center, I reached for his hand, and we shook. "Williams," he confided, "I am resigning tomorrow. I can't stand this kind of life, working in this type of environment. I am re-enlisting in the army. Is there any final thing I can do for you?" Without hesitation, I reached into my shirt and pulled out an envelope containing six or eight pages on which I had written letters to my brother, parents and sisters. I knew the mail censor would have rejected the letters if I had tried to send them out through legitimate channels. My friend, without a word, tucked them under his uniform coat, and we walked down to the control center. I never saw this remarkable guy again, but I received a letter from my brother, Dan, a couple of weeks later in which he had written, 'our friend came to have dinner with us last night. He can't find work so he is going to re-enlist in the army. Thanks for the letters'.

For the next year, I kept my job as the operator of the projector. The other guards who supervised me paled beside Ruckels. They were dyed-in-the-wool guards. The only reason I had developed the one-man clean-up crew in the first place was to have access to the archives. I should not have said 'one-man crew'. Without Ruckels, my scheme would have failed. I knew that the other guards would never permit me to scour through the records. I knew that if the lieutenants ever learned of the relationship between Ruckels and me, all hell would break loose. If the Director of the U.S. Bureau of Prisons, James V. Bennett, had ever found out that one of his men, and an Alcatraz convict, had colluded to rape and pillage a vault in the inner recesses of his personal fort it would have a far-reaching effect on the security system. It is no exaggeration that the warden and other minions would have been transferred to other institutions and demoted.

I am certain that Ruckels would have been indicted and criminally prosecuted. The secret between Ruckels and me remained just that, a secret for nearly thirty years. I have never heard from the man whom I respected so much. I hope that, if he ever reads this book, he will recognize the escapade and the author.

While I did not recognize it at the time, my clandestine relationship with my guard friend created a profound change in my attitude toward others. In this instance, I was compelled to admit there were some good guards; guards that, if given an opportunity, would have responded humanely to the problems that overwhelmed so many of the unfortunate convicts. Apparently, Ruckels must have told other guards that Nate Williams was not such a bad person once you got to know him. The problem was that there wasn't a chance to 'get to know him' better under the system of senseless segregation. And this worked both ways, so that the cons went on despising the custodial staff, and that the group of men in charge of the inmates proceeded in their blind distrust and resentment. A ceaseless carousel of mutual ignorance.

One night while I was pitching restlessly on my bunk, I heard a night guard stop in front of my cell. I laid perfectly still while his body cast an ominous shadow over my bed. He stood still for about thirty seconds. What was he up to? Before he moved on, he tossed an object onto my bed. I did not move until his footsteps were out of hearing range. I grabbed my reflector, placing it on the bars to see if he had left the tier. I could not see him. I stood for a full three minutes in the front of my cage. Pretty soon I heard him on the upper landing making his rounds. Very carefully I sat on my bunk and eyed a small package lying on the cement floor. The first thing I thought was that this son-of-a-bitch had put a 'plant' in my possession. I grabbed the alien article and was preparing to toss it over the tier. My curiosity got the better of me. I slowly opened the package. I was dumb-founded to discover a candy bar wrapped in a clean white napkin, the likes of which I had not seen since my arrest. What the hell was taking place? A candy bar in Alcatraz? And tossed into my cell by a night warder whom I didn't even know? I held the candy near the front of my cell where there was a pale light shining through. I scanned it carefully. I smelled it. I squeezed it. Finally, after much deliberation, I bit off a tiny corner. I was certain that that guard had figured out a way to poison me. It had to be one of the guards because an inmate would have one hell of a time getting a candy bar and having a guard toss it into my cell. It passed the taste-test. My next bite was much larger. I took a long time chewing it. It was the most delicious morsel of food I had had in my mouth in months and the fact that it was contraband made it more delectable. I knew the routine of the watchers so well that I judged the guard would be back shortly. Before he came back, I flushed the tell-tale napkin down the toilet. There wasn't a trace of contraband in my quarters. I sat on my bunk and shivered either from anticipation or cold. In a matter of a few minutes I heard the guard coming in the direction of B256. I was determined to see what was going on, so I faced the front of the bars. Sure enough, the guard came to my cubicle, stopped, and shined his power-ful flashlight on the floor at my feet. Quietly, he said, "Williams, what are you doing out of bed?" I fumbled for a reply. I knew that other cons would be listening, so I mumbled, "My stomach is upset." He softly said, "Ruckels", and moved on. After I crawled back under my covers, I was overcome with gratitude.

For at least two months, I received a candy bar every night. Again, the fact that all guards were not bastards impressed itself on my mind. Gradu-ally, I found that I was less inclined to scowl at the guards when we would come face to face. Inwardly, I would wonder just what kind of fellow a particular keeper was. On rare occasion, I would let my features soften when confronting a guard and I would detect a kinder countenance greeting me. Within a few months, I noticed that less personnel were apt to give me the 'dog-eye' than before.

During this particular period, I was studying psychology from the Univer-sity of California through correspondence, so I made up my mind to attempt some applied psychology on the people whom I professed to despise, the prison staff. It was a very delicate experiment because, if some of the cons saw me smiling or speaking to a guard, they might re-arrange my teeth. Most of the guards, seeing me greet them with a pleasant smile, would immediately become suspicious. I could just 'feel' them saying to them-selves, "Now what is that thug up to?" I had to be consistent if I were to be successful with my experiment. When I was alone with a guard in the Training Center, it was far easier and safer to engage that individual in conversation. He was away from other guards and I was removed from

227

other convicts, so we could be a little more civil. There was one particular guard who responded well to my overtures. Within a week or two we were at the point where we would sit on the bench, side by side, and talk freely.

Actually, I was elated to learn that these men were no different from me in their hates, disappointments, aspirations, love of families and need for companionship. It dawned on me that I had permitted my psyche to become warped, resulting in a despicable attitude toward persons whom I had never met before I became enmeshed in the tentacles of the prison system. When I would ask myself why I detested a certain man wearing a uniform, I had no rational response other than that he represented the other side of the fence. Conversely, was that why the jailers treated their charges so niggardly? I reasoned that peer pressure played an important role in the conduct and attitude of both camps. I found the experiment interesting and enlightening. One of my papers I sent in for a lesson concerned the results of my study of this subject. A week later I was shocked when the mail censor returned my lessons with a note attached that read, 'Williams, ll03, B256: Any further such letters that you attempt to smuggle out of this institution under the guise of being a lesson will result in your being punished and losing your privilege of participating in all other contact with the University of California'. I stared at the mail censor's note. I could not believe my eyes. Fury swept over me. All of the goodwill I had built up toward my fellow man was shattered. I made up my mind as to my mode of response right then. I sat down and filled out a "Request for Interview" with the Captain of The Guards. I detailed my complaint and reason for wanting to see him.

Two months later, after I had given up hope for an audience, I was held in from work one morning for an interview with the Captain. At nine o'clock, I found myself standing between two guards in front of the Captain who was seated at a desk in A Block, a vacated section of the oldest cell block on the Rock. He looked up and said, "Williams, I investigated your charges against the mail censor, Mr. Baker. You are entirely in the wrong in trying to send confidential information to a cohort outside. Personally, I think Mr. Baker would have been justified in having you thrown into solitary confinement. However, because of your exemplary conduct record, the matter will be dropped. You are dismissed."

That night I laid awake for hours trying to get things straight in my mind. The Captain had referred to my professor as my 'cohort'. Try as I did, I could not figure out what the 'confidential information' was. I learned later that everything was confidential in the eyes of those in charge of the Rock. I was terribly disturbed at what had taken place. My studies and experiments suddenly had no meaning. Even in view of this disappointing turn of events, I was determined to conduct myself properly in the presence of my keepers. I recall what Morton Sobel once told me. "Nate, when you react to the guards in a nasty and uncouth manner, you are really bringing yourself down to their level. And did it ever dawn in your thick head that maybe some of the staff might be nice people? You complain that they don't give a convict a chance. What chance do you give them?" Morton was an intelligent man whom I respected. I am certain that it was from that point on that I became determined to 'clean' up my act.

On a usual cold and foggy day on Alcatraz, Creepy Karpis, a leader of the famous Ma Barker gang, and I were walking up and down the rec yard. For no real reason, I told Creepy what Morton told me. His comments, as usual, were caustic and insulting. "Nate, do you have to get hit in the head by Big Bertha for anything to register? How in the hell you ever reached twenty-one I'll never know. Your problem is that you listen to all these ignorant young punks who want to become gangsters when they aren't capable of being a pimple on a real gangster's ass. I've watched you from the day you came in here. You strut around trying to impress the cons that are as stupid as you are. No guard in this place is responsible for your being here, so why in the hell do you want to hard-ass them? It makes it tough on them as they perform their job, it makes it hard on the cons who want to get by without any trouble and, whether you can see it, your attitude causes you to do 'hard-time'. Here is my thinking, Nate. I don't give a damn how rough you make it on yourself, but don't you cause me to do my time rougher than it already is. These very cons that are trying to impress you are the same simple-minded punks that will spill their guts on you." As he turned to walk away, he gave me a parting shot by saying, "Have a nice day, kid!" I was dumb-struck by Creepy's blast at me. I had always liked the guy and had treated him with respect. In one short minute he deflated my over-sized ego.

Some months later I was compelled to stop him in the yard and tell him how I felt about his lesson on manners toward the prison staff. It galled hell out of me to say, "Karpis, I know you were right in the dressing down you handed me. I'd like to be your friend." He stuck out his hand and we shook. Without another word he walked away.

18

Religion On The Rock

MUSINGS FROM AN ALCATRAZ CELL

The respite that the soul must have,
As I wearily end each day
Comes to me with soft relief
When on my bed I lay.

Each night I briefly flee
Across the restless bay,
And far behind I leave
The burden of a prisoner's day.

'Tis often quoted in real belief
That only imprisoned men are free
From worries that plague the human heart
But this isn't true, you see.

The human mind that cells confine
Is a greater prison by far,
Than any wall of endless stone
Or a carbon steel bar.

The tortures of the miserable life,
Those things you cannot see,
Escape the observer's first glimpse
As they inexorably sacrifice me.

Do you think of me as deprived the comfort
Of family and love,
And mitigate your conscience with,
"It's retribution from above?"

Well, let me tell of things in hell,
That you deserve to know.
Of hidden wounds inflicted red,
From which blood and tears flow.

Of injuries of the heart and soul,
That mirror the terror true,
Not overt and obvious for closed eyes,
Not supposed to be seen by you.

We know of the rules by which to live,
And of the commandments from above,
But have you forgotten in your haste
That of these the greatest is love?

So, for tonight, please escape with me,
And let me take you where
The dearest possessions on earth are found,
With those who really care.

You see, in my house at home
Steel doors don't heartlessly slam,
And insensate suspicions can't live,
For they know what I truly am.

The months rolled into endless years. Time began to mean nothing to me. There were few interruptions. Events that meant something to me in years past ceased to alert my mind. Letters from my family carried no significance. They seemed to lack vibrancy. I realized how terribly difficult it was on the family to try to write to a brother who was, for all purposes, a non-person. They knew there was nothing of which I could write. I knew of nothing that was occurring in the free world. For six years I never read a newspaper, nor a magazine that contained current events. After my fifth year, the prison administration decided to pipe in radio music. It wasn't long until, like others, I hung up my earphones and never took them down again. My weekly letters became monthly. Unknown to me, I was becoming inured to the pleasures of the free world.

It was nearly impossible for me to remember how the outside people conducted themselves. How did they dress, order food in a restaurant, dance and behave among normal persons? I was fearful I would be a freak if and when I was ever released. On rare occasions when politicians were permitted to visit my zoo, I would find myself bending over my sewing machine to avoid eye contact. We were warned to never speak to free-world visitors. On one occasion I ignored those orders. I happened to glance up from my sewing machine and thought my eyes were playing tricks on me. Standing near the front door between two guards stood one of my favorite persons; The World's Heavy Weight Champion Boxer, Rocky Marciano.

He walked with the guards down toward me, speaking to the cons as he passed. I noticed none returned his salutation, and I was sure that Rocky was embarrassed. When he got to my machine I looked him in the eyes, spoke and offered my hand. He smiled and we shook. He and I talked about his recent fight with Ezzard Charles. The two guards stood there glaring at me. We shook hands again before he was led off. In my mind I knew I was going to be picking my rear end up in the hole as soon as the guest left the Island, but I didn't care.

The following morning I was told to 'lay in' for the adjustment board. At nine the next day I found myself standing before the Captain of The Guards and two Lieutenants who comprised that silly body of men. In a sort of judicial voice, the captain said, "Williams, contrary to the rules, you spoke

232

to a visitor who was passing through the Tailor Shop. What have you to say for yourself?" I stared at the captain for a full minute before I said, "Captain, if you were in my position, and a long-time friend recognized you, stopped and offered his hand, what would you have done? There was no other way for me to respond." I was ordered to step out of the room. While I heard them discussing my case, I was absolutely dumbfounded to hear the captain say, "Men, we can't very well punish Williams for greeting an old time friend, especially when Mr. Marciano initiated the conversation I suggest we let Williams off with a warning." I had never met Rocky before in my life. In fact, if the captain had listened to me carefully, he would have been aware that I never said Rocky was an old-time friend. I simply put a supposition before him. He came to his own conclusion. When I told my friends in the yard, they had a hearty laugh.

When I first arrived there, I would spend hours watching the beautiful yachts sail through San Francisco Bay. Because I was a pilot, planes taking off from the International Airport were of particular interest to me. I cannot recall how long it was before the planes and yachts began to disappear from my eyes and mind, but they left slowly, almost imperceptibly.

Mental and physical relief came in the form of a fight, a killing or an attempted escape. Such happenings afforded us a desperately needed diversion. It didn't matter if a man was maimed, injured or killed. In fact, nothing was of importance that didn't create a diversion, that didn't take our minds off the lethal monotony. It is because of this type of treatment that many men become stir-crazy and are eventually released into a vulnerable society. They are time bombs waiting to explode without warning or reason. And then when this occurs, the citizens get up in arms and demand more convictions and longer sentences. The hue and cry for the death penalty becomes louder. It would have been quite simple to defuse the bomb through the expediency of common sense and humane treatment, something beyond the ken of the impenetrable cliques of wardens and guards.

When the guard brought around the mail one evening, he handed me an official envelope marked, 'Warden's Office'. I gazed at it for a long time. I was nearly fearful to open it. When I did, I couldn't believe my eyes. The memo stated, 'Tomorrow morning you will be kept in from your work detail for the purpose of a visit at 9:00 A.M. Your mother, Blanche Williams, has been granted the privilege of visiting you for one hour. (signed) Warden Paul J. Madigan'. I couldn't believe that my mother, a refined and delicate lady, could bring herself to see me under the terribly harsh and cruel conditions imposed on the visitors of the inmates. I never dreamed that any member of my family would ever visit Alcatraz, least of all my mother. She was such a proud and sensitive person. Had it ever crossed my mind, I would have written Dad and begged him to forestall such a possibility. Yet, here I was going to be confronted by the one person I loved the most, and wanted to see the least. There was no way I could deny Mom a visit. She was elderly and frail. It crossed my mind that if I were to reject her, I might never see her again. As matters stood, my chances of seeing her again, under any circumstances, were remote. I was nearly forty years of age and serving a twenty-five year sentence. Even if I lived for the full term, there was very little chance she would survive. Morpheus was elusive that night.

The next morning as I stood shaving, my hands were shaking uncontrollably. My face was haggard and I felt I must have aged ten years since my imprisonment. When I had finished, I slapped my face hard on both cheeks. I wanted to restore some color to my complexion which had adopted the familiar prison pallor. I combed my hair with more care. At least I didn't want to shock her with my haggard look. Suddenly, I wanted more than ever to appear like I did when I last saw her. I was striving desperately to soften the shock I knew she would suffer.

My preparation was interrupted by the sound of my steel door slamming open at the same time the guard bellowed, "OK, Williams, out for your visit." I don't recall going down to the lower landing nor walking toward the front of the cellhouse. I wanted to hide in shame. My mother at least had the fortitude to come see me, and here I was lacking the guts to greet her. At the end of the cellhouse, for the first time, I got a glimpse of the cruel manner in which the visiting room had been designed. I walked up to the steel wall and saw a very narrow slit of glass. It was probably three inches wide and six inches long. Below the glass was a sheet of steel which had a number of holes punched through it. The holes were offset so you could not view your visitor other than through the glass. The way I was positioned, I could not see the upper part of my Mother's body, just from her mouth to the top of her head. I would rather die than go through what I faced the next minute. It seemed a long time before my Mother could grasp how the visit was going to be conducted. She must have been under the impression that we were going to be permitted to embrace. She looked at me through the saddest eyes I have ever seen and, at the same instant must have grasped the cruel reality that our last contact had taken place years before. To this day, I think much of her will to live left her. She could not fathom how this could be. She turned toward the guard and held out both hands. He moved quickly to her side and held her quietly. Instantly another one of the guards entered the door and pushed a chair under her. I was utterly helpless as I watched this scenario unfold.

As luck would have it, both prison chaplains were coming into the main section of the penitentiary. They were The Reverend Peter McCormack and Father Joseph Scannell, two men who reshaped my life from that day on. They could see what had taken place, and moved to Mom's side. I continued to stare, impotently. The two ministers talked affectionately to her. In a few minutes they had quieted her down. After she had regained her composure, she stood bravely, walked over to the phone on her side of the wall and spoke into the speaker. "I feel so silly, son. I think I became ill from the trip, but I feel great now. It is so nice to see you."

For the next hour, we talked about the family. She gave me news about my daughter, Muriel; how she was doing in school and all of the other little kid things. Finally, we were told that the visit was terminated. Mom and I blew kisses to each other. She left. As I was leaving I glanced through the little window and caught a glimpse of both chaplains escorting her out. I remember being so thankful that they were there. I skipped my dinner that night and my breakfast the next morning. I had wept all night.

234

Because I had not reported for work, the guards ran a double count on me, and kept a constant running count throughout the entire day. Notwithstanding they knew I had laid in, the rules said a fifteen minute check will be maintained whenever an inmate is away from his assignment, whether it be work, hospital or cell detainment. I was so ragged out that I tried to sleep during the day after my visit.

With the guard walking by and waking me every fifteen minutes, I didn't stand a chance in hell of getting any rest. That evening I was famished, so I ate a full meal. When night fell, I was afraid I would spend another restless night, but that wasn't the case. I went to bed thinking about the awful experience of the previous day. Until morning I was not aware of anything.

I had made up my mind that I was going to have to either get my mind and emotions in order, or make a bid for the nuthouse. Right after breakfast, I stopped by the lieutenant's desk and requested permission to remain in my cell for the remainder of the day. He was aware what had taken place with my mother, so he granted my request. In the comparative quiet of the cellhouse after the work crews had left, I was able to gather my wits. There was a strong determination in me to improve things in my life. I used to say, "What the hell does it matter? I'll never live to walk hand-in-hand with Muriel. My sister, in a recent letter, quoted Reverend McCormack's comment in a communication he had sent her five months after my mother had visited in which he wrote, "Each time Nate and I visit, he invariably gets on the subject of his daughter. He surely has his heart set on that child. It will be a terrible blow for him if anything should ever estrange the two of them." On an outside chance, if a miracle occurred and I was freed, too many years would have lapsed. I could never expect her to look on me as her father. I made the decision that day to put her out of my mind as much as humanly possible. I had to go from here.

I wrote down all the pertinent things that I had to do to re-shape my shattered existence. I knew that I would run into many obstacles on my reformation trip. Over and over I repeated, "Things will go bad. Do not let them dissuade you from your goal. This is the most important journey of your life. It may be your last opportunity. You are your own worst enemy." I started the rebuilding process in my cell that morning.

I was in the midst of deep thought and planning when I was startled by my cage door sliding open. I dropped my pencil and pad and waited for the guard to call me out, but the door just stayed open. I had never seen this happen before. I was determined to remain on my bunk until either I was called out or the door was slammed shut. I caught the sound of someone walking toward my cell. A shadow fell across the door and stood still. I glanced up to see the Protestant and Catholic Ministers standing at the head of my bunk. The Reverend Peter McCormack was the first to speak. "Nate, Father Scannell and I would appreciate talking with you. We will not impose on you. We know of your hatred for authority. We don't represent the prison system in any sense of the word. May we come in and sit on your bunk with you?"

I looked McCormack over carefully. He was a small man, quite elderly with thinning grey hair. He had the kindest blue eyes I had ever seen. I

235

fought myself because I was starting to like this person. While he was waiting for my answer, he smiled a kind and gentle smile. It was the first time in many months that a kind look had been directed to me. I turned my attention to Father Joseph Scannell. He was a tall and slender man, and appeared to be in delicate health. He, too, was balding. He had a kind of attractive grin. What the hell was coming over me? I was attracted to both pastors. But I wasn't going to give them the satisfaction of knowing my feelings. I looked them over for a long time. They waited for me to speak, and I did. "I want you two to know that I didn't send for you. I am not a Christian, and I don't intend to become one. If you want to talk to me and will omit the sermonizing, I'll listen. One more thing, don't you pull the Bible on me or I'll bounce you out of my quarters. Now what do you want?" Neither of my visitors flinched or changed expression. "Nate," began Father Scannell, "the records show that you are from a Protestant family, so I should let Peter explain just why we're here. However, you have deprived me of the privilege of talking about my beloved Jesus Christ. Of course, that means Peter, also, is going to be very limited in his scope of conversation. To put it in your vernacular, both of us are in a hell of a mess, aren't we? I would like to urge you to do one thing, Nate. Get rid of the hatred that is consuming you. If you don't, you're not going to survive." I liked this fellow still more.

Peter spoke up: "We were walking through the visiting area when your Mother went into a slight shock. At first we didn't know what had taken place, but we were concerned for her." Before he could continue, I asked, "Why should you be concerned? Isn't God in your corner? All you had to do was pray and everything would have been O.K. Right?" Without a moment's hesitation, Peter continued, "Yes! And I did pray for all I was worth. I was afraid she would go into a deep shock, and at her age, that could have proven fatal. Jesus succored her immediately." I stood over him in a bellicose manner and yelled, "Remember, Sky Pilot, you were not to bring up anything about Jesus." Peter stood up, looked me in the eye and coolly said, "My dear friend, it was you who brought up the religious issue when you asked me why I didn't pray. I simply responded to your question. I want to continue so your mind will be at ease. I took your Mother home with me that night and kept her all the next day. She, my wife and I got along fabulously. We learned to love that very dear person. She telephoned your family. They had a good visit." He sat back down on the bunk and simply looked at me. He could not have stopped me more effectively if he had struck me in the pit of my stomach. My first encounter with this man, and he bested me. Without another word, both men rose and bid me good-bye.

Long after they left, I gave much thought to the purpose of their visit. They hadn't tried to convert me. I was greatly comforted knowing that they had seen to my mother's welfare. That was a nice thing to do. That evening I chastised myself for the ill manner in which I treated them. One of my good intentions was to conduct myself in a more gentlemanly way. I sure blew that resolution all to hell. The two chaplains usually showed up in the yard twice a week and mingled with the cons. I had observed how at ease they were. I was struck by how many of the joint's most notorious men walked and talked with the two men of the cloth. Frankly, prior to this past week, I would have been embarrassed to be seen talking to a preacher.

A few days later, I was playing dominoes with the Trigger Man of Murder, Incorporated, when Benji Domingo signaled that he wanted to talk with me. We met on the upper steps of the yard. He started right out. "Ya know, Nate, we got two real nice guys as preachers in here. Us cons are behind them." He stopped and waited for me to say something but I refused to take the bait. Angrily he continued, "Word spread around the joint about the tough time you had with your Mother. All of us have gone through that, so we felt pretty bad for you. One of the guards that caught your Mother as she was falling is alright. When he saw the Good Men coming in, he grabbed them and asked them to attend to your Mom. Creepy and I saw the Bible Boys in chapel the next day and we asked them to go see you. Word has it that you treated them badly. We don't like that, Nate. We can excuse that under the circumstances. Listen careful, old boy, don't get carried away with your tough-guy complex where Peter McCormack and Joseph Scannell are concerned. It would be a shame if we had to perform a pre-frontal lobotomy on your melon." Before I could answer, he was down the steps and talking to Bumpy Johnson. I was concerned with Benji's comments. These guys play for keeps in here, and I knew that I had been warned. It had been my intention to apologize to the ministers even before Benji gave me that bit of advice. I also wanted to find out the name of the guard who had steadied my Mother in the visiting room. I owed some thank yous.

The guard's voice boomed throughout the cavernous cellhouse, "Alright you Bible-thumpers, out for church services. Get your asses in gear." His comments encouraged inmates to make catcalls from their cells deriding those who wanted to go to church. One of the cons called out in a sarcastic tone of voice, "Our warden who art in heaven, give us this day our daily bread and water." It was my intention to go to the chapel to get out of cell confinement. At least, I convinced myself that that was what motivated me on that particular Sunday morning. In retrospect, I had been feeling badly about the way I had mistreated Father Scannell and Reverend Peter McCormack and I was looking for a way I could engage them in conversation and, eventually, apologize for my conduct.

On the evening before this particular church call-out, I had a session with myself. By the time it was over, I thought less of Nathan Glenn Williams. I had spent years bitching about the nasty attitude of anyone connected with prisons and here I had committed the very injustices of which I had complained. Truly, wasn't I looking for a modicum of respect? Yet, I refused to give consideration to persons who had befriended my mother. If I weren't trying to become more of a gentleman, I would say to myself, "Nate, you are a no-good jackass." Instead, I used the word onager, but it meant the same.

When my door slid open, I moved out to join the line of Bible- thumping criminals. The services were held in the same room where Ruckels and I had raided the secret file cabinets. Being Alcatraz, with an image to maintain, we were lined up in front of a huge steel gate and, after we were very carefully frisked, we were passed up one flight of stairs. I observed that

237

about every third or fourth inmate was jerked from the line, taken aside, stripped down and given the humiliating anal search for contraband. What a way to prepare for worship! And, if that wasn't bad enough, when I seated myself on the hard wooden bench, I glanced up at the gun gallery behind the steel mesh to see the barrel of a machine gun peeking down. I guess they were prepared to peacefully help us on our way to heaven, or to blast us along the way. I recall wondering how the pastor could comfortably conduct a sermon of love under the ominous gaze of a trigger-happy guard. In the corner of the room was an old upright Baldwin with the ivories chipped away. A con by the moniker of Old Folks, beat out religious tunes and I mean he really beat them out. On the outside, it would have been illegal to disturb the peace with what we passed off as singing. By the time the sermon was over, I had developed what was almost an affection for the minister. He was sincere and compassionate. He cared for us and every con in the congregation knew it. When he was through, he came over and embraced me. I was embarrassed. He whispered, "I received a beautiful letter from your Mother and sister. When it is safe, I will bring it in to you." I stammered, "Pastor, I want to ask your pardon for the way I treated you and Father Scannell. I am ashamed of myself. Will you please tell Father Scannell that I............" I got no farther because a guard walked up to me and ordered, "Move it out, Williams."

When I went to bed that evening, I felt relieved and comfortable. I attributed it to the fact that I knew I had to face the Sky Pilots and do the proper thing by them. It was during this period I wrote:

THE SAINTS WHO HAVE NEVER BEEN CAUGHT

When some fellow yields to temptation,
And breaks a conventional law,
They look for no good in his make-up,
But God how they look for a flaw.
None will ask how tempted,
Nor allow for the battle he has fought,
His name becomes food for the jackals,
For those who have never been caught.

He has sinned, they thundered
And by his example be taught,
That his footsteps lead to destruction
Cry the Saints who have never been caught.

I am a sinner, Oh Lord, and I know it,
I am weak, I blunder and I fail,
I am tossed on life's stormy ocean,
Like a ship embroiled in a gale;
I am willing to trust in thy mercy;
And keep the commandments they taught;
But deliver me, Oh Lord, from the judgement;
Of the Saints who have never been caught.

In the morning, my outlook was much improved. An opportunity to talk with Father Scannell presented itself the following Saturday in the yard. In fact, it was he who walked briskly to where I was talking to a group of friends. When I saw him approach, I excused myself and met him halfway. He extended his hand and inquired, "Nate, my friend, Peter told me he had received a nice letter from your family. Well, he is not ahead of me because I got one also. I will be by your cell in a day or two and will let you read it. How have you been doing?" I have rarely met a finer man. He was sensitive to the things that were dear to me. His smile was warm and infectious, his handshake firm and real. He told me all about his family and activities. He talked more than I did because I had a paucity of concerns about which I could gab. He understood this and continued his rapid-fire input. By the time the yard period was over, I felt as though I had known this gentleman for many years.

For many months I attended both the Catholic and Protestant services. It was my testimony to two Christians. There must have been a subtle change in my attitude toward the staff and other inmates, a change I did not recognize. It was brought to my attention in a letter from my Mom and Dad. They had quoted a paragraph of a recent letter from Reverend McCormack in which he had written, "As chaplain, may I tell you that my regard for Nathan is not for anything he may have done for me. It is for his own sake, that he is here in an environment that tests the quality of any man's character. To quote an opinion generally expressed recently at one of our Board meetings, 'he is one of the best inmates we have'. His personality has gained for him the respect of all. As Chaplain, I get very close to many of the men. Nathan, as a regular attendant at the worship services I lead here, is a great strength to me. He speaks well of my efforts and tries to get his fellow prisoners to share in the good things the church has to offer. As his instructor, I find him a very apt student, one who is diligent in his studies and consistent in his attitudes. I see him every week and have a chance to confer with him. At such times he tells me of things he hears from home." That letter from the pastor was a source of comfort to my parents.

I was surprised to find that many of the Island's most notorious miscreants would not dream of missing a chance to climb the stairs every Sunday and absorb the atmosphere of Peter and Joseph. It would be impossible to recount the multitude of favors they did for the inmates. Beyond doubt, many of those favors were illegal in the eyes of the custodial-minded. Peter and Joseph would take uncensored letters in and out of the confines of Alcatraz. Both of our pastors made it clear that they would not smuggle anything in or out that smacked of drugs or weapons.

In the case of Peter, he made more than one trip to Seattle to visit my family and tell them things I couldn't write about. One time I told him how the cons managed to get by the mail censor. He was amazed to learn that we would pen messages in urine on the backsides of our stationary, which contained no writing. Members of the family would receive a letter and read the innocuous message on the front page, then would turn the page over, put it face down on the ironing board and apply a very warm iron. As clear as day, secret writing would appear; a simple and juvenile trick that any 10 year old boy knew of. So many of their iron-clad procedures were easily thwarted. It must have been disconcerting to Mail Censor Baker trying to figure how the cons managed to learn so many things that were verboten. He was certain that the guards were smuggling messages in and out and, in some instances, they were. In most cases, he was inadvertently putting the Alcatraz "Censored" stamp on each piece of contraband that went through his office. The inmates referred to this method of sending secret messages as the "Special Delivery By Urine Express". If the censor had ever learned what the cons were doing to his precious mail, he would have had a stroke.

Through the grapevine, the convicts received word that their beloved friend, The Reverend Peter McCormack, had been forbidden to ever set foot on the Island he loved to refer to as his place of redemption. At first we all accepted the news as gossip. However, I fired a urine-coded letter to my brother, Dan. It was a one-liner which instructed him to call Peter. Before his reply could get back, the dismissal of our friend was confirmed. This is what the pastor had written my sister, Marjorie: "In response to your inquiry about my being ostracized from Alcatraz; well, it is a long story. For a long time now I have been manifesting my concern for the men in a manner not approved by the "big brass". Also, I dared to protest against some of the procedures, the injustices and, in my judgement, the cruelties committed. So on the last Sunday of October, I was called into the office of the warden and without any apologies, that officer announced my discharge from the office of Chaplain. I tried to have him state a reason and he refused, other than to say I was restricted from the island permanently. In some manner the news got out and the papers in big headlines announced 'Row on Alcatraz, Chaplain Discharged'. Of course I was besieged with phone calls from all quarters to give a story, but not knowing what I might be charged with, I refrained from discussing the matter. In a few days the papers managed to get contact with the warden and his statement was to the effect that I was 'too old and too zealous for the spiritual welfare of the inmates'. Now, after a lapse of two months and, since no further accusations have been made, I can tell you the reason for my discharge.

There is a certain prisoner there by the name of Morton Sobel. In some way his name was mentioned during the Julius and Ethel Rosenberg trial. A perjurer linked him up with the Rosenbergs. After a lengthy trial, Sobel was sentenced to Alcatraz for 32 years. In the meantime, friends of Mr. Sobel have been working to get a rehearing of his case, and many prominent citizens of all walks of life have petitioned the President to release him. A petition was prepared and signed by over 7,000 people; lawyers, educators, scientists, ministers, Roman Catholic priests and others. I was invited by Mrs. Sobel, the wife of Morton, to sign this petition. Knowing Mrs. Sobel intimately and getting firsthand information from her as to the abuses she and her husband were subjected to, in order to try to force from them testimony that would implicate innocent people, I agreed. In other words, they were being pressured to perjure themselves. They refused to do so. As a result, Morton Sobel has been an inmate at Alcatraz for over six years. I signed the petition and, though this has not been stated by the Warden, this is the reason for my dismissal.

Needless to say, I was terribly hurt at the time, as were all my friends, including Nate. I have learned that there is no such thing as redress when you deal with prison authorities, and if some of those in authority had their way, I feel I might be an associate with Nate and the others of my friends at Alcatraz in the drudgery of their lives. There is nothing more that I can say, other than I miss my association with Nate and the others very much. To repeat what I have stated many times, the period of time spent with the men on Alcatraz has been the most rewarding years of my ministry. There was so much in the association with these men that gave me great satisfaction as I watched them being changed, through the ministry of the Word and the power of God working in the lives of a number of them. Let me leave with you a little poem I ran across:

> In men whom men condemn as ill,
> I find so much of goodness still.
>
> In men whom men pronounce divine,
> I find so much of sin and blot.
>
> I hesitate to draw the line
> Between the two, when God has not."

The warden was alerted that the prisoners might riot for what he had done. Precautions were set up immediately. Services were cancelled for two weeks. When they were restored, neither Catholic nor Protestant would attend. Of course, this did not bother the authorities. So far as the Prison Bureau was concerned, religious services were a nuisance and a waste of time. Their contention was that criminals are beyond redemption.

A week or two later, Father Scannell appeared in the yard. A group of hurt and angry inmates immediately gathered around him. He climbed the stairs and, with the inmates' urinal as his pulpit, he raised his hands to quiet the clamoring men. The tower guards in their gun-cages, aware that some-thing unusual was taking places, stepped along the wall, cradled their rifles in a threatening manner and watched the scene below. The unarmed guards who were down among the irate cons were in an untenable and dangerous position. As always in such cases as this, they gathered together and huddled beneath a gun tower for mutual protection. They knew that the fire power would be directed to their defense if the captives made a move on them. There was a potential for mayhem and death if a wrong word or move had ignited the flammable fabric of the convicts' tempers. An eerie quiet had settled over the recreation area.

As I looked up and saw Father Scannell poised in such an unlikely setting, I thought of the verse in the Bible which read, in part, "I was in prison and you visited me..." The restless men waited for Father Scannell to begin, and as soon as he did, his words had a calming effect on the audience gathered below. "My dear friends, I am painfully aware of how deeply you feel the loss of The Reverend Peter McCormack. An hour ago, I met with him at his church and he prayed - not for himself, but for you and your families. He urged me to come over here and to remind you that while he cannot be with you in person, he is with you in spirit. He pleads with you to remember all that he advocated as you journey through life. Walk hand in hand with Jesus Christ, and you will be freed. Many of you are not Catholics, but I beg you, in the absence of a minister of your faith, please feel welcome to join me in worship each Sunday. Do not boycott the only temple of faith we have on this sod. At least we know it is built on solid rock." A ripple of laughter spread through the crowd below him at this unintended pun. "I want you to join me in prayer." I looked around at this unbelievable sight. The nations' most deadly, almost to a man, bowed their heads. I am sure they weren't acting in a reverential mood as much as out of the profound respect they felt for Father Joseph Scannell. A few days later, a black Muslim told me that he bowed his head as more of a display of his hatred for the established authority than for respect of the Catholic Church. He added, "I do think that the priest is one goddam good guy, but he should have been a Muslim."

The following Sunday, more men attended the Catholic service than ever before in the history of Alcatraz. The powers that be were fully aware that there was an inordinate number of inmates turning out for that service. They responded in kind. The chapel was heavily over-loaded with guards. Instead of one gunman in the cage along the wall, there were two. So far as the number of cons in the congregation were concerned, they, too, I am sure, were just making their support known and were voicing their anger at the dismissal of The Reverend Peter McCormack. Credit should have gone to the priest for having prevented a full-fledged riot. I did not know how long we would be without the Protestant services. Whoever did take McCormack's place would have a hell of a time filling his shoes. The cons would be very skeptical. Being a suspicious body of men, it could be months before any credence would be placed in a new minister.

One Sunday after services, the priest asked me if I would remain behind until the main body of inmates had returned to their cells. He had secured the permission of the Lieutenant-In-Charge for me to do so. After he had taken off his robe, he asked if I would mind washing the glasses and trays that were used for communion. I was pleased to be given the opportunity. It was at this time he told me the reason Peter had been so shabbily dismissed. Rumor had it that he was fraternizing with the convicts.

You would have to understand the tight physical restriction imposed on all inmates in Alcatraz. Other than inmate movement necessary to go to work, to the dining room and to the rec yard, there was absolutely no freedom given any con on any other occasion. No inmate moved unescorted! Ever! I was dumbfounded when I was told I could take the communion-service tray, unescorted, to the kitchen for cleaning purposes. On my first trip, I was nervous walking along the 500 feet Broadway corridor leading to the kitchen. Apparently the path had been cleared through the maze of catwalks and cellhouse guards. I was waved on my way at each check-point. At no time was I out of observance, however. No matter which way I glanced, I would see a guard watching me either directly or through a mirror. When I got to the kitchen door, a key was passed down to a guard on the cellhouse level so that he could open the huge steel gate separating the mess hall from the men's quarters. In the kitchen, I was searched and then passed on to the dish-washing section. I performed my task in about fifteen minutes. As I started to leave, the civilian chef said, "Williams, sit down at that table until I can escort you to the main gate." I sat down, and was shocked when an inmate brought me a cup of coffee and a piece of cake. I couldn't believe my eyes, nor stomach. This was the most relaxed dining atmosphere I had experienced in more than three years!

In the yard a few days afterward, the inmate who had served me the coffee and cake said that Father Scannell had called ahead and asked the chef if he could 'give Williams a treat'. I was particularly hard struck by the firing of my dear friend, Peter McCormack. I missed the many hours we had talked. While the new Protestant minister turned out to be a concerned and dedicated individual, there was no chance he could take McCormack's place. The fact that Peter did many favors for me was not the primary reason I so acutely felt his departure. I had learned to love the guy like a mentor and father. I realized I would have to occupy my mind, and avoid concentrating on negative thoughts.

The following Saturday, during yard privileges, I sought out my buddy, Creepy Karpis, and told him of my concern. He urged me to develop good reading and studying habits. "Remember what I told you when you first came in," he remonstrated. "Keep developing your mind and you will find you don't have time to develop jelly in your brain and become stir-crazy. Every solid con in here kept on an even keel by doing as I have advised you to do. All of us lose something or someone dear. You can't sky-dive off the third tier because of that loss. A lot of us are hurt by the loss of the Sky-Pilot." While we were talking, Chicago Blackie sauntered over and sort of included himself. He agreed with the suggestion given by Creepy. "You know, Nate, you have always had a leaning toward the study of law. Why don't you ask the Captain Of The Guards for an interview, and when he calls you out, ask him for permission to take a correspondence course from the LaSalle Extension University? You can get a bona fide LL.B. I once read that many practicing attorneys got their degrees through LaSalle. You've got all the time in the world. When you talk to him, you can bet your keister he'll hit the roof, and you may have to go over his head. Every con in here will be watching the outcome of your request. They dream of throwing up their own roadblocks. That's why they are stir-crazy."

That evening I decided to follow Chicago Blackie's advice. Very carefully, I wrote my request to the captain. "Captain Latimer: I would appreciate the courtesy of an interview with you for the following purpose. As the records will show, I have spent many months taking advantage of the limited correspondence courses available to us. I would like your permission to take a course in law from the LaSalle Extension University. Respectfully yours, Nathan G. Williams, 1103AZ, B256."

Three weeks passed before I received a response from the Captain. It was very brief and to the point. "Williams: Request denied." There was no explanation. When I showed the note to Harmon, he simply commented, "Goddam it, Nate, what the hell did you expect?" I shot back at him angrily, "I expected the courtesy of an explanation for the refusal, that is what I

243

expected." When I told Morton Sobel about the reply, he made a suggestion. "Why don't you go over his head and make the request of Warden Paul J. Madigan? When you truly want something from these people, or anyone else, you have to keep pressing. The brass balls of any business generally will not extend the courtesy of recognizing the wishes of a peon. In a place like this, they are much more dictatorial because they regard you as less than a peon. If you really want to study law, you will make an effort."

That evening, I sent a request slip in to the warden, asking the same privilege I had sought of the Captain. Three days later, I was surprised to be advised by the cellhouse guard that I was to be held in from work because the warden wanted to see me. The very fact that he took the time to call me out made me feel good.

The following noon I stood in front of the warden's desk; that is I and three guards. As usual, I was placed in such a position between the guards and the warden that I could be waylaid if I made a move toward Madigan. In more than one case, an irate con had tried to put his hands around the gullet of a staff member. I stood waiting for Madigan to say something. Instead, he just looked over the top of his spectacles and stared at me. Finally, he said, "Williams, you have got to be joking. With all the trouble we get from you inmates, do you really expect me to approve such a request?" I started to answer, but was cut off as he continued. "Even if I were inclined to approve the course, I would have to contact, James V. Bennett, the Director of the Federal Bureau of Prisons and present the proposal to him. If I were that stupid, I would find my posterior doing guard duty in a tower in Siberia. My answer in an emphatic NO!. You are dismissed." I did not give him the satisfaction of knowing' how disappointed I was.

The grapevine had spread the news of my attempt, and the entire inmate population was anxiously awaiting my arrival in the rec yard. Rather than explaining to each individual what had taken place, I climbed to the top of the steep stairs leading to the yard, turned toward the office in general and gave a middle finger flip. By nature, I was a tenacious person and I made up my mind then and there to pursue the matter all the way to Washington, D.C.

A week later, I got a hell of an idea. Why not write my Dad via the Urine Express and explain what had taken place this past month? It might be futile, but at least I could be a fly in the ointment. What could the authorities do about my persistence, send me to the dreaded Rock? I very carefully composed a letter to Dad, and then sat back. I knew my dad was a fighter. I also knew that he knew his way around politicians. A week later, I got a brief answer from him. He had simply written, "Dear Son, your mother and I are pleased to learn that you are going to continue with your studies. We will do whatever is permissible. Love, Mom and Dad." After all had settled down in the cellhouse that night and the landings were clear of guards, I took my Dad's letter, held a match just close enough beneath it so it wouldn't burn and watched the message take shape between the inked lines. It read: "Be patient as I work on the problem. It may take months. I will keep you abreast of my progress or the lack thereof. I will be in D.C.

seeking an interview with James V. Bennett. He may not grant it. If I can't get satisfaction there, I will contact William O. Douglas, U.S. Supreme Court Justice."

Four months elapsed before I got word about the La Salle course. When it came I got it from an unexpected source. After work one afternoon, I was surprised to look up and see the mail censor, Baker, looming in front of my hotel suite. He was holding a large manila envelope in his hand. His face was livid with anger. In a low and ominous voice he said, "Williams, I have a letter here from the Director. It is his formal approval for you to enroll in a course of law from the LaSalle Extension University. Nate, how in the hell did you swing that?" That was the first time a staffer had used my first name. "Well, Mr. Baker, you know that letters to the Director are to go straight through to him without being censored, so naturally you weren't aware that I had written him with regard to taking the course." Baker fumed and retorted, "I can't understand what is going on here. This is Alcatraz, not a girls' reformatory. I never thought I'd live to see the day when the Bureau would approve such a thing. Now every thug in the joint will start studying some foolish subject." He stomped off.

Inwardly, I was in seventh heaven, but I kept my mouth clamped. I did not want to create any more animosity than he already carried in his heart, and for a good reason. He had a maniacal hatred of all cons on Alcatraz. During the 1946 riot, Baker and other guards had been captured by the rioting inmates and were locked in a cell. The rampaging men had secured a rifle, pistol and plenty of ammunition. When the inmates realized that their chances of escape were futile, their crazy leader, Cretzer, walked up to the penned up guards and emptied the pistol into their bodies. Two died. Baker caught a slug near his knee and was crippled for life. I can understand his anger.

Notwithstanding I had received permission for the course from the highest authority, my material was not delivered to my cell for eleven weeks. I knew this delay was a retaliatory move. I talked again with Morton Sobel, Alvin 'Creepy' Karpis and Harmon Waley as to what they felt my next move should be. Each agreed that I should not stir up any trouble, but bide my time. Creepy was right when he said, "You are dealing with unscrupulous and devious people, Nate. Play the waiting game with them. They will try to get you to blow your top. Keep cool and wait."

Three months from the day I heard from Baker, the material necessary to start the course arrived. I was told to report to the Captain's desk and pick it up. I hurried back to my bunk with the cardboard box. I was anxious to examine the contents. My happiness was mingled with pain and anger when I looked through the contents. There was a note from the Captain which had been taped to my copy of Black's Law Dictionary. It read; "We are enclosing just the amount of material you will need to start your course. You are fully aware of the rule that forbids an inmate to have more than one book, other than the Bible, in his cell. I am granting you the special privilege of having your first lesson book and the Law Dictionary. If any of this material is found in the possession of another inmate, you will be severely disciplined and your study material will be confiscated. Further, you are not to assist any inmate in the preparation of legal matters." I was bitterly disappointed when I opened the dictionary to see that the censor had stamped in big black letters on more than a dozen pages throughout the book.

The ink from the stamp was wet and messy. It had soaked through two pages and obliterated many words. This was just the beginning of four years of the harassment of which Creepy had spoken.

19

Hall Of Frame

It seemed that from the day I started applying myself to the study of law, I became oblivious to the trials and travails of the guards, the inmates and even to the Hunk of Rock where I lived. Minor irritants were no longer worthy of my attention. I was blissfully absorbed in my schooling. I think what really took place at this time was the life-saving preoccupation of attaining an LL.B. I permitted myself to become so profoundly engrossed in the pursuit of this goal that I began neglecting my friends. However, I did not neglect going to church. I had a hang-up that I owed this time to Peter McCormack. My neglect of my friends became so obvious to Father Scannell that he came to my cell one evening and commented on the fact. "I think that what you are doing, Nate, is commendable, but you must set some time aside for your friends and for relaxation. Take my advice, friend; the brain needs some diversion or else you will burn out." I took his advice and started returning to a more normal routine; that is, if you can call observing fighting, knifings, assaults and escape attempts 'normal'.

The hours I spent in my cubicle studying were hours of welcome respite. Even my precious moments of privacy with Muriel became less and less important. Occasionally, in despair, I would find myself wondering why I was striving for the LL.B. Here I was nearing my fortieth year, serving a long prison term without hope of parole, and I had set my mind on a meaningless achievement. I began to lose sight of the necessity of occupying my time and mind, and the unseen benefits derived from 'escaping' through improvement. The "Trigger Man" for Murder, Inc., once told me, "When you spend hours reading or studying, those hours serve you, you don't serve them. That's the only way you can beat the government out of this time."

Tearing myself away from my books, as suggested by Father Scannell, was more difficult than I had anticipated. For the first time in my life, I decided to allot a space for all the necessary things I had to do. It took discipline, something of which I had very little. Other than my studying, the greatest pleasure I experienced was sitting in the prison yard on the upper cement steps with my closest companions whom I referred to as 'The Unholy Three'. The first was Abie "The Trigger" Chapman who was reputed to be the chief assassin for the Mafia. His other sideline profession was his connection with Murder, Inc. In that capacity, he told me that his function was to eliminate people who had incurred the wrath of a Murder, Inc. He emphasized that 'eliminate' didn't always result in the death of the victim. Methods of elimination could be accomplished by breaking a leg or

247

two, dismembering of a foot or finger or administering a near-fatal beating. The nature of the 'treatment' depended on the wishes of the client and how much he was willing to dish out.

Abie was truly one of those who defied description. I saw him as a short, homely man, about fifty. In the five years I knew him, he never combed his hair nor zipped up his pants. His eyes were colorless. He had no formal education, but was intelligent and extremely well-read. He was never without a smile, and yet there was no warmth to his countenance. Instead of looking at you, he gazed through you. He was as lethal as an asp. I never heard anybody accuse him of having any morals. It was through our mutual interest of playing dominoes that I met Trigger. If he hadn't been an inveterate cheat, we never would have become close acquaintances. Even at our innocent game of dominoes, where there were no wagers, I caught him cheating. The first time I let it pass. The next time I jumped up, kicked over the board and called him a stinking cheat. "One more time, Trigger, and I am going to re-arrange your dentures." He looked up at me and said, "I have no doubt you are capable of doing just that, but before you do, write your mother a farewell letter." At the time of this confrontation, I did not know of his reputation. As he returned my glare, I swear that he had the look of an executioner, which, of course, he was. During dinner that night, Creepy told me all about Trigger. "The funny thing about Trigger," Karpis continued, "is that the guys in here like him." This was Karpis's way of saying, that if trouble comes between you and him, the population will side with him. The following Saturday in the yard, I saw Trigger making his way toward me. I was alerted for trouble and was ready to defend myself. I believed he might be going to try to shiv me. I had no weapon but was ready to plant a boot right in between his legs. He totally disarmed me by saying, "Nate, you are the only guy in here who offers me any competition at dominoes. Let's forget our stupid quarrel and kill time, not each other, by playing the game." I was still wary of his motive, but responded, "OK, Trigger, but don't let me catch you cheating me again." He smiled and said, "I'll try not to get caught." From that time on, until he and I left Alcatraz, we played our favorite game. I had no doubt that he cheated me regularly. He couldn't help it.

This is the place for a final paragraph on Trigger. When he was eventually released from federal custody, he moved to California. Over the next twenty years, I tried to get in contact with Abie. For some reason or another, maybe by design, I couldn't make personal contact. I tried going through criminal channels, to no avail. I gave up trying to arrange a meeting between us. Surely, through the grapevine, he knew of my efforts to reach him, so I had to conclude he was not interested. Twenty seven years later, word reached me from a Criminal Research Analyst, Robert Bates of Oregon City, Oregon, as well as from a former Alcatraz guard, that a very interesting development involving Trigger was being aired in a federal court in San Francisco. Robert Bates sent news clippings of the trial. The United States District Attorney accused U.S. District Judge Robert Aguilar of eight felony accounts of using his office as a "racketeering enterprise" to obstruct justice. The part of surprising interest to me was that Trigger was named as a co-defendant. Apparently Trigger was back in the rackets and, if he was, he naturally wanted to avoid contact with past acquaintances. I could not understand a federal judge being criminally involved with a character like Abie Chapman until I learned that he was related to the jurist by marriage. It became obvious that Trigger had been travelling with some affluent and politically powerful people. At this writing, the final outcome of his case hasn't been determined. Abie is now 83 years of age.

The second party of the Unholy Three was Alvin 'Creepy' Karpis, a member of the notorious Ma Barker gang. He was nicknamed 'Creepy' by F.B.I. Director J. Edgar Hoover. Where he came up with that name is beyond me. There was nothing creepy about Al Karpis. His criminal career started in the early 30's and ended with his incarceration on Alcatraz. He had the distinction of having served more time on the Rock than any other inmate, a total of 26 consecutive years. He was one of the best read and most intelligent men on the Island. Under such terrible circumstances, that fact is a monument to his innate intelligence. There is no question that he was a very dangerous gangster. Only God knows how many banks he had robbed, or persons he had kidnapped. The Ma Barker gang was directly connected with the actual slaying of four or five men and, during the shootouts in which those men were dispatched, Karpis himself was never accused of being a killer. Even in his youth, he traveled with the most elite gangsters. He was a trusted confidant of Al Capone, with whom he served time on Alcatraz. Old-timers on the Rock told me that Creepy avoided Capone during their incarceration. Whenever I would try to engage him in any conversation concerning Al Capone, he would let me know, without uttering a word, that I was on verboten ground. He was a compassionate man and a natural counselor. During some of my roughest times, I sought his counsel. He was adamant in his suggestion that I "steer clear of the dingbats in this nuthouse. Do your own time and keep away from the troublemakers."

The third member was a man of whom I learned very little. He was the leader of Detroit's Purple Mob. His name was Louie, and his claim to fame was that he was a cinch connection for machine guns and other arsenal. At that particular time, the main priority of the FBI was to 'get Louie off the streets'. He was captured and found guilty of possession of a goodly number of Thompson sub-machine guns, the favorite weapon of hoodlums in the 1920'S and 1930'S. He wound up in the Hoover Iron-Bar Hotel in San Francisco Bay. Louie and I worked together in the tailor shop. We were physically close, but never truly buddies. In fact, I knew of no one he trusted or confided in. That alone earned him the respect of other inmates and most of the staff. How this group came to be referred to as the Unholy Three I will never know. One thing these man had in common was that each, in all the years they served, had never admitted to ever breaking the law. In their vernacular, they echoed one another in steadfastly contending they were framed. Many years later, while I was having dinner with Paul J. Madigan, a former warden of Alcatraz, he made an interesting observation: "Those three should have been inducted into an Alcatraz "HALL OF FRAME".

My studies helped me survive the deadly monotony, and those studies were interrupted at regular interludes by the inevitable eruptions of bestial violence. One of the pastimes the Unholy Three and I would enjoy with a degree of regularity was when the tourists would be sailing by our haven. The tour guide would be delivering a colorful spiel about the history of the prison and society's most deadly enemies who had been put away by Hoover and his gang. The tour boat was permitted to come within 200 yards of the Island. Any closer and they would be fired upon. There was a huge sign cautioning boats to stay beyond that limit. On a calm day when the boat filled with curious tourists got as close as it dared, the spieler's voice would carry clearly across the water and to the ears of the very men who were the subject of conversation. It was a comedy to all of us who sat on the upper steps and listened to the BS. "Now, ladies and gentlemen, you are but a few yards from the home of the dregs of society, the famous Alcatraz. Some of the very criminals of whom I speak are watching you from the recreation yard this very moment. Those of you who have binoculars might be able to see them. In that very yard sat Al Capone, Machine Gun Kelly and many other desperate men. At this time, undoubtedly you are being observed by Alvin Creepy Karpis and other members of the Ma Barker gang." From there he would go into a lengthy history of Alcatraz Island until the boat would pull around the Rock and fade from view.

At the mention of Karpis' name, the cons in the yard would start cheering Creepy. We would pat him on the back and ask for his autograph. Alvin was embarrassed at times, but he said nothing.

When young and gullible inmates would arrive, an old-timer by the name of Jackson would latch on to one of them and engage him in conversation. Eventually, he would direct the talk to include Al Capone and, to impress the greenhorn, he would refer to him as Scarface or 'my old buddy, Al'. The new con would be all eyes and ears. About this time, Jackson would pull out an old corncob pipe, stuff the bowl with tobacco, light up and leisurely puff away. As if he were about to bestow a great privilege on the newcomer, he would offer him the pipe and ask, "How'd you like to smoke the very pipe that Scarface used for five years?" An aura of hero worship would glow in the eyes of the sucker. Just wait until he could tell his buddies that he smoked from the very pipe that belonged to Al Capone. Eventually, the bait would be dropped. "Say, feller, I kind of like you. Tell you what, I am scheduled to be transferred from this joint in a couple of months. How'd you like to buy this antique pipe? I can let you have it for your ration of cigarettes until I leave or for three months, whichever comes first." By the time the sucker found he had been had, he'd be too ashamed to tell anyone. A few years down the line he would be pulling the same game on someone else. Jackson confided in me that he had sold a dozen 'Scarface Capone Corncobs'. The crazy thing about it is, some of the suckers were guys who had been around these joints for years.

Al Capone was crazy and had syphilis. In Alcatraz he was a nothing. Let me tell you what happened to him one day. Al and Harmon Waley, the famous Weyerhauser kidnapper, were in the music room practicing. Harmon was on the trombone and Al on the banjo. They got into a bitter argument after Al called Harmon a 'baby-grabbin' fruiter. This was in reference to Harmon's kidnapping caper. Before the guard could get between them, Harmon rapped his trombone around Capone's gourd. That was the funniest thing to happen in here in a year. Instances like these were life-savers in that they offered diversion without violence.

Stories related by the HALL OF FRAMERS were interesting and varied. Most were non-fictional, though amplified upon. If I had any questions as to their being based in fact, I would seek out my most trusted companion, Alvin Karpis. He had the unique habit of putting his forefinger alongside his nose if he wanted to convey to me that there was room for doubt. Never would he imply that the story-teller was not being truthful. If the tale had a grain of truth, he would always start out by saying, "Now, Nate, as I heard it, it occurred this way..." And then he would tell the story as he knew it to be. If he wanted to impress you with the fact that it was pure horse manure, he would say, "Don't ask me if that particular fabrication was true. Suffice it to say that it was put out by the FBI." That was Karpis' way of filing it in the category of lies. Some of the stories are worth trying to recall.

George Philip Weyerhaeuser, the seven year old son of the lumber magnate of Seattle, Washington, disappeared on his way home from school on May 24, 1936. The following day, a ransom note was delivered to the Weyerhaeuser mansion in which the kidnappers demanded $200,000 to secure the youngster's safe release. They had given the boy's father specific instructions as to how they could be contacted. As instructed, Weyerhaeuser put an ad the local paper which read; 'Due to publicity beyond our control, please indicate another method of reaching you. Hurry. Relieve an anxious mother'. Contact was managed, and the family paid the amount demanded. The boy was released unharmed about a week later. The person who masterminded the snatch was a young man named Harmon M. Waley. He was captured, along with his 19 year old wife, a week later in Utah. Apparently he involved his partner, William 'Yakima' Dainard on May 7, 1936. Both were sentenced to a long term and ended up on Alcatraz. Dainard became insane and was transferred to the United States Hospital For Federal Prisoners in Springfield, Missouri. He died shortly afterward. Harmon was moved to a federal prison on McNeil Island about twenty years later. From there he was freed after another three years.

During Harmon's Rock time, he and I became chums, along with JB, another bank robber who had hit the same bank thirty days after I had. JB and I listened to Harmon's endless litany of detail about the kidnapping. It was almost as if he had a compulsion to 'get it off his chest'. Harmon said the week they had the boy in their keeping was a gruesome period in which Dainard wanted to kill the boy and dump his body in a river. This very suggestion repulsed Harmon and he bitterly opposed Dainard's plot. As he told JB and me, "You know, guys, I got attached to the kid, and there was no way in hell I was going to stand by and see him slaughtered. He was really a nice boy who was unfortunate enough to have rich parents. Dainard and I quarreled bitterly. I imagined that my partner might slay the victim while I slept, so I kept myself between George and Dainard. I was relieved when we collected our money, split it and 'Yakima' went his own way." JB and I placed a lot of credence in Harmon's story. We knew that Harmon was

251

basically a gentle person who could not stand violence in any form.

Incidentally, it might be interesting to note that Harmon was caught in the cross-fire between the guards and the armed convicts during the prison riot in 1946. He wasn't involved in the actual conflict. To protect himself from the thousands of bullets which were flying around, he crawled as far under his bunk as possible. However, being a big man, his posterior protruded from under his fortress. Need I tell you where a stray slug caught him?

After his release in the mid-70's, Waley married a very wealthy woman. She died four years later, leaving her wealth to her husband. JB, Harmon and I kept in close contact for years after our release. About 1985, Harmon drove out to JB's home in a new small camper he had purchased. He calmly told JB, "I'm leaving. It is my intention to travel all over this country until I have seen every inch of it. I don't want to contact you or Nate, or anyone else. Some day they'll find me along the highway in my camper." Both JB and I gave little credence to what he had said. We thought that he was in one of his moods, and that somewhere down the line, Harmon would drive up. If he plans to do so, he had better hurry because at this writing he is about eighty years of age, if he is still living.

When I was a little boy, my mother always cautioned me to be careful with whom I associated. Her letters to me in Alcatraz were so sweet and caring. Inevitably, she would close them with this admonition; 'Now, son, be certain to practice good health habits. And remember, you are judged by your associates, so do not walk in the company of persons of bad repute. You will not be lonely if you keep your eyes on Jesus. Even though you are in prison, you are truly as free as a bird if you trust and obey Him'. I never told her that finding persons of good repute would be like finding the proverbial needle in the hay stack. Yet, I found some very dear and dependable men in the cellhouses who had numbers stamped on their backs. It was common to hear them say, "You may believe what I tell you because I have nothing left but my word." It would be injudicious to take that statement seriously. I could have written this reply to my mother; 'Dear Mom, I associate with some very well-educated gentlemen in here, so don't you fret that I might fall into bad hands'. She would have welcomed such a letter, but Dad would have seen through it. It wasn't that I sought to deceive her. I wanted to put her mind at ease.

I have found it very difficult to tell people of the heinous crimes some of my fellow prisoners had committed and, in the next breath, assure them that there were those I could trust with my life. Paradoxical men are both among the convicts and in the pews of churches. How do you respond to a person who asks, "Nate, you tell me of the Trigger Man of Murder, Incorporated, whose sole occupation was killing or maiming men, women or children on orders from his chief. Imagine breaking both kneecaps of a man you don't even know, and for a few paltry dollars? Yet when you talk of this beast, you seemed to hold him in high esteem." How in hell can I convince a Square John that, once in prison, you adapt to the society in which you are cast? You want to play chess with the Bird Man Of Alcatraz? Do you stop to ask him how many men he has slain?. No! That fact becomes inconsequential.

The important thing is that you want to kill a few hours playing a game. At this point in our existence, what the Bird Man did wasn't vital to our few hours of relaxation. Existence is the key word.

Quite often the Unholy Three were joined by others in their sort of 'inner-circle' get-togethers. It wasn't that the three for whom the group was named were esoteric and were isolating themselves from the regular population. They were, however, coldly discriminating. They simply did not encourage 'strays' infringing on their turf. There wasn't a chance that a stool pigeon or a child molester would penetrate their armor. There was an iron-clad caste system. Unless you were known or highly recommended by a respected member of the circle, there wasn't a chance in hell you would be accepted. I considered myself fortunate because I had committed a bank robbery with Arlo and Crazy Cretzer, two respected cons who vouched for me. The vouching didn't necessarily mean a verbal recommendation. Simply being seen talking with these men was an implicit stamp of approval. At that time and, in my ignorance, I reveled in my so-called position with this body of men. Later I learned that many of those 'accepted' individuals were the dregs of prison society, more perfidious than the well-known rats.

I spent months on my law studies. The staff continued to harass me by holding up my lessons for days on end. On more than a few occasions, my instructors would write me demanding that I get my lessons in on time. There wasn't any way I could write them and tell them that I did have the work in on time, but that the mail censor simply derailed them by holding them for days. Finally, I decided to send my brother, Dan, a letter via the Urine Express and explain the problem I was having. About three weeks after I wrote him, I received an answer in which he let me know that he called one of my instructors and told him what was taking place. He wrote, "I don't think you will be having any more trouble from that source." And I didn't. The instructor was aware of the impediments being thrown in my way. The books continued to be stamped and defaced. Oddly enough, that petty kind of conduct no longer irritated me. As Trigger commented, "If you are getting an education from them, what the hell does it matter how they mess the books up? Once you get your degree, you will be rid of them."

One evening when the night hack was making his rounds, he stopped by and informed me that my brother was coming to visit me the following day. Notwithstanding Dan was a Square John and was always chewing me out for being 'so damned worthless', he and I were particularly close. Even though my sister and he were subjected to the vilest of strategies utilized by the FBI, neither of the two deserted me. Our meeting the following morning was not so traumatic as the one with my mother. Mom was a sensitive person and well along in years, and seeing me in a place like the federal pen at Alcatraz proved too much for her to handle. Not so with Dan. While he had never been arrested nor spent an hour in jail, he had led a pretty physically rugged life in his youth. While I was 'borrowing' funds from an occasional bank, Dan had been a deputy sheriff in the county in which I had made my last strike. When I was arrested for the latest bank caper, he was dragged over the coals by FBI agents in Seattle. Their conduct was so reprehensible that at one point he was alerted to the fact that they might try to 'frame' him.

He was instructing an FBI agent in the science of Judo and Jujitsu when my fiasco engulfed him. After class one afternoon, Dan complained bitterly about the unconscionable tactics the FBI employed against him and my sister. His student simply cautioned, "Dan, be careful of those people. I want you to visit your former instructor, 'Jujitsu' Jorgenson." He was referring to Sven Jorgenson, a respected Seattle police officer of many years. Sven was an authority in the skills of martial arts and directed the Seattle School of Judo/Juijitsu. During the years he instructed my brother in his quest for the Black Belt, they had become good friends. Dan was puzzled by the agent's suggestion that he should talk with Sven. However, after he had talked with Sven for a brief time and Sven confirmed the danger of dealing with the F.B.I., Dan was thankful for the agent's advice.

I was concerned that Dan might start spouting off over the taping of our conversation, in which case our visit would be terminated. The first thing I said when he lifted the phone that connected us was, "Dan, be careful what you say. We are censored and taped." He simply smiled and nodded his head. Our allotted hour passed quickly. We talked about family matters and of mutual friends. I wanted to ask about Muriel but I felt he was uncomfortable on that subject. When he stood up to go, he asked, "Have you any idea if you will be transferred to another more humane penitentiary in the foreseeable future and, if so, when?" I could offer no encouragement. It was too painful for me to tell him that some of my fellow inmates had been waiting ten, fifteen and twenty years for a transfer, during which time they no longer had a family, friends or hope. When I glanced up, he was gone.

After each visit, I went into a depression that lasted for nearly a week. Little wonder that inmates discouraged loved ones from visiting. Some people had come to visit just so they could go back home and tell their friends, "Man, I was on the Rock." Big deal! As usual, when I got back from seeing Dan, I was besieged with questions from my friends wanting to know 'what is new out there'? They were starved for some information as to what was taking place. Bear in mind that these men had been deprived of newspapers, radios or any news magazines for years. As I think back on those years, I wonder what the purpose was for cutting human beings off from the world. What purpose did such restrictions serve?

Instead of months, years now began to pass unnoticed. It was necessary for me to put the thought of time out of my mind. Many old-timers had told me that after a certain length of time, I would be numb to the months and then to the years. Earlier I could not envision such a thing taking place. It did. Another inmate, the Green Lizard, told me that after he had been on the Island for eleven years, he actually forgot, momentarily, what year it was. That statement was backed up by a number of men who had passed their second decade nested away among the seagulls. While I served less than six years on my Island hideaway, I began to relate to 'forgetting the sweet taste of hope'. Now I understood how others had inured themselves and became oblivious to pangs of freedom. I became angry with myself when I noticed that months had raced by, and I had not thought of Muriel. I never dreamed I would enjoy this sort of 'freedom' from memories of my daughter. I guess, to retain my sanity, I forced her from my present life, but always kept a place for her in my fondest memories. There were others who were dear to me. Before long, I began to put them out of my mind.

About three months after Dan came to see me, a non-member of the family dropped in unexpectedly. At least I had not been informed of his pending visit by the administration. It was a total surprise to me when the cellhouse guard told me to lay in from work one morning.

At nine o'clock, my door was activated and I stepped out on the landing and stood waiting for an instruction from the guard at the lever box. "Head for the visiting stall, Williams", he yelled. Normally, an inmate is told who is visiting him a day in advance. It was an absolute right (one of the few we had) to reject a visitor. To my knowledge, none had ever been rejected. I wondered who could possibly be coming to see me and, on my trip to the visiting stall, a dozen names ran through my mind. My visitor turned out to be Marky Barrett, a very loyal correspondent from Seattle. He was accompanied by his lovely wife, Dorothy. Marky was the only one permitted to write me other than immediate members of my family. His letters had been a blessing for many months. I never dreamed he would even consider going to the expense of dropping in on that godless piece of terrain to see a person who, by the commission of a crime, had humiliated him. I attended the same church as Marky and Dorothy, The Free Methodist Church of Seattle. It would be safe to wager that the skirts of that institution were sullied for the first time by my escapade. You can imagine the furor and gossip it created when members of that staid congregation awoke one morning and read of the bank heist perpetrated by one 'Nathan Williams'.

For the third time since my imprisonment on Alcatraz, I was staring through the hazy blue bullet-proof glass trying to bring my visitors into view. When my eyes adjusted to the unnatural light, I was delighted to see my friends, Marky and Dorothy. Marky always wore a smile. Though he had never been condemnatory in any way in his letters, I expected a chewing out now that we were face-to-face. I cautioned myself to hold my temper if he decided to give me a lecture on the virtues of honesty. That never transpired and I was ashamed of myself for ever having that apprehension. Being genuine Christians, they discreetly took every opportunity to let me know of their faith.

After they left, I suffered the usual depression that such visits inflicted on me. Inmates swarmed on me in the yard asking such questions as, "What kind of clothes were they wearing? How did they wear their hair?" The things of importance to us were the things the average person takes for granted. When the famous movie actor, Edward G. Robinson, walked through the shops in the company of the warden, I am sure he was not aware of the interest we had in his clothing. Nor do I believe he was aware that some of those very inmates had gone more than twenty years without any contact with the outside world. The rare visits from people who visited their kin in prison were the only connections we had with 'what was going on in the outside world'. There was a paucity of information penetrating the iron wall.

My sister, Marjorie, was another loyal family member who wrote me regularly. She must have known how necessary it was to my sanity to receive letters. Those letters were received weekly and they afforded me hours of reading and re-reading. I could not wait for my 'letter- writing day' so I could answer her communications. Her letters were a beautiful respite from the killing drudgery of existence on Alcatraz. So, when I received word that she would be in San Francisco in a week and would be over to see me, I was ecstatic. The week deliberately dragged its feet. The hurt on both sides is so terrible sometimes that an hour of visiting drags into an eternity. Not so with Marjorie. She brought good cheer and much news concerning friends and family. I vividly recall asking her questions about Muriel. Until she had left, I did not realize how evasive her replies had been. But I do know that I was glad that the glass between us was hazy. She could not see the tears that burnt my eyes. I was at the point of giving up my visiting privileges. The pain was too much to bear.

I realized how much heartache it must have caused my family to have to visit under such cruel conditions. As a result, I composed the following letter to Warden Paul J. Madigan: 'Dear Warden; From this date forward, I would appreciate it if you would spare me the suffering of visiting under the conditions both my family and I find so offensive. Unless you grant my family and me the courtesy of visiting under pleasant and humane circumstances, I would greatly appreciate having you reject overtures from my family for visiting privileges. All parties involved except, of course, the guards, suffer irreparable damage by trying to communicate under such contrived conditions without feeling or sensitivity. In order that you might better understand what I am trying to convey, I am enclosing a packet of letters I have received from my Mother, Brother and Sister after they have visited me. I can no longer hurt them. I hereby forfeit my right to have visitors during the remainder of my time on Alcatraz. Respectfully yours, Nathan G. Williams, ll03AZ, B256.' By the time I finished this letter, I was sick at heart.

Two days later I was standing in front of the warden's desk. I fully expected to be buried in the 'hole'. He just looked at me for a full minute, and then waved an impatient arm toward his guards and ordered, "Men, stand outside until I call you." They were puzzled by his dismissal. He looked at them again and quietly assured them, "It's OK men. I want to talk with this inmate privately." Reluctantly, they eased out the door. He started out as though he had a burden to get off his chest. "Williams, I am going to call you out again in ten days. And by that time, I am sure you will find visiting more pleasant. Do you understand me?' I nodded, uncertain as to what he meant. "Dismissed," he said. I was in a quandary for the next week. I didn't know what to expect. I was certain of one thing; he was up to no good. By now I was incapable of trusting anyone. When I told the Unholy Three what had taken place, they did not believe me. They acted as though I had 'blown my top', and made me think I was headed for the loony bin.

I became quite friendly with the young fellow who had robbed the same bank I had clipped thirty days previously. He confided in me that he felt I was responsible for his being in prison. Inasmuch as I had never heard of this guy before we met in jail, I questioned his reasoning. He promptly told me, "Well, Nate, I woke up one morning and read in the paper where you and your buddy hit the bank and waltzed away with fifty grand. I figured I could do the same thing. And, to boot, I lived in the area of the bank and knew the roads in and around the county. I had a couple of kids and was having a rough time of it so I talked myself into it. I made a few practice runs, built up my courage and I hit the bank about the same time in the morning as you did. I got the loot alright, got in my car and headed for the tall timber. What do you know, the bank manager was so angry about your job that he bought a pistol and vowed he would shoot the next person who tried to rip off his bank. I was that next person. By the time he followed me out of the joint, I was in my car and was pulling out of the parking lot. Bam! Bam! The moron busted a couple of caps in my direction. One of the slugs ripped through the trunk of my vehicle. From then on things went from bad to worse, and here I am in this toilet bowl with you." I had to laugh at the way JB told his story. I had to ask this kid, "How in the hell do you figure that I am partially responsible for your robbing the bank, getting caught and coming to a halt on this Island? Where do I fit in this crazy pattern of events?" He bristled up and shouted, "Damn it, if you hadn't pulled the first caper I wouldn't have been encouraged to try my hand at it."

As I got to know JB, I could see why he would be the kind of person who would be willing to try anything for excitement. He had his share of moxie and was overloaded with guts. His quick temper and his natural ability with his fists got him into hot water with the staff and, in one case, with a fellow much larger than himself. Like many confrontations in this madhouse, it took very little to set off a violent reaction. I only know that each was striving to dislodge the head of the other. I also know that they were aware that a pair of rifles in the hands of tower guards were sighted at their hearts. That knowledge didn't seem to dampen their enthusiasm for continued mayhem. Eventually, three guards charged in between the two. JB disappeared into the hole and I didn't see him for a long time. When he came out, he was as cocky as ever.

JB was one of the few people to whom I told of my interview with the warden and what the warden had said. JB had a keen mind and was good at analyzing. We made a thousand guesses as to what the warden meant when he told me, "Williams, I am going to call you out again in ten days. By that time, I am sure that you will find visiting more pleasant." Finally, JB came up with what seemed to be the most logical explanation. "It looks to me like they are going to change the visiting conditions."

Throughout my life, I have had premonitions of events about to occur. On this particular Monday morning I awakened in a very agitated state. I was nervous and edgy. I could not eat my breakfast. I felt as if a catastrophe were going to happen, one that would adversely affect me. When the 'work bell' sounded, I lined up in the yard with my crew. The crew bosses were counting their responsibilities. Lieutenant Ordway was standing in his usual imperious manner with his size 15's, their toes pointing upward and outward. The tower guards had left their stations and placed themselves at strategic positions along the wall overlooking the lines of convicts. Their guns were cradled in their arms. As soon as the count was satisfied, the guards called into the control room, and the huge steel gate leading to the shops creaked and groaned as it was opened. The line of about one hundred convicts started down the very steep steps to the industry buildings below. I figured my nerves would settle by the time the tailor shop door slammed behind me. The only thing I could think to do was to submerge myself in the work which was stacked on my sewing machine. Almost as one, each man seated himself at his station, and the hum of the machines began.

Fifteen minutes after we settled into our routine, Ed Burns, the civilian supervisor/guard sauntered up to my machine. He leaned over the stack of shirt collars I was assembling and pretended to be counting and arranging them. It was a normal procedure so no one paid any attention to him. Unexpectedly, he held up a couple of pieces of material and said to me very quietly, "Nate, keep on working. Listen to what I have to say, but don't respond or look surprised. Show no reaction." Immediately he continued, "You and about ten other guys are being transferred to the federal prison at McNeil Island, Washington tomorrow morning." I broke out in a cold sweat and started shaking. I went to the drinking fountain and drank at least two pints of water. It was impossible for me to continue sewing shirt collars. I couldn't sew a straight line. In fact, I was almost unable to function. Ed Burns could see I was almost in a state of shock . He came over and yelled, "Nate, come over here and unload this bolt of cloth onto Louie's cutting table." He was giving me something physical to do until I could recover my composure. He eased himself close to me under the pretext of trying to help me and murmured, "You'll be OK, Nate."

I was walking on air. A transfer from the Rock was almost as good as a release from all confinement. In the yard, I waited until JB came beside me and we entered the cellhouse together. When it was safe, I quietly told him what I had learned. He looked at me and said, "Well, we now know what the warden was trying to tell you. I am glad for you, Nate, and wish I were going with you. Maybe I'll make it on the next chain." I felt sorry for JB. I knew I was going to miss him. I had really got attached to this guy. I asked JB not to mention what I had told him. A transfer of convicts to or from Alcatraz was one of the Bureau's most guarded secrets. They were always fearful some gang members might learn of the movement and way-lay the chain in an effort to free the shackled cargo. It had been done before.

I began to have doubts about my transfer. Maybe Ed Burns had been misinformed. There was nothing I could do but suffer through the wait. At the end of the work shift that day, Ed Burns indicated he wanted me to bring up the tail end of the line with him. He quietly told me, "Nate, I am happy for you. I have always felt you should have never been here. I am going to have my congregation pray for you. May God bless you. Good bye."

At mealtime, JB and I managed to share our table with six other cronies. What we had to say was done with gestures and glances. Just think; I would be living in a cell just 30 miles from my daughter! About 4:00 A.M., a guard quietly came to my cell and whispered, "Williams, you and some other men are leaving this institution in one hour. Take your personal property and stand by the door. When I open it, walk down the tier and go to the front gate." As I was getting my things together, I heard other doors being opened. I could not tell who the other lucky ones were. However, the unusual noise in the middle of the night alerted other cons. Suddenly, one of the men yelled, "Transfer! Transfer!" All hell broke loose. Every sleeping inmate was awakened and started screaming. Someone down the landing from me guessed from the noise my door made that I was one of the men leaving and he called out, "Nate, you ragged-assed bank robber, are you on the chain?" I yelled back, "Yes!" Another spoke out with, "When you get out, get a hold of a gal and give it to her for me." One by one, the men going on the chain showed up at the front gate. I was elated to see JB waiting with his pillowcase filled. And damned if 'Triggerman' wasn't there. The officials realized that the only way they could get the cellhouse quieted down was to move us out of the building. So along with a dozen guards, we were headed into an outer room. Almost as if by signal, the cons who remained behind fell silent.

In an hour, we were chained and loaded into the tiny hold of the prison yacht, Warden Johnston; the very same boat in which some of us had arrived six years previously. However, we were far more jovial leaving the Rock than when we were arriving. Understandably, our mental attitude was better. After all, weren't we leaving a hell of a prison and going to a more heavenly penitentiary? We managed to joke on the trip to San Francisco. At Fort Mason, an army bus was waiting to take us to the International Airport. By the time we were loaded on the old uncomfortable Immigration Service C47, it was nearly seven o'clock. What a motley crew rode that junker as it rumbled down the runway! On one side of the cabin were seven penitentiary guards. On the other side were eleven chain-ladened desperados. It struck me as odd that the cons were joking and laughing as the plane rumbled down the runway, while the guards were glum-faced and sour. I don't know whether it was by design or not as the craft banked sharply and circled our former island home. Even from the sky, it was a horrible looking piece of ugly rock. As soon as the plane reached an altitude of about twenty thousand feet, it leveled off and hit a steady course. The guards rose from their seats and passed sandwiches out to us. Damn, but they tasted good. After we had filled our bellies, most of us lit up cigarettes or cigars. The drone of the engines lulled me to sleep.

I don't know how long I had slept when I was awakened by men yelling, "The plane's on fire." There was a hell of a rattling of chains. The guards and the co pilot grabbed fire extinguishers, rushed to the Triggerman's seat and doused it with foam. Smoke had filled the cabin. I remember thinking what an awful way to go down. The fire was contained in a matter of minutes. When everyone had settled down, the pilot came from the cockpit, walked to the Triggerman's seat and started chewing him out. The Trigger looked him in the eyes and said, "You shitty-assed army scum, you are not talking to some dog-faced punk. Get back in that cockpit!"

With that, he spit fully into the officer's face. Before he could make another move, three of the guards landed on him and got him quieted down. The pilot was purple with rage and made threatening gestures toward the chained convict. The guard in charge got in between the flyer and Trigger and said to the former, "Don't stir these men up." The offended officer shouted, "I'm in charge of this plane! I'm the captain!" The guard looked him fully in the eyes and said, "I'm in charge of the prisoners. You fly to your destination, and I'll handle the men." Frankly, we enjoyed the encounter. We landed at the Sea-Tac International Airport about an hour after the ruckus between the captain and Triggerman Abie.

20

Transfer

As soon as we landed, the plane taxied to a secluded and heavily secured hangar at the south end of the field. From our windows, we could see a bevy of prison guards, police, airport security personnel and sundry other feeders from the public trough. There must have been a total of thirty men awaiting our arrival. Official vehicles were strategically situated to thwart any avenue of escape. When the plane's engines were cut, a large passenger bus detached itself from the others and drove right up to the craft's discharge door. I don't know how many times they rehearsed the act, but they were efficient. Inside the plane, the guards ordered us to stand in the aisle until all our fetters were examined to make sure none of us had slipped a cuff or leg iron.

When they were satisfied that we were securely trussed, we were instructed to go to the door which had been opened, and to stand at the top of the steps until the guards who had accompanied us could position themselves along the steep stairs before we started down. It would have been easy to fall and, if one did, it would have been a domino effect for the whole bunch. The chains as they clanged on the steel steps caused a horrendous racket. When we were on terra firma, the entire contingent of police converged on us.

In a matter of five minutes, the bus and its cargo was on its way toward the federal penitentiary at McNeil Island, thirty-five miles south. As the prison bus pulled onto the dock where the Island boat was waiting for us, I remembered it as it had been six years previously when I first started my journey. The hold of the boat was larger than the Alcatraz's Warden Johnston so our trip to the 'other side' was not so rough. And, too, going to McNeil was just like going home compared to the Rock, so we were a laughing galley of slaves. Guards met us with their standard display of fire power. In a matter of minutes, we were processed and slapped into the fish tanks. The inmates greeted us with hooting, hollering and other falderal. After all, this chain was from Alcatraz and, believe it or not, men from the Big House were highly respected by cons from the lesser pens. The younger inmates idolized what they called the 'epitome' among crooks. I had had young prisoners tell me how passionately they wanted to get to the Big House In The Bay. In their ignorance, they wanted the reputation of being an 'Alumnus' of the world's most famous lock-up. It was futile for me to tell them of the pain and unspeakable suffering meted out by the people who created and developed the 'special treatment for special convicts in a special

261

place of incarceration by a specially trained staff of insensate guards'.

I tried to explain how long lasting such a reputation was. If they came out mentally and physically intact, they would have a stigma that only the Rock could, indelibly, stamp on them. In addition to this dim future, I pointed out, once you got the reputation of having been on Alcatraz, you were a sitting duck for any trigger-happy cop who might want to make a name for himself. Whenever I had the opportunity, I would speak to the younger inmates and attempt to give them the facts about that Island bastille. Some actually became angry when I let them know that many Rock inmates had become stir-crazy. There was no way they could understand it when I told them that the routine on Alcatraz had reduced normal men to vegetables. The need to get out of Alcatraz was an all-consuming drive of every man I had met on the Island. It was common for many of them to attempt to get a transfer by the most despised method; that of snitching on their fellow men. Suicide was one certain way to be freed and, by that route five of them 'went home'. Also, there were untold numbers that left the Rock via the insane asylum. Zombies represented a fair share of the population. Not a few of them simply ended it all by making a run for it, only to be blasted off the cyclone fence that separated them from a watery grave. Some were 'pardoned' by a friend who plunged a knife in their backs. I tried every method I could think of to let them know that there was only one life more horrible than that of imprisonment and that was being caged on Alcatraz. At this time, it is proper for me to point out that I spent time with convicts who had served interminable years on The Rock and, when released, they recovered themselves and went on to become solid citizens. I later became friends with some Alcatraz guards in the free world, and found them to be understanding and responsible people.

My return to McNeil was nearly like being released to the free world. I could go about my assignment without having a guard traipse along. On one occasion, I was instructed to go to the electronics building about two blocks from the main cellhouse. Here, twenty years later, I can recall how great it was to be able to walk that distance in one single line without seeing an armed guard in a tower. In some instances I found myself overwhelmed by the degree of freedom I was enjoying. Notwithstanding the cells were of steel and concrete, they were larger in size than those on the Rock. I had a cellmate with whom I could communicate, a radio and fewer bulls making endless intrusions on my privacy.

Even under the best of conditions in living quarters, there is a problem of one nature or another that always arises. My cellmate was a great guy and he and I got along really well. However, my attention was drawn to a very eerie and weird fellow who celled near us. I asked my cellmate who this inmate was, and why he seemed bereft of friends, even associates. He explained, "That guy you're referring to is Charles Manson. I don't know the guy too well and I don't want to get acquainted. At night he chants funny things aloud to himself. He'll go three or four days without eating or leaving his cell other than to go to work. Cons who pass his cage tell me that they see him standing on his head when they go to the mess hall, and he is still in that position when they return. He's been here about six months or so and has yet to speak to more than a dozen men. The guy is too creepy for me to get near. Some of the younger inmates are afraid of him." Once Manson sat at the same table that my friends and I occupied at a meal. I had a chance to examine him more closely because when he would eat he would keep his head not less than four inches from his plate, not looking up once. His hair was as long as rules permitted and he was never cleanly shaven. Throughout the meal, he kept muttering unintelligibly to himself.

A few years after I had been freed, I was visiting with Jacob Parker, the former warden of McNeil Island. I brought up the subject of Charles Manson to Jake. He threw his hands in the air and said, "Oh, not that dingbat again. Let me tell you an interesting thing that took place with him while I was the superintendent. You remember Steve Bell? He was a great big guy. Well one day Bell stopped me in the hallway and told me that Manson had stolen his Christmas package. I couldn't believe this big guy complaining to me about such a thing. I asked him why he didn't punch Manson in the face. He looked at me in abject fear. 'I'm afraid of that nut. He can hypnotize you in a glance and make you jump off the tier. And another thing, Mr. Parker. I know for a fact that Manson put the hex on Ronald Torgremson. The next day, Ron nearly choked to death on a chicken bone. I happened to glance at Manson and he was rolling his eyes up in his head, looking at the ceiling and chanting.' Manson belongs in an insane asylum."

Not too many years later in Hollywood, Charles Manson, and three women he had under his spell, murdered Sharon Tate, an aspiring actress, and seven others. The home where they were murdered was spattered with blood and bizarre sayings on the walls. One of his statements after capture was, "I have X'ed myself from your world." And to prove that he and his followers were rejecting the world that rejected him, he carved a hideous X on his forehead. To show you the influence he held over his female cohorts, they too disfigured themselves by carving an X on their foreheads.

After dinner, I could go to the library to read and study, or to the social hall to hear a lecture delivered by a professor from Pacific Lutheran University. There were many 'freedoms' to enjoy. Until I began to make comparisons with Alcatraz, I realized how cruelly confining and vicious Alcatraz was. And yet, after six years in that cage, I adapted and was able to tolerate each day as being a normal existence. It took a great deal of undoing to accept the laxity of this new environment. The prison on this Island sat on the edge of the bay with forests surrounding the background. When in the yard, I could see deer grazing within a few yards. When the deer multiplied too rapidly, they were shot by guards and the venison was served to the inmates. Seeing them was pleasant. Eating them was better. Outside visitors were commonplace.

I was temporarily assigned to work in the laundry. During this thirty day period, I was being observed by the staff. Following that job, I was put to work in the cannery. And the man who worked across the bench from me sorting fruit and vegetables was none other than Dave Beck, the former General President of The International Brotherhood of Teamsters. One thing about being in a federal penitentiary was the opportunity to mingle with internationally prominent people. I soon learned that they, too, had itchy fingers and an irresistible urge to enrich their coffers with other persons' money. Underneath the skin, we really aren't that much different and, in confinement, that fact became more obvious. I was aware that one glaring distinction between Beck and me was that he was a millionaire and I was a pauper. For that reason he was treated with deference, as were other prisoners who had high political connections.

Months after I left the cannery, I was approached by an inmate lackey who acted as a front man for Beck. He had heard that I had a connection to smuggle uncensored letters from the joint. He said, "Nate, I have a heavy packet of legal documents I want to send to an attorney in Seattle. This is a favor for a pretty big con in here. Can you get them mailed without going through the censor's office? I can get a nice piece of change put to your account in the office in exchange." Naturally, I was very cautious and asked, "Just who in this 'Big' con? For all I know, you could be setting me up for a bust." He replied, "I can't tell you that, Nate, but if you keep your eyes open you can accurately conclude who he is." I talked the proposition over with JB, the only man in the pen whom I trusted. A few days later he and I were watching a ball game in the yard. JB nodded toward two men who were sitting in the bleachers. One was the lackey, the other was Beck. The conclusion was made.

I made contact with the lackey and a few days later, a runner handed me a large manila envelope. It was addressed to a well-known Seattle attorney. The most difficult part of my job was to get a package that large smuggled from the main institution to my mule on the prison tug. JB had been assigned as a truck driver. In that position, he went all over the Island unescorted. Often he had cargo to be taken to the dock where the tug tied up. I called on JB and sought his help. "Sure, I'll help you," he volunteered. "Get the package to the storehouse and see that McLeod handles it." It was a long time later that I learned how so many things got by the eagle-eyed guards whose job it was to shake down everything that went through the gate from the inside. In the case of the packet I sent, it was simply taped to the bottom of a garbage can, placed on JB's truck and was on its way.

It was weeks after I reached McNeil that my law books and lessons arrived. As a result of the delay, I was behind in my scheduled classes. The resentment that I experienced when I first received permission to take the course followed me to this institution. There were subtle attempts to discourage me from continuing my studies. All material had to go through the department of education where the director, Pete Phenneger, would have it sidetracked. When I would request an interview with him to find out where my lessons were, he would refuse to see me for a couple of weeks. I was always afraid that LaSalle would decide I was too much of a nuisance and cancel me out. That was the hope of the officials. I decided to ask my brother to assist me. On a visit, I explained what was taking place. He said he would try to contact the school and describe the type of people they were dealing with, and explain their purpose for causing me the trouble.

Three weeks after Dan's visit, I got a letter from the director at LaSalle in which he wrote in part; 'We have been advised of the unusual circumstances under which you are studying for your LL.B., and we want to assure you that you will be given ample time in which to prepare your lessons. With the determination you have displayed to date, we are confident you will prevail. It is regrettable that you have run into so many impediments.' Immediately, upon receipt of this letter, Phenneger called me to his office. He thrust a copy of my letter under my nose and screamed, "Williams, what does this letter mean?" I read it slowly, pretending it was the first time I had seen it. When I handed it back to him, I said, "I guess just what it says." Phenneger, continued, "I want to know if the school is under the impression that we are deliberately detaining your incoming and outgoing letters?" I thought his inquiry over for a moment and replied, "Well, if my lessons are completed on time, as would be indicated by the date on each one, and they took three weeks getting to Chicago, surely they would conclude that the lessons were being sidetracked somewhere along the line. Mr. Phenneger, those instructors are aware that I am an inmate in a federal penitentiary and that everything is censored coming into and going out of the prison. Logically, where could the material be slowed down?" I thought that he was going to choke. After he had recovered his composure, he made a thinly veiled threat. "Maybe you found Alcatraz more compliant?" His message didn't go by me, and I was concerned for some time that I would be returned to that place reserved for 'recalcitrant' inmates. I treaded carefully from there on out. I noticed, however, that my study material flowed with little interruption from then on out. In fact, a few months after my confrontation with the little man, he called me to his office and asked me to teach English to the inmates in evening classes. I accepted.

Eighteen months later I completed the law course and was advised that the exams for my final testing would be mailed within a month. My instructor suggested that I bone up because those tests were rugged. I was further advised that the testing had to be under the direction of an attorney or a court representative. I was stymied. Where could I get an attorney who would be willing to come to the Island and supervise me during the examination? If I were to hire one, it would cost me a fortune, and I didn't have a penny. The testing would take a few days under the rules of visiting. Suddenly, I got an idea. U.S. District Court Judge Boldt of Tacoma had been interested in a group of self-help inmates who had formed a club called the Self-Improvement Group, commonly referred to as SIG. Judge Boldt was an avid supporter and made numerous trips to meet with us. He was instrumental in getting the nation's most well-known insurance magnate, Clement W. Stone, to come to the west coast for the purpose of addressing SIG. It might be interesting to note here that twenty-five years later I met Stone at a reception in Washington, D.C. at the Sam Rayburn Building. He did not remember me but he readily recalled his visit to the Federal Penitentiary on McNeil Island. At one of our SIG meetings, I cornered Judge Boldt and told him of my attempt to get an LL.B. degree from LaSalle. He was genuinely interested and complimented me on my initiative. On a number of occasions when he would be visiting, he would seek me out and ask me how my studies were coming along. It dawned upon me that I might be successful in getting him to send a federal court official to monitor my tests.

I wrote him a letter and told him of my predicament. He response was prompt and greatly appreciated. He volunteered to 'sit over' my exams if I could make arrangements to fit them in with his schedule.

The officials at the institution felt it would be the better part of wisdom to put on a front of willingness to accommodate the judge. The date was set for two months down the road. I needed plenty of time to cram. Another bombshell was dropped in my lap. When I asked to have my entire library of law books in my cell, I was given an emphatic 'NO'. I made a personal request of the Associate Warden for special privileges under the unusual circumstances. He called me to his office and said, "You are fully aware of the rule that you can't have more than four books in your cell at one time, and that includes the Bible. I refuse to make an exception." I was not aware of any such rule with regard to the number of books permitted in a cell. As a matter of fact, I had had as many as eight books in my possession at one time, and was never tagged for it. The associate's attitude left me with one alternative. I appealed to the Warden. That gentleman refused to even speak with me.

Four months later, under the supervision of Judge Boldt, I took the test and passed. I earned my coveted LL.B. in spite of the impediments strewn in my path. I was so proud of the certificate, I asked the cellhouse guard for permission to hang it on my cell wall. He gave me permission and from that time until I left he referred to my quarters as the LAW OFFICES OF NATE WILLIAMS. One of his pleasures was to stop by my cage when making his rounds and sarcastically comment, "There is one thing for certain, Barrister Williams, we know your office rent has been paid in advance for twenty-five years. I'll bet no other attorney in the country can make that statement. However, there are two amenities you cannot lay claim to; a female secretary and a telephone. From the number of clients and cases you have since you started practicing, I can't see where you'll need either a phone or a secretary. Of course, you could use a secretary for other more important functions, I'll bet."

When influential and important visitors from the outside were being given the Red Carpet tour, you could be assured of two things: they would be accompanied by either the warden or his associate, and that an inmate would precede the visitors by a few minutes by running down the landing calling out, 'Be on your toes. Visitors up.'

One morning a runner ran by my cell calling out the usual message. I always felt like a monkey in a zoo being observed by morbidly curious people, so I would lay on my bunk and pretend to be reading a book. That is exactly what I did on this occasion. I could hear them tromping down the cellhouse corridor. As they neared my 'office', I turned my face to the wall and buried my face deeper into my book. My purpose was to be inconspicuous and hope these politicians would hurry on by. No such luck. The group of five men stopped directly in front of my personal territory. Out boomed a voice that I immediately recognized as the warden's. "Nate, stand up here. I want you to meet some congressman who are investigating various prisons in the federal system." I did as I was told. One by one, the warden introduced me to each congressman. The names meant nothing to me. I found I was embarrassed and humiliated. The real shocker came when the warden made his next comment. "Gentlemen, I want you to meet the only federal prisoner who has earned an LL.B. while being imprisoned. Nate, here, has persevered under some stringent conditions on Alcatraz, and has taken advantage of the educational programs made possible by the Federal Bureau of Prisons. While it is against the policy of this institution, we have permitted him to display his certificate on the wall of his cell. Take it down, Nate, and let them feast their eyes on your achievement." One by one, they pretended to be interested in the document. Each offered his congratulations.

When the body of men moved out of ear-shot, I flung myself on my bunk and began beating the straw pad with my fists out of sheer frustration. The very official who had introduced me to the public trough-men, was the same person who had refused to give me permission to have more than four books in my cell. And here he was pretending to have exposed me to educational opportunities, when in reality, he created one of the impediments that had rained on my head. I felt as though I were colluding with him in deceiving the congressional investigators from Washington D.C. My first inclination was to write a letter to the members of congress to whom I had been introduced, and bring the deception to light. After sleeping on it, I decided to just 'do my own time'.

One morning when I attempted to get out of bed, I found I was unable to rise without a great deal of excruciating pain. I could not figure out what was wrong. Actually, I was suffering partial paralysis that became more aggravated as the morning went on. By mid-morning, a couple of guards came to my cell to find out why I had not reported to detail. When they saw I was unable to move, they summoned the MTA. In a half an hour I was under the X-ray machine. The technician could find nothing from his film. When the doctor arrived from his residence on the Island, the pain in my back had subsided somewhat. He gave me a number of physical tests and could not find anything wrong. Oddly enough, by noon I was able to walk to my job. For a month I was plagued by twinges of discomfort and muscle spasms, but none were as disabling as the first onset I experienced.

A few weeks later, I started to rise from my chair at work and found I could not move. I was hospitalized and subjected to a series of tests. It was determined that I had a slipped disc. For weeks I was kept in traction. It was during this protracted hospital stay that I was advised that I had two visitors scheduled to see me that afternoon. Having not been advised who the visitors were, I assumed they must be members of my family. I was pleasantly surprised when my loyal friend, Marky Barrett and The Reverend Robert Fine (whom I had not met previously) were ushered into my hospital room. At this time I was heavily sedated and am certain that I didn't make too much sense as I prated foolishly. I do recall how pleased and appreciative I was to see Marky again. Throughout my entire period of incarceration, Marky had proved to be a solid and concerned friend. He wrote regularly and his letters and visits buoyed my sagging spirits. This visit again lifted my spirits and I dreaded to see them go.

My condition deteriorated so much that a specialist was called from the

Tacoma General Hospital. I was comfortable under the examination of a qualified doctor. After a perfunctory test, he took a towel from the cabinet and wrapped it around my neck. Instinctively, I grabbed at the towel. He laughed and said, "Easy, Mr Williams. I'm going to put some pressure on your neck, but I promise I won't garrote you." Before I could respond, he tightened the towel around my throat and applied pressure. A sharp pain shot through my lower spine and down my left leg. The doctor stood up and told the institutional doctor, "This man is suffering from a ruptured disc. He should be taken to the Tacoma General Hospital for a myelogram. If you will make the arrangements to bring him to the hospital and call my office to let me know when you will be there, I'll have a specialist on hand. Will you order a strong pain killer, and keep him sedated?" I could see that the two government doctors resented this authority. They were so accustomed to issuing orders to helpless inmate patients that it galled them to have a physician of this man's stature telling them what to do. Considering that they had made a dozen exams and could not pinpoint the problem, it must have been embarrassing to have this outside doctor diagnose the problem in ten minutes.

Notwithstanding the urgency expressed by the neurosurgeon, it was a week before arrangements for my transfer were approved. The comedy of errors that resulted from my trip to the free world was worthy of a Broadway stand. The doctor came to my bedside and announced, "Williams, you're scheduled to be at the Tacoma hospital by ten thirty this morning. Take a bath and be ready to travel in an hour. There will be a caseworker and two guards accompanying you. You will be taken over in the prison's ambulance. You will not get your shot of MS unless the doctor over there orders it."

In less than an hour I was given the usual 'bath' in cuffs and chains, was placed on a gurney and slid into the archaic ambulance. On the way to the dock, the driver failed to negotiate a sharp turn, The vehicle slid into a ditch and rolled over on its side. I wound up face down partially under the dashboard. The mattress was on top of me. The caseworker was sitting on my feet and the guard was nearly upside down in a corner. As painful as it was, I had to laugh.

What followed was really crazy. The officials' first concern was that I did not use this accident in an escape attempt. The guard grabbed my arm from his awkward position and called to the caseworker, "It's OK, I've got Williams. Send the driver for help." Almost immediately, my friend, JB, who was a truck driver on the Island, drove upon the scene. He was afraid someone might be hurt so he jumped from his vehicle and ripped the driver's door open. One by one, he helped all of us from the ambulance. When he spotted me, he said, "Are you OK, Nate?" I think the guard was angry that JB did not ask as to the welfare of anyone else because he yelled at JB, "Don't you talk to this prisoner. Get back to the main building and call for help." My friend, in his arrogant manner, winked at me where all could see, and said, "Sure glad you're not hurt, Nate." Before he could pull out, two prison cars drove up. Thirty minutes later I was in the prison infirmary. In a number of instances in the criminal history of this country, there have been times when gangsters have made deliveries* of prisoners from the custody of officers who are in the process of transferring convicts from one institution to another, or to and from court appearances. Many of these actions have resulted in bloodbaths. Officials used to inform prisoners beforehand when they were to be moved. The convict would get word to his buddies as to the day, date, hour and destination. Waylaying the guards and cons at some point en route was an easy task. Often, when the prisoner being moved was a stool pigeon, the deliverers would kill him during the confusion. In an effort to prevent such action on the part of the gangsters, the officials decided to keep the transfer a secret from the convict(s). As a result, an inmate was apt to be awakened in the early hours of the morning, told to pack his personal belongings and would be on his way within minutes. He would have no idea where he was going or his mode of transportation. So, unless a guard snitched the operation off, very few people were advised of the move. There have been no successful deliveries in decades. In view of the secret-transfer information, if it had not been for a friendly guard, I would have been caught unaware of the hospital's next move.

The night guard came by my hospital bed about midnight on a Sunday about a week after the ambulance fiasco and whispered, "I see on the transfer sheet that you are scheduled to be taken to Tacoma for some medical purpose. Don't mention to the MTA that I told you. I'd guess you'll be ousted about seven. I hope you have better luck than last time."

After he left, I sort of wished he hadn't told me because I could not get back to sleep. One of the inmate nurses had told me that he heard the chief doctor mention that I might have to undergo a laminectomy. At the time I had never heard of a laminectomy. But it didn't matter because I was afraid of any kind of surgery.

The ambulance came by for me early in the morning, and once again I was on my way to the boat dock and the mainland. This time, the trip was uneventful. Two different guards were in the back with me. The caseworker rode up front with the driver. When we reached the hospital, the gurney was unloaded with me still chained to it. The guards headed for the emergency entrance when I realized that they were going to take me through the milling crowd of would-be patients and nurses. I called out loud and clear, "Hey, you cops, aren't you going to take these shackles off before we go in there?" The caseworker was embarrassed as he answered for the guards, "Our instruction, Williams, were to keep you in restraints until they placed you on the table." I was infuriated. After all, I was clearly unable to walk, and really posed no problem from a security viewpoint. "Listen, you ass-hole, take me back to the joint. I am not going to go through this bull- shit. If you don't, I am going to start yelling bloody murder and I'll fight the doctors and nurses, and anyone else who tries to force me on the table." I knew they could not perform the exam without my full cooperation. One of the nurses instructed the guards to push the gurney into a room adjacent to the emergency entrance. She had been standing there and was able to grasp the whole picture. Once inside the room, she asked, "Is it necessary to keep

*forcibly freeing prisoners

269

those chains on him? There isn't any way we can do a myelogram with those things draped around him. In fact, the doctor will refuse to let you take him any farther than this room." One of the guards started to speak up, but was silenced by the all-important caseworker. "Ma'am, this prisoner is a security problem of the worst kind, and we cannot, by law, remove his cuffs and leg-irons. If you'll be patient, I'll call the warden for instructions." As the nurse started to leave the room, she called after the guard and said, "I'll get the doctor to come in and explain our position in this matter. However, I want you to know that we have done emergency operations on many men from the prison before and have never run into this situation previously."

I was enjoying the power-play I had created. I made up my mind to push this diversion to the limit. The doctor came back with the nurse before the caseworker did. He walked over to the gurney and pulled back the covers to look at my chains. Instead of saying anything to the guards, he spoke to me. "Mr. Williams, I want you to cooperate with us. We are here for the sole purpose of helping you. We are not connected with the penitentiary." It felt good to be talking with this professional man of obvious intelligence. In addition, he had addressed me as 'Mr. Williams', and I appreciated that. About this time, in walked the prison representative who had left to tele-phone the warden. He introduced himself to the doctor and they walked out of voice range and conversed. The doctor was nodding his head throughout their conversation. It appeared they had reached an agreement.

The doctor walked over to me and said in a conciliatory tone, "Mr. Williams, all us of can appreciate your feeling about being wheeled through a group of people gawking at you. So here is what we are going to do. You will be taken through that door over there and wheeled down a corridor where hospital personnel only are allowed. And when you leave, we'll take you out the same way. Is that OK with you?" I nodded my head. The doctor continued, "The officials realize that your chains will be removed through the procedure. They will be outside the door to pick you up from the table."

When we arrived in what appeared to be an X-ray room, the prison guards took off our restraints. The nurse closed the door behind them and we were alone. This was the first time in more than six years I had been anywhere near a female. She interrupted my thoughts and said, "If you'll remove your clothes and put on this gown, I'll help you up on the examining table." With that she stepped out of the room. When she returned, she was in the company of the doctor. He tested my reflexes with a rubber hammer. He stopped and looked up at me and said, "You know, you don't look like a hardened criminal to me. The guard said you had been recently trans-ferred up from Alcatraz." I waited a minute before responding. "Doctor, what does a hardened criminal look like?" He smiled and said, "Touche. Now this is a comparatively simple procedure, Mr. Williams. It is a little uncomfortable but not painful. When we are finished, I don't want you to sit or stand up for at least half an hour. If you do, you're going to suffer a giant-sized headache. When we feel it is OK for you to go, we will come in for you. Please don't get off the table." Both he and the nurse walked from the room.

Again, I was completely alone for what seemed like an eternity. I thought of escape but I knew I would be unable to walk any distance, much less run. By the time the half hour was over I thought I had been there for a week. Pretty soon a man walked in carrying my prison garb. "Here are your clothes, sir. You may dress and go." Before I could respond, he disappeared through the door.

After I dressed, I walked through the same door and found myself in unfamiliar surroundings. I walked down a long corridor, passing many nurses. It was all so strange to me. I hadn't walked 500 feet when I realized I was lost. I kept walking until I came to the main hospital entrance. Admitting and Information people ignored me. "Damn", I muttered to myself. "I am free." Only Christ knew where my keepers were. I was comfortable because everyone was ignoring me and going about their business. It was clear the prison clothes were not recognized. Suddenly a sharp pain radiated down my leg, causing me to cry out. The numb feeling was returning. I was sick with frustration. Here I was a free man and couldn't walk. I knew I was destined to go back to the island. A young fellow who had been behind the Information desk had heard me cry out, and came over to me and asked, "May I help you?" I felt so impotent, I could have cried. One chance in a lifetime and I had to muff it. I knew the guards had to be in the emergency area so I asked the fellow if he could direct me to the emergency room. "Better than that," he said, "I'll escort you there." Together we walked what seemed to be five miles. Finally he indicated a door and said, "Right through there." It was all I could do to push open the heavy door. I entered what proved to be the main entrance to the emergency room. I glanced though a large pane of glass and, lo and behold, standing outside were the three clowns who had brought me from the clink. I had to go back and I was sick.

At least here was a chance to embarrass the guards and caseworker. Gritting my teeth, I walked through the door and walked up to the startled men. They simply gaped. I sauntered up to them and asked, "Where in the hell have you guys been?" The caseworker recovered his composure first. "What in the hell is going on here? Where did you come from?" I pushed my knife in as far as I could by replying, "Shit, man, do you realize I have been running all over this complex for nearly two hours. They finished with me quite some time ago, handed me my clothes and told me I could go home. They must not have known just where my 'home' was." They were uncomfortable and I enjoyed their frustration. After that line of crap to the doctor telling him what an escape risk I was, and that I was a man considered so dangerous the government saw fit to keep me on the Rock, what fools they would have looked like if I had walked off. I envisioned the head-lines. ALCATRAZ INMATE ESCAPES!

In a matter-of-fact tone I continued leading them on. "I thought I had better look you guys up since you didn't seem interested in my where-abouts." The caseworker was incensed at my attitude and the fact I referred to them as 'you guys'. That remark was the last straw. All three snatched me up and tossed me into the ambulance. Before I could quit laughing, I was blanketed in the chains again. There was nothing left for me to do, so I snuggled in my cuffs and leg irons as the ambulance headed for McNeil

Island. Not one word was spoken by my keepers all the way back to the Steilacoom dock where the prison launch was to pick me up. I knew that if the warden ever heard of the mess they had made at the hospital, they would have lost their jobs.

By the time the boat had picked us up and transported us back to the institution, I was in unbearable pain. The prison doctor met me in the hospital hall and asked how I was doing. "I'm going to faint with pain." Nothing I ever experienced in my life was so pleasant as the sting of the needle when he injected me with morphine. In a few minutes, both pain and hunger disappeared. I slept.

A week after my trip for the myelogram, I was awakened by a rough shake on my shoulder bringing me out of a drug-induced slumber. The fellow who aroused me was the Chief MTA, McCoy. During my hospital stay, he treated me humanely. He had a good reputation among the patients. Because he was a gentleman, the general run-of-the-mill guards did not care for him. "C'mon, Nate, I want to take you to the clothing room and get you dressed out in civilian clothes. Tomorrow morning you and I are scheduled to fly the coop. No need to tell you where we are going, because I know damn well that the grapevine wised you up."

In the clothing room, I was fitted in a suit that required little alteration to make me look presentable. While I was standing in front of a mirror, I heard a strident voice I all-to-well recognized as belonging to the most miserable guard on the custody staff, Lt. Teahs. "McCoy", he bellowed, "what in the hell is Williams doing in a civilian suit?" McCoy's response was laconic. "Lt. Teahs, if you had read the switch-sheet, you would know that he is being transferred to Springfield. I am getting him dressed-out today because we are scheduled to get a plane at 4:00 A.M. tomorrow." Teahs pointed a stubby finger at McCoy and yelled, "Put that convict back in prison- issue garb. He is still a prisoner and is to remain in prison clothes at all times he is in your custody." McCoy reminded the little man that I would be traveling in a commercial plane among civilians and he felt I should not be dressed in telltale convict garb. He continued, "Williams is in such a condition as not to pose an escape danger. He is unable to walk and, without regular shots, cannot move his legs." Teahs could not stand to have his orders questioned. He turned to the clothing-room officer and said, "I am ordering you to dress this inmate in regular issue. Are you going to obey me or not?" When I was escorted back to the hospital, I was in my 'blues'.

Very early the following morning, I was adorned in the shiniest, newest and most stylish hand cuffs, leg-irons and waist chains before being escorted to the airport in the company of two guards and Mr. McCoy. One of the guards commented to the MTA, "Mac, you know the airlines will not let you go aboard with a man in chains." McCoy reached in his pocket, took out a couple of keys and unlocked all of my fetters and gave them to the guards.

A half an hour later, my traveling companion and I were 20,000 feet above McNeil Island on a southeasterly course. When we were served lunch, I was in seventh heaven. The stewardess was a dream to look at. I was embarrassed and unsure of myself. I found it difficult to answer her questions without stuttering. Yes, I would appreciate cream and sugar with my coffee. Yes, she could take my tray. Yes, I was comfortable. I even dared to go further and say, 'Thank You'. The MTA was enjoying my nervousness. To be able to hobble to the restroom alone was a milestone in my seven-year odyssey. When I returned to my seat, it was comforting to find McCoy sound asleep. It was evident he trusted me to conduct myself as a gentleman. I had made up my mind to do nothing to embarrass him. Of course, escape would have been impossible.

Our destination was Kansas City and we touched down at that airport four hours later. Before we stepped from the plane, I told the MTA that I was experiencing a great deal of discomfort. "We will go to the lavatory at the airport, Nate, and I will inject you right away. If you feel you can't make it, I will give you a shot before we leave the plane." By the time I walked the distance to the restroom, I was in excruciating pain. Within ten minutes after the shot, I felt like a new man. For the first time in more than seven years, I spoke to a representative of the prison staff in a kindly manner. " Mr. McCoy, I want you to know how much I have appreciated your consideration." He put his hand on my shoulder and squeezed it ever so lightly.

As we looked for a seat, I was amazed at the size of the airport and the bustling crowd. People were going in all directions. Luggage was stacked everywhere. Finally, we found two seats side by side. McCoy placed his bags in front of one of the seats and asked me to be seated. He said he would be back in about ten minutes. "I have to call the penitentiary at Leavenworth and ask them to send someone to pick us up. We may have to wait for an hour or so." With that he walked off. I couldn't get over the feeling of freedom. It was hard for me to fathom what had taken place in the last few hours. I experienced difficulty adjusting to the strange environment and conditions. I don't know how long the MTA was gone before I fell asleep.

It seems as of recent months I was always being awakened under somewhat unusual and stressful circumstances. I was beginning to feel I would never again wake up after I had had eight hours of sleep and was rested. Before I opened my eyes, I heard two men discussing 'the type of clothing this fellow was wearing'. One of them stated, "This guy is wearing prison issue, and he has to be the inmate we were sent to take on to Leavenworth. He has the luggage here at his feet, but he doesn't have any restraints on. Now where in Christ's name is the guard?" I was fully awake but I kept my eyes closed. Instantly, I wondered what had happened to McCoy. I had no idea how long I had been sleeping. There was one thing I knew for certain; the MTA was in much trouble when word of this got to the Bureau.

Before I could dwell on that thought any longer, one of the guards shook me. "Wake up, you. What are you doing here without an escort?" I refused to comment. If McCoy got into trouble, it would be his own fault, but I wasn't going to offer any information that might hurt him. The guard shook me again and barked, "I asked you a question!" I stared at him insolently for a full minute. "I don't know where my escort is and I don't give a damn." Angrily the guard threatened, "We'll see how tough you are when we get you to the joint." He turned to his partner and continued, "Search this smart-ass and let's get back to the prison." "Sarge, we can't just off and take this man from his assigned guard. He may have just gone to the restroom. When he gets back and finds his prisoner gone, he might alert the police and FBI. There could be a hell of a stink. And we could get our rear ends in a vice."

I glanced past the arguing guards and saw the MTA sauntering up. He didn't seem to be in any hurry, and was perfectly calm. When he got to me, he ignored them and said, "Nate, roll up your sleeve. I'm going to give you another shot." By this time, the Sarge was frothing at the mouth. "Sir", he said in the most officious voice he could muster, "I am wondering where you have been, and why this federal prisoner is not in cuffs. What is your capacity as far as this convict is concerned?" I loved McCoy's response. "First, who are you and why are you interfering with a man in my custody?" The guard colored up and pompously retorted, "You can see by my uniform that I am a Sergeant-of- the-Guards stationed at The Federal Prison at Leavenworth. I was instructed to pick you and your prisoner up and take you to the institution. While we were looking for you, I ran across this inmate sleeping on a bench. He was not in fetters as required by law, nor was he accompanied by an officer." As McCoy slowly gathered our luggage, he replied as though he was addressing the floor, "This man is in the custody of MTA McCoy, a representative of the federal hospital at Springfield. His condition is such that chains could create further damage to his already serious injury. It was I who made the decision to transport him as you see him here. He is my prisoner, not yours. When I release him to the hospital staff at Leavenworth, he will be under the care of that institution's doctor. He will be there for two days, at which time he will be released to my custody to continue our trip to Springfield. Let's head out." Without even a backward glance to the humiliated guard, he led the way to the parking area.

No one spoke a word for the hour or so it took us to reach the front of the foreboding gate of the huge penitentiary. McCoy presented my papers to the Captain. He spoke to me before he left. "Nate, I'll be back here with a US Marshal the day after tomorrow. We'll be in Springfield the following day. The nurses will give you a shot for pain every four hours. See you later."

Two days after I entered that graveyard gate, I was walking out in the charge of a US Marshal. I was not chained. In the parking lot, I met McCoy. He helped me get into the Marshal's car and before he left he said, "After your surgery, I'll see you back at McNeil Island. Keep your nose clean."

The federal officer crawled into the front seat and we were on our way. I marveled at the big Pontiac he was driving. I hadn't ridden in such luxury in years. The vehicle had amenities I had never seen before. After we had left the town of Leavenworth, the officer half-turned in his seat and said, "Williams, McCoy told me that you were not a troublesome prisoner so I am not going to chain you. By law, I can't inject you with a needle for your pain medicine, but I have plenty of pills that will do the trick when you start hurting." By looking in the rear view mirror I could examine the marshal's face. He was of Mexican extraction. He had a strong face which showed a great deal of character.

We talked very little for the first three hours of our journey. I was beginning to get hungry and, also, I had to go to the lavatory. Before I could make my wishes known, he pulled into the parking area of a small cafe. He hopped out and waited for me. When he could see I was experiencing difficulty in getting out, he took me by the arm and helped. We were no more than seated when a Mexican chef came out of the kitchen, walked over to our table and held out his hand. The marshal said something in Spanish which I didn't understand. They conversed a few minutes in their native tongue before the cook went back to the kitchen. Without asking for permission, I stood up and headed for the restroom. When I returned there was coffee on the table along with two menus. For the first time in many years I was being permitted to order my choice of food from a menu. It surprised me how little privileges like that pleased me so.

While we were eating, the officer started telling me about his career. He had been an MP in the marines. After his hitch was over, he applied for a job with the US Federal Marshal's office in Denver. He was accepted and for ten years had been transporting federal prisoners across the country. In that time, out of the hundreds he had moved about, he had lost only three. It was a record of some sort and he was proud of it. He said he had always stopped at this cafe when he was in this part of the country. "You know, Mr. Williams, you're the only ex-Alcatraz prisoner I have transferred. When I was going through your rap-sheet in the Warden's office, I was just a bit nervous. Most of you guys from the Rock have pretty rough reputations. MTA McCoy was sitting beside me while I was going through your papers, and he guessed what was going through my mind. 'Two things about this guy, Marshal; he is too damned ill to offer you trouble, and I don't think he would attempt an escape if he had a chance. While we were waiting for the guards to come after us in Kansas City, I left him alone for a full hour. I never cuffed him on the entire trip. You are in charge of him now, and I have no voice in your jurisdiction.' What he was asking was for me to forego the chains." As we were returning to the car, I thanked him and assured him once more that I would not try to escape. That night we pulled into some little town in Missouri. He took me to the local jail and made arrangements for me to spend the evening there. By mid-afternoon the following day, my papers and I were handed over to the admitting officer of the famous federal hospital. The next eight months was a horrifying experience from which I have not recovered to this day.

21

A Time To Grieve

The hospital at Springfield was a large complex which was divided into two parts in order to accommodate two categories of patients; the physically ill and the mentally ill. Before they finished with me, I thought I would be transferred to the psychiatric unit. For all I know, it might have been preferable. Surely nothing could have been as traumatic and painful as what I experienced at the hands of what passed as doctors and nurses at this zoo. None of the professional staff was answerable to any responsible authority, so they 'practiced' with immunity. There was never any fear of a legal repercussion nor a challenge to their sufficiency because the patients were convicts and, as such non-persons, were without access to the courts for legal remedy. Had I known what was in store for me, I never would have agreed to treatment at Springfield.

I was assigned to a ward which contained about ten other men. My cot was near a window and it was in that position that I observed some disturbing conditions. Pigeons were rampant all over the building. On the window sill near my bed there was pigeon excrement more that a half-inch thick. And on the same sill was a dead bird that was partially decayed. The doctors, who came by on a regular basis, could not help but see the filthy conditions. Foolishly, I mentioned the disgustingly dirty mess on the window sill to a doctor who came by to listen to complaints. Before he responded to my comment, he looked at me with disdain, examined my name card which had been attached to the bed and replied in a condescending manner, "Did you come here, Williams, to correct conditions or for surgery?" Before I could formulate an answer to his question, he moved on as he muttered to an accompanying inmate orderly, "Every new inmate who comes here for treatment has the attitude that he should be running the place. After a while, he won't even see the pigeons. He'll get used to it."

The fellow in the bed next to me listened quietly to the exchange between the doctor and me. Finally he spoke out, "Hey, Fish, you better watch your fucking mouth in this place. You get one of those freaks down on you and pretty soon they put the word out, and you're in trouble for the rest of the time you're here. By the way, the grapevine has it that you're here from the Rock. You have a buddy in a ward down the hall by the name of Robert Stroud. I guess you knew him as the Bird Man Of Alcatraz." Instantly, I took a dislike to the character and I decided to let him know it from the start. "I didn't know the Bird Man nor do I know you. Furthermore, punk, when I want your advice I'll ask for it." The following day, he was moved to another ward. I learned that he told the guard that I had threatened him.

During the next two weeks, I was given a repeat of all the previous exams I had gone through in Washington. The doctors in this hospital acted as though all the patients were malingerers and those who weren't were hop-heads who came there to get dope for their aches and pains. Consequently, it was difficult to get any kind of pain medicine. The usual treatment for pain was two APC's, a form of aspirin. Aspirin was useless in my case. Before long, I was unable to move my legs. The pain never left me. I lost track of time, so I don't know how long I had been there when they finally decided to perform a laminectomy on my spine.

As the effects of the Sodium Pentothal wore off, I became aware that I was in the critical care unit of the hospital. I was afraid and I didn't want to become fully conscious. Even in that dim state of mind, I preferred to forestall the trip back to reality and its horrors. Cautiously I tried to move my toes. They functioned so I thought I'd try my feet. They didn't function. I had the horrible feeling that I was paralyzed from the feet up. If only the doctors had told me what to expect, I would not have been so fearful of the outcome. Just a few minutes of counselling prior to the operation would have saved me hours of agony. An inmate attendant came in and took my vital signs. When he saw I was conscious, he asked, "How do you feel?" I smiled and didn't answer. When he was through with his examination, he said, "The surgery was a success, Williams. We are going to hook you up with a catheter so you can relieve your bladder. The normal functions of your body will return in a day or two. The medic has ordered painkiller for you, so when you need it just give one of us a call." There was no call button, so the patient had to call loud and often to get a response from the nurses' station. My pain killer was codeine. It worked for a very brief time but was never as effective and long-lasting as morphine.

My recovery was a long time in coming. Before I realized what happened, I was addicted to both a wheelchair and codeine. The wheelchair was my constant need and companion. I wanted the codeine to be as available as the chair. One night just after a nurse had refused to give me codeine more often than prescribed, I was approached by a convict orderly. He pulled a chair up to my bed and quietly let me know that he had a connection with the pharmacist, and could get me 'some good stuff' for a price. "What is the price?", I asked eagerly. "Well," he said, "I can get you heavy stuff three times a day for #30 canteen each month." I agreed and from that night on, I was on easy street for four months. True to his word, he would inject me with painless nights and sweet dreams. I had convinced myself that as soon as I had fully recovered I would cut the dope.

By this time, my dependence on the chair was robbing me of the exercise I needed to build up my spine and leg muscles. The cons in physical therapy worked hand in glove with those who were peddling the drugs. They verified I was getting treatment in their department and was recovering as well as could be expected. They had doctored their records to support their claim. If only a doctor had examined me at any time, he could have detected something was amiss. I would go weeks on end and never see a physician. I was anxious to be returned to McNeil Island and be near my family. I expressed this desire to an inmate orderly with whom I had become friendly. He wasn't one of the drug-pushing orderlies, thank God.

"OK, Nate, I am going to tell you how you can get back to your home state," he confided. Here is what you have to do. Kick that damn crutch of a wheelchair down the hall, and get off the dope. When you make your request to leave this place, a couple of doctors will call you in for a thorough physical. You will have to show you have responded well to their treatment. You'll be asked to walk, bend and twist the lower part of your body. If you show signs of improvement, they will recommend your transfer. You are addicted, Nate, whether or not you know it. Your toughest job will be to tell the dopers that you want no more of their drugs. Walk unassisted to the dining room and out to the yard. Go to physical therapy and demand treatment. No more faking it. Your muscles are in terrible shape. You must walk, walk and walk. Otherwise you will die in here." Before I went to bed that night, I checked my chair into the property room and exchanged it for a cane. I contacted my supplier and told him I was kicking the habit cold-turkey.

The following weeks were indescribable. I suffered with headaches, vomiting and diarrhea simultaneously. As determined as I was to walk, it was a struggle to just throw my legs over the side of the bed. Orderlies helped me stand and take a few steps. I did not realize I was not eating. After about four days of this masochistic behavior, I was so weak I couldn't have walked if I wanted to. Inmate friends helped me immeasurably. One who worked in the mess hall smuggled hot soup and crackers to me at night. It was all I could do to stomach the food. In the early mornings, I was punished with a bowl of hot cereal, milk and coffee. At noon I was fed more substantial foods. They realized what I was going through, but would not let up on me. Dozens of times I wanted to call my drug contact and order a fix.

One day the drug contact came by my bunk and sat down to talk with me. He came right to the point, "Nate, breaking the dope habit cold-turkey is a tough way to go. Its been a week since I 'fed' you, so the roughest part is over, believe me. One thing you must do is eat. Stuff your stomach until you are ready to heave it up. The process of digesting the food helps clean the poison from your system and, at the same time will strengthen you. No matter how much it hurts, get up from that bed and walk. By the way, Nate, you have a lot of friends in here. Four nights ago when I was on my way to the library, a couple of the bad ones from Alcatraz cornered me in the hallway and let me know that the priest would be performing the Supreme Unction over me if I sold you anymore of Satan's elixir, so you have no other choice but to break the habit. I'm not a Catholic, but I got their message."

From that day on, I had it easier. I could walk farther each day. At nights I could get at least five hours sleep without the terrifying nightmares that plagued me. It is true that my spine was not healing noticeably. My legs would not track. The only medicine I would accept was APC. The most difficult routine I practiced was that of exercises. My condition improved until I was able to walk in the yard every day without a cane. It was my intention to continue the therapy for at least another month before I requested a transfer. I did not want to be rejected because of lack of physical progress.

Convict orderlies ran the entire hospital. I was told that the only way I could see a doctor was to ask for an interview. I felt that it would be the better part of wisdom to seek a doctor's opinion on my progress or the lack of it. I made out a formal request to see one of the doctors.

Three weeks later a Dr. Jill called me to his office. "Doctor, I'm recovering quite well and I would appreciate being transferred to the Federal Penitentiary at McNeil Island, Washington. Apparently, exercise is the answer to my full recovery and I can take care of that in McNeil. Also, my family lives less than an hour away from the institution and I'd like to be near them." He smiled and said, "That's a logical reason for wanting to be moved. Let me give you an examination and if I feel you are fit to be sent out west, I'll make that recommendation to the Board of Medics." His exam was so much like the dozens I had had in the past that I was able to anticipate his movements before he made them. Some of the tests were so painful I wanted to cry out but I didn't dare. When I was told to bend over as far as possible, I made a miserable showing. The reflexes in my legs and feet were not responsive. His finger pressures along my spine hurt very much. I remained stoic. When he was finally through, he commented. "Well, Williams, you seem to be doing fairly well. There are areas of tenderness and there is a great deal of lack of mobility in your legs. Generally, I would say you might do as well in another hospital. I'm going to recommend that you be considered for a move within the next 60 days. However, before a final decision is made, I want to check you out again. I want you to return for treatment at physical therapy."

I didn't know whether to be elated or disappointed. The environment in this madhouse was depressing, and 60 days was a long haul. At least I took some comfort in the fact that I was going to be considered for an 'out' trip in a couple of months. I made up my mind to walk the track in the yard twice daily instead of once. I would haunt the crew in the physical therapy clinic. And the only time I would hit the sack would be at bedtime. One thing was for certain, if I didn't make the grade on the transfer, it wouldn't be because I didn't try.

One morning as I stepped from my shower, I was confronted by an old man. He was approximately 5'10' and weighed about 150 pounds. He was almost bald and was wearing a visor. His eyes were a very pale blue. The veins stood out on his forehead and hands. He was slightly bent from age. As I was drying myself, he just stood there eyeing me unblinking. His manner made me nervous. "What can I do for you,?" I asked. His voice was as I would have expected it to be; thin and high-pitched. "You're Nate Williams, aren't you?" I nodded my head. "I was sort of expecting you to drop by my ward to say hello. You've been here for six months." Before he could go any further, it hit me like a ton of bricks. The old gentleman standing before me was Robert Stroud, the famous Bird Man Of Alcatraz. He had been on the Rock while I was there, but had been in solitary confinement, so I had never seen him before. As I looked at him, oodles of statistics spun in my head. Here was the fellow who spent more years in solitary confinement than any other man in the history of this country, more than forty five years isolated from other human beings. The tomes he had written on birds and their diseases and cures were internationally acclaimed. His best known and most widely published book was DIGEST OF BIRD DISEASES. With the publication of that book, he became known as "Bird Seed" Stroud. Years later, an author by the name of Thomas E. Gaddis wrote a book detailing the life of Stroud. He captured the public's fancy by titling it "The Bird Man Of Alcatraz". Shortly after the book appeared on the shelves of thousands of stores, it was inevitable that a movie would be based on the story. Burt Lancaster starred in "The Bird Man Of Alcatraz". Actually, Stroud never worked with birds on Alcatraz. He had been confined previously at the Federal Pen at Leavenworth, and it was while he was serving time there that he was permitted to have birds, cages and laboratory paraphernalia in his cell. His writings were a result of his experiments and studies on the diseases of birds.

He was considered by the officials of the Federal Bureau of Prisons to be a very dangerous psychopath. He had already slain a guard, and they feared he would be apt to murder again, or might commit suicide. Consequently, he was shipped off to the Rock where the number 594 was stamped on his clothes and became a part of his name. He was immediately assigned a cell in solitary confinement. During my time in the Island, I never saw nor met this man. Now the famous inmate stood before me. "Frankly, Stroud," I said, "I've been so damned sick I never felt like visiting anyone. While we are on that subject, why didn't you come down to visit me?" He ignored my question and said, "When you get through, why not drop in on me and we'll cut up old touches. I understand there are three other cons from the Rock here. Two of them are so bad off they are kept in padded cells. I don't recognize the name of the third guy so I don't think I'll try to get in touch with him. Most of those buzzards are bad news."

The following evening I decided to go to Stroud's ward and gab with him. There were a myriad of tales about this oddball, some true and others just rumors. I had a rare opportunity to interview this mystery man. I did know he was a recluse who distrusted everybody, but it was by his invitation to come and see him, so he wouldn't feel I was imposing on his privacy. When I entered his ward, he was sitting alone at a table in a corner. He had his chess board and pieces spread before him. The guy was reputed to be a near-master at the game. He surprised me by jumping up and proffering his hand. "Sit down, Nate. Do you play chess?" I told him I had never played the game, that I was intimidated by it. He saw an opportunity to be my teacher. I was anxious to get "Bird Seed" to talk about himself, but I didn't want to appear to be pushing him. He gathered his chess set up and stored it under his foot locker. "Let's walk up and down the hall. I want to talk to you about some of the guys you know on Alcatraz."

He and I walked and talked until the lights blinked, indicating it was time for all patients to head for their own ward. Here was a man who had no chance to unload on anyone for nearly 45 years. He was extremely uncomfortable talking with the inmates at the Springfield hospital until I came along. There seemed to be a real camaraderie between us, partially because I was from Alcatraz also. Before I went to sleep that night, I found myself trying to psychoanalyze the guy.

Every night for weeks, the Bird Man and I either sat on his bunk and talked or walked endless miles up and down the corridor telling of our experiences. He really wasn't interested in hearing what I had to say. He wanted to spend the entire session telling me stories about his youth in Alaska and his years at Leavenworth studying about birds. That was exactly the way I wanted it. There were many writers and historians who would have envied my proximity to Robert Stroud. This unusual man was telling me stories concerning not only his free life but a detailed account of his lonely existence in a solitary cage. It was difficult for me to realize he had spent nearly a half a century alone and unable to communicate with anyone but those assigned to keep an eye on him. He graphically detailed the events surrounding the 1946 Alcatraz take-over attempt by six armed convicts. I often marveled at his intelligence and his command of the English language. It was rumored that he was unbalanced. I wondered how stable I would be if I had been subjected to those long years of loneliness.

Only once during our lengthy conversations did I ever detect a sense of personal loss or hurt, and that came about one Sunday morning while we were walking in the yard. "Nate, I know they sent me here to die. I am an old man and I have lost my will to continue. I have missed so much on this side of life that I am willing to see if there is anything worthwhile on the other side. Have you any idea how many years it has been since I have seen a child, heard a baby cry, or a dog bark, or had a glimpse of a women, or even a patch of green grass? What the hell is there left for me? And all this happened to me because I held court on a man who should have died." I held my breath, hoping he would explain that last outburst. I decided to take the bull by the horns so I asked him, "Bob, what do you mean by that last statement? After all, you did kill a man. I agree that the bureau has been unreasonably vindictive in keeping you in solitary for all these years, but how can you justify murdering that guard?" He turned those colorless eyes on me and continued his rationalizing. "Nate, my mom came to see me. I hadn't seen her in years and I really wanted to visit with her. Well, for some trumped up reason, the visiting-room rejected her request to see me. When she wrote me, she told how mean he had been to her. I felt sorry for her. She had spent all her savings to make the trip. She was very poor and was an old broken woman. I knew right then, it would be my last time to see my mother. I couldn't sleep that night so, as I laid on my bunk, I decided to hold open-court on him. I took the part of the prosecutor, judge, jury and the executioner. I found him guilty, refused him the right of appeal and sentenced him to die. I carried a concealed weapon until I could get him in the right place. And when I caught him unaware, I carried out the order of the court and sent him to meet his maker."

I was absolutely dumbfounded by his story. There wasn't anything I could do or say. He became strangely quiet. I glanced at him and saw tears dampening his cheek. I, too, wanted to weep. Without another word, he broke off our walk and left for his quarters. It was well-known that Robert Stroud was off his rocker. It was rumored that a week after we had last talked, he was caught committing oral sodomy on a young man in the library. I never saw him again.

During my noon meal one day, a guard approached my table and informed me that I was to report to the Captain's office right after lunch. One of my friends said, "You're in some kind of trouble, partner. Either that or you're going to be sent out." My spirits were lifted my his comment. I knew I was in no trouble so I must be going to be transferred. When I neared the Captain's office, a young lady said, "Williams, go right in. The Medical Board is waiting for you." Now all I had to do was impress on them how hale and hearty I was. Inside the room five men were seated around a long conference-type table. The only one I recognized was Dr. Jill. He motioned me to a vacant chair. "Williams, we are going to give you a perfunctory exam this afternoon and, depending on the results, we are going to recommend that you be returned to McNeil Island." I was elated! I was getting out of this insane asylum and would soon be near my family where I could get regular visits. "Patients leaving here do not wait for a full transfer chain. So you might have a month or two wait until a marshall is available to escort you."

I was on air for the next few days. My mental attitude was better and, accordingly, I seemed to improve physically as the days went by. Six weeks after my approval for transfer had gone through, I was told to pack my belongings as I would be leaving the hospital within the hour. I gathered my meager property and was sitting by the Captain's door within fifteen minutes. Friends dropped by to bid me farewell. Inwardly, I hoped the Bird Man would make his way down the corridor, but he didn't show. Before the hour was up, I was approached by a guard who told me to step into a nearby lavatory for a skin-search. When I came out, I was amazed to see the same Mexican marshall, Ramos Vallez, who had brought me to Springfield waiting for me. How lucky could I be? It promised to be a pleasant journey. The disappointment must have shown on my face when he started to chain me up. As he walked behind me to re-test the cuffs and waist-chain, he whispered, "Just procedure, Williams. You won't have these restraints on for long." We did not exchange words in the presence of the guards who were standing around. I spotted his car in the parking lot and actually pulled him toward it, I was so anxious to leave that horrible fortress that passed as a hospital.

After we had driven for a few hours, he pulled into a station to fuel up and let me go to the john. Before we left the restroom, he removed the restraints and permitted me to look like a human being. I rode in the front seat and we gabbed like old-time friends. "You know, Nate, the rules are that I have to leave you at a federally-approved jail when we stop at night. As much as I would like to, I can't get around that rule. When I turn in my prisoner-transfer-log, it has to reflect where you spent each night. You will be lodged in jail in Tulsa tonight."

Before he checked me in the clink he asked the receiving deputy, "Could you get my prisoner a snack?. We have travelled a long way today and he must be hungry." The deputy growled something to the effect that the kitchen was closed but he would see what he could do. The miserable bastard did get me something alright, a half-raw pork sandwich. There were fifteen guys in the jail playing checkers and cards. I refused to be the first one to break the silence and it was a couple of hours before a short bald headed man walked over to me and asked, "What's the charge, Boy?" I told him I was on transfer to the federal prison in Washington. "Where they transfer you from, Boy?" Without looking up at him I answered, "Springfield Federal Hospital. My name is Nate, not Boy." My pointed reply irritated him and I could tell there was going to be trouble. I had been dealing with this kind of jailhouse vermin for years. I eased myself off the bunk and faced him. I knew that in my weakened condition I would be no match for him, so I moved first and viciously. I ducked under his roundhouse fist and brought my knee up in his crotch. He screamed and collapsed. Fearing that his companions might take up his fight, I backed into a corner, determined to give a fair accounting of myself.

"Well, old hatchet-ass got his just deserts. Damn good job you did on him, fellow. He always causes trouble for new men who come in here. Come on out and have coffee with us." Not knowing any of these men, I was wary of their intention. I slowly stepped from the cell and seated myself at the far end of the table. In a matter of minutes, I could see that they were not going to cause me trouble. It was apparent that they had no respect for the man lying on the floor. A tall skinny individual across the table from me drawled. "I heard you tell our friend there on the floor that you were heading north to Washington. One of these days they are coming after me. I am wanted for an armed robbery in Seattle. I suppose I'll wind up at Walla Walla if I am convicted." The ice was broken so we sat up until midnight talking.

When I told them I had been in Alcatraz, they asked me dozens of questions about that place and some of the more notorious inmates. Obviously, the lore of the Rock interested everyone. Before we hit our bunks, a couple of the guys helped Baldy off the floor and into his bed. I felt sorry for him, but I knew if I hadn't moved on him first and fast, he would have beaten me. In my condition, he might have crippled me for life.

I was thankful when morning broke and I was called out of the tank in preparation for my continued trip with Marshall Vallez. The jailer who had come to the tank to escort me to the jail's office was an affable individual. He engaged me in conversation as we sat at the chief's desk. His interest was, of course, that he had a prisoner in his custody who had been on that famous island in San Francisco Bay. While we were talking, a trustee brought in a good breakfast for me. I anticipated a grilling concerning Alcatraz and some of its inmates. It was inevitable. "Williams," he began, "What was the Rock like?" God only knows how many times I had been asked that question. My answer satisfied him. "Deputy, we aren't going to be together long enough for me to respond to that question. I found the place to be a disgrace to this country. It was a viciously constructed pen, that brutalized the bodies and psyche of its inhabitants. Its effect on the staff was the same, but in a different manner. No institution like that could exist without damaging those involved in its perpetration, its very existence. It served no purpose other than to be a bastion where men could legally be mistreated. As for the inmates, there were some very dangerous men on the

Rock. By the same token, there were good men imprisoned there. There were some guards that lived on the misery of the inmates, and those individuals did their utmost to harass the prisoners. I can't lose sight of the fact that there were some damn good guards stationed there. The joint serves no purpose other than to destroy the kept and the keeper. This country should hang its head in shame." The deputy wasn't fully satisfied with my answer. "Is what you say true or are you just bitter?" I smiled and said, "Just a little bit of both." Mr. Vallez was ushered in by the chief, and in minutes we were on our way.

From Tulsa Oklahoma, we worked our way to Albuquerque. The trip was interesting to me because I had been penned up for years. I didn't realize how much I had missed the everyday things that free people see. My attention was mostly focused on any female I saw. My fantasies ran wild.

I was in the custody of a police officer who was fully armed, and who would have shot me if I tried to escape. Yet I found myself sort of attached to the guy. Wasn't he of the ilk I had vowed to hate all my life? I rationalized that he was different from the rank and file cop. But was he? The cop on the street would have arrested me and, if necessary, would have gunned me down in the process. Wouldn't this U.S. Deputy Marshall have followed the same procedure under the same set of circumstances? Contradictions swamped my mind. I was confused. Surely, at this point in time, I was ready to give a smidgeon and concede that I might be wrong. I debated with Nate Williams as the miles rolled by. As an example, I asked myself if I could have killed this likeable fellow behind the steering wheel if he tried to stop me from escaping? My response was a resounding "NO"! Could I have slain a guard on Alcatraz?. "YES"! Why could I take the life of one and not the other? Would I have taken the same drastic action against Ruckels, the guard on the Rock who had treated me so kindly? No way. In my mind, I resolved the debate by deciding that I would be selective in whom I would rub out. I would eliminate those who had abused me. It was I who had developed the despicable disposition toward them, and let that attitude manifest itself in my countenance. A bombshell of awakening shattered my mind. I found myself thanking God that I gone through the suffering of the spinal disease, submitted to surgery and was blessed with the presence of a Mexican U.S. Marshall. It was this strange set of circumstances that brought about the events that were instrumental in opening my eyes.

My reverie was interrupted by Ramos calling out, "Nate, we will be in Albuquerque in an hour or two. I thought we had better stop off for a good meal before I drop you off at the county jail. Their food is lousy. This is my hometown and I am going to stay here for a week to be with my family. I'll leave some pain medication with the jailer and tell him you're to get two pills every six hours." An hour later we finished a fine meal. Marshall Vallez permitted me to order whatever I wanted and I took advantage of him by choosing steak smothered in mushrooms. I topped that off with cherry pie a la mode. The county jail in Albuquerque was like all other such sites. As they were checking me in, the marshall and the jailer addressed one another in Spanish. I had no idea what went on between them but, whatever it was, the jailer was interested. He eyed me in a not unfriendly manner. Before my driver left, he shook my hand and said, "You can look forward to your next trip within the week. We'll be heading for California."

I was escorted down a long corridor to a big tank where there were about sixty other prisoners. About fifty percent of them were Mexicans. The rest were whites and blacks. Before the jailer locked me in the tank, he addressed a group of the inmates in Spanish. Again, I was in the dark as to what he was saying. The prisoners looked me over curiously. I began to feel like I was a freak. As soon as I was ensconced among the men in the tank, a very short white man came over to me and said, "Hey, man, if you want to, you can cell with me. At least we can communicate in our common language." I accepted his invitation and he ushered me to a double-bunked cage. He gestured to the lower bunk and let me know I could sleep there. This puzzled me because it is the rule in all jails, that the last one to enter a cell must take the upper bunk. "Why are you giving me the lower bunk?" I queried Shorty. He smiled pleasantly and advised me that the jailer had told the group that I was a very seriously injured man and there would be no roughhousing with me. He continued, "And he also said you were a notorious gangster who had been transferred from Alcatraz to a hospital in the east for surgery. I think he said they took a bullet from your spine. I figured you would be in no condition to hoist yourself into an upper bunk, so be my guest." There are instances where one inmate would pay another damn good money for a lower bunk. I took a liking to Shorty and thanked him for relinquishing his prized senior position.

After I had made up my bunk and we gabbed for a few minutes, he suggested we go out and meet some of the other prisoners. He took me among the men and introduced me to many of them. They were unusually interested in the prison from which I had been transferred. I knew the reason, but for the life of me I could not understand anyone putting an Alcatraz inmate on a pedestal.

The long week passed slowly in the Albuquerque jail. I had made friends with the fellows, so my time would have passed quickly had it not been for the terrible meals they served. My stomach was too sensitive to tolerate the spicy Mexican food. On a couple of occasions, the trustee cook prepared something more palatable for me. Even the food he fixed was enough to kill a Gila monster.

Three days later Ramos and I were pulling into Bisbee, Arizona for an evening lay-over. I was destined for the usual county jail while Ramos would be sleeping in a plush motel, drinking the best in the bar and flirting with the waitresses. My nest in the local bastille was like all the rest; hot, dirty and crawling with bugs. The minute I entered the gate and saw the heavy population of Mexicans, I knew I was again in for hot and spicy Mexican food. My stop was just for one night so I took it in stride, not that I could have done anything about it.

Ramos picked me up at seven the next morning. Right away he told me our next stop would be Los Angeles. It was a long and tiring drive. I felt sorry for him. He had to do all the driving and it began to tell on him. While he was always considerate of me, I did notice his replies to my questions were rather short. He was not a young man and I could certainly excuse him for being short-tempered at times. Throughout this long and arduous journey, Ramos proved himself to be a gentleman. I knew I would miss him when he deposited me at McNeil Island. It would have been nice if we could have corresponded, but I knew that would be impossible.

The L.A. county jail was a real switch. It was a huge warehouse of human flesh. It confined literally hundreds of inmates. In fact it had a larger population that many state prisons. Because of my reputation and the fact I had been confined on Alcatraz, I was immediately placed in the double-security unit. I was not permitted to leave the cell. My meals were brought to me in a tin bucket. The quality of the food reflected the container. I was relieved when he came after me. On the way north, the marshall told me we were going to drive to San Francisco, and would be spending the night in that city's lock-up. At his mention of the Bay city, I immediately thought of Alcatraz. To myself, I wondered if we would be able to see the Island from the highway. The thought of going near that awful place made me a little sick. It had been just over six years since I first arrived on the Rock but I never forgot the smallest detail of that entire trip by rail, and boat. Nor did I forget that horrible first night in my cell in the fish tanks. Thank God I would be ending up in Washington.

Ramos surprised me during the journey by asking me about Alcatraz. I became vitriolic in my denunciation of that institution and the type of men who could operate such a cruel den of iniquity. He listened patiently, making no comments. When I got through, he simply reminded me of the kind of criminals who made up the population on the Rock. "There were some real bad ones sent there, Nate. I know that for a fact because I personally knew some of them and the nature of their offenses. What puzzles me is that you were sent there. I've been close to you for more than two weeks now, and I can't see you as a dangerous hoodlum. I am aware of your past. If you have ever killed a man, there isn't any mention of it in your dossier. However, it contains instances of shootings in which you have been involved. And some of your buddies have been just damned mean and ugly. Based on your rap-sheet, I can see why you were a logical candidate for a cell on the Rock. I personally do not believe a man should be judged by what has been written about him. In fact, it has been a real pleasure traveling with you. Well, enough of that kind of talk.

By the way, it is my intent to spend a night in San Francisco. I have never been on the Rock, nor have I ever seen it from the mainland. If it would not bother you too much, I'd like to detour along Fisherman's Wharf and take a look at it while you're with me. I could get a running documentary from you. If you feel it would be too heavy for you to endure, I'll go to the Wharf alone. It's up to you." I assured him that I would like to see the prison from the outside. For years I had watched the tour boats, jammed with sightseers, circle the Island. They were compelled to stay outside a two hundred yard range dictated by the US government. For those of us who watched the boats and listened to the guide's spiel, it was sheer entertainment. The loudspeakers carried their voices very clearly.

Ramos picked me up from the jail before breakfast the following morning. He selected a small out-of-the-way cafe where we had breakfast. By eight o'clock, we were parked in front of Joe DiMaggio's restaurant on Fisherman's Wharf. The walk to Pier 39 took us about ten minutes. When we arrived at the dock from which the tour boats sailed, we could very clearly see the island. There were knots of the curious gazing across the Bay at that infamous penitentiary. The money makers had installed binoculars through which you could get a close-up of the pile of rock that sat off shore about a mile away. I was probably the only person in the group who had so many mixed emotions as I stared at my former home.

Ramos inserted a coin in one of the binoculars and let me get a real view of this tourists' delight. Being on the other side of the wall, I was getting a different perspective from the one so ingrained in my mind from the inside. I scanned the towers, the warden's house, the lighthouse and the dock. I watched the prison launch unload many guards and members of their families. Suddenly, my stomach started to cramp, sweat poured from my brow and I found myself becoming unreasonably angry. Ramos was quick to detect that I was having a traumatic battle within myself. He took my arm and lead me aside. "OK, Nate, that's enough. Come on, let's hit the road." I turned to him and said, "Ramos, I genuinely appreciate the opportunity you gave me here. What other inmate could have had this experience? However, we had better make ourselves scarce and damned quick."

Again we headed north. Portland, Oregon was our next destination. It was about seven hundred miles away, so we had a long trip ahead of us. We stopped only once before arriving at Klammath Falls, Oregon. I began to feel sharp pains radiating from my lower spine down to my left foot. Throughout the journey I had had some periodic numbness and pain, but it was mild and did not require a sedative. We were nearing Klammath Falls and were coming up on cafes along the highway. By the time we pulled in to one, I was suffering a great deal. He wanted to order a meal for both of us but I begged off. "I feel a little vomity so I'll take a glass of milk to coat the lining of my stomach. I am sure the medication will put me at ease and I can make the rest of the trip in comparative comfort. You go ahead and eat."

In an hour we were back on the road. He had suggested I lay down on the rear seat and get some sleep. I did as he told me, but sleep wouldn't come. We arrived at Portland at midnight. He went straight to the county jail. He got out first and opened the back door for me. When I tried to boost myself out, my legs would barely function. He helped me to a standing position and told me to brace myself against the car while he locked up. Suddenly my legs gave out and I fell to the concrete. Rather than trying to lift me, he pushed a night bell by the door to summon help. In a matter of minutes a grilled door opened and the face of a cop appeared. "What's going on here," he queried. The marshall flashed his badge on the fellow and said, "I am a U.S. Marshall and I have a prisoner to deposit here over night. He has become quite ill and I'm going to need help with him." The door slammed shut and reopened very shortly. There were two trusties with another guard who came out to assist. The guard, speaking to the trustees, ordered them to go inside and get a stretcher. As they lifted me to the stretcher, I was wracked with excruciating pain. I began vomiting. Ramos took charge immediately. "Put him in the jail-infirmary. Do not place him in a cell. He needs medical attention right away. I want a doctor to see him as soon as possible." The guard who was directing the trustees said, "We don't have a doctor here at night. We will see that he is attended to the first thing in the morning." The Marshall flared, "Tomorrow isn't satisfactory. Call a doctor from the local hospital now." The cop did not know what to do. He hesitated and finally said, "I have no authority to do that. I'll have to get permission from my superior." Ramos demanded that the hapless fellow get his boss on the phone and let him talk to the guy. During this heated exchange, the guys carrying me were having a tough time negotiating the stretcher into the small elevator. They were moving me as carefully as they could in order not to cause me further discomfort, and I appreciated their efforts. As soon as we got to the jailer's office, he dialed a number and handed the phone to Ramos. It was apparent he did not want to explain to the sheriff why he had been disturbed at this ungodly hour. The marshall harbored no fear and as soon as the 'big boy' was on the phone he said, "Sheriff, I am a U.S. Marshall here in your office. I have brought a prisoner in who has become quite sick. I want you to OK a call to the hospital requesting a doctor to come over right away." I could not hear the sheriff's response, but I did see Ramos's face cloud up. He listened a minute and then said in a cold voice. "Sheriff, if I have to arouse the local marshall on this emergency, I will do so and then I will write a full report on this incident. If something happens to my prisoner, you will have to shoulder the full responsibility. Once again, I am asking for your cooperation." He handed the phone to the jailer. After a minute or two the guy said, "Yes, chief, I'll call right now." He hung up the phone and dialed another number. I heard him tell someone that it was an emergency and that a physician was needed on the double. I was taken upstairs to the infirmary to await the medic. The deputy marshall put his hand on my shoulder and assured me, "You'll be OK now, Nate. I'll be by to pick you up early in the morning and, by this time tomorrow you will be at McNeil."

I must have dozed off, because I was next aware of a gentle voice saying, "What seems to be your problem?" I explained my surgery and the long trip we had taken the past few days. He stripped my clothes off and proceeded to give me a series of tests. He bent my knees and moved my legs in various positions. With each move, I thought I was going to faint. When he had finished, the doctor assured me that there was nothing too seriously wrong. "The prolonged journey has caused you to have muscle spasms. I'm going to give you a relaxant. In a few days, you will be able to continue your trip. I'm going to give you a shot for pain right now, and will leave instructions for you to have injections of morphine sulfate every six hours until you leave. I'll leave the results of my testing for the doctor who will see you tomorrow. Good luck."

The following morning, I was visited by the county jail doctor. He was a kind elderly man who came to the same conclusion as the other medic. "Too much riding and not enough exercise has created this problem for you. You will have to relax for a day or two." While the doctor was talking to me,

Ramos came in the room. He was beaming as he yelled, "Well, we are going to be stuck here for a few days, Nate. I'll call in every day and, as soon as I get the all-clear signal, we will make our way to home sweet home, the prison on McNeil." Before he left, I grabbed his sleeve. "Ramos, I want to thank you for the way you stood up to those cops last night. If it hadn't been for you, I would be in a hell of a mess this morning. Thank you."

Three days later I bid Ramos good-bye on the penitentiary dock as the guards cuffed me. I was back 'home', fifteen pounds lighter and in pretty sad physical condition. As the months passed, I struggled with heavy exercises, walking and running. It took three years and two more laminectomies by reputable civilian doctors to repair the damage done to my spine by the government's veterinarians in Springfield.

About four months after my return to McNeil, I was summoned to the warden's office. As soon as I entered the room where he was seated, I knew that something was afoot. He didn't hesitate to give me the sad message that my father had passed away earlier that morning. I was numb with grief. It had been my fondest dream that he would live to see me a free man again. I knew the chances of that ever materializing were slim. He was eighty-six years of age, and I still had at least ten more years to serve. I asked the warden for permission to go out to the rec yard and just walk. I was too broken-up to face my companions. He telephoned the tower guards and said, "This is Warden Madigan. Inmate Williams will have free access to the yard for the rest of the morning."

He then turned to me and in a soft voice said, "Nate, I am sorry. That is all I can say. I am assigning two officers to take you to your father's funeral. You will be leaving here the day after tomorrow. If there is anything more I can do for you, send word to me through one of the lieutenants."

As I walked around the yard, I was overcome with self- recrimination. I knew I had been a heartache to my dad for many years. I had destroyed his dreams, his will to continue. Early on the morning of the funeral, I was taken to the clothing room and fitted with a hand-me-down suit. When I met the two guards who were to be my escorts, I was angry. Both had the reputation of being miserable bastards. As soon as we reached the administration building, I was decked out in chains. We reached Seattle at noon. One of the guards, Butcher, advised me, "Williams, we are going to a cafe and get a bite to eat. Don't cause a ruckus." As they pulled into a parking lot next to an eatery, I announced, "I will not go in there with these chains." Butcher snapped, "Well, you damn well won't eat then." I just sat there and refused to be drawn into further conversation with him. Finally, one of the hacks solved the stalemate by going inside and ordering three hamburgers to go.

I began to wonder if they were going to try to take me into the funeral parlor with leg irons and cuffs on. I made up my mind to fight like hell if they tried to impose that insult on my family and me. When we parked in the space set aside for us, one of the guards informed me that they were going to take off all restraints. I was instructed to walk and sit between them. As the service was concluded, Butcher got up and covered the rear exit. The other guy walked beside me when I went forward to view my dad's body.

When it was over, they ushered me quickly out a side door and to the prison car. The chains were refitted and we were on our way. A few days after the funeral, my brother, Dan, visited me. "Are all prison personnel like those two who brought you to dad's funeral?" Out of fairness I had to reply, "No, Dan, some of them are decent persons."

Maybe it is an old wives' tale that trouble comes in double doses but it certainly held true for me. In a matter of a few months after my father's demise, word reached me that my mother had decided to follow her husband of more than fifty years. I cannot describe the feeling I experienced at the loss of my mother. I was so guilt-ridden that I thought suicide was my only answer. So far as I was concerned, the blame for their passing was due to the profligate life I had led. That fact did not mitigate my conscience then, nor has it now.

Once again, I found myself sitting in front of the warden's deck listening to a replay of his condolences. I never questioned Paul Madigan's sincerity. When he told me that I would be given permission to go to my Mom's funeral, I struck back bitterly. "Mr. Madigan, let me tell you what took place at my dad's funeral." I unloaded on him bitterly the anger that rages to this very day in my heart because of the unwarranted conduct of the two guards he assigned to accompany me on my trip to bid my Dad his last farewell. I finished my tirade with, "Can you imagine how terrible I felt without their stupid behavior? Think of how awful my family must have felt as they observed those two. Thank you for allowing me to go, Mr. Madigan, but I can't go through that again, nor do I want to submit my family to that sordid spectacle another time." During my tirade, the balding superintendent just sat at his desk with his head bowed. "Nate," he replied, using my first name, "we don't make the rules governing the transfer of prisoners. They come from the Bureau of Prisons in Washington D.C., and those rules are based on years of experience. Are you aware how many men have used funeral visits as an opportunity to escape? I would venture to say that during my thirty year career in the criminal field there have been a dozen or so who have run from the casket-side and disappeared for some time. The administration has tried to understand why a man would do this. Surely, they are grief-stricken and are not thinking clearly. But that condition isn't considered by John Q Public. They read some red-banner head line which screams, 'Dangerous convict flees guards.' They are free to prey on the public. Naturally, the Bureau bears the brunt of the citizens' reaction.

Let me be very blunt in your case. For the sake of discussion, let's say you decided to take it on the heel-and-toe from your funeral visit. In your case, let's envision the headlines. 'Ex-Alcatraz inmate escapes from custody of keepers.' What a juicy bit of news for some reporter! The heat would be piled on the head of the Director of Prisons. He isn't about to let himself be ridiculed for his policies. I have to admit that some accompanying guards overreact. Personally, Nate, I would trust you not to embarrass us. I was your warden in Alcatraz and I have observed your conduct for the past nine years. You're not a troublemaker. I will send a very feeling guard along with you if you want to attend your Mother's funeral." After Warden Madigan retired and went to Minnesota to raise orchids, and I was a free man, we corresponded on a regular basis. Before he passed away, I had the privilege of visiting him.

Under the conditions of his making, I agreed that I would like to see my Mother before she was buried. Paul Madigan kept his word. The day I was to leave for Seattle, I learned that I would be in the custody of Lieutenant Golden, a man very highly respected among the inmates and staff. Before we left the Island, he cuffed me. There were no leg irons or waist chains, just a pair of shiny handcuffs. I was devastated by the nature of the trip but I had a good feeling about my traveling guard. The first amazing thing that happened to me was his taking off the cuffs. "Williams, you could easily overpower me and escape. Please don't." I didn't respond, but I had no intention of violating this trust.

As soon as we reached Seattle, he took me to a nice restaurant and we dined in peace and camaraderie. What a difference from the last trip. When we arrived at the funeral parlor, he sat, inconspicuously, in the rear of the darkened room. "Nate, I want you to sit with your family. When the service is over, you may visit with your family as long as you wish. I will be at the car waiting for you." Before I could thank him, he disappeared.

My brothers and sisters, remembering the conduct of the two previous guards, could not believe the difference. They insisted on meeting Mr. Golden. When I introduced them to him, he was the perfect gentleman. My brother, Dan, who has always been an outspoken and somewhat brash individual, came right to the point with the Lieutenant. "Mr. Golden, we would be honored if you would have an early dinner with the family and me." Later, Dan told me he expected the officer to excuse himself from the dinner invitation, and was surprised when Lieutenant Golden answered, "I would be very pleased to accept your invitation, Dan. The last boat to the Island leaves at 6:00 P.M. today, and Nate and I have to be on it. If we can arrange that within our schedule, it would be nice to eat with you and your family." My brother made a quick call for reservations at the new Elk's restaurant on Lake Union.

The officer sat between my brothers and sisters and I sat beside my niece. After we had placed our order, I asked Mr. Golden if I could make a call. With his approval, I left the room and enjoyed a long talk with a friend. I must have been gone from the table for a half hour and I was worried that my traveling guard would be concerned as to my whereabouts. When I returned to my seat, I was pleased to hear Mr. Golden laughing at some tale my sister had told him. The dinner was great, both from the viewpoint of an excellent selection of food and the relaxed atmosphere. We had to scurry to make it to the Steilacoom dock in time to catch the return vessel. Prior to loading, the officer put the cuffs back on my wrists. It has been nearly thirty years since that event, and my remaining brother and sisters and I still remember Mr. Golden with fonds thoughts.

22

Freedom/A New Life

A long ordeal at Springfield had interrupted my study of law. From the day I began my law course, I secretly harbored the intent to prepare myself to attack the validity of my bank robbery conviction. I felt that somewhere in the arrest, indictment, conviction and sentence, I might find a flaw in the case and could seek relief in an appeal. I was aware of the slim possibility of success, but I had little to lose. The government had already taken a decade of my life and was anxious to claim another ten years.

Prisons are filled with jailhouse lawyers who, with no legal training whatever, challenged the validity of their conviction or sentence and, in a few instances, were able to gain their freedom. The courts all over the United States were flooded with habeas corpus writs. The prosecutors complained bitterly to the attorney general. They contended that being convicted of a felony deprived a convict of his civil rights and, therefore, precluded that person's privilege to exercise the inalienable rights a citizen would have to seek redress through the courts. The higher court ruled that convicted men actually retained their citizenship; that the only rights they forfeited were the right to vote or to hold public office. During the time from the filing of the suit to establish their status and, until the decision was handed down, the wardens of all institutions arbitrarily forbid inmates access to law books. Those who proceeded to defy the wardens' edict were punished by being sent to the 'hole'. The action of the higher court was, in effect, a restraining order to those officials not to interfere with convicts seeking to be heard in court. From that point on, the courts were again flooded with petitions. It is true that most of them were without merit, baseless, facetious and capricious, and were filed for the sole purpose of creating havoc in the courts. Of course, the courts refused to entertain such petitions. But the mere filing had the desired effect; inundate the courts with such filings, which had to be acknowledged. Consequently, the attorneys general were unable to respond as required by law. They did not have the manpower nor the money to withstand the onslaught. Eventually, the courts became bogged down and their calendars were back-logged for months. It was a cat and mouse game that the prisoners enjoyed immensely.

It was in this setting that I found what I felt to be a flaw in my case. At least I was confident that the sentencing judge in my case, John Bowen, had erred in my sentencing. After a conviction for bank robbery, the sentencing involves three separate charges, and each charge carries a different term to be served. All three terms are added together and the total of twenty-five years is imposed. Those separate charges and sentences are as follows: 1) Entering a bank with the intent to rob, ten years. 2) Use of a deadly weapon in the commission of the crime, ten years. 3) Taking the money from the bank, 5 years. Based upon the fact that the officials had never recovered the gun I used, I contended that the 'weapon' in my case was, in fact, a toy pistol and, therefore, could not be classified as a deadly weapon. I asked the court to set aside the sentence which stated I had used a deadly weapon, charge number 2. If the court saw fit to agree with my contention and set aside that portion of my original sentence, my term would be reduced by five years. I had already served ten years and would be eligible for parole immediately. I realized my chances were remote.

On April 2, 1963, United States District Judge William Lindberg accepted my transcript for review. I refused to accept the possibility that I could be summarily denied. Two weeks later, Judge Lindberg instructed the warden to bring me before his court. It was at this point I lost my confidence. I was fearful he would ask me to defend my position in open court and, while I was the author of the original petition, I knew I was ill-prepared to face-off with the U.S. attorneys. I asked for permission to telephone my sister. I told her of my misgivings. "Glenn, you have come this far on your own. However, the stakes are too high to gamble on the chance that you will be unable to contend successfully in the legal arena. I am going to retain Murray Guterson, the finest legal brain this side of the Mississippi. If I can get him to take the case, I will have copies of your petition in his hands right away. Just keep the faith."

A few days later I found myself in the King County Jail awaiting my court date. The following day I was told that I would be visiting with my attorney. As soon as I met Mr. Guterson, I liked him. He had the capacity to instill confidence in his clients. Anyone who had anything to do with the courts had heard of him. He was almost legendary. He was an easygoing and mild-mannered individual, but was hell-on-wheels when he started his argument. The day before my case was to be heard, he introduced me to another cracker-jack lawyer by the name of Ronald Neubauer. In one breath after the introduction, Mr. Guterson calmly stated, "Nate, Mr. Neubauer is the United States District Attorney who will be representing the government in your upcoming hearing." I wondered why in the hell my lawyer would be hobnobbing with my enemy! Apparently, concern and anger showed on my face. My attorney smiled ever so slightly and continued. "I would like to have you talk with Mr. Neubauer. You can speak to him candidly. While he is with the government, he is primarily interested that justice be done. I have talked with him at length about your life, crimes, and long imprisonment on Alcatraz." I couldn't believe my ears. For a moment, I considered firing him on the spot. Yet, I knew him to be an astute and honorable man. I decided to go along with him and, to this day, I thank God I did.

I was frank with the U.S. Attorney. He interrogated me at length about my youth, family and why I started on a life of crime. I answered him honestly. After the interview, I realized that I was a gone-gosling if Mr. Neubauer wanted to use my statements against me. He was warm and cordial after we shook hands as he prepared to leave. He simply said, "Well, Nate, we'll see you in court."

The marshall cuffed me and led me back to my cell. The outcome of this hearing was a matter of life and death so far as I was concerned, and here I had just spilled my guts to the executioner. I got little shut-eye for the next twelve hours.

I had never been more self-conscious and apprehensive in my life than I was when the marshall stopped outside the courtroom door the morning of my hearing to remove the cuffs. As he ushered me inside, I was intercepted by my attorney. He shook my hand warmly and said, "Don't be too concerned, Nate."

My attorney and I sat at the defense table; the very table at which I was seated ten years previously and heard myself sentenced to a twenty-five year term. Self-doubt crept into my mind. I found numerous reasons for the judge to deny my petition and return me to prison to spend another ten years. I nervously looked back to the persons present in the courtroom. My eyes caught a glimpse of Paul and Dan, my two brothers and my sister, Marjorie. They smiled confidently. My disturbing thoughts were interrupted when the bailiff announced the entrance of 'The Honorable Judge William J. Lindberg'. My next shock was to learn that Mr. Guterson had filed a motion for an order vacating Judgement, Sentence and Commitment of my original sentence on September 4, 1953. This action did not resemble the petition I had so painstakingly prepared months before. I didn't understand what was taking place. Both my lawyer and the government's attorney, Mr. Neubauer, were summoned to the bench where they discussed the merits of the action with Judge Lindberg. I got the feeling I was not a part of the case. The attorneys talked to each other while I sat on the hot seat. The only comforting aspect to the whole procedure was the obvious agreement between them. When they finished their conversation, they again approached the bench and talked to the judge. Apparently, I was the only confused person in the room. Before I could adjust to the rapid turn of events, the judge ordered that the Judgement, Sentence and Commitment be vacated and set aside. His order read as follows: IT IS ADJUDGED THAT THE DEFENDANT IS GUILTY AS TO COUNT 2 OF THE INFORMATION AND AS TO SAID COUNT IS CONVICTED. IT IS ADJUDGED THAT THE DEFENDANT IS HEREBY COMMITTED TO THE CUSTODY OF THE ATTORNEY GENERAL OR HIS AUTHORIZED REPRESENTATIVE FOR IMPRISONMENT FOR A TERM OF TEN (10) YEARS. THE EXECUTION OF SAID SENTENCE OF IMPRISONMENT IS HEREBY SUSPENDED AND DEFENDANT PLACED ON PROBATION FOR A PERIOD OF FIVE (5) YEARS. With that announcement, he rose and left the courtroom through his chambers.

I could not believe what I had heard. I sat there in a daze, unable to speak or move. My God, I was free! It was impossible for me to grasp the magnitude of what had taken place in the past thirty minutes. My lawyer shook my hand and said, "Nate, it is up to you now. You have an opportunity to get on with your life. If there is anything I can do for you, I urge you to call on me." He left. I had neglected to thank either attorney, but I think they understood.

It was my belief that all I had to do was to walk from the courtroom as any free person could do. When my brother and sister and I walked through the door, I was confronted by a deputy marshal. He quietly informed me that the judge had failed to sign the necessary papers to effect my immediate release. "Until we get the papers signed, you're still in the custody of the Attorney General. It is now Friday night and unless we can locate Judge Lindberg before he leaves the building, I will have to return you to McNeil Island until he returns to his chambers Monday morning. At that time, he will sign the court order and you will be freed that very day." A cold chill ran down my spine. Disappointment and anger fought for first place in my emotions. At the sight of the marshal pulling cuffs from his pocket, anger moved into first place. I stepped back and said, "Goddam it, man, you were in the courtroom and you heard what the judge said. I'm a free man. You will put those cuffs on me only after the fight." My brother realized what an impossible position in which I was putting myself. He rushed over to me and put his hand on my arm. "Glenn, if you attack this officer, you'll have an assault and battery charge against you. For once in your life, use your head. After all these years, you can stand another forty-eight hours in prison. Please don't throw everything away."

The marshal could see my position, yet he had a duty to perform. He discreetly stepped back and leaned against a wall. He knew that only an avoidance of a direct confrontation would defuse an otherwise dangerous situation. He put the cuffs out of sight. An officer of the court came over to me and quietly advised me, "Mr. Williams, I'll try to locate the judge today and ask him to return to his chambers to sign the papers. It may be that I can't reach him, in which case you'll be compelled to spend the weekend on the Island. If you create a problem here, you'll surely be returned to the institution as a parole violator, which will mean years behind the bars. Also, you'll be disappointing all those who care for you. I will ask the marshal to take you up to the holding tank without handcuffing you if you will promise not to do anything irrational. The marshal will be taking you back with other prisoners early tomorrow morning. Is it agreed?" As I followed the officer to the elevator which took us up to the cells, I felt like a sheep being led to the slaughterhouse.

All that had happened was like a dream and I was afraid I would wake up to find myself still doing an interminably long time. When I walked into the cage, I was surprised to find the door left open. This comforted me some. I started to pace up and down in my quarters. Notwithstanding the door was wide open, I still took three paces forward, turned and took three paces back as I had done ten million times on Alcatraz. I was thoroughly indoctrinated to three paces in one direction. Not one inch further. After I settled down, I began to enjoy that full realization of what had taken place in court that morning. I WAS FREE! At least I would be going on long walks, unfettered, and looking lustfully at females on the streets.

Humanity began its inroads that noon. A man walked to my cell and tossed in a newspaper. "When you get through with this, drop it on the marshal's desk." I couldn't believe my eyes nor ears. "A decent human being," I thought to myself. I sat on the edge of my bunk and read the paper from cover to cover. I stood up and went to the door of my 'home' and looked up and down the hall. Not a soul was in sight. I spotted a desk at the end of the corridor, so I strode confidently to it and deposited the paper on that desk. One who had not undergone what I had for the past decade could never understand my satisfaction at being trusted to do such a minor bidding. Confidence was slowly coming back. I laid on my bunk and fell asleep. I was awakened when a deputy entered my cell carrying a tray of hot food. "When you get through with the tray, Nate, take it to the sink in the room across the hall and rinse it out. It will be picked up by a trustee."

That afternoon my sister and brothers visited me. No guard was present. When they were ready to leave, Dan asked, "Do you want me to come to the dock at Steilacoom on Monday and drive you to Seattle?" His question sounded so unreal. "No. Thanks a lot, but I want to catch the bus by myself. I want to become independent as soon as I can, Dan." He understood. Paul reminded me that I was to spend a few weeks as a guest at his house. I was fully aware that the family wanted it that way. They further realized that the first four months of freedom was the most difficult for releasees. Potential violators usually 'fall' during that time. Having a support system on the outside enhanced a probationer's chances of a successful completion of his commitment.

At 7:30 A.M., I was awakened by a deputy and told I would be leaving for the Island in an hour. By the time I had shaved and eaten breakfast, it was time for the trip. Six other prisoners, who had just been sentenced, were herded into the holding tank to be cuffed and leg- ironed. I was amazed when the marshal pushed me aside, indicating I would not be transported in restraints. I was self-conscious when the seven of us were loaded into the penitentiary van. I was the only person not chained. The other cons eyed me with suspicion. I knew they were thinking, 'who in the hell is this dude in the suit with free hands and legs?' So far as I was concerned, I couldn't care less what they thought.

At Tacoma, the travelling guards stopped at the county jail to pick up four more cons to be added to the chain. The officers told us to get out and follow another guard into the clink. I brought up the rear with the marshals. Once inside the jail, we walked down a long hall where we lined up to go into a holding tank while the others were brought down to be hooked up to us. And at this point the damndest faux pas occurred that I have ever seen. One of the city cops who escorted us inside came to the conclusion that I was a deputy marshal because I was the only person wearing a suit. He put the men in the tank, one by one, until he came to me. He commented to me, "Marshal, will you watch these prisoners while I gather the others? It will only take me a few minutes." Inwardly, I laughed. I went along with him and assured him they would be watched carefully. He locked the men up and left me on the outside. He disappeared for about ten minutes, and then all hell broke loose. He charged back to the holding tank with four other cops and two of the federal marshals following. He was livid with anger and yelling, "There he is, the guy in the brown suit." He ran at me in a threatening manner and screamed, "You dirty con. You let me believe you were a marshal." The chief federal officer asked me if I had said I was a federal

297

agent. I told him exactly what took place and that I had not said I was a federal agent. It was a clear picture to the whole group as to what had happened. The offended cop was humiliated. All of the prisoners were loaded in the van, and we were on the final leg of our journey.

When we arrived at the prison dock, we were met by guards. I knew most of them and they were surprised to see me back. They had heard I was freed. I explained what had occurred. While they were counting the new men, one of the deputy marshals came over to me and started laughing. He told me what had taken place back at the Tacoma county jail. The young cop who had entrusted the guarding job to me came sauntering into the officers' quarters and announced that he was ready to bring the other cons down for transportation. The federal officers looked at one another in a puzzled manner. One of them turned to the city cop and asked, "Who is with the prisoners we brought in?" The city cop said, "The federal officer who was with you agreed to watch them for me." The government officer replied, "Hell, all the federal men are in this room. If you mean the man in the brown suit, he is a convicted bank robber who spent years on the Rock. He, too, is our prisoner." "With that", he continued, "we all made a dash back to the main tank. When we came upon the scene, we were puzzled until we put the scenario together. In all my years, I never ran into anything so crazy."

After the prison officials had accepted the cons along with their commitment papers, we were marched up to the main cellhouse and placed in the fish tanks. My suit was taken from me and I was dressed in institution blues. Many of my friends came by to be filled in on what happened. I got tired of explaining.

By Monday noon, an officer from Seattle came to McNeil and handed my papers to the warden. Late that afternoon, I was startled to find myself standing in the Greyhound bus depot waiting for the bus. My sudden freedom shocked me. It was a mixture of sweetness and pain. For an instant, it seemed to be unbelievably cruel to drop me off in this beehive of unfamiliar hustling and bustling. How I managed to buy my ticket and get on the right bus, I don't remember. I first became aware of the ride to Seattle when my neck became sore from so much turning from side to side to take in all the alien sights. There were new buildings, streets and most of all, lovely women. How much I had missed them! I'll bet I was the only man in the city that smelled a strange scent, that of freedom. What a glorious feeling!

The city bus ride out to my brother's home was difficult for me to negotiate. Making the correct change was a chore. My brother and his family were waiting for me to arrive. The upstairs bedroom was all my own. I had dreamed many times of being able to crawl into a bed that was devoid of iron slats for a mattress, a bed that bragged of fresh clean sheets, a pillow covered with a pillowcase and the comfort of soft warm blankets. Still, I was restless. I was so accustomed to hearing the prison noises that used to lull me to sleep. There were no flashlights blinding me four times each night while a guard counted me. There were no slamming steel doors at four in the morning to let the kitchen crew out to prepare breakfast. I didn't hear men snoring all night and cussing at whomever would listen. From out of the night came visions of my daughter, Muriel. She was only twenty-five miles from me. What was to stop me from going to see her tomorrow? Was she aware that she had a father in prison? What had my sister told her? She would be a teenager now. Would my sudden appearance on the scene interrupt her life? What would be the best way for me to handle this puzzle? It was a delicate situation with so much hinging on the outcome. The best bet would be for me to discuss it with the family.

When I awoke in the morning, I realized that I was free to get up and go for a walk. I crept from the house so as not to awaken other members of the family, quietly left by the front door and, with some uncertainty, took a deep untainted breath of fresh air and started walking. To be sure I didn't wander too far, I walked four blocks in each direction to make certain I could find my way back to the house. Dogs barked at me and the birds let me know I was disturbing them. It was so sweet.

Each day was a new adventure. I found enough confidence to go into strange restaurants and order meals without watching the guards count the silverware; to eat from dishes, not metal trays. I had to resist the habit of picking up the dishes and taking them to the kitchen. I found the staff in my selected cafe to be friendly and talkative. Within a short period of time, I screwed up enough courage to ask the receptionist for a date. When she accepted my invitation, I was uncertain where to take her. Of all places, she chose to go to a wrestling match. It is true that the idea of wrestling with her appealed to me.

On the day of my release, both of my brothers and my sister suggested I just 'take it easy and get acclimated to life in the free world.' It bothered me not to be productive. One evening at dinner, I told my brother I was going to look for a job. I followed his advice and scanned the help wanted section of the paper. There were jobs advertised, but I was not equipped to handle any that paid enough on which to survive. The only profession at which I was really skilled was bank robbery, and there were no calls for persons in that category. One of the most available jobs was driving cab, but I hadn't driven for years and had no license. The following weekend, Paul took me out early in the morning when there was little traffic and started teaching me to drive. In an hour or two I was driving well. He turned me loose with the car for another week and then told me to go to the state patrol office and apply for a driver's license. I passed the driving test, but failed the written. I crammed over the driver's manual and took the test again. Again, I failed. By this time I was frustrated and angry. I kept on driving after my brother insisted I get a learner's permit. The thought of doing this galled me to no end. I had always been an excellent driver and now I was in a primary class with kids. On my third attempt, I got the precious piece of paper.

One day, with tremendous confidence, I was sailing along one of Seattle's main thoroughfares when the silence was split by the wailing of a siren. My rear view mirror gave me the bad news. A cop was on my tail. It was kind of like the old days except I didn't have to prepare for a shoot-out. When I stopped, he strutted to the side of my car and asked for my driver's license. Without wasting time with preliminaries, he barked, "Mister, you were doing 50 miles an hour in a 30 zone. I'll have to give you a ticket." As he was writing it out, I pondered about taking off. Then I thought it over a minute and decided it would be a stupid move. He came back and handed me the ticket. I reached for my wallet and he jumped back and started to reach for his gun. By this time my wallet was in plain view. He was relieved. Obviously, he thought I was reaching for a gun. "What the hell's wrong with you? I simply want to pay for the ticket and be on my way," I growled. He looked surprised. "We don't accept money for tickets here. Where have you lived?" Without any hesitation, I answered, "In California. What has that got to do with it?" He continued, "In Washington, the traffic bureau will tell you how much the ticket will cost, and you mail that amount to them." I read the ticket carefully and finally asked. "How much will it be?" "Well," he drawled, "That will depend on how many tickets you have had in the past three years. I assured him I had not had a ticket in nearly eleven years. He smiled and said, "With a record like that, you'll be let off easy." He smiled and drove off. I smiled and drove off. Both of us were pleased, for different reasons.

Finally, I landed a job driving a dump truck. At the end of two weeks, the boss approached me and informed me that he would be unable to make the payroll for at least another two weeks. There were five of us working for him. We all agreed to wait for another two weeks. At the end of that period we received a piece of paper but it wasn't a check. It was notice that he had filed bankruptcy. So a month's work went down the drain. It wasn't the end of the world for me. I didn't want to drive truck anyway.

I finally landed a steady job driving an ambulance in Lynnwood. It was a hell of a job, but I liked the owner, Pete, and the working conditions. In less than six months, I was named as the foreman. What happened along with that promotion nearly caused my ticker to stop

As the foreman, my boss wanted me to take over much of the book work. This included making deposits and withdrawals and writing checks. He told me one morning that he wanted to take me to the Seattle First National Bank and introduce me to the president, Mr. Killian. I almost fainted. Good God, how could I get out of this one? He was the same guy from whom I had withdrawn $50,000 twelve years ago, using a gun as a withdrawal slip. Casually, I asked Pete, "How long has this Killian fellow worked there?" "Oh, I'd say about twelve years, why?" I didn't bother to answer.

The next morning, Pete and I entered the bank. I had made up my mind to face the president, come what may. We walked straight to Mr. Killian's desk. He arose to greet Pete. I stood there and held my breath. Pete extended his hand and said, "Hi, Mr. Killian, I want you to meet my new manager, Glenn Williams. I would like to have you extend the same privileges and courtesies to him as you have to me." Mr. Killian jumped up, held out his hand and beamed, "It's real nice to meet you, Mr. Williams. We want you to feel welcome here. If you need anything, just walk into my office and I am sure we can accommodate you." A few minutes later he accompanied Pete and me to the door, jovial and happy. When I had met him twelve years previously, he was not the same effervescent gentleman he was that day. His parting words were, "Drop by anytime and have

300

coffee with me."

The ambulance work lasted about a year before the inevitable happened. The city council convened one day and conjured up a bunch of ordinances to impose on the populace of Lynnwood. Only one of them affected me and that was the one that read, in general; no person convicted of a felony could secure a license to drive an ambulance or a cab in the city of Lynnwood. It became incumbent on all persons employed in either of those capacities to be fingerprinted and mugged. It mentioned that failure to comply with the ordinance was punishable by a fine and/or imprisonment.

I kept on working for three weeks before making a decision NOT to comply with that law, but to contest it. I retained an attorney and served notice of my intention. He was not too enthused over my chances of prevailing in the action. He advised me at the end of our initial interview, "Mr. Williams, so far as I can determine the council is within its right and duty to approve such an ordinance. In fact, every major city in this state has a similar ordinance. In a number of instances, the state supreme court has upheld the council's action. And we have another problem that you might consider. Your employer, if he knowingly keeps you on the job, is suscep- tible to a like punishment. I feel badly about this, Mr. Williams, because what they have dictated is that ex-felons have no right to employment in many areas of the labor market. Let me get back to you after I have had a better chance to research this matter." By the time I left the lawyer's office, I was discouraged. It wasn't as though I was in desperate financial straights that bothered me. It was the blind ignorance of a group of men and women. Now, I was beginning to see why so many men released from prisons failed in their efforts to straighten out their lives. In addition to the social stigma, there were so many legislated impediments.

I owed it to Pete, my employer, to come clean with him. The following morning I asked Pete to have breakfast with me. "Couldn't it be tomorrow, Glenn? I have a full day scheduled." My anger had been storing all night and it reflected in my sharp retort. "I don't give a damn what you have lined up for today, Pete. If it wasn't important to me, I'd rather eat with one of the corpses we took in yesterday." The guy look stunned. I had never come on so strong before. "OK, Glenn, if it's that urgent, let's go."

While we were waiting for the food to be brought, I told Pete all about my lengthy criminal career. He had not read of the ordinance that had triggered this conversation. For a full minute, he just sat there and stared at me. He exploded. "You, a bank robber? And in Alcatraz! I can't believe it, Glenn." And then he made a comment that I have heard dozens of times since then. "You don't look like a bank robber!" By the time the meal was over, I convinced him. "Pete, it appears I am going to have to leave this job." We didn't speak another word about the problem for the rest of the day. He talked the situation over with his wife. Together, they decided to ask me to stay on for a month. He said he would appear before the council to see if he couldn't post a bond and get a hearing from that body of men and secure their permission to let me work.

Three days later my attorney called me to his office. Pete had called him. The lawyer told me that he advised Pete that very few things in life were fair.

301

He called me later and said, "Here's a plan we came up with, Glenn. I'll file suit today. Until the matter comes before the local court, you'll be permitted to work. In the final analysis, you're not going to win. By the way, that guy and his wife are fond of you. He told me that you were a good employee, bank robber or not." I made up my mind I would drop the suit before it was set for hearing. I didn't tell my boss of my intention. The main reason I decided to let the matter pass was because I didn't want to face the inevitable publicity. It pained me to give up without a fight.

Since the incident took place, Pete and I became fast friends. Quite often we would talk far into the night. It was during one of these sessions that he told me something that really shook me. "A couple of years ago I resigned from the local police department where I had been a sergeant under Chief Reynolds. At that time, he was a miserable sadist. He had been a cop in Chicago. From the very beginning, he and I did not see eye-to-eye. When the opportunity arose for me to leave the force and open this business, I grabbed it. Here is the problem as I see it in your case, Glenn. If and when Reynolds gets a whiff of your past, he is going to land on you with both feet. It'll be a chance for him to create problems for me. In this small community, word will get out about your past reputation. I look for it to be leaked by your lawyer. If he doesn't let it out, you can be certain it'll be headlines when the suit is filed. The local paper here is starved for something sensational. I'm willing to wager that there hasn't been a significant banner headline since you knocked off Lynnwood's Seattle First National Bank." He chuckled at that statement.

About a week later, while I was eating breakfast, who should walk in but the chief, Greg Reynolds. I am sure the meeting was by design. He undoubtedly knew that I ate my meals at that cafe along with Pete's other employees. He walked straight to my table and, without asking for an invitation, pulled out a chair and sat down. I had learned early in life to take the initiative in delicate situations, and this was one. His first mistake was in trying to intimidate me by the stare-down game. I had had many years to practice this tactic on professionals. My eyes bored right into his without blinking. Finally, he fidgeted and said, "I'm Greg Reynolds." I never took my eyes from his, nor did I acknowledge his comment. He turned red and continued, "I've seen you around driving one of Pete's rigs. Well, I ran a check on you, Williams, and found out you are an ex-convict with an impressive record. Let me come right to the point. You, as an ex- felon, cannot drive a public vehicle in 'my town'. Before we have a problem, I'd suggest you leave this city." I was so angry that it was with great difficulty that I was able to contain myself. I finished a cup of coffee before very calmly saying, "Reynolds, this isn't 'your town'. I have a right to live and work here. As you know, I'm challenging the legality of the ordinance that would restrict me. My lawyer will answer any further questions you might have." Reynolds was enraged. He jumped up, kicked over his chair and yelled, "If any of my officers as much as sees you taking a piss, they will haul your ass down to my jail, and then we will see how tough you are." I had been around long enough to know he was dangerous. My inquiries about this reptile revealed much about the reputation of Greg Reynolds.

During a code 3 run one midnight, I saw a police vehicle approaching from the rear. I heard its siren and saw the red lights flashing. The fact that I, too, was running with red lights and siren, should have alerted the driver of the police car that I was on an emergency run. The police car pulled alongside my ambulance. The two occupants in the front seat were waving at me frantically. Not knowing what to expect, I stopped in the middle of the road and rolled my window down. The cop nearest my side jumped out and screamed, "What the hell is wrong with you? Didn't you see our lights or hear the siren?" I yelled back, "Can't you see I am on an emergency run? I can't sit here and argue with you!" I rolled up my window and started to take off. Before I could get under way, the driver of the police car pulled directly in front of the ambulance, effectively blocking me. My assistant, Roger Lovelace, kept his cool far better than I. He grabbed my arm and said, "Don't try to go around them, Glenn. They're up to something. Just take it off code 3 and sit here." At this time, both cops leaped from their car, came to the driver's side and jerked my door open. Both had their guns drawn. "Shut the motor off, Williams. If you try to move this rig, we'll blow the tires off. You're under arrest. Get out of the ambulance." As I started to get from behind the wheel, both of them yanked me out head first and threw me to the ground. They had cuffs on me quickly. I was dumbfounded. I demanded, "What are you up to? The least thing you could do would be to let me finish this run. Someone could die because of this interference." "We'll take that responsibility. Get in the prowl car. We're going to book you for reckless driving and resisting arrest." Turning to Roger, they asked him to carry on. He did just that. As I was being dumped in the back of the police car, I heard the ambulance drive off with tires squealing.

I felt sorry for Roger. Depending on the situation, he may have had a tough job handling it alone. In any event, he was the most dependable and knowledgeable first aid man on our crew. What I didn't know until later was that Roger radioed the office and told the boss what had occurred. That accounted for the fact that Pete was at police headquarters waiting for the cops and me to show up. They were surprised to see him standing before the sergeant's desk raising hell. The two cops took my cuffs off and threw me into a cell. I could hear Pete yelling, "Why did you arrest Glenn?" The two who had brought me in informed him that he could read their report and find out. "I want to go his bail right now," my boss told them. The sergeant tried to quiet the irate company owner. "Pete, you worked here long enough to know that bail can't be set until morning when the judge is here. Only the chief can let him out sooner." Pete was insistent. "Well, call the guy and let me speak to him." Reluctantly, the officer got Reynolds on the line. Apparently the sergeant had told the whole story to his superior because Reynolds ordered my release immediately with instructions for me to show up at the station in the morning.

While we were driving to the office, Pete asked me exactly what happened. "They accused me of driving recklessly. And that is bull shit! I was on a code 3 and drove as fast as I safely could. There was no traffic to speak of." He stopped at our favorite coffee spot. To our surprise, Roger pulled up. He was visibly angry. Before we could say a word, he said, "Guess what,

Glenn? That call was a false alarm." None of us spoke for a long time. Finally, Pete very quietly said, "Fellows, as sure as hell this was a put-up job to give the cops a chance to harass us." Suddenly, something came to my mind. I grabbed Pete by the arm and said, "You're right. When they pulled us off the road, one of them said, 'Shut the motor off, Williams'. It was pitch dark outside. The lights were off on the inside of my vehicle and it was impossible for them to identify anyone. How did they know I was behind the wheel? They had to have spotted us leaving the office as soon as we came out to get into our rig." The three of us sat there for a long time drinking cup after cup of coffee. As if by signal, we arose as one and left for the office and bed.

I was distressed at the turn of events and didn't get any sleep until early morning. I went back over my employment record since I was released. My first job went down the drain because my employer went broke. Now, this ambulance spot was proving too hot for me. I decided to quit, but first I wanted to talk it over with my brother and sister. The next morning I told Pete I was going to be in Seattle for the day. Marjorie and Dan agreed to meet me for lunch. I had told them briefly what my problem was. I didn't enjoy the food. They advised me to stick it out for a couple of days and, if I felt I had to leave after that, then by all means, leave. Dan was a philosophical individual and I could depend on him for reliable advice. Marjorie knew I was the sort of person who would act irrationally when I felt goaded. She was fearful I would react in a manner that might lead me right back into a life of crime. In my heart I knew that I was not going to go off the deep end. No matter how bad things got, I was determined to keep out of the tentacles of the law.

I got back to the ambulance company's office late afternoon. Pete called me into his office and spilled his guts. "Glenn, I can't prove it, but I'd bet that false alarm was turned in by the local constabulary. You have no idea how Reynolds hates me. He has no reason to dislike you, but he'll strike at me through you. Both of us are vulnerable, but your position is far more precarious than mine. In your case, he can legally cause you much trouble. Let me give you a little advice. You have more potential than you can express driving a meat wagon. For your own good, why don't you quit?" I smiled as I responded, "Pete, that's why I came back this afternoon. I intend to leave this evening. I want you to see it my way. I've just finished more than ten hard years under terrible conditions. I'd like a little peace and an opportunity to lead a normal life. I know that ex- convicts have a difficult time recovering when they are released, but I never expected so much resistance from such unexpected sources. As an example, here I am trying to make a living and I step smack-dab in the middle of a feud between a vengeful police chief and my employer. If this had happened ten years ago, I'd have gotten rid of Reynolds. I don't have those inclinations anymore, so I'll get out of this community. It's been a pleasure meeting you, and I'm sorry it turned out this way."

For the next two years I tried my hand at selling, driving truck and starting my own business. I met a nice young lady during that period, and we married. In due time, my wife announced she was pregnant. I was elated. I wanted to raise a child to its maturity, a child I could call my own. Throughout the time my wife was carrying the baby, I secretly prayed it would be a girl. My mind kept flashing back to the time Muriel was born, and to the brief three years of bliss I spent with her. This time, I was determined I wouldn't jeopardize my new baby's life or happiness. During my wife's pregnancy, I made up my mind to go into business for myself. A friend, who was a car detailer, convinced me that money could be brought in if a company were formed and it was operated in a business-like manner. I leased a lot on the main drag in Seattle and proceeded to set up Glenn's Auto Prep.

In no time at all my company was in the black. It did take most of my time, but I was confident we were on the road to financial independence. I began to take time off to enjoy myself. I purchased a beautiful car and played the big-shot around town. Eventually, I got the idea I didn't have to be on hand all the time, that it would make money whether I was there or not. After all, I had a great crew I could depend on. On one occasion, when I returned from a disastrous weekend in Las Vegas, I learned that a number of my checks had bounced. I demanded that a representative of the bank go through my books with me. It took very little time with this professional auditor to convince me that I was not only broke, but that my books were in a mess and I was in debt. If I learned one thing, it was that I was not a businessman. The silver lining of that period was the birth of my baby. It was a girl, and I was ecstatic. My wife and I decided to name her Natalie. She was a beautiful baby, blessed with excellent health.

Through an acquaintance I became involved with the Fremont Baptist Church. So far as I was concerned, the primary magnate of the church was The Reverend Norman McCue, its pastor. He reminded me of The Reverend Peter McCormack and Father Joseph Scannell, my very dear friends on Alcatraz. Norm was an intellect, sincere and dedicated to his faith. His personality drew many people to him. There are very few people with whom I have felt so relaxed and comfortable. It wasn't that he sacrificed his integrity to placate me or anyone else. On a number of occasions, I was affronted by his abrupt manner of correcting or challenging me. I found him to be the kind of gentleman who could disagree with you in no uncertain terms and, at the same time let you know that he loved you. In the years of turmoil that dogged me, he was always a stalwart to whom I could turn for guidance.

It was during my time at the church that a different direction in my life's course took place. It was at a dinner in the church's social hall where I met the guest speaker one evening. He was a Presbyterian minister by the name of Richard Simmons. His topic that evening was one of intense interest to me because it dealt with convicts. A few years before, Mr. Simmons felt called to minister to the men and women in Washington State's penal institutions. He felt they were forgotten. A number of business and Christian leaders formed a non-profit corporation which they named Job Therapy. He developed the nationally recognized Man-To-Man project. Its purpose was to get a free man involved in the life of a forgotten man in prison on a one-to-one relationship. Simmons' only requirement was that

305

the outside contact be a Christian. The civilian was to form a bond of friendship with the prisoner by visiting and counselling him. The sponsor promised that when the convict was released, he would meet the man at the gate, take him to his destination (if it was within the state), and to stand by him until he was on his feet. It soon became inevitable that the sponsor would endeavor to secure employment for the releasee. As a result of this commitment, a division of the program was developed for the sole purpose of finding jobs for ex-convicts. It was a marvelous undertaking. In a few short years, the concept was adopted by many states and Canada. Richard's wife, Barbara, felt that the women in our penitentiaries were being deprived of the same benefits as the men. She initiated a Woman-To-Woman counterpart that was an immediate success. In fact, her success was recognized by the White House.

When Mr. Simmons addressed our group at the church, I listened to every word. His purpose was to ask men to volunteer to become sponsors. After his speech, I approached him and asked to speak to him privately. I directed him to a corner of the room where we had a degree of privacy. For the first time since my release, I opened up my past to a total stranger. He was surprised and intrigued. We talked at length. Before the evening was over, he asked me to come to work with him. He advised me that they were without funds and that my work would be as a volunteer. "However, Glenn, we have a number of proposals for funding with a half dozen corporations. I'm certain we will be amply funded in a short time. I know you can't support a family by volunteering your time. As soon as our first money comes in, I'll put you on salary. A man with your past reputation will be an asset to Job Therapy." Soon I was ensconced in an office as an employee of Job Therapy, a position that led to an amazing change in my life; a transition that, if not documented, would never be accepted as valid.

Working in an area that dealt entirely with felons, releasees and their families proved to be the most interesting and fulfilling endeavor I had ever experienced. It afforded me a great sense of satisfaction. In my work, I found I was dealing with police, parole officers, judges and even prison guards. It hadn't been too long ago that I was an avowed hater of all authority. To make it more unbelievable, I was enjoying it. Among my assignments during the five years at Job Therapy, one was as a liaison between our office and the penal institutions of the state. In that capacity, I would travel to those institutions to transact Job Therapy business. I soon became acquainted with THE KEEPERS OF THE BEES and the bees themselves. I was soon on a first name basis with the staff of the institutions. Oddly enough, notwithstanding my hatred of anything that smelled of police and prisons, I thoroughly enjoyed the working relationship.

It wasn't long before my work with the cons, their families and the officials whose job it was to try to rehabilitate the felons became widespread. I had the reputation among the cons and their keepers of being a person who would not violate the confidences of either group. Many inmates would ask me to smuggle out letters, bring in drugs and in other ways break my word with the officials. From the beginning I let them know that I was in the business of trying to help them and, if I were to start breaking the confidence of either side, I would be impotent in my efforts. At first, the cons felt I was betraying the phony con-code. They refused to recognize that I wouldn't be assisting them if I started betraying them or the employees of the corrections department. I was steadfast in my determination to play the game according to my sense of fair-play. It paid off. I know of no other ex-convict that was trusted by the cons and the authorities as much as I.

On the subject of earning the trust and confidence of the penal officials, I often think of Leo Johnston, a highly respected parole officer in Seattle. It had been my wish to work in the field of corrections where I could use my experience and expertise to help prisoners and parolees. I cannot remember when I first met Leo. But I do remember the first interview he granted me. I expressed my wish and hopes of working under the umbrella of the state parole officials. Leo is the first person with whom I confided my desire. He sat back, listened to what I had to say and finally commented, " Glenn, I'm certain the state isn't, at this time, willing to consider such a proposal as you have made. In fact, I would urge you to abandon such a thought." I left his office disappointed and discouraged. After I had proven myself for two years at Job Therapy as a reliable employee in the very field in which Leo Johnston worked, I was pleased to be accepted by Leo as an individual whom he could trust and work with. To this day Leo and I have remained friends.

Robert Tropp, the former Secretary of Corrections for the state of Washington called me to his office in the state capital in Olympia and commended me for the work I had been doing. He issued me a pass to enter any state penal institution with complete movement within the system unescorted. I was inordinately proud of my new possession, not because of the pass in itself, but because it represented a total trust and acceptance. In this new career I had chosen, mountains were moved as if by some myste-rious hand. Opportunities presented themselves.

One day I received a letter from a fellow incarcerated in the state prison at Walla Walla. It read: "Dear Nate, For some time now, you've been coming over here to address classes of men who are about to be paroled. You tell them of the opportunities on the outside if we would but prepare ourselves to accept them. You exhort us not to serve time, but to make time serve us by constantly striving for self- improvement. Personally, I think you're full of crap. How many of us could get the break you got from Judge Lindberg? Well, this letter ain't about you and your speeches, its about my son. I ain't seen the kid for six years and I miss him. My ex-wife don't care if I see him, but we don't have any money to pay to get him here from Bellingham. You come over here every month or so. Will you bring him with you so we can visit? I am afraid that he will forget me unless we can get together. You probably don't understand what this means to me because I can't explain it. If you can do this for me I'll be the happiest guy in the joint and Robbie (my boy) will be happy to see his dad again. It will give me something to look forward to for the next five years I have to serve. If you can, will you write my boy's mother and tell her you will bring Robbie over here? Here is her name and address. Thanks ahead of time. Bob #27877". I actually wept when I read his plea. The letter touched my heart.

Little did Bob know what I experienced when I was separated from my daughter. I felt every hurt that Bob was suffering.

I traced the boy's mother through the name and address I had on hand. I learned that she had a telephone, so I called her. I had no idea what kind of reception I'd get. Normally, there are irreconcilable differences between man and wife when the man goes to prison. The wife is deserted, shamed and usually is left without a dime on which to live. Communication becomes impossible and a rift results that is rarely resolved. I have seen this hundreds of times over the years. It is really understandable. I held my breath as the phone rang. A woman's voice answered saying, "Hello" and nothing beyond that. I had to handle the introduction carefully because she might cut me off. "Mrs. Anderson, I am Glenn Williams with the Job Therapy corporation in Seattle. The agency for which I work is dedicated to the rehabilitation of felons. Your husband has heard of us, and he contacted my office and asked if I would call you and get your permission to take your boy to the penitentiary to visit him. I would like to discuss this possibility with you." There was such a long pause before her reply that I thought she had simply hung up on me. Finally she said, "I have no objection to Robbie seeing his father, but it isn't my intention to turn him over to a stranger. I'll be visiting my mother in Everett this coming Saturday. If you want to meet me at her home, we'll discuss it in her presence." It was agreed that I would drive to Everett and meet with her.

When I knocked at the door, I was met by an attractive woman of about thirty years of age. Standing by her side was a fine looking boy whom I took to be Robbie. Mrs. Anderson invited me in where she introduced me to both the boy and her mother. It was apparent she had talked the matter over before I got there. It was more apparent that the grandmother was against the idea of letting the youngster make the journey. It was she who spoke first. "Mr. Williams, we have gone through hell because of the crime the boy's father committed. So far as I am concerned he has forfeited his right to ever see the lad again." I was prepared for this eventuality. "Ma'am," I responded, "What you say may be right, but have you given Robbie any consideration in this matter? It won't be too long before his father will be freed. When he is, he will come looking for his son. If, at that point, he is refused visitation privileges, he has the right to go to court and seek a court order granting him those rights. I am not trying to get involved in a family matter here. My purpose is to ask Robbie's mother if she will let him go to the institution for a meeting with his dad. If she has any question about the advisability of granting the father's wish, it might be best for her to consult an attorney. I will be available at my office any time."

Turning to the boy's mother I handed her my card and thanked her for giving me the opportunity to meet with her. She surprised me by walking outside as I started to leave. I sensed that she had something to say, so I hesitated on the porch to give her time to regain her composure. "Mr. Williams," she began, "will you tell my husband that I really have no objection to his seeing his son. In fact, it might be good for both of them. It is true, I am very bitter with him for doing what he did to Robbie and me, but I must admit he was crazy about the kid. Would you be able to take me along with my son and let me see Bob? We don't have a penny to our name." Inwardly, I was elated. Her response was more than I could have hoped for. "What is your first name?" I asked. She told me her name was Carol. "Carol, you don't have to have any money for the trip. The company will pay your expenses. I'll be taking three other wives over to Walla Walla next Saturday. If you can be at my office by six in the morning, I'll be very happy to have you go with us. We will be gone for two days."

The following Saturday she was in my station wagon along with three other wives who were going to visit their husbands. Robbie and I hit if off immediately. Carol was very nervous as we drove up to the penitentiary gate. The other women consoled her. While they were signing in, I went inside ahead of the group and placed myself in a position where I could see Bob, Carol and Robbie when they met. Bob was not aware that they were even coming.

The iron gate opened from one end of the room to admit the prisoners. After they had been frisked and seated, the gate at the other end of the room swung open to admit the outside visitors. In all, there were about fifty people crammed in the small enclosure. Robbie saw his dad first. He screamed, "Daddy", broke loose from his mother, tore across the room and flung himself into his father's arms. Tears streamed down the cheeks of both. After a long embrace, Bob looked up and saw his wife. He was hesitant, as was she. Neither knew how the other would receive them. With great effort, he walked over to her and spoke. I felt sorry for her. She was so uncertain. They didn't make body contact. He led her to the seats that had been reserved. Robbie demanded his dad's full attention, making it extremely difficult for Carol and Bob to communicate. Each was very uncomfortable. I hoped that tomorrow's visit would be more relaxed. I knew that they had much to say to the other. Robbie was making a real nuisance of himself. An idea came to my mind. I walked over to where they were sitting and held my hand out to Bob. I didn't know whether or not he would be angry with me. He stood up and we shook hands. The poor guy was embarrassed. I put my plan into action. "Say, Bob, would you have any objection if I took Robbie down to the fair grounds to see the roping horses?" Robbie howled with delight. That made it easier for Carol and Bob to give their OK.

About 4:30 PM, Robbie and I returned to the prison to pick up his mother and the other women. Before going to the motel after the last Saturday visit, it was our custom to go to a favorite cafe and enjoy a spaghetti dinner, topping it off with a bottle of wine. By the time the wine was finished, the girls were relaxed and talkative. Carol looked at me and smiled warmly. It was obvious that her visit had ended on a happy note. The next day they visited all day. At 5:00 PM that night, we were rolling toward Seattle. Before Carol left for Bellingham, she confided in me that she and Bob were going to re-marry and try to make a go of it after he was released. She hugged me and whispered, "Glenn, Bob and I want to thank you for making this trip possible."

Word soon spread among the inmates that rides with me were possible. Before long, dozens of mothers, fathers, children, wives and sweethearts were calling my office to make arrangements to go to the prison. Most were indigent and had no other way to get to the institutions. I had a seven-passenger station wagon, so I was limited to the number of passengers I could accommodate. Often I would cram eight to ten adults and children in my vehicle.

It wasn't too long before I was named to the Board of Directors of Job Therapy. I felt out of place in that position. There were many prominent people serving on the Board. Among them were former Chief Justice of the State Supreme Court, Robert Utter, a former chief test pilot for the Boeing Company, in addition to attorneys, doctors and heads of many large corporations.

For a long period, I was the only ex-con in the agency. I became the brunt of many jokes and barbs, all in good humor. When word leaked out about my past, I was approached by the media for interviews. At first, I was reluctant to get before the public's eye because of my family. As always, I sought the advice of my brother, Dan, and my sister, Marjorie. Both made their views known without hesitating. Marjorie acted as the spokesman when she brought out the most salient point. "Glenn, you seem content with what you are doing. It certainly is a field you understand better than anyone in the business. You cannot keep up this type of work and hope to keep your past a secret. If you try to do that, it will come up and haunt you down the road. Let your past be known. There will be those who will condemn you, but they will be in the minority. For the first time since you came home, you appear to be more settled and satisfied. If you are concerned about the members of the family, put your worries aside. We will be proud of you. Be prepared for bitter disappointments from agitators. Eventually they will disappear. If you think you cannot stand the heat, then find another kind of employment." Dan and Marjorie made up my mind for me that evening.

Before the year was out, I had made a dozen appearances on T.V. and radio shows all over this state. Speaking engagements cropped up every week. I addressed the Elks, Lions, Kiwanis, Rotary and many lesser known civic clubs. I was comfortable lecturing classes in junior high schools, high schools and major universities and colleges throughout the state. Newspaper accounts of my past and present were published locally and out of state. My liaison work with the corrections people continued. My station wagon wore out and I was stuck for transportation. Job Therapy was in no financial position to fund a new vehicle for me. I decided to go before the Board and ask them to make a transportation department within our agency, and to give me the job of running it. I explained to the members how essential it was to keep family ties intact if we were to try to rehabilitate the men during their incarceration, and what better method than to make family visitation a possibility. I tried to impress on them that I knew of what I spoke. I had gone through the mill. The board refused to consider my request.

At about this time, the inmates of the New York penitentiary at Attica rioted and took dozens of guards as hostages. It was a tense and dangerous period that continued for a week or so. Headlines all over the world played the riot to its hilt. Many civilians blamed the New York Department of Corrections for creating the conditions that prompted the convicts to take things into their own hands. Negotiations between the feuding inmates and prison personnel failed. I made the trip to Attica to determine from that vantage point why the inmates went on the rampage. It was juvenile of me to think I could learn anything from the outside of the walls. In the first place, when I approached the compound itself, I was ordered off the state land in no uncertain words. I stayed at my hotel for two days and talked to many townspeople about the situation. Of course they were entirely behind the officials. One lady told me, "If I had my say, I'd blow every one of those cons to kingdom come." I reminded her that there were many guards among the inmates and that they too would perish.

I had been home less that a day when word was broadcast that the guards, police and national guard had stormed the prison. From the accounts, it was a slaughter. Forty inmates were slain. Later it was determined that some of the guards were slain by brother officers firing randomly. None were killed by the prisoners. It was this incident that later caused me to resign from Job Therapy and organize a non-profit and charitable agency for the purpose of transporting indigent families to the various penal institutions for visitation privileges.

23

Return To The Rock

I vowed I would die rather than return to Alcatraz. But we can't account for events which take place that result in a change of mind. As an example, who could have ever dreamt that Native American Indians in November, 1969 would invade and occupy the Rock? They declared that by virtue of some pact with the federal government many generations ago, the Island was the property of the Indians and that their occupation was legal and justified. Or who could have dreamt that the U.S. government would let the Indians' territorial grab go unchallenged?

Within a week after the event took place, I received a dozen calls from ex-Alcatraz inmates. As unreal as it may seem, I received a call from one of my buddies in Jacksonville, Florida who said, "Nate, ain't that a hell of a note about those Indians crashing the Rock? Who do they think they are? I hope Uncle Sam sends in the Marines and gets their asses off our place!" At first, I was dumbfounded by his attitude. Here was a guy who had spent twelve years in a cell on Broadway. Every day he bitched about the place, the guards, the food and his sentence. He would tell his friends that he was going to come back some night after his release and blow the whole place into the Pacific Ocean. How could he be so incensed about the Indian occupation? As for myself, I could have cared less what happened to that pile of boulders. The media milked the story for all it was worth.

A month after the Indians took control, I got an idea. I thought I'd go down there and ask them to let me visit the former penitentiary. It would be an intriguing experience and an opportunity for me to take pictures of every inch of the place. I had heard some gruesome stories of dungeons carved in the face of the rock. Horror tales ran rampant and I placed little credence in any of them. However, I had learned that Creepy Karpis was not a man to make up stories and he was one of two men who told me that he had personally done time in what he referred to as the 'Limestone Dungeons'. The other individual was Arnie K., Karpis's closest friend. He, too, had been dragged into those same cells. No amount of rehearsing could have prepared them for the detailed information they had given me. The guards denied that such dungeons ever existed.

One day the papers carried an account of the Indians burning down the former warden's residence. Other acts of vandalism were attributed to the new residents. Doors were supposed to have been ripped off the cells, copper pipes were reported to have been torn out and sold for scrap to help the Indians finance their escapade. Wooden structures were torn down and

313

used to build fires to keep them warm. The Indians maintained that those stories were rumors and that they were designed by the federal government to give them an excuse to oust the interlopers.

I had made up my mind to travel to San Francisco and try to get permission to spend some time at my old home. Everything depended upon the goodwill of the Indians. I realized that, if I were successful in getting on the Rock and taking pictures that might offend the sensitive Bureau of Prisons officials, they would try to discredit me by saying I was a disgruntled ex-inmate who was trying to embarrass the government. I decided to ask two or three respected individuals to accompany me on the proposed trek. I selected two such men who were involved with me at Job Therapy. They were Gerard Kemp, a bank manager, and David Yates, a chemist. Both had impeccable reputations. I decided not to tell them my purpose in taking them along. I simply painted a picture of the excitement of a visit to Alcatraz, a place where few civilians had ever set foot. Both were delighted that I would ask them to accompany me. I told them there was a probability that we would be denied permission to go to the Island, but that I, by virtue of the fact that I had been a prisoner on Alcatraz, would stand a good chance of getting on. They were fairly warned that the entire trip might be a waste of time. Both agreed to chance it.

The three of us took turns driving from Seattle to San Francisco. We stopped only to eat and hit the rest areas. While one was driving the other two would grab catnaps. Twenty hours later, on June 5, 1970, we checked into our motel, which was located directly across from Pier 41. There was very little preparation for the venture, which was to take place the next morning. I checked my camera, flash bulbs and film.

After a good night's sleep, we headed for Pier 40 on the Embarcadero where the Indians had set up an office. They had painted a large sign on the front of the building which read, ALCATRAZ RECEIVING DEPOT! When we entered the structure, we were confronted by an Indian who identified himself as Joseph. We told him the purpose of our visit and asked him who could give us permission to go to the Island. He was very uncooperative. Finally, he told us to locate the boat Bass Tub I at Fisherman's Wharf. We were to see a Captain Paul, the skipper of the Bass Tub. He could give us an OK to make the trip. Also he could tell us to go to hell.

I could not understand the surly attitude that greeted us at every meeting with the Indians. Captain Paul was a mean-looking person who was very suspicious of our motives. When we made our wishes known, he asked many questions. Why do you want to visit Alcatraz? Are you federal agents trying to get a foothold on the Island? We were getting nowhere with this guy, so I hit on the idea of telling him the truth about myself. I told him that I had served time on the Rock and that I wanted to go back and see how the joint looked from a free man's viewpoint. He asked me about my cell number, my inmate number, the last warden, why I was sent to such a maximum penitentiary, when I got out and how the Indians were treated. With the exception of the last question, I had no problem answering them quickly and correctly. As for his question concerning the treatment of the Indians, I told him that all prisoners on the Island were treated the same;

shamefully. He apparently wanted me to tell him that the Indians had been singled out for maltreatment, which would give their activists grist for the mill.

When Captain Paul inquired about David and Gerard, I told him that they were business people who lived in Seattle, volunteered their spare time with a charitable organization, and were interested in the history of America's most dehumanizing penal institution. The skipper of the boat obviously did not believe my story. He conferred with another Indian who openly smirked at us. I was becoming discouraged because it was becoming clear that we were not going to make the grade. During the interrogation, David and Gerard stood without comment. Eventually, the other Indians started questioning me about the description of certain cells, the hospital, gun galleries, punishment cells, the dining room and the solitary cell in which The Bird Man of Alcatraz had been isolated. I did my best to keep cool. His final question prompted me to take the initiative. What was the number of Scar Face Al Capone's cell? I could not answer that one. "Other than my own cell, I don't know the numbers of the others. I've answered each of your questions correctly and without hesitating. What reason would I want to go to the prison, other than the one I gave you?" Before he could respond, Captain Paul said, "We're fearful that the government will plant people on the Rock and try to oust us without a fight. For all we know, you could be FBI agents. And as for answering the questions, you could have rehearsed the whole tale. You don't look like a bank robber to me. If you want to come back tomorrow, we might let you take the boat over. We're going to make contact with some ex-cons who we know were inmates over there. If you're telling the truth, we'll know it by noon tomorrow." Before we left, I told him that he should know the name by which I was known on the Island, Nate Williams. I knew if he were to mention Glenn Williams, none of the ex-cons would recognize it and we would be dead in the water.

Over dinner at Joe Dimaggio's on the Wharf, we talked about the events of the past two hours. I sensed that Gerard and David were becoming apprehensive, and would just as soon head for home. They thought of the possibility that there would be trouble. Neither of them had ever experienced anything like dealing with convicts or physical confrontations, and the thought of getting involved in that manner was distasteful to them. I assured them that the worst that could happen would be getting rejected at the dock. The idea of returning without expending every effort bothered me. "Well, if you fellows want to go back to Seattle, go ahead, but I'm going to stay here until tomorrow, win, lose or draw."

At noon the following day, the three of us showed up at the pier where the Bass Tub was docked. During the night I had made up my mind; as a final effort, I would try to bribe Captain Paul. There is truth in the old adage that 'money talks'. I went aboard without my traveling companions to face the captain. I came right to the point; "Well Captain Paul," I said, "we're ready to go. I presume the guys you contacted last night gave us a clean bill of health." He took his time before saying, "You know there is a great expense in operating this boat." "How much?" I asked. I was surprised that all he asked for was fifty dollars. Before he could take another breath, I had the money under his nose. "We will be shoving off in a few minutes."

Gerard and David were beside themselves when I told them we had it made. While we were waiting, about ten Indian children and their mothers went aboard. Each was carrying supplies. During the trip, I was in the bow with my eyes glued to the ominous promontory that rose three hundred feet above the water. When I had come in chains as a prisoner, it was at night and I could see nothing. Today, I was shocked at what a horrible sight it presented. I had to fight off the tremors I was feeling. In no way could I have imagined such a physical reaction upon facing the reality of returning to my old home. I was doing so voluntarily and should have been able to handle it. I was afraid that David and Gerard would see me in this condition, but they couldn't take their eyes off the empty, ghostly-appearing vacated buildings. In a matter of a few minutes, I had regained my composure. The boat docked at the decaying pier. The Indians crowded us aside as they scrambled off and headed for a shack that was used as an office. David and Gerard preceded me.

On June 7, 1970 at 1:30 PM, I set foot on the prison property I had left exactly ten years previously. The first thing that caught my eye was a crudely painted sign on a shack that read: HOME OF THE FREE. WELCOME TO INDIANLAND ALCATRAZ! So much for my vow never to return to this ulcerous piece of real estate in San Francisco Bay. My friends looked to me for guidance. Hell, I didn't know just what to do. About that time, an Indian approached us from the shack and told us to go inside. There was a fellow sitting behind a box which served as a desk. He made us sign a sheet of paper. The man facing us said, "OK. You guys have one hour to go where you want to go. We're sending a guide along with you. Be back here on time. Don't keep the boat waiting or you'll find yourselves swimming to the mainland." He had assigned a very handsome youngster to guide us. His name was Peter. From the beginning, I set out to win Peter's confidence and friendship. When he started to tell us what the buildings were used for and where the main cell blocks were located, I thought this was the time to impress him. "Oh, yes, Peter, I know. I lived on this Island as a prisoner for years. Let's enter the cell blocks from the front. We go up past the Warden's house." Peter was surprised and let us roam at will.

The warden's mansion had been burned to the ground. Gerard and David talked between themselves, ignoring me. We entered the main offices. The warden's office had been looted and was strewn with hundreds of letters and documents which had been taken from overturned filing cabinets. I began taking pictures. Across from the warden's office were offices of lesser officials. Each had been vandalized beyond description. The control center of the institution was open. The telephone lines and what furniture was left had been destroyed. Glass had been broken from every window. The control center had housed the very latest security equipment. It had been a regular fortress protected by steel plates and bullet-proof glass.

I found the control center of particular interest to me because of a board filled with keys which fitted every lock in the institution. The keys were in numerical order, so it wasn't difficult for me to locate the key that would allow me to open the lock-box that controlled my cell. I appropriated that key along with a half-dozen others. The next room, just before entering the cellhouses, was the visiting room. The same damage had been inflicted on it. As I stepped inside, I recalled when my mother had fainted there years ago. The thought hurt me again.

When we stepped inside the huge steel doors that led to row upon row and tier upon tier of small cubicles stacked like chicken crates, nausea overcame me. I stepped to the right and looked up to the second floor and into my cell, B256. The door was partly open so I scrambled up the narrow, winding steel stairs and gazed in awe at the filthy cage in which I had spent so many years. I became angry and frustrated and tears streamed from my eyes. I turned around to find my friends and Peter standing beside me. Peter started to say, "Is this your....", when I cut him off. "Yes, Peter, this is where the United States Government placed all its puke and vomit." I stepped inside my cell and had David take four or five pictures of me inside.

From that point on, we walked all the cellhouse corridors. Good old Broadway hadn't changed. From the cellhouses, we went up the stairs to the hospital and down the hall to the room where The Bird Man Of Alcatraz had been confined.

There was a most important part of this trip that I wanted to record, and that was the existence of the limestone dungeons. From the description of the location given to me by Creepy Karpis and Arnie K., I had a good idea where they were located. At one end of the yard there was a steel door that led to the shops. My watch indicated we had about fifteen minutes to get back to the dock. Directly outside the door, I started to turn to the right to get to the area under the hospital where the dungeons had been dug. Before I could get started, Peter called out, "Sir, if you want to get to the holes, I can show you a safer and quicker way. Follow me." Like a goat, he scrambled along a little-used path that I had not seen. He led us along the wall until we came to a sort of mesa. It was overgrown with high bushes and weeds.

"There they are," shouted Peter as he pointed to an open tunnel. We made our way to a most eerie sight. The tunnel was dug from the earth with no supports. It went into the hillside for about twenty feet. On each side of the tunnel a cave had been hollowed out. Each one was about fifteen feet long, ten feet wide and less than six feet high. The Indians had torn off the large wooden doors and let them lie partly inside. It was pitch dark inside. I was afraid to grope my way in, but I forced myself to do so. David took pictures of me standing inside. The flash served to give us a brief view of the dungeons. Before we left, I had pictures of each of us inside. I was fortified with the evidence I so badly wanted. Creepy and Arnie K. had told the truth. The guards who had sworn that there were no such caverns had either lied or were truly unaware of their existence. After all, Creepy had been on the Rock for twenty-six years, and he did say that the dungeons had not been used for the last decade of his time on Alcatraz. When I had visited ex-warden Paul Madigan in Minnesota just prior to his death, he told me that there were old ammunition dumps carved in a number of places on the Island.

We had heard the warning whistle of the Bass Tub, so we rushed to get to the dock. When it landed, there were about fifteen Indians who busied themselves unloading supplies. From the looks of their activity, it seemed they were preparing for a siege or a long stay. The most difficult problem they encountered was the lack of water. It had to be hauled from the mainland in containers. We later learned that sympathetic people on the other side hauled all sorts of supplies to the Indians. I thought that the government would have put up a blockade to dissuade activists from helping to sustain the Indians. It appeared that the officials reasoned that any action they might take would make them look bad. They were confident that in a short time the Indians would find living on the bleak and unforgiving pile of boulders untenable.

As we sat on a bench waiting for them to signal the three of us to go aboard, I was already planning a second trip as soon as possible. There were many items I wanted to appropriate and take home as souvenirs. Suddenly I got an idea. Why not pave the road for a future trip by buttering up the people who were obviously in charge? I already knew that the skipper of the boat was on the take. I left my two companions and sauntered into the office-shack. Sure enough old sourpuss was still behind the desk. I walked over to him and thanked him for permitting us to come over even though he had nothing to do with our being there. I continued, "I have a reason to hate this government, too. I share your cause and want to contribute to your stay here." With that, I pulled out my wallet and gave him twenty dollars, my last penny. For the first time, his severe countenance relaxed and a slight smile crossed his face. It is amazing what a few greenbacks can do. I went on to say that I intended to write a book and wanted to be able to return to Alcatraz very soon to gather information for my manuscript. For the first time he spoke my language loud and clear. "When you come back, look me up and I will grease the road for you." I assured him I would, in return, grease his palm. Money is the universal tongue.

As we were heading back to San Francisco, I stood at the stern and watched the grim penitentiary fade in the background. It was extremely hard for me to understand how I could have come back to such a place, and be prepared to return again. I rationalized that such journeys were essential to the completion of my book. Had I known what was waiting for me on my next visit, I would have shunned the Island.

The pictures we had snapped on our visit to the Rock were developed right away. They turned out to be very clear and distinct. I was afraid of losing them so I had five copies developed. So far as I knew those snapshots could very well be the only ones I would ever be able to get in my possession. And, as I had told the Indian when we left Alcatraz, it was my intention to include in my autobiography my experiences on Alcatraz.

After I had been home a week, I started the ball rolling for my return trip. I planned to take a large briefcase on my next Alcatraz visit. If given half a chance, I was going to fill it with whatever I could grab from under the noses of the present caretakers. I wanted to spend at least a full day rummaging around the old homestead. One thing was for certain, it was going to take cash to 'buy' my round trip ticket on the Bass Tub. It would be easy for the skipper of the boat to assume I was well-healed and he might demand an exorbitant amount. And in addition to the skipper, I had promised the guy on the Island that I was prepared to help their cause on my next trip down. In realty, I didn't know whether to take along one hundred or five hundred bucks. It dawned on me that the Indians might not want me to take anything off the Island. I didn't know what to expect.

I had a friend, Jim Hearst, who was the manager of the local Bankers Life And Casualty Insurance company. Jim had talked with Gerard and David and was excited with the possibility that he, too, might be able to visit the vacated prison. Gerard and David had painted a romantic picture of their adventure. I noticed, however, that when I invited them to make a second trip, they had reasons for not going again. I really wanted company on my upcoming trek so I invited Jim to accompany me. I also told him that there might be an expense involved in addition to our airfare, motel, taxi and meals. Five weeks after my first trip to the island, the plane to San Francisco, transporting Jim and me, landed at the International Airport. We checked into our motel at 5:50 P. M., too late to contact the Bass Tub or to go to the Alcatraz Receiving Depot at Pier 40.

The next morning, Jim and I were on Fisherman's Wharf looking for a place to have breakfast. By 8:00 o'clock we had finished a leisurely meal and headed for the dock where the Bass Tub was tied up. Not only was the skipper at the helm, there was a beehive of activity surrounding the boat. TV cameras and reporters were everywhere. Captain Paul was yelling at the reporters, "I don't give a f—k who you are, you are not going to board this vessel!" A dozen or so Indians with packs on their backs were trying to get through the crowd so they could get on deck. My heart sank. Did this mean Jim and I were going to be kept off the Rock? I decided to bull my way through and to hell with the consequences. I grabbed Jim by the arm and pulled him with me as we mingled with the boarding Indians. As we stepped on deck, the skipper spotted me and called out, "You there, come up to the cabin." I was relieved that he hadn't tossed us off.

The small engine kicked over and the boat pulled away from the pier. When I had an opportunity, I slipped Captain Paul a C-note. He pocketed the money quickly. After we were well on our way, I asked the skipper, "What was all the fuss with the TV people?" He advised me that a child had been playing on an upper landing in the main cellhouse and had fallen fifteen feet to the concrete floor. I later learned that she never regained consciousness, and died sixty hours from the time of the accident.

For the second time within a month, I stepped on the prison pier. I was overcome by the same sense of despair. Jim realized that a change had come over me and he asked me if I was ill. I explained what my problem was. He had a sensible answer to my problem, but he hadn't experienced the problem. I understood his logic when he consoled me with what he would do if the roles were reversed. "You seem to have lost sight of the fact that you came of your own volition this time. You came as a free man and you will leave with no strings attached. All the way down here, Glenn, you complained that you might not be able to get us on the Island. Well, here we are, and damned if you haven't got a long face. Frankly, I'm enjoying myself."

He walked over to the shack. I hurried after him because I was afraid he might alienate those sensitive souls who controlled our movements here.

The same man I had given the money to when I left last time was behind the desk again. Before he could open his mouth, I handed him an envelope in which there were two fifty-dollar bills. A flash of disappointment crossed his features. Sensing this I said, "When we get ready to leave I'll double that amount." This was getting too rich for my blood and my purse. Without speaking, he motioned for me to place my briefcase on the desk. I was reluctant to do so but had no other choice. Jim and I watched as he rifled through it, All he found was candy, a camera, a note pad and my flashlight. To make certain he did not put too restrictive a time limit on us, I reminded him that I would be gathering material for my book and would need the entire day. "The last boat leaves for the mainland at six o'clock tonight and if you're not on it, you'll be sleeping here. You can make arrangements for another commercial boat to pick you up if you want to pay them. If you decide to go that route, get word to Captain Paul before he leaves." It dawned on me that that might be a good idea so I approached the skipper and asked him if he would make arrangements for a pick-up vessel to be here at 8:00 PM. Paul was happy for the opportunity and said, "Sure, I'll have one here at that hour, but you'll have to come up with two hundred dollars right now." I talked him into taking a check. Jim and I started the steep climb up to the top of the Rock.

By the time we had reached the burned-out shell that had once been the home of the wardens, I had forgotten the dread that had swept over me when we first landed. We went through every destroyed room of the burned house. Either the Indians had stripped it clean, or the officials never left anything when they departed. From there we went up to the offices which had been maliciously destroyed. On the floor of the warden's office there were hundreds of official letters, memos and records. I gathered a handful and stuffed them in my case. In a few minutes we were in the room where I had operated the movie projector. We crawled up the steep ladder that led to a vacated gun gallery where the armed guards stood watch over the worshippers during the Sunday services. I surveyed the areas that heretofore had been accessible to gun guards alone. What would the old-time guards think if they knew that a former inmate was now treading in their personal sanctums? I remember thinking, "My God, how time alters everything!" From there, Jim and I went straight to B256, my old cage. I wanted to take something from the cell, but there was nothing left. We rampaged through the inmate's dining room, hospital and D-Block punishment cellhouse.

We had a lot more ground to cover, so we made a beeline to the yard, down the steep stairs to the shop-line where most of the cons worked. In the tailor shop, I stood where my old sewing machine had been anchored to the floor. During this entire tour, I explained everything to Jim. He was fascinated and made notes of his own. We covered the furniture shop, glove factory and the old net-making facility. In each workshop, I thought of friends who had worked there and wondered where they were at this time. I knew that most were in other penitentiaries or were dead, some by

320

execution, some by the makeshift shivs of vengeful cons, and a few by their own hands. My next and most important stop was the limestone dungeons. This time I had brought a flashlight that would enable me to examine the interior. On the way up the incline, I told Jim about the caves he was going to be seeing. He could not believe they existed and he asked, "Glenn, I was led to believe that this country had the most advanced and humane prisons in the world. But as I see this evidence to the contrary, it disturbs me. How in the world can a person subject his fellowman to such barbarity?" He was getting a firsthand picture that told him far more than I could. Before he would believe that this government had placed the Bird Man Of Alcatraz in solitary confinement for more that forty years, it was necessary for him to read documents that supported what I had told him.

By the time we reached the tunnel leading into the holes, we had to rest. It was getting late and we were hungry. I shared my candy bars with Jim. My travelling companion was a younger man than I so he was anxious to push on. I refused to budge until I had rested for a half hour. When my energy returned, he and I made our way into the tunnel and to the doors of the holes. I said nothing as Jim examined the huge wooden doors which had been ripped from their hinges. Across each door was a strip of iron that served as reinforcement. Jim stared into the cavernous darkness of the dungeons but could see nothing. He asked for the flashlight and flooded the interior of the rooms. That was the first time I had seen the inside. I took the light and stepped into the depths of the cave we had been examining. I am only five feet, eight inches tall and yet I could not stand erect. That meant that the inmates had to keep bent over during their confinement. I could see that there was no limestone, so I wondered why the inmates referred to the holes as limestone dungeons. When I questioned Arnie K., he told me that whenever they had to urinate, a noxious odor would rise from the floor and burn their eyes. From that, they assumed that their quarters were carved from limestone. I called to Jim and told him to come on in and see the caves from the inside. He refused to budge. He covered up by saying he suffered from claustrophobia. "Won't you at least come close enough to get pictures of me while I'm in here?" I asked. Reluctantly, he edged toward the opening and shot six or seven pictures.

Both of us were relieved to leave that area and go to the stairs that led to the catwalks above the yard. From that position, I could imagine how the guards felt as they patrolled. For the millionth time, I asked myself how a man could accept that kind of work. While we were up there, we stepped into the towers that sheltered the guards in inclement weather, which was most of the time. The lights from across the bay were flickering on. A fog began creeping in and covering the Rock in an eerie shroud. It was time for us to get to the pier. Our chartered boat would be there to pick us up in half an hour.

From the top of the roadway that descended to the landing, we could see bonfires at the pier. The closer we got to our destination, the more we heard yelling, whooping and war cries. Jim commented, "They must be having some sort of celebration." When we had reached the level, Jim and I stayed in the darkness and witnessed the strange sight. Plainly there had been some drinking. A fight broke out between two Indians. It was quickly broken up. The more we observed the group, the more obvious it became that many were drunk. Jim and I didn't want to become embroiled in a melee, yet we had to be at the dock in a few minutes. I suggested that we saunter across the flat, make our way to where our boat would dock, and draw as little attention to ourselves as possible.

We were pretty well to the dock when we were seen. Three or four of the men made their way toward us. Their manner of approach indicated that trouble was heading our way. Their friends had stopped their dancing and whooping and watched us. "Jim," I said, "don't face them in an antagonistic way, and let me do the talking." As they came abreast of us, the leader called out, "What are you doing here?" I replied, "We were given permission to come to the Island and do research work on a manuscript." All three grabbed us. I was struck from behind and knocked nearly unconscious. I rolled to a side in time to see three or four start beating Jim. In no time at all his face was a bloody mess. I became so angry that I tossed my briefcase away from me and struggled to my feet. If we were going to be beaten, I was damn sure going to fight to the best of my ability. I never got clear up before I was floored again. At this point, the others started calling to their comrades and telling them to let us alone. Our attackers stopped their punching and kicking. I felt my wallet being ripped from my pocket and my watch being torn from my wrist. At that moment, a brilliant searchlight cut through the night and focused on Jim and me lying on the ground. The skipper of the boat started blasting his fog horn steadily. Most of the Indians faded into the fog. Jim helped me up and we made our way to the boat which had docked. I pulled away from him and ran back to retrieve my precious briefcase. The captain of the boat helped us aboard. He bellowed, "What the hell were they trying to do to you guys?" It was obvious so I didn't bother to answer. He showed us where the head was.

Jim and I washed up as best we could. I walked back to the pilot house and explained to the skipper and his two-man crew. "How could you two be so stupid as to go over there alone. You're goddam lucky they didn't toss you into the bay. So far as those Indians are concerned, all white men look like Custer."

When we walked into the motel lobby, the surprised clerk said, "Were you robbed?" I truthfully responded, "Yes." He reached for the phone saying, "I'll call the cops." I told him that the affair had already been reported, and that all we wanted to do was get washed up and go to bed. Jim gave me hell as soon as we got to our room. "Why did you tell the clerk that the matter had already been reported?" I was sore, tired and angry as I snapped, "Listen to me. I came here for one purpose. My briefcase contains that purpose. I am thankful they didn't keep the case or destroy the contents. If the cops got involved, they might want to confiscate the briefcase, and we might never get it back." I soaked in the tub and crawled into bed. I ached so badly I could hardly turn over.

In the morning, Jim and I both were so stiff we had trouble shaving. My face looked like chopped beef. Jim was quite certain he had sustained a broken rib. After a hearty breakfast, which took an hour to chew, things looked better. "What did they take from you, Jim?" I asked. "They got my watch. Am I glad they didn't get my wallet," he answered. "How about you?" Glumly I told him I had lost my wallet, watch and pride. That afternoon two bruised and cut passengers boarded a plane for Seattle.

By the time my two-week vacation was over, the black and blue color of my face gave way to my normal complexion. However, my anger did not subside. I wrote letters to the Indian 'chiefs', of which there were at least ten, and told them of the assault and robbery which had taken place earlier that month. There were no responses. The letters had not been returned, so I knew they had been received. One of my dearest friends was an Indian professional wrestler by the name of Don Eagle. He was no typical modern day grunt and groan actor of questionable ability. He was from the era of legitimate wrestling. His ability and recognition resulted in his performing before the crown heads of Europe. He was, in brief, an Indian of outstanding quality. Don Eagle, during a ceremony at the Tulalip Indian Reservation, was my family's guest. At dinner that night, I told him what had happened to Jim and me on Alcatraz. He became very angry. He roared, "Damn, here we are trying to elevate the misconception and image of Native Americans, and some liquor-loaded morons pull a stunt like this. I'll tell you one thing, when I am in Frisco next month, I'll confront the parties responsible for beating you and your companion. Believe me, you'll hear from someone."

A month after Jim and I had been assaulted and robbed, a whole series of events began occurring. Don Eagle called me from the Bay area and informed me that he had demanded a meeting with the leaders of the various tribes involved with the Alcatraz takeover. They swore that a beating and robbery never took place. But Don Eagle had done his homework before meeting with the upper echelon. He had questioned others who had been on the Island at the time, and they stated that the two 'palefaces' had started the fight. Don Eagle said he knew they lied for two reasons. Why would two men jump fifteen men? He also knew that I wasn't the type to arbitrarily seek trouble, particularly when my one desire was to get off the Island with the loot I had in my briefcase.

On June 30th, I received a letter from a fellow whose name was Grey Eagle. It was written on an Indian letterhead and read as follows:

ALCATRAZ RECEIVING DEPOT
INDIANS OF ALL TRIBES
PIER 40
EMBARCADERO
San Francisco, Ca 94117

Mr. Glenn Williams
Employment Counselor Job Therapy, Inc.
2210 No. 45th
Seattle, Washington

Dear Mr. Williams:

This letter and apology, while written by me, is truly from all Indians of All Tribes.

We learned that you and your friend had been mistreated and robbed by our brothers while you were our guests on INDIANLAND ALCATRAZ. The conduct of our brothers was inexcusable under normal circumstances,and doubly so when such a friend of the Indians as you were so shamefully treated. Other uninvited white men have been thrown off theIsland; You can understand the Indian thinking in this matter.

You are invited to return to Alcatraz and gather material with which to complete your book. I beg you to reveal the truth with regard to the terrible treatment the Indians received while imprisoned with you under such disgraceful conditions.

The material we delivered to you at Fisherman's Wharf was our legal property. We transferred it to you to be used in your book.There is much more which the government abandoned that you may pick up at our Receiving Depot. We want this to be all over the country in order that the people can see just how rotten the Justice Department is.

You will be honored to know that the Council has declared you the only true WARDEN OF INDIAN LAND ALCATRAZ..; all others were trespassers, and were there by illegal authority.

We look forward to your return.

Your friend,

Grey Eagle

Three weeks after receipt of that letter, my wife, Thelma called me and said that a crazy thing had just occurred. Apparently, my daughter, Natalie was playing on the front porch when she was surprised by a bright red VW van pulling up in front of the house. She was more surprised when a large, dark-visaged man with long braided iron-grey hair, wearing a beautifully beaded doe skin jacket, walked up to the house. She ran inside calling her mother. At the door, the man said, "I am Mr. Eagle from San Francisco. Is Mr. Williams here?" My wife told him I was at work. She gave him the address and he left. Natalie, wild-eyed, asked her mother, "Were those real Indians in the car, Mama?" Thelma nodded. "Just like the ones your Daddy visited in California. We have the pictures of them that he took."

After she hung up, I wondered what was taking place. I had had all I wanted to do with Indians for awhile. I had no more than dismissed the incident from my mind when I heard my secretary call out, "Glenn, come out here and see what we have in front of the office." Having a general idea, I rushed to the front window just in time to see a red Microbus pull up in a No Parking Zone. The side door slid back and out poured eight Indians who were putting on full regalia as they walked up to the front office. The leader was carrying a headband decorated with bright feathers. Three others toting Safeway shopping bags followed the chief. They stopped at the secretary's desk and asked to see Mr. Williams. She indicated the office in which I could be found. By this time, the entire office staff was in the hallway watching the unusual sight.

I stepped into the hallway and confronted the group. "I am Glenn Williams. May I help you?" The most imposing of the group walked up to me, extended his hand and announced, "I am Chief Grey Eagle, Mr. Williams. We have a presentation to make." While he was speaking, he donned his head feathers. The others wore moccasins, leather pants and shark's tooth necklaces. As if on a signal, they staged a whooping, heel-stomping Indian dance. It was very colorful. As the wild sounds penetrated the building, my office began filling with staff and clients. The dance stopped as quickly as it had started. Grey Eagle handed me a beaded leather tube containing a scroll. It was a proclamation from the Indian Council, appointing 'Mr. Nate Williams' the first legal Warden of Alcatraz. I was bewildered. A short fat warrior-like individual said, "We would like to have the office cleared. We wish to Pow Wow and smoke a peace pipe." When the others had left my office, the Indians began speaking in their native tongue, of which I didn't understand a word. When they had finished, it was obvious they were preparing to leave. I found my voice long enough to say, "I am honored." The last thing Grey Eagle said was, "This is in atonement for the abuse our brothers gave you and your friend during your visit to Indianland Alcatraz." As their bus pulled away, I noticed two things about it; it had a New York license plate and a parking violation ticket under the windshield wiper. There was little work completed at my office that day. Thirty-five staff members had been treated to an entertainment unparalleled in their recollection, and mine.

A month after the colorful ceremony had taken place in my office, I received an official post office departmental envelope. To my amazement, it contained what was left of the contents of my wallet which had been taken from me on the Alcatraz dock. Inside was a brief note which stated that the contents were found on Fisherman's Wharf. The plastic card-holders contained my credit card, pilot's license and social security card.

On my return to Seattle from that fateful day on the Rock, I had been so busy I didn't have the time to examine the contents of the letters and memorabilia I had purloined from the offices of the upper echelon staff on the Island. While my wife and daughter were going to visit relatives on the weekend, I decided to go through my trove. When I opened the briefcase, I was filled with anticipation at what I might have gathered. My best expectations were fulfilled. For a reason I will never understand, the prison bureau had abandoned very personal and important letters and inter-departmental memos. There were dozens of letters of security-laden information which had been exchanged between the various wardens of the vacated prison and the Director Of The Federal Bureau of Prisons. Most of the communications were between the Director James V. Bennett and wardens Swope and Madigan. They dealt with such delicate information as inmate transfers and the disciplining of certain recalcitrant convicts and disobedient guards.

One letter of interest to me concerned Warden Madigan's dismissal of my dear friend, The Reverend Peter McCormack. The reason for his discharge was that he was too friendly with potentially dangerous convicts such as the famous Morton Sobel, Alvin Karpis and Harmon Waley, the kidnapper of George Weyerhaueser. It seemed that somewhere down the line, the pastor questioned the propriety of continuing the inhumane solitary confinement of Robert Stroud. The Stroud incident alone would have assured the release of Peter McCormack, because of the cat and mouse game Bennett loved to play with the Bird Man, the Bird Man being the mouse. Bennett could have ordered Stroud's release into the general inmate population any time he wished. The enormous pressure from interested parties around the world, urging the government to stop the senseless 'solitary caging of a human being', failed to budge Bennett. The Bird Man spent forty five years in solitary confinement, more than any other convict.

There were many letters of interest that I had taken from the warden's office. Among them was a letter from a sixteen year old high school student who was doing a paper for her social studies class. She had written Warden Madigan and asked if he would tell her what the average IQ of the inmates was. I thought the request was cute. I decided to write her at the address she had given on her letter, although it had been penned twelve years earlier. I explained to her how I happened to fall into possession of her letter. It took six weeks for a reply to come back. It was from a lady in New Jersey with a different name. She was happy to have heard from me. She told me that she vividly remembered writing the letter. She had since married and was living in New Jersey. She thanked me profusely.

There was a request from a Bobbie in London who said he was a 'collector of locks'. He asked if the warden could send him a lock that was used to 'detain violent criminals produced in the United States'. A Lady asked for a nail from one of the buildings. Another wanted a piece of the Rock, 'not too large' so she could use it as a doorstop in her home. There were a dozen such correspondences, all wanting some part of the prison. Madigan's responses were all verbatim et literatim. Dear So and So: I was pleased to receive your letter of last week. I must advise you that the rules and regulations issued by the Department of Justice forbid me from responding to your specific request. Yours truly, Warden Paul Madigan.

In the pre-dawn hours of June 11, 1971, fifteen remaining Indians on the Island were awakened to find that about a dozen government agents had landed with instructions to oust all Indians found on the Rock. The surprise raid caught them off guard, and the fight they had promised to wage never materialized. They surrendered meekly and were evacuated in a brief time. Instead of arresting them, the government lodged them in a hotel on the mainland. In a matter of days, they disappeared from the Bay area, and the Battle of Alcatraz was over.

The Indians left their mark of fire and vandalism on the prison buildings. Some of the structures were so badly damaged it was necessary to raze them. Rumors ran rampant that the Island was up for sale. Offers had been made to buy it to establish a Monte Carlo-type gambling casino. Entrepreneurs from around the country were supposed to have made bids for the purchase of the twenty-one acre pile of rocks in the Bay. One millionaire wanted to restore the prison to its original appearance, fill the cells with wax figures of the most famous inmates, and use it as a tourist trap. Lamar Hunt, one of the richest men in the United States, made an offer to the City and County of San Francisco. It was accepted. Hunt's proposal was to level the Island of all buildings and to develop a huge commercial complex. The outcry of the citizens in the area was loud, long and effective. Secretary of the Interior, Walter Hickel, squashed the Hunt proposal. His action eventually resulted in the Island being put under the jurisdiction of the National Park Service. For months thereafter, Alcatraz Island, alone with its memories and ghosts, remained unattended and desolate. In my mind I was certain that the Island, and the magnetic name of Alcatraz, would fade into history. I was mistaken.

On a visit to Newark, New Jersey, in the early part of 1973, I was surprised to see a headline of a newspaper which read: ALCATRAZ DESIGNATED TO BE OPENED TO TOURISTS! I could not believe my eyes. How could anyone in his right mind think that such a vile place would attract tourists? Six months after that article appeared, I received a letter from the National Park Service inviting me to consider acting as a guide to the tourists who were beginning to flood Alcatraz. The Service felt that having a former Alcatraz convict leading the tours would lend more spice and authenticity to the program. I would have been pleased to act in that capacity but I had to refuse because of my job in Seattle. Other former inmates received similar letters. To my knowledge, most found reasons to reject the invitation. The Service was able to enlist former inmate M. Rausch. M's old buddies who had been on the Rock with him watched his progress avidly. They didn't have long to watch because he was terminated after a very brief stint. Rumors had it that he had a difficult time with the truth when relating his experiences on the prison. His vitriolic denunciation of the guards, maltreatment (real or imagined) and general abusive conditions condoned by the Federal Bureau of Prisons left many of the tourists, Park Rangers and ex-Alcatraz employees disturbed. He was told that that wasn't the reason he had been retained, and was summarily discharged. In a brief time, it was obvious that America's Devil's Island was destined to become a major tourist attraction. Its horrible history, spread worldwide, assured it that distinction.

24

Bus Driver

I decided to leave Job Therapy and form my own non-profit agency to provide transportation and counseling to the families of men incarcerated in the Washington State Penitentiary. In memory of the men who lost their lives in the New York prison riot at ATTICA, I registered my agency under the name of ATTICA. Throughout my years of imprisonment, I had observed prisoners deteriorating for a number of reasons. But the main reason they gave for tossing in the towel, was the separation from their families. The separation in itself is understandable, but to deprive a man from seeing his loved ones for years on end will soon destroy his will to continue. They are the only contact he has with reality.

The majority leave their families in a worsened financial dilemma than when they were with them. On the outside, the families exist on the crumbs they can get from the state. The thought of being financially able to travel to visit with the husband/father is out of the question. Oddly enough the inmate does not seem to understand the poverty-stricken condition in which the family finds itself. He thinks he is being deserted and conveys his anger by writing accusatory letters to his wife, mother or dad. They, in turn, are hurt and frustrated and respond irately. Generally, they make the mistake of telling the incarcerated person that he is responsible for all the woes they are experiencing. While this probably is true, it is something the imprisoned man knows, but can't stand to face. Before long, all communication ceases. If there was ever a chance for rehabilitation to set in, there isn't any fertile ground within the inmate. I have seen men thrive well in their cages as long as they have had frequent contact with their loved ones; more so if they are allowed to visit with them. One cannot overemphasize the importance of continued family contact.

Washington State Governor Dan Evans was very progressive on prison reform. In 1970, I was privileged to address a subcommittee of the state legislature on subjects related to a new approach to rehabilitation. The lawmakers seemed to be receptive to my ideas until I broached the subject of conjugal visits. They cooled noticeably when I appealed to them to consider the subject for debate. Today, conjugal visits are common in nearly every penal institution in the country. However, his administration did advance programs such as furloughs for inmates serving long sentences.

There was an ill-conceived experiment which called for well-meaning citizens to take a lifer home for a family-oriented dinner. The inmates dubbed it 'Take A Lifer To Dinner'. The program no sooner got off the ground than Joseph St. Peter, a lifer dining with a family, excused himself from the dinner table to go to the bathroom. He made an exit through the lavatory window and managed to get to Tacoma. Apparently, before approving St. Peter for the visit, officials forgot to review his history, which would have revealed a long list of escapes and attempted escapes. Some methods he employed to get over the walls were ingenious. Now, all of a sudden, his keepers decided to drive him to town to eat with a freeman and his family. It was never determined just how St. Peter got to Tacoma from Walla Walla. It is known, however, that when he arrived in Tacoma, he walked into a pawn shop and confronted the manager. During his attempted robbery, he and the fellow exchanged words, words that alerted the pawnbroker's wife, who was in a back room, to the fact that a robbery was in progress. The plucky woman grabbed a pistol from a drawer, parted the curtains between the two rooms and opened fire on St. Peter. It appeared from the evidence she wounded the robber. During the shootout, St. Peter shot her husband to death. The public outcry was deafening. Citizens wanted to know how this dangerous criminal got away from his prison and wound up in Tacoma and there wasn't even a mention of his escape. Governor Evans' programs came under attack from the media.

Shortly following the St. Peter incident, another convict was given a five-day furlough to visit his family. He stole a car and was halted by a state patrolman for speeding. As the officer was writing out a ticket, the released man shot the patrolman. After he had fallen, mortally wounded, the man on furlough got out of the car, took the officer's gun and administered the coup de grace with the wounded man's own revolver. It was well-known that the killer had often expressed a wish to 'snuff a cop'. His final act of violence also delivered the coup de grace to Governor Evans' relaxed penal experiment.

In every penitentiary, when the officials want to let an inmate know he has a visitor, the con's name and number is announced over loudspeakers which are strategically situated all over the institution's building and rec yard. In the yard, when the speaker blares, "The following men are to report to the visiting room for visits", all activity and yelling ceases so the announcement can be heard. There is no message so sweet as to hear your name and number called. I have watched the faces of men who hoped against hope that someone cared enough to come to see them. No matter how many years pass without ever being summoned to the visiting room, the hope is still there. Some try to bury their disappointment under the guise of not giving a damn. No matter how great the disappointment, cons exist by covering up. They consider it a weakness to express their hurt. What a price to pay just to impress your fellow-men when, in reality, they cry also. There is no doubt that much irreparable psychological damage is visited upon some of the men undergoing this experience.

Probably the most graphic illustration of the degree of this damage, which I personally witnessed, was on an inmate who was affectionately known as Wagon Wheel. He was finishing up his twentieth year in the abyss known as Alcatraz. When the mail was delivered to the individual cells each night, the mailman would walk down the corridor, stop briefly as he tapped a letter on the flat bar of a cell. Every ear on the landing would be tuned to hear who got a letter. Often an inmate would call to his buddy in a cell thirty feet away and tell him of the mail and its content. Wagon Wheel, who had gone nearly two decades without hearing from a soul, would tap a heavy piece of cardboard on his bars so everyone who was listening would believe he had received a letter. After a few minutes, he would call to some friend in an adjacent cage and say, "Andy, I just got a letter from my daughter. She is graduating from high school next week. Said to tell you hello, and that she'd write you in a month or so." Invariably, Andy would call back, "Thanks, Wagon Wheel. When you answer, tell her it was nice to hear from her. By the way, she must be about seventeen years old by now." As unfeeling and cold as most cons are, never once did anyone of them remind the guy he had been locked up for twenty years. They played the game with him year in and year out. Was he damaged? Other than his fellow inmates, who gave a damn? Only a man who has gone through such an experience can appreciate the hurt created by this senseless ostracism.

I had often dreamed that I would like to develop a program whereby indigent families could visit their incarcerated loved ones. In my heart, I knew it would be beneficial to the relatives of the inmates as well as the guys inside. I harbored a deep concern about youngsters who had not seen their dads in years, if ever. Of course, if I were to have transportation, the first major piece of equipment I'd need would be a small bus. Again, I went to my eternal faucet of flowing cash, my brother and sister. Each thought I was crazy to take on such a project. Marjorie was the most vociferous. "Glenn, you're out of your mind! Do you realize what you are taking on? Where will the money come from? How will you get ongoing support?" I tried to explain that I was certain that I could get funds from the same sources as Job Therapy got theirs; churches, businesses, large corporations and private citizens. Finally, I appealed to Dan. He finally gave in and financed a small bus. I rented a one-room office, hooked up one phone, had stationery printed and ATTICA was in business.

I made a trip to the state prison at Walla Walla. The first person I discussed my plan with was the warden, B.J. Rhay. He expressed doubt about the success of the plan. However, he gave me permission to address the inmate body and tell them of my plan. It was met with much enthusiasm by the inmates. I spent four days among the inmates and sought their input. Hundreds of them wrote their families and explained the function of ATTICA. Within a week my phone was ringing off the hook. I developed a brochure that fully explained our proposed program, and mailed out 500 copies. The concept appealed to the media, and articles began appearing in nearly all the papers in the state. As a result, funding began.

The families of the inmates made reservations for the first bus to the state prison. I was a novice in this business and made many mistakes, one being overloading the reservations. When we left our office, there were 23 mothers, dads, children and wives crammed into a 20 passenger vehicle. KOMO TV had cameramen and reporters on hand to cover the event.

Six hours later, the bus pulled into the prison compound. Weary travelers were happy that the journey was over. The penitentiary staff was upset because they were not prepared to handle so many visitors at one time. The first episode was chaotic. Nevertheless, we had to start somewhere and learn from our mistakes.

Within two months, the Attica Bussing program was well on its way. To avoid overloading, I appealed to friends to make the trip in their private cars and to take as many passengers as they could safely carry. Many were willing to volunteer as drivers and use their vehicles. At the same time, they would be able to visit a penitentiary for the first time in their lives. The main assistance I had over the next five years came from my office manager, Bonnie Venny. She was a beehive of activity and energy. In addition to her natural organizational skill, she was doubly motivated by the fact her son was serving a long prison term.

In 1974, a group of cons wrote me and asked if I could arrange to bring special busses to the prison for a Christmas celebration. I felt this was a excellent idea, so once again I flew to Walla Walla to present the proposition to Superintendent Bobby Rhay. At first he was skeptical. "Williams," he asked, "how are you going to manage such a project as that? Even without your hair-brained plan, we are swamped with so many visitors that we have a difficult time processing the normal flow. I'll tell you what. If you present me with a plan that seems the least bit feasible, I'll give the Christmas party serious thought. I want to discuss it with my staff so you had better come up with a solid and workable solution. Right off hand, I want you to know that I think it is a loser."

Instead of leaving for Seattle that night, I stayed over in order to meet with the group of inmates that had approached me with the idea in the first place. I told them exactly what Bobby Rhay had said. "Now you guys had better come up with a plan that appeals to him and the staff," I advised. "Get on it right away because, if approved, I have a hell of a task trying to make preparations. Get with your families and determine how many people we are talking about. We have a miracle to perform."

Three weeks later, the inmates wrote to tell me that more than 200 family members had responded affirmatively. They wanted reservations. As soon as I got this information, my Board of Directors went to work on the details. I don't think a one of them thought we had a chance in hell of pulling this grandiose venture off. I forwarded our completed proposal to Mr. Rhay and held my breath. True to his word, he presented the proposal to his staff, and they were not adverse to the idea. They expressed some reservations and penciled in a number of changes we would have to make. The day he mailed me the revised plans, he telephoned me. "Williams, The staff and I are inclined to think your Christmas party plan has some merit. Look over the revised article which I am returning today. Conform to our changes and we will go from there. This is not to be construed as an OK." The Board and I could find nothing in the altered documents with which we couldn't live.

By November 15th, we received the approval from Superintendent Rhay and from the officials in the state's capitol at Olympia. By this time, I had driven the Attica bus on the six hundred mile round-trip for thirty consecutive weekends. I was bone weary. I asked JB, my old friend from Alcatraz, to relieve me by taking over for four trips. Thank God he agreed to do it. Not only did I need a break from the job; I had much work to do to prepare for the Attica Christmas Party.

Bonnie Venny came into my office early one morning and asked me a question that floored me. "Well, Glenn, we have one vehicle. It holds about thirty passengers. Now what are we going to do about the other one hundred and fifty who have phoned in their intent to join us on the Christmas visit?"

I was desperate. I knew that we could not recruit thirty-five cars and drivers to accommodate us. Bonnie decided to call Ruth Walsh, anchorwoman of KOMO TV, and tell her of our dilemma. On Ruth's next broadcast, she made a poignant appeal for help in getting someone to help Attica obtain three large buses and drivers. She let the public know that at least five such vehicles with drivers were in need, and asked that they call her at KOMO TV. By evening the wonder of all wonders occurred. Attica received four calls from churches, two businesses and a bus company all offering the use of a bus and driver. Each caller realized, without being asked, that there would be heavy additional expenses needed to cover the cost of fuel, food and motel space. The much needed financial assistance began to roll in.

In addition, we received publicity in the Seattle Post Intelligencer by well-known columnist Emmett Watson. His article began, "Help send a child to prison. No, that's not a 2 1/2-martini sick joke, but the slogan adopted by Attica, the very reputable prisoner-help group. Attica is trying to raise money to bus children to see their fathers in the Walla Walla pen." The article went on to list our needs and the cost of the project, as well as appealing to the public for help. The publicity generated by these sources was so widespread that we received letters and money from all over the state.

Two weeks before we were to make the big venture, Bobby Rhay called me from the pen and said he had been approached by an inmate committee which asked for permission for them to throw a Christmas Party for their kids. He informed me he had given his OK, and asked me to make the necessary arrangements at this end. When I asked Bonnie if she was up to any more hard labor to assure the success of the party. Her response, as always, was, "Sure, Glenn". She spent a week contacting churches and asking them if they would prepare small gifts for the children to receive from their fathers. When asked how many, she nonchalantly informed them she would need 300. One church said, "What kinds of presents do you want, Bonnie?" Typical of her, she replied, "If you suddenly had more than 200 kids to give gifts to, what would you select.?" When advised what we needed, Carol Dicus of Women Aglow in Walla Walla addressed the problem to her group. Days later, my office was filled with hundreds of brightly wrapped boxes.

Bonnie and I loaded the gifts in our bus and drove them to the penitentiary. They were passed among the inmates who had their kids on the list for the purpose of selecting the appropriate present according to sex and age. They prepared tags with the youngsters' names on them. Superintendent Rhay let the inmates put up a large Christmas tree.

The night before the big trip, three large buses were parked in KOMO's TV station parking lot, which was across the street from the Attica office. The drivers were to be ready to pull the rigs out, fully loaded, by 4:30 A.M. for the trip. The buses were decorated for Christmas and loaded with crates of goodies.

I placed JB in charge of the lead bus. I knew him to be a top-notch driver with a cool head. You can imagine the magnitude of our responsibility. JB and I had walkie-talkies and were in constant touch. The snow was deep and treacherous, but JB slowed the convoy down over the dangerous section of the road. When we reached the Snoqualmie Summit, JB came in on his walkie-talkie. "Nate, there are three State Patrol Cars with their lights flashing. They are signaling me to pull off at the large cafe on top. What do you want me to do?" I knew that JB, with his hot temper and his dislike of police, might get us in trouble. I radioed back, "JB, no rough talk. Signal the buses to follow you. Pull into the parking lot, keep the engines running for warmth. I am pulling around to intercept you now." Before the lead bus could stop, I had pulled ahead. I called to JB, "Go to each driver and tell them to stay with their rigs, engines running. It is below freezing out here. Keep the passengers inside." I left my vehicle and walked over to the first prowl car and demanded to know what the problem was. Before he could answer me, I saw a private state station wagon and a TV sound and camera truck park along side JB's rig. I knew most of the TV media in and around Seattle, but I did not recognize any of this crew, nor did I see their call-letters. At this point a patrol officer came up to me and politely explained what was taking place. "The governor asked us to overtake you. The Corrections Department wants a record of this event. I am sure you will be on your way in a matter of a few minutes."

TV floodlights lighted the whole mountainside. It was nearing daylight and the passengers, who had been sleeping, were awakened. Dozens of kids' faces were pressed against the windows. Turning the buses around and getting them back on the road was a chore, but within a half-hour we were lined up and picking our way down the eastern slope of the pass. At 10:30 A.M., three buses loaded with weary and anxious parents and children were pulling into the city limits of Walla Walla. Once again, the media swamped us.

The regular visiting room was set aside for this Christmas event. The room measured about 40 by 50 feet, not nearly large enough to accommodate the over 200 people who tried to jam into it. The officials allowed us to use a long corridor that helped ease the crowding. In the center of the main room was a beautifully decorated 15-foot Christmas tree. Under the base of the tree were brightly wrapped presents. Wandering around the room were three Santa Clauses. The kids didn't seem to care that there was more than the traditional St. Nick. The noise was unbearable. The youngsters were running in circles trying to get to the gifts. In order to make some semblance of order, and to get the show on the road, a guard got on the PA system and asked all parents to corral their kids and align them along the walls of the room. When this was finally accomplished, an inmate Santa

Claus started reading the names off the packages as he picked them up. It took about half an hour to get all the gifts distributed. As the kids were inspecting their presents, the parents wandered over to a long table that was covered with food. The gala event lasted four hours.

The announcement that the party was over had a solemn effect. An eerie silence crept over the room. Before they started to disperse, they began singing carols. It wouldn't have taken much to start the tears flowing. When each father walked up to embrace his loved ones, he was escorted from the room. As the children saw their dads being taken away, they started sobbing. The mothers followed suit. I watched many a dad rush from the scene so he could weep in the privacy of his own cell. As each kid was loaded on the bus, he was handed a sack containing an orange and some hard candy. In addition to this, food had been supplied for the home trip. When the inside count was okayed, we carefully counted our passengers. At a signal from the tower guard, I called to JB, "Head for home, partner."

By the time we reached the half-way mark, all the youngsters were sound asleep. As darkness set in, we turned the dome lights on. In one of the buses somebody started dancing in the aisles. Before long there were three buses containing dancing people. People in other cars, when they passed us, would stare in wonderment. Our passengers would wave at them, and they would wave in return. Gradually, fatigue overtook the exhausted families and, like their children, they soon fell asleep.

Just as we started to cross the Lake Washington Floating Bridge, JB made contact with me on the walkie-talkie, "Nate how are things going back there? Not a soul is awake here. In fact, I am damn near asleep myself. I'm exhausted! Don't you ever come up with another idea like this again." In response, I told him everything seemed to be OK. An hour later, we were unloading the buses. It was midnight. We had been up for 20 hours.

In the seven years that Attica operated, we took between 200 and 300 family members to the prison every Christmas season. When I finally left Attica, we had carried more than 15,000 loved ones to the institution. There were grand experiences and sad ones. As the years rolled by, it seemed I was called on to do much of the work that the penal staff should have performed.

Of the most dreaded experiences were the ones when I would be asked to transport an inmate to the funeral of his mother or dad, or occasionally to his child's. I would find myself hurting along with my passenger.

I had one man 'run' from the funeral parlor. He had asked me if he could go sit with the grieving family members in their shrouded-off section. I did not hesitate to give him permission. When the service was over, he did not show up with his sisters and brothers. Before the procession started to the cemetery, I asked his sister where Bob was. She looked embarrassed and stared at the ground without answering me. Her brother spoke up angrily, "He ran out the back door. So far as I am concerned, that's the dirtiest thing a man can do. How low can Bob get, running from his mother's funeral service?" Word of what he had done would get back to other cons on the inside. He would pay a hell of a price when his fellow inmates could lay hands on him. Rarely does a convict run from a funeral service. There is only one honor code among convicts and that is you do not run from a funeral or sickbed trip.

During the Attica bussing program, we rarely had unhappy times going to the pen. Coming back was a different story. For the first hour on the return route, I witnessed very little frivolity. By the time we reached the halfway point, all of us were ready for a cup of hot coffee, and cookies and milk for the kids. The brief respite seemed to lift their spirits and there was singing and telling of experiences.

I will never forget one young wife who made the trips with me for five years to visit her husband. Betty was an unusual young lady. She was rather shy and quiet, but on occasion she would go on a talking jag. Notwithstanding her stories, always true, were hilarious, she would never crack a grin. The other women in the bus would always listen quietly. When Betty was finished the others would laugh loud and long. Two incidents she related will live in my memory forever. We were returning on a particular trip and it was past midnight. On this journey Betty rode up front with me. It was snowing up a blizzard on the summit of Snoqualmie Pass, a particularly dangerous stretch of road under these conditions. Betty reached over and touched my arm, a gesture she always made when she wanted my attention. "Glenn, my Mom refuses to visit my husband. Will you talk to her before my next trip and ask her to visit him?" I had practiced a hard and fast policy of never getting involved in the passengers personal family affairs, and I reminded Betty of my reluctance to meddle in the matter. I did ask her, "Why does your mother refuse to visit your husband?"

After a moment's hesitation she replied, " Well, you know that my husband is serving time for assault and battery with a knife, don't you?" I assured her that I did. She continued, "She's mad at him, Glenn, because she's the one he stabbed." I thought the other women in the bus would never cease laughing.

One summer night, we were coming home by a different route. It was a magnificent moonlit night. As we approached a bend in the road, we could see a falls with its water cascading down about 1000 feet. It glistened like a silver needle in the night. It was breathtaking. Again, Betty was in her favorite seat beside me. I turned to her and commented, "Betty, isn't that beautiful? How would you like to be beside that falls having a picnic on a hot summer day?" She jerked around in her seat and glared at me. "Don't you talk to me about picnicing by a waterfall!" I was dumbfounded by her reaction to my question. Before I could say another word, she continued, "One day my boyfriend and I were enjoying a picnic lunch by a waterfall. It started raining heavily. We ran under a ledge into a sort of cave. I got pregnant. Don't talk to me about picnicing under a waterfall again!" And again the other passengers howled with laughter.

Her last surprise was one I could not share with others on the bus. Betty called my house one evening at midnight. She was terribly upset. "Glenn," she cried, "Do you know where I can get an abortion?" I was shocked by the question. "No, Betty, I don't. How could you get in this mess? Your husband is coming home in three weeks." I should have been prepared for some off-the-wall story. "An ex-boyfriend of mine met me on the street last week. We talked about old times and, before we parted I agreed to go to a show with him the following evening. He came to pick me up in a fancy made-over van. The seats were upholstered in lovely cloth. It was one of those fancy jobs that the studs call a 'sin bin'. When we pulled into the drive-in, I told him I wouldn't tolerate any funny stuff and that if he started it, I was going to take a cab home. After the feature had been running for about a half-hour, he suggested that we get in the more comfortable seats in the back. I'm pretty sure I'm pregnant." I couldn't laugh at this story. I felt very sorry for her. She called me again three weeks later and told me that she was not pregnant after all. Her husband was released six months later and they moved away from the area. I never heard from her again.

Our funds were running low, so I had to make pleas from all sources possible. I had heard that there was some funding from St. Patrick's church. I called and came in contact with Sister Vera Gallagher. I explained our project to her only to learn that she had heard of us. When I asked her if she could arrange some funding, she said she would try and asked me if I would bring some literature to her office. Meeting her was an eventful day in my life. She was one of the most delightful women I had ever met; intelligent, keen sense of humor and very compassionate. I asked her if she would like to take a trip with me to the prison. Without hesitation, she agreed. I wanted her to see what it was like firsthand. She was a wonderful traveling companion. As I drove onto the penitentiary compound, the first tower guard directed us to a parking area near the warden's office. I parked right under a manned tower. The guard was standing outside on the catwalk with a rifle at the ready. I sensed something was amiss. Finally, he called over his loudspeaker to a group of inmates in the prison yard whom we could not see. "Break it up down there." Apparently they did not heed his order, so he fired a shot in their midst. Sister Vera and I could hear the slug ricochet off the concrete. I was concerned about her safety and started to push her to the protection of our bus. I underestimated the plucky lady. She was pawing at her handbag to get her camera. She wanted to get a picture of what was transpiring. The guard could be seen aiming his weapon down at the men in the yard. All who met Sister Vera loved her. On our way back to Seattle, she asked if she could write an article about Attica and me. In February 1981, the Catholic Digest published her story. It was titled: Bus Man of Alcatraz.

25

Father And Daughter Reunited

During my years with Job Therapy, I met a young lady who was a volunteer secretary and employer contact with the corporation. Lorna had two young sons, Scott and Don, who were near the age of my daughter Natalie. Lorna would often care for Natalie when I wasn't able to take her with me on my trips. At this time, I had begun having almost the entire responsibility of Natalie's care due to her mother's illness. Though Lorna had not previously been exposed to working with ex-offenders and their families, she shared my interest in this field and would accompany me on treks to the institutions or speaking engagements taking notes and assisting in my scheduling. We became close friends and our friendship continued even after Lorna left Job Therapy.

Despite the satisfaction I derived from having found my niche and life's work, I was restless and had difficulty concentrating at times. Was this sense of restlessness due to the years I had been in a cage? I think so. There had to be some explanation for my inability to lie down and rest, to enjoy the beauty of nature around me, to be able to sit down with friends and talk. My friend, JB, said he was concerned about me during this period of my life. At dinner one evening he said, "Nate, for a time there I was worried that you might have a nervous breakdown." I think one of the reasons I was having a difficult time coping was the fact that whenever I had time on my hands, unpleasant memories crashed in on me and endless visions of my daughter Muriel came to the surface. I felt that I probably would never be able to lead a normal life.

I knew it wasn't normal for me to think endlessly about her. It had become a mania with me. I constantly thought of the manner in which I would approach her for the first time. How would I broach the subject of parentage when she was not even aware of my existence? How could I re-establish a relationship when, in reality, there had never been a relationship so far as she could remember?

Out of desperation, I turned to Lorna and told her the complete story of my loss of my beloved daughter. Lorna's sincere interest and compassion released years of pent-up emotion that I had kept bottled up tightly within myself. I told her how difficult it had been living within an hour's drive of Muriel and not being able to see her. I had been free six years and was no closer to getting a glimpse of her than I had been when I first entered my Alcatraz cell. I told Lorna of the pact I had made with myself. If I'd reduced it to a written contract, it probably would have been worded like this:

IN THE INTEREST OF MURIEL, WHEN I AM RELEASED I WILL
NOT MAKE CONTACT WITH HER EITHER THROUGH LETTER,
PHONE OR PERSONAL VISIT. THE REASON FOR THIS AGREE-
MENT WITH MYSELF IS THAT I DO NOT WANT TO INTERRUPT
HER LIFE IN ANY WAY WHILE SHE IS GROWING UP. THERE-
FORE, I WILL WAIT UNTIL SHE IS TWENTY- ONE YEARS OF AGE
BEFORE I SEEK A MEETING WITH HER. AND AT THAT TIME I
WILL TELL HER THAT I AM HER FATHER, AND WHAT TRAN-
SPIRED WHEN SHE WAS THREE YEARS OF AGE.

My determination, encompassed in the above quasi contract, was as
valid to me as though I had made it in a court of law. And I abided by it. But
why? Was I being realistic about this self-imposed restriction? It couldn't
be unfair to my daughter because she wasn't aware of my existence. She was
raised believing that my sister and brother-in-law were her natural parents.
I was fully aware of two things; one, I had to get her out of my mind for the
time being, and I could only accomplish this if I were to be busy every
waking hour; two, so help me God, I was going to see her again as soon as
she was of age. By the time I had unloaded on Lorna, both of us were in
tears. Her advice will never be forgotten. "Glenn, in your state of mind, you
are in no condition to act rationally at this time. Let's agree not to take any
action for at least a month. In that time, you and I can discuss what
move will be best. As things stand now, you're punishing yourself. Muriel
is not suffering." Lorna will never know how she endeared herself to me
that evening.

A few years earlier in 1969, my brother had told me that Muriel was going
to graduate from high school. I made up my mind right then that I was going
to attend the graduation exercises incognito. I reasoned that I could at least
see her without anyone knowing of my presence. It took a number of phone
calls to find out the name of the high school where the graduation exercises
would be held. On the night of the graduation, I drove to the far end of the
parking lot where I felt I would be least apt to be seen by my daughter's step-
parents, my sister and her husband. I envisioned an unpleasant encounter
if we met. I was conscious of the possibility of a confrontation, the last thing
I wanted.

Every possible negative thought entered my mind. From my vantage
point, I watched the cars start to fill the parking lot. It was getting dark and
I had a difficult time distinguishing one person from another. I realized I
would have to drive nearer the front door if I were to be able to recognize
Muriel. In addition to the darkness, I was not too certain I could tell which
one of the girls was her. After all it had been nearly sixteen years since I had
seen her. My original intent was to wait until all the parents and friends had
filed into the auditorium before I entered. In my inconspicuous suit and
dark glasses, I felt that my sister and her husband would not be able to
identify me. I was heavier than ever before, and the passing years did a snow
job on my hair.

When I noticed that the traffic entering the lot had dwindled to very few
incoming vehicles, I got out of my car and skirted the more lighted areas and

made my way to the building. By the time I mounted the few stairs and walked through the open doors, sweat was pouring down my sides and soaking my clothes. It sort of reminded me of the many times I had entered banks with the intent to rob; not nervous, but always sweating profusely. Surely I couldn't recall any bank heist that had caused me the concern and fear I was experiencing at the prospect of looking on my daughter's face for the first time in many years.

I was jarred out of my reverie by a touch on my arm. An attractive young lady was pressing a program into my hand, and at the same time was saying, "Here is your program, sir." I stepped aside and took a fleeting glance to where the graduates were seated with the hope of just one glimpse at my daughter. It was futile. I refused the program, bolted through the door and headed for my car. I drove home barely able to see through the tears that had filled my eyes. I was angry at myself for not being assertive enough to force my way down the aisle to a row nearer the front. I felt that one of the biggest milestones of Muriel's life had passed and I was deprived of witnessing it.

Later, I learned that Muriel was employed in a bank in a suburb of Seattle. I made up my mind to go to the bank and try to see her. It wasn't my intent to make myself known to her, but to just look at her. I drove to the parking lot of the bank and went in. Luckily, it was quite busy so I wasn't conspicuous. There were about five tellers and four or five other employes behind the cages. I looked from one to the other. I felt I would recognize her, but could not see anyone who looked like Muriel. She could have been out to lunch, or maybe she didn't come to work that day. Any number of excuses cropped into my mind. One thing for certain, I couldn't keep standing there and staring at the employees. I had the appearance of a man casing the joint for a heist. When I backed out from my parking space, I thought I noticed a bank employee making a note of my license number. I should not have stalled in the bank trying to locate Muriel. Wouldn't this have been a hell of a note if they had called the police and told them of this suspicious-looking man casing the joint? Of course, I was in there legitimately, but it would have been difficult trying to explain my reason for being there, especially if they ran a check on me. After that incident, I made no other effort to see her.

Muriel's twenty-first birthday anniversary was a brief month away. I again discussed with Lorna my distress and longing to be reunited with my daughter. She and I hashed over the options I had. We decided that I could not simply approach her on the street and start out by saying, "Hi, I'm your father and......." Nor could I expect her step-parents to be sympathetic to any overture along this line. It was my intention, however, to let them know what my intentions were. I wanted them to know this so that if there was a repercussion from Muriel, they would understand what had taken place. At times I thought I would drop the entire matter and let Muriel continue on with life. In my heart I knew that I could not go on this way. I bounced my idea off Lorna. "I'm going to locate and talk with Muriel's mother and tell her what I plan to do. I have feelers out to find where she lives. What do you think of that idea?" Lorna pondered the question over for a long time before offering her opinion and, when she did reply, it was with the same cool-headed deliberation.

"That might be a good thing to do. However, I wonder if her natural mother has been in touch with her. It seems improbable, or Muriel would already know that the people who raised her were not her natural parents. In that case, I'd suggest that you contact your sister and go from there. It appears to me that you need to act now or drop it altogether. Why don't you compose a letter to Muriel in which you explain its purpose and ask her to meet with you? She is of age now, and should be able to make her own decisions." I thought her suggestion was great. I was happy to have her in my corner.

That night, I agonized over the wording of the letter. So much hinged on Muriel's interpretation of what I was to write. By three the next morning, I had finished the letter I wanted to mail. It read as follows:

June 5, 1972

Dear Muriel,

For many years I have wanted to see you and talk with you. Whether I am right or wrong in waiting so long, I don't know. But for eleven of these years, it was physically impossible for me to contact you in person or by letter.

Before I wrote this letter, I discussed the advisability of doing so with your aunts, cousins, and uncles. The conclusion was that I should give you the option to re-establish the acquaintanceship with your father, which was so abruptly terminated when you were about three years old. The termination was not of my desire, and I have lived these years regretting that I could not have raised you and displayed my love for you, which has never ceased.

The situation, Muriel, is simply this: As much as I love you and want to see you, I feel I should let you make the choice whether you want to see me or not. Naturally, I hope you will give me the privilege of taking you to dinner some evening very soon and giving me the opportunity to explain why I was forced to leave you nearly nineteen years ago.

The entire responsibility of our separation must rest on my shoulders, and I am willing to accept this. No one else is to blame.

There isn't anything I can add to this unless you will give me the opportunity to do so in person.

Will you please call me at my office at 442-1510 in Seattle? In the event I am not in the office at that time, please ask

342

for my secretary, Lorna McLeod, and give her a number so I can
return your call. If you call in the evening, you may call
me at my home phone which is ME3-2442, also in Seattle.
Or if you wish to write me, would you please do so at the
above address?

While I naturally hope you will let me talk with you, I will
abide by your decision and, if I don't hear from you, I will
necessarily assume that you deem it best that we don't see
one another. And, in this event, I will not attempt to
contact you again.

Devotedly,
Your Father

Glenn Williams

P. S. You might be interested to know that you have a four and a half year
old step-sister named Natalie.

Lorna and I shared some apprehension over the wording of the letter.
After having read and re-read it half a dozen times, we cast the die and
prepared to post it. Before I arrived at the post office, Lorna laid her hand
on mine and came up with a suggestion that I thought was a gem of an idea.
"Glenn, why don't we drive by Muriel's bank and wait until she gets off? I'll
take the letter, and as soon as she leaves the bank, I'll intercept her and hand
it to her. And, if she will give me a chance, I'll tell her who the letter is from.
You can trust me to use good judgment." I was so grateful that Lorna was
with me.

We parked in an inconspicuous place across the street from Muriel's
place of employment and waited for the employees to come out. Lorna was
confident she would be able to identify her. I was not too certain. At closing
time, the girls started leaving the bank. Lorna and I stared intently at each
person. We both saw her at the same time. I started to tell Lorna that I
thought she was the girl walking in front of two others. Before I could finish
my sentence, Lorna grabbed my arm and whispered, "There she is. I know
that is Muriel." Before I could stop her, Lorna jumped from the car, crossed
the street diagonally and walked up to my daughter. When Lorna addressed
her, I could tell Muriel was startled. I watched as Lorna talked. She handed
the letter to Muriel, said something and came back to where I was parked.
I had had only a brief glimpse of her from a distance of about fifty feet, but
I would have recognized her readily. From that distance, I could tell she was
a lovely appearing young lady. I drove off choking back the tears.

I don't remember saying anything to Lorna until we were back in the city
limits. I tried to keep my voice controlled as I asked, "How did Muriel
react? What did she say?" When I glanced at her, I saw that tears had welled
in Lorna's eyes. She placed her hand over one of mine and squeezed gently.
When she spoke, there was a catch in her voice. "She was very surprised,
Glenn. I can't remember what she said, but it was very little. She took the
letter, stared at me and began crying. You know, I had the feeling she was

not unaware of what was happening, but then she couldn't have known. She thanked me and walked away." We didn't discuss it any more that evening.

Now that I had initiated the first part of my plan, I called Muriel's stepmother, my sister. She was shocked to hear from me for the first time in nearly twenty years. I came right to the point and said, "Denise, I think I had better tell you of my plan. I have waited until Muriel was of age before letting her know who I am. I did so by letter today. It is my judgment that she should know who her father is. I deliberately waited this length of time so she would be more mature and able to handle the trauma. I am aware that you may disagree with me, and may be very angry. If so, I am sorry. She might come to you about this. If she does, you will know of her concern beforehand. I have located her mother, and am contacting her today. If you want to call me, reach me through Marjorie." Denise accepted my decision with apparent calm. At least she didn't vent any anger in my direction. However, she did surprise me with her response. "Glenn, I anticipated your move some time ago. The timing is coincidental, but it so happens that I recently told Muriel the facts surrounding her parentage. She was shocked. We will see what takes place in the next few days."

I had located Muriel's mother through her employment. Without hesitation, I kept the ball rolling and called her office. I was amazed that, after all these years, I recognized her voice. I began, "This is Glenn. I'm beginning an effort to contact Muriel for the purpose of identifying myself and letting her know that I'm her father. She is of age now, and I don't want her to go on through life thinking that my sister is her natural mother. When I called Denise and told her of my intent, she took me by surprise by telling me that she had already informed Muriel of the circumstances surrounding her childhood and her adoption. The purpose of this call is to advise you that Muriel may ask me who and where her natural mother is. I would have no option but to tell her the truth. What would you want me to do with regard to this matter?" Muriel's mother was so taken aback she could not answer for a few minutes. In addition to the nature of my statement, she was totally thrown for a loop upon hearing from me after so many years. She stammered and finally blurted out, "Please tell her who I am and where I can be reached. For many years I have wanted to see her again. It has been hell for me too, Glenn." I promised I would keep her advised of my progress, but cautioned her of the possibility that our daughter might not wish to have us enter her life, in which case, I was going to abide by Muriel's decision and would demand that her mother do likewise. Before I could hang up, my ex-wife asked if we could meet and talk this over. I said, "I'll think it over and will get back to you."

Later that week we met near her office. I spotted her immediately. She was still a very attractive woman. I was embarrassed and did not know how to open a dialogue. I can't remember what was said at the beginning. I am sure it was trivia. From her conversation, I gathered that she, too, had suffered from the separation, and had entertained the thought of meeting with Muriel. The difference between her situation and mine was that she was under court order to no longer interfere with the girl's life. The court must have thought that I would be in no position to be a problem in this area, so it neglected to put a restraining order against me.

Muriel's mother asked, "Glenn, do you think we're doing the right thing?" My response was quick and to the point. "Right or wrong, I am going through with my original intent. Considering that Denise had already told Muriel she was an adopted child, I feel more determined than ever to pursue the matter. Muriel is bound to be puzzled by the turn of events, and more so after reading my letter." Then she turned to me and spoke in a very low voice, "When you see her, will you please ask her to see me also?" For a moment all my bitterness faded, and I felt a twinge of sorrow for her.

When I met Lorna that night I told her, "You mentioned that you had the feeling that Muriel was not unaware of what was happening. Well, you were correct. I found out that Denise had just informed Muriel of the details of her adoption."

More than a week passed and there was not one word from Muriel. I felt she may have decided to ignore my letter. As I drove home, I was about to give up on the chances of Muriel ever trying to get back to me. After all, she had had more than ten days to respond. This left me with the determination to go ahead with my life. I had a great deal to do and I had two choices; either give up and float with the tide or bury myself in my work.

One of my trips took me to Butte, Montana where I was scheduled to address two civic groups. As I was checking out of my hotel room, the clerk advised me that there was a long distance call for me from my office. When I dialed the number, it was answered by one of the volunteers in my office. "Mr. Williams, you had a call from your daughter this morning. She asked that I get her message to you as soon as possible. I told her that you were out of town and would be back tomorrow. She was determined that you be contacted, if possible, today. She wanted you to return her call regardless of the hour. Here is the number she left." Although I had been praying for word from her, when it finally came I was stunned. I was afraid to return her call. What would I do if she rejected my proposal that we meet? Rarely had I ever been so beset with self-doubt. My first impulse was to place a long distance call to her. Finally I decided to wait until I was back home.

When my plane landed in Seattle, I raced to a public phone and dialed her number. There was no answer, even though I let it ring a dozen times. There was nothing I could do until tomorrow. At seven o'clock the next morning, I dialed her number. She answered immediately. I could not bring myself to talk for a few seconds. When I did, I simply said, "Muriel, this is your Dad. I was out of the state when I got your message. I called last night but you weren't home." Afraid she might hang up, I continued, "I called this early because I wanted to reach you before you went to work." There was nothing more I could say until she responded. After what seemed like an eternity she spoke. "I'm not working today. Would you care to have lunch with me? If so, we could meet at the Holiday Inn in Renton." I hurriedly agreed to the place and hour.

I was unsure of myself. I called Lorna and told her what had taken place. She was beside herself with happiness. "Will you join me when I meet her, Lorna?" Her response was prompt and to the point. "It would be inappropriate, Glenn. I understand your lack of confidence and your desire for some support. I realize how important this meeting is to you. I'm certain it will turn out for the good. If she weren't amenable to your request to talk to her, she wouldn't have telephoned you. You get dressed up and fight your own battle." At the time I was perturbed with Lorna, but later was grateful to her for her good judgment.

I arrived at the Holiday Inn a half-hour early. Nerves put my stomach in a turmoil. The thought of food nauseated me. I wanted a table away from the center of the dining room, and made arrangements with the hostess for Muriel and me to be more or less isolated. It was incidental that the table was situated in such a position that I could see people entering the dining area. I went to the rest room and was returning to our table when I found myself face to face with my daughter as she was approaching the hostess' station. I mustered what little confidence I had left and walked over to her. "Hi, Muriel. I don't expect you to recognize me, but I am your dad." She appeared calm and well in control of herself. I stuck out my hand to accept hers in a handshake. It dawned on me what a formal way to greet someone whom I had been waiting years to meet. Yet, I was afraid of smothering her. She was almost like a complete stranger to me. "I have a table already selected," I stammered. "I hope it is OK with you." I led the way and seated her. Damn, but I was miserably uncertain of myself! I couldn't understand how she could be so poised. I was tremendously relieved when she broke the awkward silence by saying, "I hope you're as hungry as I am." When the waitress came to take our orders, Muriel was ready with her selection. I can't remember what I ordered or what we ate.

It had always been a practice of mine, when confronted with uncertainty, to take the bull by the horns and get right to the problem, and believe me, I was faced with a monumental problem at this setting. With no preliminaries, I blurted out, "Muriel, I know this is an uncomfortable situation for you. Please let me explain my position." I don't know how long I babbled nor do I recall what I said. To the best of my ability, I told her the true story of what had transpired in our lives over the past twenty-one years. I accepted the full responsibility for the chaos and heartache I had visited on her and my family. I assured her that I couldn't account for gambling with her future by continuing to rob banks after her birth, especially in view of the fact that I adored her from the date of her arrival. I spared her the grim details of my life on Alcatraz, and of the seemingly endless anger, frustration and pain. I ended by saying, "If you would rather not continue this relationship, Muriel, I will certainly understand and will not bother you further. I simply had to see you one more time and, for this opportunity, I am truly grateful to you."

She explained what my sister had told her regarding her parents and what had led up to their adopting her. One of the reasons she had not contacted me sooner was because she had experienced a very difficult time adjusting to the trauma created by my sister's announcement, and the receipt of my letter. She was in a quandary. I could certainly understand her being perplexed by the unbelievable turn-around her life had taken. My heart ached for her. As she spoke, I was surprised by the calmness of her voice. "It took me days to make the decision as to whether I should respond to your letter or to pack my things and start off with a new life. I decided not to run but to face the facts as they are. Now that we have talked, I am glad I met with you."

As she talked I was able to look her over carefully. She was a beautiful young lady who had inherited much of her mother's classic features. My sister had done a good job in raising her. She had impeccable manners, spoke with a well-modulated voice and used excellent English. I was impressed by her demeanor under such trying circumstances. By the time we had talked to our heart's content, it was well after two in the afternoon. Before we parted, Muriel gave me her address and phone number and asked me to call her in a couple of days. As I drove back to Seattle, I was elated. It would have been hard to find a happier guy. That evening I told Lorna of all that had taken place.

During the next two weeks, Muriel and I met often. We drove to my brother's place of business in another city. He had not seen her since she was four years of age, but he recognized her immediately. On another occasion, we visited Natalie and her mother. It was the first time she had ever met her half-sister. Natalie's mother was very ill and could not contribute much to our meeting.

It was necessary for me to drive the Attica bus to the state prison one weekend. I invited Muriel to go along on the trip. Going to visit a penitentiary was a foreign experience for my older daughter. She was uncomfortable riding with a dozen family members of imprisoned men. For her comfort, I let her ride up front with me. She was a good sport and seemed to enjoy the trek in general. Natalie accompanied us, and the two had a good chance to get acquainted.

My fondest dream had been realized one day when she addressed me as 'Dad'. I felt she had accepted me. Muriel's natural mother had been calling me and asking me to arrange a meeting with her daughter. I asked Muriel one morning if she would like to meet her natural mother. At first she was hesitant. She asked me a number of questions concerning her mother's role in this whole picture. I answered them to the best of my ability. Her toughest question was put to me bluntly and without warning. "Dad, I can understand your not contacting me for so many years. You were unable to do so. But why didn't my mother make an effort to get in touch with me? Why, after all these years, does she suddenly want to see me?" She stopped me cold with that one. I had no answer for her. I realized that our picture could not be complete until we had clarified the question of Muriel's mother.

About a week later, I contacted Muriel and asked her to have dinner with me. It was during this time that I mentioned her mother to her again. Without hesitation, Muriel said, "Yes, I would like to meet her. If you can set up some evening after work, I would be glad for the three of us to get together." When I called Muriel's mother, she was pleased with the prospect of us getting together. I set up a time for us to have dinner about a week later.

I picked Muriel up and drove her to the restaurant where we were to eat. When Muriel and I arrived, I saw her mother sitting in the reception area. I took Muriel by the arm and led her to where her mother was. It was an

347

emotion-laden meeting. Her mother stood up and put her arms around Muriel. Both were crying. After a few minutes I suggested that we find a table where we could talk freely. It was my intent to leave the two of them alone to re-establish their relationship. I interrupted and said, "Muriel and I have been together a number of times. I have told her the absolute truth concerning the time from her birth to this day. I want to leave the two of you to be together for awhile. Take your time."

I left the diner and drove to a nightclub downtown. I immediately consumed a number of strong drinks. I engaged the bartender in a lot of small talk. I simply wanted to give Muriel and her mother an opportunity to talk to their hearts' content. By the time I was ready to return to the diner, I was not certain whether I had been gone for one hour or six. Apparently they had had plenty of time to discuss whatever had been on their minds. I drove Muriel back to her apartment. I didn't ask her anything about her conversation with her mother and she didn't volunteer anything.

Now that there was an apparent happy conclusion to the separation of Muriel and me, I buried myself in my work. Due to so much publicity concerning this 'guy from Alcatraz' who was on the scene so often via the media, I was inundated with requests to speak to civic groups, churches, schools and even police-related groups. I learned that it wasn't because I was supposed to be an authority on matters related to prisons, paroles and rehabilitation as much as it was that I had been on the Rock. And that prison and its infamous occupants always carried a degree of mystique that intrigued people. Rarely did my speeches last more than twenty minutes. However, during the question and answer periods, I found myself tied up for more than an hour. The attendant notoriety and the subsequent demand on my time took me from my work. I knew that it was necessary for me to appear before groups in order to solicit funding. It wasn't long before my lecture circuit kept me out of the office for weeks on end. Some of the appointments were in remote states and cities. As a result of my prolonged absences from my office, the quality of our program suffered. To make matters worse, requests came in from adjacent states asking me to set up a similar project in their areas. It was at this point that I rejected all invitations that imposed on my time.

In addition to the heavy workload, I was confronted with the fact that my wife's health was failing. Our relationship worsened until we found it necessary to separate. Inasmuch as she was in no condition to care for Natalie, I had to assume that responsibility. Natalie and I found an apartment where we lived near her mother's home. The two of them were very close and I had no intent of coming between them. Divorce was inevitable, and that painful procedure was necessary. For my daughter's sake, I asked the court to give me custody of the youngster. It was a tough time for Natalie and me. She was too young to understand why her dad and mom no longer lived together. As often as I could, I took her over to her mother's house so they could spend time together. Just when Natalie was becoming accustomed to our new way of life, her mother passed away in her sleep. Seldom have I had to go through such agony. For a brief time, Natalie became uncontrollable. I gave notice of my intent to take a three-month leave of absence. We stayed in the city, but spent almost every waking hour doing our own thing. Gradually, we adapted to our new way of life together. When I returned to work I was re-energized and tackled problems with a renewed zest.

26

United

Devoting my time to raising Natalie and operating the Attica program made somewhat of a juggler out of me. My daughter had ridden on the bus with me for a number of years, and she was tiring of it. She was now about nine years of age and the novelty was wearing off. The question of what I was going to do with her while I made the weekly trips caused me concern. One thing was for certain, I could not compel the girl to go along as a passenger. On numerous occasions, I would ask Lorna and her two sons, Scott and Don, to come along to keep me company. While the inmates' family members were visiting at the prison, Lorna and the children and I would spend time in the motel pool or driving around the countryside. However, Lorna could not make too many trips with me because of her responsibilities at home which took up much of her weekends. She understood the problem I was having with Natalie and would take care of her during my drives.

As practically the sole driver of the Attica busing program for about six years, I was burning out. For months I had harbored the thought of developing a program which dealt with teenagers who were experiencing difficulty with the law and their schools. I felt a sense of confidence in this area because of my experience, and the fact that I had worked with juveniles when I was with the Job Therapy agency. I was torn between my loyalty to Attica and my desire to get away from it and try something more challenging. There was no question in my mind that I had to have relief from the monotonous prison visitation routine. It came down to the fact it wasn't a matter of choice. I very definitely had to make a change. I was troubled by the fact that many people were dependent on the Attica busing program. They had no other means of transportation to visit their loved ones who were incarcerated. It is true they could have taken a commercial bus, but most were indigent and had no means to pay the cost of a ticket. Ninety percent of Attica's passengers rode at no cost. As usual, when I was confronted with a problem, I always bounced it off Lorna for input. When I told her what I intended to do, she said, "Glenn, I'd like to see you turn the busing over to some dependable person. I've realized that you were beginning to burn out. For whatever reason you decide to fold Attica, you are justified in leaving it. For more than seven years you have almost single-handedly operated the agency. Not only that, you founded and funded the original project. It is true that you have had some dedicated volunteers, such as Bonnie, but she was a rarity. So, I urge you to announce to your Board of Directors your intent to leave Attica." I was pleased with Lorna's agreement.

I contacted Father Richard Stohr, a priest who had financially supported Attica for a number of years. His response was great. "Glenn, I think my church will be willing to take over the duties of your agency." Here was a dedicated and knowledgeable man who was willing and able to make a smooth transition.

With this burden lifted from my shoulders, I dived right into the development of my youth project which I named Teen Intercept. Our purpose would be to intercept youngsters who displayed a propensity to truancy and other minor misdemeanors. Our Board of Directors and Advisors included lawyers, psychiatrists, teachers, businessmen and police officials. We announced our services to the media and were pleased with their response.

Lorna was concerned that I might be developing a project that would enslave me. She had witnessed the inordinate hours I had spent in the service of Attica. She had agreed to volunteer in the area of bookkeeping and secretarial service on a limited basis. She had her regular job and had no intention of neglecting Scott and Don. Lorna never ceased to amaze me with her insight of my nature and disposition. She summed it up by advising, "Remember that you have a daughter who is going to require more and more of your time and supervision. You can't expect to take Natalie on long business trips for the purpose of 'being with her'. She will now be demanding more of your time and energy, and there must be a quality to that time and energy. What I'm really saying is this; take your work with Teen Intercept as an eight to five job. You owe the rest of the time to yourself. Also, I want you to know from the beginning just what my limitations are."

While I knew she was correct, I became miffed with her blunt way of putting it. Yet it was this very quality that endeared her to me.

By its very nature and the demand for other agencies to work in the field of juvenile delinquency, Teen Intercept was well accepted. From the beginning, we were inundated with requests for assistance. Teachers, parents, relatives and counselors referred youngsters to us for assistance. It was amazing how much we were sought out when we were needed, and how consistently we were avoided when we sought funding. Much of the time, our meager funding was not enough to pay for the office and its upkeep. We would often dip into our own pockets to help with the office rent and utilities. How we managed to function under those conditions, I'll never know. However, those five years afforded me with an education I could not have received from any other source. Working with youngsters was more appealing than expending energy into the elusive dream of rehabilitating sophisticated criminals.

In the developmental stage of Teen Intercept, Lorna proved to be a boon. While she did tell me that she did not intend to spend a great deal of time on the project, she was really responsible for the setting up of the office. Whenever she had a spare moment, she took care of the correspondence and other incidental chores. She and I worked weekends and late into the evenings. Her very presence was a constant reminder to me that she had become more than a friend and fellow worker to me. I had fallen in love with her. I found everything against me when I dreamed of asking her to marry me. I was twenty-nine years her senior and had a deplorable reputation. She was so in control of her life. I felt inferior to her in every respect. And to make matters worse, she was a beautiful young lady who had other admirers. At times, I thought I had better be satisfied with just being a friend. But how in the hell can you be 'just a friend' when you are in love?

Lorna would often invite Natalie and me to have dinner with her and Scott and Don. Inevitably, I would construe each invitation as an overture on her part. But she had a way of keeping me at arms' length. On some occasions I would ask her to join Natalie and me on trips. In every case, we got along admirably. It encouraged me that she seemed to enjoy my company. After each date, I would promise myself I was going to tell her exactly how I felt about her. But when the time came to part for the evening, I lost my fortitude.

As the months passed, I became more and more dissatisfied with my role as her friend. It surprised me that I lacked the guts to confront her with my feelings. Facing a bank full of people and robbing that bank held no fear for me. And here I stood afraid to tell a woman I was in love with her.

A business trip arose that required my going to San Francisco. When I told Lorna that I would be gone for a few days, she said, "I wish I could get away and go with you. I want a rest from the boys and the monotony of work." She could not have said anything that would have pleased me more. Impulsively, I took her hand and asked, "Why don't you join me? We can get sitters for the children. It will be good for both of us, and you can bet the children will be glad to get rid of us." I couldn't believe my ears when she told me she would ask for a few days off, get one of her friends to take care of the boys and join me. I was on cloud nine.

A week later, Lorna and I were dancing to the music of a marvelous orchestra in the Starlight Room on top of the Sir Francis Drake Hotel in San Francisco. Notwithstanding she was being dragged around the floor by the country's worst dancer, Lorna seemed to be having a great time. We dined sumptuously. It was the occasion of my lifetime and my happiness was augmented by the flow of champagne.

During the dinner, I found myself searching the night for a blinking light in the Bay that would indicate the location of Alcatraz. Lorna queried, "What are you trying to see?" I couldn't help but look at her sheepishly as I responded, "You won't believe this, but I am trying to see if I can locate my old hotel room on the Rock." She laughed hysterically. "I can't believe this! Here we are on a date in a magnificent setting and you're attempting to bring back horrible memories of the past. Where in the world could I possibly fit in this scene?" My courage, buttressed by copious quaffs of the heady drinks and an impetuous nature, encouraged me to blurt out, "I'm in love with you. I want you to fit in the scene with me by becoming my wife. Will you marry me?" I said it and a great weight was instantly lifted from my shoulders. I remembered thinking that, regardless of her answer, at least I had mustered the guts to ask her. She could do no more than crush me with a refusal. In a deliberate manner, she placed her knife and fork on the table and calmly surveyed me. She took her time in responding and, when she did, it was a quiet and simple, 'Yes'. I leaned across the table to kiss her and nearly set my hair on fire by the burning candle. Very few words were exchanged between us during the rest of the evening.

In the weeks that followed the announcement of our engagement, I was kept busy with the demands of Teen Intercept. It appeared from the beginning of the operation that I was going to be smothered with requests to speak to various audiences. It had been my hope that this kind of pattern would not materialize as it had with Attica. I understood that agencies from which I had sought financial assistance would ask me to address their boards where they could interrogate me before granting or denying donations. Our very existence depended upon the income from such agencies. Civic clubs, schools and churches made demands on my time which took me away from the actual work I wanted to do. It is true that they assisted in a financial way, but that didn't alter the fact that there were only twenty-four hours in each day and that I could expend only a certain amount of energy. I learned years before that when your very existence depends on the generosity of the public, you must remember that two things are vital to your success; publicity and their purse strings.

Each time I appeared on TV or an article appeared in the papers, more demands were made on my time. I was pleased to be recognized, but unhappy with so many demands on my time. Lorna said, "Glenn, quit complaining or get out of this kind of commitment. I notice that, when you are asked to give of your time, you fall all over yourself thanking the caller for the opportunity. Then, when you hang up the receiver, you tell me how tired you are of traveling and talking. Let me answer the phone and I'll tell them that your schedule is full but you would entertain another invitation at a future time. While I'm on the subject, I've noticed that at the conclusion of your talk, you usually invite questions. Always, the entire question and answer period is used up asking you personal questions and asking you to tell of your experiences on Alcatraz. I can understand their interest, but it is little wonder that you are worn out from speaking. People attribute your success in this field to your experience in the criminal arena. The two are interwoven. As I've told you before, you should write your autobiography. If there's that much interest, you could do well. Your story is one that should be told."

We set the date of our wedding for the earlier part of the upcoming December. When the day for the service came, I was nervous. Due to the fact that our dear friend and former pastor, Norman McCue, had left the Fremont Baptist church, Lorna and I had switched to the University Baptist church. The congregation at UBC was dedicated to social issues. They were involved in 'putting their faith to work'. This attracted Lorna and me to their midst. The Reverend Donovan Cook was the pastor. Lorna and I met with him and sought his counselling for our pending marriage. He had a tasteful sense of humor that made it easier for us to accept his counselling. He asked Lorna, "Why do you want to marry this worn-out bus driver?" During our meeting with him, we told him the date we wanted to tie the knot. His disappointment was obvious when he said, "I won't be in town to perform the ceremony. I have a commitment that will take me from the state." We, too, were disappointed. We had become attached to Donovan.

Lorna and I agreed that we would ask Reverend Norman McCue to marry us. We were delighted when he agreed to do so. The wedding took place December 2, 1977. We had decided to make it a quiet ceremony with only family members attending. The ceremony was simple. My intended wife was radiantly beautiful as we stood before the Reverend McCue. I was so damn nervous I couldn't recall what the minister was saying. Fortunately, I remembered to say 'I Do' at the appropriate time. I was relieved when the vows were ended. Lorna's brother, Don, and his wife were kind enough to take care of our children so we could enjoy a brief weekend honeymoon in Vancouver, B.C.

The morning of our departure from our hotel, we decided to eat breakfast in the hotel dining room. Throughout my life I have always had premonitions that seemed to come to pass. On our way down in the elevator, I had the eerie feeling that we were going to meet someone I had known from years before. When the elevator reached the bottom floor, we started down a partition that separated the hallway from the dining room. I could not believe my eyes. Elmer Fjermadal, an ex- employee from the federal penitentiary at McNeil Island, was seated with an attractive lady at one of the tables. He and his wife were celebrating their wedding anniversary. I remembered Elmer with fond memories. He was the instructor of the furniture shop and I was one of his inmate charges. He was a rare individual. He had been able to keep his perspective on life under stressful circumstances. He was remarkable in that he managed to maintain a humane attitude toward the convicts. He was respected by every inmate with whom he came in contact. I had never heard anyone make a disparaging remark about Elmer. If I had to meet anyone from the past, I was delighted that it was Elmer. As Lorna and I were making our way toward his table, he saw me and stood up to greet us. It was a pleasure to introduce him to Lorna. In turn, he introduced us to his wife. When I told him the occasion of our being there, he smiled broadly and congratulated Lorna and me.

27

Presidential Pardon

In August 1978, without my knowledge, Lorna had written a letter to President Jimmy Carter asking him to issue me a pardon. She had listed a dozen reasons why she felt I deserved one. One day, a large envelope arrived from the U.S. Attorney General's office addressed to her. After she had read the contents, it became apparent that she was obviously distressed. I said, "What's the problem, Lorna? If something is bothering you, why don't you tell me and we'll work on it together. Let's not keep secrets from each other." She finally broke down and said, "Honey, I wrote to President Carter and asked him to consider issuing you a pardon. Today I received a packet from the U. S. Pardon Attorney. There were a number of forms enclosed that involved answering dozens of questions. Naturally, I can't answer them. I wanted to surprise you. I was naive enough to think that President Carter would simply send you a pardon. After all, you've been free for more than fifteen years. You have an excellent record. I didn't dream it was going to be such a complicated procedure." She started crying.

I felt sorry for her and gathered her in my arms in an effort to comfort her. When she quieted down, I explained a few facts to her. "In the first place, Lorna, to my knowledge, no prisoner on Alcatraz has ever received a presidential pardon. It is unheard of. You'll never know how much I appreciate and love you, more so now because of this effort on your part. So far as I am concerned, darling, I am not remotely interested in a pardon. I have served the time and owe no man." Her response was quick and left no doubt about her feelings on the subject. "I don't feel you're being fair in not considering my feelings and those of the children when they become older. You certainly deserve a pardon. Your record for the past fifteen years must account for something." When I realized how much this meant to Lorna, I decided to cooperate.

The questions and forms seemed endless. A requirement from the Pardon Attorney was that I was to get three letters of recommendation supporting my pardon application. When I was retained by the Job Therapy Corporation, I met a superior court judge, Robert Utter. He was a warm and humane person, a man of impeccable integrity, respected and highly regarded by all with whom he came in contact. I became acquainted with Judge Utter and had the opportunity to associate closely with him. Notwithstanding I was a recently released bank robber, Judge Utter treated me with respect. One of the last official acts of the Governor of the state of Washington, Dan Evans, was to appoint Judge Utter to the State Supreme

Court. Because of Judge Utter's stature, the appointment met with widespread public approval. I decided to ask Judge Utter if he would write a letter of recommendation to President Carter.

Another man of equal stature and respect, who also served on the Board of Directors of Job Therapy, was Leeon Aller, Jr., M.D. He, too, befriended me at every turn of the road. He constantly exhorted me to keep striving, and to devote my life to helping others. I became fast friends with both of these gentlemen. It was my intention to seek the same assistance from Doctor Aller.

The third individual whom I intended to approach for the same purpose was my dear friend and pastor, The Reverend Donovan Cook of the University Baptist Church. Pastor Cook, Judge Utter and Doctor Aller all were stalwart and highly respected men. I felt fortunate to be able to count them as friends. Each one had substantially contributed to my reformation.

A week after I had completed the questionnaire from Washington, D.C., I found myself sitting with Chief Justice Robert Utter in his chambers where he had so graciously agreed to grant me an interview. I came right to the point. "Bob, I am making a plea for a presidential pardon from Jimmy Carter. It was initiated by Lorna, but this phase of it has to be handled by me. You have known me for a number of years. Both of us served on the Board of Directors of Job Therapy, were co- speakers on a number of occasions and have been friends. You are fully aware of my past. I must get recommendations from three reputable citizens. It's my intention to also seek help from Dr. Aller. Will you furnish a letter of recommendation for me?" I was not surprised by the Justice's warm and spontaneous reply. "Glenn, I would be pleased to do so, and I am happy that you called on me for this purpose." I left his office encouraged, and wondered how such a steadfast citizen could so wholeheartedly come to my assistance.

A few days later I met with Doctor Aller in his Family Medical Clinic. I explained the reason for my visit. He response was prompt and heartwarming. "I am pleased that you came to me for support, Glenn. I believe that if any person in your circumstances deserves a pardon, you're that person. I'll prepare a strong letter of support. You may depend on that." As I left his office, I began to wonder why I had doubts that the individuals I had contacted would hesitate to respond affirmatively. It was at this point that I began to realize that I must have considered myself unworthy of the consideration of my fellow man. Surely this attitude was a result of the many years I had lived in the unreal world of criminals. I recalled my hatred of judges because they represented the law. Yet, the only one with whom I associated turned out to be a true friend, one willing to help me at a crucial time.

The day following my visit with Doctor Aller, I called Donovan Cook and asked him to have lunch with me. He agreed, and when the meal was over, I told him of my pardon application, the three letters of recommendation I needed, and the willingness of Judge Utter and Doctor Aller to write in my behalf. Donovan was elated at the prospect of a pardon and said, "Glenn, if you hadn't asked me to be a party to your effort I would have been disappointed. God bless Lorna for having the faith in you that is shared by the members of our congregation." I was overwhelmed by the response of all three men. Still, I was certain that no president in his right mind was going to pardon a man from Alcatraz.

After the requirements of the Pardon Attorney were met, the documents were returned for his consideration. As I understood the procedure, if the Pardon Attorney felt the application was unworthy of presidential consideration, it would never be forwarded to the executive offices. The Pardon Attorney functioned as a sort of one-man screening committee to protect the chief executive from being inundated with requests. I felt that my application would be 'flushed'. Nevertheless, Lorna was determined to press on with the matter regardless of my negative attitude. So the documents were sent by certified mail. That wife of mine was thorough and determined.

Lorna didn't comment on it for months, though I know she watched the mailbox every day. She made no reference to the application in any of our conversations. I knew that every month that passed she became more disappointed and discouraged. Yet, her faith never wavered. Because of my love, devotion and appreciation of Lorna, I didn't go on my usual tirade of denunciation of the bureaucracy. The more time that passed without word from Washington, D.C., the angrier I became. Throughout the entire nine months that elapsed since the forwarding of the application, Lorna continued to avoid mention of the unreasonable length of time the officials were taking to respond. It was apparent she was not accustomed to dealing with government bureaucracy.

One morning at breakfast, Lorna was tight-lipped and perturbed to such an extent that I asked her if something was wrong. She didn't answer me directly, but said in an offhand manner, "I'm going to take the day off. There are some things I want to do. I'll be back in time to fix dinner." I felt constrained from asking her where she was going. If she had wanted me to know, she would have told me. I later learned that she had gone to the state capitol to see Judge Utter. When she was ushered into his chambers, he sensed she was distraught. In his kind way, he invited her to be seated and asked, "What can I do for you, Lorna?" Without hesitation, my wife poured out her discouragement and frustration and asked if there was some way Judge Utter could help. He agreed to send a letter to Washington State Senator Magnusen in Washington, D.C., with a copy to Lorna. True to his word, we received the copy shortly thereafter.

The months rolled on. It was December 22, 1980, and with Christmas a few days away, our energies were directed toward preparing for our annual trip to Lorna's parents' home to celebrate the holidays. Along with the exchange of gifts and Christmas greetings, the adults enjoyed the laughter of the children as they opened their presents. We left for home late on Christmas Eve. The kids were exhausted and by the time we had driven ten miles, they fell asleep in the rear seat. Lorna laid her head on my shoulder and dozed off. An hour later, she woke up just as I was pulling into our driveway. While she was rousing the children and herding them into the house, I crossed the street and picked up our mail. Inasmuch as the postal department had delivered mail on Christmas eve, our box was overloaded.

I put the mail on the dining room table and went in the other room to take off my overcoat. I had no more than laid it across the bed than I heard a sharp cry from my wife. She was standing in the middle of the room with tears streaming down her cheeks. She was holding a large envelope which she had opened. Without a word she handed me the contents. I was puzzled as I stared at the legal document. The first few words I read left me shocked. They were: JIMMY CARTER, PRESIDENT OF THE UNITED STATES OF AMERICA; TO ALL TO WHOM THESE PRESENTS SHALL COME, GREETINGS; BE IT KNOWN, THAT THIS DAY THE PRESIDENT HAS GRANTED UNTO NATHAN GLENN WILLIAMS A FULL AND UNCONDITIONAL PARDON. I didn't seem capable of absorbing the full meaning of the presidential proclamation. Lorna sat at the table with her head bowed and sobbed. I sat beside her and put my arms around her shoulders. Both of us wept. Previously I had told her that I didn't give a tinker's damn about a pardon, but when I actually received it, I was overcome with joy. We called the family and many of our friends the next morning, and told them the good news. They, too, were overjoyed.

Over the years, I had had many contacts with reporters, TV personalities and persons connected with radio broadcasting. The inevitable happened. Local papers printed stories about the 'guy from Alcatraz who had received a presidential pardon'. The publicity generated more speaking engagements and TV appearances than I could accommodate.

An interesting sidelight to the entire two year ordeal became known when the neighbors read of my pardon. Apparently, the FBI investigated Glenn Williams before the president would take an affirmative action in the matter, really looking into my past over the last decade. Agents interviewed my neighbors, friends, employer and acquaintances. The strange thing was that no one mentioned to me the inquiries the FBI had made until it became known that I was, in fact, pardoned.

A retired FBI agent told me that the Seattle bureau was confident that I would never receive executive consideration. He said one of his agent buddies told him, "Can you imagine giving a pardon to a man with his criminal past? And, on top of it all, this thug was on Alcatraz. He must really be crazy to even dream of such a thing. He's lucky just to be out of the joint." The retired agent and I were in a cafe having coffee about a week after I received the big news. I had to get in my digs. "Chuck, why don't you tell your friends at the bureau that this 'crazy thug' got his pardon from President Jimmy Carter?" The retiree sipped his coffee and replied, "Hell, those guys can read. I don't have to rub their noses in it. The fellow that was so damn certain you would be rejected was astounded. He told his boss, "How an ex-con off the Rock can get a presidential pardon, I'll never know. If J. Edgar Hoover was alive, he'd hang himself."

The tension of long hours of work and the anxiety while waiting for months for word from Washington, D.C. had left us emotionally drained. On top of everything else, the three kids were wearing us to a frazzle. It was a good excuse for us to take a vacation, something we had never had. Lorna and I began to plan a trip to Europe. I had heard there was an International Symposium on Crime and Delinquency in Holland, so I pressured her to consider spending at least three days in that country so I could attend the event. "You attend the affair, Glenn. I don't want to hear or see anything related to prisons while on vacation. This prison, crime and delinquency thing is your bag, not mine."

A few months later, we placed the kids at a farm camp and were on our way to Europe, a first for both of us. Before departing Seattle, while we were waiting in the airport coffee shop, an announcer on the TV told of Nancy Reagan sending a very expensive finger bowl to Prince Charles and Diana for their wedding gift. The astronomical price she paid for the bowl infuriated me. I don't know what got into me. I went to the phone, called my secretary and told her I wanted her to go to the 88 cent store and buy a finger bowl. I instructed her to mail it to Prince Charles in London in care of the Buckingham Palace. She was to send a card with it and sign my name. In addition, I told her to put my home number as the return address. It took some convincing to make her believe that I was serious. I asked her not to pay over one dollar for the bowl. I made her promise me that she would do as instructed and do it immediately. As our plane was taxiing down the runway, I chuckled to myself.

We landed at London's Heathrow Airport nine hours later. From there, a few hours after that, our plane was circling Amsterdam preparing to land at Schiphol Airport. I wanted to find out where the symposium was being held and when. Finding someone with whom we could communicate became a constant challenge. I approached a police officer and asked him if he spoke English. He smiled affably and led Lorna and me across the airport ticketing office and deposited us in front of a young lady behind the car rental desk. He spoke to her in the native tongue and gestured toward us. She asked, "May I be of help to you?" I inquired, "We want to know where the International Council On Crime and Delinquency is being held and when." She picked up the phone and talked to a person on the other end of the line. When she had finished, she turned to us and said, "The group is meeting in Den Haag. They will be in session for two more days."

I thanked her and told her we were scheduled to pick up a car. She took down the required information, asked for our international driving permit and had us in a car within a few minutes.

The freeway to The Hague was just a few blocks from the airport. As I pulled onto the freeway, I got the surprise of my life. The cars were going so fast I couldn't get off the on-ramp. When I finally made it, I goosed the car up to seventy miles an hour to keep up with the traffic. At that speed, the cars zipped past us. It didn't take me long to realize that traffic 'loitered' at eighty miles an hour on this freeway they called the Autobahn. We followed the signs to Den Haag. I don't recall how long it took us to get there, but I was happy to get off the rat-race and on to safe and sane street driving. Trying to find our hotel was another challenge. We were continually seeking out people who spoke English. After what seemed forever travelling in circles, I pulled in front of a cab and pointed to the name Des Indes Hotel on the paper we carried. The cab driver signaled us to pull in behind him, and he had us in front of our hotel in minutes. That afternoon, Lorna and I fell into bed exhausted. We awoke to jovial singing in the pub located just outside our window. We joined the merriment a short time later.

The cost of our room included our breakfast, which we thought was going to be the typical continental breakfast of coffee and sweet rolls. It turned out to be a fabulous feast. While we were eating, Lorna reminded me that she was not going to the symposium but, instead, was going to spend the day visiting museums and art galleries. We agreed to meet at the hotel for dinner that evening.

The cabbie dropped me off at an old but magnificent building which had been converted into a sort of convention hall. When I entered through the massive carved and ornate doors, I was stopped by a man in a uniform that had so many medals pinned on it I don't see how he could carry them around. He spoke in Dutch and, as usual, I replied in English. He motioned for me to be seated. He disappeared down a hall, returning in a few minutes with a distinguished Chinese gentleman in tow. The oriental bowed and asked, "May we be of assistance?" I explained that I was visiting from the U.S. and had just arrived yesterday. I further told him I was involved with the criminal justice system and wanted to attend the meeting. "Where are you from in the United States?" he asked. When I replied that I was from Washington, I was amazed with his change of demeanor. He spoke a few words to the doorman. The doorman graciously ushered me into the great hall. I understood very little of what was going on and felt that my attendance was a waste of time. When I rose to leave, I found myself face to face with the oriental who had spoke the magic words that gained me entry. "It was a pleasure to have you join us, sir. It is an honor that Washington sent a representative from its Justice Department." I stared in disbelief. He extended his hand which I shook briskly.

All the way back to my hotel I was in a quandary. I explained to Lorna what had taken place. She said, "Glenn, I know why they were so cordial to you. They thought when you said you were from Washington that you meant Washington, D.C." Lorna wanted to take a tour of the area surrounding Den Haag. I wasn't interested in guided tours, so I told her I was going to visit Holland's primary institution for first offenders.

In order to find the location of that reformatory, I went to the local police station to get my bearings, and try to determine the possibility of my visiting the reformatory. I had difficulty making myself understood. Finally, at my request, one of the officers got on the phone and contacted someone who spoke English. He spoke in Dutch for a few minutes and then handed me the receiver. I explained, very carefully, the purpose of my going to the police station. He told me to put the officer back on the phone. After the official hung up he was all smiles. To my amazement he directed me to a police vehicle, held the door open and motioned for me to get inside. We drove along a waterfront for maybe ten miles until we came to an area that had the name Den Haag Scheveningen on a signpost at the community's outskirts. A few more blocks and the police car pulled into a long string of very old buildings. The only inkling I got that it was a penal institution was the fact that the main door was locked. When the Dutch policeman knocked, a small door slid open. There were a few words exchanged, and then the massive door swung open. The person who admitted us was dressed in a light grey uniform. He spoke to the officer for a minute, then smiled warmly at me and held his hand out. My escort indicated I was to follow the uniformed gentleman.

As the guard ushered me down long hallways, I passed many shop-like buildings in which young men were working, obviously inmates. We passed through a carpenter shop, a tailor shop and a print shop. I am certain the inmates knew I was a stranger in the country because of their curiosity. Maybe my clothes were different. As they chatted among themselves, I never heard one word of my native tongue. They laughed and grinned at me in every shop.

From the shop line, we entered an area that proved to be the administrative offices. When we stopped in front of a pane-glassed door, the guard knocked. At a signal from within, the door swung open, and I was face to face with a man who most certainly was a person of importance. He was an extremely handsome fellow. The man behind the desk sprung to his feet, came directly to me and reached out his hand. He shocked me when he addressed me in impeccable English. "Mr. Williams, we are pleased to have you as our guest." He knew my name and I understood him. We had a common language between us. As he invited me to sit down, he rang a bell on his desk.

When the door opened again, an elderly woman came in with tea. My host continued. "I am the Governor of this facility. It is my understanding that you have come from Washington for the purpose of looking our system over." Here was that same misunderstanding about which Washington I came from. I tried to explain to him that I was from Washington State. He nodded and smiled broadly. I don't think my comment about the state of Washington registered with him. "Yes," I advised him, "I would very much appreciate going through your institution." He stood, took a hat off the shelf by his desk and said, "I'll personally take you through our facility."

I was tremendously impressed over the difference between our reformatory and theirs, and the kindness and concern of their staff as compared with the cold and suspicious attitude of the guards in the U.S. I learned that instead of being called warden, their chief-of- staff was referred to as Governor. I saw no evidence of bars or armed guards. My questions were answered civilly and honestly. The tour took us through every shop. Without being asked, the workers came over to me and handed me samples of their crafts. The tour ended in the community dining room. Food was served at a table where staff and inmates ate next to each other, and ate the same kind of food. I could tell from the relaxed attitude of the prisoners that eating at the same table as the staff was customary; this was unheard of in the U.S.

As I was conducted to the door leading to the street, the Governor said, "I will have our postal clerk drop you off at your hotel. He goes in for the mail at this time." I turned to him, shook his hand and said, "I can't express my appreciation to you and your staff for the courtesy you have extended. If you ever come to Washington state, please look me up and I will arrange for you to take a tour of our prisons. Incidentally, if this is Holland's minimum confinement reformatory, where do you keep your maximum security convicts?" He told me that there was a more restricted penitentiary on the outskirts of Amsterdam, and that, if I were in that city, he would call the Governor of that prison and arrange for me to have an interview with him. I thanked him again, handed him my business card and stepped into the waiting truck. On the ride back to the hotel, I reflected on what I had seen. The persons in charge of their inmates were not sullen nor defensive. They were immaculately uniformed and had a very professional bearing. During the tour, the Governor had told me that each officer, referred to as a counselor, was well-educated and screened. They had to have a propensity for dealing with men and women. In their profession, they were well-respected in their communities and by their charges. What a contrast to the guards, convicts and prisons in the United States.

We wanted to take in as much of Europe as we could in our limited time, so instead of going directly back to Amsterdam where I could visit their maximum security facility, Lorna made her feelings known in a very few words. "I didn't come all the way to Europe to visit prisons and talk to guards. I want to go to Brussels and then on to Paris to see some of the sights. Before we head for home we can spend some time going through the prison you are referring to."

Brussels was a beautiful city with more history and places of interest than I could have imagined. We spent hours going through castle-like buildings and museums. The following day we took a train to Paris. Knowing nothing about needing reservations, we ran into a hell of a storm. The train we boarded had standing room only. It was so crowded that it was impossible to go to the restroom. Numerous young back-packers had their gear laying in the aisles, so a person could not walk or stretch. However, we were fortunate enough to meet a friendly older couple from Brussels who owned a summer home in southern France. Seeing our dilemma, they insisted that we take turns sharing their seats. Three of us would sit at a time in the reserved seats and one would take a turn standing for awhile.

When we pulled into the train station in Paris, we were exhausted. Our plan was to spend the day in Paris and take an evening train back to Brussels. We spent a pleasant day at the Eiffel Tower, but saw little else. The most beautiful sight I saw when we got back to Brussels was our bed.

It seemed to me that my wife could not get enough of sightseeing. She spent the next day visiting art galleries. I told her I would rather sit on the lawn and watch the grass grow. She returned to our hotel that evening just as I was preparing to have dinner alone. "I was going to tell you about the famous paintings I saw," she said, "but you wouldn't have enjoyed them. They weren't behind bars." I ignored the thrust.

Our return trip to Amsterdam was a leisurely one. We enjoyed the Belgium, German and Dutch countryside. The spotlessly clean small German towns were especially appealing and the windmills of Holland were right out of National Geographic.

The night we arrived in Amsterdam, we spent several hours in the hotel's lounge listening to an accomplished pianist. In the morning, Lorna was more than pleased to accompany me to the penitentiary. As she said the

364

night before, "I'm not objecting to spending some time visiting penal institutions with you, but I don't want to go home and tell my friends that I spent two weeks in Europe visiting prisons. I know that that's your profession, Glenn, but there is a limit."

The desk clerk listened as I told him where I wanted to go. He gave us instructions in detail. But he didn't take into consideration that I could not read street signs, so I became lost. The trip took us twice as long as it normally would have. We spent a good deal of time stopping and asking, "Do you speak English? We're trying to locate such and such". At a service station where we stopped in search of an English speaking person, a police car drove up to the gas pump. I jumped from my car and started speaking in my tongue. He was patient, but lost in trying to understand me. An idea crossed my mind. I pulled out my wallet and extracted the calling card of the Governor of the Scheveningen institution. The officer peered at it for a full minute before a smile broke across his features. He stepped from his car and pointed to a complex of large beautiful buildings about two blocks from our position. The buildings rose more than ten stories high and resembled apartments in an affluent neighborhood. I hesitated, but the officer was determined that that was the place I wanted to find. I was in no position to argue, so I thanked him and drove toward the place he had directed. Even as we drove up to the front door, I was uncertain. By the time I had brought the vehicle to a halt, a uniformed officer stepped to our car, and asked us something in Dutch. I resorted to the calling card I had shown the police officer. He motioned us to a parking area and waited for us to return.

The officer escorted us through the large doors and to an elevator. It rose several stories before it stopped. It was at this point that I realized we were in a secured building. We stepped into a glass cage. Our guide pressed a series of buttons and a door opened to admit us into an office building. We were led to an office in which there were about ten clerk-secretaries. There was a very friendly atmosphere permeating the whole area. We walked to the end of a long hallway and into an office where a young man was sitting behind a desk. Not wanting to go through the hassle of non-communication, I didn't wait for him to say anything. I extended my hand and started right out, "Sir, I'm Glenn Williams and this is my wife, Lorna." Before I could say another word, he immediately stood up and offered his hand. He said, "You two must be the visitors from the United States. The Governor from Scheveningen called a few days ago and said you would be by. I understand that you are involved with the criminal justice system in America, and that you wish to tour our facility. I am the Associate Governor, and I welcome you." Again Lorna and I were surprised and pleased by the manner in which we were received.

Before we began the tour, I asked the associate, "May I take pictures?" He advised me it was permissible, but that if I snapped any of the inmates or counselors, I must first get their approval. He assured me that snapshots of the rooms, hallways, dining area and practically every aspect of the buildings themselves were permissible. The freedom of movement was unbelievable. I was accustomed to the rigid rules and regulations imposed by our penal authorities.

I was struck by the structure of their prison buildings. Not once did we see bars, armed guards or any evidence that we were inside a maximum security penitentiary. As we were led through the buildings, I kept waiting for bells and slamming iron doors which are so prevalent in the institutions of our country. Most of the structures were connected, but on a few occasions we passed out of doors to reach other destinations. It became apparent that the next building we entered was, indeed, the place where the men were confined. The first thing Lorna and I noticed was the control center. It sat in the center of a very wide hallway. The control panel was a series of cameras and buttons. From the operator's position, he could view every room, nook and cranny of the building. He could communicate with every occupant of every room. No loudspeaker blared out while we were there. The hallways were spotless. Smartly-dressed women were evident in number. They walked unescorted down the hallways. I asked the officer in the control center if I could take a picture of the nerve center. He looked at the Associate Governor for approval, then nodded his head. The doors were closed while we went through, but not by design. Most of the inmates were working and were not in that particular area. A few wandered up and down the hall, stopping to speak to both female and male counselors. I could not believe how comfortable my wife and I felt.

When we had finished seeing that area, the associate told us that each area was the same and that time would preclude our seeing them all. From there, we saw the spacious gymnasium, dining room, schoolrooms and chapel. From our upper viewpoint, we could see inmates in a number of yards playing handball and tennis. The complex of buildings was so situated that each building formed a play area. No walls, razor-wire fences or gun towers.

Our escort asked us to accompany him to his office so he could take care of any pressing business. He apologized and said, "I must turn you over to one of my assistants for the afternoon portion of your visit. Other obligations are going to keep me busy for the rest of the day. I want you and Mrs. Williams to know that it was a pleasure to meet and be with you." Once again, he stood and offered his hand to Lorna and me.

Our escort for the afternoon was a Mr. VanAgan, the Assistant Governor. He advised us that we were permitted to see any part of the premises, but I had some questions I wanted to ask. He took us to a sort of coffee-break room and said he would answer any questions if he had the answers. I asked, "Mr. VanAgan, how long has it been since an inmate has attacked or killed a staff person?" He said he had been there fifteen years and had never heard of such an attack. In response to how many attempted escapes take place over a year's time, he told us that one resident had walked away from a transporting officer four years ago. I asked, "What sort of punishment is meted out for serious offenses"? He replied, "Generally, we remove the resident from the work privilege list, confine him to his room for a period of time and restrict him of all privileges except visiting. As a rule, this type of punishment continues for one or two months, depending on the gravity of the offense." I had to interrupt at this point. "Mr. VanAgan, why do you not take the visiting privileges from a resident who had violated certain rules? It is a common practice in our country." He hesitated a moment, then enlightened me on the intelligent and humane method Holland has of handling its inmates. "In Holland, the law forbids the taking of visiting privileges. By law, it isn't a privilege, but a right protected by our constitution. And our individual thinking seems to be that, while the resident has misbehaved, we have no right to punish the families of the residents. Even if we had the authority to impose such punishment, we don't believe it is in the interest of the resident nor his family." "One final question, Mr. VanAgan. What is your limit on isolating a resident who proves intractable?" I asked. He hesitated then said, "If one of our charges proves to be intractable over a lengthy period of time, he is taken before a Board of Counselors, and a psychologist assists them in their efforts to find a solution that will best serve the resident. Often we refer him to our psychiatrist who is empowered with the authority to recommend that the offender be hospitalized. Further punishment is out of the question."

If I intended to shock our escort with my next line of questioning, I was due to be disappointed. "Have you ever heard of The Bird Man of Alcatraz, Robert Stroud?" I was advised that every student of sociology in Holland is familiar with the name and the case. I continued, "Are you aware that he was placed in solitary confinement where he remained for forty-four years?" He answered quickly, "Yes, and I am aware that the penal authorities in America judged him to be a psychopathic killer." He went on, "In Holland, that type of punishment could never take place." The length and type of questioning to which I had subjected him seemed to make him uncomfortable. Finally, I asked him if I could go to the area in which a resident would be locked up.

He was happy to direct us to a unit in another building. To us it seemed to be an exact replica of the other units with rooms on each side of a hall. He led us to a room that had been stripped of all furnishings. It was neat and clean and had a large plate glass window that looked over the city of Amsterdam. I made note of this fact as I had done of all I had seen and heard.

As we prepared to leave, I took special pains to let Mr. VanAgan know how deeply we appreciated him and the Associate Governor. Just before I started to walk to my car, he asked, "Mr. Williams, do you know a warden in the Washington state penitentiary by the name of B.J. Rhay?" I couldn't believe my ears. I replied, "Bobby Rhay and I have been friends for many years. How did you happen to know him?" Mr. VanAgan smiled. "He visited here a couple of years ago. I was one of his escorts. If you see him, please convey my best wishes to him."

I guess I was lost in thought all the way back to our hotel. My wife broke the unusual silence by asking, "Why the solemn face?" I explained to her that I could not believe the difference of attitude and treatment of Holland's prisoners as opposed to ours. I told her I had talked to many penologists who had informed me of the modern method employed in Holland, Sweden, Norway and Denmark in the treatment of their convicts. More than forty years ago, April Anthony, an attorney in San Francisco in a speech before a Kiwanis Club said, "The United States is fifty years behind the Netherlands in their treatment of convicted men and women. The Netherlands has accomplished this feat by taking the profit out of the warehousing of human beings." Lorna appeared to be disturbed by my comments. She asked, "Do you think we're making any advances in this field?" I assured her that I saw nothing to indicate there was a change on the horizon.

When we walked into our hotel lobby, it was filled with tourists who had come to Europe for the wedding of Prince Charles and Diana, which was to take place the following day. The next day we joined the other hotel guests at afternoon tea in a large, luxuriously decorated room set up with a television to view the royal wedding.

Our departure from Europe was complicated by President Reagan's firing all the Air Traffic Control personnel in the United States. This act caused hundred of flights to the USA to be cancelled. There was an unbelievable jam at all airports in the United states. Incoming traffic was at a standstill. Upon our arrival from Holland to Heathrow, we found that airport in a mess. Hundreds of stranded passengers were laying on the floor. There was little room to walk anywhere.

We were lucky to get a cab to take us to our hotel. Lorna and I were gravely concerned. Our kids were at a farm camp and were to be picked up on a specific date, and we were not sure if we would be able to get out of England in a week. Phone lines were jammed. We couldn't call anyone in the U.S. to ask them to pick up our kids. Lorna, who is the calmer one in our family, said, "Glenn, there is nothing we can do but wait this out. Let's take advantage of the time we have. Let's tour Westminister Abbey and see the changing of the guards at Buckingham Palace." We heard that a few planes were now able to take off for America. Retired and substitute air controllers had agreed to man the towers. Heathrow was still jammed from the huge backlog, but was thinning out after each plane departure.

On our way to see the changing of the guards at Buckingham Palace, our tour bus passed a line of people at least a mile long and eight abreast filing into a building about a half-mile from the Palace.

I asked the guide what the lineup was all about and she said, "They're waiting to view the wedding gifts the royal couple received. It is the custom that whenever there is a royal wedding, the gifts are put on display for the commoners to see." Suddenly, I remembered the finger bowl I had sent to Chuck and Di. I started laughing. When I could catch my breath, I whispered to my wife, "Do you know that those people are going in to see the finger bowl that I sent? Wouldn't it be a sight to see my dollar finger bowl among all those gorgeous gifts from around the world?" She refused to answer me.

Neither Lorna nor I had ever seen an event as colorful as the changing of the guard. The crowd was absolutely silent as the horses pranced in precision drill. Upon our return to the hotel, we learned that the airline office had called from Heathrow. When I returned the call, I was told that we were booked for a morning flight out.

By ten o'clock the next morning, we were in the air heading for home. There was not an extra seat left on the plane. It was crowded, but we were relieved to be headed home. Ten hours later, we touched down at the Sea-Tac International Airport in Seattle. Of course it was raining!

28

ALCATRAZ AGAIN!

One evening when I returned from the office, I was confronted by a wife who had that 'I-want-to talk-with-you' look. Normally, under such circumstances, I am subjected to a lecture. She was holding a letter which had arrived that afternoon. She stuck it under my nose. I glanced at the return address on the envelope and lost my breath. I saw there was no actual return address, but instead two words which would have assured its return from anywhere in the world; BUCKINGHAM PALACE. I nervously opened the envelope. The single sheet of stationery read:

Buckingham Palace

From: Rear-Admiral Sir Hugh Janion KCVO

21st September 1981

Dear Mr. Williams,

The Prince and Princess of Wales have asked me to send you their sincere thanks for the useful glass oven dish you have sent.

Their Royal Highnesses much appreciate your kind thought in sending this gift and ask me to thank you most warmly.

Yours Sincerely,

Hugh Janion

I began to laugh. I could not control myself. To think I would receive a thank you from Buckingham Palace for something that was sent in jest. When I settled down, I noticed that Lorna was smiling ever so slightly. She said, "Glenn, you're crazy! Naturally, the proper thing to do is to acknowledge receipt of a gift, and that is what the royal family did in this instance. They have no way of knowing that the 'oven dish' was sent as a joke, in bad taste so far as I am concerned, or whether some nutty American was sincere in forwarding a cheap glass dish to the Prince and Princess." A few days later she was displaying the letter to our family and friends. The letter, royal seal and all, has a prominent place in our scrapbook.

A close friend, who is also a psychiatrist, and I were having a serious discussion over dinner late one evening. He brought up the subject of my relentlessly driving myself. His manner in doing so was kind and done in my best interest. "You push yourself too hard. I've watched you over the

369

years and have come to a conclusion I feel compelled to share with you. It is my considered opinion that you are motivated because of your guilt over the injuries you have inflicted on your family and friends. You're wasting your time, Glenn. Nothing can atone for what you have done. And not one member of your family or friends would want you to carry a burden you can't lay down. It would serve no purpose to them, and can only result in destroying you. You're striving for an acceptance that you have already received, but you refuse to recognize that acceptance. You have devoted yourself to your fellow man for nearly twenty years. You've received recognition as an authority in your field. In the interest of Lorna and the children and yourself, I urge you to learn to relax, slow down and smell the roses before those flowers are placed on your grave." I was so angry that, had he and I not been close friends for so long, I would have severed our relationship right there. He saw that I was greatly disturbed by his comments. He excused himself before I did something unreasonable.

I remained seated, mulling over what he had said. It took some time before I realized he was telling the truth. I simply had a difficult time facing the facts that were so obvious. My mood became reminiscent. My mind flew back to the time I had been called into the warden's office and informed that my beloved father had died. He assured me that I would be able to go to the funeral. I should have rejected the opportunity. Little did my family members understand the hurt and guilt I suffered as I looked at my dad in his casket. Here was a gentleman that had devoted his life to his children. He asked nothing more than they be honest. I turned out to be an outlaw. For a long time after he was buried, I suffered from self-reproach. As the months passed, I forced him from my memory. For a brief time, I was comfortable in the dream that, when I was released, I would make a success of myself in memory of him.

About a year after Dad's passing, I was called into the same warden's office again and told that my mother had passed away. I had always felt that I was truly an unemotional and tough hombre who could face any diversity. As I stood by my mother's casket and gazed at her, I was unable to stop the tears. Good Lord, here was the second beloved parent who left this world without her fondest wish being realized, that she would live to see me back in the family fold. The only shallow comfort I could muster was that she would not suffer anymore. Just as my friend had said this evening, I refused to let the past go into the past and stay there.

Unconsciously or not, I was driving myself unmercifully in an attempt to clear myself of the guilt that I carried. In truth, I was not aware of the underlying reason for my inability to slow down. I believe Lorna knew what I was doing, although she never mentioned it. I never told her until this writing what our friend had said. She then advised me that she had felt this to be true all along.

The summer of 1983, we decided to go on a vacation with our younger son, Don. Don was l4 years of age and really interested in travel. When he learned of our trip, he insisted on planning the itinerary. The main portion of the trip was to visit Yellowstone National Park. We went through Deer Lodge, the home of the Montana State penitentiary. Lorna commented, "I might have known that we would include a prison in our trip." I retorted, "Oh, come on, Lorna. Don and you made up the route and the places of interest we were to visit. I knew that Deer Lodge was in Montana, but I didn't know we were necessarily going through that town. However, honey, I would like to visit the joint as long as we are going to be there."

Don and Lorna walked my legs off taking in the sights at Yellowstone. From there, we drove to Jackson Hole, Wyoming. We were not prepared for the insufferable heat in that area in July. The thermometer registered 109 degrees. It was suffocating and made the three of us sick. Our only hope was to get an air conditioned hotel room. We learned that there were precious few hotel rooms, and the only one we could find had no air conditioning. Without hesitation, we headed for the coast of California.

What a blessing it was to enter the outskirts of San Francisco. Don had gathered brochures from the motel lobby. After lunch, he examined the brochures and marked off places that would appeal to tourists. To this very day, Lorna swears that during this entire trip, I had planned to make Alcatraz one of our stops. I must admit that during our drive to the coast, I did give thought to my old home. I suggested that she and Don visit other points of interest and I would go to the Rock alone. To my surprise she and Don voiced strong objections to my suggestion. Both assured me that they were also interested in visiting Alcatraz.

We hustled over to the Alcatraz pier to board the sightseeing vessel. As we approached the ticket window, we were surprised to see a double line of tourists extending more than fifty feet from the window. I didn't know what to make of it. I made my way to the front of the line and inquired about cost and the time we should board. An employee of the Red And White Fleet, the authorized carrier of passengers to Alcatraz, told us that there was no way we could make the trip today, and maybe not even tomorrow. We could not imagine so many people going to see a vacated penitentiary. He was patient as he explained a fact that left me staring in disbelief. "This is the largest single tourist attraction in California. It's absolutely necessary to make reservations at least one day in advance of the day you plan to go over. I would suggest that you get in the line and purchase your tickets for tomorrow."

Lorna's interest was now really whetted. She was more anxious than I to see what was of so much attraction. I could have never dreamed that average citizens would want to 'tread that painful mile', an expression that cons used among themselves to describe their trek in chains up the steep climb to the cellhouse. We looked at the line and it seemed to have grown in the few minutes we had spoken to the Red And White employee. Lorna said, "Darling, let's stay over a day or two, if necessary. I want to tell my friends at home that I have been on Alcatraz." Immediately, Don voiced agreement. Naturally, I was all for it. We waited in the long line and were able to purchase tickets for the next morning.

We spent the rest of the afternoon visiting Telegraph Hill and riding the Cable Cars. Before we went to sleep, Lorna said, "Glenn, you've led a very interesting, though profligate, life. As Doctor Aller once told me, 'Glenn is the one of a very few ex-cons who has succeeded on the outside, despite almost insurmountable odds. Just coming out of prison makes the chances of success remote, but when you add that to the fact that he was on Alcatraz, success is not in the average con's vocabulary'. Again, I urge you to write your autobiography. Not next week, but tomorrow. I want you to start taking notes in preparation. I'll help you every step of the way." I hugged her, and gave her my promise.

Early the following morning, we ate breakfast and hurried to Pier 41, from which the boat left. At least we thought we were early, but there were more than two hundred passengers already standing at the boarding gate. On that first boat, I counted nearly three hundred and fifty passengers, and I learned that other boats left regularly all day long, seven days a week.

Before our boat departed, I had been watching a handsome, grey-haired man mingle among the crewmen and passengers. He seemed to know everyone. In his Red And White Fleet uniform he was an imposing, rather dignified, figure. He had a voice you could hear clearly from one end of the boat to the other. I watched and listened to him and then realized he must be a tour guide. When he would make a comment to somebody about things on the Rock, Don would turn to me and ask, "Is that the way it was?"

The trip to the Island took about ten minutes. Shortly before we landed at the dock, the uniformed gentleman made his way directly to me. He introduced himself as Frank Heaney. I told him who I was and, in turn, introduced him to Lorna and Don. I admired his straightforwardness when he inquired, "Are you an ex-employee from the prison bureau, Mr. Williams?" I looked him straight in the eyes and replied, "No, Mr. Heaney, I am an ex-Alcatraz inmate revisiting my old homestead." He actually seemed pleased to hear this, and by the time the boat had docked, we were talking like old-time friends. I learned that he had been a former guard, at the age of 21, the youngest guard on Alcatraz. His tenure was before my time. He had worked on the island for about a year. Lorna and I took an instant liking to him.

As the boat groaned against the dock, I looked up at the familiar scene. Try as I did, I could not prevent the sharp aching in the pit of my stomach. It was the same pain that I experienced when I first went to the prison in chains, and on each occasion when I landed while the Indians were in charge. Now, here it was plaguing me again. I glanced at Lorna and Don as they walked up the gangplank to the landing. Neither smiled. They actually appeared distressed at the sight of the foreboding buildings and the ominous gun tower that loomed more than sixty feet into the sky. Lorna's features were taut and drawn. I asked her if she was OK. She assured me that she was. Admittedly, she wondered how I could have survived in such surroundings. "Lorna, you haven't seen anything yet. You'll be going up to the cellhouses and seeing more disturbing sights than there are here. Please prepare yourself for what is to come. Remember, I'm a free man now. The pain of the imprisonment is past." She recovered her composure and told me something of what I had not been aware.

"Honey, Don and I watched your face as we were crossing the bay, and both of us were upset by your pained expression. I think you were living some very depressing moments of your life over again. I wonder if these visits are bad for you, Glenn?" I admitted the obvious. It was difficult, if not impossible, for me to conceal the dread that seemed to strike at my stomach. I tried to convince myself that all the bad memories should be in the past, that they no longer presented a problem for me. This was my third trip to the Rock since I had been released, and you would have thought I would get accustomed to it, knowing that I could leave at will.

Mr. Heaney approached from the Park Rangers' shack and asked me to come to the office and meet with the Alcatroopers, as the rangers were called. I accompanied him and was introduced to six rangers. "One of the reasons these rangers want to meet you, Glenn," he explained, "is to ask you some questions. They're trying to gather as much factual information as they can. A number of ex-guards have volunteered information, but the personnel here wants to hear it from both sides. It's their job to guide tours on the Island, and they are asked hundreds of questions. There are many answers they don't have. Is it OK with you?" I assured him I would be pleased to help where I could. I listened to their spiel to hundreds of visitors, and found them knowledgeable as a result of their study of the history of the prison, its inmates and staff. They refused to let their biases embitter their description of the most famous criminal who had done time on the Island. I found that my description of some of the men with whom I had done time was far more harsh and vindictive than any of those descriptions given by the Alcatroopers.

I had a question I wanted to ask Mr. Heaney, so I cornered him before he took the return boat. "Mr. Heaney, when you sought me out on the boat coming over, I am certain that you knew I was an ex. How did you pick me out, or am I that obvious?" He smiled and replied, "First, may I call you Glenn or Nate, whichever you prefer? In turn, I would appreciate having you call me by my first name. One of the people coming over with us came running up to me and said she had heard a lady in the line talking to a boy, about his stepfather's having done a number of years on the Rock. Naturally, I was interested, so I asked her to point you out. No, you were not a bit obvious. In fact, I said to myself 'that fellow isn't the type you'd find on Alcatraz as a prisoner'. More than likely she had misunderstood you, or you were giving the lady with you a snow job. In any event, I had to ask you." He left to board his vessel, and I walked over to join Lorna and Don for our steep climb to the top of the hill.

During this particular period, in the infancy of the Alcatraz Tour Project, it was the policy of each ranger to take a group on a personalized trek. The ranger would give a brief talk telling a little of the history of the prison and its inmates and then would lead the group on a prearranged tour. As the ranger for our group gave his talk, I felt compelled to tell my wife that he was mistaken regarding certain points. When our group was standing in front of the punishment cells, and he was telling the group about the details of the use of those cells, I quietly told my wife a detail that didn't fit his description. Apparently, I was speaking louder than I realized, because the ranger gave me a sharp look of disapproval. A lady standing next to me asked, "Sir, how do you know so much about this place?" Before I could silence Don, be spoke up loud and clear. "My step dad served lots of time here as a bank robber." A number of others had heard his remark. I was embarrassed. The ranger was doing an excellent job. I was hoping he wouldn't think I was downgrading him. Finally, he addressed me in a loud and clear voice. "Sir, if I am making any mistakes in my presentation, and you know I'm wrong, I would be happy to have you correct me." This situation required delicate handling. I answered him as openly as I could when I said, "I find your knowledge of the complete details of this Island to be remarkably accurate. This group is fortunate to have you conducting this tour. I served a number of years in this prison and, as a result, am very familiar with certain aspects that you could not possibly know. I am sorry to have disrupted this tour." The Alcatrooper smiled broadly and asked if I would please correct him on any erroneous statements he might make.

During the rest of the tour, he encouraged us to walk by his side. Throughout the remainder of our trek, I was stopped by members of our group asking me for pictures and autographs. Before we left, I sought out our guide and apologized. He said he was pleased to have met me and asked me to come to the shack and meet with his buddies and superiors. I told him that I had spent quite some time with them when the boat had docked.

Lorna and Don wanted to be locked up in the solitary confinement cells. They were grim faced, nervous and glad to get out of the cage. I was over my despondency and enjoying the venture. While my family was there, I made up my mind they were going to witness as much of the grim details that were permissible. It was impossible to take them to the dungeons. The Prison Bureau had said they didn't exist, so the rangers were compelled to put up barriers to the halls and stairways with signs that read: Danger. Due To Deterioration, This Section Of the Building Is Closed. I had no doubt that areas of the institution were in bad shape. I had taken pictures of those dungeons and, when I confronted old-time guards with proof of their existence, they contended that those holes were used during the army occupation to store ammunition. Be that as it may, I knew prisoners who had been cooped up in those holes, dungeons that they described in intimate detail before I ever saw them. To be as familiar as they were with those crypts, they would have to have been locked up in them. As one inmate put it, "I nearly died in the dungeons that didn't exist."

It wasn't that I had any startling information to reveal. I simply wanted my family to be fully aware of the nature and extent of the punishment that was meted out. By the time our tour was completed, Lorna and Don were treated to actual sights I had described. They were very well informed of most of the details surrounding the true history of the cruel and inhuman punishment, so successfully concealed, suffered by those men on the Rock. What was surprising to me was their quick recovery from the effects of their visit. Both assured me that it was an experience they would not have missed for the world.

29

"Mr. President"

My volunteer work for non-profit agencies was rewarding in that it gave me a sense of self-worth. In all my life, I had never given of myself or of any material property I possessed. I had sailed through life always on the take. The thought of giving was foreign to me. When I looked back on the years I had devoted to Job Therapy, Attica, Teen Intercept and volunteering with the Food Bank, I fully realized that my life had been enriched beyond measure. Those years had been spent without remuneration, yet I felt I had been well-paid. There isn't any dollar value I could place on the work I had done.

My work with the Food Bank was perhaps the most rewarding. There is a good feeling about delivering groceries for hungry people. I was blessed with a wife who was kind and helpful. However, there were times Lorna would be impatient when I would get home late at night. There was one occasion when she was particularly put out with me. I had been picking up groceries for the Food Bank late into the evening. As I backed the car into our driveway, she turned the porch light on. Then she disappeared into the living room as I started to unload groceries to be sorted and re-bagged to go to the warehouse. For the first time, she did not appear on the scene to assist me. About halfway through the unloading, I figured I would ask her to help. I walked into the living room and found her in a wispy sheer negligee. The only light was from two candles in sterling silver candle-holders on the coffee table. On that table were two champagne glasses, a bottle of un-opened champagne, a single red rose and an envelope with my name on it. On the davenport was my wife. I stood there gaping in wonderment. Without a word, she handed me a lovely card which read: Happy Anniversary, Glenn. It dawned on me that this was our wedding anniversary. What can a man say at a time like this? I stuttered and offered a weak excuse about forgetting. That was years ago, and she has never let me forget it. I don't think I have ever forgotten our anniversary since.

On March 16, 1983 I received the prestigious Jefferson Award, which was sponsored by the American Institute for Public Service in Washington, D.C. The presentation was made at the Sheraton Hotel at a meeting of the Seattle Downtown Rotary Club. Here I was, an Alcatraz alumnus, selected with five others from among 121 nominees. I felt out of my element among such prominent citizens. There are very few possessions I have that I treasure as much as the bronze medallion I received that day. On it was inscribed, GLENN WILLIAMS: IN RECOGNITION FOR OUTSTANDING PUB-

LIC SERVICE. Congratulatory letters came from friends Amos Reed, Secretary, Department of Corrections; Robert Utter, Chief Justice of the State Supreme Court, and Ralph Munro, Secretary of State.

The same month, I received the following letter from the Governor of the State of Washington. It read as follows:

State of Washington

John Spellman, Governor   Office of the Governor

March 29, 1983

Mr. Glenn Williams
2212 - 15th West
Seattle, WA 98119

Dear Mr. Williams:

It gives me great pleasure to inform you that you have
been selected to receive a Governor's Distinguished
Volunteer Award for 1983. Your volunteer service is
an asset to your community and to the citizens of
Washington. I applaud your contribution.

Mrs. Spellman and I invite you to be recognized for the
work you have done during WASHINGTON VOLUNTEER
WEEK at a special Governor's Distinguished Volunteers Award
Ceremony in the House of Representatives Chamber of the
Legislative Building in Olympia at noon on Tuesday,
April 19, 1983. A reception at the Executive Mansion
will immediately follow.

I hope that you can be present. Mrs. Spellman and I
look forward to seeing you.

With best wishes,

Sincerely,

Governor John Spellman

The Award Ceremony was very impressive. Following the ceremony and the presentation by the Governor, Lorna and I were privileged to attend the reception in the Governor's mansion. I was impressed by the graciousness of the Chief Executive and his lovely wife. In a scrapbook put together by Lorna are two pictures from that memorable occasion of which we are very proud. One is of Governor and Mrs. Spellman, my wife, Lorna, and me. The other photo is of my friend, Ralph Munro, Secretary of State and myself.

In 1984, once again, Lorna and I were Rotary's honored guests at the Community Service Award Program. Among the guests were my brother, Dan, and our four children. This was the first occasion to which my family had been invited.

1984 seemed to be the year I was destined to be kept busy responding to invitations to address various audiences throughout the United States. However, none were as welcome as the request I received from Norm Chamberlain, Program Director of the American Correctional Association. In a call to my office, Norm asked me if I would be the keynote speaker at the Plenary Session of the Association's ll4th Congress of Correction in San Antonio, Texas. I was absolutely thrilled to be considered for such an honor. I accepted immediately. The prospect was made more appealing when he told me that my wife was invited to accompany me.

A week later, Lorna and I were guests at the beautiful La Mansion Hotel on the bank of the San Antonio River. No expense was spared to make us comfortable. In Alcatraz, the guards did not welcome me with imported wines, a basket of fruit and chocolate candies, so you can see I was not accustomed to luxury. However, I became adept at accepting such amenities.

Lorna suggested that we visit the Convention Center, where I was scheduled to speak on the following day. The session had begun its program that morning. Until we arrived, I was not aware that there were over four thousand members convening. A huge banner hanging on the wall as we entered the main building took our eyes. ATTENTION MEMBERS; ON THE LOWER LEVEL, WILL BE THE LARGEST DISPLAY OF THE LATEST SECURITY DEVICES FOR PRISON OFFICIALS AND POLICE. My wife was not too interested in spending her time looking over such paraphernalia, but to placate me, she agreed to go along.

Both of us were astounded by the magnitude of the display. They had set up booths for each company that was huckstering its wares. I must have had the appearance of a buyer. From the very first booth, one attendant or another would button-hole me and begin a sales pitch. To make it more interesting, and to learn about the restraining devices, I played the part of a buyer. Every possible invention with which to immobilize prisoners was in one section or another. Among the items displayed were new types of handcuffs, leg irons, gas guns and straight jackets. One of the largest exhibits was a prison bus. The salesman, showing the advantages of his product, cornered Lorna and me and, without any delay, began extolling the virtues of his company's 'safest and most comfortable prisoner transportation bus ever manufactured'. He showed how the cage, by rearranging the movable steel mesh walls, could accommodate more occupants, separate the violence-prone convicts from the more docile. "And," he went on, "this can be accomplished with a minimum of effort and time. The driver and the guard could ride in maximum comfort and security. If, by any chance, one of the prisoners managed to slip his handcuffs, the driver could release a bulletproof sheet of glass to seal off the driver's compartment. Do you have any questions?" I assured him that I did. "You mentioned that in the event a prisoner slipped his handcuffs, the driver could take a counter-move to protect himself. Just a minute ago, my wife and I were talking to a gentleman who sold the very latest in handcuffs and he told us it would be impossible to slip out of the new version of his product." The salesman laughed and moved on to another prospect.

The last stand at which we stopped offered a 'gadget' that was so far ahead of its time it didn't stand a chance of being accepted. However, it has since been utilized as the very latest device to track and keep track of parolees and probationers. It was a band of leather which was to be locked around the releasee's waist. Attached to the band were electronic gadgets which sent signals to a central receiving station. The person receiving the signals could tell by the strength of the signal whether the releasee was within a certain jurisdiction to which he had been assigned. If the signal was weak, it told the receiver that that person was either out of his area or was on his way out. He could immediately warn the officials that the person on parole was in the act of absconding. Believe it or not, it was rejected by most officials as being too much like putting a 'bell on cattle'.

It was just too inhumane. Five years later, a more sophisticated version of the 'cow bell' was being used in most states. It is hailed as being an infallible method by which officials can keep hourly tabs on persons who are under supervision. The device now has the more palatable name of Electronic Home Monitoring Device. Even Lorna, who was adverse to going through what she termed, the convicts' torture chambers, became interested in the contrivances. It was an appalling experience and an education for her.

On the morning I was scheduled to speak, Lorna and I walked from our hotel, along the lovely San Antonio River bank, to the Convention Center where I was to address the Plenary Session. Besides wanting to enjoy the beauty of the river running through the middle of the city, I had another reason I wanted to walk instead of taking a cab; that was to try to rid myself of the nervousness that had overwhelmed me that morning. I did not admit it to Lorna, but I was terrified at the prospect of standing before a group of more than one thousand experts in the fields of law, psychology and criminology. I knew the audience would consist of judges, prosecuting attorneys, wardens, guards, social workers, FBI agents, chiefs of police, sheriffs and related professions. Every person present was there by virtue of his vocation and reputation. And who was their guest speaker? None other than a man whose only qualifications were that he had spent years robbing banks, and trying to figure a way to escape from the clutches of the very people to whom he was to speak.

Anxious not be too early, my wife and I stopped for a cup of coffee. I was stalling until Lorna said, "Glenn, you won't want to walk in a room that is already filled with people. Let's get a move on while traffic is milling around." She led the way into a very large auditorium which was already filling up with association members. On our way to the raised podium, Lorna veered off and took a seat in the front row near the microphones. It was comforting to have her so near me. As I mounted the steps to take a seat near Norm Chamberlain, I felt my legs go weak. I had addressed hundreds of audiences and had never experienced any compunction. But for some reason, I was extremely apprehensive. I could not account for it. It was a relief to shake Norm's hand. He introduced me to Anthony Travisono, Executive Director of the American Correctional Association. We had a few minutes to talk among ourselves, and the camaraderie I felt with these two gentlemen had the effect of relaxing me.

The time came for Norm to introduce me. His laudatory remarks embarrassed me. He referred to me in such glowing terms that I was beginning to wonder if I was the person to whom he was referring. I glanced down at Lorna. She appeared so fresh and confident. When I rose to begin my talk, I was politely applauded. I can't recall what I said. It seemed that I was just running my mouth. There had been no time limit put on me. I found myself wishing Norm had restricted me to five minutes. Half an hour later I was through. To my astonishment, the entire audience rose to their feet and gave me a prolonged and vigorous standing ovation. It was the most pleasant sound I had ever heard. Again I sought Lorna's face. She had joined the others in the applause. Her smile was radiant. People from the audience came to the podium to thank me personally.

As Lorna and I were preparing to leave, a man walked up to me and said, "Mr. Williams, you're the first speaker who came here with such unique qualifications. I'm an architect who specializes in building maximum security prisons. Sometime I would like to talk to you and get some ideas how I might better accomplish the erecting of a penitentiary more escape-proof than Alcatraz." I told him that I would be pleased to talk with him. "However, sir, I feel I would be betraying many of my friends who have devoted a lifetime amplifying on the skills of Harry Houdini."

The last man to congratulate me handed me his calling card. He, too, was an architect who specialized in designing prisons. He thrust out his hand and said, "I am Sol DeLano of San Francisco. I often thought of the improvements I could make on the Island of Alcatraz. I could transform it into a park of unimaginable beauty so far as the land is concerned. The project could be accomplished in such a manner that the trees and shrubs would conceal the monstrosity the government erected there. Now, mind you, Mr. Williams, this could be done without sacrificing the security of the institution. A transformation of this nature would quiet the rumblings of the citizens of the Bay area who want the prison closed. Actually, it would increase the number of tourists who flock on the boats to circle the Island." I listened patiently until he finished then told him, "Surely you're aware that Alcatraz is no longer a penitentiary and, if I am correctly informed, it already attracts many thousands of visitors monthly in its present state and condition." He was quick to say he had heard rumors to the effect that the state of California was going to buy the property and erect a fortress-like prison such as never has been imagined in the world. He continued, "One of the reasons the government closed the Rock was because of the expense of having to carry water to the Island by barge. I'm certain the state would lay a huge water pipe from San Francisco." I bade him good-bye, saying that my wife and I had had a very tiring day, and wanted to get to our hotel for some rest. When she and I were out of earshot, Lorna looked at me and said, "I've heard everything."

The next day, we took in some of the local historical sights. We visited the Alamo Shrine and some of the local missions. Our last evening there, we took advantage of our time alone without the kids and sat at a table on the patio adjoining the hotel sipping drinks and being serenaded by Mexican guitarists and singers. We ended the evening by having dinner at a nearby restaurant that featured flamenco dancers and a talented guitarist. The next morning Lorna and I were on the plane heading for Seattle. A month after our San Antonio trip, Mr. Travisono presented me with a handsome commemorative plaque, a gift from the members of the American Correctional Association.

A number of months passed in which I had time to settle down to a more normal life. However, that tranquility came to an end with the nationwide publicity that announced a program initiated by Nancy Reagan. It was supposed to have been a one-of-a-kind national project for the purpose of redirecting our youth away from the scourge of drugs which was sweeping the nation. Nancy referred to it as the Chemical People Project. The details were skimpy as to how the effort would be coordinated. The announcement certainly resulted in a big send-off from the media. I was particularly interested in Nancy Reagan's involvement in this area, realizing it would take a monumental effort from the upper echelon of government if anything good was to be accomplished. While the President's wife was not 'in' government, it was implied that the President would be behind her. In fact, it was expressly stated that he gave his approval after considering the possible political ramifications.

One morning as I was parking my car in front of my office, I was surprised to see my secretary running to greet me. She was out of breath as she gasped, "Glenn, there is a call from Washington, D.C., and they're on hold." By the time I got to my desk, I, too, was breathless. I picked up the phone and said, "Glenn Williams speaking." I thought it was one of my friends calling to give me hell. A feminine voice came on the line saying, "Mr. Williams, this is Mrs. Reagan's social secretary. She has asked me to request your presence at breakfast on.........." That was as far as she got. I was in a bit of pique on that morning and was in no mood for what I thought was a gag. I responded, "Yes, I would be happy to have breakfast with Nancy, but she will have to come to Seattle. My schedule is too full for me to be taking any trips." The lady came back on the line with, "Sir, it is her intent to be in Seattle for the introduction of her Chemical People Program. You will be receiving a formal invitation from Mrs. Reagan in a few days, and we hope you will be available for the breakfast." The phone clicked and went dead. Silently, I cursed myself for making a fool of myself.

Within a few days, the invitation to the Nancy Reagan breakfast arrived. It gave the date and hour I was to be at the Seattle Westin Hotel. On that morning, I arrived early. It was interesting to watch the security personnel place armed officers at strategic intervals. The entrance was filled with city policemen. The streets surrounding the building were barricaded. Only police vehicles were in evidence. As I approached the door to the lobby, I was confronted by a secret serviceman. Politely he asked, "May I help you?" I showed him my invitation. I was then directed to a hallway on an upper floor. When the escalator reached that level, I saw at least twenty others who were obviously her guests. A lady was placing name tags on each of us. We were ushered into a lavishly furnished dining room. What I thought was going to be a limited number of diners, turned out to be a large affair.

Shortly after we were seated, in came Nancy Reagan flanked by so many men and women, she wasn't too much in evidence. The usual speeches took up at least an hour. During the talks, breakfast was served. When we had finished eating, Nancy was introduced. She explained what she wanted to accomplish with her Chemical People program. All through my experience in dealing with juveniles, as well as adults, I strongly believed the real culprit was drugs. I was willing to be a crusader against drug pushers and addicts. As we filed out past Nancy Reagan's seat, she greeted each of us. When she shook my hand she said, "It was a pleasure to have you with us, Mr. Wilson." I glanced at my name tag. In large letters, it read MR. WILLIAMS.

Within two months, the program seemed to be at an end. It wasn't funded or organized. Four meetings were held in my office. At the first meeting, fifteen people were there, at the second, six and at the third, four. None showed up at the last get-together. I contacted friends in other states and learned that the Chemical People Project had no offices or phones. None were even listed in directories. When it was introduced, I was confident it would fly. I was very disappointed.

For more than a year, I had been working on my autobiography. There always seemed to be some interruption; the progress was very slow. Lorna, who had been pushing and prodding me to work more steadily on the book, was becoming more insistent. She had a cunning way of motivating me. "You're no longer a kid, Glenn, so get on the ball. I'm tired of hearing you say you will have it finished in no time. May I remind you that you told Ralph Munro in 1970 that you were thinking of writing your life history, and he urged you to do so? I am going to contact him and tell him you are still 'thinking'." I reminded her that, from the time I had first decided to start the book, many things took place that were of importance to the manuscript. She bounced back with, "Certainly. But I don't want your obituary to be one of them." I pondered the consequences of assault and battery, and decided to hold my peace. In moments of serious thought, I often felt that I had a story that would be interesting to write about. So, sporadically, I made notes. I had thousands of notes, but no organized outline.

At my age, I should not be subjected to what happened to me in April of 1984. My work had stacked up so high on my desk that, on this particular morning, I had attacked it before 6:00. There was no one else in the office this early, so I felt I could accomplish a great deal before the others started to arrive. The phone rang and I cursed to myself. "Who could be bothering me at this hour?" It was an effort to be polite as I inquired, "Hello. May I help you?"

I cradled the phone on my shoulder so I could keep on working, and waited for the message. A lady with a very refined voice and phone manner asked, "Is this Mr. Williams?" I assured her it was. I nearly fell out of my swivel chair when she continued, "Mr. Williams, I am President Reagan's social secretary. The purpose of this call is to tell you that you have been invited to have lunch with the President and receive a volunteer award at the White House on May 7th of this year." Before she went any further with her spiel, I started to retort testily, "Tell Ronnie that I will be scheduled that day, but if he wants to take Air Force One out for the following day, I can give him an hour or two." I nearly committed the same faux pas that I did when the call came concerning breakfast with Nancy Reagan. I held my tongue. However, I did express disbelief. "I can understand your hesitancy, Mr. Williams. You may not believe it, but yours is not the first expression of disbelief I have heard. There are two ways I can assure you that this is a bona fide invitation; I can give you my phone number and have you call back, or you can wait to receive the written invitation which will be mailed out this week." I was at a loss for words. Stuttering replaced my normal voice. "I have friends who pull practical jokes on me, and I was sure that this was one of those occasions. I would be honored to have lunch with President Reagan."

Immediately, I got on the phone to tell Lorna what had taken place. She, knowing what a practical joker I am, was skeptical. However, she could tell by my awed tone of voice that I was serious. I told her we'd talk about it at dinner that evening.

I was sitting at my desk stunned when my secretary walked in. She took one look at me and asked, "What's wrong, Glenn? You look pale." Before I replied, I took the pile of papers in front of me and swept them into a drawer. I knew full well that there would be no more tasks completed by me that day. "Bonnie, I want to take you out for breakfast. I haven't eaten yet, and I cannot function until I have my coffee." While I was waiting for my ham and eggs, I told her about the phone call. "Do you believe me?" She smiled and told me, "Yes I do. You see, I wrote the President more than three months ago. I told him about your unbelievable past, your striving to atone, your successful efforts in helping ex-cons, and of your own personal recovery. I even told him that former President Jimmy Carter granted you a full and unconditional pardon. I stated that you were the only ex-Alcatraz inmate ever to receive a presidential pardon. I'm happy for you." I thanked her profusely.

That evening, Lorna joined me for dinner at our favorite restaurant, Louie's Cuisine Of China. It seemed that on every occasion to celebrate, my family and I always chose Louie's, one of Seattle's finest Chinese restaurants. It was an appropriate setting to discuss the phone call from Washington. I asked to be seated at a more remote table away from the traffic. Art Louie smiled and said, "Either this is your anniversary or your wife's payday. In either case, I'll wager that Lorna pays for the meal." We sipped our cocktails before I began discussing the Washington D.C. invitation. "Are you sure that it isn't one of your friends pulling your leg?" she asked. I told her that the lady who called had offered to give me her phone number, and that I could call back for verification. That seemed to satisfy my wife. However, she said she would not tell any of her friends, nor actually believe it, until we had the invitation in our hands. A week after I had received the call from D.C., an envelope came with the return address as THE WHITE HOUSE. I pulled the card from the envelope and read:

THE PRESIDENT

requests the pleasure of your company

382

at luncheon

On Monday, May 7, 1984

at eleven-fifteen o'clock

Please Enter Southeast Gate

It was official that I had been invited to have lunch with President Ronald Reagan. A few days later, I received a packet containing many details of the event. Two airline tickets were enclosed. Lorna and I were delighted to learn that I could bring one guest. I teased my wife and told her that I wanted to take a former girlfriend.

As though it were coordinated, numerous news stories by syndicated columnists, public service announcements by major radio networks and TV outlets nationwide carried the story. Some of the headlines read: "FROM HARDCORE CRIMINAL TO LUNCH WITH PRESIDENT REAGAN", "CRIMINAL-TURNED-HERO TO HAVE LUNCH WITH PRESIDENT REAGAN", "FORMER ALCATRAZ INMATE TO DINE WITH PRESIDENT" and "QUEEN ANNE BASED DRUG PROJECT EARNS PRESIDENTIAL ACCLAIM". As my wife scanned the headlines, she commented, "Aren't these more refreshing than previous headlines of the past which depicted you as an incorrigible bank robber?"

Each TV station and newspaper carried stories of their local recipient, but the one I most appreciated was written in my hometown paper, The Wenatchee World. It is amazing where paths cross with old friends and acquaintances as the decades pass. The Executive Editor of The Wenatchee World, and the Editor and Publisher, Robert W. Woods and Wilfred R. Woods, respectively, were men with whom I had attended school in my youth. Fifty five years later, I met Bob Woods in the Washington state capital where he and I were being honored as recipients of the Governor's Volunteer Award. When his name and his position as Executive Editor of The Wenatchee World was announced, I knew that he had to be my old school friend. I made it a point to confront him over tea at the Governor's mansion. Of course we would never have recognized each other. Without hesitation, I told him who I was and the circumstances under which I remembered him. I explained that I was Wenatchee's bad boy, where I went from that period of my life and what I did. Out front I told him that I had spent a lengthy term on Alcatraz. He simply stared at me in disbelief. He asked the logical question, "What are you doing here?" I filled him in with the details of my life since I was released, and told him of my full and unconditional pardon from President Carter. By this time, the reporter part of him took over, and he took a pad from his pocket and made notes as I talked. A week later, I received in the mail a copy of The Wenatchee World. In it was an article under his by-line. Using the vernacular of the Apple Capitol of the world, he headlined the article, One 'Bad Apple' Turns Into 'Extra Fancy'. He wrote of the highlights of my life including the fact that I was to have lunch with President Reagan.

Even as far away as Worcester, Massachusetts, the staid and conservative Paul Revere Companies, for whom Lorna worked as the Seattle agency office supervisor, occupied the first page of their in-house newspaper to headline the story of her husband's Presidential Award for volunteer work. I asked Lorna how her home office became aware of the Presidential invitation because I knew Lorna was always hesitant to mention my criminal past until people got to know me well. She advised me, "Fay Setran, our friend who works in the agency with me, told the visiting home office auditor the story. In his enthusiasm, he carried the story back to Worcester and the company publicity department."

Friends from across the U.S. called to congratulate me. One of the most crazy calls came from my Alcatraz buddy, JB. He asked, "Nate, will you put the pressure on Ronnie for a pardon for me? I know you can swing it, fella."

The month we waited for the actual flight to Washington was the longest month I ever experienced, with the exception of a month before my release from the Rock. But that day arrived, and Lorna and I boarded our plane for the journey. We were two happy people. We had clipped a picture from the local paper of the only other person selected from Washington state, and recognized her on our flight. She was as excited as Lorna and I were. The most thrilling part of the flight was our final approach to the Dulles International Airport as we circled over the Capitol. Lorna commented, "In about twenty-four hours, we will be dining with President Ronald Reagan in The White House. I must be dreaming."

Persons who helped with the coordinating of the award event were on hand to drive us to the J.W. Marriott Hotel, where reservations had been made to accommodate the winners of the award. Including their spouses, there were about twenty guests. The opulence of the lobby of our hotel took my breath away. Before the night was over, we had been told that the J.W. Marriott was the guest house chosen by senators, congressmen and visiting dignitaries. The magnificent chandelier glistened like a thousand diamonds. The other appointments were equally impressive, all done in good taste. I was surprised that the government would house us in such luxury. My mind has always had an odd way of making comparisons, as it did in this instance; as an example it flashed back to thirty years ago when the same government ensconced on an idyllic Island in San Francisco Bay, a hostelry recognized for its security and indescribable social amenities.

We went to a meeting that evening with our coordinators. We were told when and where we were to meet the following morning. We were taught an interesting lesson in etiquette by some person who knew just how you are expected to act in the presence of the President. Until she came along, I was confident I'd experience no problem with meeting the chief executive. After she got through, I was paranoid.

As a precautionary measure, we were told not to walk any distance in Washington, D.C. alone at night. Our advisor ended the warning with, "The is one of the most criminal-ridden cities in the country." Inasmuch as the government was picking up the tab, Lorna and I decided to eat in the luxurious restaurant adjacent to the hotel. We sampled every exotic item on the menu, most of which we could not pronounce. My wife and I didn't see the tab. Thank God! We slept soundly the night before out trek to the White House.

When we woke up on the morning of our luncheon appointment, neither Lorna nor I were hungry. In addition to the late heavy dinner the previous evening, we were nervous with excitement and anticipation. I was certain that the other award winners were in the same boat. We were to leave for the White House at ten o'clock, so we had a couple of hours to kill. Lorna said she wanted to take a tour of our hotel surroundings. While she was doing this, I read the Washington Post. Lo and behold, it carried a lengthy story about the Presidential Awards program at the White House. As I was struggling with the crossword puzzle, my wife returned from her tour. With another hour to pass, we had tea and coffee in the hotel's cafe. Before we had finished, our names were called over the public address system. Our driver was waiting for us in the lobby.

The trip to the White House took only a few minutes. We were deposited at the Southeast Gate. At least fifty men and women were milling around waiting for admission. I walked over to a policeman and struck up a conversation with him. He knew what we were there for, so when I asked him why there were so many people when less than twenty award winners were invited, he laughed loudly and said, "Every political hanger-on shows up on such occasions. Their very lifeblood depends on being seen entering or leaving the White House. And only God knows how many Secret Servicemen are mingling with the crowd. Then you have a dozen or more reporters. TV cameramen and their helpers are in the group also. An event of this nature makes for excellent media coverage. As a rule, when ten people are invited to the White House, from out of nowhere three dozen show up. They have to be people of means or security would oust them. Believe me, the Secret Service misses nothing."

Within minutes after my conversation with the officer, the massive gate leading to the While House grounds swung open. Three or four plainclothes men stood on each side of the gate. About ten feet inside there was a table set up. A man standing beside the table with a portable P.A. system announced, "Those of you with passes line up in front of the table. All others, step off the premises."

It was interesting to note that very few left. I could not guess how many remained. Lorna and I were at least twentieth in line. From the number of men watching the group in front of the table, I am certain a sparrow could not have approached the White House without being apprehended. It would have been easier to crack the mint at Fort Knox than to get past that barricade. When it was our turn to face the interrogator seated in front of us, Lorna was ahead of me. He eyed her carefully, asked for her invitation, eyed her again, asked for her social security number, which he compared with the one on her invitation. He nodded his head and Lorna walked around the table and lined up with the others. I was subjected to the same procedure. Within half an hour, our group was told to follow the uniformed guard.

The door through which we were to enter had an Alcatraz-like appearance. Directly inside the door, we were brought face to face with a large mechanical stool pigeon (the name convicts put on a similar device used to screen moving inmates). If anybody had been carrying a piece of metal, an alarm would have sounded. We were stripped of anything that might activate the detector. Once the officials were satisfied that we were clean, they led us up a flight of stairs to a room where we were to be briefed. The only thing I remembered being said was, "When you enter the dining room, you will find your name on a place setting on one of the tables. Please seat yourself at that table. We ask you to remain seated until the band strikes up 'Hail To The Chief'. At the time the President enters the room, you will be expected to stand and applaud him. Wait until he is seated before you sit down. You are not to get up from your table until the ceremony is over and the President prepares to leave, at which time you may stand and applaud him until he has left the room. Those who will be called to the podium to receive their commendations and medallions will be permitted to stand."

Only when the man was through talking did I notice that the room was decorated and painted in a soft blue hue. The luxurious furniture was of matching color. I missed the significance of the color scheme until we were guided through a number of adjacent rooms, each of a different color.

While the other recipients and I were getting our briefing, Lorna and the other guests were having refreshments in one of the adjoining rooms. Leave it up to Lorna to meet a celebrity by the name of Nanette Fabray, a prominent actress who had starred in Hollywood at the time Ronald Reagan was in his prime. She was still a lovely lady who appeared to be ten years younger than she actually was. To this day, one of Lorna's prized possessions is a snapshot taken with Nanette.

Prior to going into the dining room, we were escorted on an in- depth tour of the White House. As I stood in awe at the resplendency of the carpets, murals, furniture and the huge decorative urns, I then, for the first time in my life, could understand the absolute necessity of taxes upon taxes being levied. Spaced at regular intervals were members representing every branch of the armed services. It was truly impressive. I cannot possibly describe the splendor of the dining room. Waiters stood at attention at their stations. Strategically deployed around the room were men dressed alike in dark blue suits. From their demeanor, I figured them to be secret service operatives whose sole purpose was to protect Ronald Reagan. I counted about ten whom I was certain were guards. Lorna and I did not share the same table, but I caught her eye and nodded toward an opposite wall where there were dozens of TV cameramen and their assistants. Reporters were everywhere. It reminded me of what the officer had said before we entered the grounds. "An event of this nature makes for excellent media coverage."

While I was occupied casing the joint, the band began playing that familiar tune, Hail To The Chief. Immediately two men on each side of a door stiffened to attention. I had no idea where the President would come in, so I simply watched where most eyes were glued. Sure enough, the door was opened by two aides and, as though in trained unison, everyone in the room stood and clapped loudly as the President of the United States entered, accompanied by a retinue of a dozen men.

While I had never been a Ronald Reagan fan, I had to admit he carried a magnetic air about him. His personality seemed to be directed to each person in the room. The sweeping manner with which he waved his hand made you think he was personally saluting you. His smile was warm and sincere. He was strikingly handsome. Lorna's table was so situated that the President had to pass much closer to her than to me. She was so busy ogling Ronald Reagan for the rest of the evening, I could not catch her eye again. A twinge of jealousy swept over me.

As soon as the President was seated, the waiters moved with precision and began serving the food. I noted that the waiters were all tall black men in contrasting white jackets and black trousers. They were very well-rehearsed. It was amazing how quickly they had the food before each diner. About three years prior to my sitting at that table, I read where Nancy purchased an $8,000 set of china to replace the existing White House china. I would not recognize expensive china from the dishes purchased at Woolworths. However, I wanted to say I had eaten from the finest china available. I don't know whether it was because I was eating with the President of the United States, or because it was free, that it was the best prepared and tastiest meal I had ever consumed. The menu read:

LUNCHEON
The President's
Volunteer/Action Awards

Cold Shrimp Bisque
Cheese Twists

Supreme of Chicken in Orange Sauce
Wild Rice
Green Beans Amandine

Lime Mousse

Frefethen Johannisberg Reisling 1982

THE WHITE HOUSE
Monday, May 7, 1984

Throughout the entire meal, I noticed that all eyes seemed to be on the President. He was chatting affably with his dinner partners. Occasionally he would speak to someone at another table. I don't remember how long the meal lasted, but as soon as I had finished my lime mousse, the waiter was at my side to clear the plates. This was a signal to me that the 'main event' was going to take place shortly. Try as I did, I couldn't help but be nervous. All of the joking I did previously about how I was going to act when I came face-to-face with Ronald Reagan, proved to be just that, joking. I glanced at Lorna and was comforted by her smile of confidence. I wondered if she was aware that I really dreaded the next hour. She had a way of seeing through me and my facades. My return 'thumbs-up' gesture did not impress her. I found myself wishing she were at my table so I could squeeze her hand.

A number of men arose from the table at which the President was dining. I recognized former Governor George Romney of Minnesota to be the first person to stand. He stepped back so the President could precede him to the podium. Governor Romney proved to be a very capable emcee. He told the gathering that the purpose of this dinner was to bestow national recognition and honors to a group of dedicated men and women who had served their fellow men unstintingly and without thought of benefit to themselves. He then introduced the President of The United States, whom he said would personally greet, commend and present to each individual a medallion bearing the signature of the Chief of State.

When Ronald Reagan rose to step to the podium, his first few words were drowned out by the thunderous applause of the assemblage of persons. I remember hoping that we would be called alphabetically to accept our accolades. I was uncomfortable with the thought that, quite possibly, I might be summoned first. Another fear that overcame me was that each of us might be asked to say a few words. Damn, but this award thing was taking its toll on me. Again, I looked in my wife's direction. She was still clapping for all she was worth.

The President's talk was brief and to the point. He reiterated what Governor Romney had said and stated, "The distinguished Governor George Romney will assist me in the presentations." On a table beside the podium were boxes which held the medallions. Governor Romney stepped to the mike and called out the name of the first recipient. As the lady approached the few steps leading up to the podium, she was very graciously greeted by President Reagan, who extended his hand in a warm gesture of welcome and congratulation. It was so apparent that he had a way of relaxing those whom he knew were apprehensive. He spoke to each one, calling them by their first name. Once again, I thanked God that there were others preceding me. As each person shook hands with the President, TV cameras whirred and flash bulbs exploded from the reporters section. It was apparent the President was talking briefly to each recipient. However, they were too far from the microphone for me to catch their response.

Prior to the dinner, each guest had been handed a brochure. On the cover was the Presidential Seal. Emblazoned across the front were the words, THE PRESIDENT'S VOLUNTEER ACTION AWARDS, 1984. From across the United States, 2500 nominations were received. Of that number, twelve individuals and seven corporations were selected to receive this most prestigious award for volunteer service. My picture and a description of my volunteer work, as well as mention of my tenure on Alcatraz, were included.

I estimated that each presentation took less than three minutes, so within twenty minutes, I was standing in front of the President shaking his hand. My nerves had settled down and, oddly enough, I was comfortable with this warm personality. Governor Romney gave a brief outline of my history including mention of my term on Alcatraz. He then went on to praise me for my work.

Since my release from the Rock, I had never hidden my past. My record had been printed in dozens of newspapers across the country giving, in great detail, my full criminal history. I had appeared on numerous TV programs and talk shows over a period of twenty years and, not once did I give second thought to the fact that my past had been revealed. I was inured to embarrassment or shame. No man can erase the past by concealment. It struck me strangely that a twinge of resentment swept through me when Governor Romney made pointed reference to Alcatraz. He did so with no rancor. He was simply quoting what had been announced previously. Nevertheless, when the name of that disgraceful prison was mentioned, I detected a hush falling over the room. As the President shook my hand, he said, "Glenn, I am very proud of what you have done with your life and what you have given the citizens of this country." I thanked him and then said, "Mr. President, I bring you greetings from the Honorable John Spellman, Governor of the State of Washington." As I turned to exit, Governor Romney took my arm and asked me to face the camera so a frontal photograph could be taken. I jokingly told him that the post office had many of them on hand. As I walked back to my table, I was surprised how many men and women reached out to shake my hand.

Those at my table asked me to autograph their menus or programs. One lovely elderly lady leaned over and quietly whispered, "You don't look like a bank robber." I squeezed her hand in appreciation. As the guests rose from their seats to leave, I was approached by a White House correspondent. He requested my appearance at a press conference on the White House lawn. I was shocked. A press conference on the White House lawn! I responded, "You must have a dearth of newsworthy stories to be calling on me." He laughed and replied, "Not so. You are the first ex-Alcatraz inmate I have ever met. And you don't really fit the mold." Just as he took me by the arm to lead me out, Lorna walked up and gave me a warm embrace. " I am so proud of you, Glenn," she said quietly. I introduced her to the reporter and told her I was on my way out to a news conference. If it hadn't been for the reporter leading the way, I would have been lost in the maze of halls, doors and rooms leading to the beautifully manicured grounds.

I had heard of the news conferences given on the White House lawn, but I was totally unprepared for what faced me. There were a battery of reporters representing the Washington Post, The New York Times and the Christian Science Monitor. One aggressive reporter, without asking my permission, took the box in which I was carrying my medallion and draped the medal around my neck by the red, white and blue ribbon to which it was attached. Flash bulbs nearly blinded me. I have no idea how many reporters were questioning me at the same time. Nor do I remember what their questions were. I vividly recall, however, that the one question of paramount interest concerned Alcatraz and whether I personally knew Al Capone, Baby Face Nelson, Machine Gun Kelly, John Dillinger, Creepy Karpis, and a host of others. My responses were yes and no; some I did and some I did not.

A reporter from the National Enquirer asked if he could do a story on me when I returned to Seattle. Before I could respond, Lorna, from out of the background, informed the man that she handled such matters in Seattle, and we would entertain his request at a future date. Later I asked Lorna why she had made that statement to the reporter. She said, "You can do without publicity from a publication of that sort." Dan Sutherland, a reporter from the Christian Science Monitor's Washington News Bureau asked if he could contact me in Seattle for a story. Less than a month later, he interviewed me over the phone.

By two o'clock that afternoon, Lorna and I had returned to our room. We both were exhausted but elated. We sat and made our plans for the rest of our trip. We wanted to visit the museum at the Smithsonian Institute, the many monuments and, above all, I insisted that we take a tour of the FBI headquarters. "After all," I kidded her, "I did contribute to some of its history." As I was removing my suit jacket, we became aware of the medallion around my neck. It was the first opportunity we had to examine it in detail. It had come in a Tiffany box and classic drawstring bag typical of Tiffany creations. The box was lined with deep blue velvet. On the lid of the box, printed in silver, were the words, THE PRESIDENT'S VOLUN-TEER ACTION AWARD. Neither Lorna nor I had realized, initially, that Tiffany had created this sterling silver medallion expressly for the presentation. The face was engraved with the Presidential seal and the back of the medal was personalized with the recipient's name and the President's signature. Throughout my career, I have received a number of plaques and other articles of recognition, but this medallion was to become the most treasured.

That afternoon Lorna and I were invited to the offices of the Senators from Washington State, Dan Evans and Slade Gorton. They were lavish in their praise of the work we had done in the volunteer area of Washington state. I had met Dan Evans when he was the governor of Washington. On one occasion, he had presented me with a commendation in recognition of the work I had done in the criminal justice division. Before we left, they had their official photographer take pictures of the senators and us. From their offices we went to meet with our Washington State Representative, Joel Pritchard, and also had our picture taken with him.

Later in the afternoon, Lorna and I toured some of the D.C. places of interest. I don't think there was a monument in the capitol we missed. An interesting part of our tour was the two hours we spent in the Smithsonian Institute. We had to hurry back to our hotel and freshen up for a reception being held that evening in the Sam Rayburn Building to honor the volunteers. By the time we arrived at the reception, the hall in which it was held was filled with many people. Other than one or two recipients of the award, Lorna and I did not know a soul. We were subjected to a few long speeches.

During the course of the evening, I heard someone address one of the guests as W. Clement Stone. The name took me back to twenty-five years ago. W. Clement Stone is one of the giants of the insurance industry. While I was a convict on McNeil Island, I was the program director of a group we call The Self-Improvement Group. It was organized by the Catholic chaplain and some of the inmates. Its purpose was to encourage the inmates to pursue goals of self- improvement. Often we would invite successful men to come to the Island to be our guest speaker at our weekly get-together. I had read about W. Clement Stone and his remarkable career, so I took a chance and wrote him requesting his presence at one of our meetings. The warden, who had to approve all who came to the prison, laughed aloud and said, "Williams, I have to admit, you shoot for top guns. Stone is a multimillionaire who resides over a huge conglomerate of insurance companies. Are you of the impression he will just drop his empire and come to a prison to exhort some cons to better their way of life?" Even before I took the letter out for the warden's approval, I felt I was asking too much. Nevertheless, I couldn't lose by making the effort. I sent it.

To the amazement of everyone, including the warden, W. Clement Stone graciously accepted our invitation. He arrived on schedule and delivered one of the most dynamic talks we had ever heard. After the meeting, he had dinner with the cons. Before leaving, he told me that he genuinely appreciated the invitation, and that being with us was one of the highlights of his career.

Now, a quarter of a century later, W. Clement Stone was meeting with some of the most prominent dignitaries in government. I scanned practically every man in the room, but couldn't see anyone who resembled the man whom I had met many years ago. I knew he would be quite elderly, so I sought out those with grey hair. Also, I remember him as a man just a little over five feet tall. Eventually I narrowed it down to one person. He was a fellow with coal black hair and a thin black moustache. I looked him over carefully, but could not imagine that he might be Mr. Stone. I did the next best thing. I approached an officer and asked him if he knew a Mr. Stone and, if he was present. "Certainly," the uniformed man boomed, "Everyone knows Mr Stone. There he is over by the faucet." I looked over to where he had indicated and, sure enough, it was the small black-haired man whom I had seen before. I told Lorna the story of his prison visitation. I walked nearer to get a better look. Yes, it was W. Clement Stone. His hair and moustache were dyed black. Therefore, he appeared to be much younger than his eighty years. He had to be the fellow I had met long ago.

Lorna was reluctant to have me ask him if he was W. Clement Stone. Nevertheless, I walked up to him, excused myself and asked, "Sir, are you W. Clement Stone?" He drew back, puffed himself up to his full height and answered in a somewhat imperious manner, "Yes. May I be of assistance to you?" Not being a shy person, I came right to the point. "I was imprisoned in the federal penitentiary on McNeil Island, Washington about twenty-five years ago. At that time, I wrote you a letter and asked you to come and speak to a group of us convicts. When we got your letter of acceptance, we were a happy lot. None of us forgot how kind you were to interrupt your busy schedule, fly 3000 miles and meet with us. Later in the day, you sat in the inmates' dining room and enjoyed a meal with us. I heard your name mentioned a few minutes ago. I made up my mind to thank you again, twenty-five years later." The gentleman's face beamed. He was beside himself when he said, "Yes, I remember the incident. It was a highlight in my career. I'm sorry that I can't remember you, but I recall that venture. My, this is unbelievable!"

During his brief response, he kept pumping my hand. Then his face brightened again, and he made an interesting observation. "Why you are the chap who was presented an award at the White House this morning! You have every right to be proud." Lorna had been standing off to my side. I called her over and introduced him to her. Working for a life insurance company and being fully aware of W. Clement Stone's importance to the history of life insurance, Lorna was impressed. Mr. Stone graciously accepted my request to pose for a picture with Lorna. Lorna has that picture hanging in our office at home.

By the time we got back to our room, there were two exhausted persons who tumbled into bed. The next morning, totally rested and refreshed, we rose to greet the day. Since Uncle Sam was footing the bill and we would soon be leaving this luxurious hotel, I decided that Lorna should have breakfast served in bed, a luxury she has never before or since experienced. At first she was reluctant, but then agreed only if she had time to freshen up and put on some make-up. While she was getting ready, I called room service and ordered fresh fruit, scrambled eggs, toast and chilled fruit juice. She was sitting nervously in bed when I responded to a rap on the door and admitted a bellhop. Right off the bat, I asked him if he would be so kind as to serve her breakfast in bed so I could get a picture of it. He laughed heartily and said he would be happy to serve such a charming lady in bed. He was a handsome Mexican dressed nattily in his uniform. His manner in serving the breakfast showed he had performed this service before. Lorna was embarrassed. I snapped two or three pictures for her to show her family and friends.

We had decided to spend a few more days in the vicinity at our own expense, so we checked into the Holiday Inn in Arlington, Virginia. We selected that area because we had two very dear friends and members of our church who had moved to Arlington. We called Collin and Linda Tong as soon as we were settled in our new quarters. They were delighted to hear from us. They knew we were going to be in Washington D.C., as well as the occasion for our visit, and they were anxious to see us. Inasmuch as they had to go to work, we made arrangements to meet that evening for dinner in a quaint French restaurant. That suited our schedule because I wanted to go back into the capitol.

There was no way I would leave that city without touring the FBI headquarters. When our cab dropped us off in front of the J. Edgar Hoover Building, I found it to be cold, foreboding and without expression. In fact, it had a sort of prison appearance. Lorna and I joined the tour group going through the building. The guide had apparently rehearsed her lines so thoroughly that she never deviated from the lesson she had been taught; what to say and what not to say. I found her lauding of the FBI nauseating. Lorna sensed that I wanted to challenge her statements concerning some of the gangsters whom I had known personally. She cautioned me to keep my remarks to myself.

It was inevitable that we would be shown dozens of different types of deadly weapons which had been confiscated from gangsters. We were permitted to view the famous laboratory from behind glass walls. Throughout the entire tour I waited for the best part of all; the rogues' gallery. At the end of the tour, we came to a wall that was covered with pictures of many of the nations' number one criminals. A lady behind us commented to her husband, "Just look at those killers. Wouldn't it be terrible to meet them in an alley?" I had to smile and, to myself, I agreed with her assessment.

Before leaving, we were treated to a demonstration of marksmanship. I was thrilled by this prospect. We gathered in a small theater. There were seats to accommodate fifty people. In front of us was bullet-proof glass. It was so dark we could not see anything beyond the partition. As soon as we were seated, lights beyond the dark glass were turned on, and it lighted up so we could see everything in the firing range. A full-sized silhouette of a man hung on an overhead automatically-operated transit wire. At the press of a button, the target could be moved farther back or nearer the instructor. A man walked into view and began addressing the audience through a sound system. He was wearing a billed cap with the initials FBI across the front, and a jacket which appeared to be bulletproof. He did need protection, I assumed, from ricocheting slugs. He introduced himself and informed us that he was the firearms instructor for the FBI, and that he would give us a brief demonstration of his skills. "I will," he advised, "use revolvers and a sub-machine gun. We are very adept at other types of weapons such as rifles and shotguns, but time will not permit the full gamut of firearms display. You will hear the muted sound of the guns being fired via our sound system."

The man's skill was unbelievable. From all ranges, he riddled the silhouetted target in the heart and chest area. The explosive sounds of the guns being fired added a realistic touch to the demonstration. It was a brief but impressive display of the most skillful use of firearms I have ever seen. I was always proud of my marksmanship but, when this fellow was through, I was relegated to the class of marksmen who occasionally brings home a rabbit.

Before we left, the instructor walked through a door and talked with us briefly. "Are there any questions?", he asked. Lorna, fearing I would make some brash comment, grasped my arm. I spoke out anyway and made a request of this sharpshooter. "Sir, I would greatly appreciate the target which you riddled. Would that be possible?" He was very polite and obliging. "We do not get many such requests, but I see no reason why I can't send you this target. Please leave your name and address and I will see what I can do. However, I cannot assure you I will be permitted to send it to you." I had been home less than a month when I received a letter from the FBI firearms instructor, Lewis L. Padula, in which he stated, "I was able to secure permission to send you the target used in my demonstration before your group. It will arrive under separate cover within a few days." True to his word, the target was sent to me.

That evening while Lorna and I were enjoying dinner with our friends, Collin and Linda Tong, I dominated the conversation with stories of my life leading up to the climax at the White House. Linda managed to get me to close my mouth long enough for her to make a statement. "Glenn, why don't you finish that book you're always talking about? Your life has so many documented and interesting tales it would be a best seller." Lorna, who had been after me for years to pen an autobiography, gave me that I-told-you-so look. I began working again on the book as soon as we got home. Being a great procrastinator, it took me six years to finish it. I found it very difficult to research events that occurred more than sixty years ago and to relive many of the difficult times.

30

EPILOGUE

Upon our return from Washington, D.C. we found our mailbox jammed with cards and letters of congratulations. We were pleased to hear from so many well-wishers. In addition to our being deluged by friends, requests to make public appearances started coming in. At this point, we decided that I could not continue to make speeches for the sole purpose of being an entertainer. I had learned from experience that there is a great deal of expense connected to travel and accommodations, and that many agencies and clubs were profiting from my appearances. I realized that I could no longer afford to give my services gratis. However, I continued to speak without compensation to churches, non-profit agencies, youth groups and high schools.

There continued to be a strong 'fixation' about the Island that attracted attention to any convention taking place in the Bay area. When it was decided by the Federal Bureau of Prisons that Alcatraz would be used as a super maximum prison for incorrigible criminals, every agency in San Francisco screamed their objection. Among the more vociferous in their objection was the San Francisco Chapter of the Federal Bar Association. And yet, in 1984, to celebrate the fiftieth anniversary of the establishment of Alcatraz as a high-security penitentiary, that same chapter sent out invitations to Lawyers' Club Members and their guests to attend a private after-hours tour of the Island. I was asked to attend the event in the capacity of a speaker and guide. Attached to the 'invitation' was a request that I send my check in the amount of $37.50. I called the event chairman, Assistant District Attorney Michael Tonsing, and objected strenuously to being charged. When I reminded the lady who answered the phone that I was to be a guest speaker and guide, I was told there had been a mistake and it was too late to correct it. I was asked to send my invitation along with my check, and was told that I would be reimbursed. "Well, in addition to myself, I am bringing a Michael Kroll as my guest." She assured me that my guest would be welcome. Michael Kroll is a free-lance writer from the Bay area who volunteered to critique my autobiography. I telephoned Michael and told him he was to be a guest of the Federal Bar Association. I explained the circumstances and asked him to pick me up at the airport. He inquired, "How did you arrange that, Nate? You bet I'll pick you up. I look forward to attending such a prestigious event. I'm going to take my notebook along. Maybe I can get a story."

Michael met my plane at the airport and we drove hurriedly to Pier 41, arriving just in time to join the other passengers. The ferry was filled to capacity by the time the group was loaded. The person who was checking the list before boarding couldn't find our names. I argued that I was a guest, and that I was to act as a guide. "As for Mr. Kroll, he was approved as my guest." She could not locate us on the roster. She asked, "Are you with the National Park Service? It states here that that agency is furnishing the guides. They're already on board." Testily, I replied, "No, madam, I am not with the Park Service. I was invited to come here from Seattle for the purpose I explained before." Finally, the lady decided to let us board. I had no reason to expect further problems with our admission to the events of the evening. Michael made a statement that made me more apprehensive when he said, "It certainly is unusual that they would invite you, and then not include you as a passenger on the ferry."

We were still mulling over the mix-up when the boat docked at the Island. The Rock had been lit up for the occasion, but the lights created an eerie scene. As soon as we left the boat, I cornered one of the Park Service Rangers and explained what had happened. While he was looking through his roster, another Ranger who recognized me said, "Nate, I'm surprised to see you here tonight. Are you with this bunch?" I explained my situation one more time. He turned to the man who was still trying to find me listed and said, "Nate has been on the Island a number of times and has acted as an unofficial guide. If he wants to lead some of the members, it's OK. He knows more about this Island than any of us."

While this dialogue was taking place, I noticed Michael talking to a young lady who had cameras slung over her shoulder. As I started to walk away, he caught me by the arm and introduced me to her. "Nate, I want you to meet Harriet Chiang. Harriet is the Staff Writer for The Recorder, which is the official newspaper of the U.S. District Court. I told her about your history, and she's anxious to write an article about you and your presence here." I said, "I would be delighted to cooperate with you on the article, Harriet." Instead of guiding people around the Island, Harriet, Michael and I spent a wonderful evening traipsing around the grounds on our own. Harriet questioned me sharply and in detail. Her questions were relevant and intelligent. She took pictures of me in front of my old cell, and leaning on the burned out wall of the warden's former residence. She told me she had never had the opportunity to talk to an ex-inmate of the Rock, and that she felt she was now better equipped to understand both sides of the divergent stories about Alcatraz. She remained with Michael and me for the rest of the evening.

After the boat returned from Alactraz that evening, Michael and I walked to his car. From there we drove to the lovely Ferry Plaza Restaurant, where the Bar Association dinner was to be held. We parked his little 1977 Datsun among the Mercedes Benz's, Cadillacs and Jaguars. We were greeted by a receptionist who asked for our invitation. Very patiently, I explained the circumstances of my being there. My name was not on the guests' roster nor on the speakers' agenda. I turned to my friend and groaned, "Oh, God, not again." I wasted no time in requesting to speak to the Chairman of Events, Michael Tonsing. She asked me to excuse her for a moment or two. Very shortly, she returned with a distinguished looking gentleman. Without hesitation he said, "Welcome, Mr. Williams. I'm sorry about the confusion. Come right in. We have a place all set up for you." I never said a word. I simply put my hand on Michael's arm and guided him past the receptionist.

I estimated that there were at least five hundred people in attendance. It was apparent that the members of the bar and their guests were persons of prestige and wealth. I was surprised that I was not introduced to the program chairman who was responsible for the order in which speakers would be called. The members were very friendly to Michael and me. We were included in their conversations, but somehow I felt we were not really in the inner circle.

A man walked up to my table and said, "Sir, I feel as though I know you from somewhere. I'm Ralph Blake." A chunk of ice lodged in my stomach. I had recognized him as a former guard on Alcatraz, but I couldn't recall his name. I handled the incident in the manner I found most comfortable; head on. "Mr. Blake, I'm Nate Williams. While I recognize you, until you told me, I couldn't remember your name. I was an inmate on the Rock when you were assigned there." His jaw dropped. I knew he was wondering how I could have been invited to an affair of this nature. He recovered his composure and said, "Now, I remember you. That was some time ago, wasn't it?" Michael grinned and commented, "It's a small world."

I had not had time to read the program until the meal was finished. I scanned through it and was surprised that my name had been omitted from the list of speakers and guides. I was at a loss to understand why I was not on the roster. When the program chairman made the introduction of speakers and guides, my name was not called. I noted that Mr. Blake had been listed. However, when the last speaker had finished, neither Ralph Blake nor I, had been called. One of the members of the bar arose and explained that the evening had gone by too rapidly to permit further entertainment. Michael melted my rising temper by saying, "What do you care? You got a good meal. Did you ever dream, while you were in your cell, that some evening you would experience a night like this?" I observed to my friend, "We certainly enjoyed Harriet's company more than those whom I was scheduled to guide." Michael was beside himself with enthusiasm. "She is respected among the writers of this community, and you can bet she'll write a very interesting story about you and your experiences."

On the third day of January, 1985, I was surprised to get a letter from Washington, D.C. Again, the return address simply read: THE WHITE HOUSE, WASHINGTON, D.C.

In Honor of
the President of the United States
and Mrs. Reagan
the Vice President of the United States
and Mrs. Bush
The Committee for
the 50th American Presidential Inaugural
requests the honor of your company

at the
Inaugural Ball
Monday evening the twenty-first of January
one thousand nine hundred and eighty-five
in the City of Washington

Black Tie   eight o'clock
Please respond to
THE SOCIAL SECRETARY
THE WHITE HOUSE
at your earliest convenience
giving date of birth and social security number
(202) 456-2510

To this day, I don't understand why I was selected to receive an invitation from the WHITE HOUSE to attend the Presidential Inaugural Ball. I've never been a political person. I have never made a contribution to any political party. In addition, I am a Democrat. Yet a Republican governor and a Republican president had selected me for recognition. And now, this invitation from The White House. I responded, assuring the social secretary that I would be in attendance and expressed appreciation for the invitation. I regretted that Lorna was not included.

I flew out of Seattle on January 20th. By that time, the mercury had dipped to seven degrees below in Washington, D.C. I dreaded the extreme cold. I assured my wife that I would remain indoors during the entire affair. I promised her I'd take a taxi everywhere I went.

It was bitterly cold as my plane landed at the International Airport in Arlington. Lorna had insisted that I take an overcoat. Walking the few feet from the airport to a taxi left me chilled to the bone. On the twenty-first, I remained inside all day. Twice I ventured down to the lobby to visit with other guests, and to pick up a couple of papers which were filled with the details of the Inaugural Ball. The usual parade and marching bands had to be cancelled because of the cold. According to the TV report that afternoon, only a handful of persons cancelled their trip. Every room in the hotel in which I was staying was taken. At seven-thirty in the evening, I showered, shaved and donned my tuxedo. Because there were so many demands for transportation, each cab that pulled up to the door had to be filled. By this time, I learned that there were three or four locations at which the ball would be celebrated. I was relegated to the one being held at the Smithsonian Institute.

At the Ball, it took an inordinately long time to have my pass checked and approved for entry. As we entered the door to the Institute, we were told to remove our coats, hand them to the cloakroom girls and to proceed through a fluoroscope check-point. On each side of that device were three or four solemn-looking individuals who had to be still more security. After I had passed through the detector, I glanced back and watched the secret service agents pat down the garments that were given up for hanging in the cloakroom.

I wandered all through the buildings. Many of the halls and rooms were off limits. I searched all through the crowd hoping I would find someone I knew. There was a small dance floor roped off. A few couples danced to an orchestra. So far as I could tell, this was going to be one dull evening. To break the monotony, I went to one of the many small bars that had been spaced at intervals. I ordered a Tom Collins and paid the ridiculous price of $5.00. If the bartender had put any liquor in the glass, it evaporated before I could get it to my lips. To make matters worse, there were no chairs on which to be seated.

To pass the time, I walked to the entrance through which I had come. It was situated in a hall and was not so crowded. I noticed a tall handsome gentleman standing off to himself observing the guests. He had every appearance of being a Secret Service agent. I walked over to him and struck up a conversation. He was amiable and easy to talk to. We touched on the size of the group and how many states were represented among them. Finally, I asked, "How in the world could you hope to protect the Chief of State with such a large conglomeration milling round?" He grinned and replied, "Sir, we know every person in this crowd. Each has been subjected to a background check. Believe me, no shady persons are in this gathering." I nearly swallowed my tongue. I often wondered if he knew more about me than I realized. "Another thing," I continued, "I'm here by a special invitation from the President. Why, then, was I searched, fluoroscoped and subjected to such scrutiny?" In a response that was dead serious, he said, "Sir, everyone is here by special invitation." At that moment, a lady was walking by. I asked her if she would use my camera to take a picture of the Secret Serviceman and me. I turned to the fellow and said, "Does that meet with your approval, sir?" He smiled broadly, put his arm over my shoulder and replied, "It would be a pleasure." She took two shots. I thanked the gentleman and walked back into the main section.

There was one other event that took place which angered me. I took an elevator to the second floor to use the lavatory. Standing at the elevator were three or four more guards. Going in was no problem, but when men would come out, they were searched by a portable 'mechanical stool pigeon' before they were permitted to enter the elevator going down to the main ballroom. When it was my turn to be scanned, the instrument emitted a loud buzzing. Before I could explain that I had a steel rod in my spine, I was jostled into a restroom by the agents. I resented being handled in such a manner and I complained bitterly. "Sir, we'll have to ask you to strip off your clothes so we can do a more thorough search." Defiantly, I replied, "And if I refuse?" A short man, who apparently was the superior officer, very coolly answered, "If you refuse, then we'll have to call security and have you taken to the city jail where you may be assured you will be searched." I submitted to the stripping and search. It was obvious from the long scar on my spine that I did, indeed, have metal inserted in that area. I was allowed to enter the elevator and go to the lower floor. When I cooled off, I knew that the agents had acted properly.

I drifted toward the bandstand to better hear the music. As soon as I got there, lo and behold, a familiar face appeared from the tightly packed assemblage. It was Senator Claude Pepper of Louisiana. I intercepted him and introduced myself. He possessed the grace and charm that is so evident in southern gentlemen. Yet, I knew that the garrulous old gentleman was a hell-cat on wheels when roused. For once, I met a man that could talk me under the table, and he did just that. It was a pleasure to have someone to listen to. It was nearing eleven o'clock and I had been wondering when the President and his entourage would stop by to greet their supporters. I asked Mr. Pepper if he had any idea when they would appear. He grinned like a fox and answered, "No, but let me give you a little bit of an education. They never announce just when he will come on the scene, nor through which door. I have a hunch it won't be too long. The people are tired and will start to thin out pretty soon. Now, you see that plug in the bandmaster's ear? Well, keep an eye on him. When the President is about to enter, it will be announced to the bandmaster through his hearing device. They do that so he will strike up 'Hail To The Chief' as President Reagan appears. If you watch the bandmaster closely, he will tip off the door through which the President will enter by glancing toward it. Also, he will interrupt the musicians and alert them. It's a well-rehearsed procedure; one that I've been watching for many years."

Mr. Pepper had no more than quit talking than I heard the bandmaster tapping on his music stand. Before I could get my wits about me, 'Hail To The Chief' filled the auditorium. Not fifteen feet away from us a door swung open and in filed a dozen plainclothesmen. Then I saw the Reagans and Bushes follow. Without a moment's hesitation, the gentleman from Louisiana pushed his way through the throng and approached the President with outstretched hand. The President was trying to make his way to the bandstand. The secret Servicemen were clearing a path for him and Vice President Bush and his wife. I did as many around me. I shoved my way through the group and managed to shake the President's and Vice President's hands. When the party reached the raised stand, they mounted it, and the four of them waved to the wildly cheering men and women. As if on cue, the band started playing a waltz. I knew the end of the evening was nearing, so I made my way to the exit. I looked back and saw the President and his wife Nancy and George Bush and Barbara dancing.

My plane arrived in Seattle the next day. As exciting as the whole venture was, I was tired and happy to be with my family again.

I didn't expect to receive any more communication from the nation's capitol, and I expressed this to Lorna. I noticed a smile breaking at the corners of her mouth. She said, "Glenn, I have an envelope in the car for you. " When we got in the car, she handed me a large envelope with that familiar return address, THE WHITE HOUSE. I simply stared at it. While the enclosure carried the seal of the REPUBLICAN NATIONAL COM-MITTEE, there was no indication that I was invited to attend any more functions. However, I must admit I was dumbfounded as I read the wording of the document.

President Ronald Wilson Reagan,
Senator Paul Laxalt, General Chairman,
and

Frank Fahrenkopf, National Chairman,
on behalf of the
Republican National Committee
cordially invite you to become a member of
the 500 Club
and to attend a private briefing
with Administration officials and
Republican Congressional leaders

To this day, I'll never know what prompted this prestigious assemblage of Republican leaders to invite Nathan Glenn Williams, a Democrat, to become a member of their elite 500 Club.

I received yet another letter from the capitol. It was from a representative of the State Department. The lady wrote that an official visitor from France, Paulette Nevoux, was going to be in the United States to study this country's juvenile delinquency programs and the methods in which we were attacking that problem. She expressed her desire to visit the Pacific Northwest. I was asked to be her host. I was delighted for the opportunity. Two weeks later, a call came from a Dr. Joanna Dezio of New York. Doctor Dezio had been assigned by the State Department to be Paulette Nevoux's official translator. She and Mademoiselle Nevoux would be arriving in Seattle on Friday and hoped that I could spend a few days with them. On the specified day, I went to their hotel to pick them up. The clerk started to ring their room when a lady approached me and said, "I heard you asking the clerk to call our room. I am Doctor Dezio. Mademoiselle Nevoux will be here shortly. May we sit and talk for a few minutes?" She went on to advise me that Mme. Nevoux did not speak nor understand English. From what I gathered after my conversation with the doctor, Mme. Nevoux was involved with the juvenile criminal system of France and was, in some minor role, connected with President Mitterand's cabinet. Mme. Nevoux stepped from the elevator as we were talking. Before I was introduced, Doctor Dezio spoke to her in French. Mme. offered her hand in greeting. At first it was clumsy trying to communicate through an interpreter. However, as time went on, our system of communication went quite smoothly.

Mme. Nevoux seemed more interested in my personal observations that she did in dry statistics. Nothing was indicated that my guests had been made aware of my criminal past. Throughout our time together, I wondered about that possibility. I wondered why the State Department referred Mme. Nevoux to me. I had no reputation on the national level to distinguish me. I concluded that a phone call from the Department to Seattle resulted in the name of my agency, Teen Intercept, being mentioned. Locally, it was a well-known and established agency. In any case, I enjoyed this particular assignment.

On the final day of their visit, I told them about my experiences in my youth at the Green Hill College. I recalled the months I had spent there when it was known as WSTS, Washington State Training School. I decided to tell Mme. Nevoux and Doctor Dezio of my experience as a twelve year old boy incarcerated in that abusive institution. I told them of the unbearable beatings, the sexual abuse of the inmates by the guards and, finally, of my escape from their clutches. When I was through, there was a puzzled expression on Mme.'s face. When she did speak, the translator told me that Mme. wanted to know if such conditions still existed at the training school. I assured her that they did not.

I decided to take my guests out to lunch at Louie's Cuisine of China on the last day of their stay. Doctors Thomas Deal and Trish Lipscomb, members of our church and dear friends, had agreed to sponsor a French exchange student. They were unable to meet the young man at the airport on his arrival, and they asked Lorna and me to pick him up. He stayed with our family for a few days and we became very fond of him. The experience was very rewarding. The student's name was Pierre, and he spoke quite good English, at least enough to make himself understood. Our son, Don, who was studying French in school, was excited at the prospect of a French visitor. Inasmuch as Tom and his wife, Trish, were not going to be home for a few days, we had the opportunity to have Pierre stay at our home. It was during this time that my guests, Mme. Nevoux and Doctor Dezio and I were going to have lunch at Louie's. I thought it would be nice to invite Pierre to join us. I explained to him that one of my guests was from France. Mme. Nevoux was happy to have one of her fellow men dine with us. She and Pierre began speaking in fluent French. It was pleasant hearing them converse in that beautiful language.

Before I was to take the two of them to the airport for their return trip, I took them by my wife's office. The three of them talked for only a few minutes because we had to hurry to catch the plane. On our way to the airport, Mme. Nevoux and Doctor Dezio talked at length between themselves. When it was time for us to say good-bye, Doctor Nevoux said that Mme. Nevoux extended an invitation for me to visit France as her guest.

Seventy times, my birthday anniversary had been celebrated. On some occasions, the celebration took place in my mind only because I was in some dingy cell or hole. Nevertheless, seventy of them slipped past. On my seventy-first, my wife said she wanted us to spend the weekend in San Francisco. She had one proviso; that we would not go near Alcatraz. Seventy-one years after I was born, to the day, she and I landed at the International Airport. For the next two days, we rode the cable cars, visited Telegraph Hill, Fisherman's Wharf, shopped at the markets that we always found so quaint and interesting, went to Candlestick Park and crossed the Oakland Bay and Golden Gate bridges a dozen times. We dined at many of the city's fine restaurants. In the evenings we danced at the Top of the Sir Francis Drake Hotel.

The last day of our visit, we took a final ride on the Cable Car. It wasn't pre-planned, but the car took us to the top of a hill that offered a magnificent view of San Francisco Bay. Right out in the center of the bay was an Island that was so familiar. I stared at it longingly. Lorna groaned and reminded me of the proviso. We were not to intermingle that prison with our tour. I commented, "Honey, we have done about everything we can do in town. What's wrong with a little visit around the bay?" An hour later, she and I were trudging Alcatraz's terrain. When we left the Island, she said, "I might have known that I couldn't keep you from going over there. Well, it's your birthday and if you want to spend part of it in your old cell, I guess I shouldn't complain."

Among my friends, I have a special young lady named Karen Mechler-Lovelace. She is a diminutive and pretty girl who is five feet tall and weighs less than one hundred pounds. Karen was indirectly responsible for bringing about one of the most memorable celebrations I have ever attended; my 25th year of living the life of a free man, a quarter of a century on the streets for the first time in my life. Karen is a bubbly sort of person who loves to dream up parties and events for all occasions. As I learned later, when Karen heard that on April 1988, I would have been out of prison for 25 years, she suggested to my wife that a party be thrown to celebrate my twenty-five years of freedom. "You know how Glenn loves parties and celebrations of all kinds," Karen reminded Lorna. The two of them got their heads together and planned a party, and decided they would invite a few of my closest friends. Karen started out suggesting about a dozen people. As they started preparing the list of names, each would think of another person who 'just had to be invited'. Gradually the roster grew to more than fifty people. Lorna reminded Karen that there were many members of our church, University Baptist, to which I was attached, and I would be disappointed if they weren't invited. The end result was that the two of them came up with a list of more than one hundred guests. Lorna and Karen were trying to make the arrangements for the party without my being aware of what was going on. Somewhere along the line I learned about the shindig. My first reaction was the prohibitive cost entailed. Lorna overrode my objection. "Glenn, this is a big occasion. How many people can celebrate being out of Alcatraz for twenty-five years?" I enjoyed her sense of humor.

My wife chose to have the event take place at The Windjammer, on Shilshole Bay. Because of the large number of guests, she had to rent the Crow's Nest, a dining room which overlooked the water. Lorna spent many hours preparing the decorations and invitations. She found some napkins and paper plates that were striped like a convict's uniform. They were perfect for the occasion.

Our friend, Louise Ellis, one of the best cake bakers and decorators in the city, has been baking cakes for numerous occasions for many customers in the Seattle area. My wife called Louise and placed an order. Louise outdid herself. She made the cake in the shape of Alcatraz Island with a prison mounted on the top and surrounded by water. With only a photo, Louise produced a remarkable likeness of the famous prison. She had placed the walls and gun towers in their proper places. It was truly a work of art. I wanted to have it frozen so I could keep it. If we had been able to find a baker to produce a cake comparable to Louise's, I am sure it would have cost more than a hundred dollars. Being Louise, who has a heart as big as all outdoors, she insisted that we accept the cake as a gift. In addition, she graciously spent the entire time cutting and serving cake to the guests.

An assortment of guests attended. There was JB, the only other ex from the Rock, exes from other institutions, police officers, retired guards from federal prisons, doctors, attorneys, teachers, a nun, ministers, a judge, a

403

retired warden, a retired FBI agent, neighbors, friends from Lorna's and my places of employment, Donovan Cook, my pastor and dozens of church friends. Steve McKenzie, a musician from our church composed and sang a song dedicated to me. Dr. Leeon Aller played the harmonica. Donovan spoke and roasted me unmercifully. He mentioned that I was the church moderator, but for understandable reasons the Board would not elect me to the Board of Trustees. When JB saw the Alcatraz cake, he couldn't believe his eyes. That piece of artwork was the attention-getter. Pictures of it were taken by many guests. It was an evening I will never forget.

It was a relief to have a lighter schedule, more time to devote to my family, and to do things I wanted to do. However, I was not prepared to get involved in areas of dangerous ventures until I got a call from my friend, Jay Cascio, a television personality with KING Broadcasting. Jay had done a couple of TV programs concerning my past, so when he called, I was not expecting to be set up. He told me he had made a parachute jump a week earlier. He elaborated on what a great thrill it was. Then he caught me off guard and said he would like me to be on his program "EVENING", in which I would be filmed doing a tandem jump with, and under the auspices of Mark Scott, a veteran of this sport, with more than 2000 jumps under his belt. Jay was always of the opinion that I was an impulsive individual, not too blessed with good judgment. My acceptance of his proposition confirmed his original opinion of me.

The week before I was scheduled to skydive, I experienced a number of sleepless nights. I even entertained the idea of reneging or conferring with my psychiatrist. Surely, at 72, I was suffering some sort of aberration; either that or Jay was one hell of a salesman. I never breathed a word to my wife of my intention, or she would have solved the problem by having me committed. On the day of the dive, I met my tandem partner, Mark. Only then did I know what a tandem jump consisted of. An instructor harnesses himself behind a student in such a manner that they parachute as one. The student does not have a parachute. He depends upon the instructor to pull the rip cord and both float safely (hopefully) to earth. I derived little comfort knowing that if something went wrong, I would not be alone. Mark taught me how to leave the plane, control myself while descending, land, and to pretend I was cool and collected. He commented on how quiet I was prior to boarding the jump-plane. He didn't know how difficult it was for me to talk when my teeth were chattering like a machine gun. As the plane climbed to 11,000 feet, I went through a gamut of emotions. And all through this adventure, Lorna was sitting at her desk where she was employed, not knowing what her irresponsible husband was up to.

When we attained the altitude at which we were to leave the plane, the pilot opened the door.

Mark asked, "Are you ready to jump, Glenn?" With the wind rushing by, he couldn't hear me scream, "NO! Let me out." He did as I asked, and I found myself 'out' and falling from two miles up. We 'free fell' for 45 seconds before engaging the main chute. The snap of the harness against my chest hurt but, at the same time, felt good. It slowed our descent rate from 125 miles an hour to a mere 25 Mph. Besides Mark, the pilot and myself, there was another man going aloft with us. He was wearing a parachute and had a camera attached to the side of his helmet. I learned later that he dived from the plane as soon as Mark and I cleared. Very expertly, he did a free fall until he was parallel with Mark and me. He pulled his rip cord at the exact time we had. I first noticed him when he maneuvered to my right at the same altitude, and not 25 feet from me. He was completely relaxed and smiled encouragingly at me. I thought I returned his smile, but when I saw the picture on TV, I was actually grimacing. How can you smile when you are paralyzed with fear? After he had taped about three minutes, and we were near the landing target, he pulled away from us. The fellow was a master of his profession of aerial photography. About 1,000 feet above the target, I saw Jay and his cameraman taking pictures as we neared the ground. He waved, and I responded with an air of bravado I didn't feel. When he struck the grass, I bounced a few times on my posterior, dragging poor Mark along. It is amazing how one's bravery returns when he is safe from any danger. I unstraped my harness and strutted over to where the TV crewmen were standing.

Jay told me that it would be a week before the program would be airing. That made me quite happy, because I would be in St. Louis on a speaking engagement when it showed on TV. Before I left, very sneakily, I asked Lorna if she would watch the broadcast. I gave her the date and hour. She asked me what the nature of the program was. I replied, "Oh, it's a few minute show on which I am appearing." She had seen me on TV enough not to be overly curious, but she promised to watch it. On the evening it was to air, I phoned Lorna from Wichita and reminded her. I don't want to go into detail regarding her reaction when she picked me up at the airport a few days later. Succinctly, it amounted to 'you are insane, Hubby'.

It seemed that every time I got a phone call from the east coast, it always amounted to more than a casual phone conversation from some friend. The call I got early one morning proved my point. It was from Doctor Richard Korn, a professor at the John J. College of Criminal Justice in New York. He said he has a friend who is the director of Daedalus Production, Inc. "Nate, she is into social issues at this point. She's gathering a great deal of footage on the conditions of prisons in this country, much to the chagrin of the authorities. Well, she wants to do a documentary on Alcatraz. I told her about you, and she's interested in having you appear in the documentary. She'll be contacting you if you are amenable to the idea. Her name is Nina Rosenblum." A week after Richard Korn's call, I heard from Ms. Rosenblum. She explained the nature of her work, and of her consuming interest in social issues. Her interests ran parallel to mine. I was impressed by her obvious dedication and intelligence, and I assured her I'd be happy to cooperate.

A month later, Lorna and I met Nina and members of her television crew on the Alcatraz docks. From the moment my wife and I met her, we liked her. She surmounted a number of obstacles prior to being given permission by the Golden Gate National Recreation area, under whose supervision Alcatraz Island had been placed, before being permitted to do the filming on the Rock. One of the impediments was the requirement that she have a million dollar insurance policy. Nina was a persistent sort of individual who cleared every roadblock, one by one, as they arose. Eventually, she and her crew were on the Island with all the paraphernalia required to do a large-scale scene-shooting production. Lorna and I stayed away from Nina and the crew during their preparations. We didn't want to impede her in any way.

While my wife and I were standing near the Rangers' shack, a member of Nina's crew ran up to me and said, "Nate, we're having a problem with one of the Alcatroopers. She is saying we can't go here, we can't go there, we can't do this and we can't do that. If we're so restricted, there is no way we can function." I was at a loss. I had no authority over the Park Service's operation or its employees. Nevertheless, I sought out the ranger who had given the crew such restrictive perimeters in which to work. That is when I met Nancy Bernard. Like myself, she was short of stature and, I think, a rather stubborn lady. I introduced myself to her and was given a look that seemed to say, 'and who are you'? While I was perturbed by her restrictions and attitude, I liked her immediately. I asked about the boundaries she had placed on the crew. She promptly retorted, "Those aren't my boundaries, Mr. Williams. They are the limitations imposed by the Park Service and they apply to everybody who comes on this Island. I simply enforce them." I felt she might be a volatile young lady, so I tried being tactful. "What puzzles me Ms. Bernard, is that I am permitted to go to many of the areas that you say are out of bounds. Why could I do so and the television crew be restricted?" I held my breath. Nancy looked me full in the eyes and said, "When were you ever allowed to go into forbidden zones?. I've been here for months and have never seen you in those areas?" I went for broke and said, "Nancy, I've guided tours here unofficially for many months. In fact, I even showed the Indians around this penitentiary." She asked, "In what capacity did you do this?" I pulled her aside, as though in confidence, and told her that, before she was even born, I had been imprisoned on the Island for a number of years, that I returned when the Indians occupied my former home and that I had been asked by the government to act as an official tourist guide. Little by little, Nancy relented and the crew was allowed to shoot scenes in the vital sections that were so essential to a successful production. She accompanied me for the rest of the day. She was standing by when it was my turn to be filmed walking up the famed Broadway.

During the walk up Broadway, I was to leisurely amble from one end of the corridor to the other toward the cameramen, all the while appearing to be interested in what was in the cells. Apparently, I was to appear to be reminiscing about the past when I was an inmate and walked that same corridor. Nina kept ordering me back time and time again to do the scene over. Every time I had to do a repeat, the crew would have to yell at the tourists and ask them to clear the area. On the last take, I heard a young girl ask her friend, "What's going on here?" Her friend replied, "It's a film crew from Hollywood. They're doing a movie." The young lady looked me over with contempt and said, "That guy ain't no actor!"

Before the day was over, Nancy and Lorna had become friends. My wife gave Nancy a run-down on my career. When the time came for Daedalus

Productions to leave the Island, Nancy asked if we could talk. She said she wanted to get some history about the Island and its inmates. At the time we boarded the boat, she introduced me to her friend, Donna Middlemist, a volunteer with the Park Service. Donna is probably the most knowledgeable person on the Rock concerning the entire history of Alcatraz, its inmates and physical structure. The Park Department is very fortunate to have such well-informed employees as Nancy Bernard and Donna. Donna is a former school teacher who learned the art of continued studying, and applied that knowledge to researching the prison. Consequently, when there are questions concerning the lore of Alcatraz, one of the two has the answer.

When Lorna and I saw Nina off, we felt we were bidding a dear friend good-bye. The end result of Nina's efforts were in evidence as one viewed her profound and gripping film documentary.

Nancy Bernard called my home one summer evening in 1988 and told me that she was in the process of preparing a new project that was being designed for the entertainment and education of the visitors to the Island. Where she ever came up with this idea, I will never know. It was their plan to ask a group of retired guards and an equal number of ex-Alcatrazites to greet and speak to the tourists. Each side was to give its opinion of the institution. The ex-guards would answer questions from the audience, as would the cons. The visitors would be advised that they were being treated to an unusual opportunity to hear from both sides of the debate, and they would be asked to direct questions to the speakers. Both the cons and guards would be asked to give their personal opinions and viewpoints. Of course, the cons would have a far different viewpoint than the guards. I suspected that Nancy and Donna got their heads together and concocted the scheme.

Other than those of us who were so close to the problem, few could imagine the hard work and long hours both Donna and Nancy expended. Here were two ladies attempting to get hardened cons from the street to associate with the very guards who were ready to shoot them if the occasion demanded. On the flip side of the coin, they were expecting those ex-guards to confront the very cons they had to lock up every night, and search their persons and cells on a regular basis. They had to bear in mind that the cons, if they could be convinced to make a volunteer appearance back on the despised bastille, would be in a position to 'lay it on' the guards with impunity. From my experience and viewpoint, I could envision many problems. I had doubts that Nancy could get more than two or three Alcatraz alumni to show up. In the first place, there aren't too many of us alive and/or on the streets. Those who are would probably rebel at the thought of returning to the Island. But I had to admit it was an intriguing plan and, if it went smoothly, it would be an educational sort of thing as well as immensely interesting to civilians to be able to see the reaction of the guards and inmates, former enemies. I agreed to be there for the event a nd assured them of my cooperation. I admired the innovation and spunk these two had.

Nancy asked the question I was afraid she would pose, "Nate, can you give me the names and addresses of some former Rock inmates so I can invite them?" I had to refuse to do this without their permission. However, I promised to do the next best thing. "Nancy, I'll contact a few and ask them to call you, or I will get their OK to let you have their phone numbers. I'll get back to you." I called my old Buddy, JB and explained the proposition to him. I thought he was going to come right out to my house and do me bodily harm. "Nate," he roared, "how in the hell could we be expected to meet with former guards? There may be some that show up whom I hated." After an hour of begging, he agreed to make the trip with me.

Nancy and Donna, in the meantime, were contacting ex-guards who lived in the Bay area. According to the coordinators, there were many questions from those whose job it was to keep us on the Island against our will. Apparently, the questions were of the same nature as those the ex-cons asked. Would it be prudent for them to face men whom they previously considered the most dangerous in the U.S.? Nancy and Donna had more success recruiting the men who wore the uniforms than I had in getting any exes. That was understandable, because many of the guards retired when the prison was closed, and they stayed in the vicinity. The cons were spread all over the country in various other federal joints. The very few who were ever released either returned to a life of crime or hibernated in remote areas of the country. The last thing they wanted was publicity. I wrote Nancy and told her I was able to get only one other ex. With JB's approval I gave her his name, address and phone number. She had been able to convince Leon 'Whitey' Thompson, #1465AZ to join JB and me. I think there were five guards including the former Captain of The Guards, Phil Bergen, who agreed to show up. We were outnumbered.

At eight o'clock on the morning we were scheduled to catch the boat to the Rock, JB, his wife, and Lorna and I were standing apart from the hundreds of tourists who were waiting to catch the same boat. JB and I wanted to scan the crowd to see if we could recognize some of the guards. About ten yards from us was another small group of eight or ten men. JB was the first to spot one of the old-time guards in that bunch. When he drew my attention to the fellow, I saw another among them under whom I had served time. For the life of us, neither could recall their names. This wasn't unusual because inmates seldom had any conversation with the guards.

Donna came over to where we were standing and told us the boat was ready to take on passengers. She then went over to the guards and advised them it was time to move toward the loading platform. Just as we got to the ramp, I looked up in time to see one of the officers smile and raise his hand toward me in a sort of half-hearted salute. I could understand his uneasiness because I felt the same way. I felt it was time to determine exactly where we stood with one another, so I left my friends and approached him and the other officers. I put my hand out to the one I recognized as Bert Garrett and said, "Good morning, Mr. Garrett. It has been so long I wasn't certain it was you." He smiled amiably and replied, "It has been a long time, Nate. Gosh, I can't believe you're grey-haired. I think you left here in '60, about twenty-four years ago. Do you recognize the others of us who worked here?" I had to admit the only one I remembered was Phil Bergen. Phil was very congenial, as were the rest. I hailed JB and asked him to 'come over and renew acquaintances'. Then I introduced them to JB's wife and Lorna. By the time the boat pulled out for the trip, all of us were chatting like long-lost friends.

JB was right in the middle of the conversation, completely relaxed. Our reservations about how we would be accepted were put at ease.

Nancy and Donna were pleased at how well we were communicating. Both confessed they were a bit apprehensive at first. We were each handed a program. The visitors were aware that there would be ex- Alcatraz cons and Guards among them and that they would be willing to answer questions. As we split up, I was approached by a young Park Ranger who said Frank Heaney had told him about JB and me. He said he would like to interview me alone when the tour was over. It seemed he was doing some research work for the department. While we were talking, a boy of about twelve asked the Ranger, "Could you point out one of the ex-inmates who will be here today? Will he be wearing anything that will let us know what he is?" The Ranger smiled, laid his hand on my shoulder and told the youngster, "This man here knows who they are. You stick with him and he'll introduce you to them." The boy and I went into the main cellhouse where we located JB. I called JB over and said. "JB, this young man would like to meet you."

I looked at the boy who had turned beet red. He had wanted to see 'one of those guys', and was embarrassed when he was introduced. When I left JB and him, they were talking up a storm. As I was walking to the isolation cells, Nancy and Donna intercepted me. They had a sandy-haired fellow in tow. Nancy asked, "Nate, do you remember this man?" I really cased the fellow, but couldn't place him. She grinned and said, "This is Whitey Thompson. He served time here with you. The reason you don't remember him is that he came on the Rock only a week or two before they transferred you out. Anyway, I wanted you two to meet." Whitey and I talked at length before it came time to speak to tourists in different areas of the joint. I learned later that Whitey had written a book titled 'Last Train To Alcatraz'. It was a success from the day it was published.

I was told that there were more than 3500 tourists on the first day of the inmate-guard project. JB, Whitey and I autographed hundreds of programs and books. On the return boat, the inmates and guards were on a first name basis. We agreed to get together on the following and last day of the event. At dinner that night, our wives asked JB and me some penetrating questions. JB's wife led the interrogation by asking, "Why is it you fellows who hated the guards with such vehemence, even to the point you wanted to assault them, today were laughing and joking with them?" JB and I looked at one another. That was a toughie, but I offered what I thought was a reasonable explanation. During their training and indoctrination to become guards, they were taught that the cons were there for all types of nefarious crimes. The officials were told to bear in mind that the inmates were, in many instances, intelligent, cunning, ruthless and potentially dangerous; that they would do anything to set up an escape route, get drugs or other kinds of contraband. And all this would be accomplished at the expense of the guards' occupation and reputation, maybe even his life. There was one cardinal rule: do not trust nor fraternize with any inmate. To top off the scare tactic, they were advised that their lives, and the lives of their fellow guards would be put in jeopardy unless they obeyed the teachings of the instructors. On the other side of the fence, the convicts were taught by older cons that they must never trust nor associate with a guard. He was bad news. In fact they were not to be seen talking to an official. To do so would put them suspect of ratting on another con. There was a flaw in this training. The guards and the inmates were human beings with the frailty of being human beings. Certain inmates would take a liking to a particular guard, and a guard would take a liking to a specific inmate. That was inevitable. Supposedly, Alcatraz had the best trained personnel in the system. Yet, guards in that institution were drawn into friendships with some inmates. That was the case with some convicts. I wrote of two who used to carry letters, uncensored, to my family and friends. They would bring me candy, a commodity that many inmates had not seen in years. They would bring me information from the 'front office' that was forbidden to fall into the hands of the prisoners. They did this of their own free will. They could not have hoped to gain any material advantage, because I had nothing to exchange. In order to avoid a relationship of this nature, all guards were transferred from one job to another every ninety days. This was done to prevent a friendship from developing over a prolonged period.

"That sounds like a reasonable explanation," my wife commented. I reminded JB that both of us upheld the convict code for all the years we were incarcerated. Still, we associated with guards on the outside. They were guests of our families. To this very day, I have close friends who are retired wardens. Everything goes into full circle. When I was operating my Teen Intercept program, a former guard of Alcatraz who was aware of my project, came to me and asked my help in getting his grandson's life straightened out. Today he is an engineer with Boeing. His grandad and I are friends. On the Rock, we were foes.

On the surface, I feel good with what I've done with my life, but in the reality of night I fight horrendous and nightmarish battles as I struggle with my conscience. My friends see me as the epitome of success, a man who, by the dint of his own strength and determination, overcame the stigma of a sordid criminal past. When I look into the mirror as I'm shaving, I see a weak and guilt-ridden image. Among my friends, I'm an open book, a book that has a colorful jacket, pages that are filled with selected pictures and of good deeds that portray me as 'one hell-of-a guy'. The book jacket was selected to impress others. The pictures are touched up and unreal, like the publicity photos of show people and politicians. If I were seen as I truly am, the sand under my feet would shift and I would crumble. It's uncomfortable living with myself because I have to adopt a Jekyll and Hyde personality. I have become so adept at this dual role that I have lost sight of which in me is good and which is bad. The struggle isn't worth the effort. I envy the openness and sincerity of little children before they begin practicing the coquetry they absorb from their contact with adults. They sleep while I toss restlessly.

Those on whom I visited profound anguish throughout their lives are no longer here, so it is too late to make amends. From the day of my birth, I am sure that my beloved parents dreamed of the joy and pleasure I would bring them for the rest of their living days. I was their hope of the future. Instead, from my pre-teen years, I disgraced and humiliated them. I proceeded through my life with ruthless disregard for their lives. It would be redundant to recount the atrocities I committed in my inexorable drive to destroy myself and them. The grievous hurt I caused my family throughout their lives is indescribable and unpardonable. Yet, they are here and I can make every effort to atone for my noxious behavior. But Mom and Dad are beyond hearing my entreaties. If they could have been here to share in the good things that have been heaped on me in the form of accolades, commendations and honors, my reformation would have been more complete and meaningful.

Lorna asked me what I was thinking of when President Reagan publicly commended me for the years of work I performed for my fellow men. I replied, "I wish to God that my parents were here to share in this ceremony." This was my constant prayer and, each time I would address an audience and hear their applause, my silent petition would be the same. Society, by a gesture of the President's signature on an unconditional pardon, has forgiven me. That pardon has not quieted my restlessness or eased my guilt. The pardon I would have coveted would be the one only my parents could have conferred. If I could turn back the clock and beg the forgiveness of my Mother and Dad, I would be a more complete man.

When I go flying alone, I experience a sense of complete freedom. I am up there among the clouds with my Creator where I can, uninterruptedly, express my amazement at the turn my life has taken, and give thanks to Him. I am lost in wonderment at the changes in my thinking. Guards are no longer vicious animals. Many are my confidants and friends. Unbelievably, we greet one another in an embrace. I have no one whom I have to impress with my toughness. I am free to stand among others and smile in trust and confidence. And I can shout out my expressions of thankfulness for a lovely wife and children, at the privilege I have of enjoying my brother and sisters, and friends. In the bright skies, the sun shines without the stripes that were so indelibly stamped on my mind as it shined through the prison bars for so many wasted years. As the time for making radio contact in preparation for landing instructions approaches, my reverie disappears and I come back to earth, hopefully a rejuvenated man.